SAP® BW

A Step-by-Step Guide

Biao Fu, Ph.D.
Henry Fu, P.E.

Addison-Wesley

Boston • San Francisco • New York • Toronto • Montreal
London • Munich • Paris • Madrid
Capetown • Sydney • Tokyo • Singapore • Mexico City

The publisher offers discounts on this book when ordered in quantity for bulk purchases and special sales. For more information, please contact:

U.S. Corporate and Government Sales
(800) 382-3419
corpsales@pearsontechgroup.com

For sales outside of the U.S., please contact:

International Sales
(317) 581-3793
international@pearsontechgroup.com

Visit Addison-Wesley on the Web: www.awprofessional.com

Library of Congress Cataloging-in-Publication Data

Fu, Biao.
SAP BW : a step-by-step guide / Biao Fu, Henry Fu.
p. cm.
Includes bibliographical references and index.
ISBN 0-201-70366-1 (alk. paper)
1. SAP Business information warehouse. 2. Data warehousing. 3. Management information systems. 4. Business—Computer programs. I. Fu, Biao. II. Title.

HF5548.4.B875 F8 2002
650'.0285'5785—dc21

2002066530

Pearson Education, Inc.
Rights and Contracts Department
75 Arlington Street, Suite 300
Boston, MA 02116
Fax: (617) 848-7047

ISBN: 0-201-70366-1
Text printed on recycled paper
1 2 3 4 5 6 7 8 9 10—CRS—0605040302
First printing, July 2002

To

Xiqiang and Huizhong, our parents

Anna, Biao's daughter

George, Henry's son

Contents

Preface

Book Objective

This book is a how-to guide. It uses step-by-step procedures with captured screen shots to illustrate SAP BW's functionalities. Although the book focuses on the core SAP BW technology, it also discusses other SAP technologies, such as Basis, ABAP (Advanced Business Application Programming), and ALE (Application Link Enabling) when necessary. It does not, however, discuss third-party reporting tools and BAPI (Business Application Programming Interface).

Intended Audience

This book is written for BW implementation teams and other individuals who need a product to understand the data warehousing concept.

Prerequisites

BW is built on the Basis 3-tier architecture and coded in the ABAP language. ALE and BAPI are used to link BW with SAP systems (R/3 or BW) and non-SAP systems.

This book, however, does not require readers have knowledge in these areas. Instead, BW has made the development of a data warehouse so easy that people with minimal experience in database design and computer programming can use it.

Book Structure

This book is organized into two parts:

- Part I contains guided tours. We start from a simplified business scenario, then illustrate how to create an InfoCube, load data into the InfoCube, check the accuracy of the loaded data, create queries to generate reports, and manage user authorization.

- Part II focuses on advanced topics, such as InfoCube design techniques, aggregates, multi-cubes, operational data store (ODS), Business Content, generic R/3 data extraction, data maintenance, performance tuning, and object transport.

The appendices introduce ASAP (Accelerated SAP) for BW, one of the derivatives of the ASAP implementation methodology developed by SAP, and give an overview of the Basis 3-tier architecture.

Conventions Used in This Book

High-Level Procedures

Most chapters are organized so that they present a high-level procedure for completing a particular task. For example, the contents of Chapter 2, Creating an InfoCube, are as follows:

2.1 Creating an InfoArea
2.2 Creating InfoObject Catalogs
2.3 Creating InfoObjects—Characteristics
2.4 Creating InfoObjects—Key Figures
2.5 Creating an InfoCube
2.6 Summary

The corresponding high-level procedure for creating an InfoCube is as follows:

FIGURE 0.1 A HIGH-LEVEL PROCEDURE

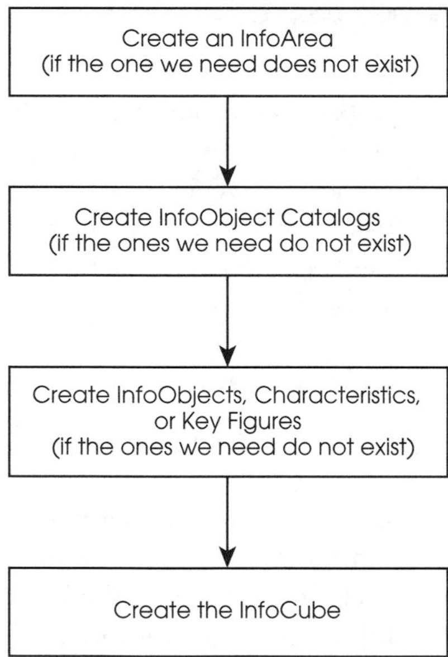

Almost always, you can complete a task in many ways. In such cases, we will select a strategy that shows better logical dependency.

Work Instructions and Screen Captures

Each step in the high-level procedure involves many substeps. Whenever possible, we will use captured screen shots to illustrate these substeps. Following is an example of how to start BW Administrator Workbench:

Step 1 After logging on to the BW system, run transaction *RSA1*, or double-click *Administrator Workbench*.

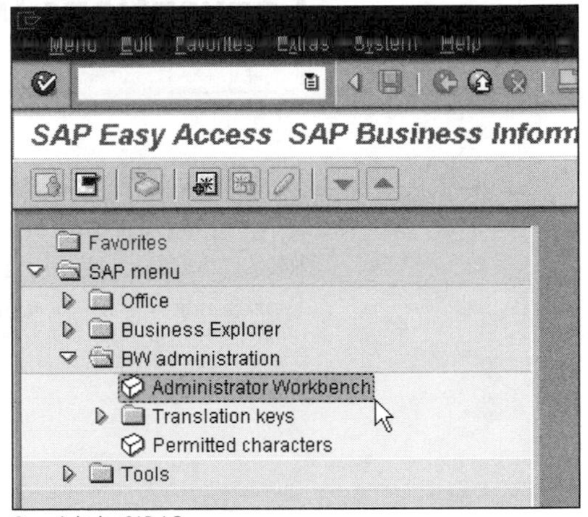

SCREEN 2.1

Each screen is assigned a unique number, which is then used to reference the screen from other locations in the book. In this example, the screen number is 2.1, where "2" is the chapter number and "1" indicates that it is the first screen in that chapter.

Key words, such as *RSA1* and *Administrator Workbench*, are shown in italic for easy distinction.

Caution Due to the differences among BW releases and patches, the screens in your system may appear somewhat different from the screens illustrated in this book. BW is becoming more stable, so these differences should be small.

Transaction Codes

In SAP, transaction codes are the technical names of menu items or ABAP programs. Transactions can be used as shortcuts to screens we want to open. For example, to start Administrator Workbench, we can either (1) double-click the menu item *Administrator Workbench* or (2) type *RSA1* in the transaction field RSA1 and then click . The transaction field appears in the upper-left corner of a SAPGUI window.

To display transaction codes for all menu items, in Screen 2.1 select the menu item *Extras* → *Setting*, check the option *Display technical names* in the pop-up window as shown in Screen 0.1, and then click to continue.

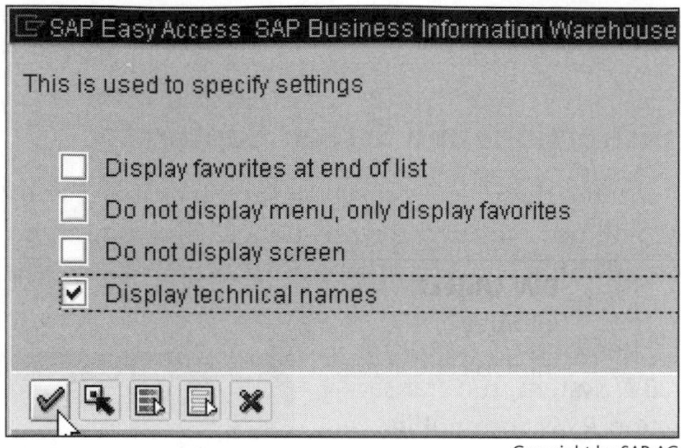

SCREEN 0.1

Screen 0.2 shows the result. Here transaction codes are displayed at the leaf level of the menu item tree structure. For example, the transaction codes RSA1, RRC1, RRC2, RRC3, and RSKC correspond to the menu items *Administrator Workbench*, *Create*, *Change*, *Display*, and *Permitted Characters*, respectively.

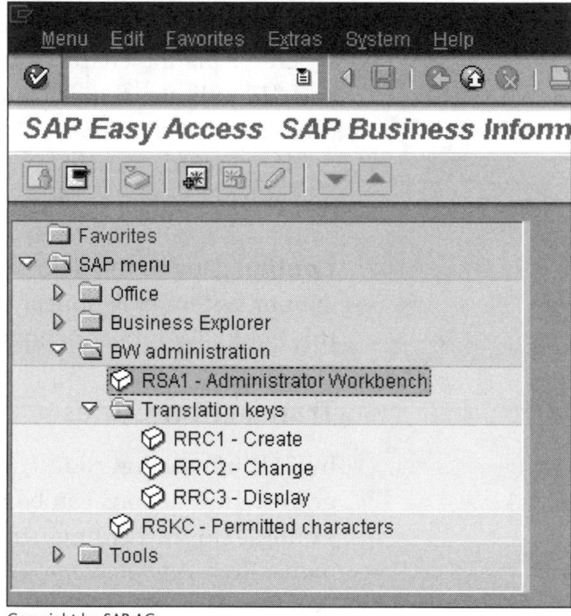

SCREEN 0.2

To find the transaction code for a particular screen, select the menu item *System* → *Status* of the screen. The transaction code will be displayed in a field called *Transaction*.

Legends

BW implements good visual aesthetics. That is, different icons and their colors represent different objects and their status.

If the legend icon is visible in a screen, clicking it enables us to see the meaning of each icon in that screen. Table 0.1 provides some examples.

TABLE 0.1 EXAMPLE OBJECT ICONS

Icon	BW Object
	InfoArea
	InfoObject Catalog
	Characteristic (green for active, gray for inactive)
	Key Figure (green for active, gray for inactive)
	InfoCube

Icons are also used to represent command buttons in BW. Table 0.2 offers some examples.

TABLE 0.2 FREQUENTLY USED COMMAND ICONS

Icon	Command
	Create
	Save
	Delete
	Change
	Display
	Display—change switch
	Detail
	Check
	Activate
	Generate
	Continue
	Cancel
	Execute
	Refresh
	Display table contents
	Look up
	Enter
	Back to the previous screen

Object Names and Descriptions

We can give any name to an object as long as the name does not exceed the length limit set by BW. This name, which is often referred to as the technical name, uniquely identifies an object.

BW prefixes the number 0 to the names of the objects delivered with Business Content. For this reason, we will begin our object names with an alphabetical letter.

The object description can be a free sentence.

Consider the following example. The characteristic is named *IO_MAT* and its description is *Material number*.

Step 2 Enter a name and a description, and then click ✔ to continue.

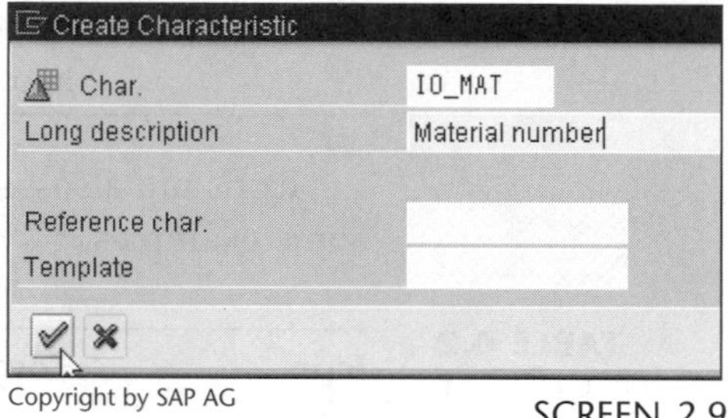

SCREEN 2.9

Caution Name all BW objects consistently. Very often, renaming an object means that you must delete and recreate the object. When other BW objects depend on that object, you may have to delete and re-create the depending objects as well.

Field Descriptions and F1 Help

To keep the description of each step in a procedure short and clear, we do not describe all fields or options in a screen. If needed, you can check the BW online documentation for more information. Perhaps even more convenient, you can select the field and then press the F1 function key to display an online help file. The online help file for the field *Reference char.* of Screen 2.9 is shown in Screen 0.3.

Terminology

BW objects and terms encountered in each chapter are summarized in the last section of each chapter, not necessarily the first place we use these objects and terms.

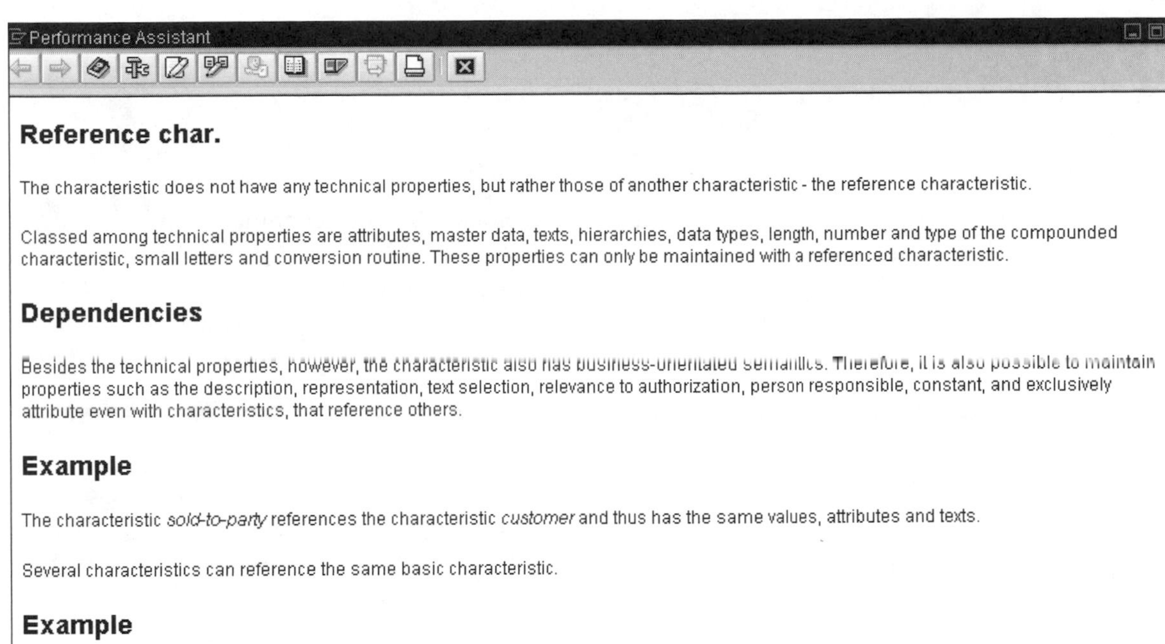

Performance Assistant
Reference char.
The characteristic does not have any technical properties, but rather those of another characteristic - the reference characteristic.
Classed among technical properties are attributes, master data, texts, hierarchies, data types, length, number and type of the compounded characteristic, small letters and conversion routine. These properties can only be maintained with a referenced characteristic.
Dependencies
Besides the technical properties, however, the characteristic also has business-oriented semantics. Therefore, it is also possible to maintain properties such as the description, representation, text selection, relevance to authorization, person responsible, constant, and exclusively attribute even with characteristics, that reference others.
Example
The characteristic sold-to-party references the characteristic customer and thus has the same values, attributes and texts.
Several characteristics can reference the same basic characteristic.
Example
The characteristic sender cost center and receiver cost center reference the characteristic cost center .

SCREEN 0.3

For Further Information

A list of materials for further reading appears at the end of each chapter. To avoid duplication among chapters, here we give two very important resources that apply to SAP BW in general:

- *SAP Library: Business Information Warehouse:* The online documentation is delivered with the BW installation CDs.
- *ASAP for BW Accelerators*: Accelerators are documents, templates, tips, and tricks on specific topics. Their titles are listed in Appendix A, and the files can be downloaded from http://service.sap.com/bw/. An OSS (Online Service System) ID from SAP is required to access this Web site.

Acknowledgments

Many individuals made this book possible, directly and indirectly. In particular, we want to thank:

- Addison-Wesley executive editor Mary O'Brien; editors Alicia Carey, Mariann Kourafas, and Stacie Parillo; production editor Melissa Panagos; and copyeditor Jill Hobbs.

Our first complete draft was completed one year ago. Then, when we were about to send it out for the final review, our laptop was stolen in a hotel breakfast area, together with the backup CD. Without a hard copy of the draft, we decided to start all over again. Stacie sent us the original draft of several chapters that she had, and Mary gave us time to recover the loss. Together, they encouraged us to finish the book.

We learned a hard lesson.

- Our reviewers:
  - Capers Jones of Software Productivity Research, Inc.
  - Claire Radice of Getronics
  - Dr. Guido Schroeder of SAP America
  - José A. Hernández of realTech Spain
  - Prof. Dr. Peter Cunningham of University of Port Elizabeth, South Africa
  - Dr. Peter C. Patton of Lawson Software
  - Todd Levine of Supply Access, Inc.
  - Vladimir Berelson of Cap Gemini Ernst & Young
  - William S. Girling of Institute for Data Research

They corrected our errors, gave us advice, and proofread the drafts word by word.

- Our friends, colleagues, and clients:
  - Bill Clarke of Texaco
  - Dan Spaulding of KPMG Consulting
  - Ed Sawyer, Jennie Marquez, and Stewart Wiens of Motorola
  - Kafeel Khan, Mike Eames, Monica Bittner, Philippe Tanguy, and Shelley Rossell of PricewaterhouseCoopers
  - Kristen Cheyney of Micron Technology
  - Minako Ishii and Satoru Akahori of Sony
  - Peer Gribbohm of Ernst & Young
  - Robert Freeman of Fuguji LLC

Peer Gribbohm led me to the data warehousing and the SAP BW worlds. Mike Eames and Shelley Rossell provided me with an SAP Basis and SAP BW teaching position at PricewaterhouseCoopers (PwC) Global Training Center. Robert Freeman spent several months with us proofreading and tuning the book's language.

Clients offered us project opportunities. Friends and colleagues made these challenging opportunities a fun experience, and they were always there when we needed help.

- Our college and graduate school professors:
  - Prof. Gengdong Cheng of Dalian University of Technology, Dalian, China
  - Prof. Lingcheng Zhao of Northwestern Polytechnic University, Xi'an, China
  - Prof. Prabhat Hajela of Rensselaer Polytechnic Institute, Troy, New York
  - Prof. Zhongtuo Wang of Dalian University of Technology, Dalian, China

Besides sharing their knowledge with us, they taught us how to tackle technical problems effectively. These skills helped us enormously, in both our academic and professional endeavors, after we developed interest in information technology.

Of course, we are responsible for any errors and omissions. And we will be glad to hear from any reader who wishes to make constructive comments. We can be reached at biao.fu@fuguji.com

Part I

Contents

Guided Tours

In Part I, we will tour basic SAP BW (Business Information Warehouse) functionalities using a simplified business scenario—sales analysis.

After introducing the basic concept of data warehousing and giving an overview of BW, we create a data warehouse using BW and load data into it. We then check data quality before creating queries and reports (or workbooks, as they are called in BW). Next, we demonstrate how to use an SAP tool called Profile Generator to manage user authorization.

After finishing the guided tours, we will appreciate BW's ease of use and get ready to explore other BW functionalities.

Chapter 1

Business Scenario and SAP BW

The objective of **data warehousing** is to analyze data from diverse sources to support decision making. To achieve this goal, we face two challenges:

- Poor system performance. A data warehouse usually contains a large volume of data. It is not an easy job to retrieve data quickly from the data warehouse for analysis purposes. For this reason, the data warehouse design uses a special technique called a **star schema**.
- Difficulties in extracting, transferring, transforming, and loading (**ETTL**) data from diverse sources into a data warehouse. Data must be cleansed before being used. ETTL has been frequently cited as being responsible for the failures of many data warehousing projects. You would feel the pain if you had ever tried to analyze SAP R/3 data without using SAP BW.

SAP R/3 is an ERP (Enterprise Resources Planning) system that most large companies in the world use to manage their business transactions. Before the introduction of SAP BW in 1997, ETTL of SAP R/3 data into a data warehouse seemed an unthinkable task. This macro-environment explained the urgency with which SAP R/3 customers sought a data warehousing solution. The result is SAP BW from SAP, the developer of SAP R/3.

In this chapter we will introduce the basic concept of data warehousing. We will also discuss what **SAP BW (Business Information Warehouse)** is, explain why we need it, examine its architecture, and define Business Content.

First, we use sales analysis as an example to introduce the basic concept of data warehousing.

1.1 Sales Analysis—A Business Scenario

Suppose that you are a sales manager, who is responsible for planning and implementing sales strategy. Your tasks include the following:

- Monitoring and forecasting sales demands and pricing trends
- Managing sales objectives and coordinating the sales force and distributors
- Reviewing the sales activities of each representative, office, and region

Suppose also that you have the data in Tables 1.1 through 1.3 available about your firm's materials, customers, and sales organization.

TABLE 1.1 MATERIALS

Material Number	Material Name	Material Description
MAT001	TEA	Ice tea
MAT002	COFFEE	Hot coffee
MAT003	COOKIE	Fortune cookie
MAT004	DESK	Computer desk
MAT005	TABLE	Dining table
MAT006	CHAIR	Leather chair
MAT007	BENCH	Wood bench
MAT008	PEN	Black pen
MAT009	PAPER	White paper
MAT010	CORN	America corn
MAT011	RICE	Asia rice
MAT012	APPLE	New York apple
MAT013	GRAPEFRUIT	Florida grapefruit
MAT014	PEACH	Washington peach
MAT015	ORANGE	California orange

TABLE 1.2
CUSTOMERS

Customer ID	Customer Name	Customer Address
CUST001	Reliable Transportation Company	1 Transport Drive, Atlanta, GA 23002
CUST002	Finance One Corp	2 Finance Avenue, New York, NY, 10001
CUST003	Cool Book Publishers	3 Book Street, Boston, MA 02110
CUST004	However Forever Energy, Inc.	4 Energy Park, Houston, TX 35004
CUST005	Easy Computing Company	5 Computer Way, Dallas, TX 36543
CUST006	United Suppliers, Inc.	6 Suppliers Street, Chicago, IL 61114
CUST007	Mobile Communications, Inc.	7 Electronics District, Chicago, IL 62643
CUST008	Sports Motor Company	8 Motor Drive, Detroit, MI 55953
CUST009	Swan Stores	9 Riverside Road, Denver, CO 45692
CUST010	Hollywood Studio	10 Media Drive, Los Angeles, CA 78543
CUST011	One Source Technologies, Inc.	11 Technology Way, San Francisco, CA 73285
CUST012	Airspace Industries, Inc.	12 Air Lane, Seattle, WA 83476

TABLE 1.3
SALES ORGANIZATION

Sales Region	Sales Office	Sales Representative	Sales Representative ID
EAST	ATLANTA	John	SREP01
	NEW YORK	Steve	SREP02
		Mary	SREP03
MIDWEST	DALLAS	Michael	SREP04
		Lisa	SREP05
	CHICAGO	Kevin	SREP06
		Chris	SREP07
WEST	DENVER*	Sam	SREP08
	LOS ANGELES	Eugene	SREP09
	SEATTLE	Mark	SREP10

*Prior to January 1, 2000, the Denver office was in the Midwest region.

You also have three years of sales data, as shown in Table 1.4.

TABLE 1.4 SALES DATA

Customer ID	Sales Representative ID	Material Number	Per Unit Sales Price	Unit of Measure	Quantity Sold	Transaction Date
CUST001	SREP01	MAT001	2	Case	1	19980304
CUST002	SREP02	MAT002	2	Case	2	19990526
CUST002	SREP02	MAT003	5	Case	3	19990730
CUST003	SREP03	MAT003	5	Case	4	20000101
CUST004	SREP04	MAT004	50	Each	5	19991023
CUST004	SREP04	MAT005	100	Each	6	19980904
CUST004	SREP04	MAT005	100	Each	7	19980529
CUST005	SREP05	MAT006	200	Each	8	19991108
CUST006	SREP06	MAT007	20	Each	9	20000408
CUST007	SREP07	MAT008	3	Dozen	10	20000901
CUST007	SREP07	MAT008	3	Dozen	1	19990424
CUST008	SREP08	MAT008	3	Dozen	2	19980328
CUST008	SREP08	MAT009	2	Case	3	19980203
CUST008	SREP08	MAT010	1	U.S. pound	4	19991104
CUST009	SREP09	MAT011	1.5	U.S. pound	5	20000407
CUST010	SREP10	MAT011	1.5	U.S. pound	6	20000701
CUST010	SREP10	MAT011	1.5	U.S. pound	7	19990924
CUST010	SREP10	MAT012	2	U.S. pound	8	19991224
CUST010	SREP10	MAT013	3	Case	9	20000308
CUST011	SREP10	MAT014	1	U.S. pound	10	19980627
CUST012	SREP11	MAT014	2	U.S. pound	1	19991209
CUST012	SREP11	MAT015	3	Case	2	19980221
CUST012	SREP11	MAT015	2	Case	3	20000705
CUST012	SREP11	MAT015	3.5	Case	4	20001225

The data in these tables represent a simplified business scenario. In the real world, you might have years of data and millions of records.

To succeed in the face of fierce market competition, you need to have a complete and up-to-date picture of your business and your business environment. The challenge lies in making the best use of data in decision support. In decision support, you need to perform many kinds of analysis.

This type of **online analytical processing (OLAP)** consumes a lot of computer resources because of the size of data. It cannot be carried out on an **online transaction processing (OLTP)** system, such as a sales management system. Instead, we need a dedicated system, which is the data warehouse.

1.2 Basic Concept of Data Warehousing

A data warehouse is a system with its own database. It draws data from diverse sources and is designed to support query and analysis. To facilitate data retrieval for analytical processing, we use a special database design technique called a star schema.

1.2.1 Star Schema

The concept of a star schema is not new; indeed, it has been used in industry for years. For the data in the previous section, we can create a star schema like that shown in Figure 1.1.

The star schema derives its name from its graphical representation—that is, it looks like a star. A **fact table** appears in the middle of the graphic, along with several surrounding **dimension tables**. The central fact table is usually very large, measured in gigabytes. It is the table from which we retrieve the interesting data. The size of the dimension tables amounts to only 1 to 5 percent of the size of the fact table. Common dimensions are unit and time, which are not shown in Figure 1.1. Foreign keys tie the fact table to the dimension tables. Keep in mind that dimension tables are not required to be normalized and that they can contain redundant data.

As indicated in Table 1.3, the sales organization changes over time. The dimension to which it belongs—sales rep dimension—is called the **slowly changing dimension**.

FIGURE 1.1
STAR SCHEMA

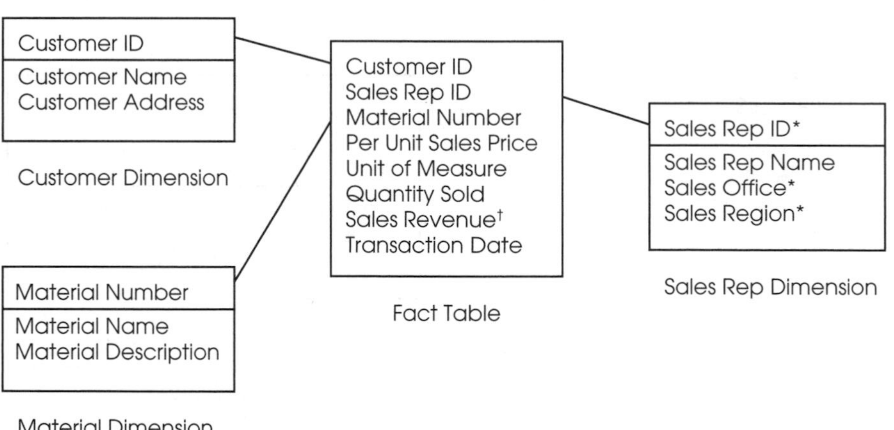

*Sales Region, Sales Office, and Sales Rep ID are in a hierarchy as shown in Table 1.3.
†Sales Revenue = Per Unit Sales Price × Quantity Sold.

The following steps explain how a star schema works to calculate the total quantity sold in the Midwest region:

1. From the sales rep dimension, select all sales rep IDs in the Midwest region.
2. From the fact table, select and summarize all quantity sold by the sales rep IDs of Step 1.

1.2.2 ETTL—Extracting, Transferring, Transforming, and Loading Data

Besides the difference in designing the database, building a data warehouse involves a critical task that does not arise in building an OLTP system: to extract, transfer, transform, and load (ETTL) data from diverse data sources into the data warehouse (Figure 1.2).

In data extraction, we move data out of source systems, such as an SAP R/3 system. The challenge during this step is to identify the right data. A good knowledge of the source systems is absolutely necessary to accomplish this task.

In data transfer, we move a large amount of data regularly from different source systems to the data warehouse. Here the challenges are to plan a realistic schedule and to have reliable and fast networks.

In data transformation, we format data so that it can be represented consistently in the data warehouse. For example, we might need to convert an entity with multiple names (such as AT&T, ATT, or Bell) into an entity with a single

FIGURE 1.2
ETTL PROCESS

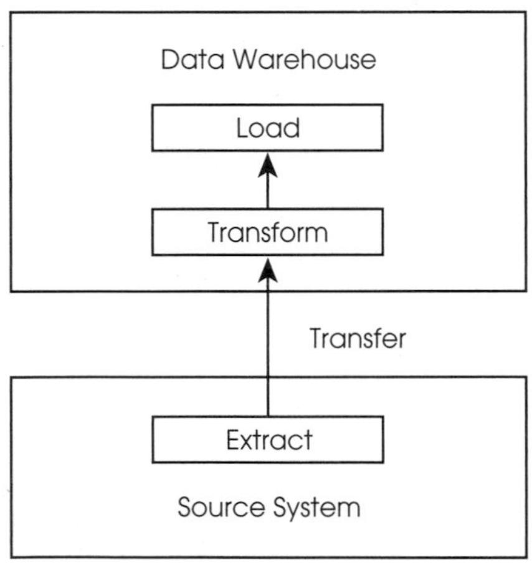

name (such as AT&T). The original data might reside in different databases using different data types, or in different file formats in different file systems. Some are case sensitive; others may be case insensitive.

In data loading, we load data into the fact tables correctly and quickly. The challenge at this step is to develop a robust error-handling procedure.

ETTL is a complex and time-consuming task. Any error can jeopardize data quality, which directly affects business decision making. Because of this fact and for other reasons, most data warehousing projects experience difficulties finishing on time or on budget.

To get a feeling for the challenges involved in ETTL, let's study SAP R/3 as an example. SAP R/3 is a leading ERP (Enterprise Resources Planning) system. According to SAP, the SAP R/3 developer, as of October 2000, some 30,000 SAP R/3 systems were installed worldwide that had 10 million users. SAP R/3 includes several modules, such as SD (sales and distribution), MM (materials management), PP (production planning), FI (financial accounting), and HR (human resources). Basically, you can use SAP R/3 to run your entire business.

SAP R/3's rich business functionality leads to a complex database design. In fact, this system has approximately 10,000 database tables. In addition to the complexity of the relations among these tables, the tables and their columns sometimes don't even have explicit English descriptions. For many years, using the SAP R/3 data for business decision support had been a constant problem.

Recognizing this problem, SAP decided to develop a data warehousing solution to help its customers. The result is SAP Business Information Warehouse, or BW. Since the announcement of its launch in June 1997, BW has drawn intense interest. According to SAP, as of October 2000, more than 1000 SAP BW systems were installed worldwide.

In this book, we will demonstrate how SAP BW implements the star schema and tackles the ETTL challenges.

1.3 BW—An SAP Data Warehousing Solution

BW is an end-to-end data warehousing solution that uses preexisting SAP technologies. BW is built on the Basis 3-tier architecture and coded in the ABAP (Advanced Business Application Programming) language. It uses ALE (Application Link Enabling) and BAPI (Business Application Programming Interface) to link BW with SAP systems and non-SAP systems.

1.3.1 BW Architecture

Figure 1.3 shows the BW architecture at the highest level. This architecture has three layers:

1. The top layer is the reporting environment. It can be **BW Business Explorer (BEx)** or a third-party reporting tool. BEx consists of two components:
   - **BEx Analyzer**
   - **BEx Browser**

   BEx Analyzer is Microsoft Excel with a BW add-in. Thanks to its easy-to-use graphical interface, it allows users to create queries without coding SQL statements. BEx Browser works much like an information center, allowing users to organize and access all kinds of information. Third-party reporting tools connect with BW OLAP Processor through **ODBO (OLE DB for OLAP)**.

FIGURE 1.3 BW ARCHITECTURE

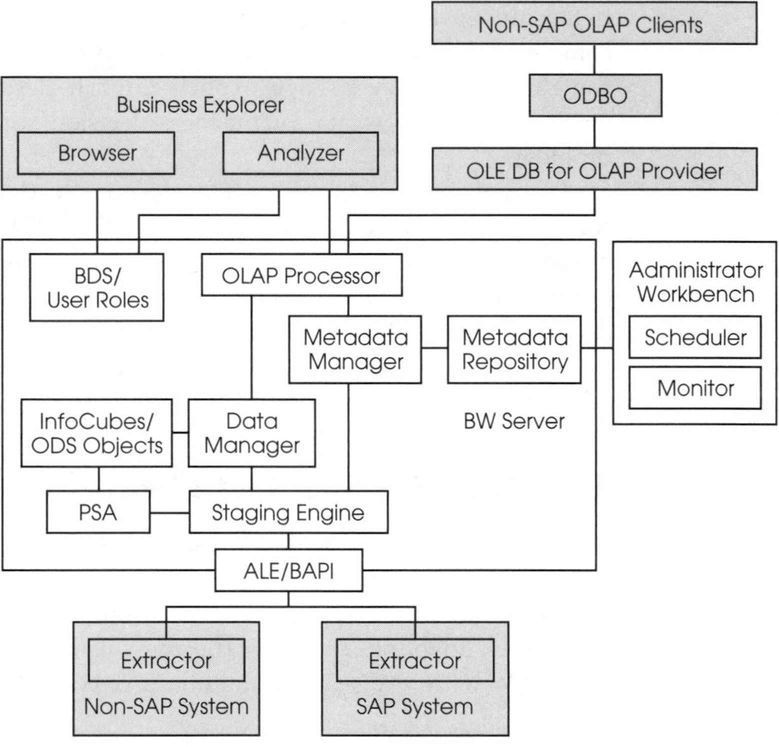

Source: Adapted from SAP BW online documentation.

2. The middle layer, **BW Server**, carries out three tasks:
   - Administering the BW system
   - Storing data
   - Retrieving data according to users' requests

   We will detail BW Server's components next.
3. The bottom layer consists of **source systems**, which can be R/3 systems, BW systems, flat files, and other systems. If the source systems are SAP systems, an SAP component called **Plug-In** must be installed in the source systems. The Plug-In contains **extractors**. An extractor is a set of ABAP programs, database tables, and other objects that BW uses to extract data from the SAP systems. BW connects with SAP systems (R/3 or BW) and flat files via ALE; it connects with non-SAP systems via BAPI.

   The middle-layer BW Server consists of the following components:
   - Administrator Workbench, including BW Scheduler and BW Monitor
   - Metadata Repository and Metadata Manager
   - Staging Engine
   - PSA (Persistent Staging Area)
   - ODS (Operational Data Store) Objects
   - InfoCubes
   - Data Manager
   - OLAP Processor
   - BDS (Business Document Services)
   - User Roles

Administrator Workbench maintains meta-data and all BW objects. It has two components:

- **BW Scheduler** for scheduling jobs to load data
- **BW Monitor** for monitoring the status of data loads

This book mainly focuses on Administrator Workbench.

Metadata Repository contains information about the data warehouse. Meta-data comprise data about data. Metadata Repository contains two types of meta-data: business-related (for example, definitions and descriptions used for reporting) and technical (for example, structure and mapping rules used for data extraction and transformation). We use **Metadata Manager** to maintain Metadata Repository.

Staging Engine implements data mapping and transformation. Triggered by BW Scheduler, it sends requests to a source system for data loading. The source system then selects and transfers data into BW.

PSA (Persistent Staging Area) stores data in the original format while being imported from the source system. PSA allows for quality check before the data are loaded into their destinations, such as ODS Objects or InfoCubes.

ODS (Operational Data Store) Objects allow us to build a multilayer structure for operational data reporting. They are not based on the star schema and are used primarily for detail reporting, rather than for dimensional analysis.

InfoCubes are the fact tables and their associated dimension tables in a star schema.

Data Manager maintains data in ODS Objects and InfoCubes and tells the OLAP Processor what data are available for reporting.

OLAP Processor is the analytical processing engine. It retrieves data from the database, and it analyzes and presents those data according to users' requests.

BDS (Business Document Services) stores documents. The documents can appear in various formats, such as Microsoft Word, Excel, PowerPoint, PDF, and HTML. BEx Analyzer saves query results, or MS Excel files, as workbooks in the BDS.

User Roles are a concept used in SAP authorization management. BW organizes BDS documents according to User Roles. Only users assigned to a particular User Role can access the documents associated with that User Role.

Table 1.5 indicates where each of these components is discussed in this book. As noted in the Preface, this book does *not* discuss third-party reporting tools and BAPI.

TABLE 1.5 CHAPTERS DETAILING BW COMPONENTS

Components	**Chapters**
Business Explorer: • Analyzer and Browser	Chapter 5, Creating Queries and Workbooks
Non-SAP OLAP Clients	Not covered
ODBO	
OLE DB for OLAP Provider	
Extractor: • ALE	Chapter 3, Loading Data into the InfoCube, on how to load data from flat files Chapter 10, Business Content, on how to load data from R/3 systems Chapter 11, Generic R/3 Data Extraction
BAPI	Not covered
Administrator Workbench	The entire book, although not explicitly mentioned
BW Scheduler	Chapter 3, Loading Data into the InfoCube, on BW Scheduler
BW Monitor	Chapter 4, Checking Data Quality, on BW Monitor

Components	Chapters
Metadata Repository	The entire book, although not explicitly mentioned
Metadata Manager	
Staging Engine	Chapter 3, Loading Data into the InfoCube
	PSA
	Chapter 4, Checking Data Quality
ODS Objects	Chapter 9, Operational Data Store (ODS)
InfoCubes	Chapter 2, Creating an InfoCube
	Chapter 7, InfoCube Design
	Chapter 8, Aggregates and Multi-Cubes
Data Manager	Chapter 12, Data Maintenance
OLAP Processor	Chapter 13, Performance Tuning
BDS	Chapter 5, Creating Queries and Workbooks
User Roles	Chapter 6, Managing User Authorization

1.3.2 BW Business Content

One of the BW's strongest selling points is its **Business Content**. Business Content contains standard reports and other associated objects. For example, BW provides you, the sales manager, with the following standard reports:

Quotation Processing

- Quotation success rates per sales area
- Quotation tracking per sales area
- General quotation information per sales area

Order Processing

- Monthly incoming orders and revenue
- Sales values
- Billing documents
- Order, delivery, and sales quantities
- Fulfillment rates
- Credit memos
- Proportion of returns to incoming orders
- Returns per customer
- Quantity and values of returns
- Product analysis
- Product profitability analysis

Delivery

- Delivery delays per sales area
- Average delivery processing times

Analyses and Comparisons

- Sales/cost analysis
- Top customers
- Distribution channel analysis
- Product profitability analysis
- Weekly deliveries
- Monthly deliveries
- Incoming orders analysis
- Sales figures comparison
- Returns per customer
- Product analysis
- Monthly incoming orders and revenue

Administrative and Management Functions

- Cost center: plan/actual/variance
- Cost center: responsible for orders, projects, and networks
- Order reports
- WBS Element: plan/actual/variance
- Cost center: plan/actual/variance
- Cost center: hit list of actual variances
- Cost center: actual costs per quarter
- Cost center: capacity-related headcount

Chapter 10 discusses Business Content in detail.

When necessary, we can also use a function, called **Generic Data Extraction**, to extract R/3 data that cannot be extracted with the standard Business Content. Chapter 11 discusses this function in detail.

1.3.3 BW in mySAP.com

BW is evolving rapidly. Knowing its future helps us plan BW projects and their scopes. Here, we give a brief overview of BW's position in mySAP.com.

mySAP.com is SAP's e-business platform that aims to achieve the collaboration among businesses using the Internet technology. It consists of three components:

- mySAP Technology
- mySAP Services
- mySAP Hosted Solutions

As shown in Figure 1.4, mySAP Technology includes a portal infrastructure for user-centric collaboration, a Web Application Server for providing Web services, and an exchange infrastructure for process-centric collaboration. The portal infrastructure has a component called mySAP Business Intelligence; it is the same BW but is located in the mySAP.com platform. Using mySAP Technology, SAP develops e-business solutions, such as mySAP Supply Chain Management (mySAP SCM), mySAP Customer Relationship Management (mySAP CRM), and mySAP Product Lifecycle Management (mySAP PLM).

mySAP Services are the services and support that SAP offers to its customers. They range from business analysis, technology implementation, and training to system support. The services and support available from http://service.sap.com/bw/ are good examples of mySAP Services.

mySAP Hosted Solutions are the outsourcing services from SAP. With these solutions, customers do not need to maintain physical machines and networks.

FIGURE 1.4
MYSAP TECHNOLOGY AND MYSAP SOLUTIONS

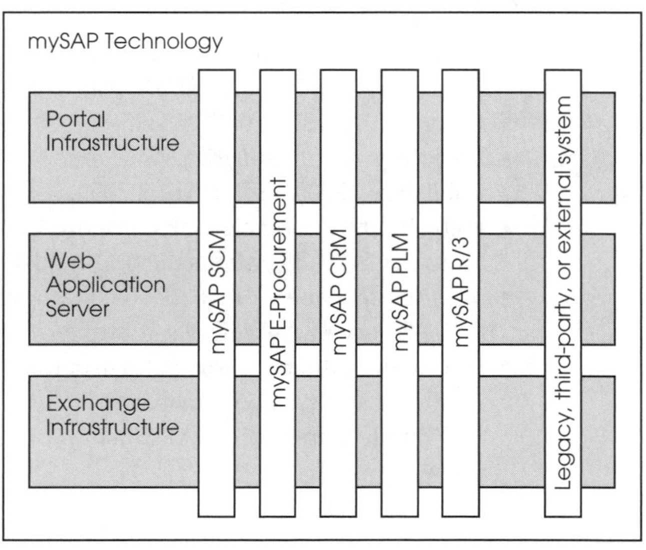

Source: Adapted from SAP white paper, "mySAP Technology for Open E-Business Integration—Overview."

1.4 Summary

This chapter introduced the basic concept of data warehousing and discussed what SAP BW is, why we need it, its architecture, and what Business Content is. Later chapters will discuss these subjects in more details.

Key Terms

Term	Description
Data warehouse	A data warehouse is a dedicated reporting and analysis environment based on the star schema database design technique that requires paying special attention to the data ETTL process.
Star schema	A star schema is a technique used in the data warehouse database design that aims to help data retrieval for online analytical processing.
ETTL	ETTL represents one of the most challenging tasks in building a data warehouse. It involves the process of extracting, transforming, transferring, and loading data correctly and quickly.
BW	BW is a data warehousing solution from SAP.

For Further Information

- Book: *The Data Warehouse Lifecycle Toolkit: Expert Methods for Designing, Developing, and Deploying Data Warehouses,* by Ralph Kimball. John Wiley & Sons, 1998. ISBN: 0471255475.
- Book: *Business Information Warehouse for SAP,* by Naeem Hashmi. Prima Publishing, 2000. ISBN: 0761523359.
- Web site: http://service.sap.com/bw/ is the official BW Web site maintained by SAP. It contains the original BW materials.
- SAP white paper: "mySAP Technology for Open E-Business Integration—Overview." Available at http://www.sap.com/.
- SAP white paper: "Portal Infrastructure: People-Centric Collaboration." Available at http://www.sap.com/.
- SAP white paper: "mySAP Business Intelligence." Available at http://www.sap.com/.

Next . . .

We will create an InfoCube that implements the Figure 1.1 star schema.

Chapter 2

Creating an InfoCube

In BW, Customer ID, Material Number, Sales Representative ID, Unit of Measure, and Transaction Date are called **characteristics**. Customer Name and Customer Address are **attributes** of Customer ID, although they are characteristics as well. Per Unit Sales Price, Quantity Sold, and Sales Revenue are referred to as **key figures**. Characteristics and key figures are collectively termed **InfoObjects**.

A key figure can be an attribute of a characteristic. For instance, Per Unit Sales Price can be an attribute of Material Number. In our examples, Per Unit Sales Price is a fact table key figure. In the real world, such decisions are made during the data warehouse design phase. Chapter 7 provides some guidelines for making such decisions.

InfoObjects are analogous to bricks. We use these objects to build **InfoCubes**. An InfoCube comprises the fact table and its associated dimension tables in a star schema.

In this chapter, we will demonstrate how to create an InfoCube that implements the star schema from Figure 1.1. We start from creating an **InfoArea**. An InfoArea is analogous to a construction site, on which we build InfoCubes.

2.1 Creating an InfoArea

In BW, InfoAreas are the branches and nodes of a tree structure. InfoCubes are listed under the branches and nodes. The relationship of InfoAreas to InfoCubes in BW resembles the relationship of directories to files in an operating system. Let's create an InfoArea first, before constructing the InfoCube.

Work Instructions

Step 1 After logging on to the BW system, run transaction *RSA1*, or double-click *Administrator Workbench.*

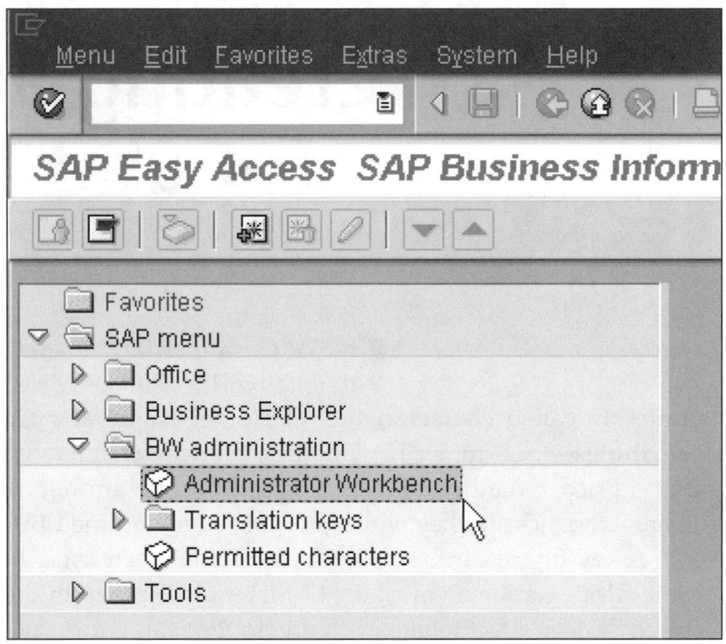

SCREEN 2.1

Step 2 In the new window, click *Data targets* under *Modelling* in the left panel. In the right panel, right-click *InfoObjects* and select *Create InfoArea. . . .*

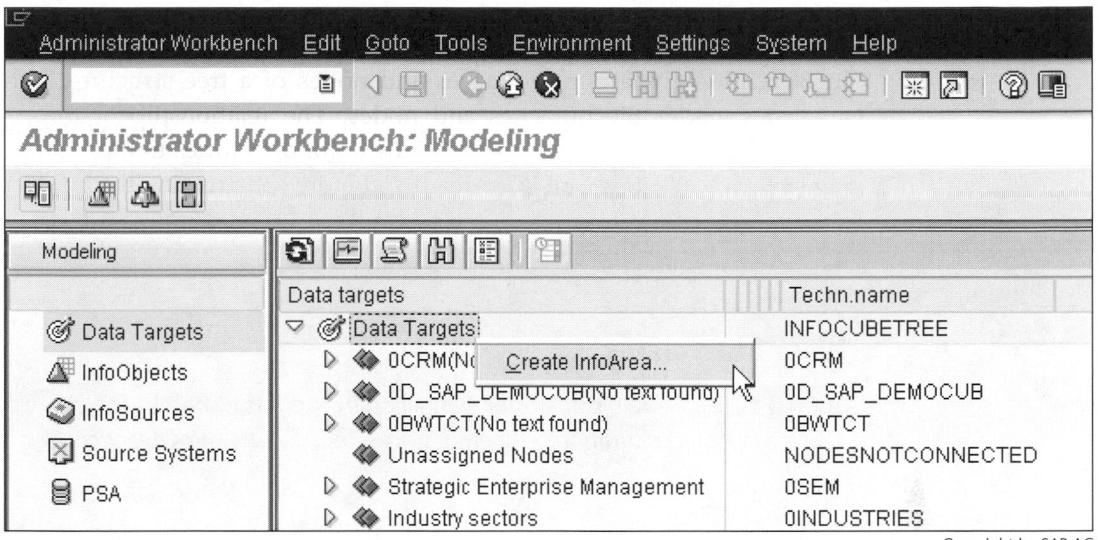

SCREEN 2.2

Note: In BW, InfoCubes and ODS Objects are collectively called **data targets**.

Step 3 Enter a name and a description for the InfoArea, and then click ✔ to continue.

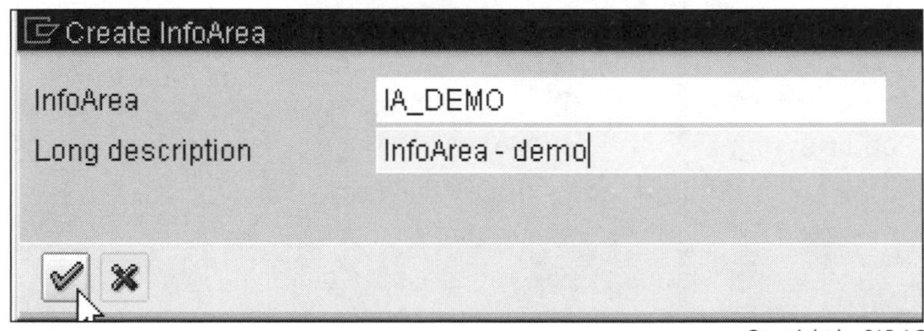

SCREEN 2.3

Result

The InfoArea has been created as shown in Screen 2.4.

2.2 Creating InfoObject Catalogs

Before we can create an InfoCube, we must have InfoObjects. Before we can create InfoObjects, however, we must have InfoObject Catalogs. Because characteristics and key figures are different types of objects, we organize them within their own separate folders, which are called **InfoObject Catalogs**. Like InfoCubes, InfoObject Catalogs are listed under InfoAreas.

Having created an InfoArea in Section 2.1, let's now create InfoObject Catalogs to hold characteristics and key figures.

Work Instructions

Step 1 Click *InfoObjects* under *Modelling* in the left panel. In the right panel, right-click *InfoArea – demo*, and select *Create InfoObject catalog. . . .*

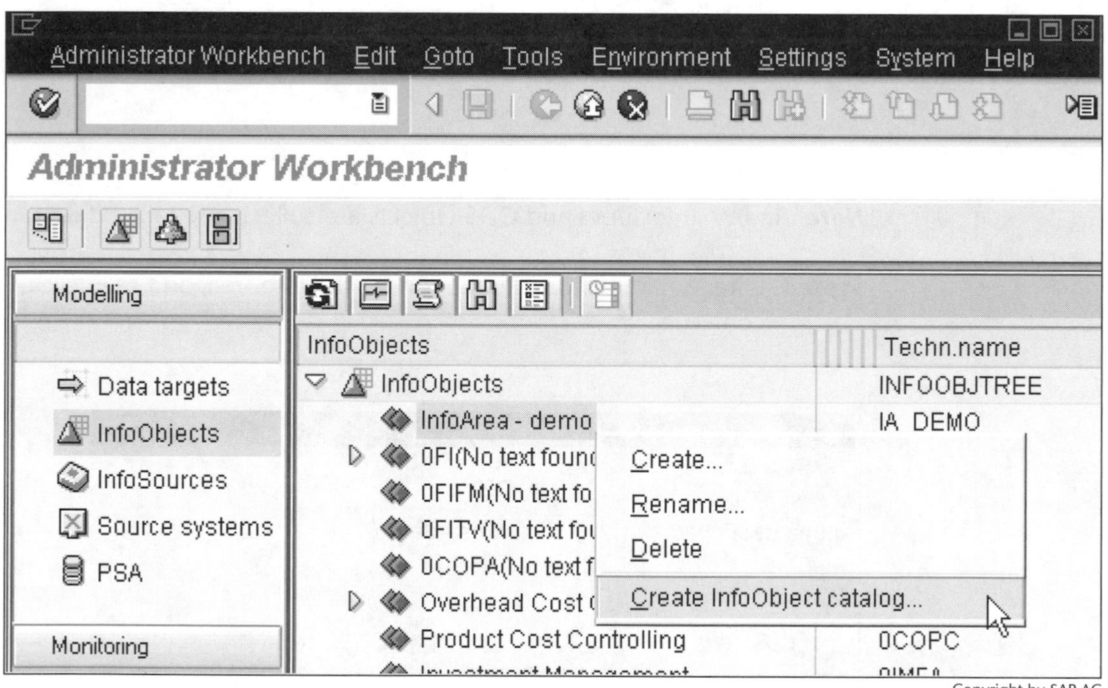

SCREEN 2.4

Step 2 Enter a name and a description for the InfoObject Catalog, select the option *Char.*, and then click [icon] to create the InfoObject Catalog.

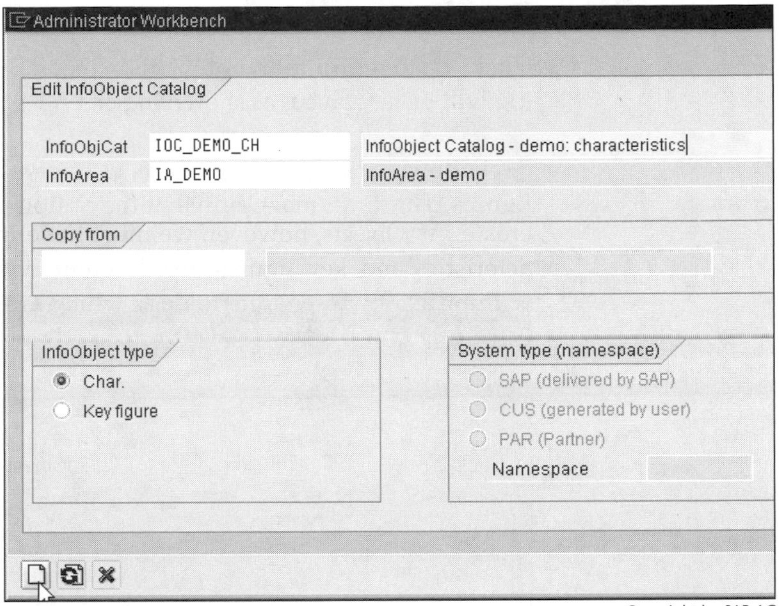

SCREEN 2.5

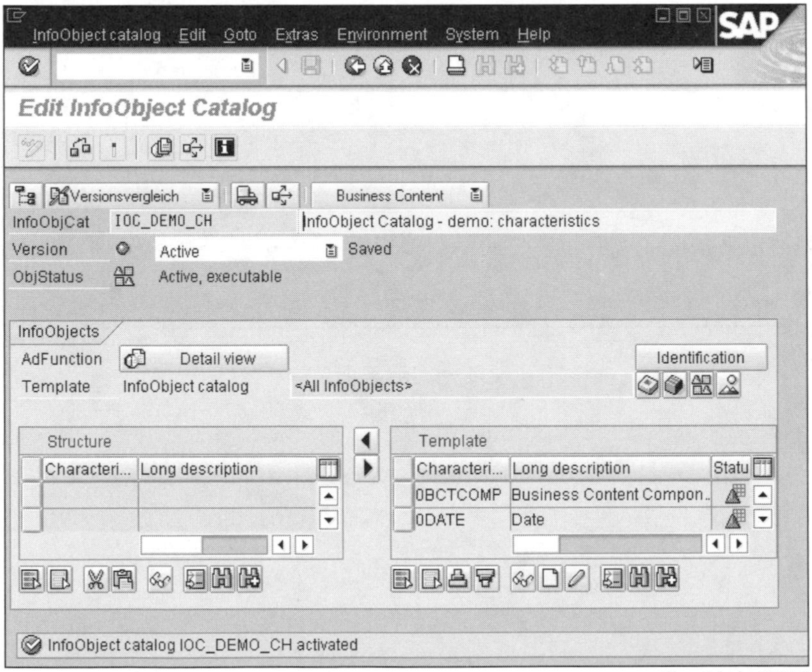

Step 3 In the new window, click [icon] to check the InfoObject Catalog. If it is valid, click [icon] to activate the InfoObject Catalog. Once the activation process is finished, the status message *InfoObject catalog IOC_DEMO_CH activated* appears at the bottom of the screen.

SCREEN 2.6

Result

Click to return to the previous screen. The newly created InfoObject Catalog will be displayed, as shown in Screen 2.8.

Following the same procedure, we create an InfoObject Catalog to hold key figures. This time, make sure that the option *Key figure* is selected (Screen 2.7).

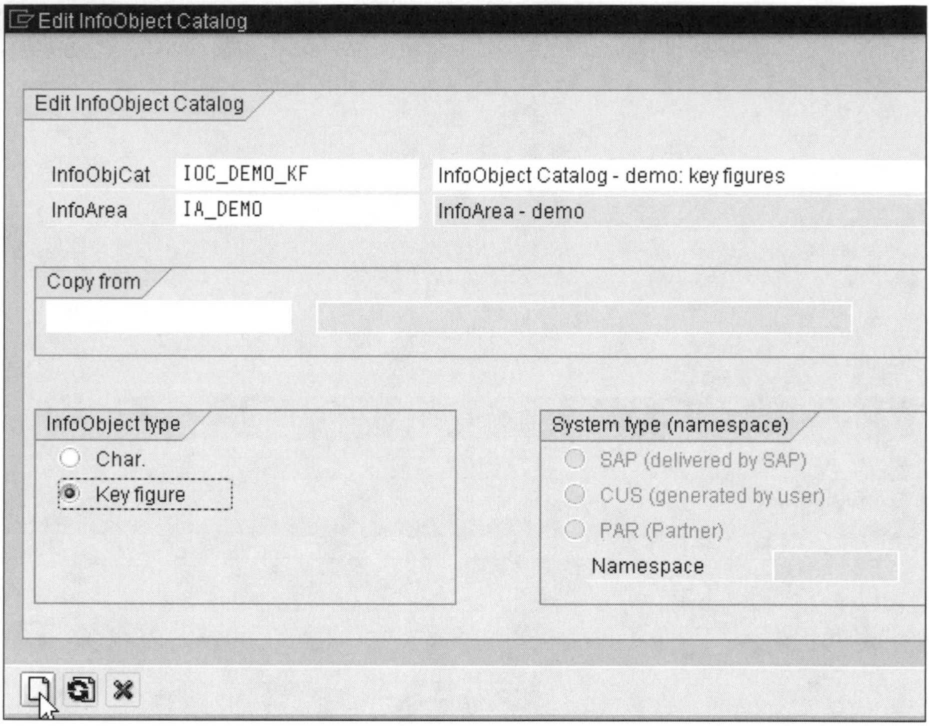

SCREEN 2.7

2.3 Creating InfoObjects—Characteristics

Now we are ready to create characteristics.

Work Instructions

Step 1 Right-click *InfoObject Catalog – demo: characteristics*, and then select *Create InfoObject. . . .*

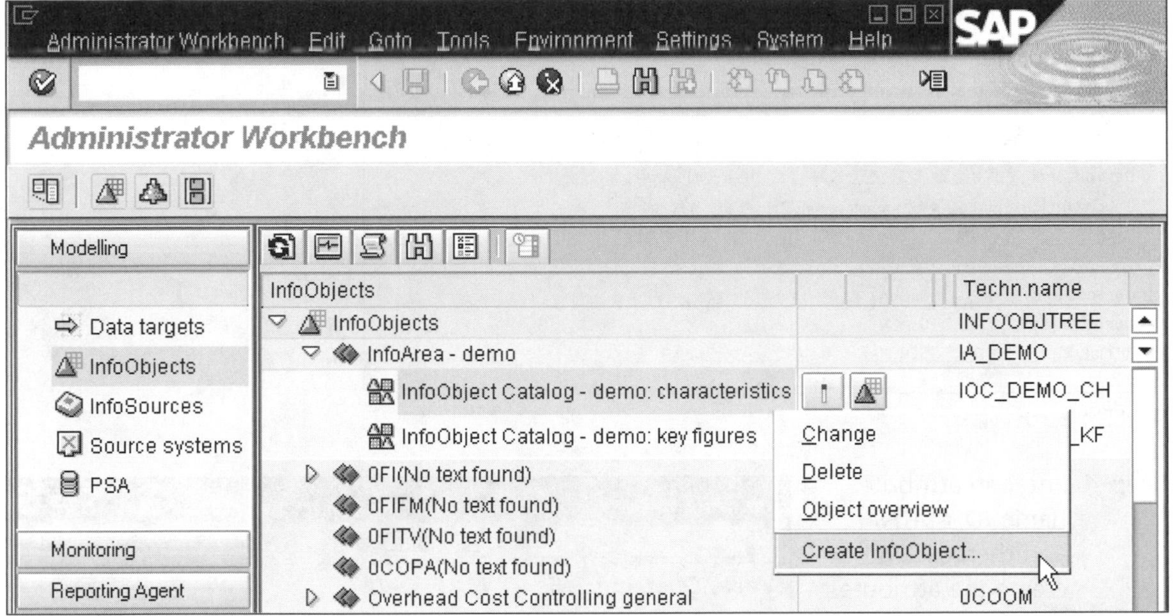

SCREEN 2.8

Step 2 Enter a name and a description, and then click ✔ to continue.

Create Characteristic
Char. IO_MAT
Long description Material number
Reference char.
Template

SCREEN 2.9

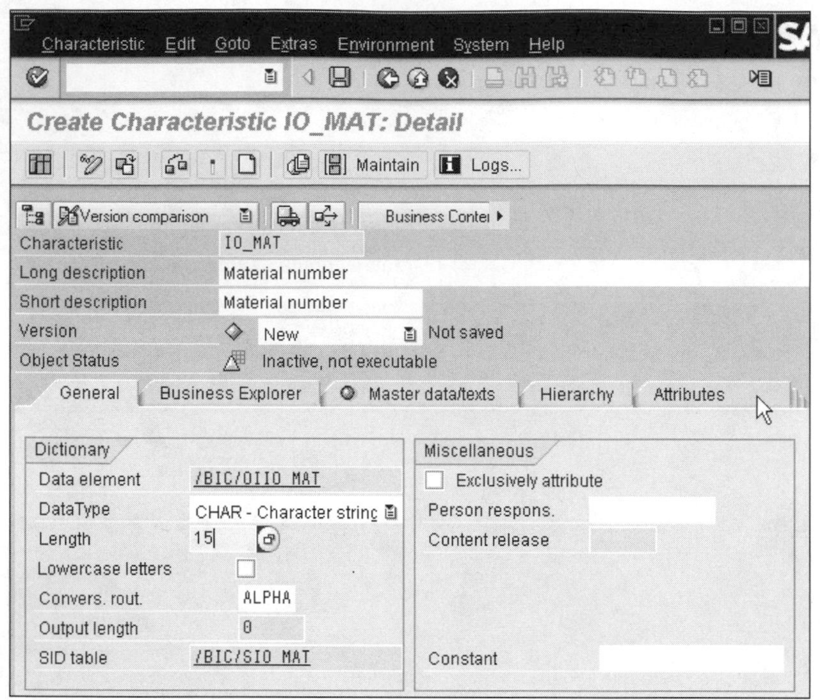

SCREEN 2.10

Step 3 Select *CHAR* as the *DataType*, enter *15* for the field *Length*, and then click the tab *Attributes*.

Step 4 Enter an attribute name *IO_MATNM*, and then click ☐ to create the attribute.

Note: Notice that IO_MATNM is underlined. In BW, the underline works like a hyperlink. After IO_MATNM is created, when you click IO_MATNM, the hyperlink will lead you to IO_MATNM's detail definition window.

SCREEN 2.11

Step 5 Select the option *Create attribute as characteristic*, and then click ✔ to continue.

Note: Section 11.3, "Creating a Characteristic in BW," discusses an example of the key figure attribute.

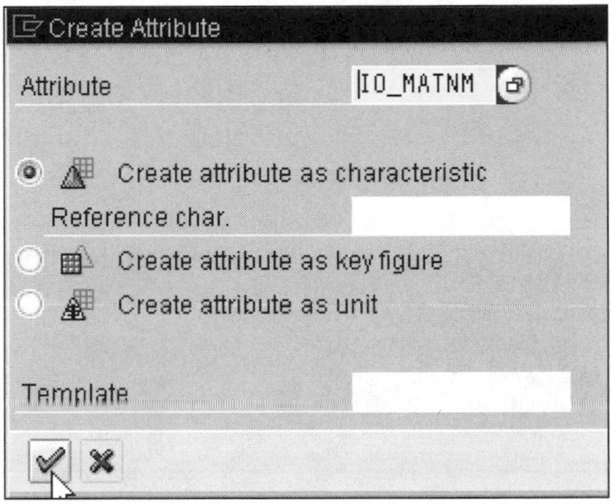

Create Attribute

Attribute IO_MATNM

Create attribute as characteristic

Reference char.

Create attribute as key figure

Create attribute as unit

Template

SCREEN 2.12

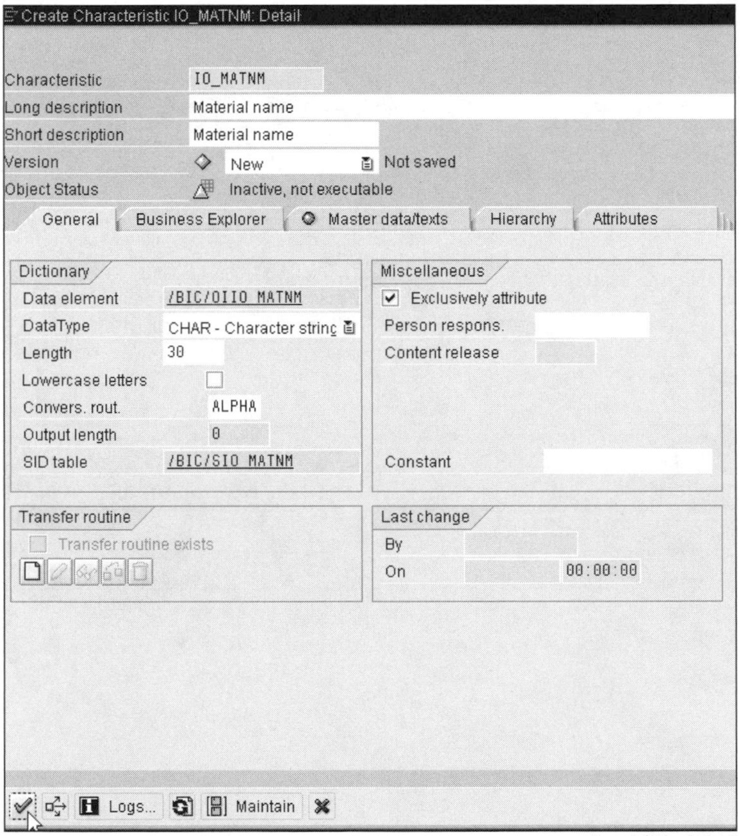

Create Characteristic IO_MATNM: Detail

Characteristic IO_MATNM

Long description Material name

Short description Material name

Version New Not saved

Object Status Inactive, not executable

General | Business Explorer | Master data/texts | Hierarchy | Attributes

Dictionary

Data element /BIC/OIIO_MATNM

DataType CHAR - Character string

Length 30

Lowercase letters

Convers. rout. ALPHA

Output length 0

SID table /BIC/SIO_MATNM

Miscellaneous

Exclusively attribute

Person respons.

Content release

Constant

Transfer routine

Transfer routine exists

Last change

By

On 00:00:00

Logs... Maintain

SCREEN 2.13

Step 6 Select *CHAR* as the *DataType*, and then enter *30* for the field *Length*. Notice that the option *Exclusively attribute* is selected by default. Click ✔ to continue.

Note: If *Exclusively attribute* is selected, the attribute IO_MATNM can be used only as a **display attribute**, not as a **navigational attribute**. Section 7.2, "InfoCube Design Alternative I—Time-Dependent Navigational Attributes," discusses an example of the navigation attributes.

Selecting *Exclusively attribute* allows you to select *Lowercase letters.* If the option *Lowercase letters* is selected, the attribute can accept lowercase letters in data to be loaded.

If the option *Lowercase letters* is selected, no **master data tables, text tables**, or another level of attributes underneath are allowed. Section 7.1, "BW Star Schema," describes master data tables and text tables, and explains how they relate to a characteristic.

Step 7 Click to check the characteristic. If it is valid, click to activate the characteristic.

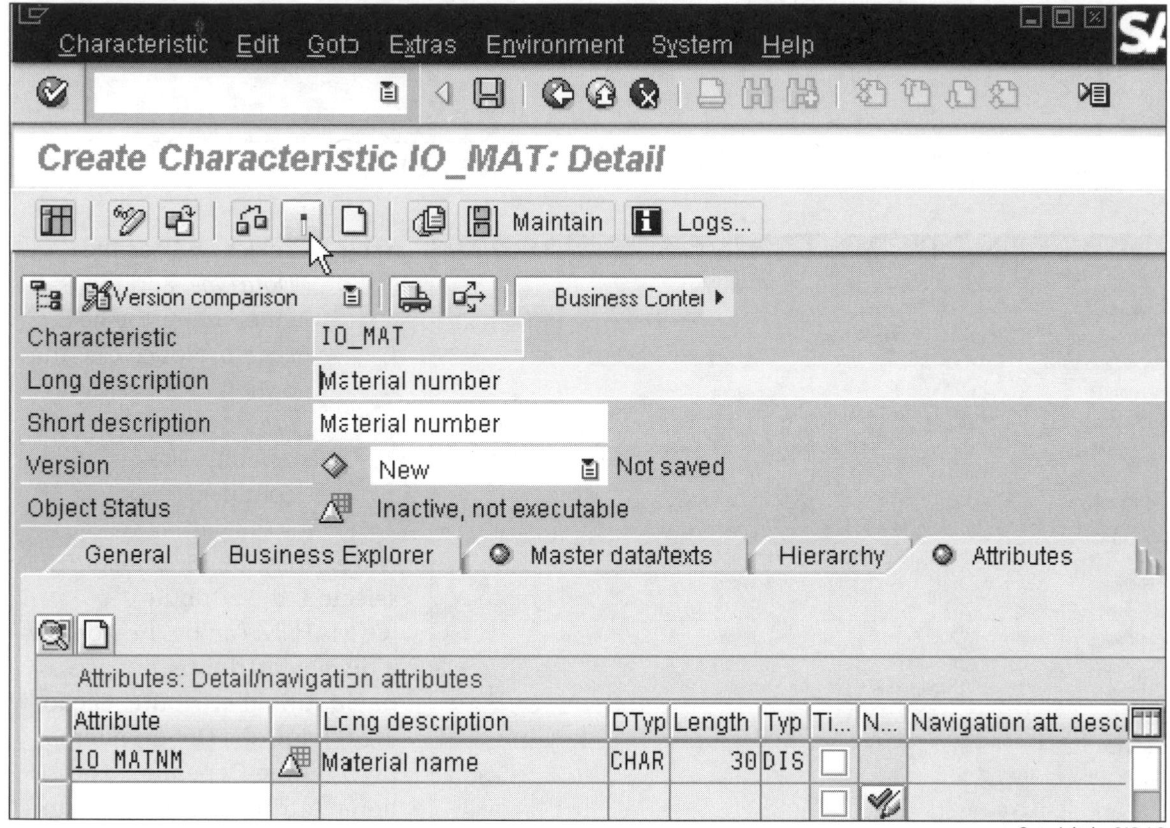

SCREEN 2.14

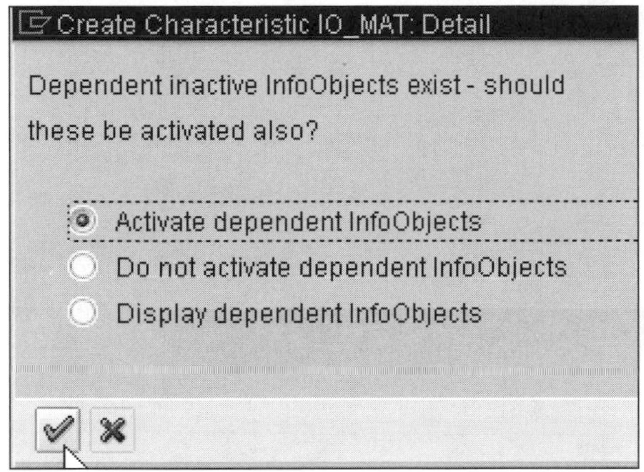

SCREEN 2.15

Step 8 A window is displayed asking whether you want to activate dependent InfoObjects. In our example, the dependent InfoObject is IO_MATNM.

Click ✔ to activate IO_MAT and IO_MATNM.

Result

You have now created the characteristic IO_MAT and its attribute IO_MATNM. A status message *All InfoObject(s) activated* will appear at the bottom of Screen 2.14.

Note: Saving an InfoObject means saving its properties, or meta-data. You have not yet created its physical database objects, such as tables.

Activating an InfoObject will create the relevant database objects. After activating IO_MAT, the names of the newly created master data table and text table are displayed under the *Master data/texts* tab (Screen 2.16). The name of the master data table is /BIC/PIO_MAT, and the name of the text table is /BIC/TIO_MAT.

Notice the prefix /BIC/ in the database object names. BW prefixes /BI0/ to the names of database objects of Business Content objects, and it prefixes /BIC/ to the names of database objects of customer-created BW objects.

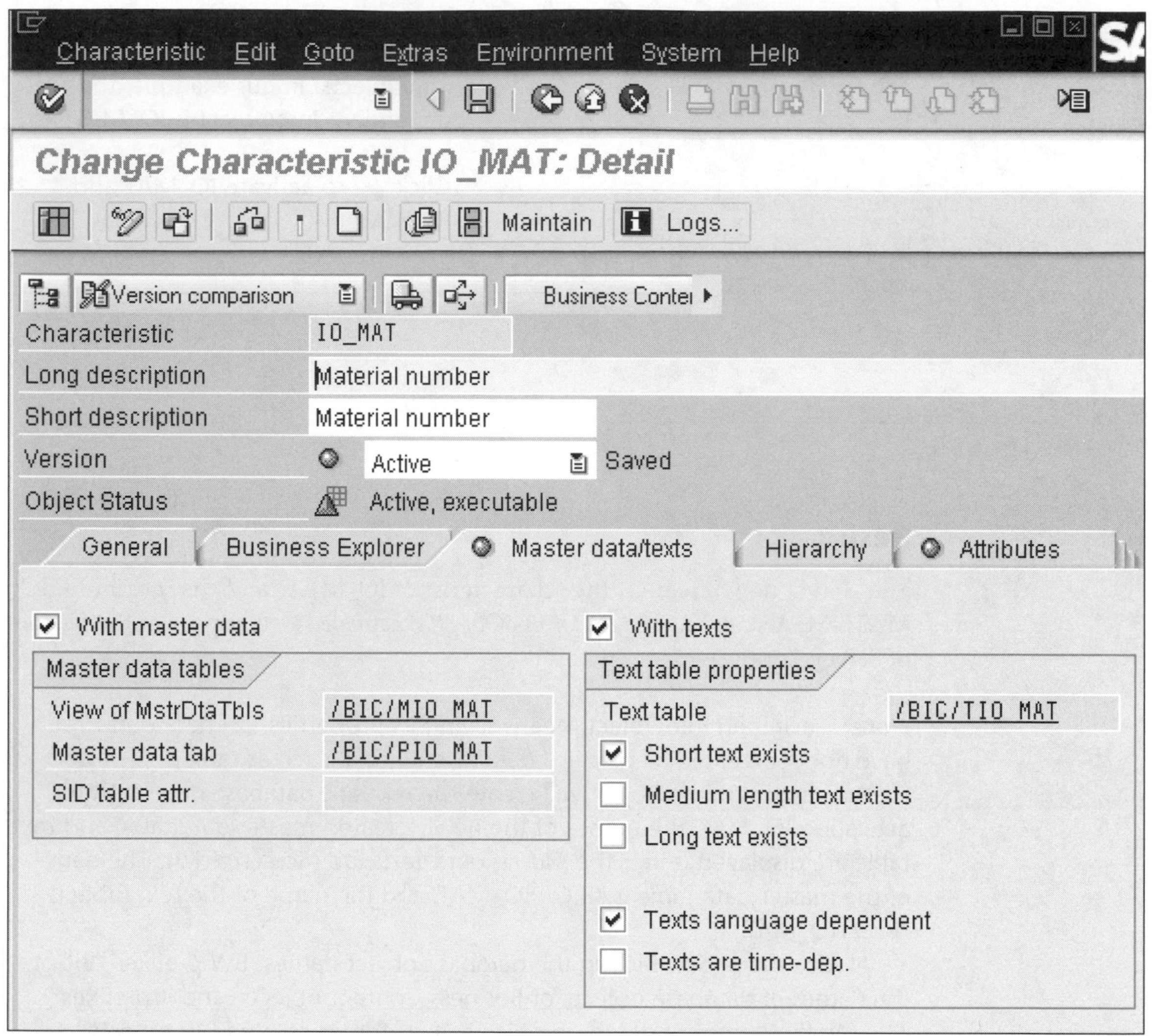

SCREEN 2.16

Repeat the preceding steps to create the other characteristics listed in Table 2.1.

TABLE 2.1 CHARACTERISTICS

Characteristics Name and Description	Assigned to	DataType	Length	Exclusively Attribute?	Lowercase Letters?
IO_MAT Material number		CHAR	15	No	No
IO_MATNM Material name	IO_MAT	CHAR	30	Yes	No
IO_CUST Customer ID		CHAR	15	No	No
IO_CUSTNM Customer name	IO_CUST	CHAR	40	Yes	Yes
IO_CUSTAD Customer addresss	IO_CUST	CHAR	60	Yes	Yes
IO_SREP Sales representative ID		CHAR	15	No	No
IO_SREPNM Sales representative name	IO_SREP	CHAR	40	Yes	Yes
IO_SOFF Sales office		CHAR	30	No	No
IO_SREG Sales region		CHAR	30	No	No

The column "Assigned to" specifies the characteristic to which an attribute is assigned. For example, IO_MATNM is an attribute of IO_MAT.

The *Material Description* in Table 1.1 will be treated as IO_MAT's text, as shown in Table 3.2 in Section 3.4, "Creating InfoPackages to Load Characteristic Data." We do not need to create a characteristic for it.

IO_SREG and IO_SOFF are created as independent characteristics, instead of IO_SREP's attributes. Section 3.6, "Entering the Master Data, Text, and Hierarchy Manually," explains how to link IO_SOFF and IO_SREG to IO_SREP via a sales organization hierarchy. Section 7.2, "InfoCube Design Alternative I—Time-Dependent Navigational Attributes," discusses a new InfoCube design in which IO_SOFF and IO_SREG are IO_SREP's attributes.

BW provides characteristics for units of measure and time. We do not need to create them.

From Administrator Workbench, we can verify that the characteristics in Table 2.1 have been created (Screen 2.17) by clicking *InfoArea – demo*, and then clicking *InfoObject Catalog – demo: characteristics.*

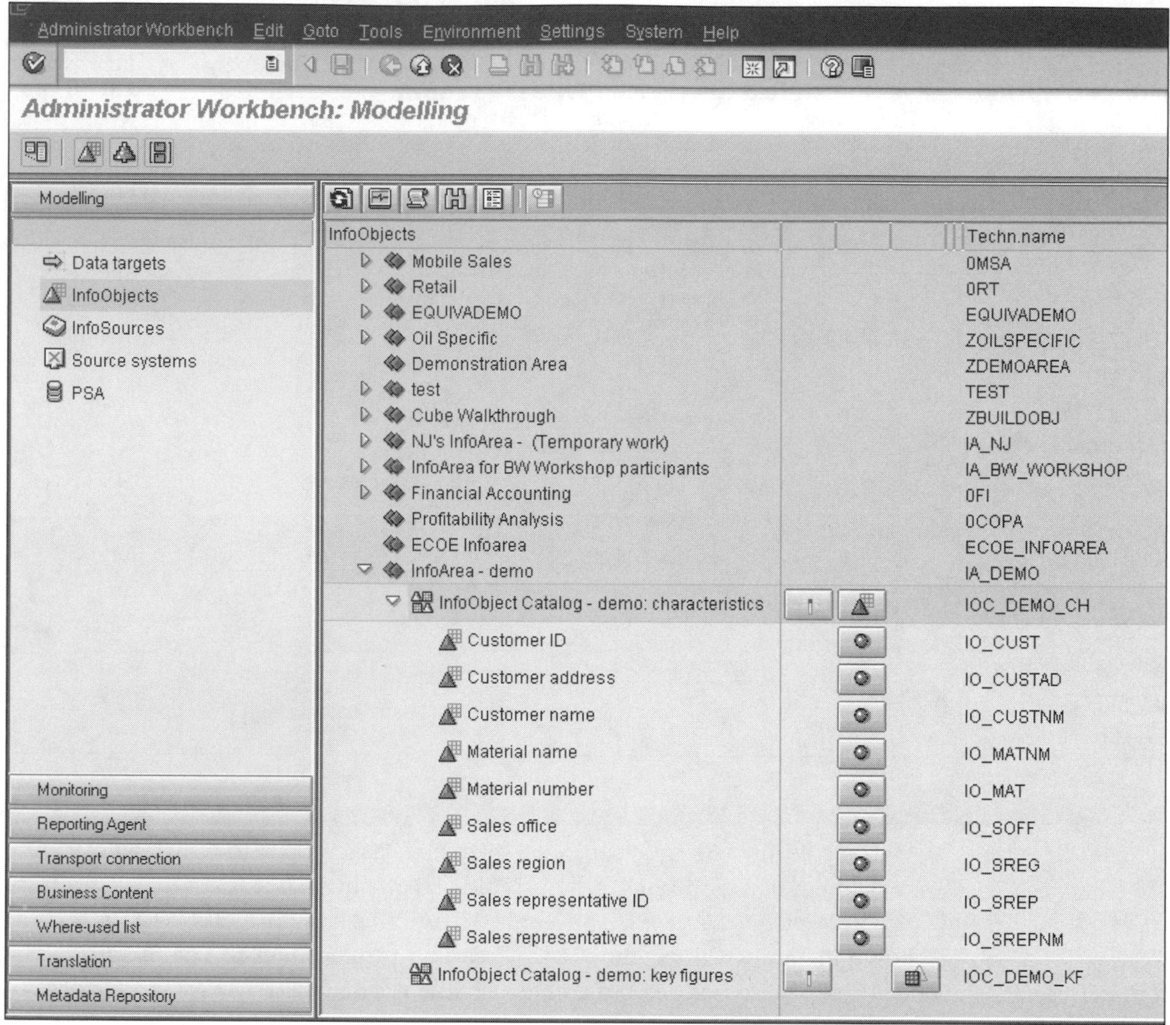

SCREEN 2.17

2.4 Creating InfoObjects—Key Figures

Next, we start to create the key figures.

Work Instructions

Step 1 Right-click *InfoObject Catalog – demo: key figures*, and then select *Create InfoObject*.

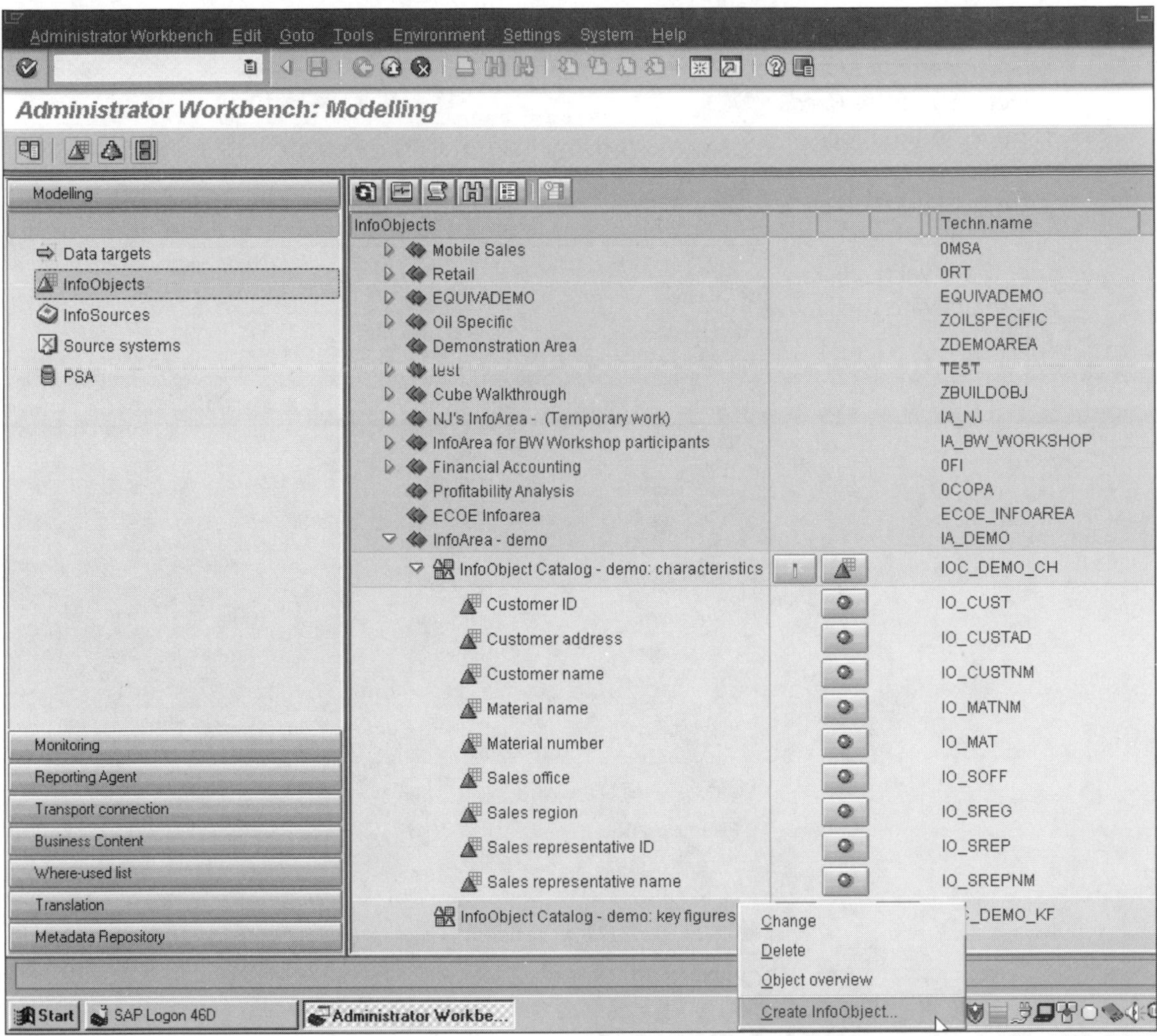

SCREEN 2.18

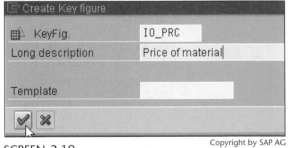

Step 2 Enter a name and a description, and then click ✔ to continue.

Create Key figure

KeyFig.	IO_PRC
Long description	Price of material
Template	

SCREEN 2.19

Step 3 Select *Amount* in the block *Type/data type*, select *USD* as the *Fixed currency* in the block *Currency/unit of measure*, and then click to check the key figure. If it is valid, click to activate the key figure.

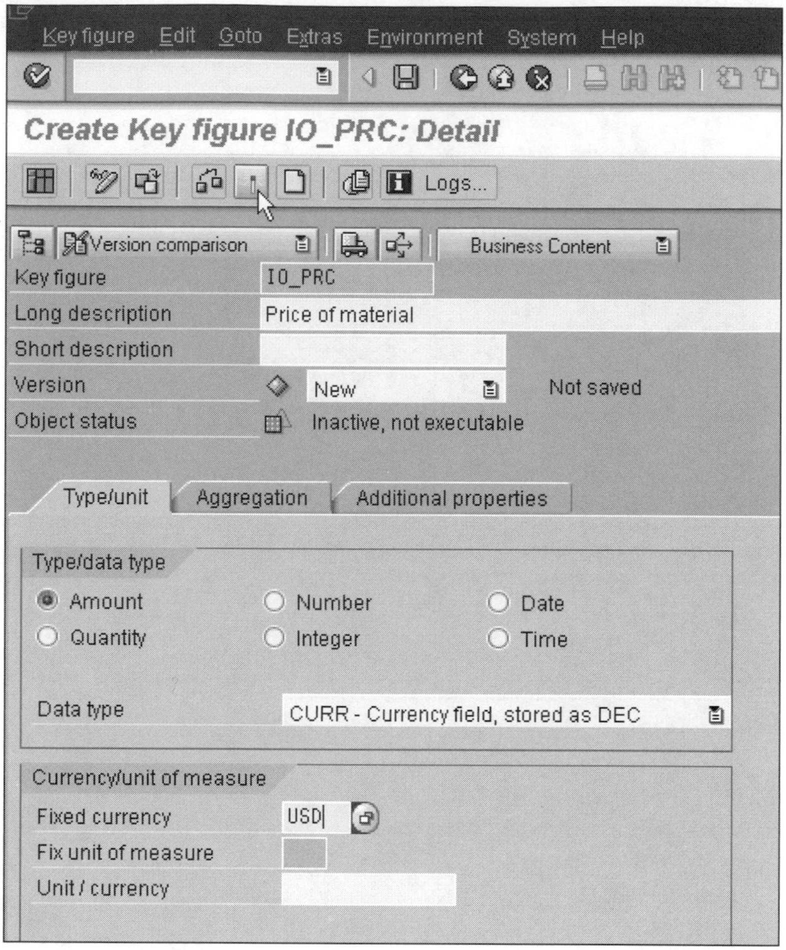

SCREEN 2.20

Result

You have created the key figure IO_PRC. A status message *All InfoObject(s) activated* will appear at the bottom of Screen 2.20.

Repeat the preceding steps to create other key figures listed in Table 2.2.

TABLE 2.2
KEY FIGURES

Key Figure Name and Description	Type/Data Type	Currency/Unit of Measure
IO_PRC Price of material	Amount	Fixed currency: USD
IO_QUAN Sales quantity	Quantity	Unit/currency: 0UNIT
IO_REV Sales revenue	Amount	Fixed currency: USD

From Administrator Workbench, we can verify that the key figures in Table 2.2 have been created (Screen 2.21) by clicking *InfoArea – demo*, and then clicking *InfoObject Catalog – demo: key figures*.

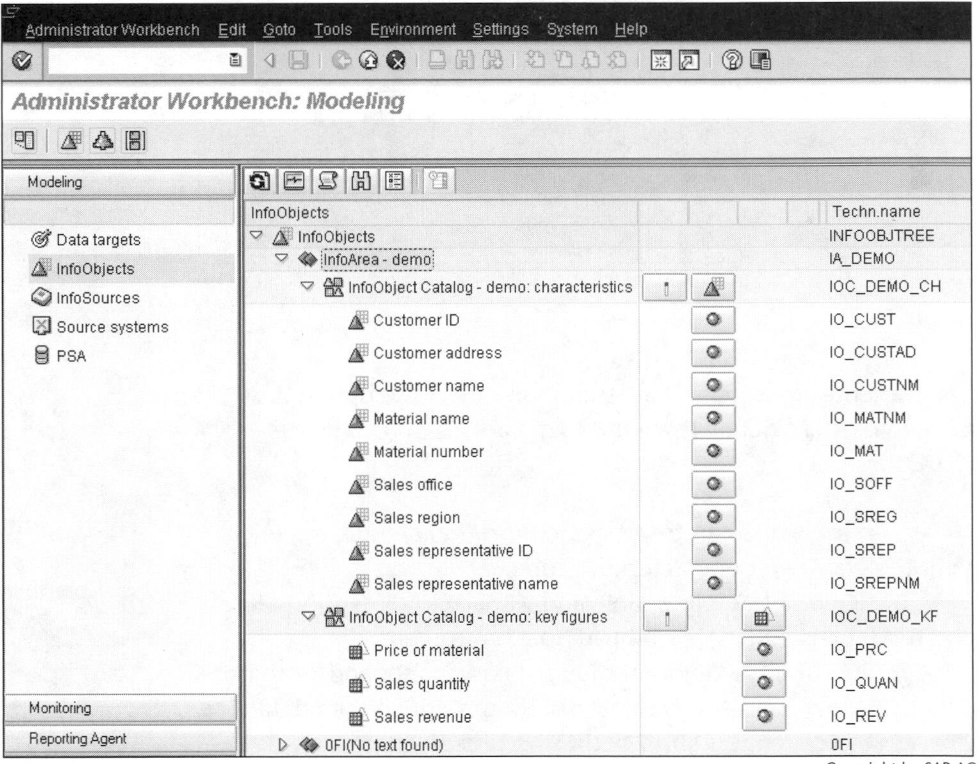

SCREEN 2.21

Having created the necessary InfoObjects, we now continue to create the InfoCube.

2.5 Creating an InfoCube

The following steps demonstrate how to create an InfoCube, the fact table and associated dimension tables, for the sales data shown in Table 1.4.

Work Instructions

Step 1 Select *Data targets* under *Modelling* in the left panel. In the right panel, right-click *InfoArea – demo* and then select *Create InfoCube. . . .*

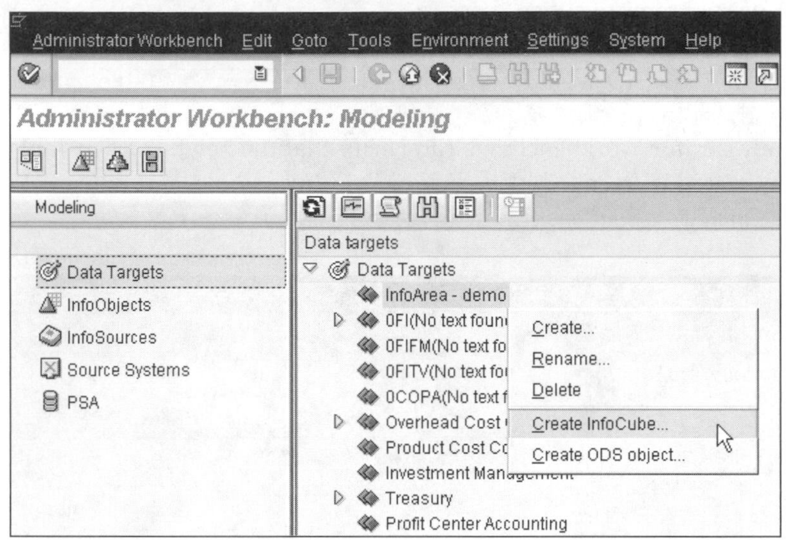

SCREEN 2.22

Step 2 Enter a name and a description, select the option *Basic Cube* in block *InfoCube type*, and then click [create icon] to create the InfoCube.

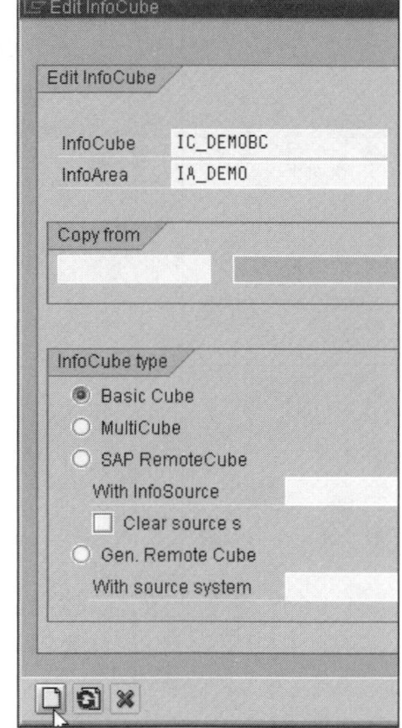

SCREEN 2.23

Note: An InfoCube can be a basic cube, a multi-cube, an SAP remote cube, or a general remote cube.

A **basic cube** has a fact table and associated dimension tables, and it contains data. We are building a basic cube.

A **multi-cube** is a union of multiple basic cubes and/or remote cubes to allow cross-subject analysis. It does not contain data. See Chapter 8, Aggregates and Multi-Cubes, for an example.

A **remote cube** does not contain data; instead, the data reside in the source system. A remote cube is analogous to a channel, allowing users to access the data using BEx. As a consequence, querying the data leads to poor performance.

If the source system is an SAP system, we need to select the option *SAP RemoteCube.* Otherwise, we need to select the option *Gen. Remote Cube.* This book will not discuss remote cubes.

Step 3 Select *IO_CUST*, *IO_MAT*, and *IO_SREP* from the *Template* table, and move them to the *Structure* table by clicking ◀.

Next, click the *Dimensions . . .* button to create dimensions and assign these characteristics to the dimensions.

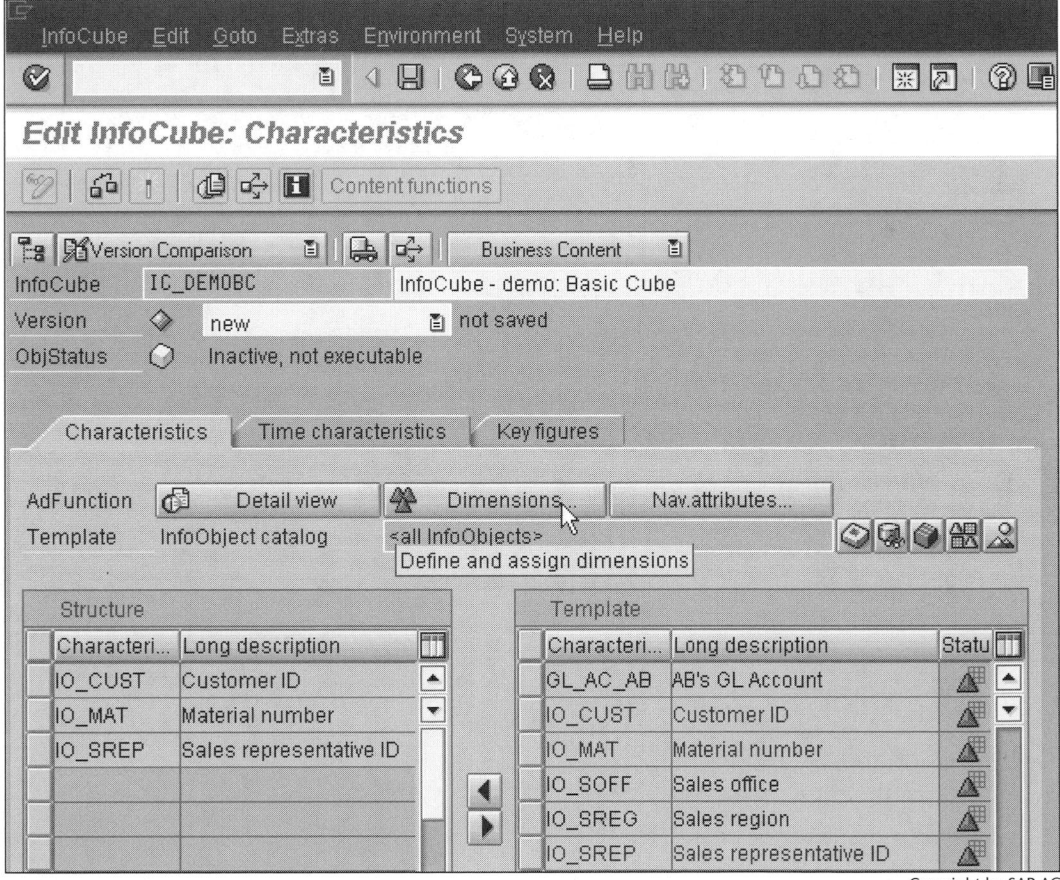

SCREEN 2.24

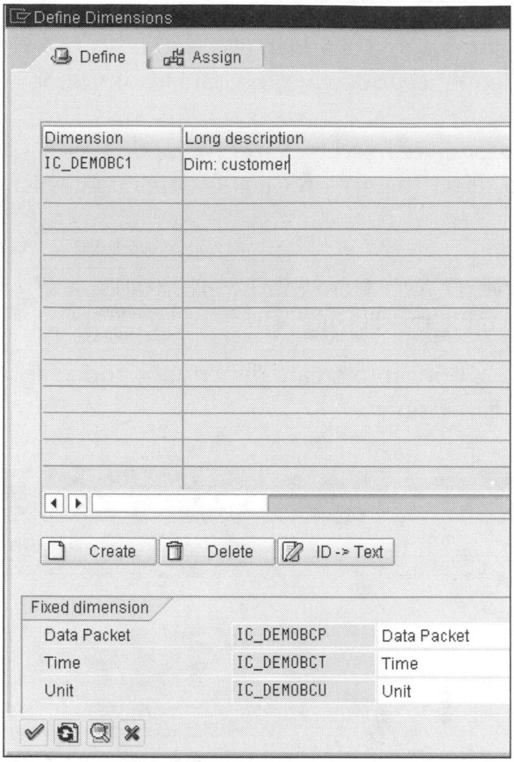

SCREEN 2.25

Step 4 Click Create, and then enter a description for the dimension.

Note: BW automatically assigns technical names to each dimension with the format <InfoCube name><Number starting from 1>.

Fixed dimension <InfoCube name><P|T|U> is reserved for Data Packet, Time, and Unit. Section 12.2.3, "Data Load Requests," discusses the Data Packet dimension.

A dimension uses a key column in the fact table. In most databases, a table can have a maximum of 16 key columns. Therefore, BW mandates that an InfoCube can have a maximum of 16 dimensions: three are reserved for Data Packet, Time, and Unit; the remaining 13 are left for us to use.

Repeat the same procedure to create two other dimensions. Next, click the *Assign* tab to assign the characteristics to the dimensions.

Step 5 Select a characteristic in the *Characteristics and assigned dimension* block, select a dimension to which the characteristic will be assigned in the *Dimensions* block, and then click Assign to assign the characteristic to the dimension.

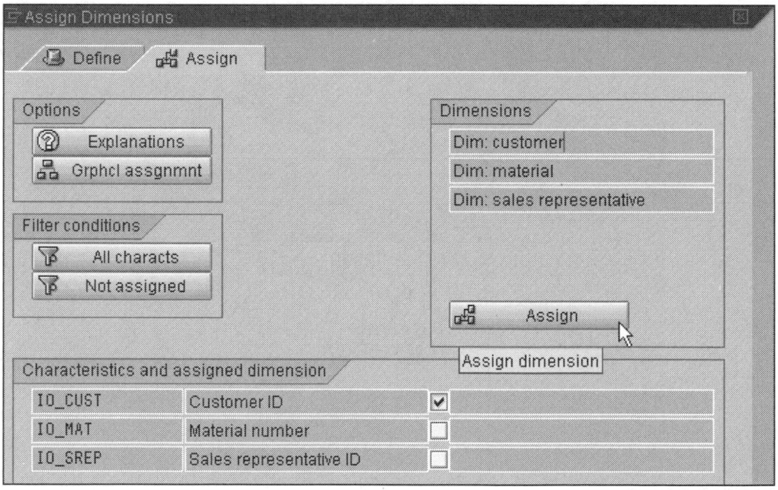

SCREEN 2.26

Step 6 After assigning all three characteristics to their dimensions, click ✔ to continue.

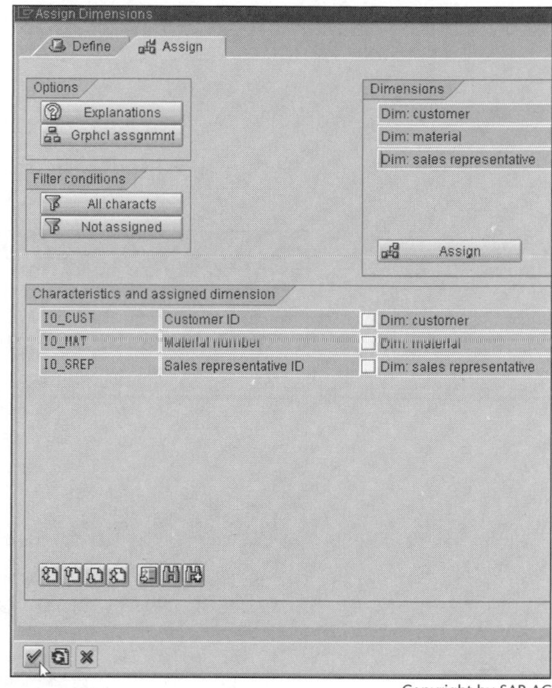

SCREEN 2.27

Step 7 Select the *Time characteristics* tab, select *0CALDAY* from the *Template* table, and move it to the *Structure* table by clicking ◀.

SCREEN 2.28

Step 8 Select the *Key figures* tab, select *IO_PRC*, *IO_QUAN*, and *IO_REV* from the *Template* table and move them to the *Structure* table by clicking .

Next, click to check the InfoCube. If it is valid, click to activate the InfoCube.

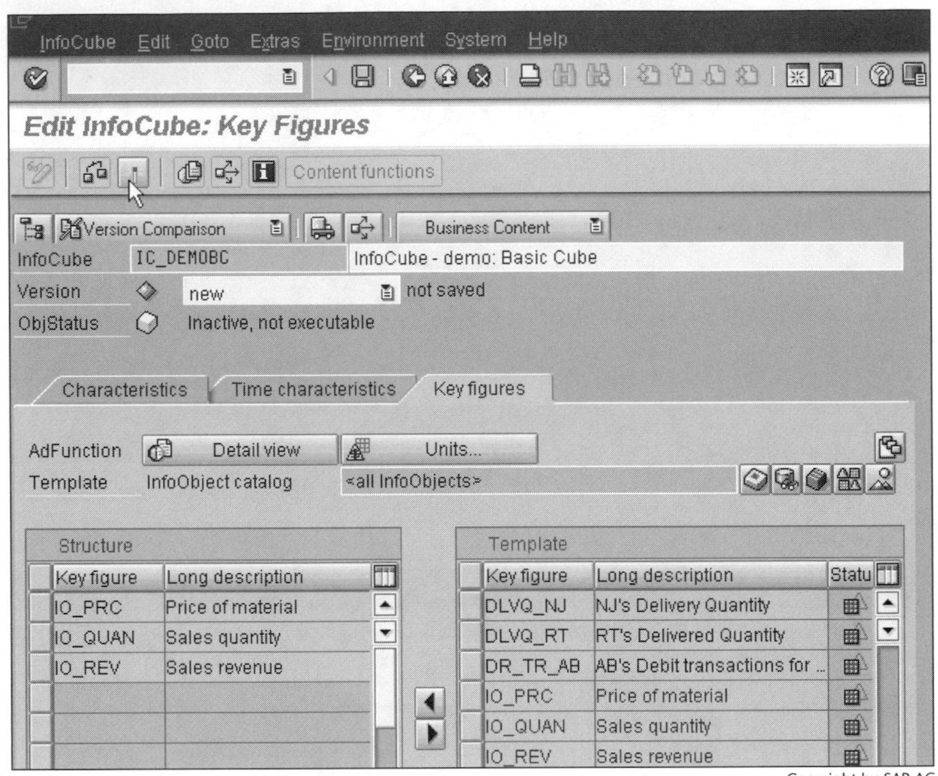

SCREEN 2.29

Result

You have created the InfoCube IC_DEMOBC. A status message *InfoCube IC_DEMOBC activated* will appear at the bottom of Screen 2.29.

2.6 Summary

In this chapter, we created an InfoCube. To display its data model, you can right-click *InfoCube – demo: Basic Cube*, then select *Display data model . . .* (Screen 2.30).

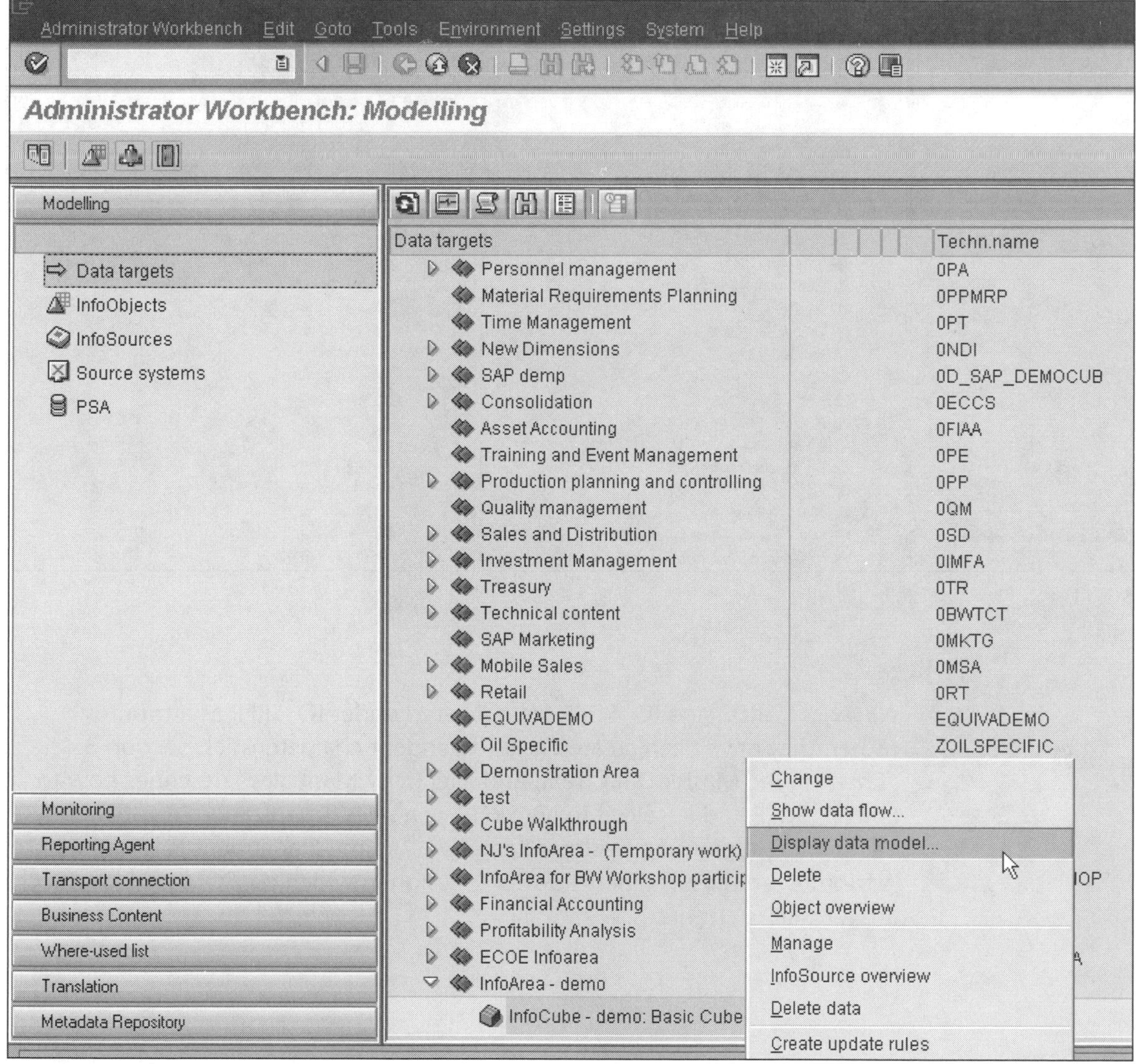

SCREEN 2.30

The data model appears in the right panel of Screen 2.31.

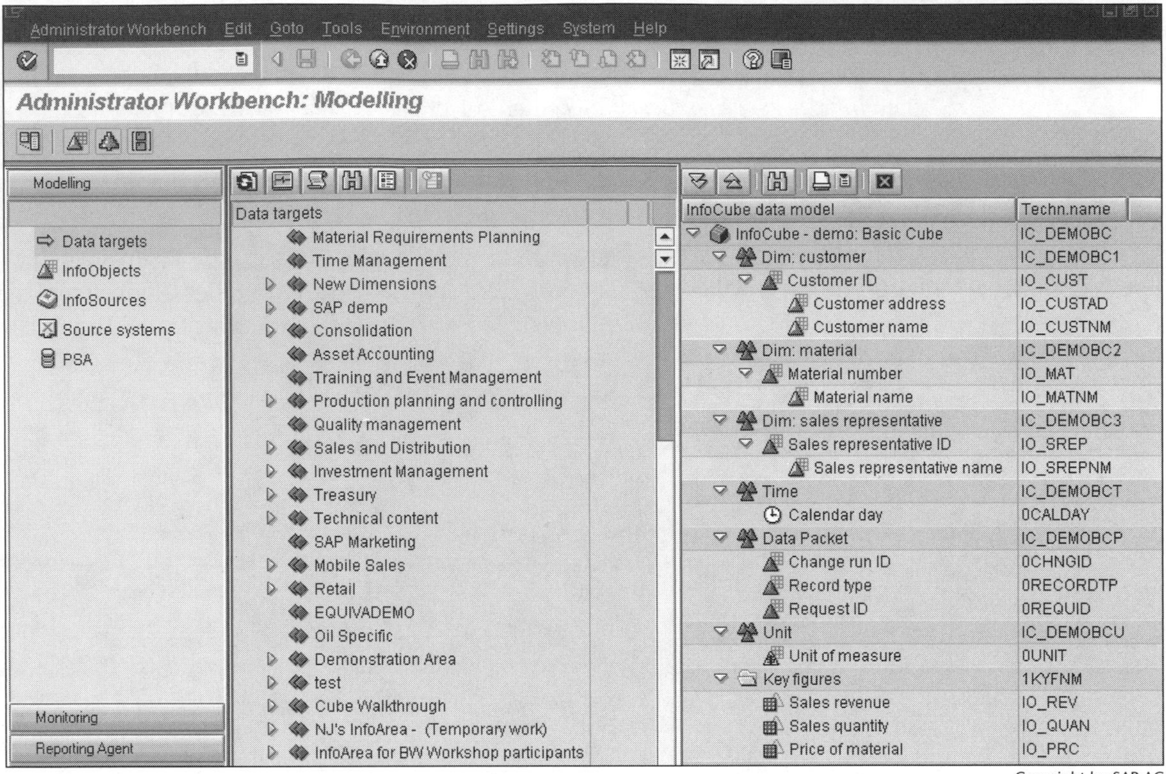

SCREEN 2.31

Note: IO_SREG and IO_SOFF are not listed under IO_SREP as attributes; rather, they have been created as independent characteristics. Section 3.6, "Entering the Master Data, Text, and Hierarchy Manually," describes how to link IO_SOFF and IO_SREG to IO_SREP via a sales organization hierarchy. Section 7.2, "InfoCube Design Alternative I—Time-Dependent Navigational Attributes," discusses a new InfoCube design in which IO_SOFF and IO_SREG are IO_SREP's attributes.

Key Terms

Term	Description
Key figure	Key figures are numeric values or quantities, such as Per Unit Sales Price, Quantity Sold, and Sales Revenue. The maximum number of characters allowed for the technical name is 9.
Characteristic	Characteristics are descriptions of key figures, such as Customer ID, Material Number, Sales Representative ID, Unit of Measure, and Transaction Date. The maximum number of characters allowed for the technical name is 9.
InfoObject	In BW, key figures and characteristics are collectively called InfoObjects.
InfoObject Catalog	InfoObject Catalogs are used to organize InfoObjects. Two types of InfoObject Catalogs exist: one for characteristics and one for key figures. The maximum number of characters allowed for the technical name is 30.
InfoArea	InfoAreas are used to organize InfoCubes and InfoObjects. Each InfoCube is assigned to an InfoArea. Through an InfoObject Catalog, each InfoObject is assigned to an InfoArea as well. The maximum number of characters allowed for the technical name is 30.
InfoCube	An InfoCube consists of a fact table and its associated dimension tables in the star schema. The maximum number of characters allowed for the technical name is 30.

Next . . .

We will load the data described in Chapter 1, Business Scenario and SAP BW, into the InfoCube.

Chapter 3

Loading Data into the InfoCube

In Chapter 2, we created an InfoCube. In this chapter, we will demonstrate how to load the data described in Chapter 1 into this InfoCube. From a data integrity and load performance point of view, we will load the characteristic data (Tables 1.1 through 1.3) before the transaction data (Table 1.4).

Data reside in source systems. In the example used in this chapter, the data reside in our PC in four Microsoft Excel files. To set up a protocol to ensure that BW knows where to find these files and how to extract the data, we must define a **source system** in BW. To schedule a load, we must also define a BW object called **InfoPackage**.

For the InfoPackage to know the structure of the data's destination (either a characteristic or an InfoCube), we must define yet another BW object called **InfoSource**. If the destination is an InfoCube, after the data pass through the

InfoSource, BW allows us to aggregate key figures. In BW, this aggregation procedure is called an **update rule**.

With this background information in mind, now let's define a source system so BW knows where to find the data.

3.1 Creating a Source System

A BW system can accept data from all kinds of source systems, such as the following:

- R/3 systems
- BW systems
- Flat files
- External systems through third-party ETTL tools

The following procedure shows how to create a flat file source system. Chapter 10, Business Content, describes how to create an R/3 source system.

Work Instructions

Step 1 Select *Source systems* under *Modelling* in the left panel. In the right panel, right-click *Source systems* and select *Create. . . .*

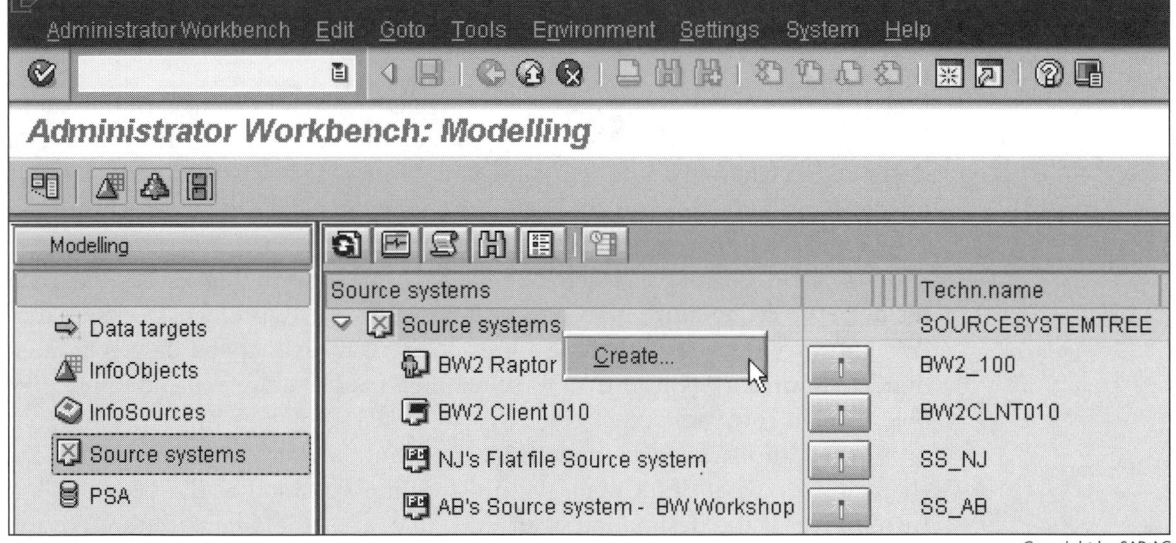

SCREEN 3.1

Step 2 Select the *FileSystem, manual meta data, data using file inte* option, and then click to continue.

SCREEN 3.2

Select Source System Type

SAP R/3, automatic creation (from release 3.

SAP R/3, manual creation (from release 3.0D)

BW Business Information Warehouse

FileSystem, manual meta data, data using file inte

Ext.System, data and meta data transfer-staging

Step 3 Enter a name and a description for the source system, and then click to create the source system.

SCREEN 3.3

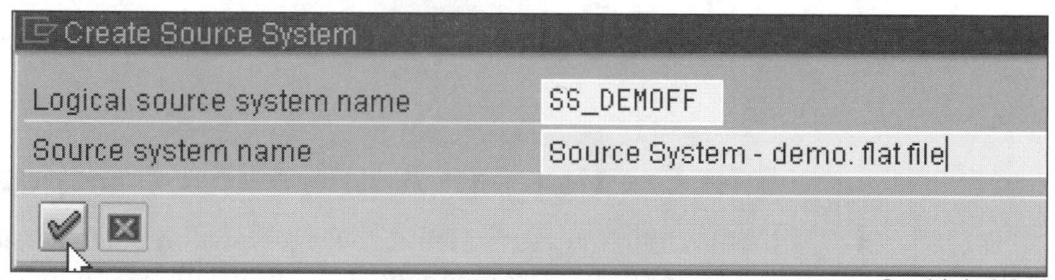

Result

You have created the source system. A status message *Source system SS_DEMOFF creation successful finished* will appear at the bottom of Screen 3.4.

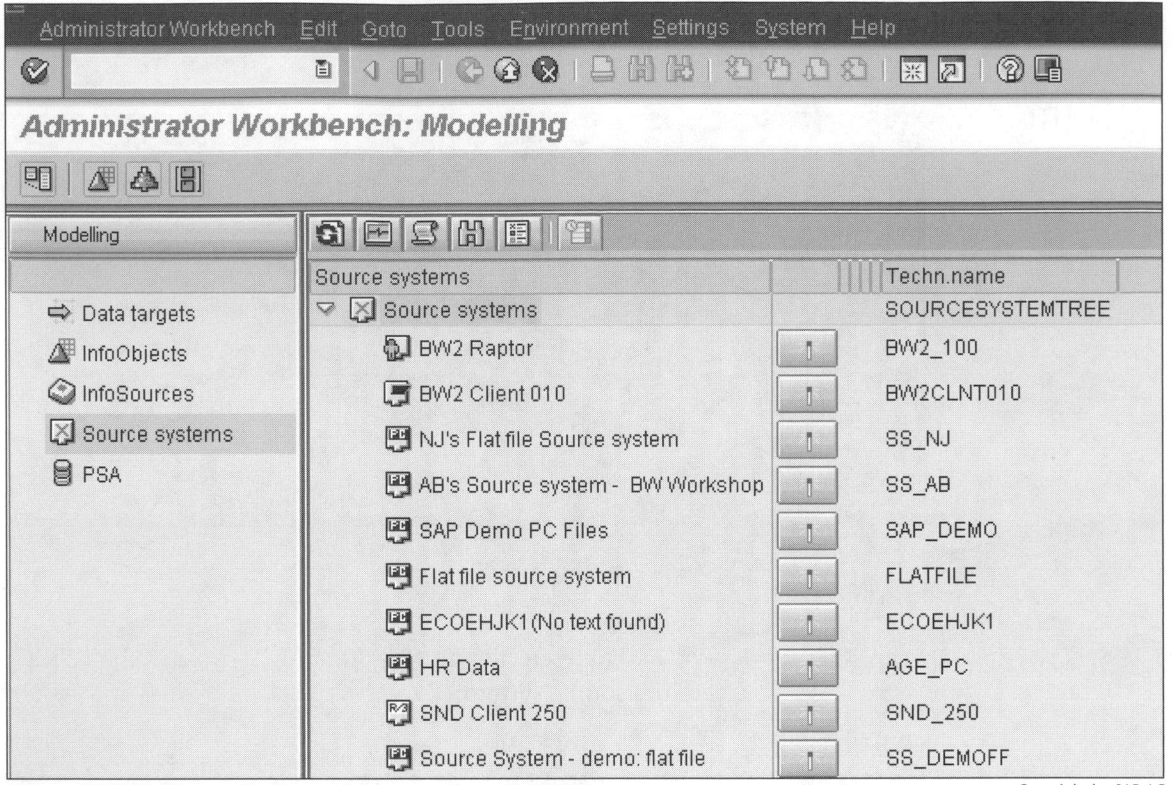

SCREEN 3.4

3.2 Creating an Application Component

In BW, InfoSources and InfoPackages are organized using a tree structure called **application components**. The application components are analogous to the InfoAreas for InfoCubes. Next, we create an application component.

Work Instructions

Step 1 Select *InfoSources* under *Modelling* in the left panel. In the right panel, right-click *InfoSources* and select *Create application component. . . .*

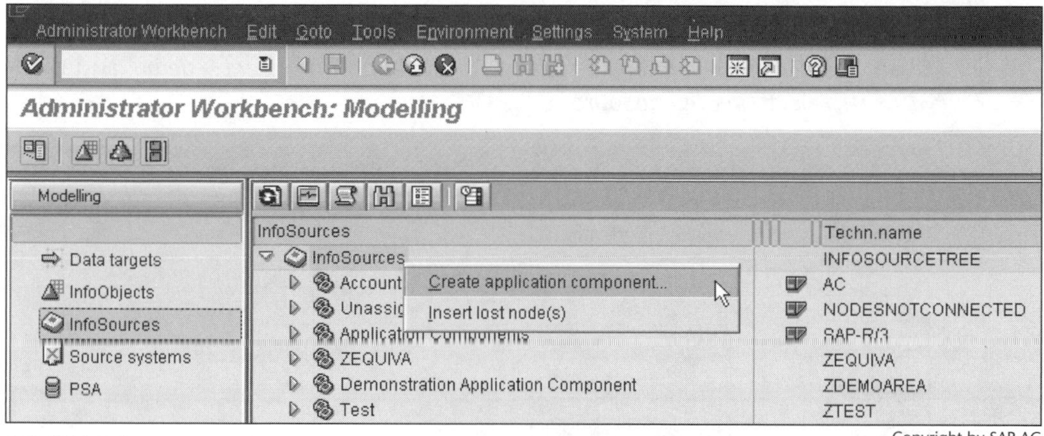

Copyright by SAP AG

SCREEN 3.5

Step 2 Enter a name and a description for the application component, and then click ✔ to continue.

Copyright by SAP AG

SCREEN 3.6

Result

The application component has been created, as shown in Screen 3.7.

Note: BW adds a prefix of "Z" to the technical names of application components, unlike the naming system used for other BW objects.

3.3 Creating an InfoSource for Characteristic Data

In Chapter 1, we learned that ETTL is a challenging task. BW uses InfoSources and **transfer rules** to define the mapping and transformation rules that govern the ETTL process.

In this section, we use IO_MAT as an example to show how to define an InfoSource and transfer rules for characteristic data. In Section 3.6, we will discuss how to define an InfoSource and transfer rules for transaction data.

Work Instructions

Step 1 Right-click the newly created *Application Component – demo*, and then select *Create InfoSource. . . .*

SCREEN 3.7

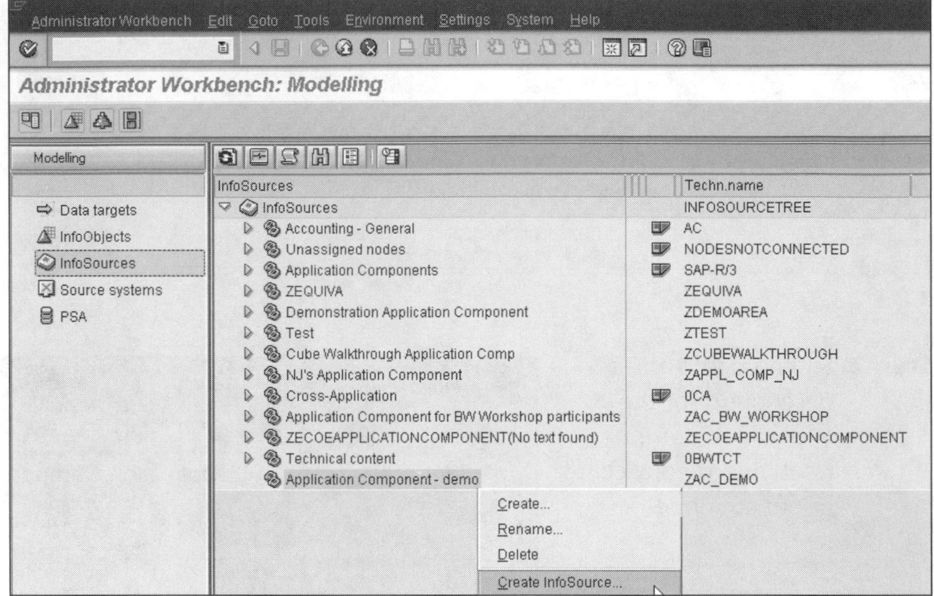

Copyright by SAP AG

Step 2 Select the option *Master data/texts/hierarchies*, and then click ✓ to continue.

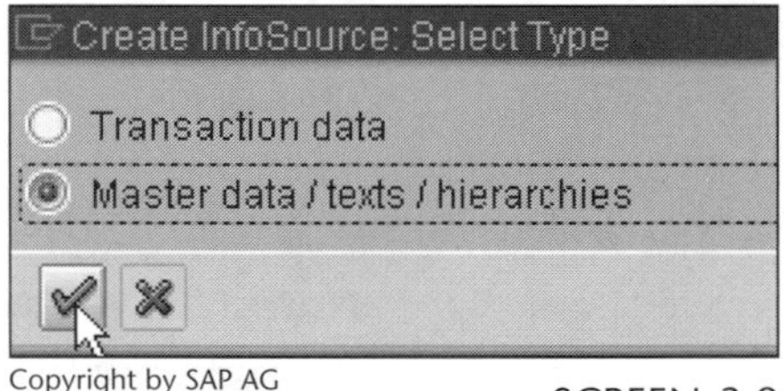

Copyright by SAP AG

SCREEN 3.8

Note: In BW, characteristic data can consist of master data, texts, and hierarchies. Selecting this option ensures that the InfoSource to be created will apply to a characteristic. Section 7.1, "BW Star Schema," discusses master data, texts, and hierarchies and explains their relationships to characteristics.

SCREEN 3.9

Copyright by SAP AG

Step 3 Enter IO_MAT, and then click ✓ to continue.

Step 4 Click ✓) to pass the message.

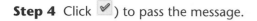

Information
InfoSource IO_MAT (Master data) assigned to
application component ZAC_DEMO

SCREEN 3.10

Step 5 Now we need to tell the newly created InfoSource where to find the data and what the transfer rules are. Right-click *Material number*, and then select *Assign DataSource. . . .*

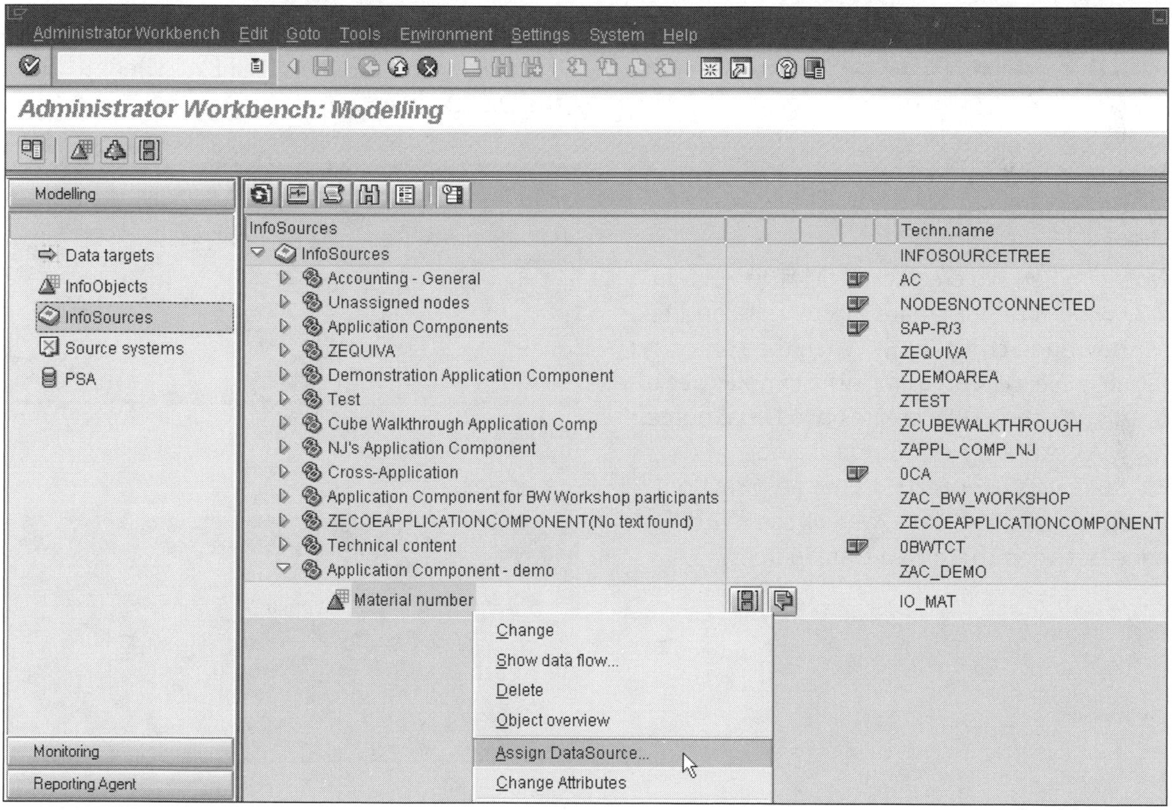

Administrator Workbench Edit Goto Tools Environment Settings System Help
Administrator Workbench: Modelling
Modelling
Data targets
InfoObjects
InfoSources
Source systems
PSA
Monitoring
Reporting Agent

InfoSources	Techn.name
InfoSources	INFOSOURCETREE
Accounting - General	AC
Unassigned nodes	NODESNOTCONNECTED
Application Components	SAP-R/3
ZEQUIVA	ZEQUIVA
Demonstration Application Component	ZDEMOAREA
Test	ZTEST
Cube Walkthrough Application Comp	ZCUBEWALKTHROUGH
NJ's Application Component	ZAPPL_COMP_NJ
Cross-Application	0CA
Application Component for BW Workshop participants	ZAC_BW_WORKSHOP
ZECOEAPPLICATIONCOMPONENT(No text found)	ZECOEAPPLICATIONCOMPONENT
Technical content	0BWTCT
Application Component - demo	ZAC_DEMO
Material number	IO_MAT

Change
Show data flow...
Delete
Object overview
Assign DataSource...
Change Attributes

SCREEN 3.11

Note: A **DataSource** is not only a structure in which source system fields are logically grouped together, but also an object that contains ETTL-related information. Four types of DataSources exist:

- DataSources for transaction data
- DataSources for characteristic attributes
- DataSources for characteristic texts
- DataSources for characteristic hierarchies

Chapter 11, Generic R/3 Data Extraction, discusses how to create a DataSource.

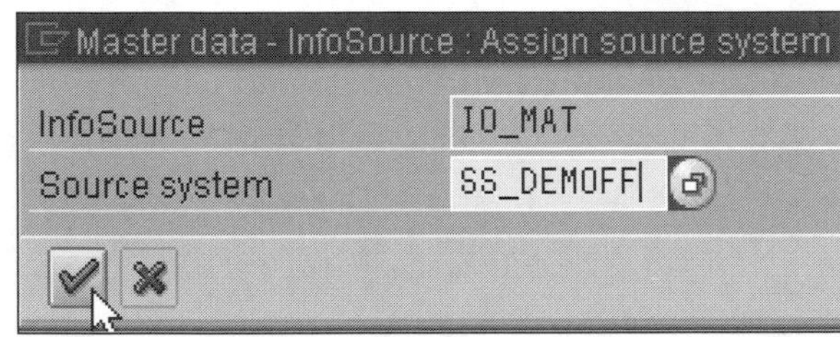

SCREEN 3.12 Copyright by SAP AG

Step 6 Enter the source system created in Section 3.1, *SS_DEMOFF*, in the field *Source system*, and then click ✔ to continue.

Note: DataSources are associated with source systems, so we must first tell BW where to find the DataSources.

Step 7 Click Yes to pass these two messages.

Note: When we created IO_MAT in Section 2.3, we elected to create master data and texts as shown in Screen 2.16. When the source system is a file system, as in this example, because of this selection, BW creates two DataSources: IO_MAT_ATTR for master data, and IO_MAT_TEXT for texts. In the next section, when we load the data, we will see the difference between these two DataSources.

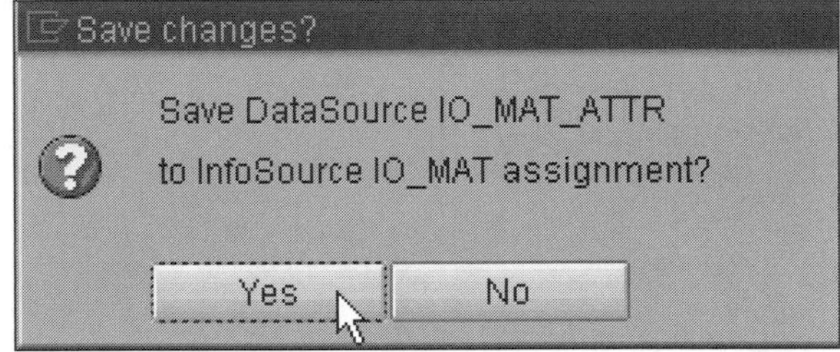

SCREEN 3.13 Copyright by SAP AG

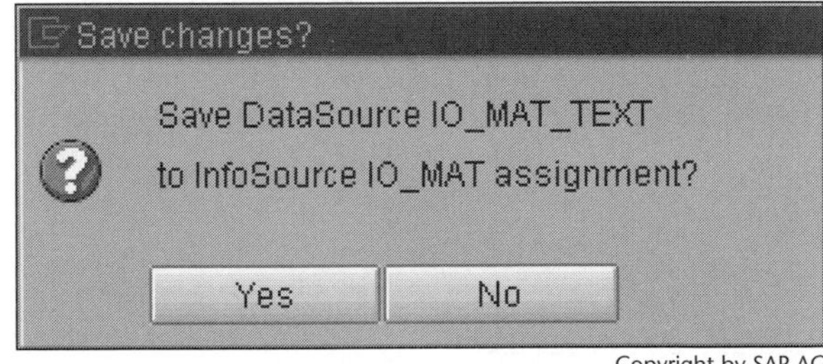

SCREEN 3.14 Copyright by SAP AG

Step 8 Click to activate the transfer rules.

Note: The icon in the *Tp* column indicates that the transfer rule is a simple one-to-one mapping. By default, BW defines simple one-to-one transfer rules. In this case, we accept the default definition. We will show how to use ABAP to define transfer rules in Section 3.7, "Creating an InfoSource for Transaction Data."

SCREEN 3.15

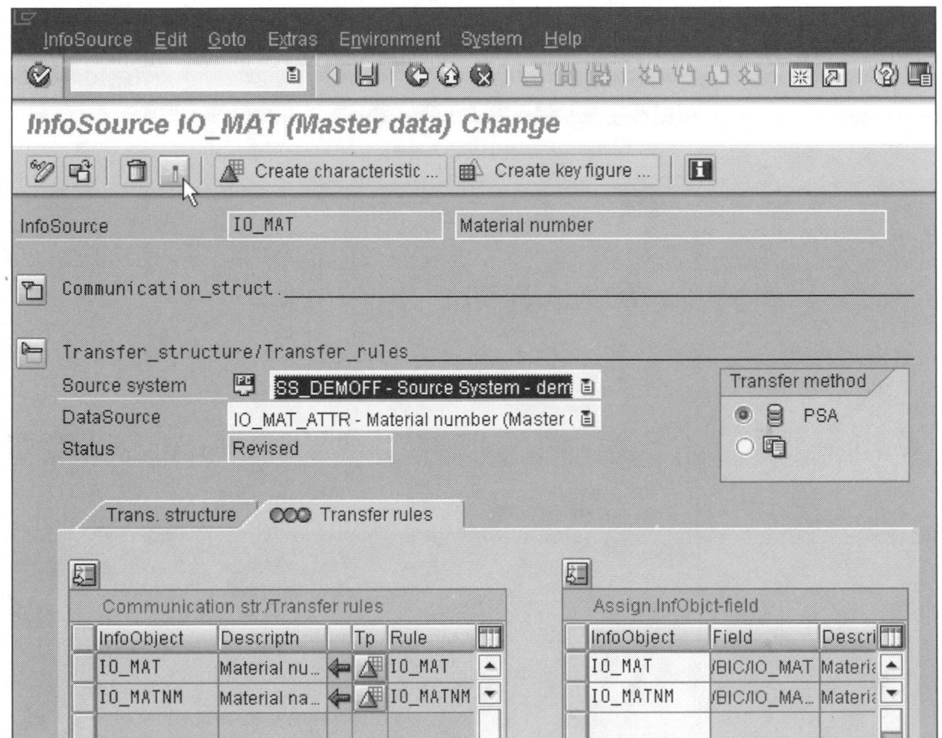

Result

We have created an InfoSource and transfer rules. A status message *Transfer rules IO_MAT_ATTR_AH activated* will appear at the bottom of Screen 3.15.

Now that the InfoSource and transfer rules are in place, we can create InfoPackages to load the characteristic data.

3.4 Creating InfoPackages to Load Characteristic Data

BW uses InfoPackages to define how to select data, and when to transfer and load the data. In BW, a characteristic can consist of three data components:

- Master data, or attributes as they are sometimes called
- Text
- Hierarchy

Section 7.1, "BW Star Schema," discusses master data, texts, and hierarchies and explains their relationships to characteristics.

Each part requires an InfoPackage. This section describes how to create InfoPackages to load master data and text. The next section covers entering master data and text manually.

Work Instructions

Step 1 Right-click *Source System – demo: flat file*, and then select *Create InfoPackage. . . .*

SCREEN 3.16

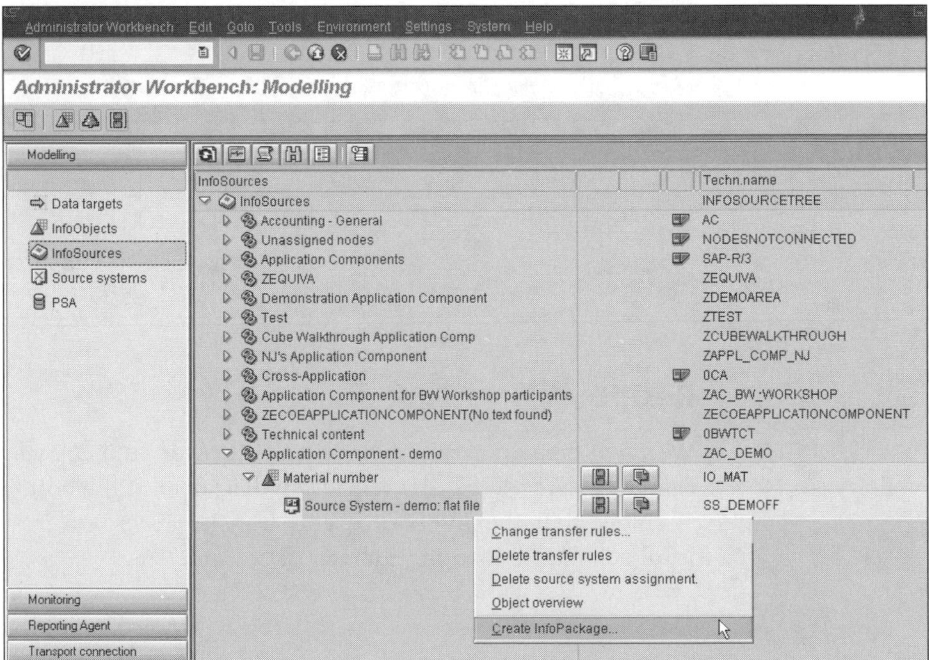

Step 2 Select the DataSource *Material number (Master data)*, enter a description for the InfoPackage, and then click ✔ to continue.

SCREEN 3.17

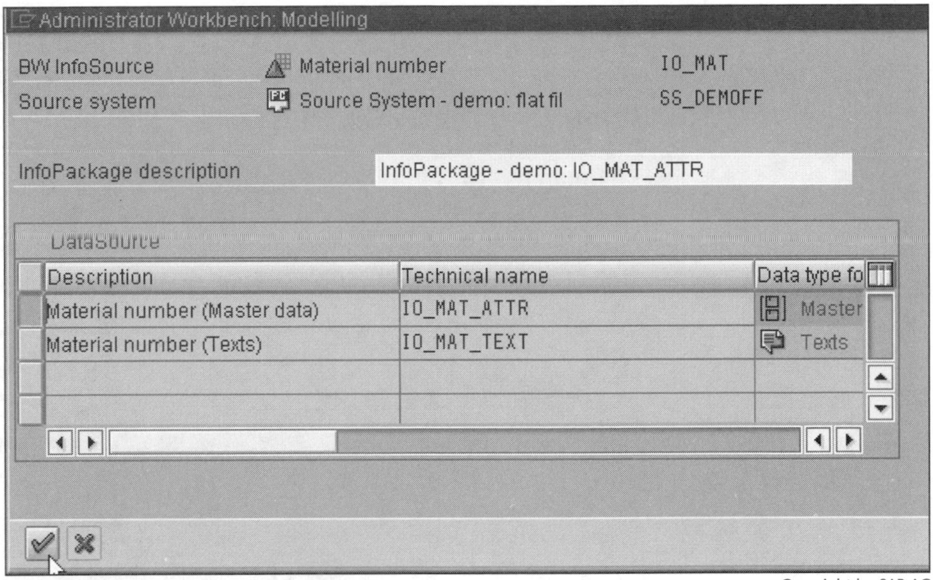

Copyright by SAP AG

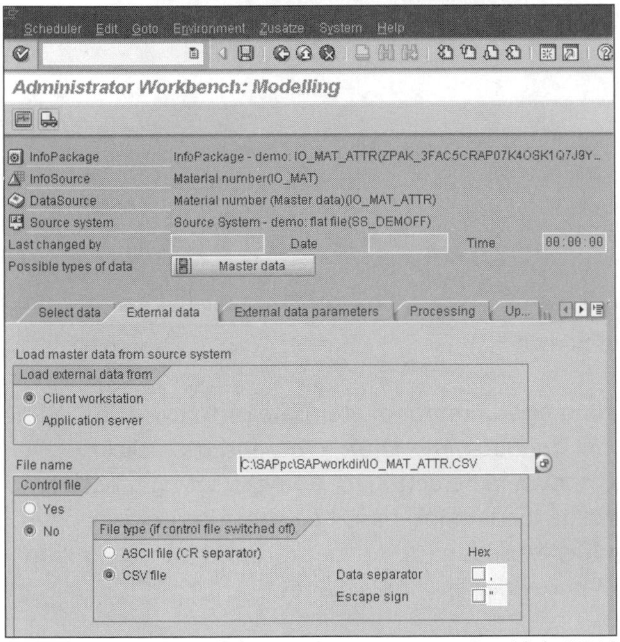

Step 3 Click the *External data* tab. Select options as shown in the screen. Enter a file name with a path. The file contains the data given in Table 3.1.

Note: The data file can reside on a front-end computer (or *Client workstation* as it is called here) or one of the application servers in the SAP Basis three-tier architecture. In our example, IO_MAT_ATTR.CSV resides in our front-end computer. For better loading performance, it is recommended that you place data files in application server computers.

Copyright by SAP AG

SCREEN 3.18

Step 4 Click the *Schedule* tab, select the option *Start data load immediately*, and then click to load data.

SCREEN 3.19

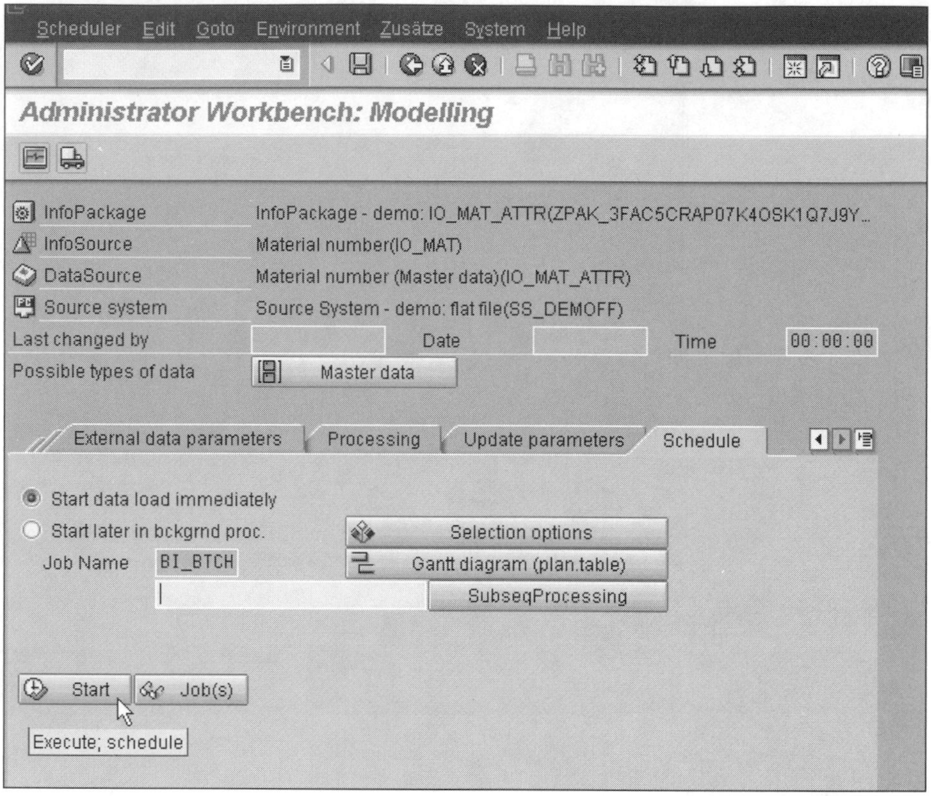

Result

The staging engine starts to load the data. A status message *Data was requested* will appear at the bottom of Screen 3.19.

Note: To schedule the loading operation for a later date or to execute loading periodically, select the option *Start later in bckgrnd proc*, and then click . A pop-up window appears, as shown in Screen 3.20. You can set up a background process to start the data loading job based on the criteria specified in Screen 3.20. The same window is used in R/3 for background job scheduling. In essence, BW Scheduler is embedded in InfoPackages.

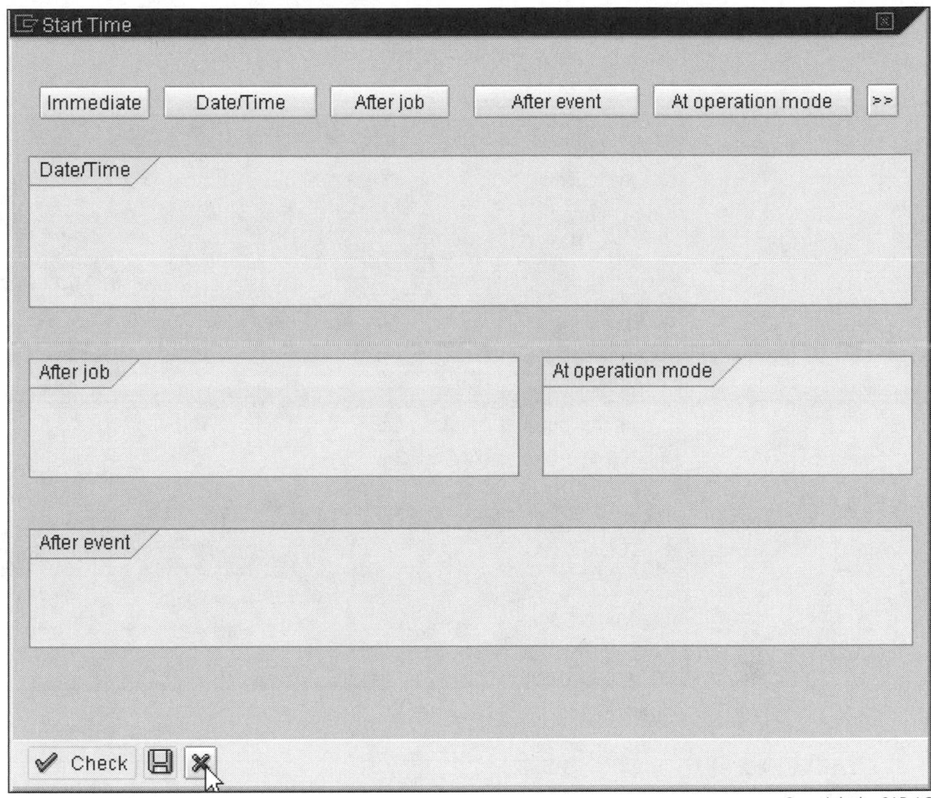

SCREEN 3.20

TABLE 3.1 MATERIAL NUMBER—MASTER DATA

MAT001	TEA
MAT002	COFFEE
MAT003	COOKIE
MAT004	DESK
MAT005	TABLE
MAT006	CHAIR
MAT007	BENCH
MAT008	PEN
MAT009	PAPER
MAT010	CORN
MAT011	RICE
MAT012	APPLE
MAT013	GRAPEFRUIT
MAT014	PEACH
MAT015	ORANGE

By repeating this procedure and selecting *DataSource Material number (Texts)* (Screen 3.21), we can load the texts in Table 3.2.

SCREEN 3.21

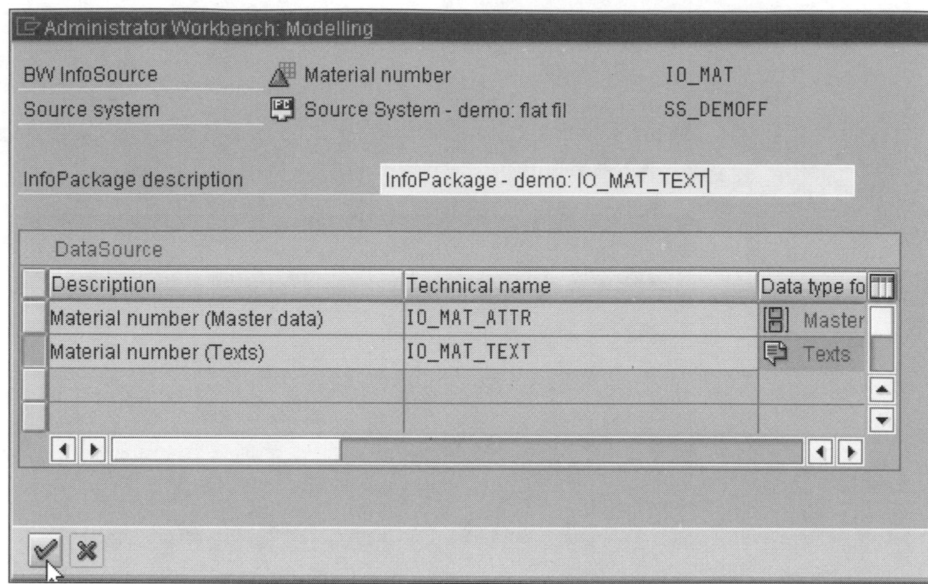

TABLE 3.2 MATERIAL NUMBER—TEXTS

E	MAT001	Ice tea
E	MAT002	Hot coffee
E	MAT003	Fortune cookie
E	MAT004	Computer desk
E	MAT005	Dining table
E	MAT006	Leather chair
E	MAT007	Wood bench
E	MAT008	Black pen
E	MAT009	White paper
E	MAT010	America corn
E	MAT011	Asia rice
E	MAT012	New York apple
E	MAT013	Florida grapefruit
E	MAT014	Washington peach
E	MAT015	California orange

The first column specifies the language of the texts, with "E" indicating English.

3.5 Checking Loaded Characteristic Data

Before we check the loaded characteristic data, let's confirm that the load operation was successful.

Work Instructions

Step 1 Click [icon] to view the status of the data load. It leads us to BW Monitor.

SCREEN 3.22

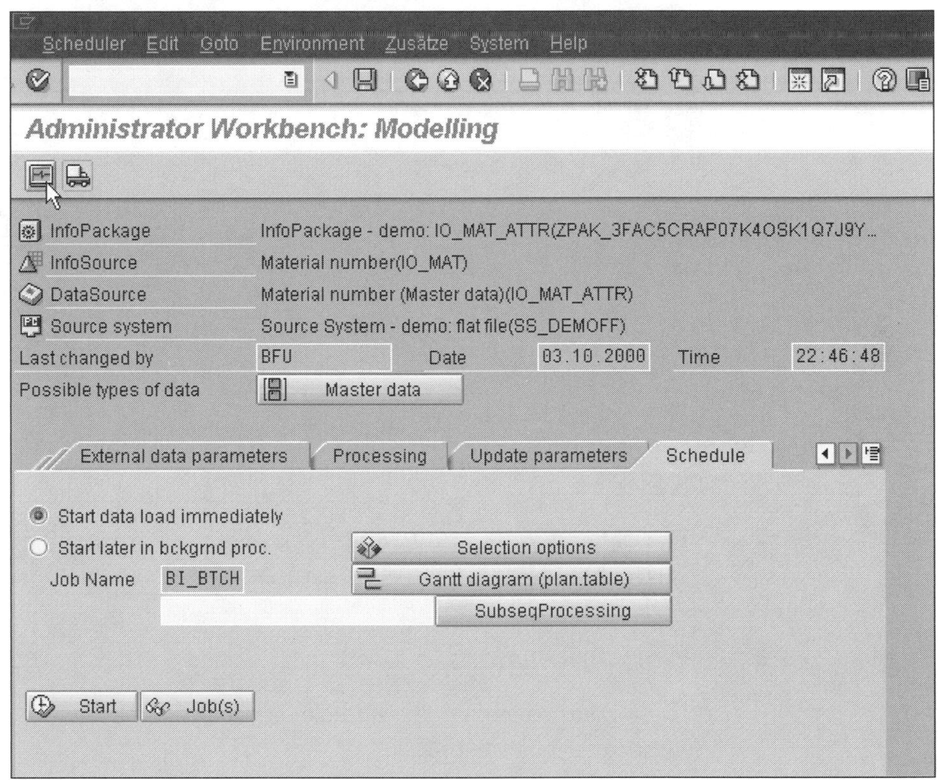

Step 2 Click [icon] to view the status of all data loads triggered by this InfoPackage.

SCREEN 3.23

Step 3 Green lights in the left panel indicate that the data have been loaded successfully.

SCREEN 3.24

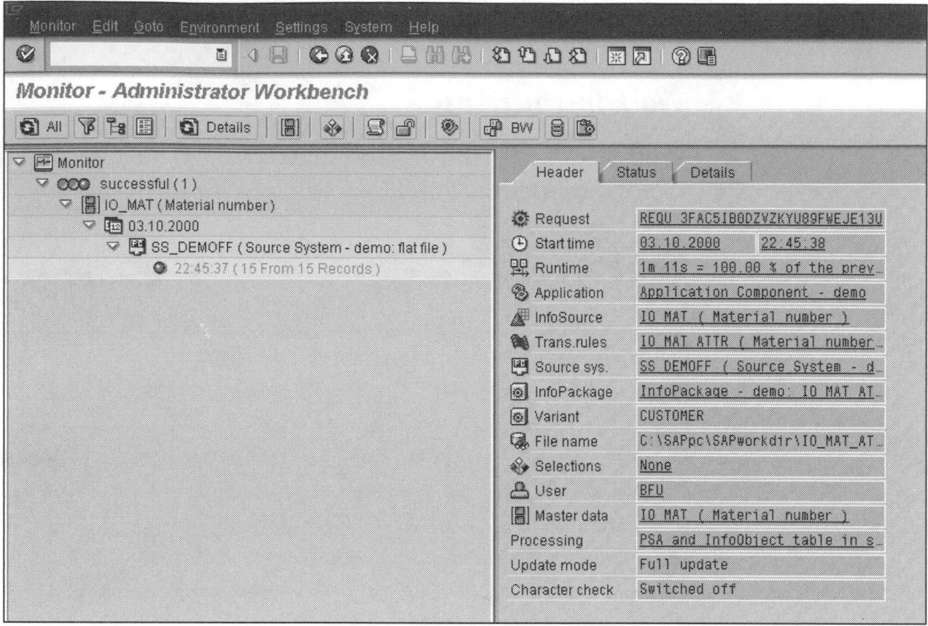

Result

The data are now in IO_MAT. Next, we will display the IO_MAT contents to verify that the data have been loaded correctly.

Work Instructions

The loaded characteristic data can be displayed in many ways. The next set of steps describes one of them.

Step 1 Right-click the characteristic *Material number*, and then select *Maintain master data*.

Note: The two under *Material number* indicate the InfoPackages we created in Section 3.4.

SCREEN 3.25

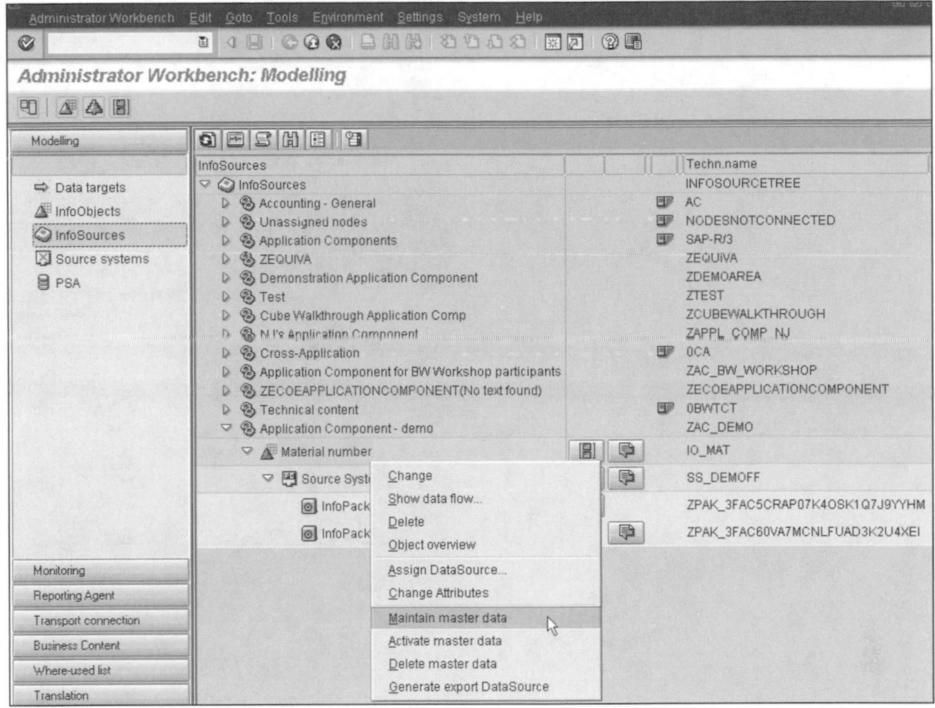

Program Edit Goto System Help

Characteristic IO_MAT - Maintain master data: Selection

Material number | to

Language key EN

Material name | to

Maximum no. of hits 1,000

SCREEN 3.26

Step 2 Click [icon] to display the contents.

Note: To see only some of the data in IO_MAT, we can use the text fields in this screen to specify selection conditions. For example, the selection conditions in this screen specify that a maximum of 1,000 entries with texts in English will be displayed.

Result

The loaded data—both master data and texts—are displayed in Screen 3.27; they are correct.

SCREEN 3.27

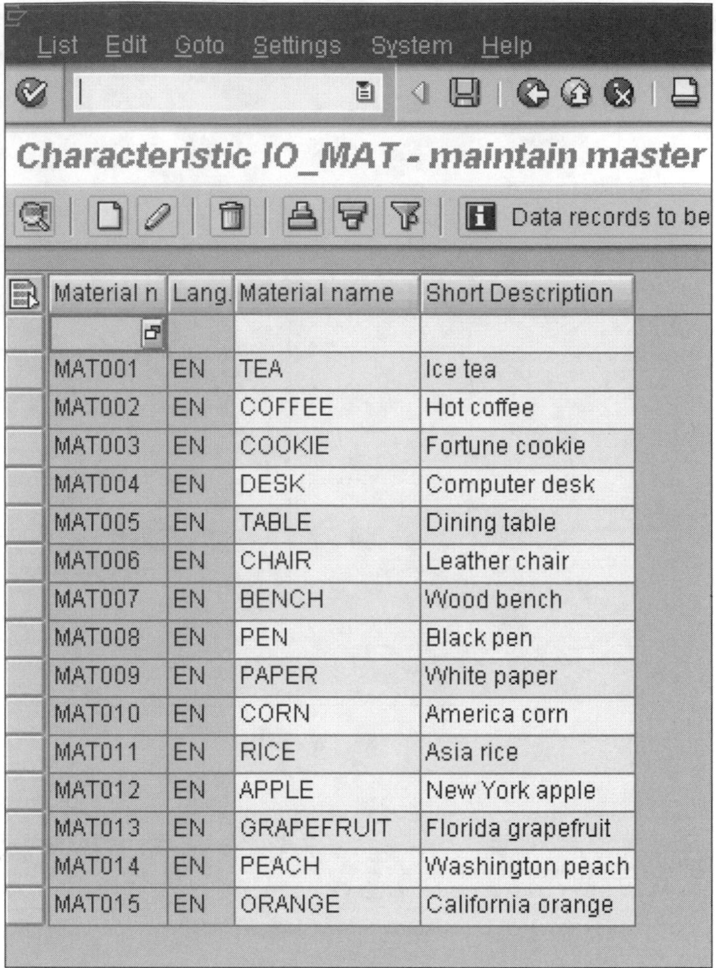

Material n	Lang.	Material name	Short Description
MAT001	EN	TEA	Ice tea
MAT002	EN	COFFEE	Hot coffee
MAT003	EN	COOKIE	Fortune cookie
MAT004	EN	DESK	Computer desk
MAT005	EN	TABLE	Dining table
MAT006	EN	CHAIR	Leather chair
MAT007	EN	BENCH	Wood bench
MAT008	EN	PEN	Black pen
MAT009	EN	PAPER	White paper
MAT010	EN	CORN	America corn
MAT011	EN	RICE	Asia rice
MAT012	EN	APPLE	New York apple
MAT013	EN	GRAPEFRUIT	Florida grapefruit
MAT014	EN	PEACH	Washington peach
MAT015	EN	ORANGE	California orange

Chapter 4 discusses how to check data quality in an InfoCube.

3.6 Entering the Master Data, Text, and Hierarchy Manually

Using the procedure given in Section 3.5, we can not only display characteristic data, but also enter new data and change existing data. In this section, we use a different technique. First, we show how to enter master data and texts for characteristic IO_SREG. Then, we describe how to create a hierarchy for IO_SREP.

3.6.1 Master Data and Text

Work Instructions

Step 1 Select *InfoObjects* under *Modelling* in the left panel, right-click *Sales region,* and then select *Maintain master data* in the right panel.

SCREEN 3.28

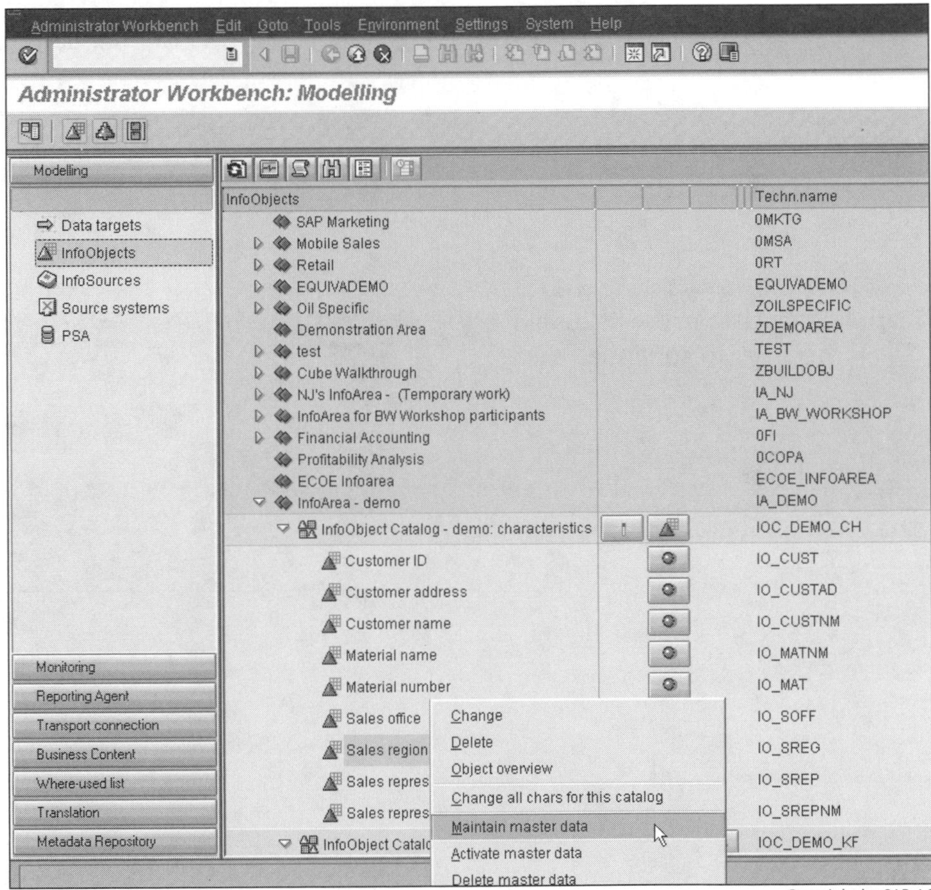

Program Edit Goto System Help
Characteristic IO_SREG - Maintain master data: Selection
Sales region
Language key
EN
Maximum no. of hits
1,000

SCREEN 3.29

Step 2 Click to display master data.

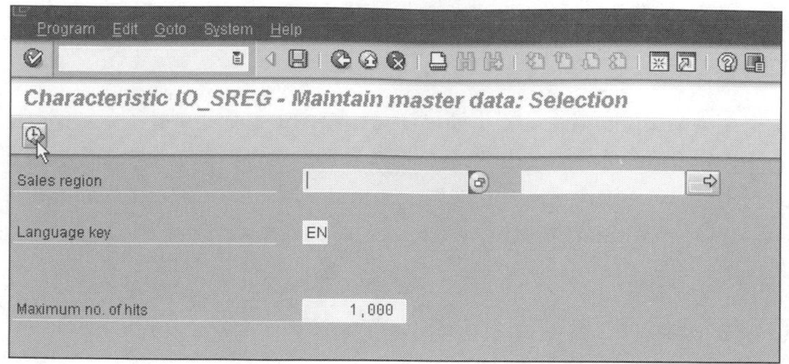

Step 3 Click to create a record.

List Edit Goto Settings System Help
Characteristic IO_SREG - maintain master data: List
Data records to be edited
Sales regi
L
Descriptn

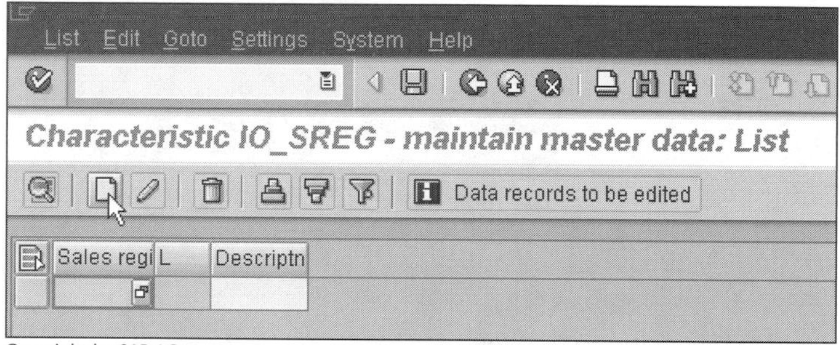

SCREEN 3.30

Step 4 Enter data in the fields and click to continue.

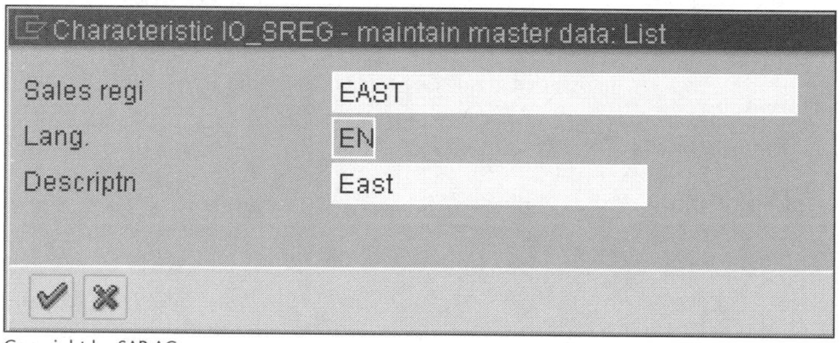

Characteristic IO_SREG - maintain master data: List
Sales regi
EAST
Lang.
EN
Descriptn
East

SCREEN 3.31

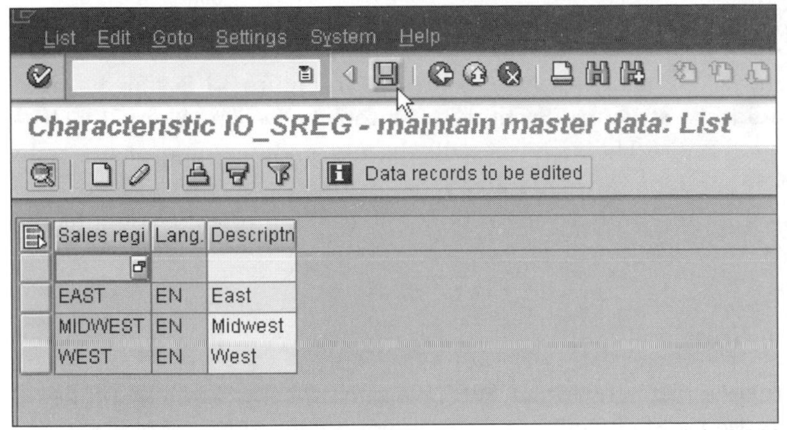

SCREEN 3.32

Step 5 Repeat Steps 3 and 4 to enter two more records, and then click [save icon] to save the data into the database.

Result

You have entered data into IO_SREG. A status message *Data has been saved* will appear at the bottom of Screen 3.32.

Repeat the same procedure to enter data into IO_SOFF.

3.6.2 Hierarchy

Table 1.3 is actually a hierarchy. It should look like the hierarchy depicted in Figure 3.1 when we visualize the table data.

FIGURE 3.1 TIME-DEPENDENT HIERARCHY STRUCTURES

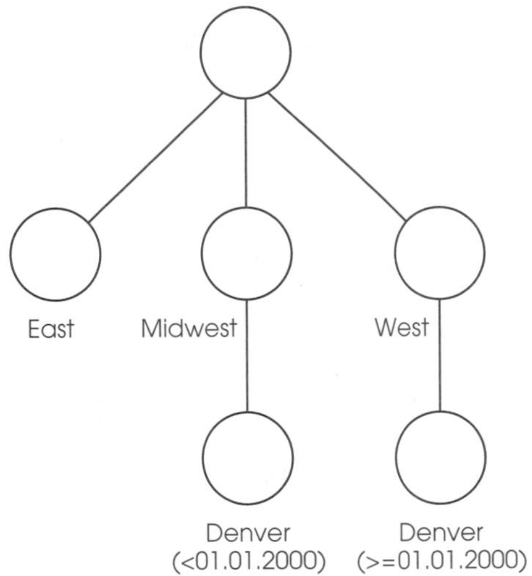

This hierarchy indicates the Denver office was in the Midwest region before January 1, 2000. On and after January 1, 2000, the Denver office was part of the West region. In BW, a hierarchy such as the one in Figure 3.1 is called a **time-dependent hierarchy structure**. Section 7.4, "InfoCube Design Alternative III—Time-Dependent Entire Hierarchies," will discuss another type of hierarchy called a **time-dependent entire hierarchy**.

The following procedure describes how to create a time-dependent hierarchy structure for IO_SREP.

Work Instructions

Step 1 To create a hierarchy for IO_SREP, we must specify hierarchy properties in the IO_SREP definition. To modify the IO_SREP definition, double-click InfoObject *Sales representative ID.*

SCREEN 3.33

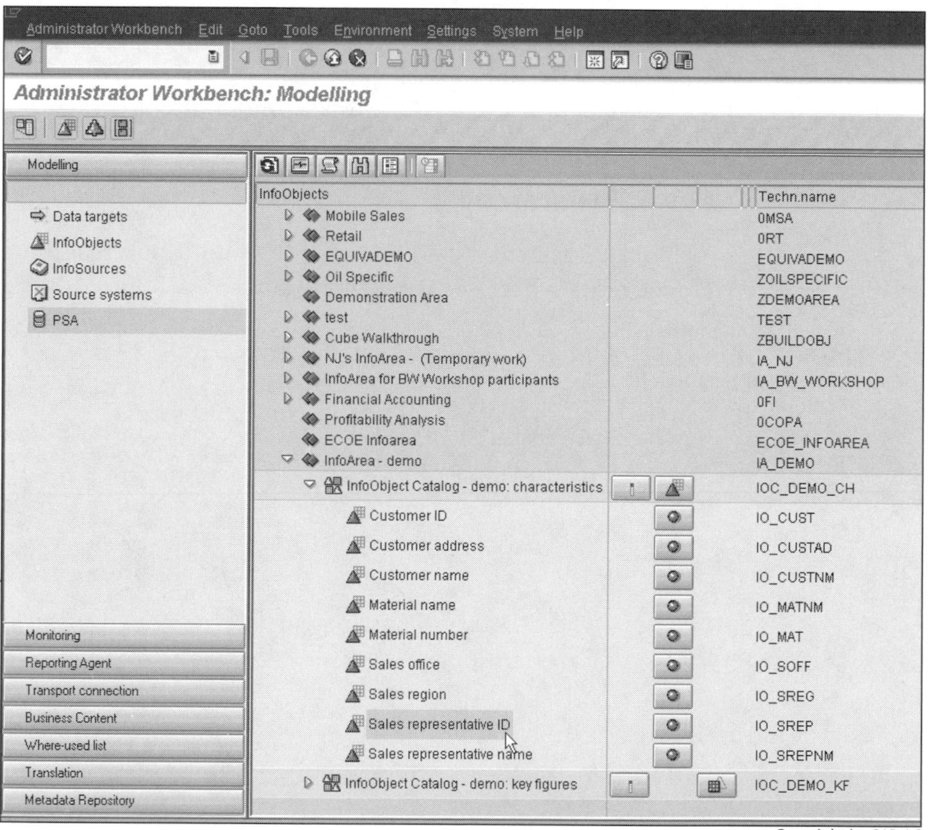

Step 2 Under the *Hierarchy* tab, select the option *with hierarchies*, and then select the option *Hierarchy structure time-dependent*.

Next, click to check it. If it is valid, click to activate the modification.

Note: The activation will create three database tables for this hierarchy: /BIC/HIO_SREP (hierarchy table), /BIC/KIO_SREP (hierarchy SID table), and /BIC/IIO_SREP (SID hierarchy structure).

Besides DataSources for master data (IO_SREP_ATTR) and texts (IO_SREP_TEXT), IO_SREP will work with a third DataSource, IO_SREP_HIER. With IO_SREP_HIER, we can use an InfoPackage to load hierarchy data as well.

Section 7.4, "InfoCube Design Alternative III—Time-Dependent Entire Hierarchies," gives an example of *Entire hierarchy is time-dependent*.

SCREEN 3.34

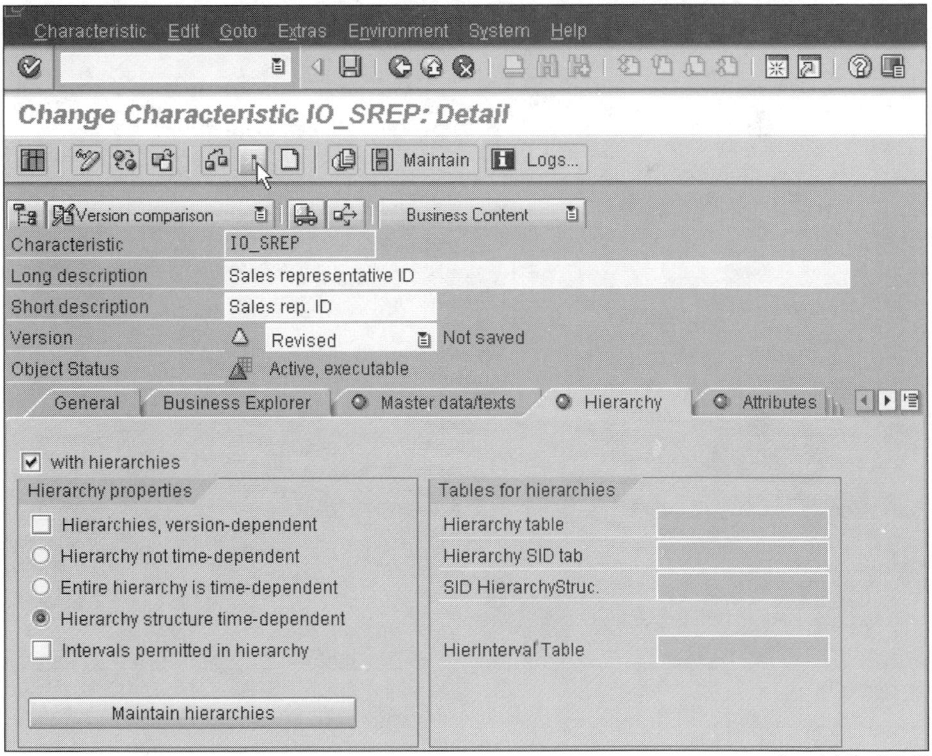

Step 3 In the *Administrator Workbench: Modelling* window, right-click the characteristic InfoObject *Sales representative ID*, and then select *Create hierarchy. . . .*

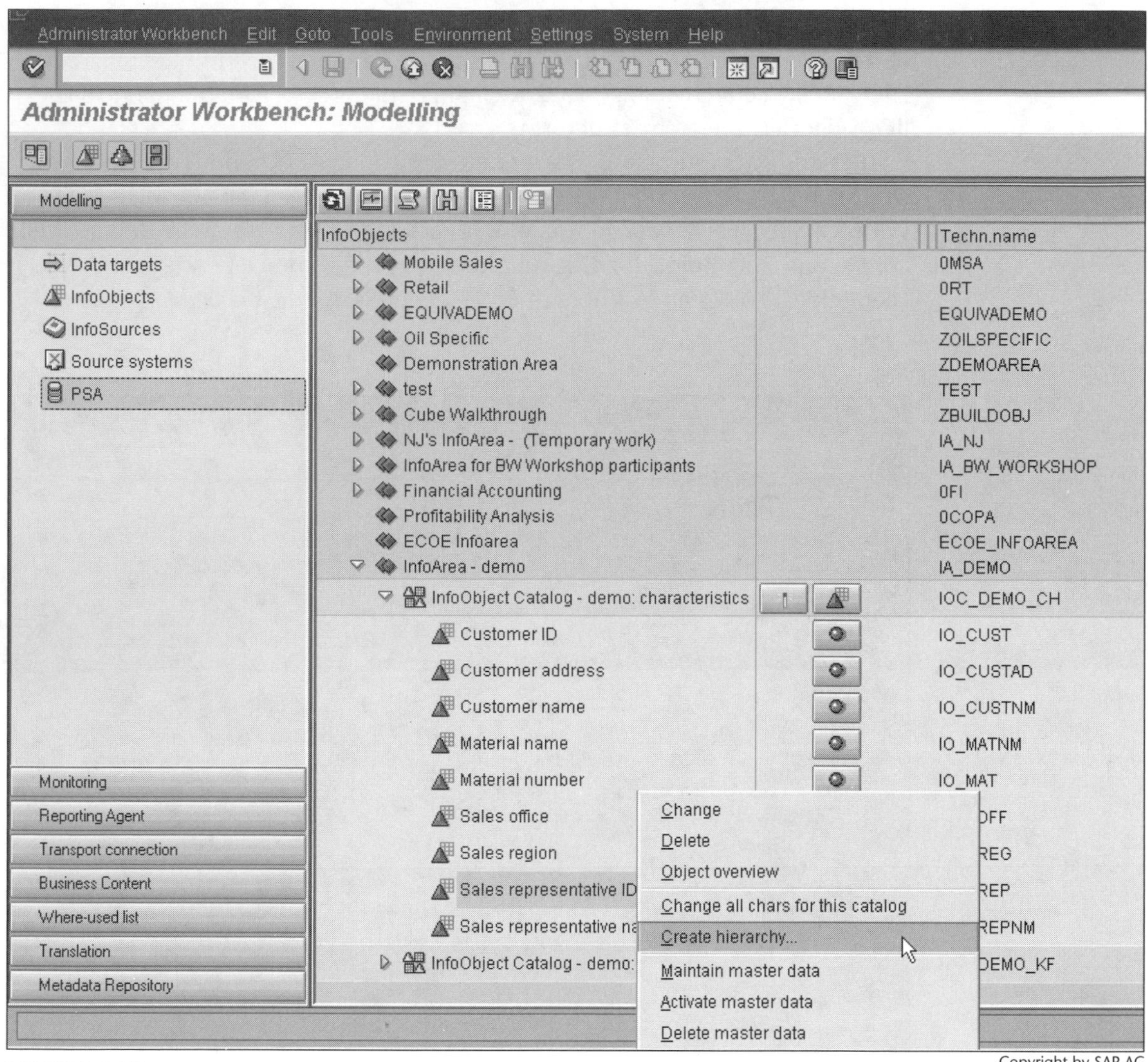

SCREEN 3.35

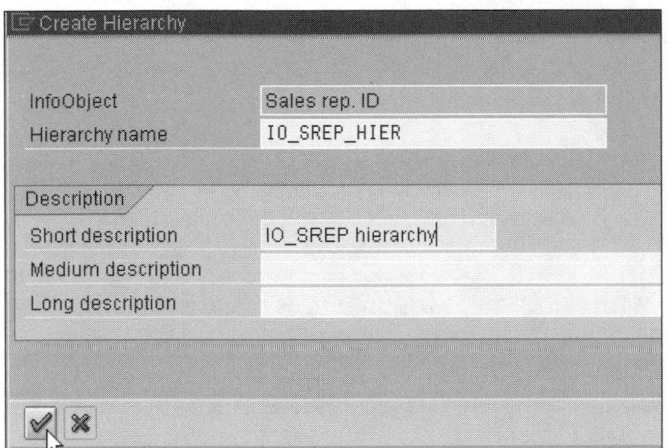

Copyright by SAP AG

SCREEN 3.36

Step 4 Enter a name and a description, and then click ✓ to continue.

Step 5 Right-click *IO_SREP hierarchy,* and then select *Insert characteristic node. . . .*

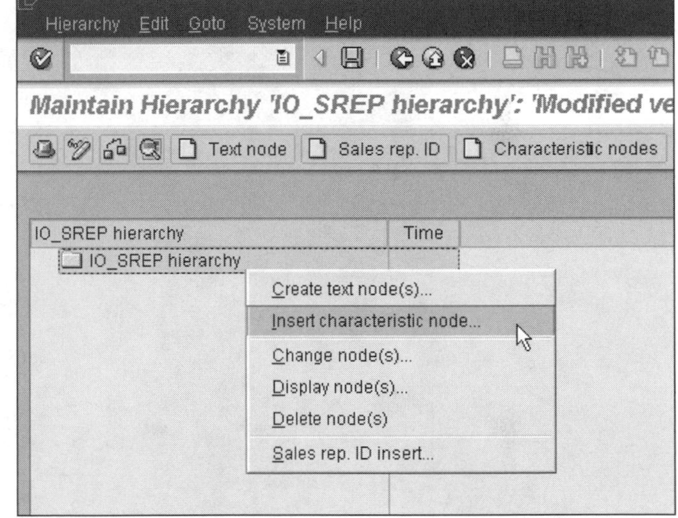

Copyright by SAP AG

SCREEN 3.37

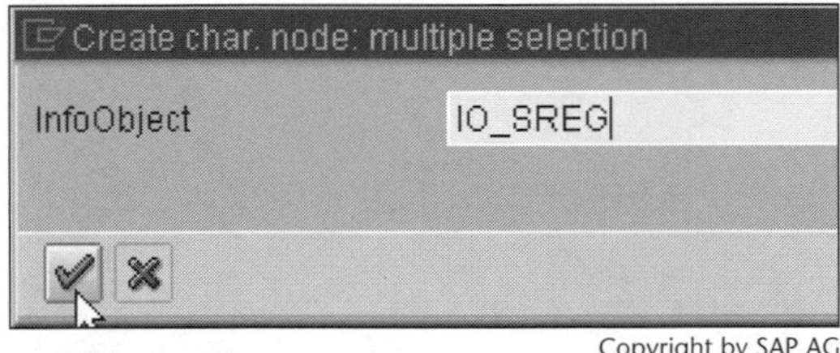

Copyright by SAP AG

SCREEN 3.38

Step 6 Enter *IO_SREG*, and then click ✓ to continue. Here we use IO_SREG data to create the hierarchy nodes.

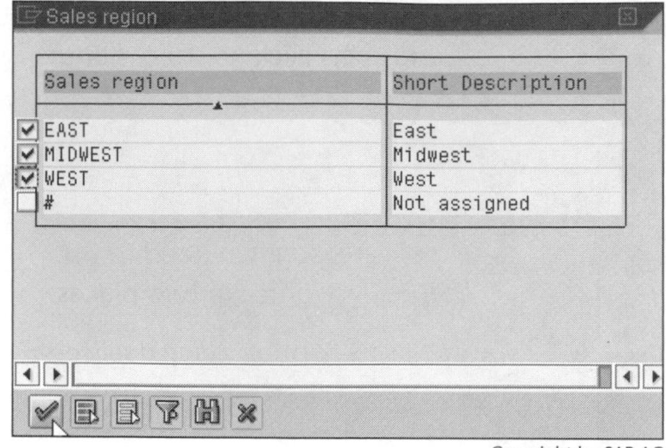

SCREEN 3.39

Step 7 Select all three regions, and then click ✓ to continue.

Step 8 Three regions are displayed under *IO_SREP hierarchy*.

To assign offices to each region, right-click one of the regions and repeat Steps 5, 6 (enter *IO_SOFF* instead of IO_SREG), and 7. This screen shows that Denver, Los Angeles, and Seattle will be assigned to the West region.

SCREEN 3.40

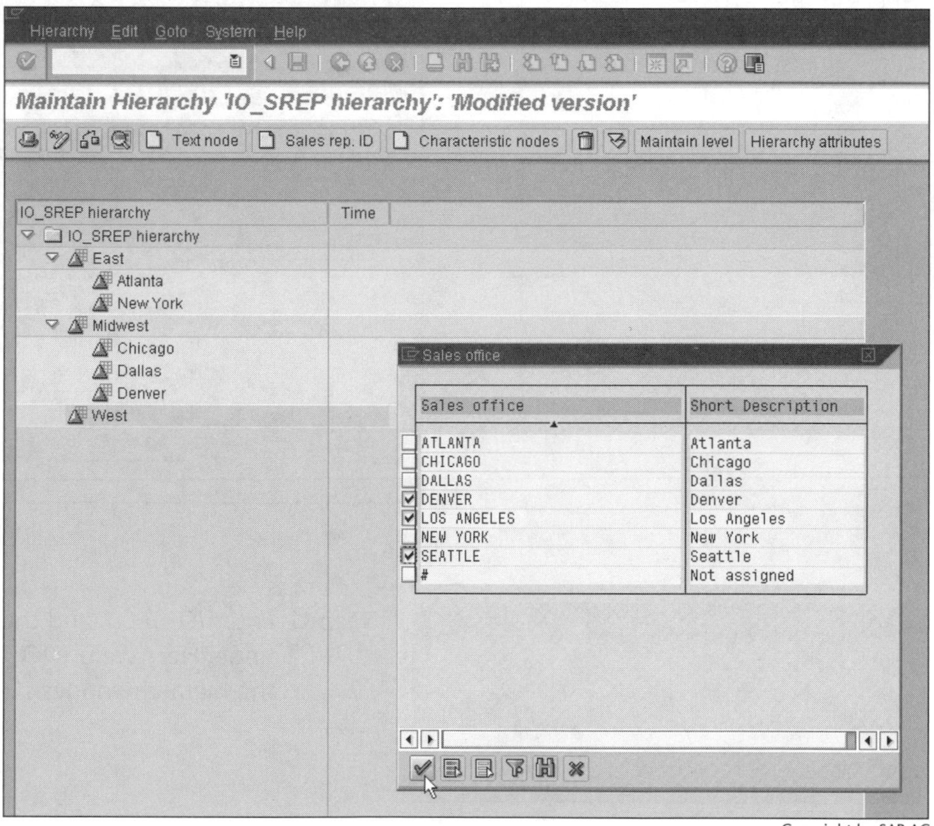

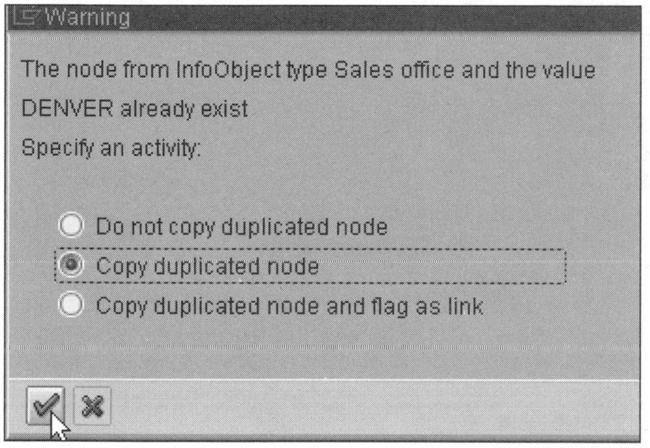

SCREEN 3.41

Step 9 Because the Denver office is already assigned to the Midwest region, we see this message. As noted in Chapter 1, the Denver office was part of the Midwest region before January 1, 2000. For this reason, we need to put the Denver office in two places.

Select the option *Copy duplicated node*, and then click ✔ to continue.

Step 10 Now we need to specify the valid date periods for the Denver office. Right-click the first *Denver* in the Midwest region, and then select *Change node(s). . . .*

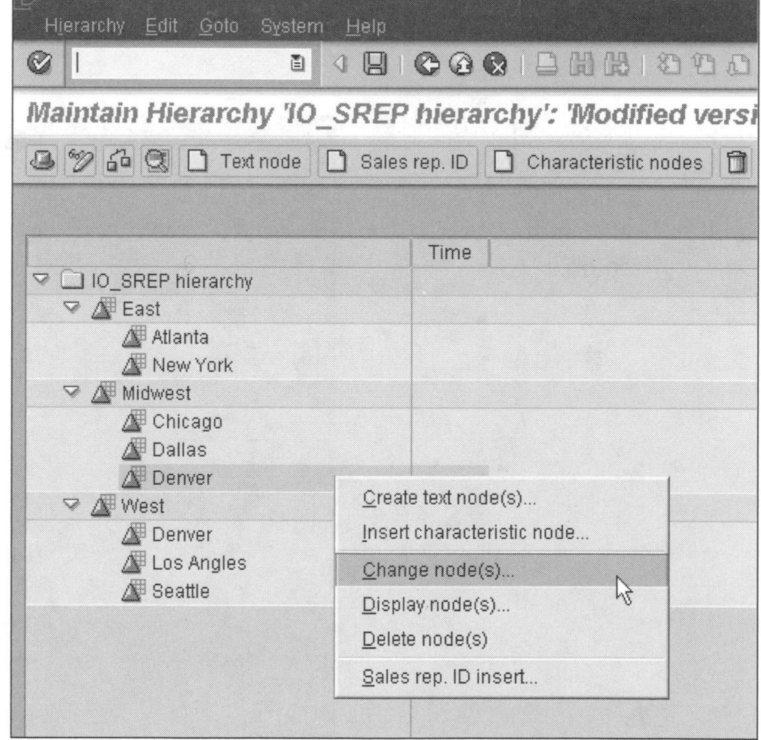

SCREEN 3.42

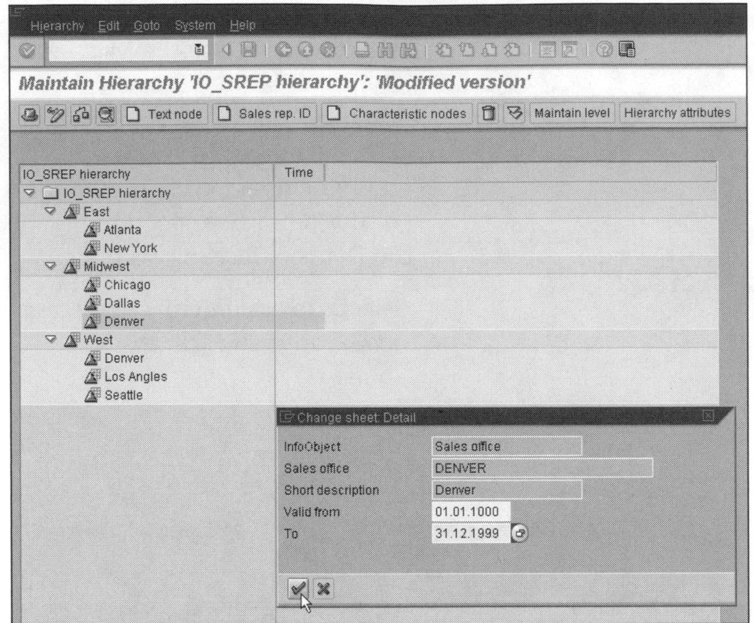

SCREEN 3.43

Step 11 Enter dates in *Valid from* and *To*, and then click ✔ to continue.

Step 12 Repeat Steps 10 and 11 to specify valid dates for the Denver office in the West region.

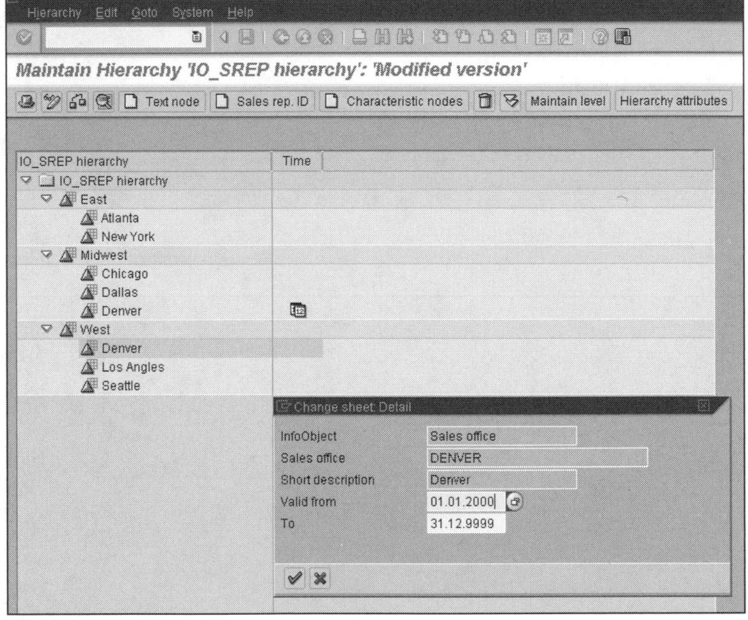

SCREEN 3.44

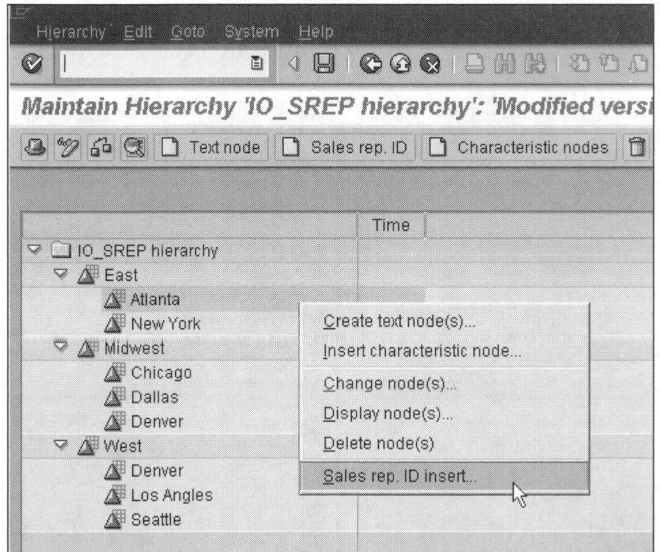

SCREEN 3.45 Copyright by SAP AG

Step 13 Next, we assign sales representatives to each sales office.

At the hierarchy leaf level, we can either insert IO_SREP values following the previous steps or right-click an IO_SOFF value, such as Atlanta in the East region, and then select *Sales rep. ID insert. . . .* We take the second approach.

Step 14 After assigning sales representatives to each sales office, click to save the hierarchy. Now we need to activate the hierarchy before we can use it.

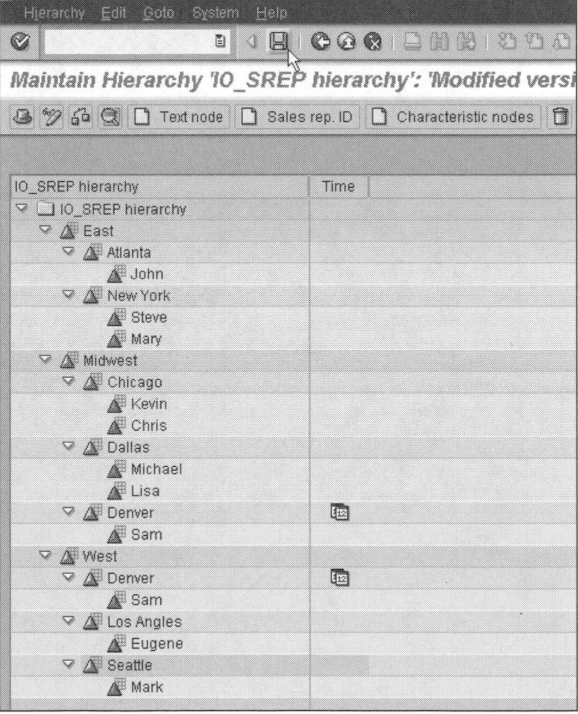

SCREEN 3.46 Copyright by SAP AG

Step 15 In the *Administrator Workbench: Modelling* window, right-click the newly created hierarchy *IO_SREP hierarchy*, and then select *Activate*.

SCREEN 3.47

Result

You have created the hierarchy. Its color will change from gray to green.

Now that we have loaded and entered all characteristic data, it is time to load the transaction data.

3.7 Creating an InfoSource for Transaction Data

In Section 3.3, we used BW's default simple one-to-one mappings for characteristic data. In this section, we will write a transfer rule in the ABAP language.

Table 1.4 lists the material per unit sales price and quantity sold. It does not provide any sales revenue data, however. To improve future query performance, it is recommended that we calculate the sales revenue and save this result in the fact table, rather than calculate the sales revenue during a query run. The database design in Figure 1.1 reflects this idea, and the following procedure shows how to implement it.

Work Instructions

Step 1 In the *Administrator Workbench: Modelling* window, select *InfoSources* under *Modelling* in the left panel, right-click *Application Component – demo*, and then select *Create InfoSource. . . .*

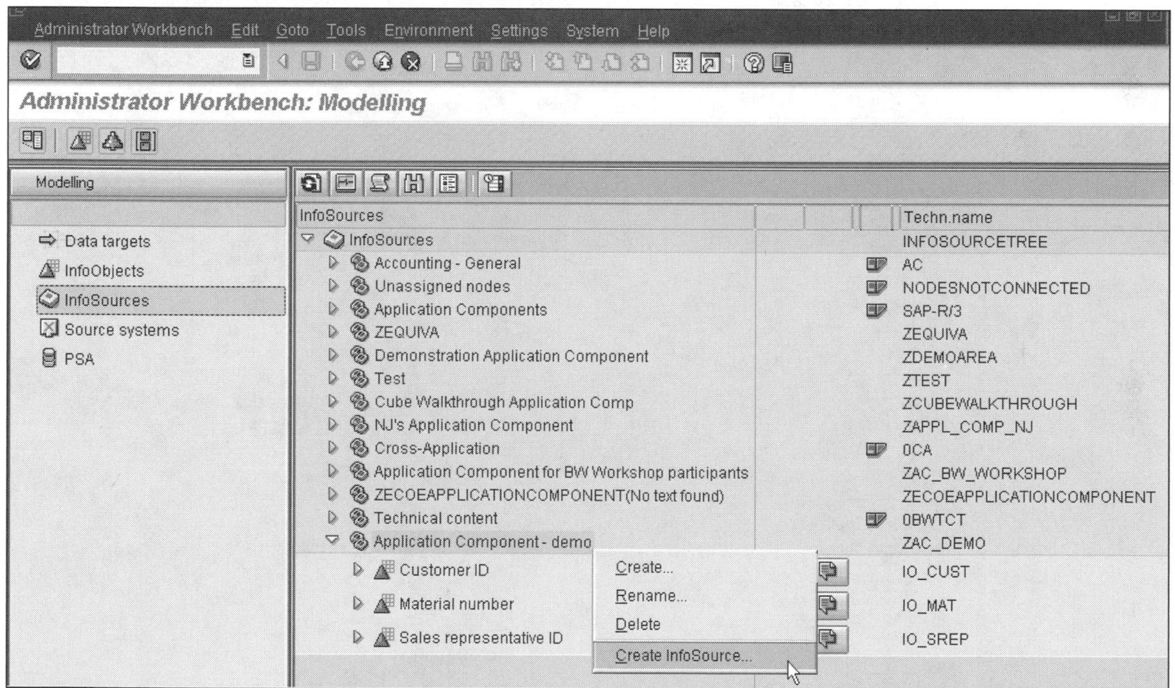

SCREEN 3.48

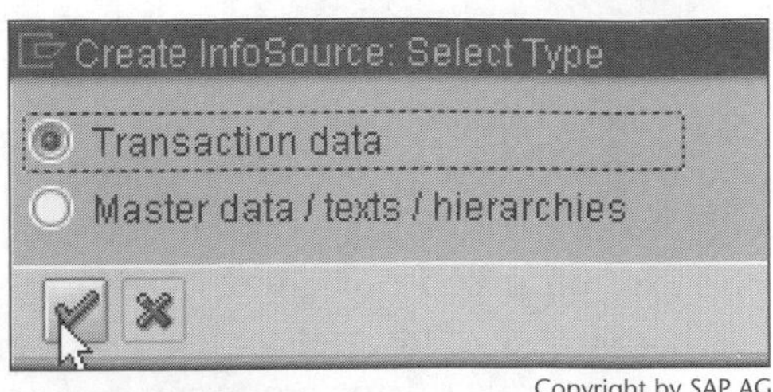

SCREEN 3.49

Step 2 Select the option *Transaction data*, and then click ✔ to continue.

Step 3 Enter a name and a description, and then click ✔ to continue.

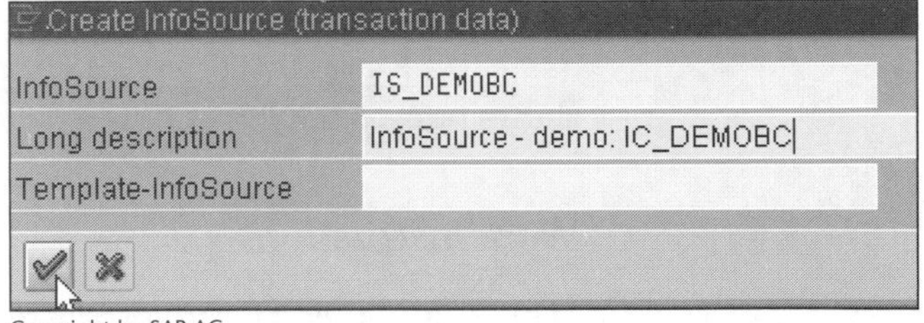

SCREEN 3.50

Step 4 The InfoSource is displayed but is not active yet. Double-click the InfoSource to create a communication structure.

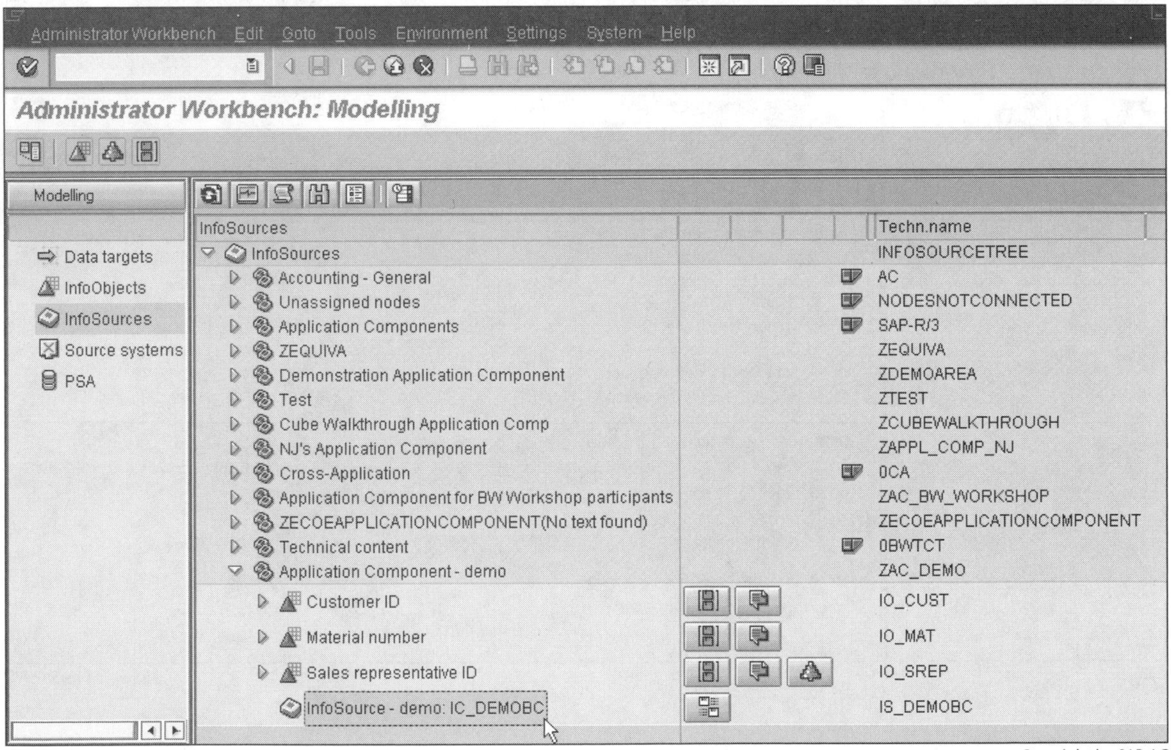

SCREEN 3.51

Note: In Section 3.3, we skipped this step. BW created a communication structure for us automatically based on the characteristic attribute information.

A communication structure is needed here so that the data passed by an InfoPackage can feed multiple InfoCubes. See the note for Screen 3.70.

Step 5 Enter InfoObjects as shown, and then click [icon] to save and activate the communication structure

SCREEN 3.52

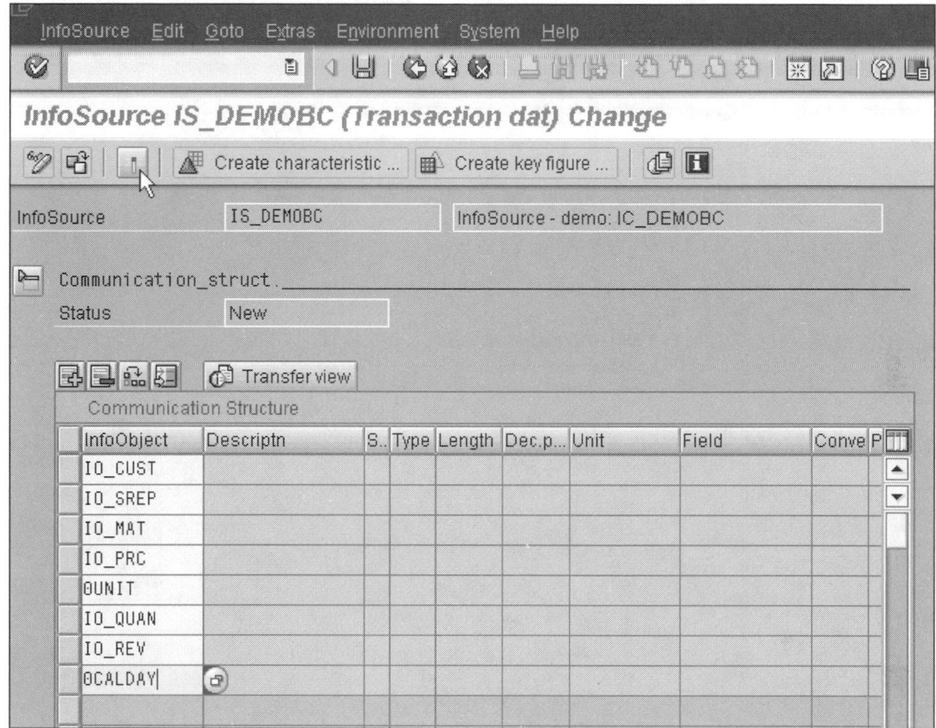

Result

You have created the communication structure. A status message *Communication Struct. IS_DEMOBC activated* will appear at the bottom of Screen 3.52. Now we can clearly see that an InfoSource is simply a communication structure.

Next, let's create the transfer rules.

Work Instructions

Step 1 In the *Administrator Workbench: Modelling* window, right-click the *InfoSource – demo: IC_DEMOBC,* and then select *Assign DataSource. . . .*

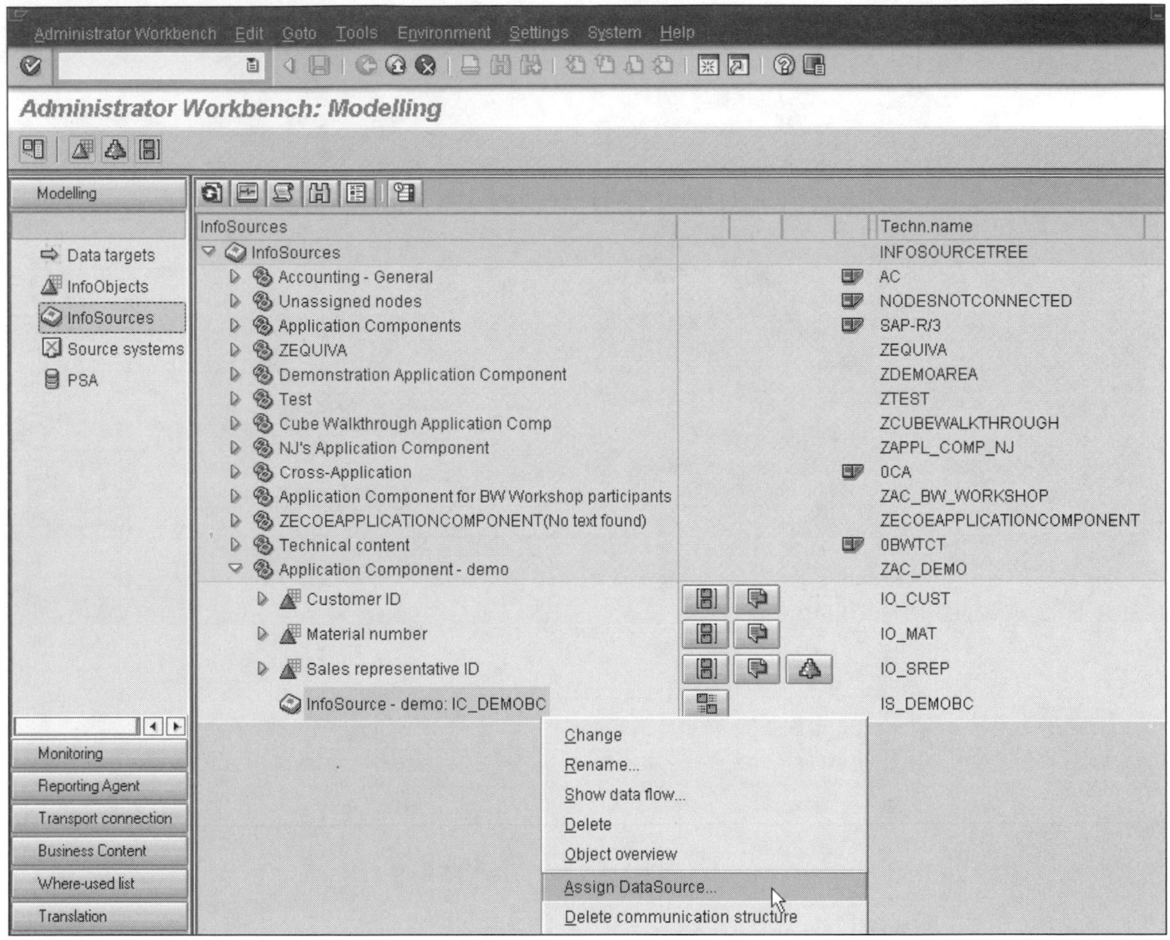

SCREEN 3.53

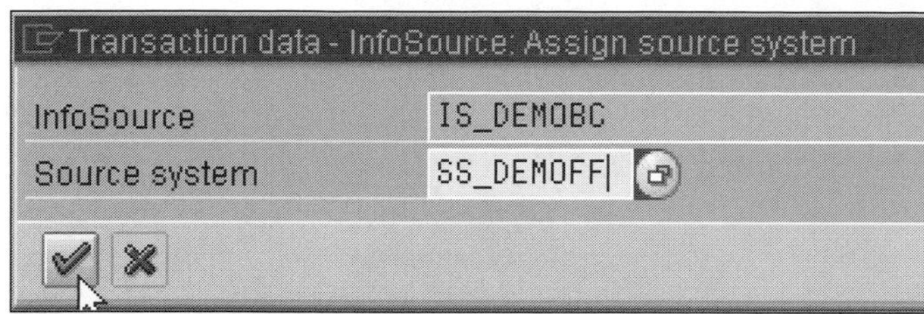

SCREEN 3.54

Step 2 Enter *SS_DEMOFF* in the field *Source system*, and then click ✓ to continue.

Step 3 Click Yes to pass the message.

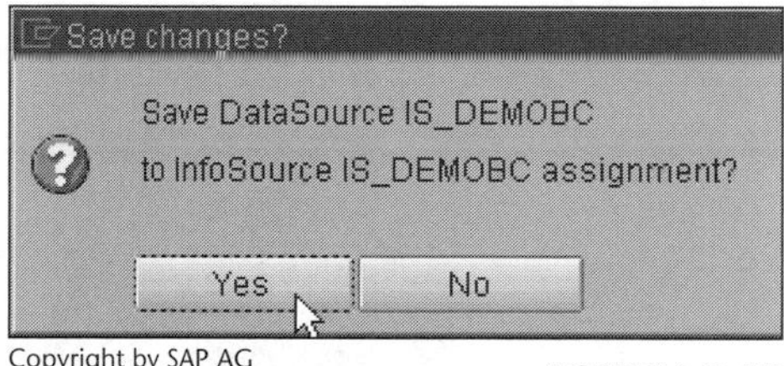

SCREEN 3.55

InfoSource IS_DEMOBC (Transaction dat) Change

InfoSource: IS_DEMOBC — InfoSource - demo: IC_DEMOBC

Communication_struct.

Transfer_structure/Transfer_rules

Source system: SS_DEMOFF - Source System - dem

DataSource: IS_DEMOBC - InfoSource - demo: IC_DEM

Status: Revised(not save...

Transfer method: PSA

Trans. structure | Transfer rules

DeltaPrcss: Only full upload (delta only using ODS) — Open bal.

Only char

Transfer view

Transfer structure

Field	InfoObject	Sel...	Descriptn	S..	Type	Length	Dec.p...	Unit	Co
/BIC/IO_C...	IO_CUST	☑	Customer ID		CHAR	15			AL
/BIC/IO_S...	IO_SREP	☑	Sales rep. ID		CHAR	15			AL
/BIC/IO_M...	IO_MAT	☑	Material number		CHAR	15			AL
/BIC/IO_P...	IO_PRC	☐	Price of material		CHAR	17	2		
UNIT	0UNIT	☐	Unit of measure		UNIT	3			CU
/BIC/IO_Q...	IO_QUAN	☐	Sales quantity		CHAR	17	3	UNIT	
/BIC/IO_R...	IO_REV	☐	Sales revenue		CHAR	17	2		
CALDAY	0CALDAY	☑	Calendar day		CHAR	8			

SCREEN 3.56

Step 4 BW proposes a transfer structure based on the information of the communication structure. Under the *Trans. structure* tab, check four fields in the *Selection* column. You can use these four fields as selection conditions when loading data using an InfoPackage.

Note: A **transfer structure** maps DataSource fields to InfoSource InfoObjects.

Step 5 Under the *Transfer rules* tab, the simple one-to-one mappings appear in the left table, called *Communication str./Transfer rules*. Click at the intersection of *IO_REV* and *Tp* to replace the one-to-one mapping with an ABAP transfer rule for the sales revenue calculation.

SCREEN 3.57

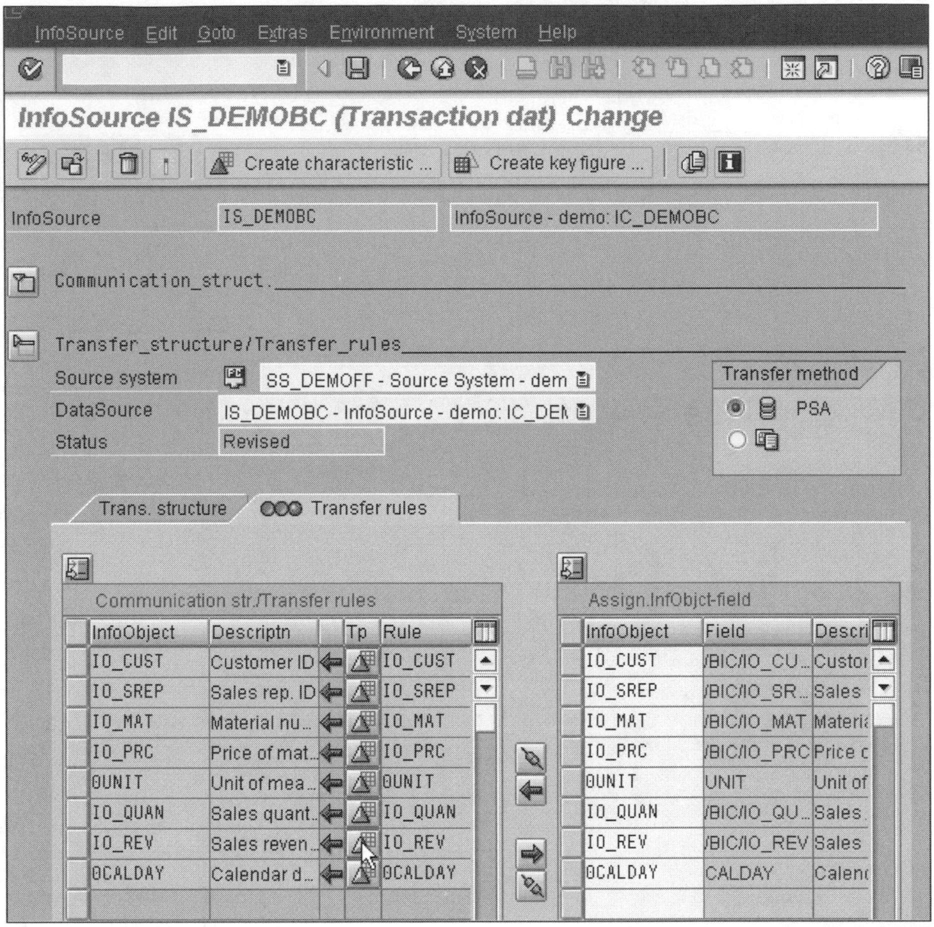

Step 6 In the pop-up window, select the option *@9WQLocalA*, and then click to create an ABAP transfer rule.

Note: The first option, *InfoObject,* is the default—the simple one-to-one mapping. The second option, , allows us to specify a constant. The third option, @9WQLocalA, enables us to define an ABAP transfer rule.

SCREEN 3.58

Edit Transfer Rules
InfoSource IS_DEMOBC
InfoObject comStr. IO_REV
Source system SS_DEMOFF
Transfer rules
InfoObject IO_REV
@9V\QLocal A
Create routine

Step 7 Enter a name for the *Transfer routine*, select the option *All fields*, and then click ✔ to continue.

Note: In BW, the ABAP transfer rule is called a transfer routine.

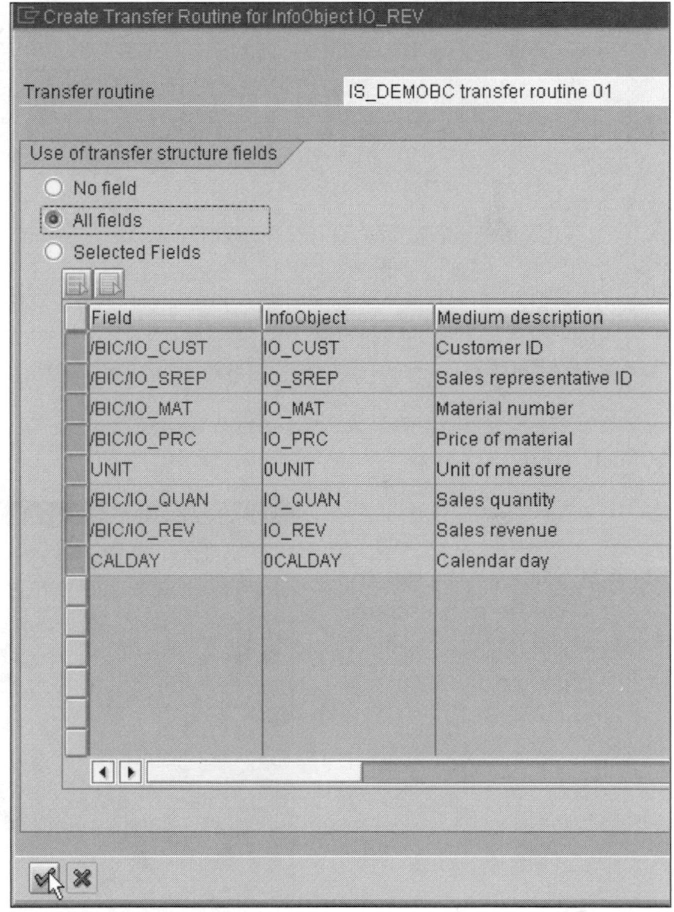

SCREEN 3.59

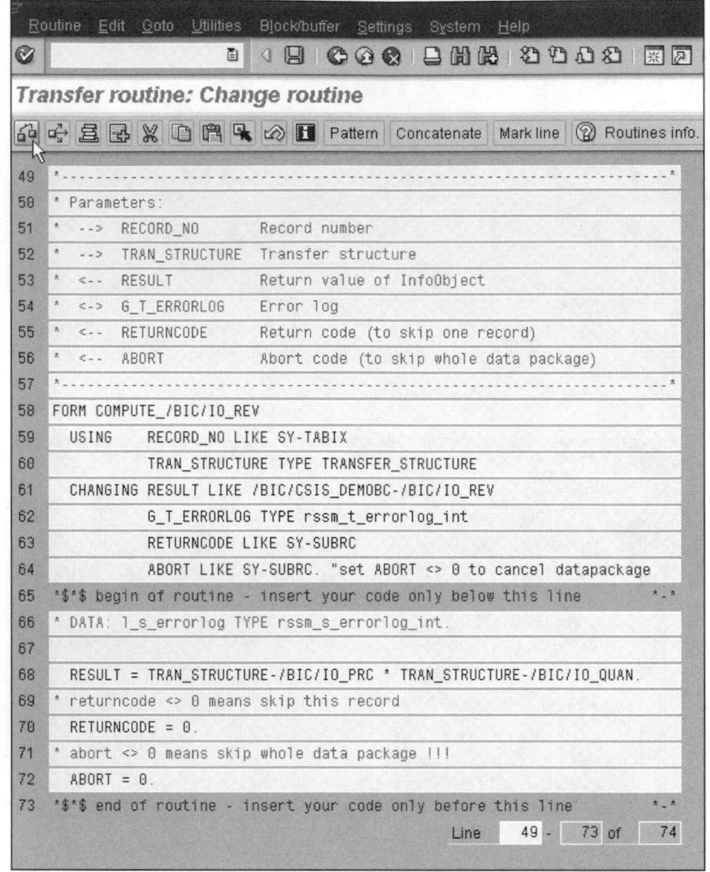

Routine Edit Goto Utilities Block/buffer Settings System Help
Transfer routine: Change routine
Pattern Concatenate Mark line Routines info.
49 *--*
50 * Parameters:
51 * --> RECORD_NO Record number
52 * --> TRAN_STRUCTURE Transfer structure
53 * <-- RESULT Return value of InfoObject
54 * <-> G_T_ERRORLOG Error log
55 * <-- RETURNCODE Return code (to skip one record)
56 * <-- ABORT Abort code (to skip whole data package)
57 *--*
58 FORM COMPUTE_/BIC/IO_REV
59 USING RECORD_NO LIKE SY-TABIX
60 TRAN_STRUCTURE TYPE TRANSFER_STRUCTURE
61 CHANGING RESULT LIKE /BIC/CSIS_DEMOBC-/BIC/IO_REV
62 G_T_ERRORLOG TYPE rssm_t_errorlog_int
63 RETURNCODE LIKE SY-SUBRC
64 ABORT LIKE SY-SUBRC. "set ABORT <> 0 to cancel datapackage
65 *$*$ begin of routine - insert your code only below this line *-*
66 * DATA: l_s_errorlog TYPE rssm_s_errorlog_int.
67
68 RESULT = TRAN_STRUCTURE-/BIC/IO_PRC * TRAN_STRUCTURE-/BIC/IO_QUAN.
69 * returncode <> 0 means skip this record
70 RETURNCODE = 0.
71 * abort <> 0 means skip whole data package !!!
72 ABORT = 0.
73 *$*$ end of routine - insert your code only before this line *-*
Line 49 - 73 of 74

SCREEN 3.60

Step 8 Scroll down the ABAP routine, to the right of *RESULT* = enter *TRAN_STRUCTURE-/BIC/IO_PRC * TRAN_STRUCTURE-/BIC/IO_QUAN*. The statement should appear as shown on line 68. This ABAP statement specifies how we calculate IO_REV, the *RESULT*, from IO_PRC and IO_QUAN.

Click [check icon] to check the ABAP routine. If it is valid, click [save icon] to save it.

Step 9 Click [✓] to return to the main screen.

Edit Transfer Rules
InfoSource IS_DEMOBC
InfoObject comStr. IO_REV
Source system SS_DEMOFF
Transfer rules
InfoObject
@9V\QLocal A IS_DEMOBC transfer routine 01

SCREEN 3.61

Step 10 The cell icon changes from to . Click to activate all transfer rules.

SCREEN 3.62

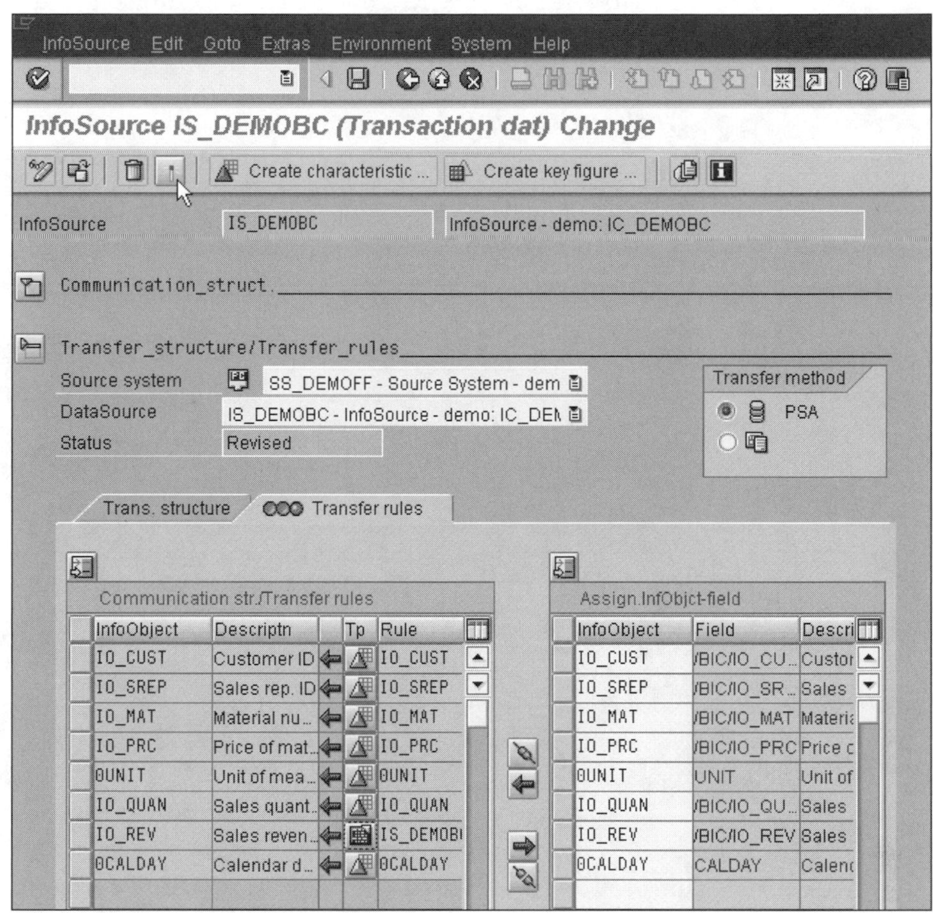

Result

You have created transfer rules. A status message *Transfer rules IS_DEMOBC_AH activated* will appear at the bottom of Screen 3.62.

3.8 Creating Update Rules for the InfoCube

Before creating an InfoPackage to load the transaction data, we must define rules for the InfoCube IC_DEMBC that determine how data will be updated. In BW, these rules are called update rules.

Work Instructions

Step 1 Select *Data targets* under *Modelling* in the left panel, right-click *InfoCube – demo: Basic Cube,* and select *Create update rules* in the right panel.

SCREEN 3.63

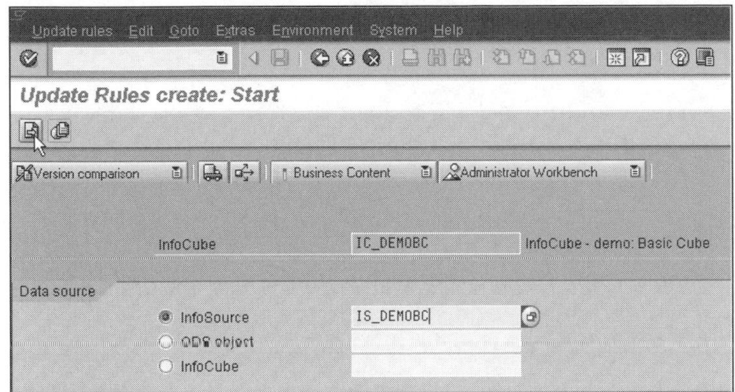

SCREEN 3.64

Step 2 In the *Data source* block, select the option *InfoSource*, enter the newly created *IS_DEMOBC*, and then click [icon] to move to the next screen.

Step 3 Accept the default update rules. Click [icon] to check the update rules. If they are valid, click [icon] to activate them.

Note: Section 9.2, "Preparing to Load Data into the ODS Object, Then into an InfoCube," describes how to use ABAP to define an update rule.

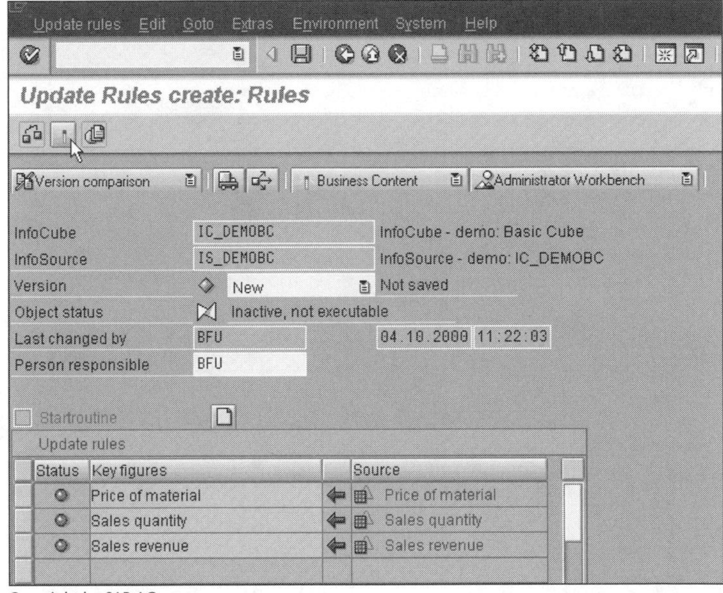

SCREEN 3.65

Result

You have created the update rules. A status message *Update rules were successfully activated* will appear at the bottom of Screen 3.65.

Note: BW release 3.0A allows you to create update rules for a characteristic's master data and text as well.

3.9 Create an InfoPackage to Load Transaction Data

Now we are ready to create an InfoPackage to load the transaction data. In this InfoPackage, we will specify how and when to load data.

Work Instructions

Step 1 Right-click *Source System – demo: flat file*, and then select *Create InfoPackage. . . .*

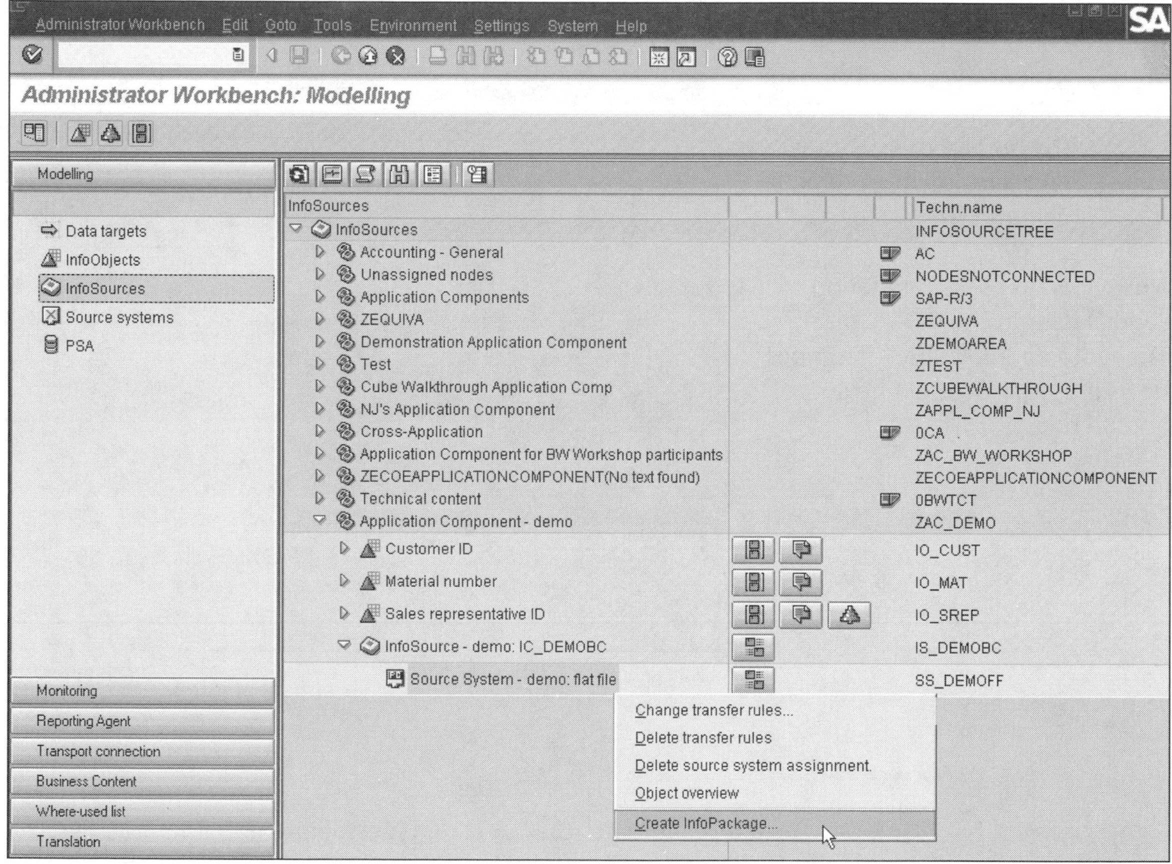

SCREEN 3.66

Step 2 Select DataSource *InfoSource Demo: IC_DEMOBC*, enter a description for the InfoPackage, and then click ✔ to continue.

SCREEN 3.67

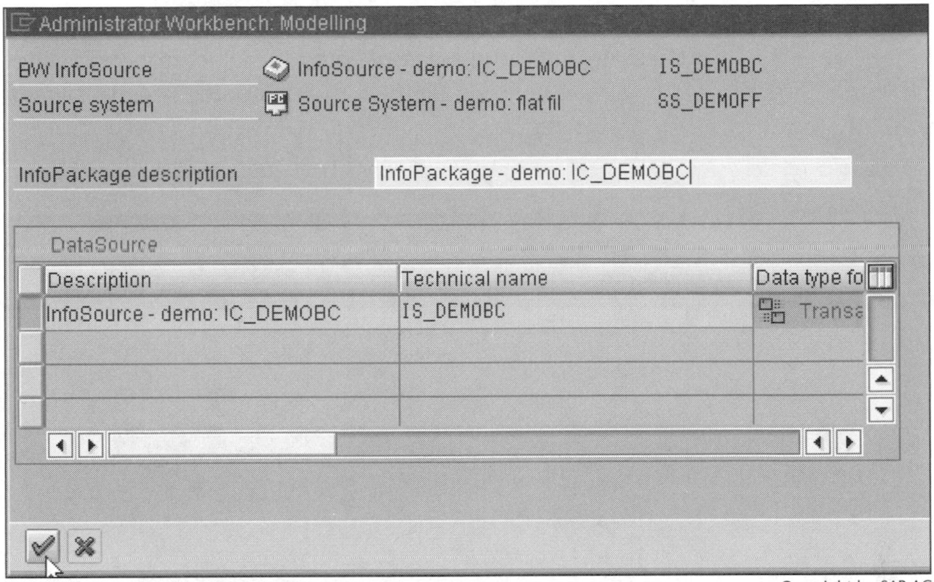

Administrator Workbench: Modelling

BW InfoSource	InfoSource - demo: IC_DEMOBC	IS_DEMOBC
Source system	Source System - demo: flat fil	SS_DEMOFF

InfoPackage description: InfoPackage - demo: IC_DEMOBC

DataSource

Description	Technical name	Data type fo
InfoSource - demo: IC_DEMOBC	IS_DEMOBC	Transa

Step 3 Under the *Select data* tab, note the fields we selected in Screen 3.56. We can use the selection condition on 0CALDAY to load 1999 data first, 2000 data second, and 2001 data last. If we do not enter anything, all of the data will be loaded together in one data load request. Because we do not have a large volume of data, we load them all together.

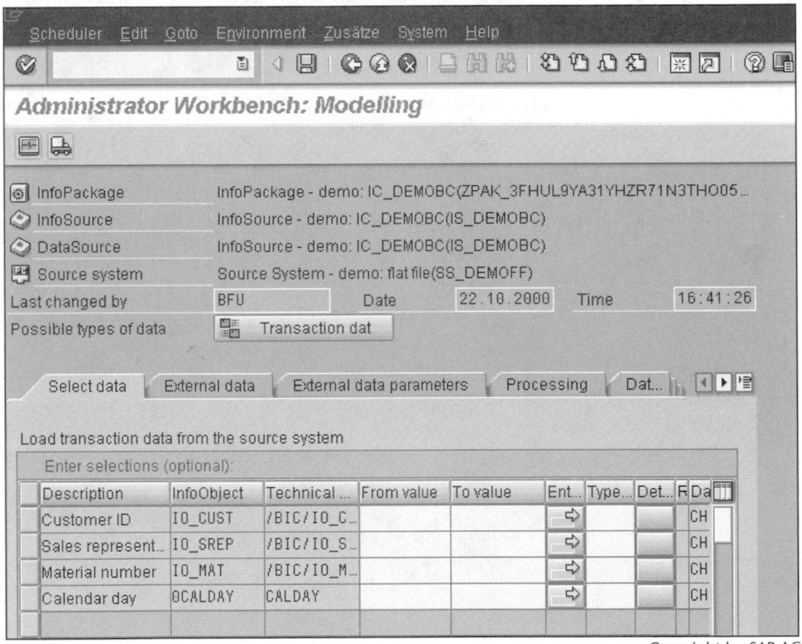

Scheduler Edit Goto Environment Zusätze System Help

Administrator Workbench: Modelling

InfoPackage	InfoPackage - demo: IC_DEMOBC(ZPAK_3FHUL9YA31YHZR71N3THO05...
InfoSource	InfoSource - demo: IC_DEMOBC(IS_DEMOBC)
DataSource	InfoSource - demo: IC_DEMOBC(IS_DEMOBC)
Source system	Source System - demo: flat file(SS_DEMOFF)
Last changed by	BFU Date 22.10.2000 Time 16:41:26
Possible types of data	Transaction dat

Select data | External data | External data parameters | Processing | Dat...

Load transaction data from the source system

Enter selections (optional):

Description	InfoObject	Technical ...	From value	To value	Ent...	Type...	Det...	R	Da
Customer ID	IO_CUST	/BIC/IO_C...			⇨				CH
Sales represent...	IO_SREP	/BIC/IO_S...			⇨				CH
Material number	IO_MAT	/BIC/IO_M...			⇨				CH
Calendar day	0CALDAY	CALDAY			⇨				CH

SCREEN 3.68

Note: 0CALDAY (Calendar day) is the characteristic in Screen 2.28 that represents the Transaction Date in Table 1.4. We also included it in the InfoSource definition.

Step 4 Under the *External data* tab, select options as shown in the screen, and enter a file name with a path. The file contains the data from Table 3.3.

SCREEN 3.69

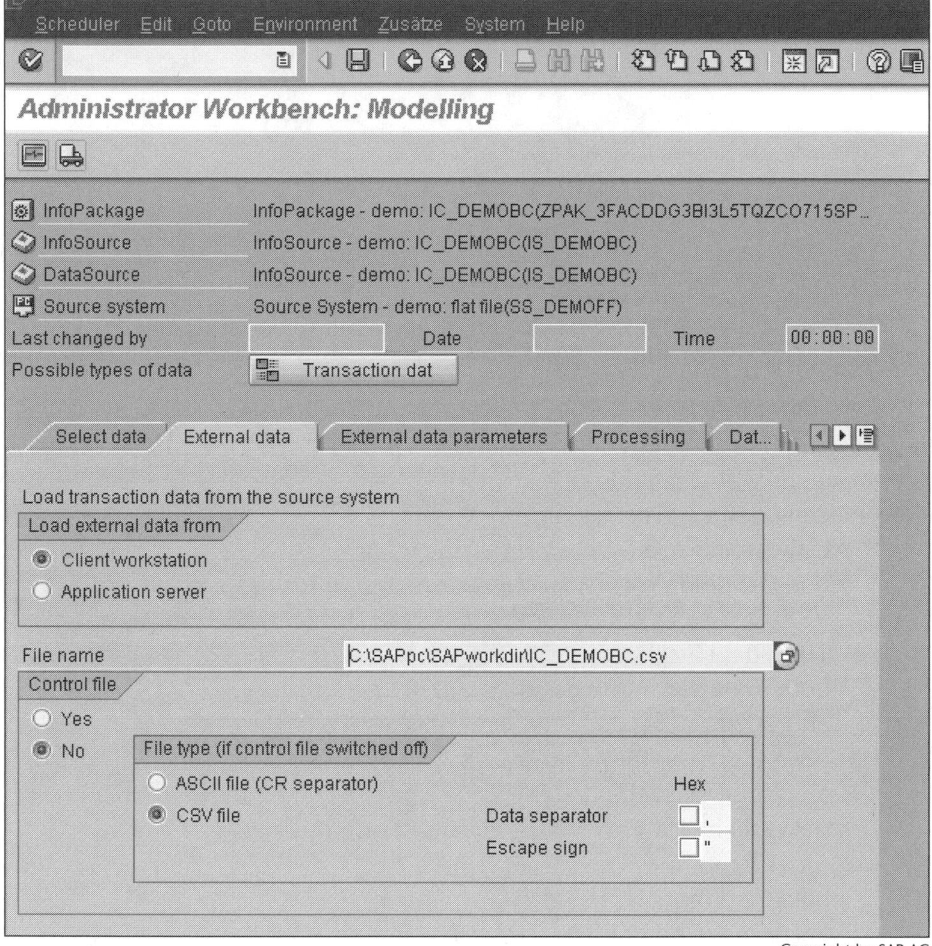

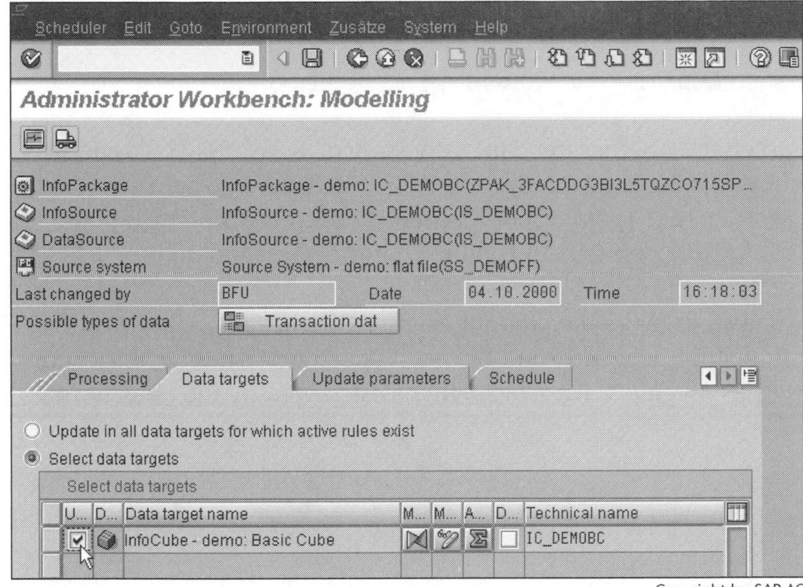

SCREEN 3.70

Step 5 Under the *Data targets* tab, select the option *Select data targets*, and then select the first row for our InfoCube IC_DEMOBC.

Note: If the InfoSource appears in the update rules for other InfoCubes, all of the InfoCubes will be listed in the table. We can then specify into which InfoCubes we want to load the data.

STEP 6 Under the *Schedule* tab, select the option *Start data load immediately*, and then click [icon] to load the data.

SCREEN 3.71

Result

A status message *Data was requested* will appear at the bottom of Screen 3.71.

Note: We can check whether the data were loaded successfully by using BW Monitor as shown in Screen 3.22. Section 4.1, "Checking InfoCube Contents," and Section 12.2.1, "InfoCube Contents," both describe techniques for checking the InfoCube contents to confirm that the data loading process worked correctly.

Table 3.3 shows the sales data for our example. In the table, CS, EA, and DZ are abbreviations for Case, Each, and Dozen, respectively. The IO_REV column will hold the sales revenue data, which will be calculated by the transfer rule.

TABLE 3.3 SALES DATA

IO_CUST	IO_SREP	IO_MAT	IO_PRC	0UNIT	IO_QUAN	IO_REV	0CALDAY
CUST001	SREP01	MAT001	2	CS	1		19980304
CUST002	SREP02	MAT002	2	CS	2		19990526
CUST002	SREP02	MAT003	5	CS	3		19990730
CUST003	SREP03	MAT003	5	CS	4		20000101
CUST004	SREP04	MAT004	50	EA	5		19991023
CUST004	SREP04	MAT005	100	EA	6		19980904
CUST004	SREP04	MAT005	100	EA	7		19980529
CUST005	SREP05	MAT006	200	EA	8		19991108
CUST006	SREP06	MAT007	20	EA	9		20000408
CUST007	SREP07	MAT008	3	DZ	10		20000901
CUST007	SREP07	MAT008	3	DZ	1		19990424
CUST008	SREP08	MAT008	3	DZ	2		19980328
CUST008	SREP08	MAT009	2	CS	3		19980203
CUST008	SREP08	MAT010	1	LB	4		19991104
CUST009	SREP09	MAT011	1.5	LB	5		20000407
CUST010	SREP10	MAT011	1.5	LB	6		20000701
CUST010	SREP10	MAT011	1.5	LB	7		19990924
CUST010	SREP10	MAT012	2	LB	8		19991224
CUST010	SREP10	MAT013	3	CS	9		20000308
CUST011	SREP10	MAT014	1	LB	10		19980627
CUST012	SREP11	MAT014	2	LB	1		19991209
CUST012	SREP11	MAT015	3	CS	2		19980221
CUST012	SREP11	MAT015	2	CS	3		20000705
CUST012	SREP11	MAT015	3.5	CS	4		20001225

3.10 Summary

In this chapter, we loaded the data described in Chapter 1 into the characteristics and InfoCube we created in Chapter 2. Figure 3.2 shows the many ways in which data can flow into a destination in BW. In this chapter, we followed the path linked via solid lines. The rest of this book will discuss the other paths.

FIGURE 3.2 DATA FLOW

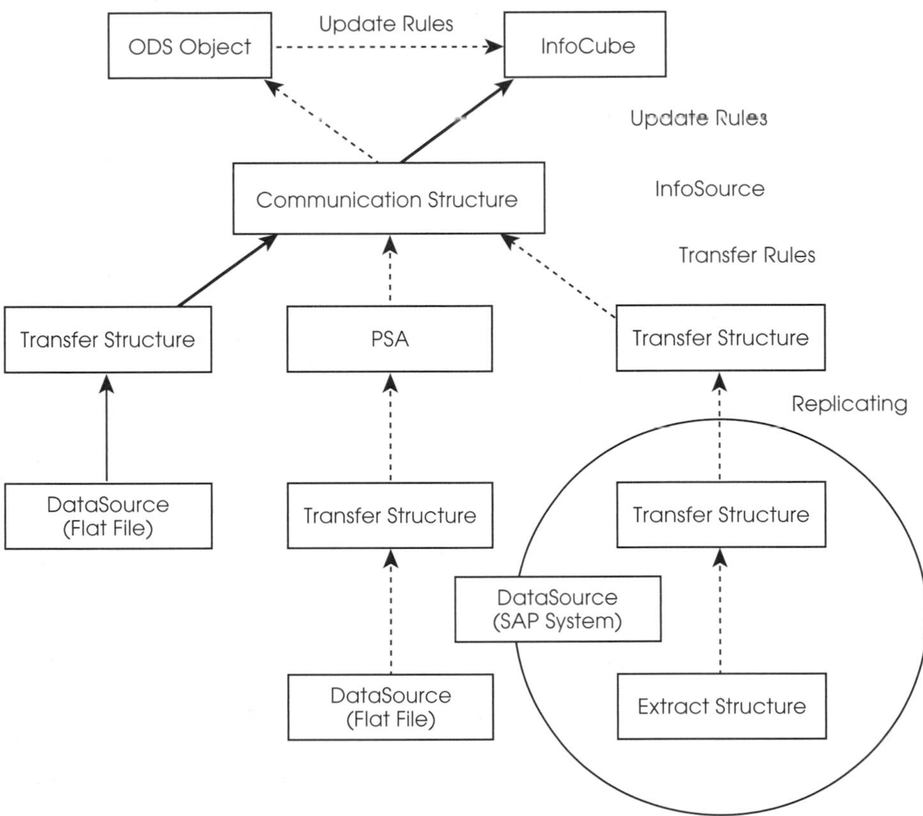

Key Terms

Term	Description
Source system	A source system is a protocol that enables BW to know where to find data and how to extract those data. When the source system is a non-SAP system, such as a flat file or a third-party tool, the maximum number of characters allowed for the

	technical name is 10. When the source system is an SAP system, either R/3 or BW, its technical name matches its logical system name. The maximum number of characters allowed for the technical name is 32.
Application component	Application components are used to organize InfoSources. They are analogous to the InfoAreas in InfoCubes. The maximum number of characters allowed for the technical name is 32.
InfoSource	An InfoSource is a structure in which InfoObjects are logically grouped together. InfoCubes and characteristics interface with InfoSources to get source system data. The maximum number of characters allowed for the technical name is 32.
Communication structure	The communication structure serves as the structure in the InfoSource.
DataSource	A DataSource is not only a structure in which source system fields are logically grouped together, but also an object that contains ETTL-related information. Four types of DataSources exist: • DataSources for transaction data • DataSources for characteristic attributes • DataSources for characteristic texts • DataSources for characteristic hierarchies The maximum number of characters allowed for the DataSources technical name is 32.
Transfer structure	A transfer structure maps DataSource fields to InfoSource InfoObjects.
Transfer rule	Transfer rules specify how DataSource fields map to InfoSource InfoObjects.
InfoPackage	An InfoPackage specifies when and how to load data from a given source system. BW generates a 30-digit code starting with ZPAK as an InfoPackage's technical name.
Update rule	An update rule specifies how data will be updated into a target. The data target can be an InfoCube or an ODS object. If the update rule is

	applied to data from an InfoSource, its technical name will match the InfoSource's technical name. If the update rule is applied to data from an ODS object, its technical name will match the ODS object's technical name prefixed with number 8.
BW Scheduler	BW Scheduler specifies when to load data. It relies on the same techniques used for scheduling R/3 background jobs.
BW Monitor	BW Monitor displays data load status and provides assistance in troubleshooting if errors occur.

Next . . .

We will check the loaded transaction data.

Chapter 4

Checking Data Quality

In Chapter 3, we loaded the data from Chapter 1 into the characteristics and the InfoCube created in Chapter 2. In addition, we checked characteristic contents. In this chapter, we will demonstrate how to check InfoCube contents. Having correct data in BW is the ultimate goal when loading data.

In Chapter 3, we also used BW Monitor to check whether data were loaded successfully. In this chapter, we will demonstrate how to use BW Monitor to diagnose errors when a data load fails.

Once data are loaded into their destinations, removing the data from their destination is not an easy task, as we will learn in Chapter 12, Data Maintenance. BW provides **PSA (Persistent Staging Area),** a place where we can display and check data before they are loaded into their destinations; we will learn how to use PSA in this chapter.

4.1 Checking InfoCube Contents

You can check InfoCube contents in several ways. One technique is introduced here; another method will be discussed in Section 12.2.1, "InfoCube Contents."

Work Instructions

Step 1 In the *Administrator Workbench: Modelling* window, right-click *InfoCube – demo: Basic Cube*, and then select *Manage*.

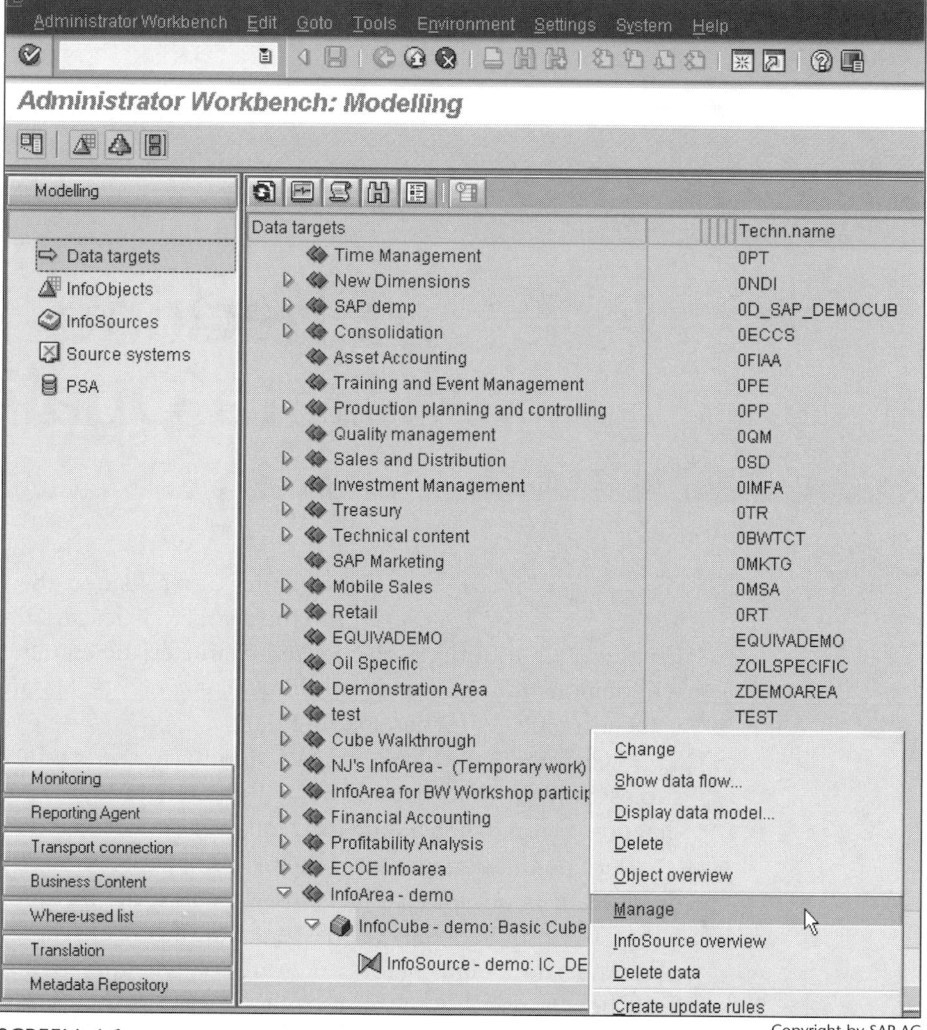

SCREEN 4.1

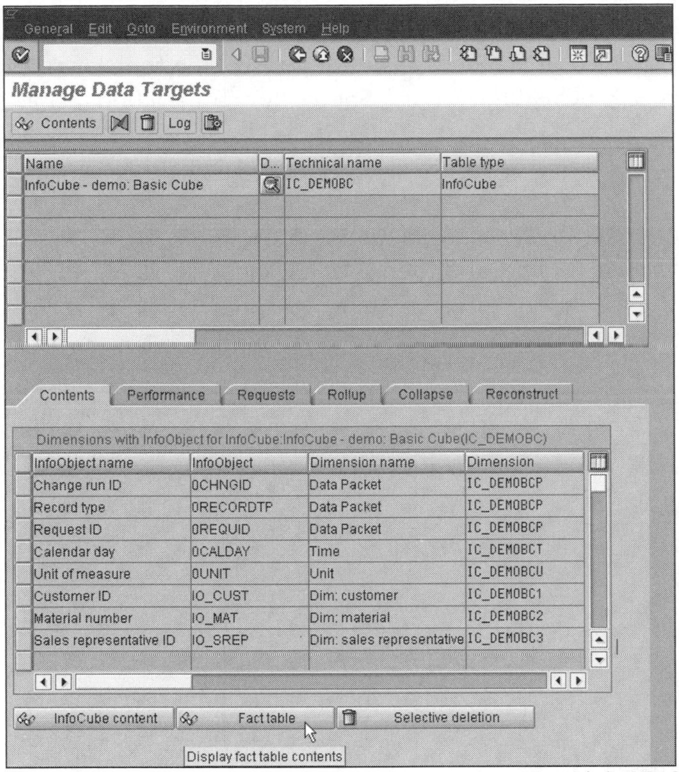

Step 2 Under *Contents* tab, click Fact table.

SCREEN 4.2

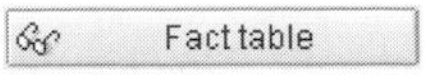

Step 3 Click to display the data.

Note: BW uses </BIC|/BI0>/F<InfoCube name> to name an InfoCube's fact table in the database.

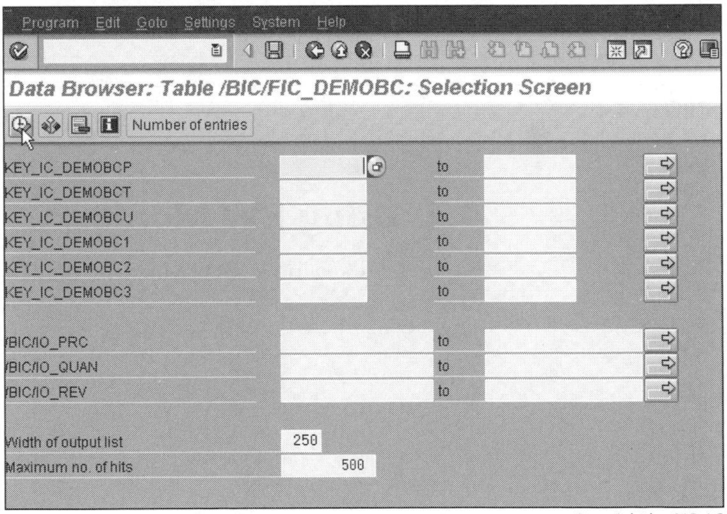

SCREEN 4.3

Result

The loaded data are displayed in Screen 4.4. As we can see, the transfer rules we created in Section 3.7, "Creating an InfoSource for Transaction Data," worked correctly.

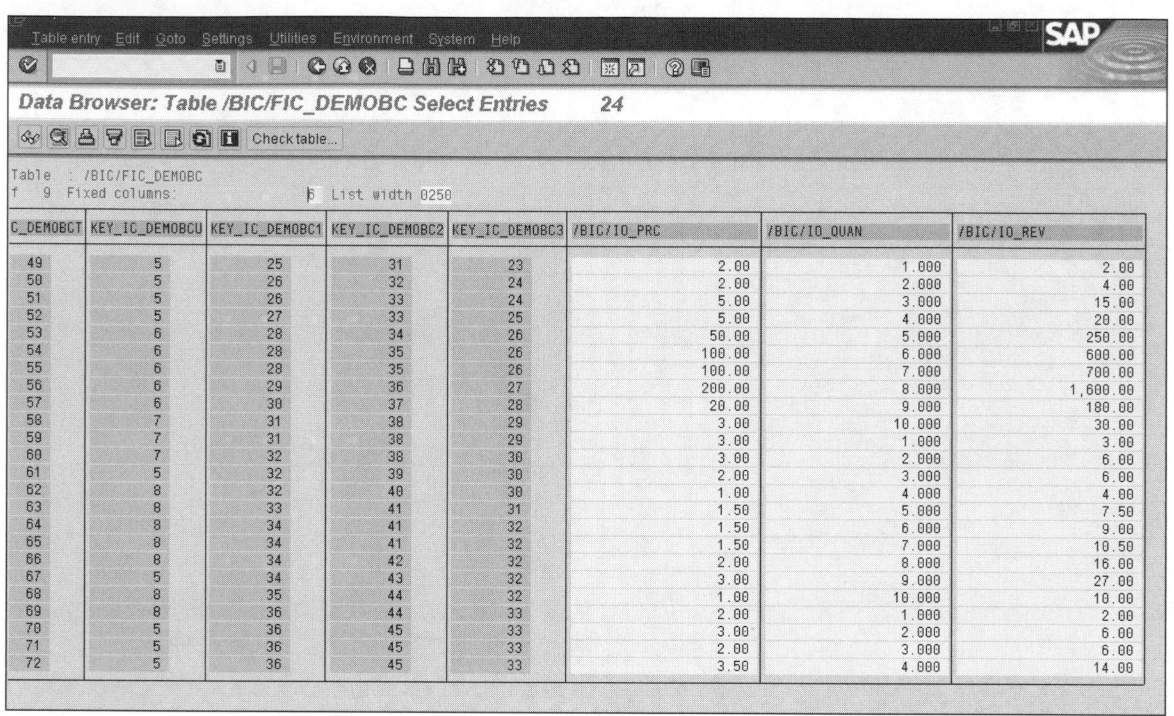

C_DEMOBCT	KEY_IC_DEMOBCU	KEY_IC_DEMOBC1	KEY_IC_DEMOBC2	KEY_IC_DEMOBC3	/BIC/IO_PRC	/BIC/IO_QUAN	/BIC/IO_REV
49	5	25	31	23	2.00	1.000	2.00
50	5	26	32	24	2.00	2.000	4.00
51	5	26	33	24	5.00	3.000	15.00
52	5	27	33	25	5.00	4.000	20.00
53	6	28	34	26	50.00	5.000	250.00
54	6	28	35	26	100.00	6.000	600.00
55	6	28	35	26	100.00	7.000	700.00
56	6	29	36	27	200.00	8.000	1,600.00
57	6	30	37	28	20.00	9.000	180.00
58	7	31	38	29	3.00	10.000	30.00
59	7	31	38	29	3.00	1.000	3.00
60	7	32	38	30	3.00	2.000	6.00
61	5	32	39	30	2.00	3.000	6.00
62	8	32	40	30	1.00	4.000	4.00
63	8	33	41	31	1.50	5.000	7.50
64	8	34	41	32	1.50	6.000	9.00
65	8	34	41	32	1.50	7.000	10.50
66	8	34	42	32	2.00	8.000	16.00
67	5	34	43	32	3.00	9.000	27.00
68	8	35	44	32	1.00	10.000	10.00
69	8	36	44	33	2.00	1.000	2.00
70	5	36	45	33	3.00	2.000	6.00
71	5	36	45	33	2.00	3.000	6.00
72	5	36	45	33	3.50	4.000	14.00

SCREEN 4.4

4.2 Using BW Monitor

Next, let's see how BW Monitor can help us troubleshoot during the ETTL process.

Work Instructions

Step 1 Select *InfoCube – demo: Basic Cube*, and then click [icon].

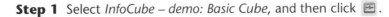

SCREEN 4.5

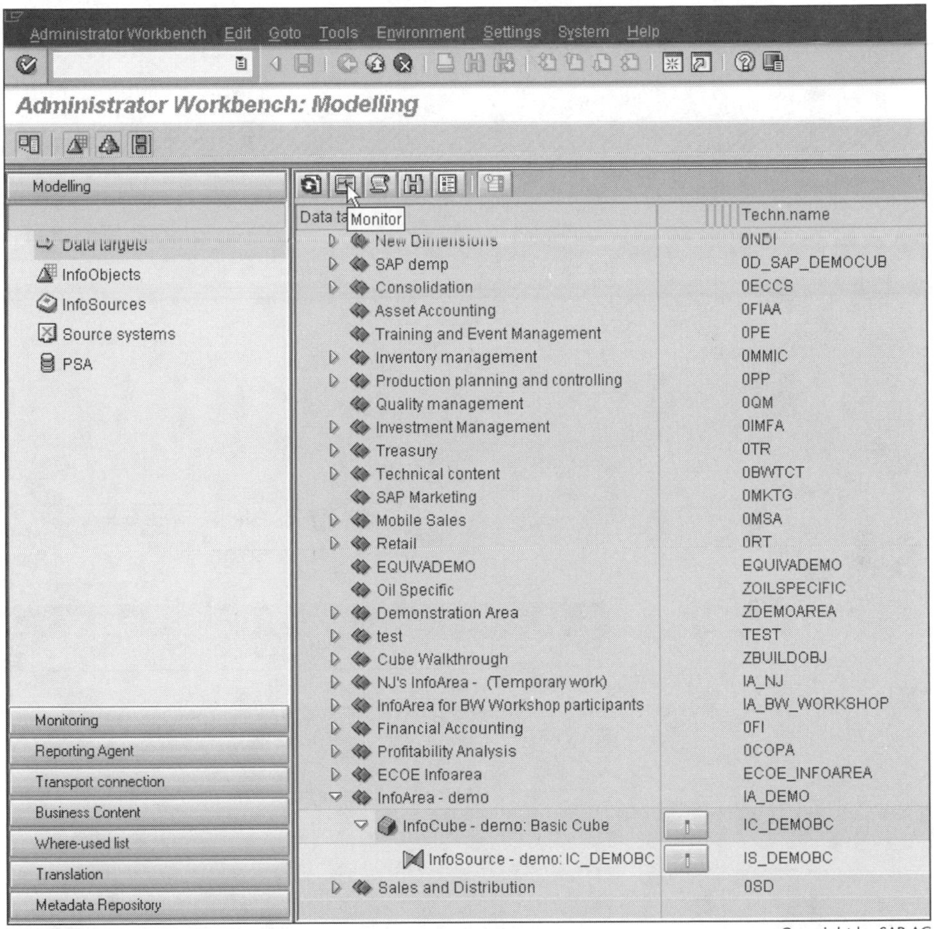

Step 2 Leave *Selection date* blank to list the status of all data loads into this InfoCube. Click [icon] to continue.

SCREEN 4.6

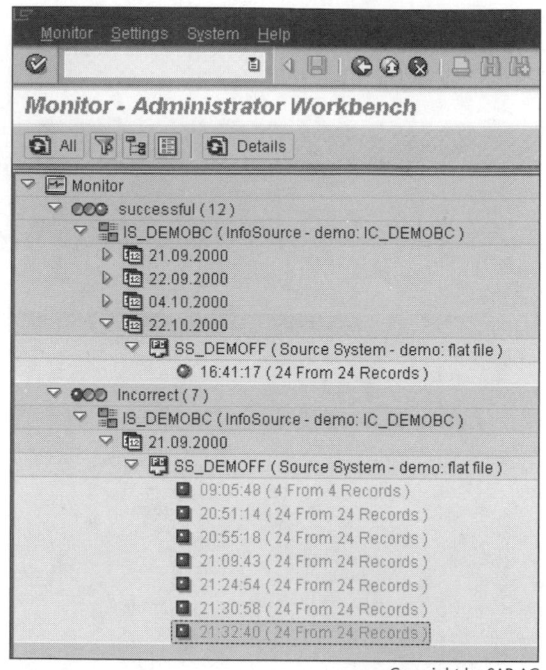

SCREEN 4.7

Step 3 We see the status of all data loads (12 successful, 7 failed), plus date/time information, the number of records selected from the source system, and the number of records coming into the BW system.

Double-click the last failed load operation to get its details.

Step 4 Click Error message to display the error.

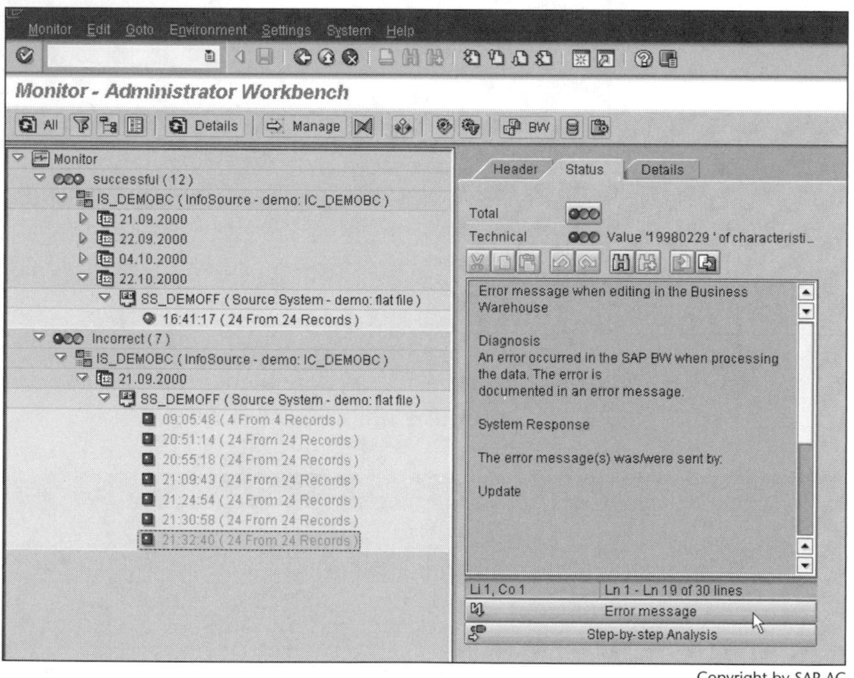

SCREEN 4.8

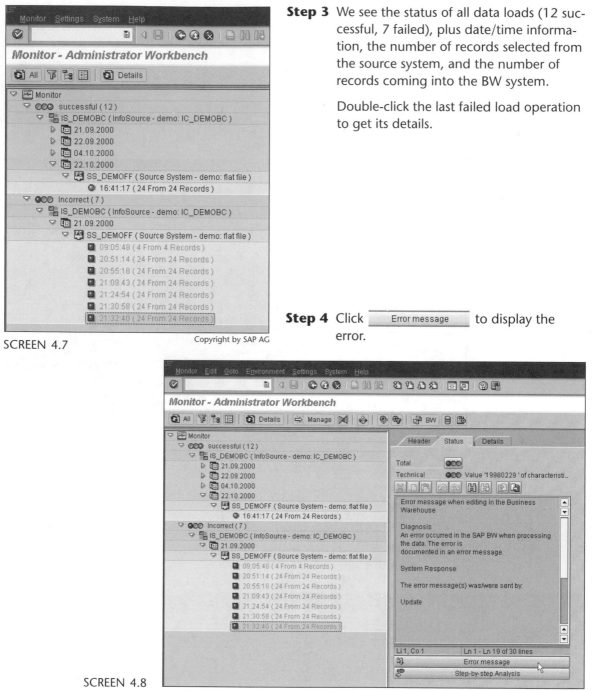

Step 5 Review the error message.

SCREEN 4.9

Monitor messages

Type	Message Text	ID	No.	LTxt
■	Value '19980229 ' of characteristic 0DATE is not plausible	BRAIN	27	

Step 6 Under the *Details* tab, notice how the data flowed and where the error occurred.

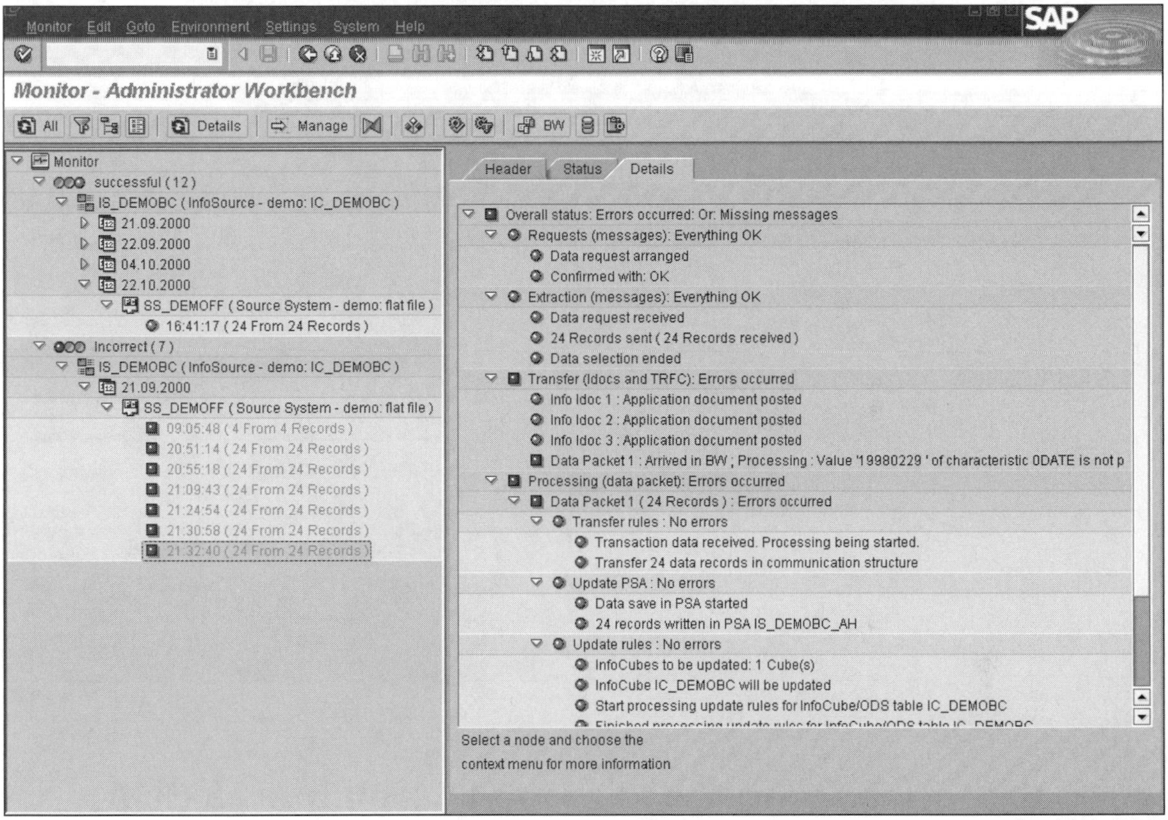

SCREEN 4.10

Result

You have learned how to use BW Monitor to display the status of data loads and to find out when, where, and how errors (if any arose) occurred.

To examine the status of other data loads, we can click [filter icon] in Screen 4.10. In the new screen, we can specify selection conditions to display the status of the data loads in which we are interested (Screen 4.11). For example, by clicking User... in the *Further selections* block, we can specify user-related selection conditions.

SCREEN 4.11

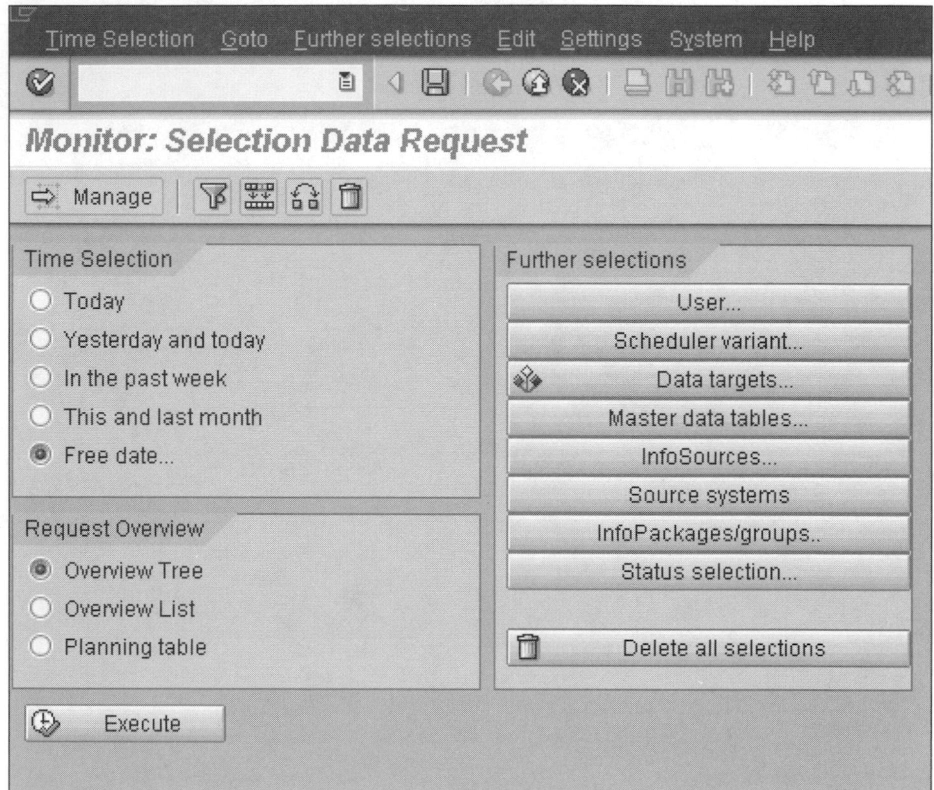

4.3 Using the Persistent Staging Area (PSA)

PSA stores data in its original source system format. In this way, it gives us a chance to examine the data before we send them into their destination—either characteristics, ODS objects, or InfoCubes.

Work Instructions

Step 1 Reload the data from Table 3.3. This time, in the InfoPackage created in Section 3.9, under the *Processing* tab, select the option *Only PSA*, instead of the default *PSA and then into data targets (packet by packet)*.

SCREEN 4.12

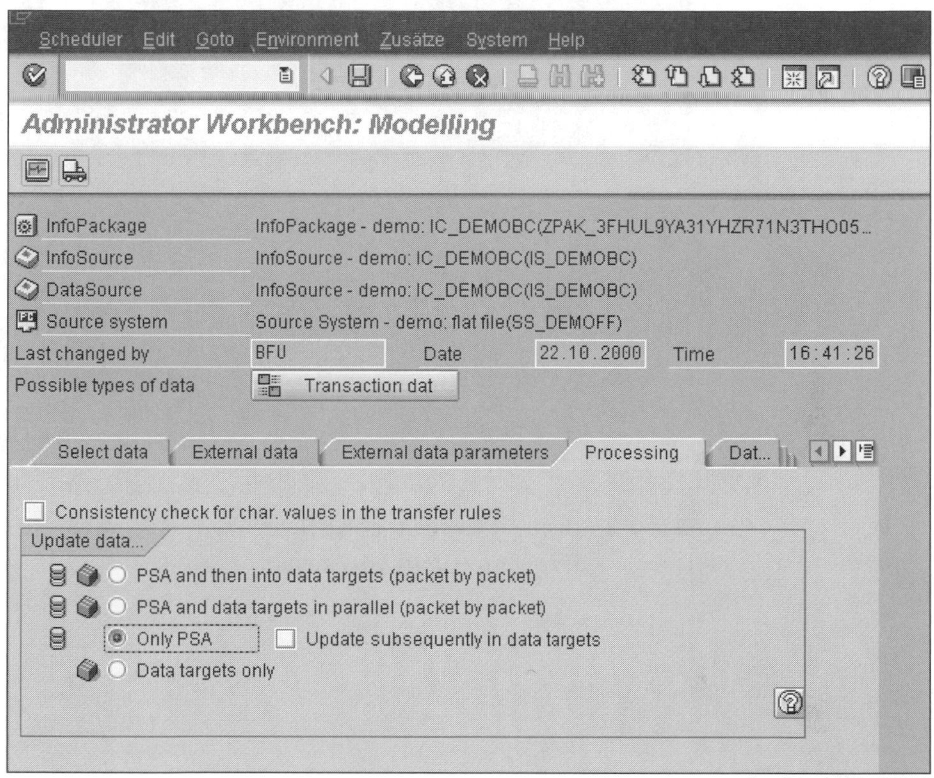

Step 2 Start the data loading process as shown in Screen 3.71. After the *Data was requested* message appears at the bottom of the screen, click as shown in Screen 3.22. A green light appears next to the data load request, which indicates that the job was successful.

Next, click to display the PSA data.

SCREEN 4.13

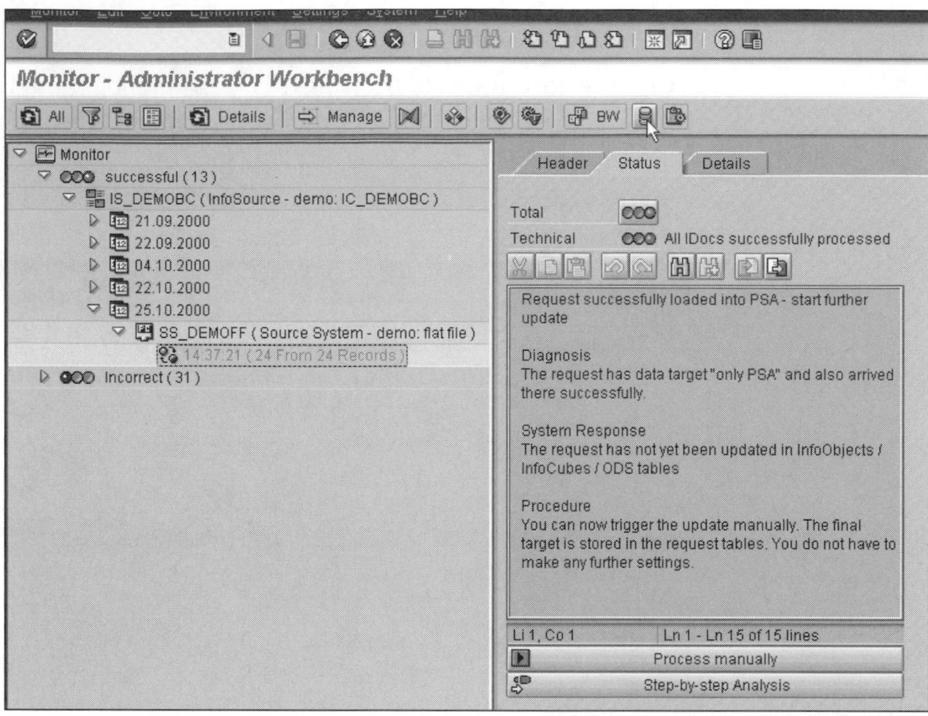

Step 3 Click ✔ to see records 1 to 1000. BW sets this range by default.

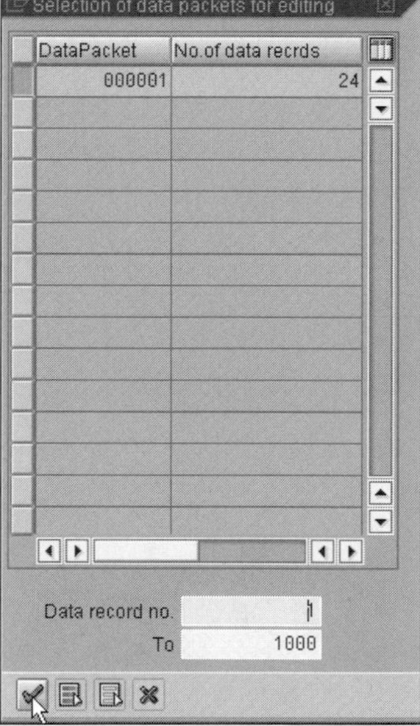

SCREEN 4.14

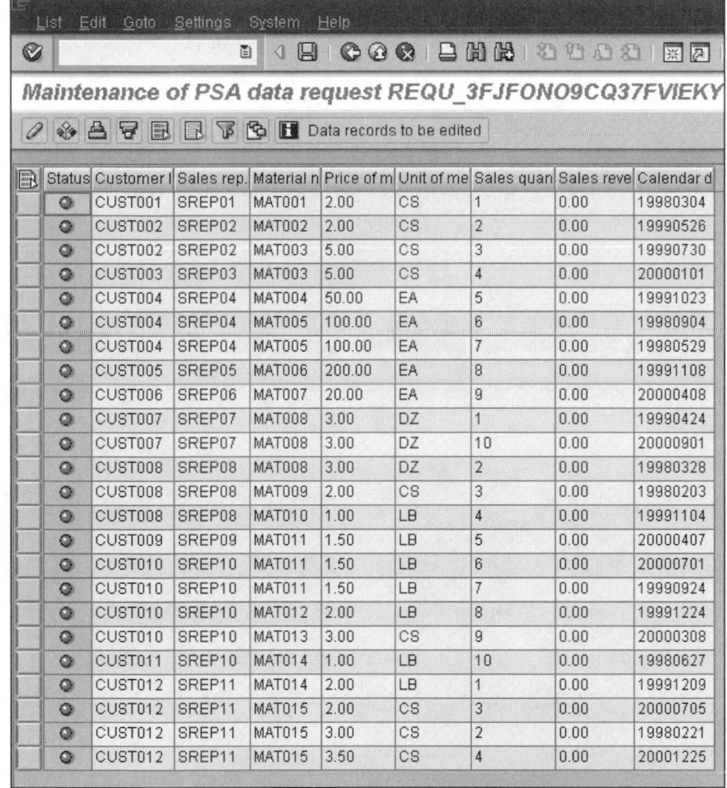

Status	Customer I	Sales rep.	Material n	Price of m	Unit of me	Sales quan	Sales reve	Calendar d
	CUST001	SREP01	MAT001	2.00	CS	1	0.00	19980304
	CUST002	SREP02	MAT002	2.00	CS	2	0.00	19990526
	CUST002	SREP02	MAT003	5.00	CS	3	0.00	19990730
	CUST003	SREP03	MAT003	5.00	CS	4	0.00	20000101
	CUST004	SREP04	MAT004	50.00	EA	5	0.00	19991023
	CUST004	SREP04	MAT005	100.00	EA	6	0.00	19980904
	CUST004	SREP04	MAT005	100.00	EA	7	0.00	19980529
	CUST005	SREP05	MAT006	200.00	EA	8	0.00	19991108
	CUST006	SREP06	MAT007	20.00	EA	9	0.00	20000408
	CUST007	SREP07	MAT008	3.00	DZ	1	0.00	19990424
	CUST007	SREP07	MAT008	3.00	DZ	10	0.00	20000901
	CUST008	SREP08	MAT008	3.00	DZ	2	0.00	19980328
	CUST008	SREP08	MAT009	2.00	CS	3	0.00	19980203
	CUST008	SREP08	MAT010	1.00	LB	4	0.00	19991104
	CUST009	SREP09	MAT011	1.50	LB	5	0.00	20000407
	CUST010	SREP10	MAT011	1.50	LB	6	0.00	20000701
	CUST010	SREP10	MAT011	1.50	LB	7	0.00	19990924
	CUST010	SREP10	MAT012	2.00	LB	8	0.00	19991224
	CUST010	SREP10	MAT013	3.00	CS	9	0.00	20000308
	CUST011	SREP10	MAT014	1.00	LB	10	0.00	19980627
	CUST012	SREP11	MAT014	2.00	LB	1	0.00	19991209
	CUST012	SREP11	MAT015	2.00	CS	3	0.00	20000705
	CUST012	SREP11	MAT015	3.00	CS	2	0.00	19980221
	CUST012	SREP11	MAT015	3.50	CS	4	0.00	20001225

SCREEN 4.15

Step 4 Review the 24 records stored in PSA. To modify one of them, you select the record and then click ✎. Notice the zeros in the *Sales revenue* column; their presence indicates that the transfer rules have not yet been applied to the PSA data.

Step 5 After checking the data in PSA, now we can send the data to IC_DEMOBC.

In the *Administrator Workbench: Modelling* window, notice the load request *InfoPackage – demo: IC_DEMOBC (25.10.2000)* in the right panel. Right-click the request, and then select *Start the update immediately*.

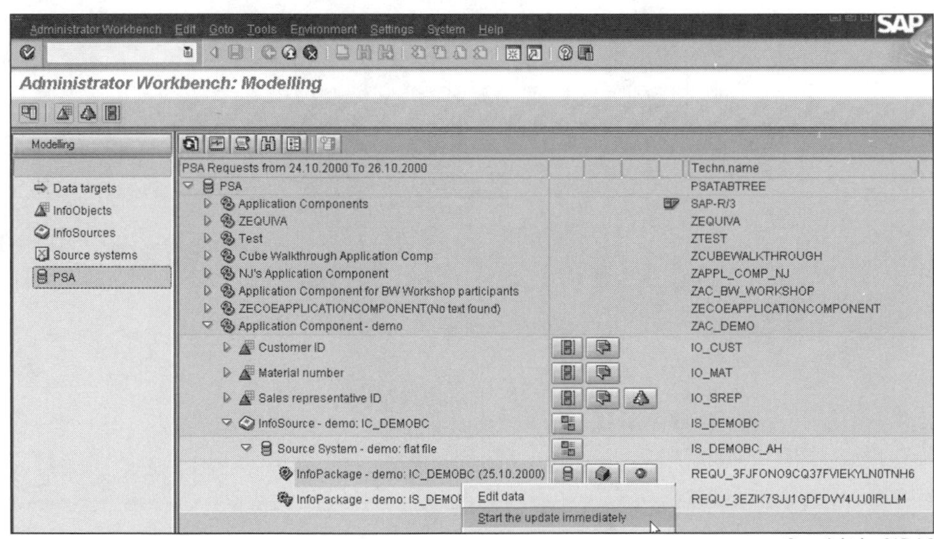

SCREEN 4.16

Step 6 In the *Administrator Workbench: Modelling* window, right-click *InfoCube – demo: Basic Cube*, and then select *Manage* (Screens 4.1 and 4.2).

Under the *Requests* tab, notice the status of the data loads. The first row shows the status of the data load in Step 5. Click [icon] in the first row, which returns you to BW Monitor. You will see that the load from PSA into IC_DEMOBC was successful.

SCREEN 4.17

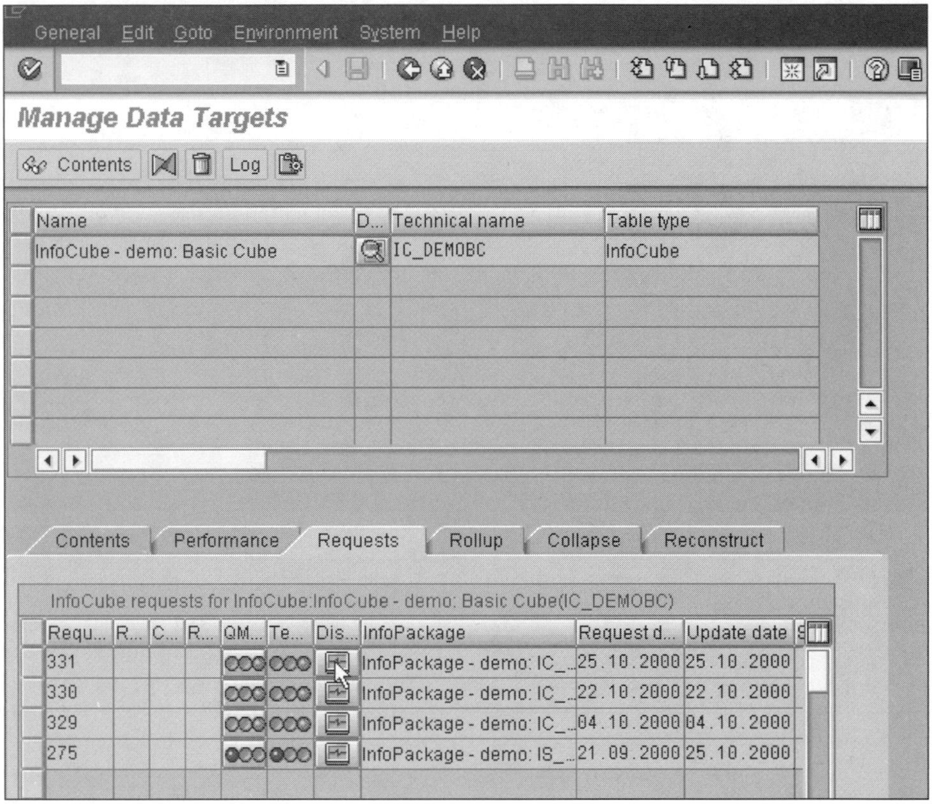

General Edit Goto Environment System Help

Manage Data Targets

Contents | Log

Name	D...	Technical name	Table type
InfoCube - demo: Basic Cube		IC_DEMOBC	InfoCube

Contents | Performance | Requests | Rollup | Collapse | Reconstruct

InfoCube requests for InfoCube:InfoCube - demo: Basic Cube(IC_DEMOBC)

Requ...	R...	C...	R...	QM...	Te...	Dis...	InfoPackage	Request d...	Update date
331							InfoPackage - demo: IC_...	25.10.2000	25.10.2000
330							InfoPackage - demo: IC_...	22.10.2000	22.10.2000
329							InfoPackage - demo: IC_...	04.10.2000	04.10.2000
275							InfoPackage - demo: IS_...	21.09.2000	25.10.2000

Result

You have loaded data into IC_DEMOBC via PSA. Using PSA, you verified that the data were loaded correctly into BW.

4.4 Summary

In this chapter, we checked InfoCube contents, used BW Monitor to analyze data loads, and used PSA to check data before they were sent to a destination InfoCube.

Figure 4.1 shows how data flow in BW. In this chapter, we followed the path linked via solid lines. Later chapters in this book will discuss the other paths.

FIGURE 4.1
DATA FLOW

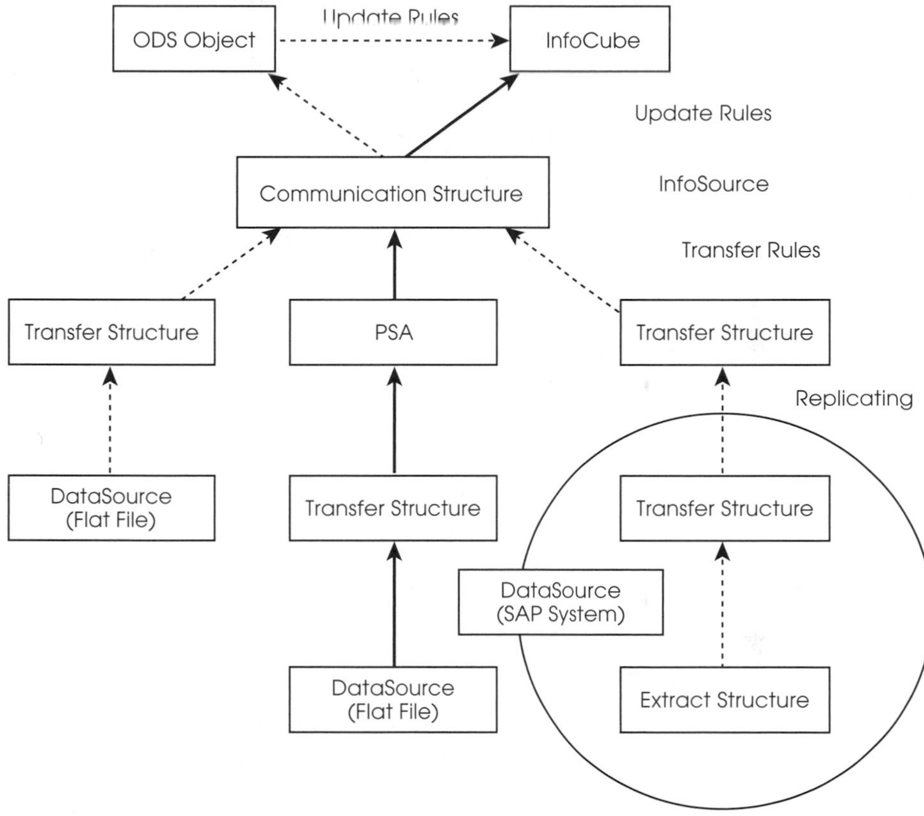

Key Terms

Term	Description
PSA	PSA is a data staging area in BW. It allows us to check data in an intermediate location, before they are sent to their destinations in BW.

Next . . .

We will create queries on the InfoCube to generate reports.

Chapter 5

Creating Queries and Workbooks

In Chapter 2, we created an InfoCube; in Chapter 3, we loaded data into it. In this chapter, we will create queries and reports using the BW presentation tool called **Business Explorer (BEx)**. BEx consists of two applications: **BEx Analyzer**, which you use to create queries and reports, and **BEx Browser**, which you use to organize reports. We will work with both applications in this chapter. We will also demonstrate how to create and use **variables**.

5.1 Creating a Query Using BEx Analyzer

The following steps demonstrate how to create a query.

Work Instructions

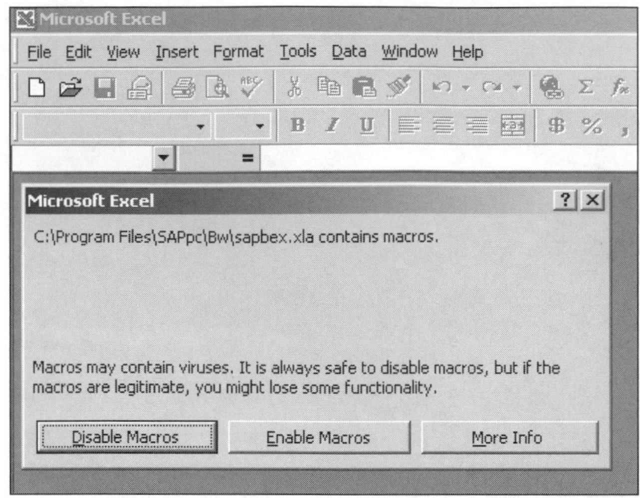

SCREEN 5.1

Step 1 Open SAP Business Explorer Analyzer by selecting *Start* ➜ *Programs* ➜ *SAP Frontend* ➜ *SAP Business Explorer Analyzer* from Windows, and then clicking Enable Macros .

Note: BEx requires the gateway service to communicate with the SAP application server. Appendix B, SAP Basis Overview, discusses the gateway service and the SAP application server.

Step 2 Click [Open icon] to open or create a query.

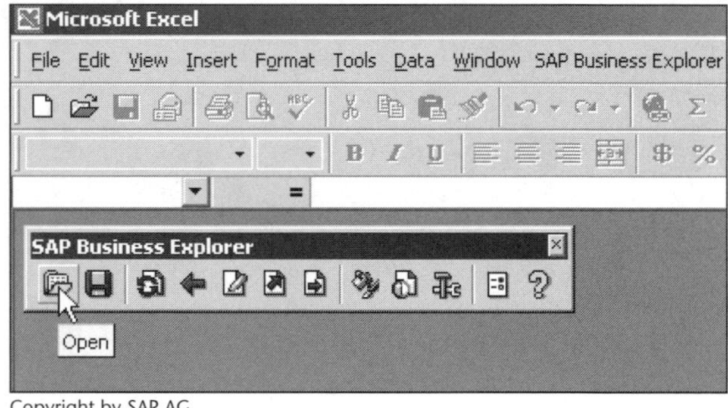

SCREEN 5.2

Step 3 We need to log on to the BW system. Select the system that contains our InfoCube, and then click OK to continue.

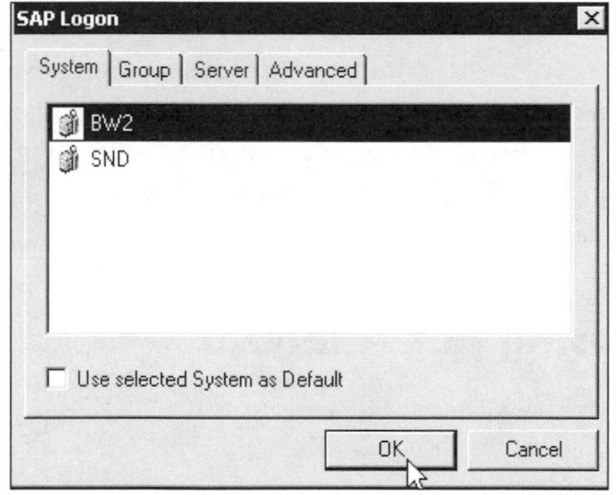

SCREEN 5.3

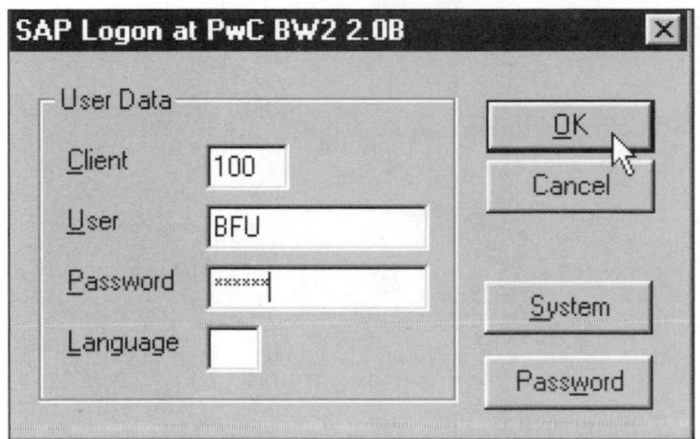

SCREEN 5.4

Step 4 Enter the correct user ID and password, and then click OK to continue.

Step 5 We have not created any workbooks yet. Click Queries to display queries or create a query

SCREEN 5.5

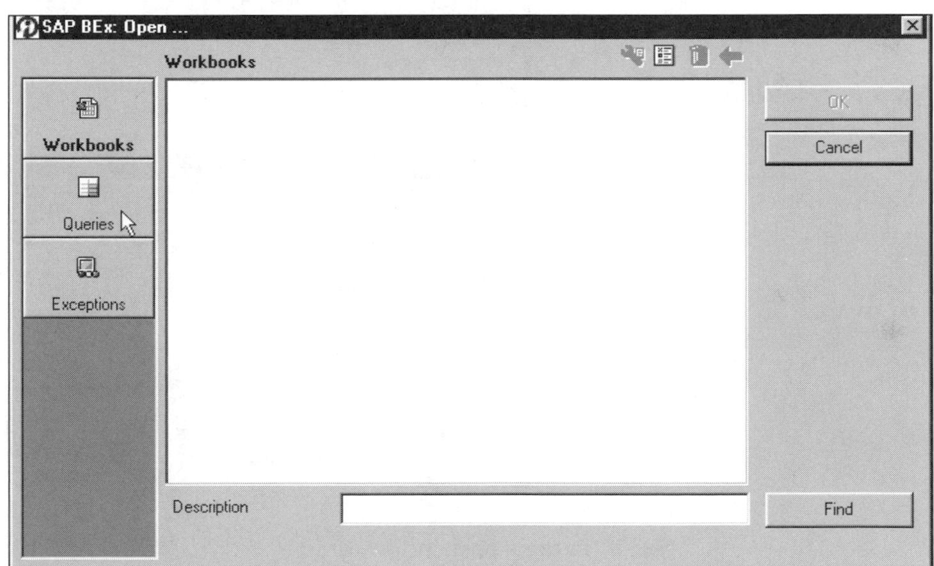

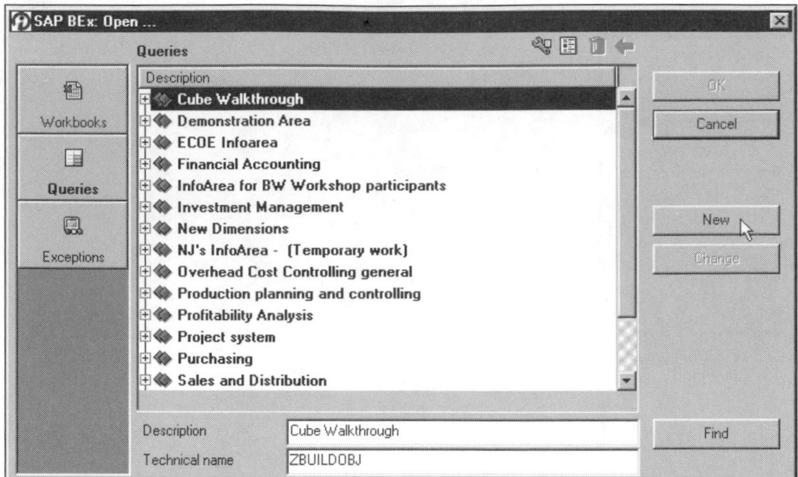

SCREEN 5.6

Step 6 Review the list of InfoAreas that is displayed. Our *InfoArea—demo* does not appear in the list because it has only one InfoCube, which does not have a query yet. Click New to create a query.

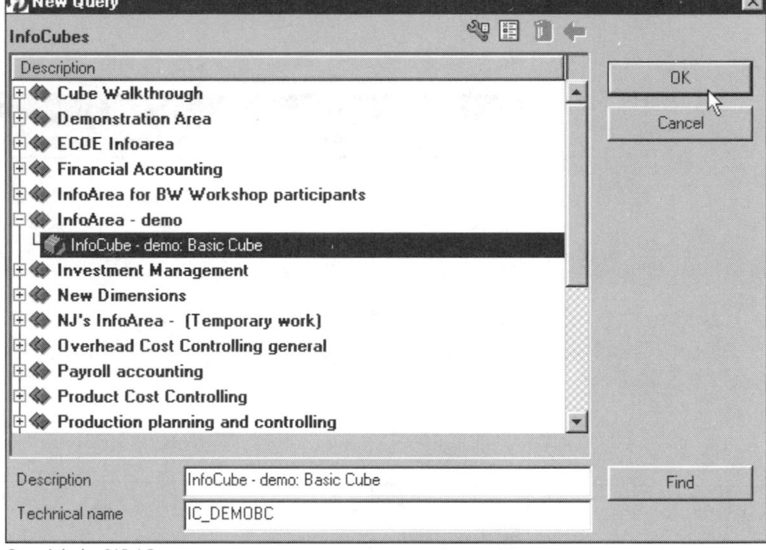

SCREEN 5.7

Step 7 Select our InfoCube, and then click OK to open a query design window.

Step 8 In the new window, drag and drop three key figures to the *Columns* panel, characteristic *Sales rep. ID* to the *Rows* panel, and three other characteristics to the *Free characteristics* panel.

If desired, you can click the save-and-run icon to save and run the query. The result will not display *Sales rep. ID* in the hierarchy we created in Section 3.6, “Entering the Master Data, Text, and Hierarchy Manually,” however.

To display the hierarchy in the query result, right-click *Sales rep. ID* and select *Properties.*

SCREEN 5.8

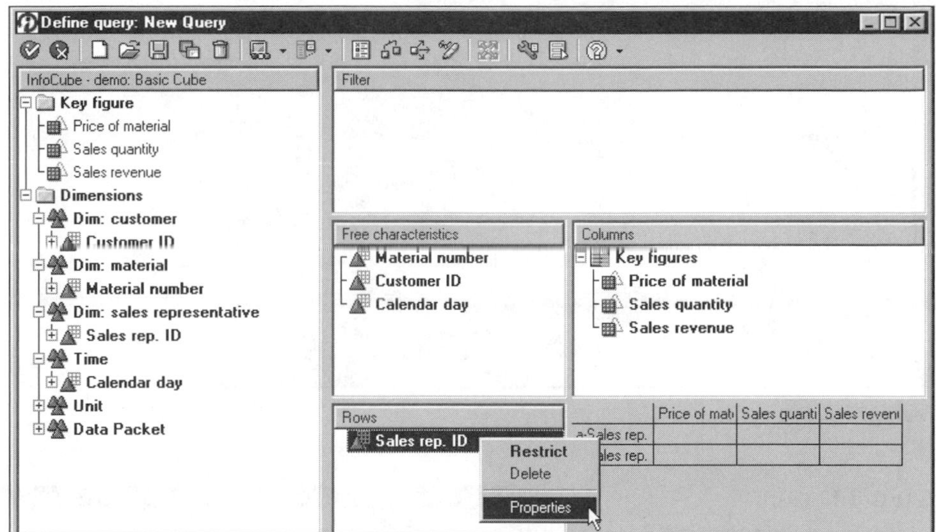

Step 9 Click to list the hierarchies associated with the characteristic.

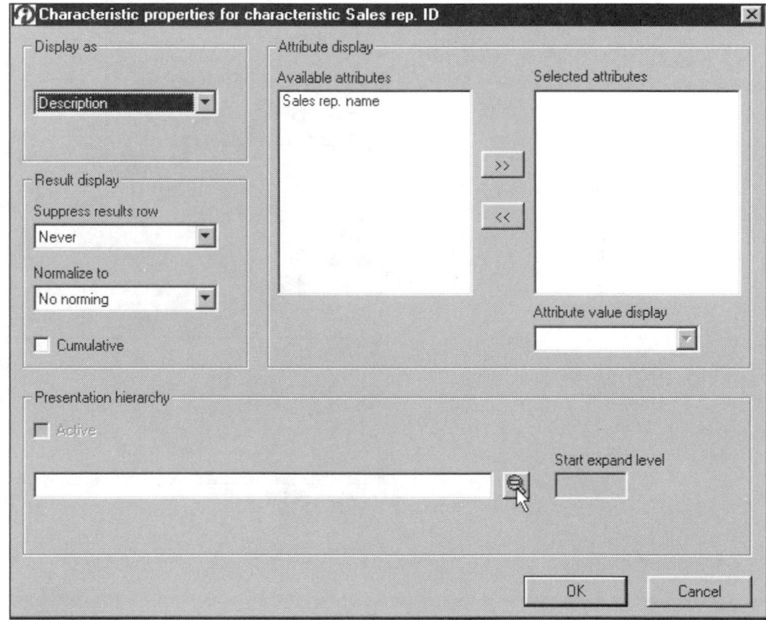

SCREEN 5.9

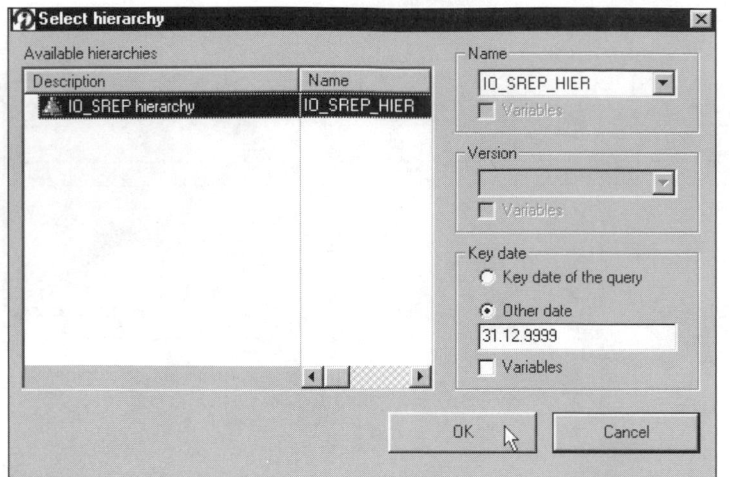

SCREEN 5.10

Step 10 In the pop-up window, select *IO_SREP hierarchy,* which we created in Section 3.6, and then click OK. Notice the date *31.12.9999* in the *Key date* block.

Step 11 Click OK to continue.

Characteristic properties for characteristic Sales rep. ID

Display as

Description

Result display

Suppress results row

Never

Normalize to

No norming

Cumulative

Attribute display

Available attributes

Sales rep. name

Selected attributes

Attribute value display

Presentation hierarchy

Active

IO_SREP hierarchy

Start expand level

3

OK

Cancel

SCREEN 5.11

Step 12 Click ✓ to save and execute the query.

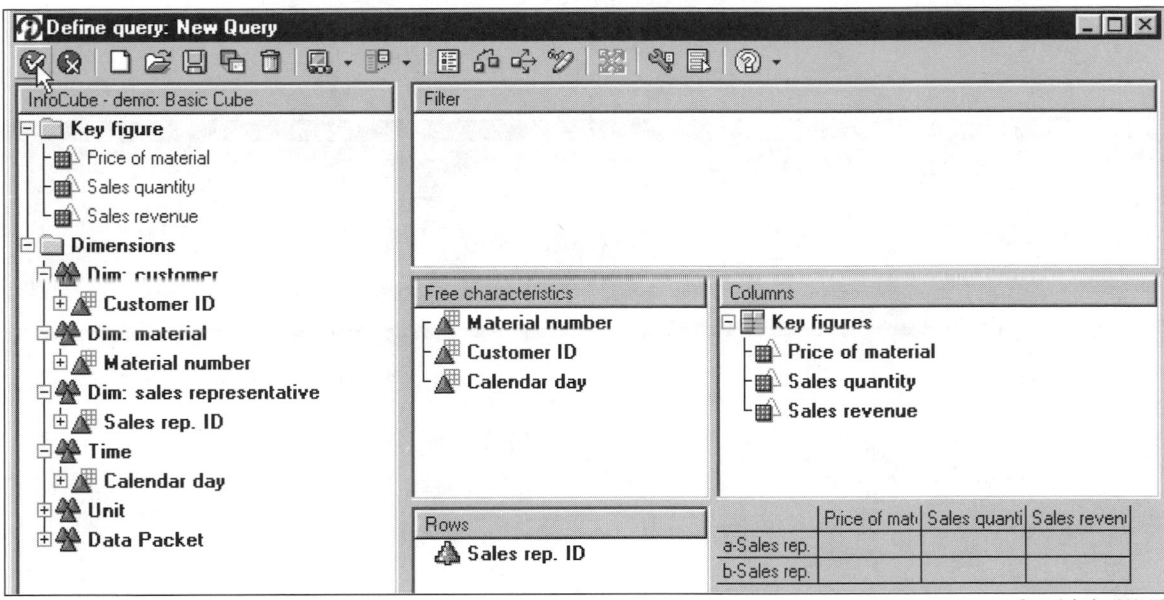

SCREEN 5.12

Step 13 Enter a technical name and a description, and then click ✓. We use a simple format <InfoCube name>_Q<two-digit number> to name the query, where "Q" stands for query.

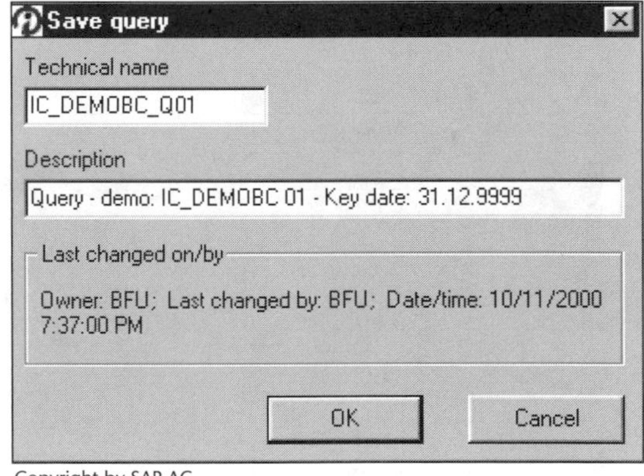

SCREEN 5.13

Step 14 An Excel file is opened and populated with the query result. Examine the query result:

1. The *Sales rep. ID* data appear in column A. The Step 8 free characteristics data are not visible.
2. In the Chicago office, materials sold by Kevin are in unit EA, and those sold by Chris are in unit DZ. It is not appropriate to generate a total by combining EA and DZ, so the cell for the Chicago office contains *.

3. Besides the three regions, another node appears at the same hierarchy level called *Not assgnd Sales rep. ID (s)* with *SREP11* under it. The reason is that SREP11 is not in the sales organization (Table 1.3) although he or she made sales (Table 1.4).

Microsoft Excel - Book1

File Edit View Insert Format Tools Data Window SAP Business Explorer Help

A9 = Sales rep. ID

	A	B	C	D
1	Query - demo: IC_DEMOBC 01 - Key date: 31.12.9999			
2				
3	Material number			
4	Customer ID			
5	Calendar day			
6	Key figures			
7	Sales rep. ID			
8				
9	Sales rep. ID	**Price of material**	**Sales quantity**	**Sales revenue**
10	Overall result	**$ 517.00**	*	**$ 3,528.00**
11	▽ **IO_SREP hierarchy**	$ 506.50	*	$ 3,500.00
12	▽ **East**	$ 14.00	10 CS	$ 41.00
13	▷ **Atlanta**	$ 2.00	1 CS	$ 2.00
14	▷ **New York**	$ 12.00	9 CS	$ 39.00
15	▽ **Midwest**	$ 476.00	*	$ 3,363.00
16	▽ **Chicago**	$ 26.00	*	$ 213.00
17	**Kevin**	$ 20.00	9 EA	$ 180.00
18	**Chris**	$ 6.00	11 DZ	$ 33.00
19	▷ **Dallas**	$ 450.00	26 EA	$ 3,150.00
20	▽ **West**	$ 16.50	*	$ 96.00
21	▷ **Denver**	$ 6.00	*	$ 16.00
22	▷ **Los Angles**	$ 1.50	5 LB	$ 7.50
23	▷ **Seattle**	$ 9.00	*	$ 72.50
24	**Not assgnd. Sales rep. ID (s)**	$ 10.50	*	$ 28.00
25	**SREP11**	$ 10.50	*	$ 28.00
26				

SCREEN 5.14

Step 15 Double-click the free characteristics *Material number, Customer ID,* and *Calendar day*, which produces a new query result.

Microsoft Excel - Book1

Query - demo: IC_DEMOBC 01 - Key date: 31.12.9999

Material number
Customer ID
Calendar day
Key figures
Sales rep. ID

Material number	Customer ID	Calendar day	Price of material	Sales quantity	Sales revenue
America corn	**Sports Motor Company**	**04.11.1999**	$ 1.00	4 LB	$ 4.00
		Result	**$ 1.00**	**4 LB**	**$ 4.00**
	Result	Result	**$ 1.00**	**4 LB**	**$ 4.00**
Asia rice	**Hoolywood Studio**	**24.09.1999**	$ 1.50	7 LB	$ 10.50
		01.07.2000	$ 1.50	6 LB	$ 9.00
		Result	**$ 3.00**	**13 LB**	**$ 19.50**
	Swan Stores	**07.04.2000**	$ 1.50	5 LB	$ 7.50
		Result	**$ 1.50**	**5 LB**	**$ 7.50**
	Result	Result	**$ 4.50**	**18 LB**	**$ 27.00**
Black pen	**Mobile Communication**	**24.04.1999**	$ 3.00	1 DZ	$ 3.00
		01.09.2000	$ 3.00	10 DZ	$ 30.00
		Result	**$ 6.00**	**11 DZ**	**$ 33.00**
	Sports Motor Company	**28.03.1998**	$ 3.00	2 DZ	$ 6.00
		Result	**$ 3.00**	**2 DZ**	**$ 6.00**
	Result	Result	**$ 9.00**	**13 DZ**	**$ 39.00**
California orange	**Airspace Industries,**	**21.02.1998**	$ 3.00	2 CS	$ 6.00
		05.07.2000	$ 2.00	3 CS	$ 6.00

Copyright by SAP AG

SCREEN 5.15

Note: Free characteristics allow for drill-down. Use of free characteristics with an appropriate query read mode reduces the I/O volume for the initial query result, thereby improving query performance. Section 13.3.1, "Query Read Mode," discusses three types of query read modes.

Step 16 To save the query result, click [save icon], and then select *Save as new workbook. . . .* In BW, the saved Excel file with the query result is called a **workbook**. Section 5.2 demonstrates how to access and open the workbook using three different methods.

	A	B	C	D
1	Query - demo: IC_DEMOBC 01 - Key date: 31.12.9999			
2				
3	Material number			
4	Customer ID			
5	Calendar day			
6	Key figures			
7	Sales rep. ID			
8				
9	Sales rep. ID	Price of material	Sales quantity	Sales revenue
10	Overall result	**$ 517.00**	*	**$ 3,528.00**
11	▽ IO_SREP hierarchy	$ 506.50	*	$ 3,500.00
12	▽ East	$ 14.00	10 CS	$ 41.00
13	▷ Atlanta	$ 2.00	1 CS	$ 2.00
14	▷ New York	$ 12.00	9 CS	$ 39.00
15	▽ Midwest	$ 476.00	*	$ 3,363.00
16	▽ Chicago	$ 26.00	*	$ 213.00
17	Kevin	$ 20.00	9 EA	$ 180.00
18	Chris	$ 6.00	11 DZ	$ 33.00
19	▷ Dallas	$ 450.00	26 EA	$ 3,150.00
20	▽ West	$ 16.50	*	$ 96.00
21	▷ Denver	$ 6.00	*	$ 16.00
22	▷ Los Angeles	$ 1.50	5 LB	$ 7.50
23	▷ Seattle	$ 9.00	*	$ 72.50
24	Not assgnd. Sales rep. ID (s)	$ 10.50	*	$ 28.00
25	SREP11	$ 10.50	*	$ 28.00
26				

SCREEN 5.16

Note: Workbooks are saved as Binary Large Objects (BLOBs) in the database. A BLOB is a special data type that stores blocks of unstructured data (such as text, graphic images, video clips, and sound waveforms) in the database. In addition, it allows for efficient, random, piecewise access to the data.

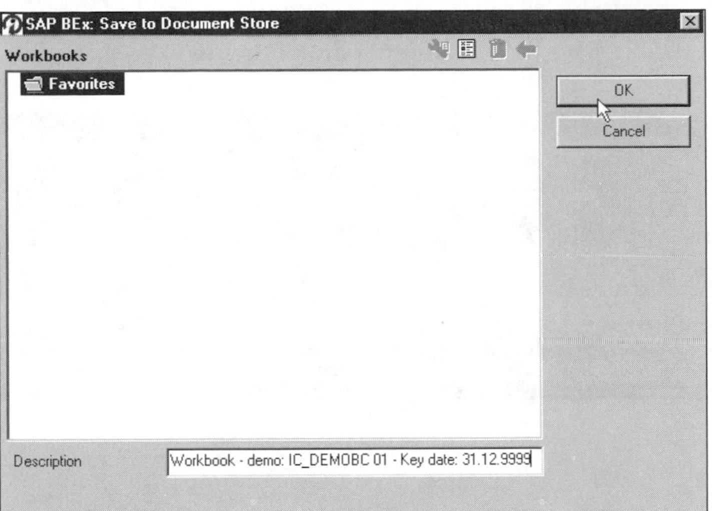

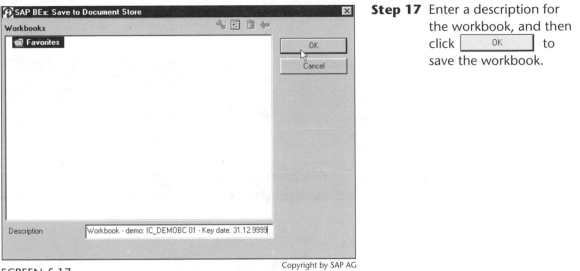

SCREEN 5.17

Step 17 Enter a description for the workbook, and then click [OK] to save the workbook.

Step 18 Let's create a new query assuming that the Denver office is still in the Midwest region. Recall that in Chapter 1, we noted that before January 1, 2000, the Denver office belonged to the Midwest region.

Create another query by repeating the previous steps, but this time replace the key date 31.12.**9999** in Screen 5.10 with *31.12.**1999***.

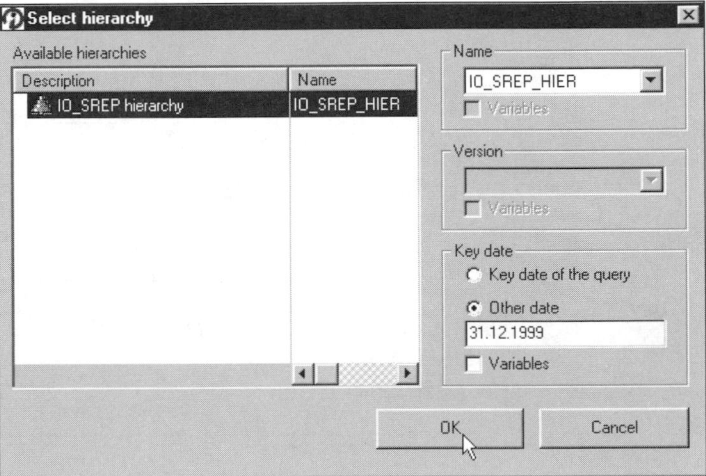

SCREEN 5.18

Step 19 Run the query. In the result, the Denver office is listed under the Midwest region. Save this query result as another workbook.

Microsoft Excel - Book5

File Edit View Insert Format Tools Data Window SAP Business Explorer Help

A9 = Sales rep. ID

Query - demo: IC_DEMOBC 02 - Key date: 31.12.1999

Material number
Customer ID
Calendar day
Key figures
Sales rep. ID

Sales rep. ID	Price of material	Sales quantity	Sales revenue
Overall result	**$ 517.00**	*	**$ 3,528.00**
▽ **IO_SREP hierarchy**	$ 506.50	*	$ 3,500.00
▽ **East**	$ 14.00	10 CS	$ 41.00
▷ **Atlanta**	$ 2.00	1 CS	$ 2.00
▷ **New York**	$ 12.00	9 CS	$ 39.00
▽ **Midwest**	$ 482.00	*	$ 3,379.00
▷ **Chicago**	$ 26.00	*	$ 213.00
▷ **Dallas**	$ 450.00	26 EA	$ 3,150.00
▷ **Denver**	$ 6.00	*	$ 16.00
▽ **West**	$ 10.50	*	$ 80.00
▷ **Los Angeles**	$ 1.50	5 LB	$ 7.50
▷ **Seattle**	$ 9.00	*	$ 72.50
Not assgnd. Sales rep. ID (s)	$ 10.50	*	$ 28.00

SCREEN 5.19

Result

You created two queries with different key dates and saved the query results as workbooks.

Note: In the data warehousing world, the key date 31.12.9999 query result (Screen 5.14) is often referred to as a **today-is-yesterday** scenario, and the key date 31.12.1999 query result (Screen 5.14) is known as a **yesterday-is-**

today scenario. In Section 7.3, "InfoCube Design Alternative II—Dimension Characteristics," we will encounter two other scenarios, **yesterday-or-today** and **yesterday-and-today.** These scenarios are developed to validate and analyze data when the situation involves a slowly changing dimension.

5.2 Organizing Workbooks Using BEx Browser

After saving the two workbooks in Section 5.1, we can reopen them using any of the following three methods.

Method 1: BEx Analyzer

If we now click [Workbooks] in Screen 5.20, we see the saved workbooks. If we double-click either of the workbooks, BEx Analyzer will open, and the saved workbook will be displayed.

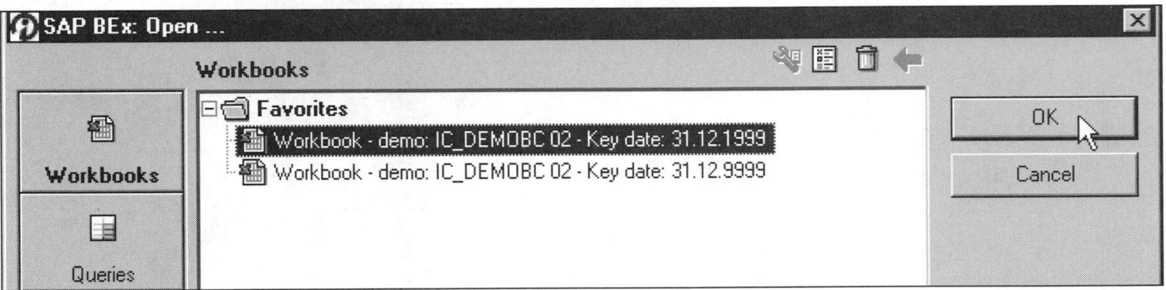

SCREEN 5.20

Method 2: SAP GUI

Logging on to BW from SAP GUI, we see the workbooks listed under the *Favorites* folder (Screen 5.21). If we double-click either of them, BEx Analyzer will open, and the saved workbook will be displayed.

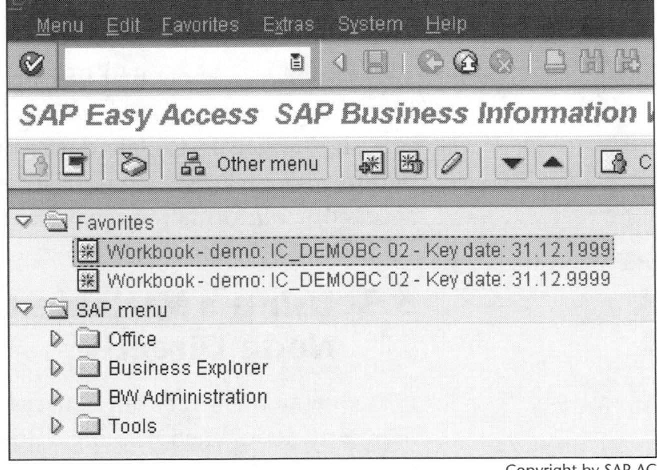

SCREEN 5.21

Method 3: BEx Browser

If we launch BEx Browser by selecting *Start* ➜ *Programs* ➜ *SAP Frontend* ➜ *SAP Business Explorer Browser* from Windows and log on to the BW system, we see the two workbooks displayed as Favorites (Screen 5.22). If we double-click either one of them, BEx Analyzer will open, and the workbook will be displayed.

SCREEN 5.22

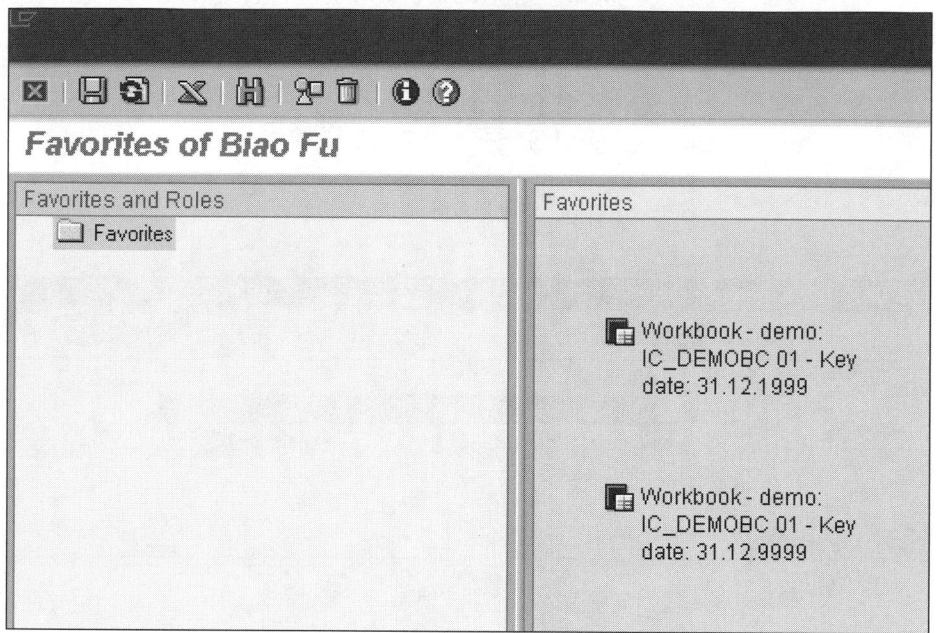

For now, we know that BEx Browser is just a workbook organizer and that BEx Analyzer displays our query results. After we open a workbook, we can refresh it to get up-to-date data from the database by clicking [refresh icon] on the toolbar. In Chapter 6, Managing User Authorization, we will demonstrate how to access other information resources from BEx Browser.

5.3 Using a Variable to Access a Hierarchy Node Directly

If the hierarchy is very large, users might want to jump directly to a particular hierarchy node when running a query. One way of achieving this goal is to use variables. Next, we describe a procedure to create a variable.

Work Instructions

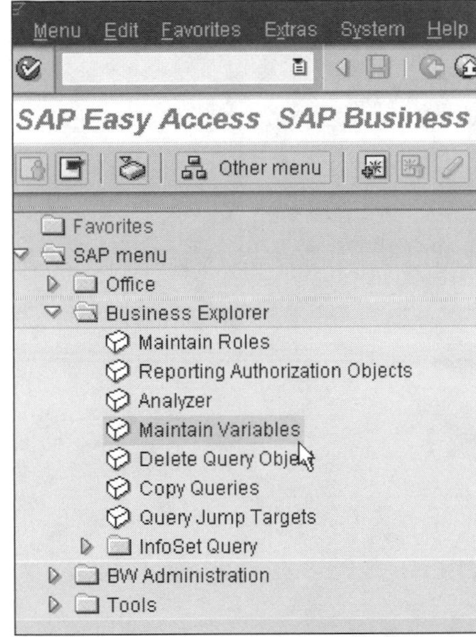

SCREEN 5.23

Step 1 Log on to the BW system, and then click *Maintain Variables* or run transaction *RSZV*.

Step 2 Change the display mode to the create/change mode by clicking .

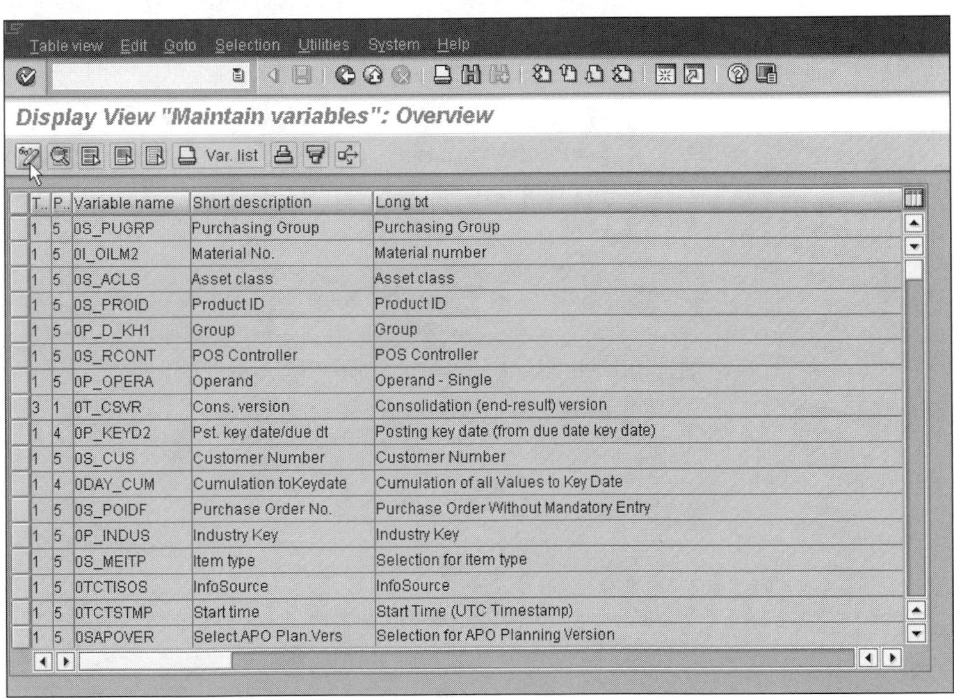

T..	P..	Variable name	Short description	Long txt
1	5	0S_PUGRP	Purchasing Group	Purchasing Group
1	5	0I_OILM2	Material No.	Material number
1	5	0S_ACLS	Asset class	Asset class
1	5	0S_PROID	Product ID	Product ID
1	5	0P_D_KH1	Group	Group
1	5	0S_RCONT	POS Controller	POS Controller
1	5	0P_OPERA	Operand	Operand - Single
3	1	0T_CSVR	Cons. version	Consolidation (end-result) version
1	4	0P_KEYD2	Pst. key date/due dt	Posting key date (from due date key date)
1	5	0S_CUS	Customer Number	Customer Number
1	4	0DAY_CUM	Cumulation toKeydate	Cumulation of all Values to Key Date
1	5	0S_POIDF	Purchase Order No.	Purchase Order Without Mandatory Entry
1	5	0P_INDUS	Industry Key	Industry Key
1	5	0S_MEITP	Item type	Selection for item type
1	5	0TCTISOS	InfoSource	InfoSource
1	5	0TCTSTMP	Start time	Start Time (UTC Timestamp)
1	5	0SAPOVER	Select.APO Plan.Vers	Selection for APO Planning Version

SCREEN 5.24

Step 3 Click New entries to create a new variable.

SCREEN 5.25

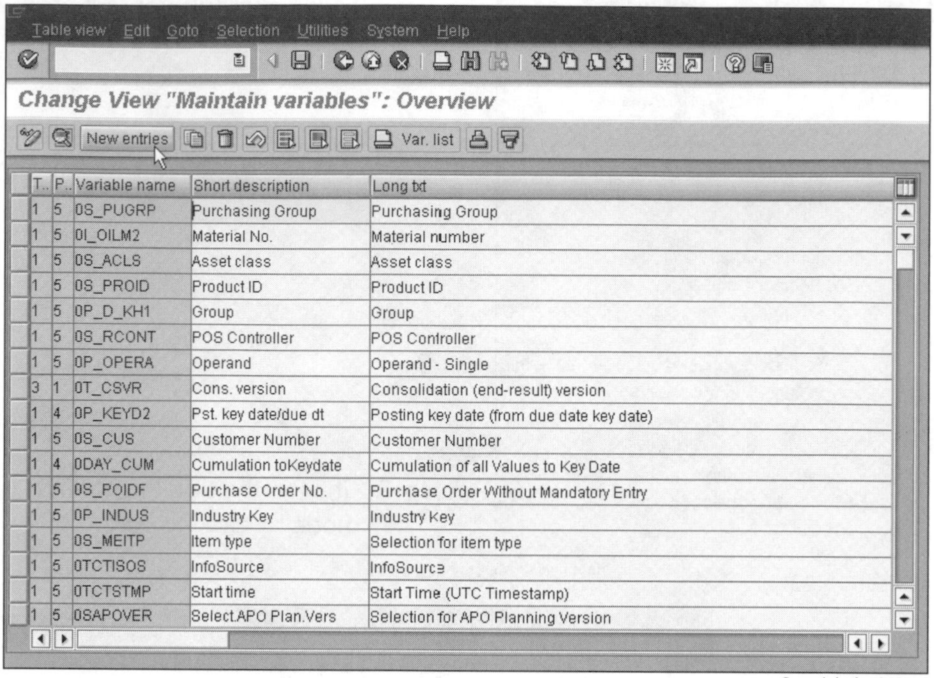

Table view Edit Goto Selection Utilities System Help

Change View "Maintain variables": Overview

New entries Var. list

T..	P..	Variable name	Short description	Long txt
1	5	0S_PUGRP	Purchasing Group	Purchasing Group
1	5	0I_OILM2	Material No.	Material number
1	5	0S_ACLS	Asset class	Asset class
1	5	0S_PROID	Product ID	Product ID
1	5	0P_D_KH1	Group	Group
1	5	0S_RCONT	POS Controller	POS Controller
1	5	0P_OPERA	Operand	Operand - Single
3	1	0T_CSVR	Cons. version	Consolidation (end-result) version
1	4	0P_KEYD2	Pst. key date/due dt	Posting key date (from due date key date)
1	5	0S_CUS	Customer Number	Customer Number
1	4	0DAY_CUM	Cumulation toKeydate	Cumulation of all Values to Key Date
1	5	0S_POIDF	Purchase Order No.	Purchase Order Without Mandatory Entry
1	5	0P_INDUS	Industry Key	Industry Key
1	5	0S_MEITP	Item type	Selection for item type
1	5	0TCTISOS	InfoSource	InfoSource
1	5	0TCTSTMP	Start time	Start Time (UTC Timestamp)
1	5	0SAPOVER	Select.APO Plan.Vers	Selection for APO Planning Version

Step 4 Name the variable as *V_SREG*. After entering the other basic information requested, click ✓ to provide more information.

SCREEN 5.26

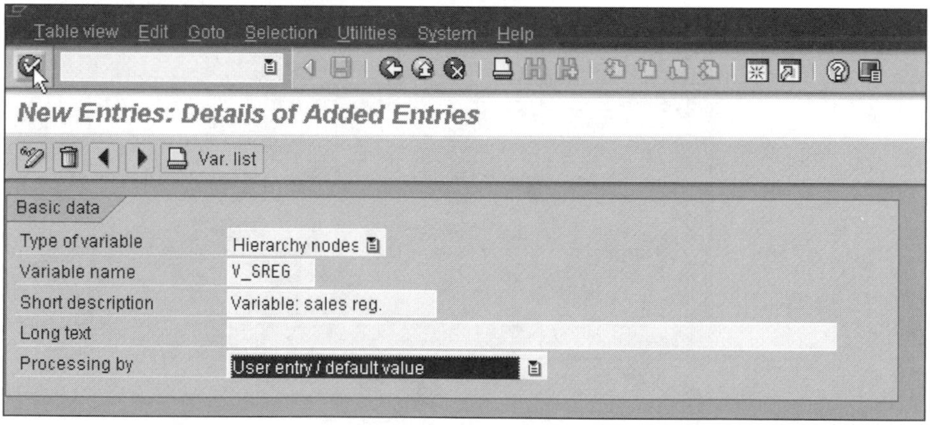

Table view Edit Goto Selection Utilities System Help

New Entries: Details of Added Entries

Var. list

Basic data

Type of variable	Hierarchy nodes
Variable name	V_SREG
Short description	Variable: sales reg.
Long text	
Processing by	User entry / default value

Step 5 Enter *IO_SREP* in the field *Characteristic,* as it is associated with the hierarchy. Make other selections as shown in the screen, and then click [save icon] to save the variable.

SCREEN 5.27

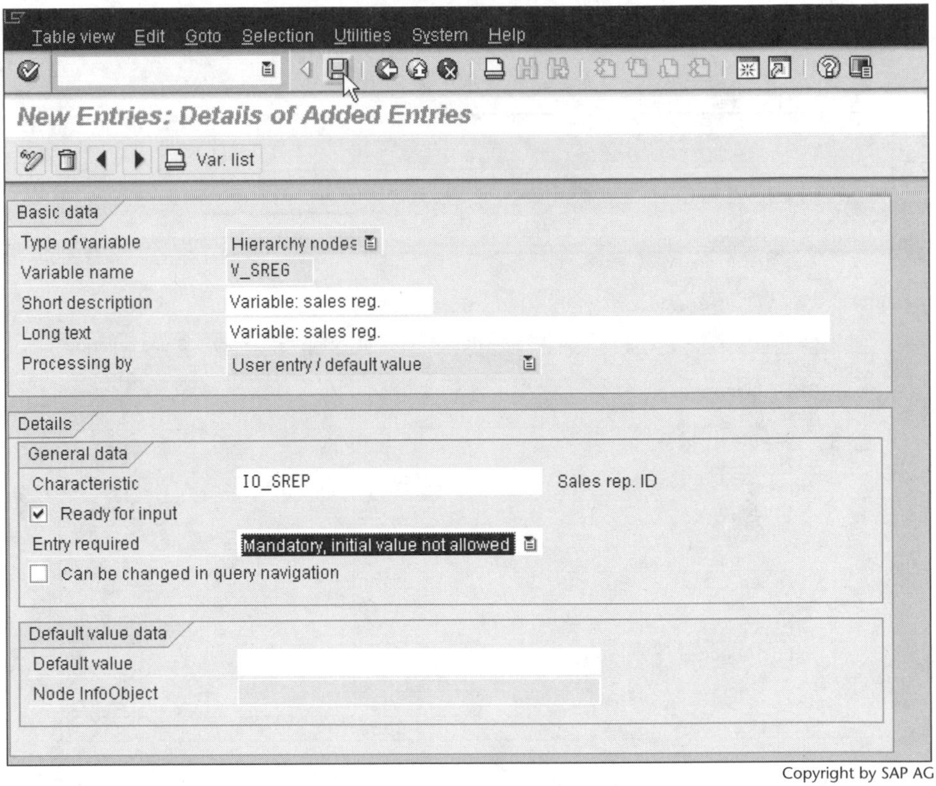

Copyright by SAP AG

Next, we will use the new variable to enhance the query IC_DEMOBC_Q01 created in Section 5.1.

Step 6 Return to the query created in Screen 5.14. Select ✎, and then select *Change query (global definition). . . .*

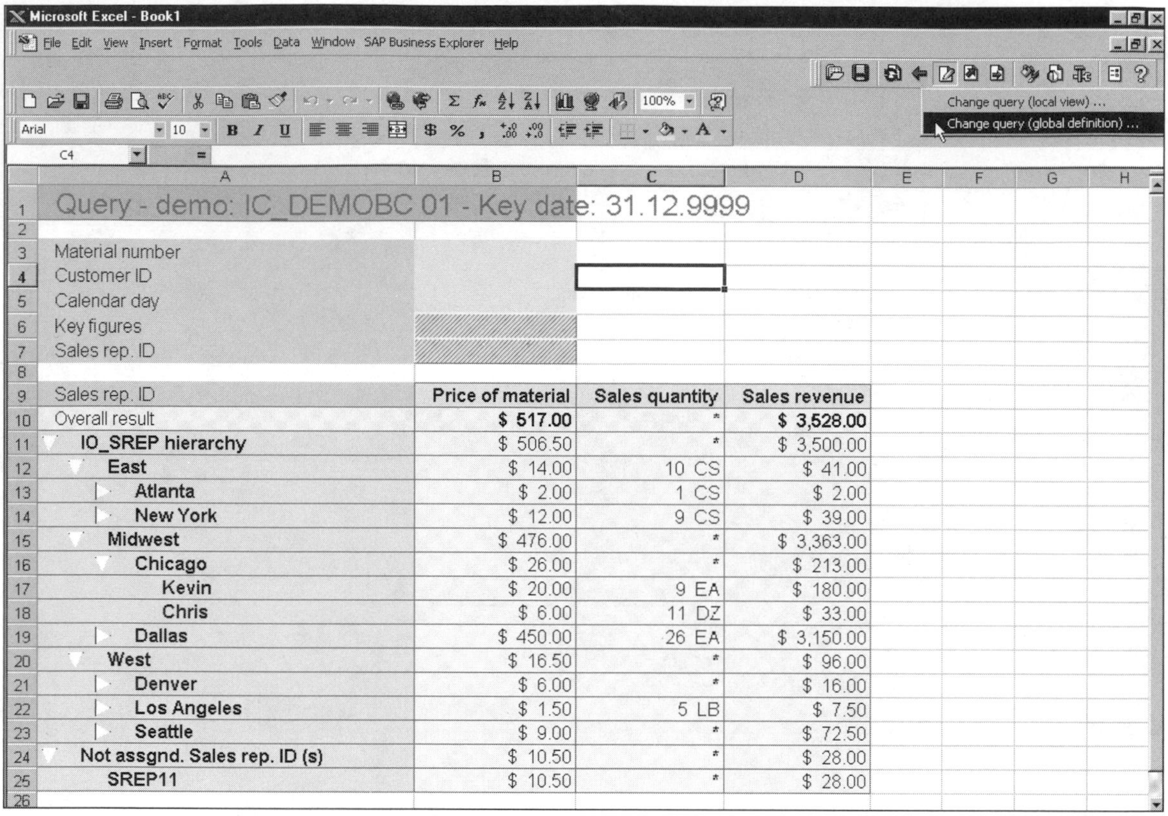

Microsoft Excel - Book1

File Edit View Insert Format Tools Data Window SAP Business Explorer Help

Change query (local view) ...

Change query (global definition) ...

Query - demo: IC_DEMOBC 01 - Key date: 31.12.9999

Material number
Customer ID
Calendar day
Key figures
Sales rep. ID

Sales rep. ID	Price of material	Sales quantity	Sales revenue
Overall result	**$ 517.00**	*	**$ 3,528.00**
IO_SREP hierarchy	$ 506.50	*	$ 3,500.00
East	$ 14.00	10 CS	$ 41.00
Atlanta	$ 2.00	1 CS	$ 2.00
New York	$ 12.00	9 CS	$ 39.00
Midwest	$ 476.00	*	$ 3,363.00
Chicago	$ 26.00	*	$ 213.00
Kevin	$ 20.00	9 EA	$ 180.00
Chris	$ 6.00	11 DZ	$ 33.00
Dallas	$ 450.00	26 EA	$ 3,150.00
West	$ 16.50	*	$ 96.00
Denver	$ 6.00	*	$ 16.00
Los Angeles	$ 1.50	5 LB	$ 7.50
Seattle	$ 9.00	*	$ 72.50
Not assgnd. Sales rep. ID (s)	$ 10.50	*	$ 28.00
SREP11	$ 10.50	*	$ 28.00

SCREEN 5.28

Step 7 Right-click *Sales rep. ID,* and then select *Restrict.*

SCREEN 5.29

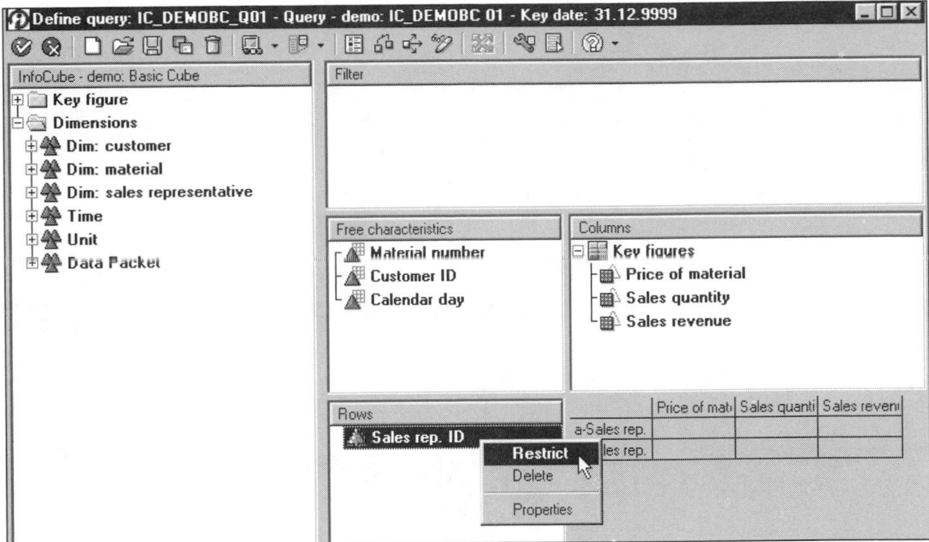

Step 8 Select *Variable: sales reg.* from the left window and move it to the right window by clicking [→]. Next, click [OK] to continue.

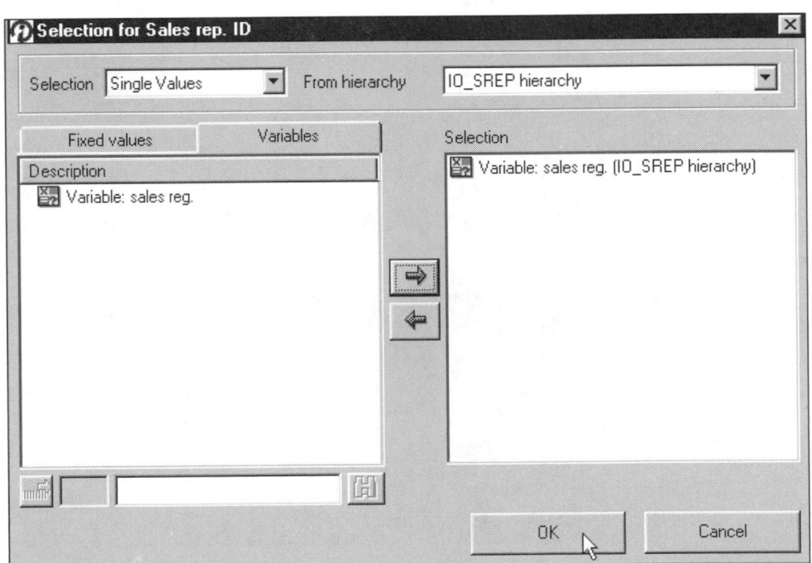

SCREEN 5.30

Step 9 Click [icon] to save and execute the query.

SCREEN 5.31

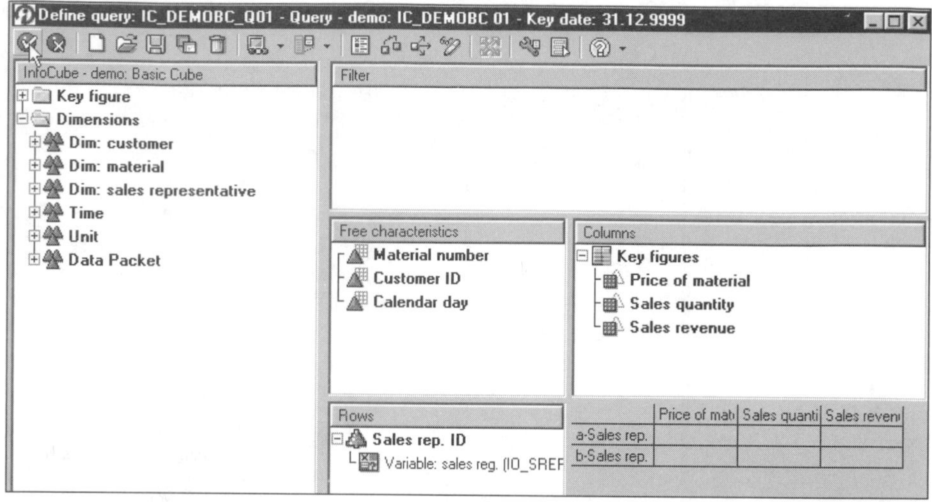

Step 10 Click [Yes] to save the query.

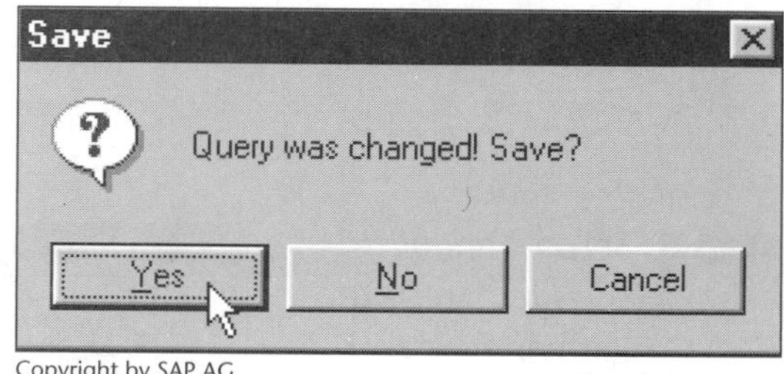

SCREEN 5.32

Step 11 Click [icon] to display the hierarchy nodes.

SCREEN 5.33

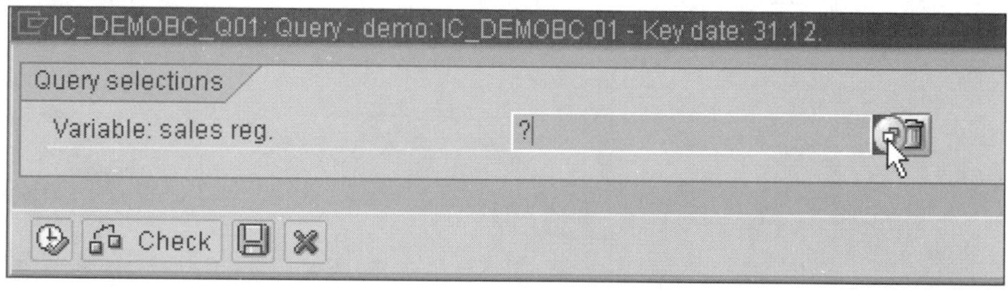

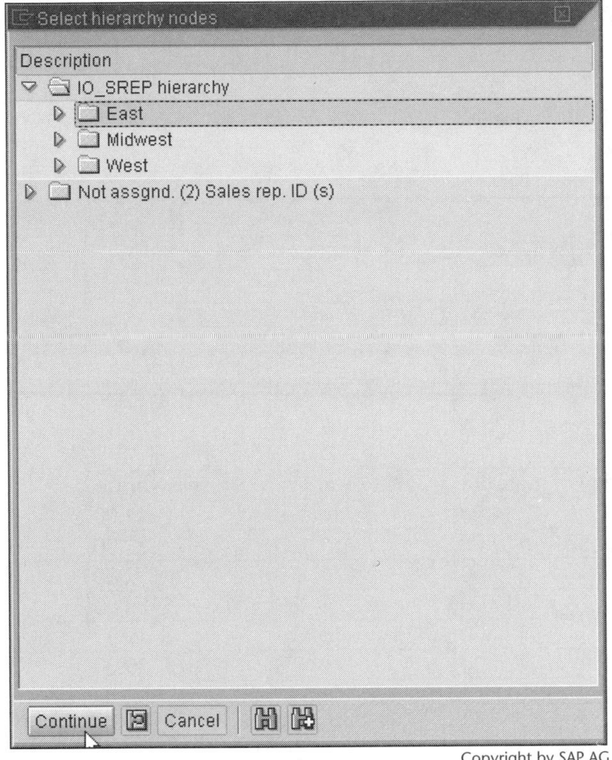

SCREEN 5.34

Copyright by SAP AG

Step 12 Select *East,* and then click Continue .

Step 13 Click [icon] to continue.

SCREEN 5.35

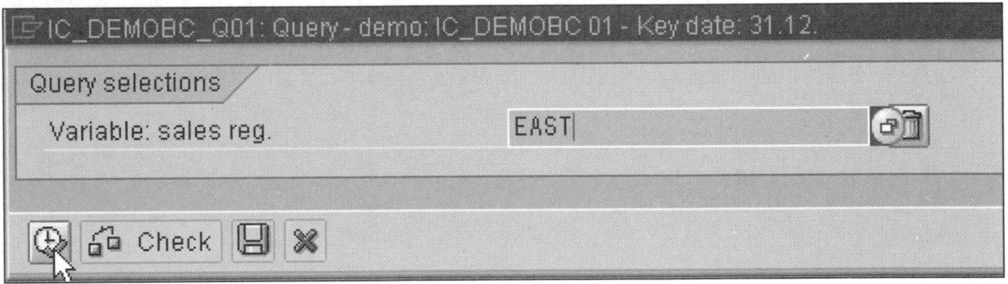

Copyright by SAP AG

Result

The query result (Screen 5.36) contains only the East region data.

Microsoft Excel - Book3

File Edit View Insert Format Tools Data Window SAP Business Explorer Help

A9 = Sales rep. ID

	A	B	C	D	E
1	Query - demo: IC_DEMOBC 01 - Key date: 31.12.9999				
2					
3	Material number				
4	Customer ID				
5	Calendar day				
6	Key figures				
7	Sales rep. ID				
8					
9	Sales rep. ID	**Price of material**	**Sales quantity**	**Sales revenue**	
10	**East**	$ 14.00	10 CS	$ 41.00	
11	**Atlanta**	$ 2.00	1 CS	$ 2.00	
12	**John**	$ 2.00	1 CS	$ 2.00	
13	**New York**	$ 12.00	9 CS	$ 39.00	
14	**Steve**	$ 7.00	5 CS	$ 19.00	
15	**Mary**	$ 5.00	4 CS	$ 20.00	
16					

SCREEN 5.36

5.4 Summary

In this chapter, we examined the basic features of BEx. We also learned how to create queries and workbooks using BEx Analyzer and how to access workbooks from BEx Browser. Figure 5.1 illustrates this process.

FIGURE 5.1
QUERY AND WORKBOOK

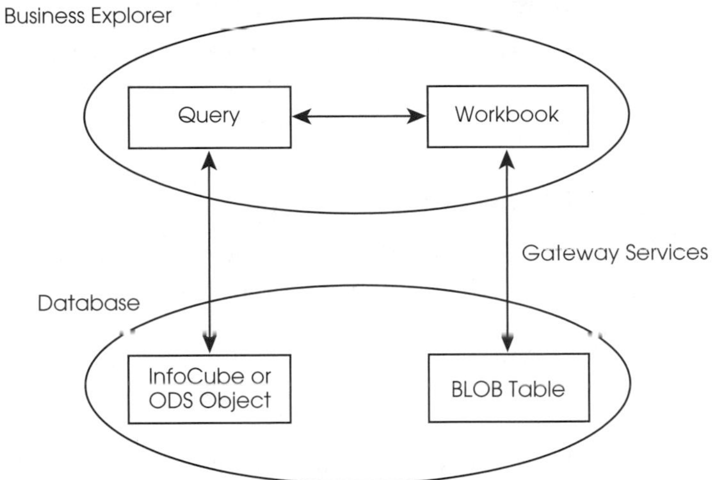

In this chapter, we also demonstrated how to create and use variables.

Key Terms

Term	Description
Query	A BW query is a selection of characteristics and key figures for the analysis of the data in an InfoCube. A query refers to only one InfoCube, and its result is presented in a BEx Excel worksheet. The maximum number of characters allowed for the technical name is 30.
Workbook	A BW workbook is an Excel file with a BEx query result saved in BDS. BW assigns a 25-digit ID to each workbook. Users only need to name a workbook's title.
Drill-down	Drill-down is a user navigation step intended to obtain further detailed information.
Free characteristic	A free characteristic is a characteristic in a query used for drill-downs. It is not displayed in the initial result of a query run.

Term	Description
Variable	A variable is a query parameter that gets its value from user input or takes a default value set by the variable creator.

For Further Information

- Book: *SAP BW Reporting Made Easy 2.0B/2.1C,* by SAP Labs, Inc., Simplification Group. Johnson Printing Service, 2001. ISBN: 1-893570-66-5.

This book demonstrates the use of several additional BEx features:

Filters
You use filters to restrict characteristics to single values, value intervals, hierarchy nodes, or variables.

Restricted Key Figures
Similar to the filters on characteristics, restricted key figures are key figures with restricted values.

Calculated Key Figures
Key figures can be calculated using a formula. For example, we can implement the Figure 1.1 formula to obtain the sales revenue.

Next . . .

We will create authorization profiles to manage the access to the InfoCube data. In addition, we will examine some other features of BEx Browser.

Chapter 6

Managing User Authorization

Security is an essential element of any information system. BW is no exception to this rule. It uses an R/3 utility called **Profile Generator** to manage authorization. In this chapter, we will demonstrate how to use this utility.

The foundation of SAP authorization management is based on **authorization objects**. These objects define what a user can do, and to which SAP objects. Such a definition is called **authorization**. For example, the authorization in Table 6.1 allows users with that authorization to display and execute—but not change—the queries IC_DEMOBC_Q01 and IC_DEMOBC_Q02. This authorization is defined using authorization object S_RS_COMP.

TABLE 6.1 AN AUTHORIZATION FROM AUTHORIZATION OBJECT S_RS_COMP

S_RS_COMP Field	Field Description	Field Value
ACTVT	Activity	Display, Execute
RSINFOAREA	InfoArea	*
RSINFOCUBE	InfoCube	*
RSZCOMPID	Name (ID) of a reporting component	IC_DEMOBC_Q01, IC_DEMOBC_Q02
RSZCOMPTP	Type of a reporting component	Query

Multiple authorizations are combined to create an **authorization profile**. In SAP, an authorization profile is assigned to a **user role**. Users assigned to the role have the authorizations to execute the defined business activities.

In this chapter, we will use Profile Generator to create user roles and assign users to the roles. In addition, we will demonstrate how to run R/3 transactions and access Web sites from BEx Browser. Although the sales manager described in Chapter 1 may not need this function, we cover it here so that we can introduce an advanced feature powered by the integration of BEx Browser and Profile Generator. Let's start with a demonstration of the Profile Generator.

6.1 Creating an Authorization Profile Using Profile Generator

With Profile Generator, SAP has made authorization management very easy. First, we will create an authorization profile for a role. All users in that role can run queries but cannot change the queries.

Prerequisites

Three users U_EAST, U_MIDWEST, and U_WEST have been created through transaction *SU01*.

Work Instructions

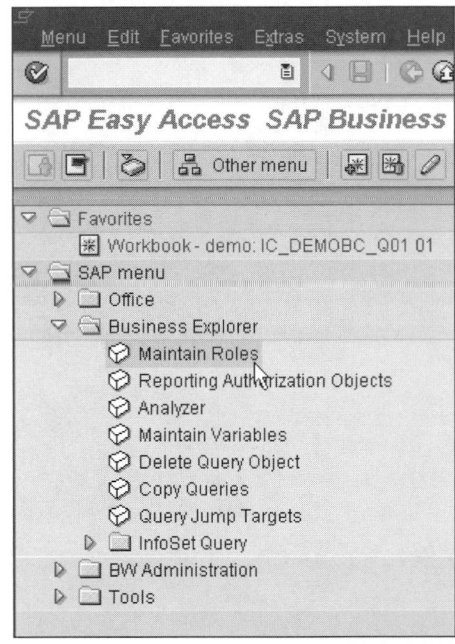

SCREEN 6.1

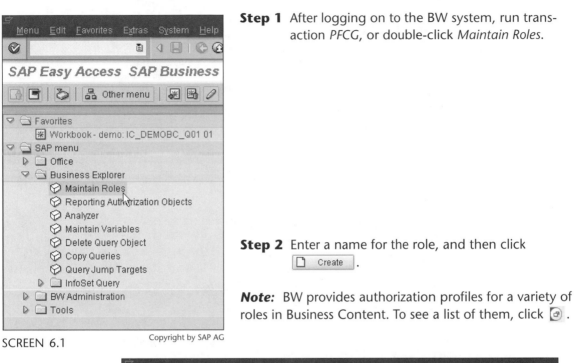

Step 1 After logging on to the BW system, run transaction *PFCG*, or double-click *Maintain Roles.*

Step 2 Enter a name for the role, and then click Create.

Note: BW provides authorization profiles for a variety of roles in Business Content. To see a list of them, click the icon shown.

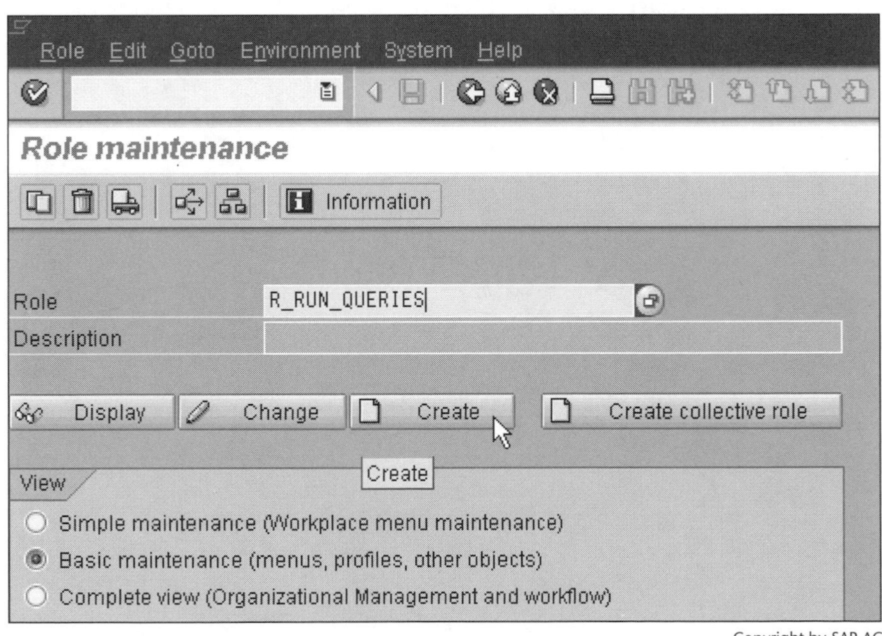

SCREEN 6.2

Step 3 Click the *Authorizations* tab.

SCREEN 6.3

Copyright by SAP AG

Step 4 Click Yes to save the role and continue.

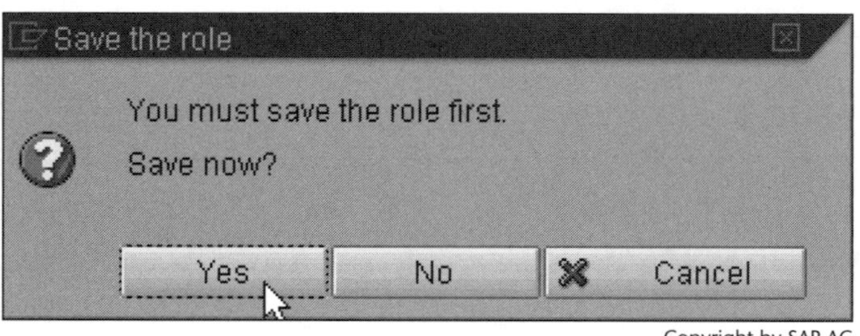

SCREEN 6.4

Copyright by SAP AG

Step 5 Click [change icon] to *Change authorization data.*

SCREEN 6.5

Step 6 Select the template *S_RS_RREPU,* and then click [Adopt reference].

Note BW provides authorization templates for a variety of roles in Business Content. *S_RS_PPEPU* is one of them, for query display and execution.

SCREEN 6.6

Step 7 The new window shows all authorizations for this role. For example, the users assigned to the *R_RUN_QUERIES* role can *Display, Execute, Enter, Include,* and *Assign Calculated key figure, Query, Restricted key figure,* and *Template structure.*

Note: If we expand other nodes, we will see other authorizations granted to this role.

To change an authorization field value, click next to the field. In our example, the reporting component *Query* has the activity *Execute* in two places. Let's remove *Query* from the first one.

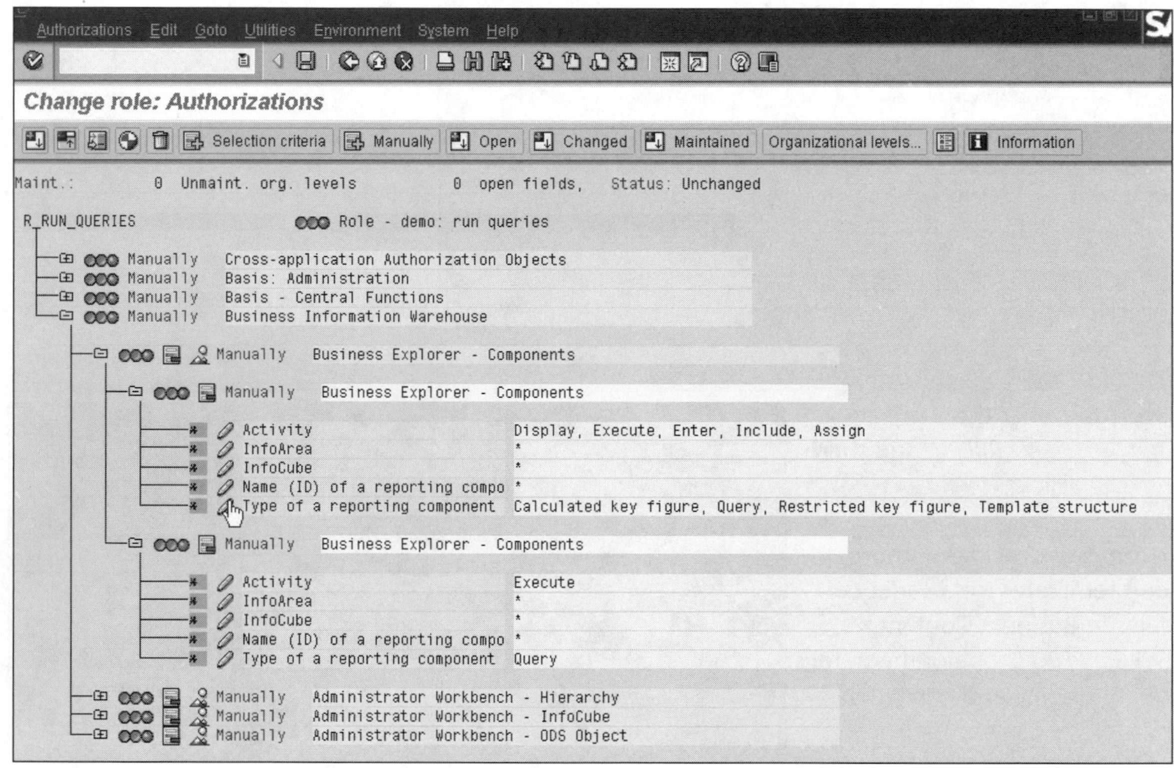

SCREEN 6.7

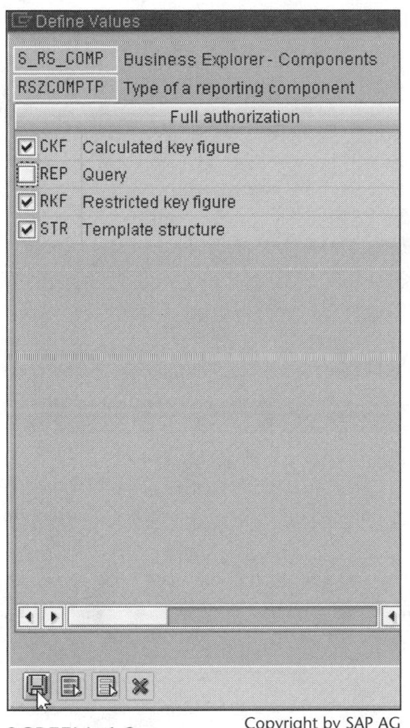

SCREEN 6.8

Step 8 Deselect *REP* for *Query,* and then click [save icon] to continue.

Note: *S_RS_COMP* is an authorization object; *RSZCOMPTP* is one of its fields. In this field we specify objects on which users can perform activities.

Step 9 Click [generate icon] to generate the profile.

SCREEN 6.9

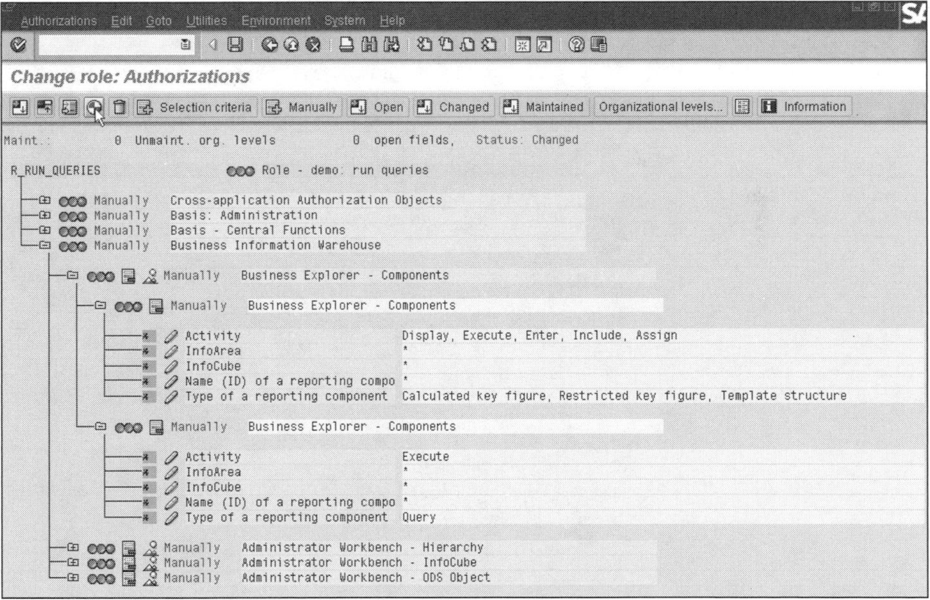

Step 10 Enter a name and a description, and then click ✔ to continue.

SCREEN 6.10

Assign Profile Name for Generated Authorization Profile

You can change the default profile name here

Profile name AP_R_QUERY

You will not be able to change this profile name later

Text Authorization Profile for role R_RUN_QUERIES

Step 11 The status light of the *Authorizations* tab turns green (the red square becomes a green circle). Click the *User* tab to assign users to this role.

SCREEN 6.11

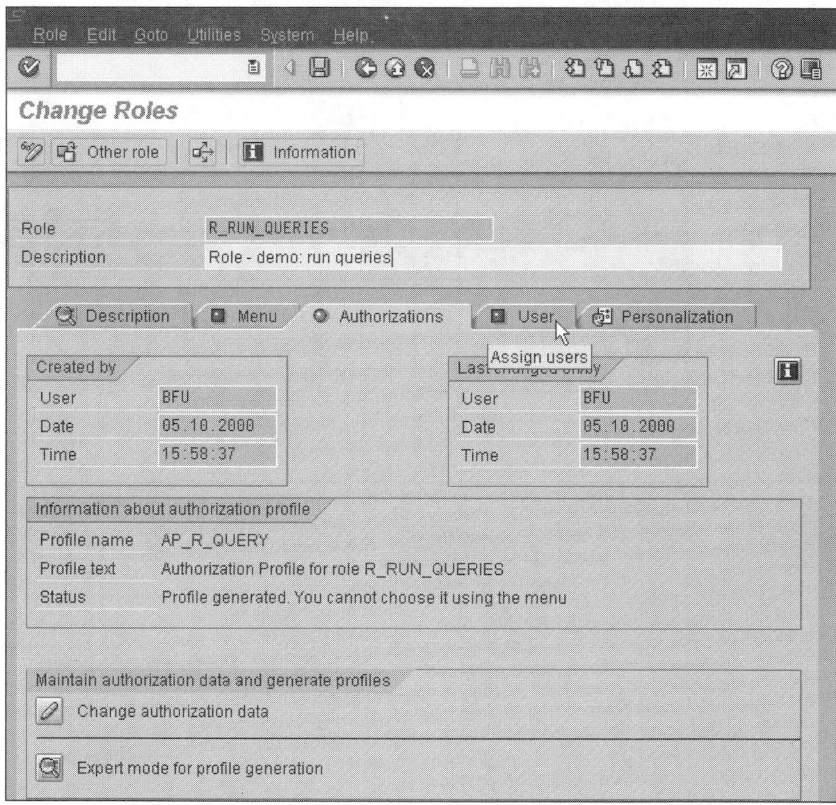

Step 12 Enter three users: one from the East region, one from the Midwest region, and one from the West region.

Click [User compare] to add the authorization profile to the users' master data.

SCREEN 6.12

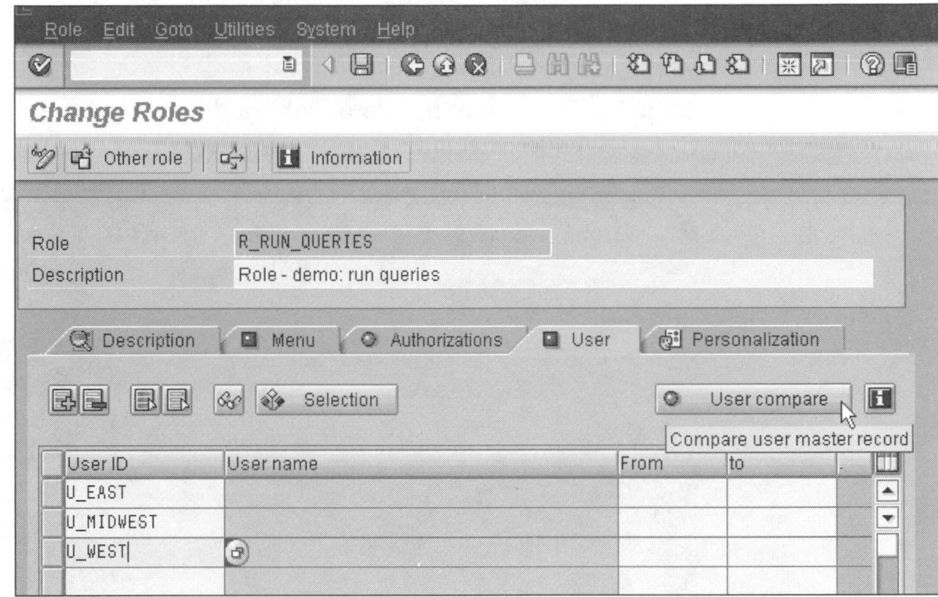

Copyright by SAP AG

Step 13 Click [Complete compare] to continue.

SCREEN 6.13

Compare Role User Master Record

Last comparison

User BFU
Date 05.10.2000
Time 15:55:07

Complete adjustment

User
Date
Time 00:00:00

Information for user master comparison

Status User assignment has changed since the last save

Complete compare | Expert mode for compare | Information

Copyright by SAP AG

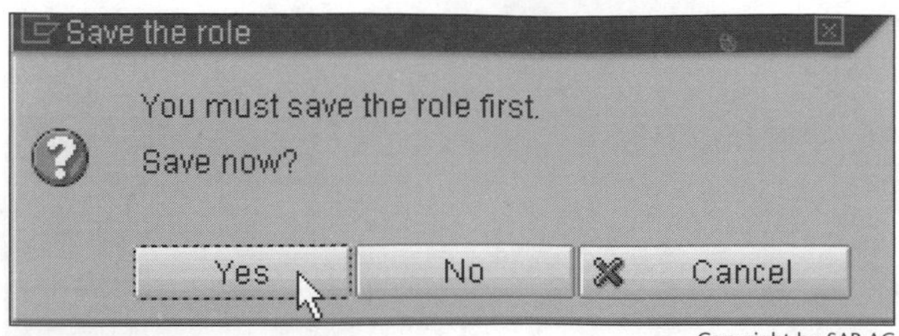

SCREEN 6.14

Step 14 Click [Yes] to save the role.

Step 15 Notice that the status light of the *User* tab turns green (the red square becomes a green circle).

SCREEN 6.15

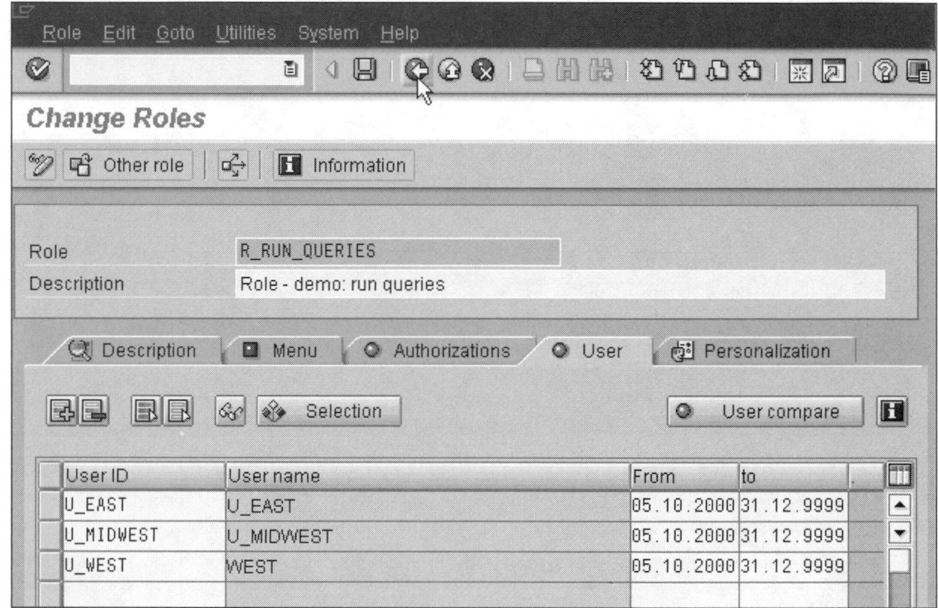

Result

You have created the role *R_RUN_QUERIES* and its corresponding authorization profile *AP_R_QUERY*. Also, you have assigned three users to this role. To verify that the role and assignments are correct, run transaction *SU01* to display user U_WEST's master data. Under the tab *Roles,* review the role to which this user is assigned (Screen 6.16). Under the tab *Profiles,* notice the user's authorization profile (Screen 6.17).

SCREEN 6.16

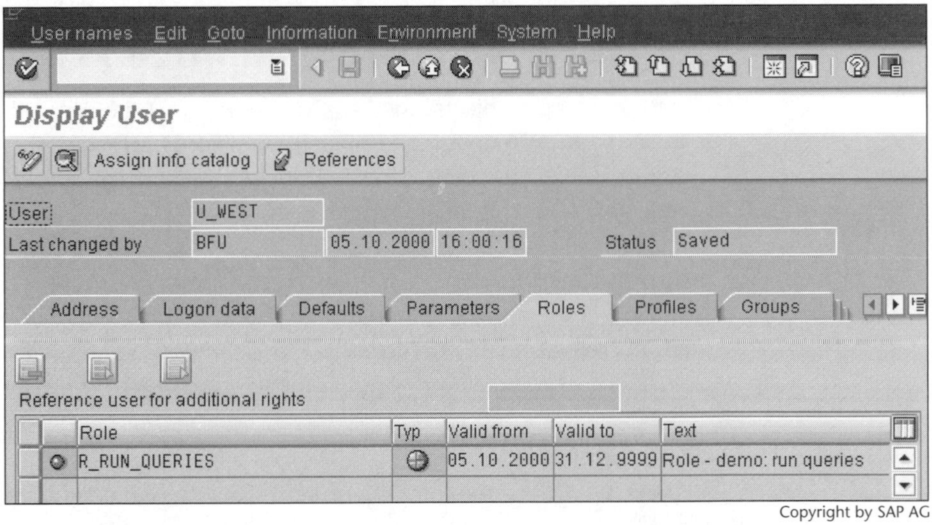

SCREEN 6.17

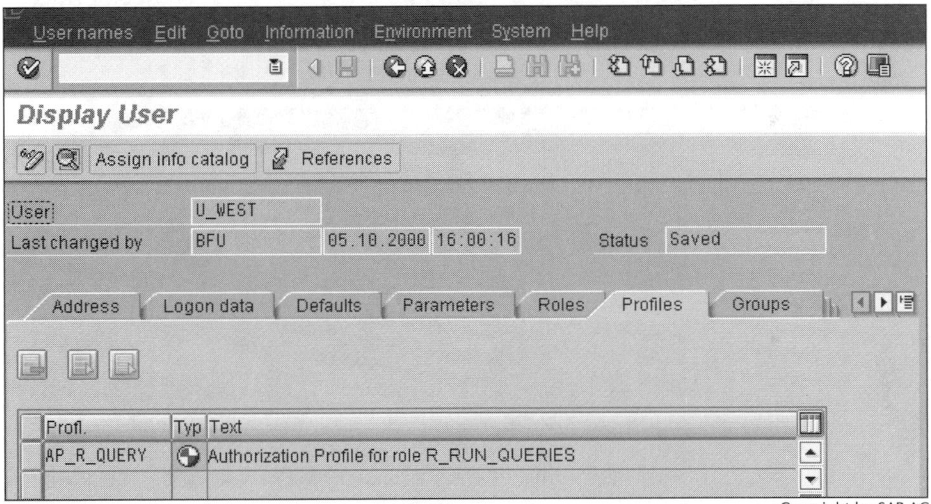

From this example, we get an idea of how BW manages its authorization. Each role has an authorization profile. Users assigned to a particular role have all authorizations included in the authorization profile. A user can be assigned to multiple roles. The user derives his or her authorizations from the roles to which he or she is assigned.

6.2 Creating an Authorization Object to Control User Access to the InfoCube Data

Authorization objects, such as the one in Screen 6.8, are the foundation of SAP authorization management. For this reason, SAP provides many authorization objects for most conceivable activities that users might perform on R/3 and BW objects. Nevertheless, in BW, we almost always need to create our own authorization objects. For example, the sales manager might decide that it is not appropriate for users in one sales region to view another region's sales data. In this case, the appropriate authorization object is not available from SAP, so we must create one by ourselves.

Before we create our own authorization object, we need to do a few things.

Prerequisites

Step 1 Modify the InfoObject *IO_SREP* to make it be authorization relevant.

Open the InfoObject *IO_SREP*, and then select the option *Authorization Relevant* in the *General settings* block under the *Business Explorer* tab. Click [icon] to check the new InfoObject definition. If it is valid, click [icon] to activate the change.

SCREEN 6.18

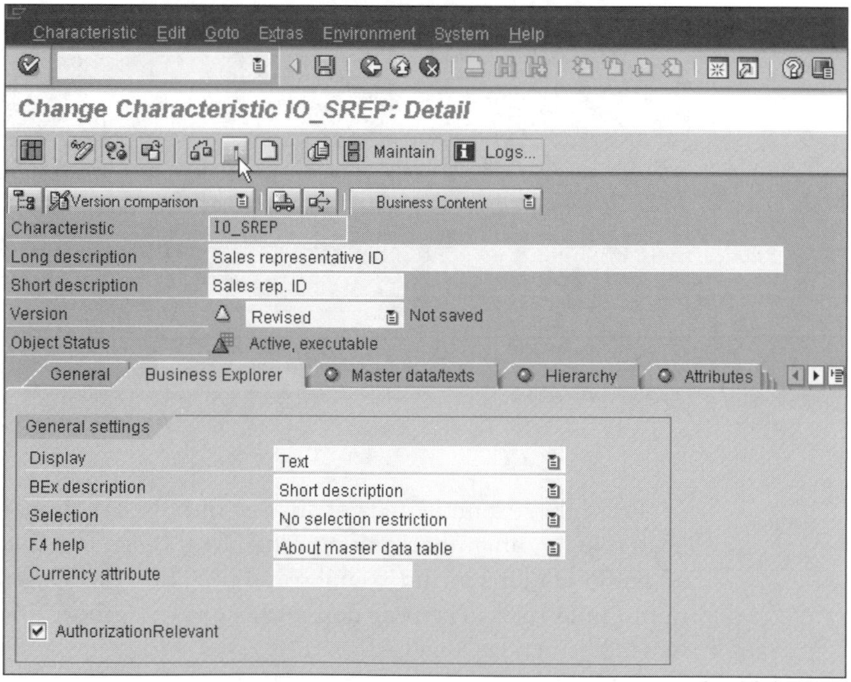

Characteristic Edit Goto Extras Environment System Help

Change Characteristic IO_SREP: Detail

Maintain Logs...

Version comparison Business Content

Characteristic	IO_SREP
Long description	Sales representative ID
Short description	Sales rep. ID
Version	Revised Not saved
Object Status	Active, executable

General | Business Explorer | Master data/texts | Hierarchy | Attributes

General settings

Display	Text
BEx description	Short description
Selection	No selection restriction
F4 help	About master data table
Currency attribute	

☑ AuthorizationRelevant

Step 2 Make sure that the InfoObject 0TCTAUTHH is available.

Note: If the InfoObject 0TCTAUTHH is not available, follow the instructions in Section 10.4, "Installing Business Content and Loading R/3 Data," to install it.

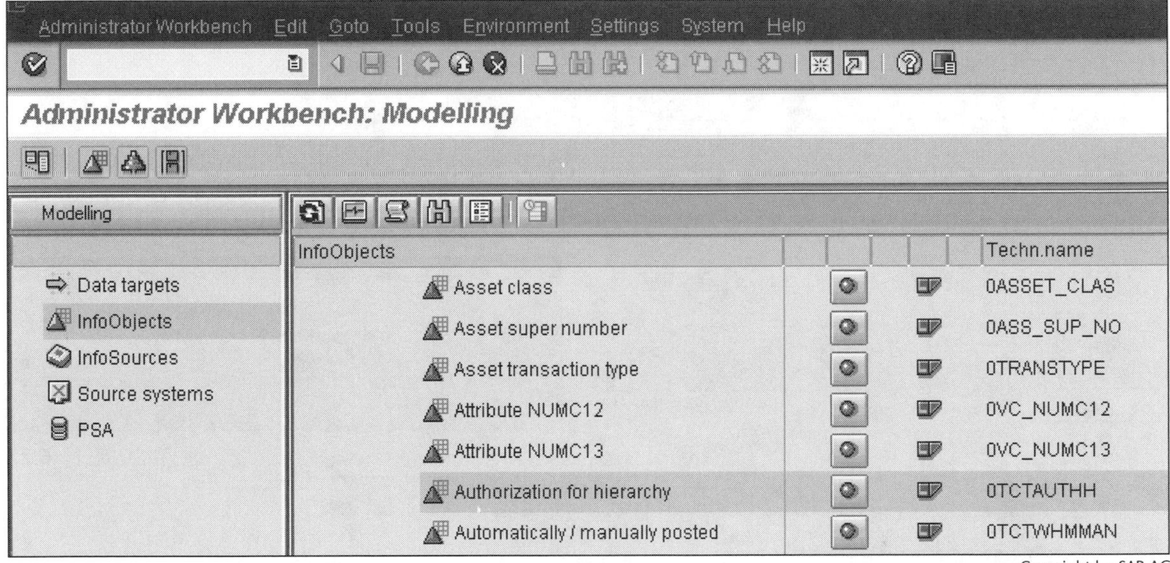

SCREEN 6.19

Now, we can create our authorization object.

Work Instructions

Step 1 Log on to BW, and then either double-click *Reporting Authorization Objects* or run transaction *RSSM*.

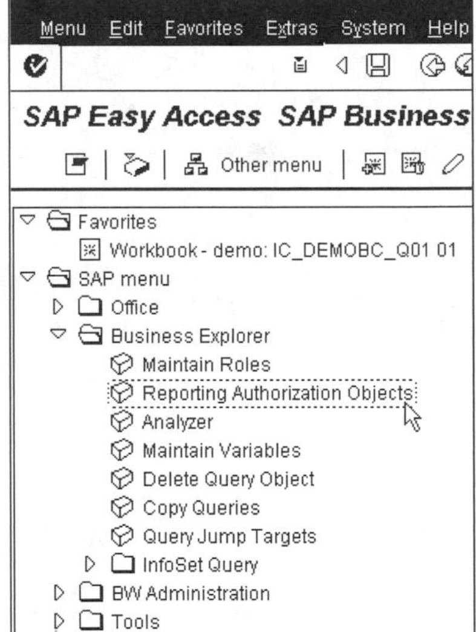

SCREEN 6.20

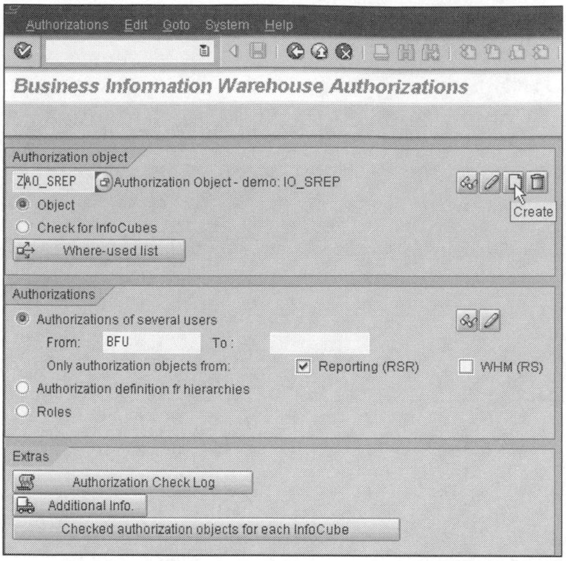

SCREEN 6.21

Copyright by SAP AG

Step 2 Enter a name, make sure the *Object* option is selected, and then click [icon] to create the authorization object.

Note: The names of customer-developed authorization objects must begin with *Y* or *Z*.

Step 3 In the pop-up window, enter a description and then click [icon] to continue.

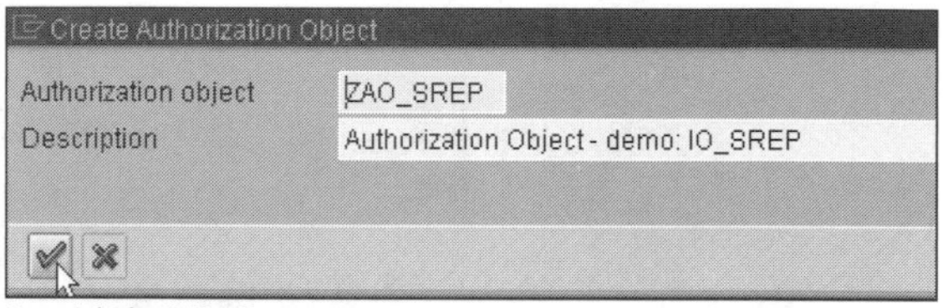

Copyright by SAP AG

SCREEN 6.22

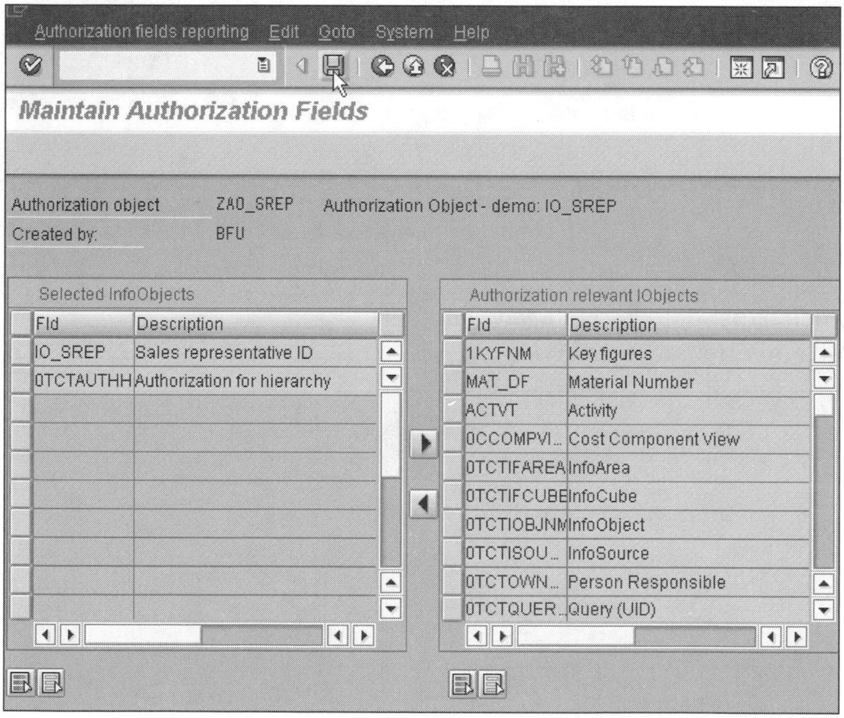

Step 4 Select *IO_SREP* and *0TCTAUTHH* from the *Authorization relevant | Objects* window. Move them to the left window by clicking [icon]. Click [icon] to save the changes.

SCREEN 6.23

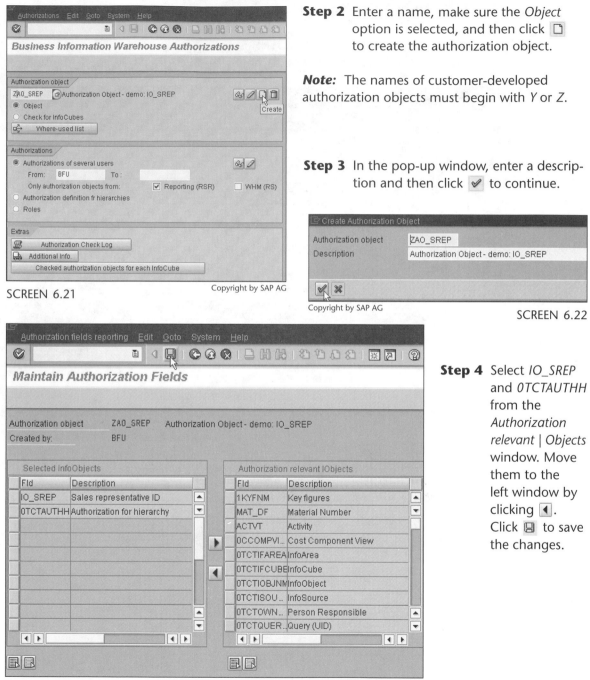

Copyright by SAP AG

Step 5 For demonstration purposes, click Local object to save the authorization object as a local object so it will not be transported to other systems.

Note: See Section 14.2, "Development Class," for more information on *$TMP* and local objects.

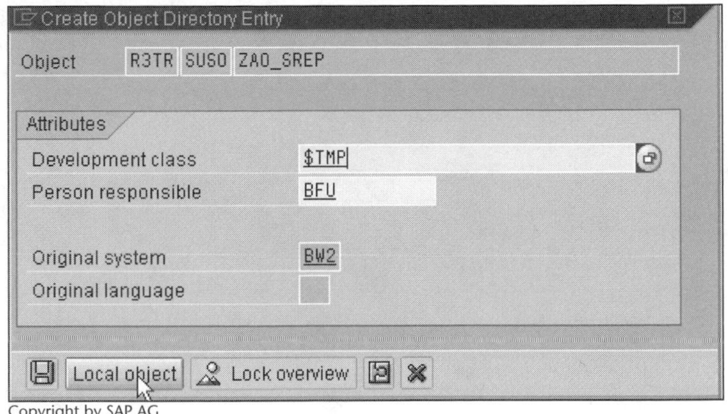

SCREEN 6.24

A status message *Authorization object ZAO_SREP saved* will appear at the bottom of Screen 6.23.

The authorization object has been created with two fields, IO_SREP and 0TCTAUTHH.

Next, we will specify the InfoCubes to which this authorization object will apply.

Step 6 Select the *Check for InfoCubes* option, and then click the change icon to change the authorization object.

SCREEN 6.25

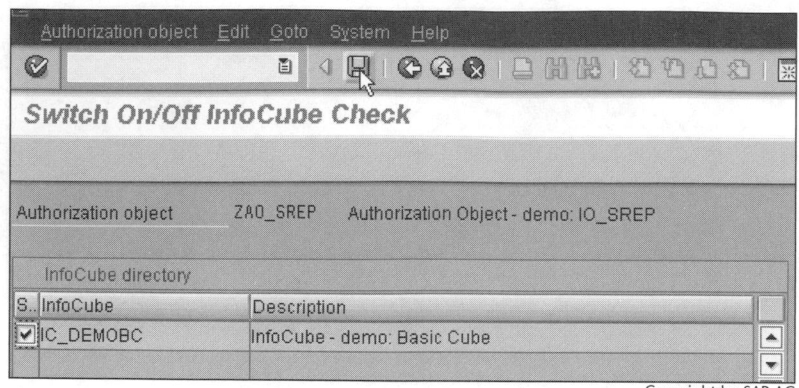

SCREEN 6.26 Copyright by SAP AG

Step 7 Select *IC_DEMOBC*, and then click [save icon] to save the authorization object.

Note: Only one InfoCube depends on InfoObject IO_SREP. Otherwise, more dependent InfoCubes would be listed.

Next, we need to create an authorization for each region.

Step 8 Select the option *Authorization definition fr hierarchies*, and then click [change icon] to create an authorization.

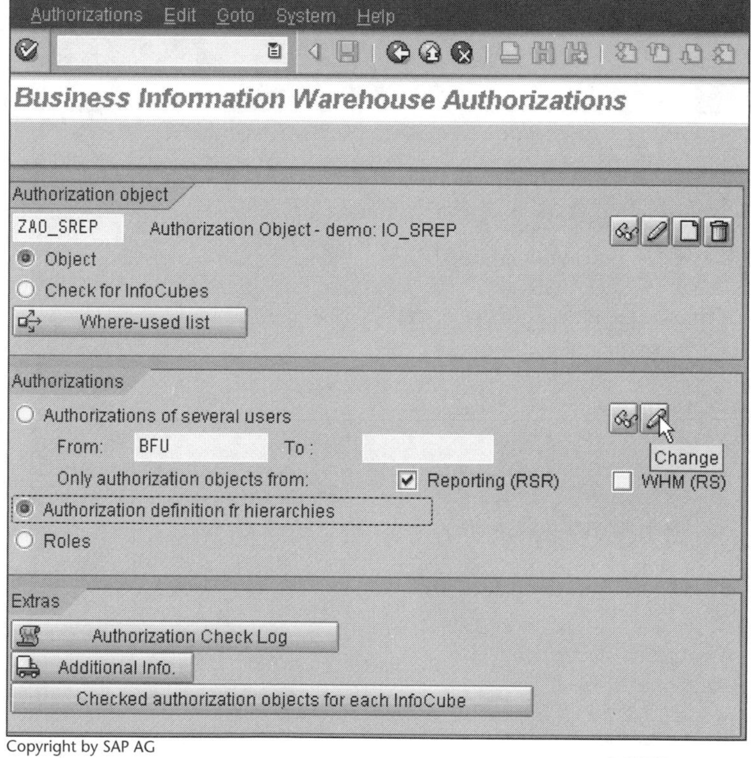

Copyright by SAP AG

SCREEN 6.27

Step 9 Enter a name for the authorization and provide other information as shown in Screen 6.28. Click [icon] to look up the available *Type of authorization.*

Note: Except for the name of the authorization, you can populate all fields by clicking [icon] and choosing one item from the list.

SCREEN 6.28

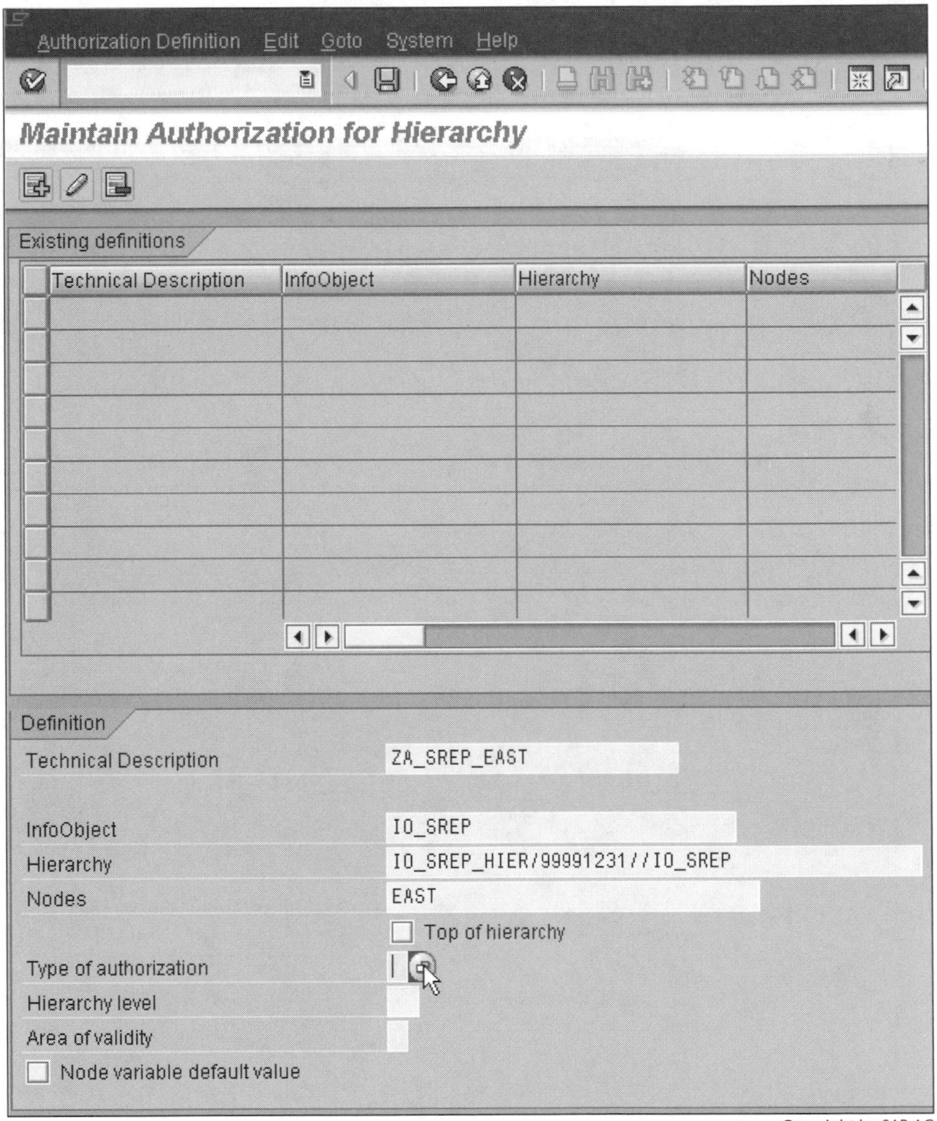

Authorization Definition Edit Goto System Help

Maintain Authorization for Hierarchy

Existing definitions

Technical Description	InfoObject	Hierarchy	Nodes

Definition

Technical Description ZA_SREP_EAST

InfoObject IO_SREP

Hierarchy IO_SREP_HIER/99991231//IO_SREP

Nodes EAST

Top of hierarchy

Type of authorization

Hierarchy level

Area of validity

Node variable default value

(1) 4 Entries found
Ty... Copy ...
Short text
0
Only the node
1
Subtree below nodes
2
Subtree below nodes to level (incl.)
3
Complete hierarchy

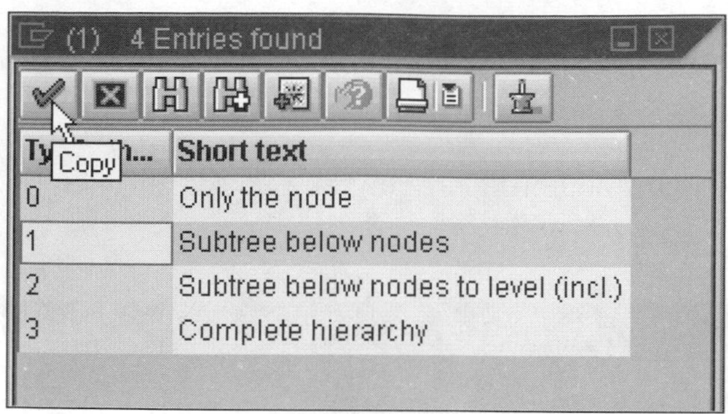

SCREEN 6.29

Step 10 Select *1* for *Subtree below nodes,* and then click ✔ to continue.

Step 11 Click 💾 to save the authorization.

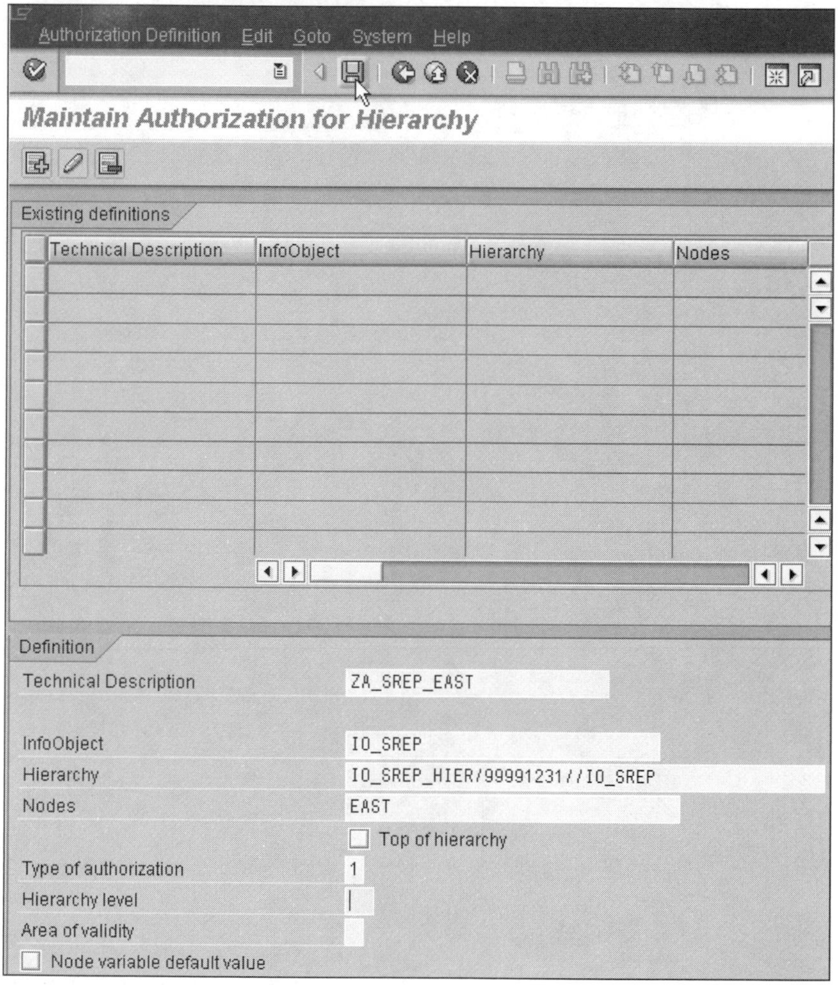

Authorization Definition Edit Goto System Help
Maintain Authorization for Hierarchy
Existing definitions
Technical Description
InfoObject
Hierarchy
Nodes
Definition
Technical Description
ZA_SREP_EAST
InfoObject
IO_SREP
Hierarchy
IO_SREP_HIER/99991231//IO_SREP
Nodes
EAST
Top of hierarchy
Type of authorization
1
Hierarchy level
Area of validity
Node variable default value

SCREEN 6.30

Result

You have created the authorization using the newly created authorization object.

We use the same method to create an authorization for the West region (Screen 6.31).

SCREEN 6.31

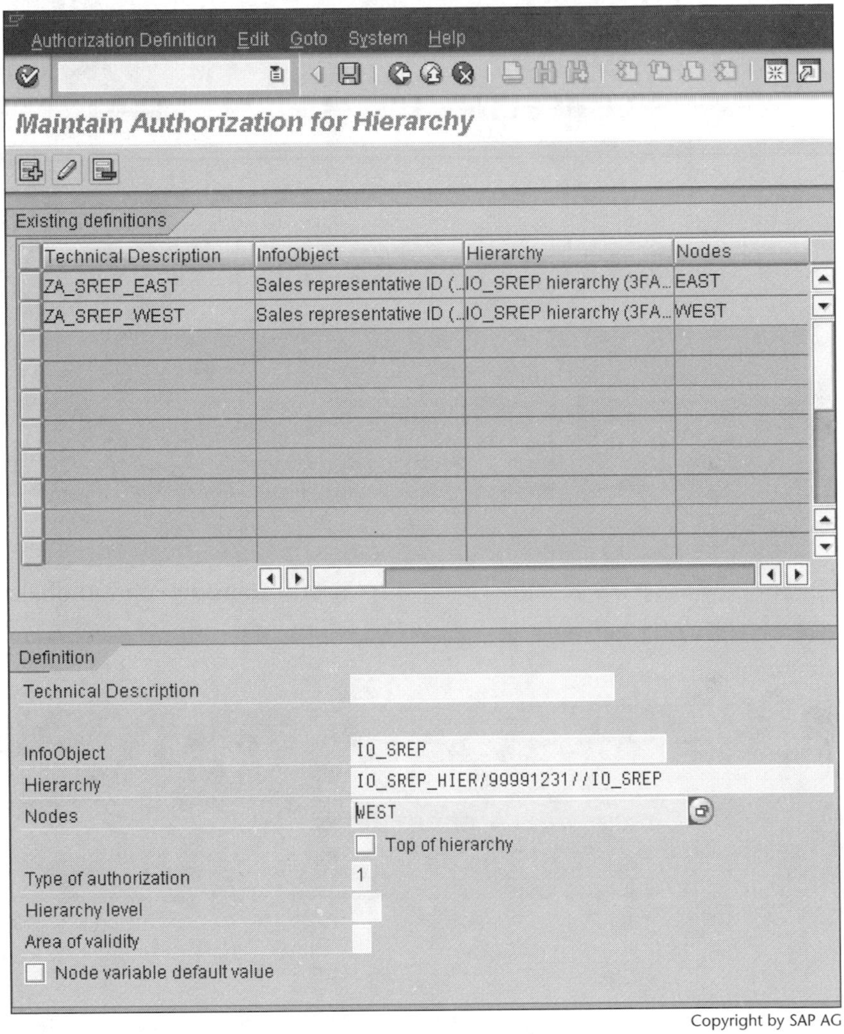

Authorization Definition Edit Goto System Help

Maintain Authorization for Hierarchy

Existing definitions

Technical Description	InfoObject	Hierarchy	Nodes
ZA_SREP_EAST	Sales representative ID (...	IO_SREP hierarchy (3FA...	EAST
ZA_SREP_WEST	Sales representative ID (...	IO_SREP hierarchy (3FA...	WEST

Definition

Technical Description

InfoObject IO_SREP

Hierarchy IO_SREP_HIER/99991231//IO_SREP

Nodes WEST

Top of hierarchy

Type of authorization 1

Hierarchy level

Area of validity

Node variable default value

Now we can use the authorization object and the authorizations to create an authorization profile for a role. The users assigned to this role and the role created in Section 6.1 can access only the East region's sales information.

Step 12 Repeat the steps from Screen 6.1 to Screen 6.5 to create a role called *R_RUN_SREP_EAST*. This time, however, click [Do not select templates] because we will use our own authorization object.

SCREEN 6.32

Choose Template

Template	Text for Template
SAP_ADM_AU	Administration: Authorization data administrator
SAP_ADM_PR	Administration: Authorization profile administrator
SAP_ADM_US	Administration: User administrator
SAP_ALL	Complete authorization with all authorization objects
SAP_PRINT	Print Authorization
SAP_USER_B	Basis authorizations for users
S_RS_RDEAD	BW role: Administrator (development system)
S_RS_RDEMO	BW role: Modeler (development system)
S_RS_ROPAD	BW role: Administrator (productive system)
S_RS_ROPOP	BW role: Operator (productive system)
S_RS_RREDE	BW role: Reporting developer (development system)

Adopt reference | Do not select templates

Step 13 Click [Manually] to insert our authorization object.

SCREEN 6.33

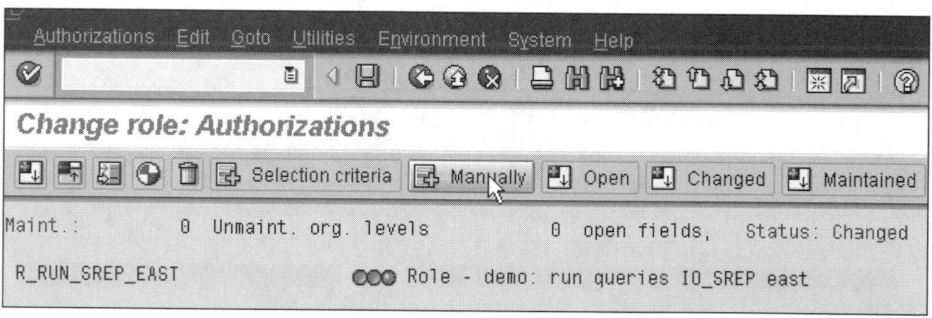

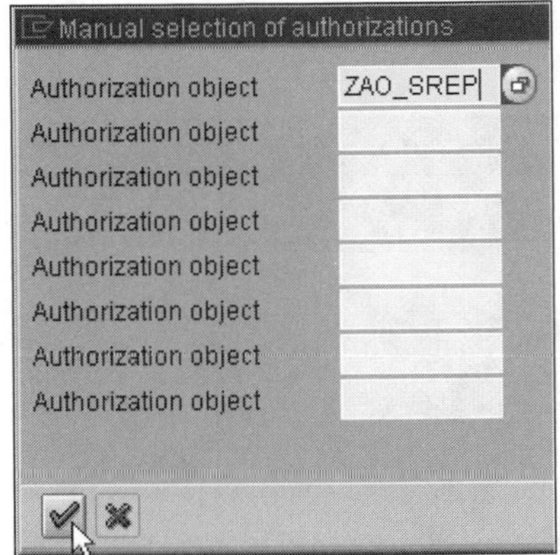

Copyright by SAP AG

SCREEN 6.34

Step 14 Enter *ZAO_SREP* as the authorization object, and then click ✔ to continue.

Step 15 Click ✎ to add authorizations to the *Authorization for hierarchy* field.

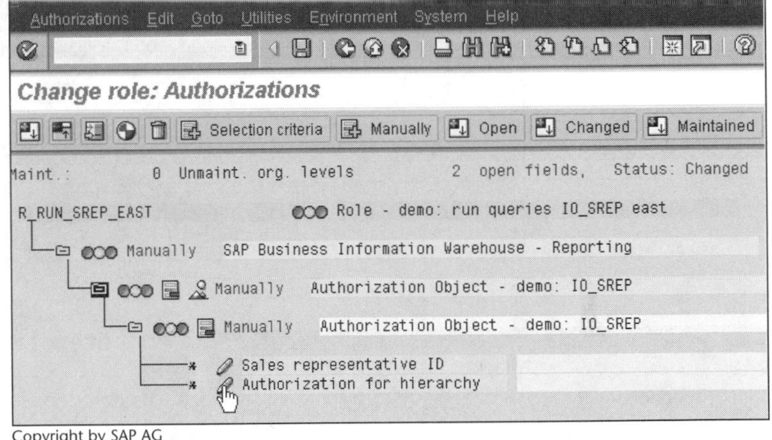

Copyright by SAP AG

SCREEN 6.35

Step 16 Enter *ZA_SREP_EAST*, an authorization created previously, and then click 💾 to continue.

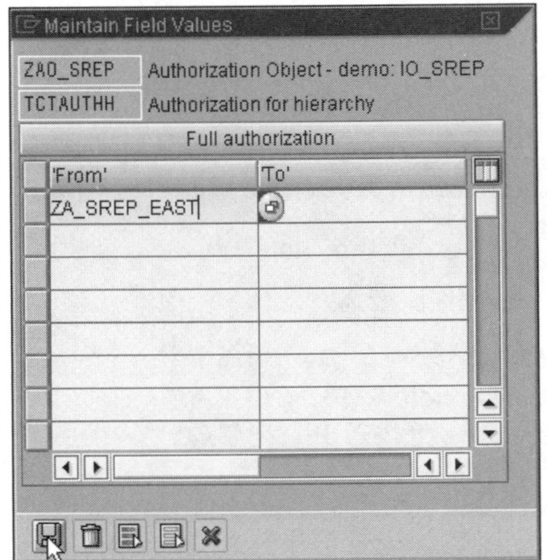

Copyright by SAP AG

SCREEN 6.36

Step 17 Click [icon] to generate the authorization profile for the role.

SCREEN 6.37

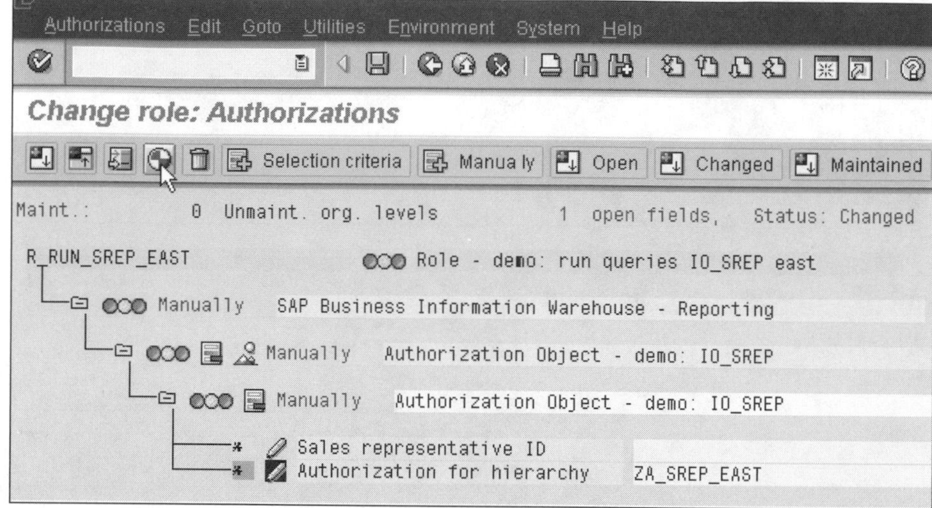

Copyright by SAP AG

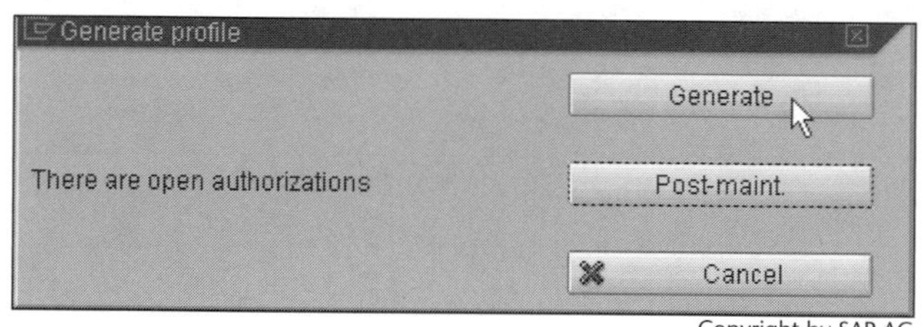

Copyright by SAP AG

SCREEN 6.38

Step 18 This message indicates that the *Sales rep. ID* field has no values. Click [Generate] to continue.

Step 19 Enter a name and a description, and then click [✓] to continue.

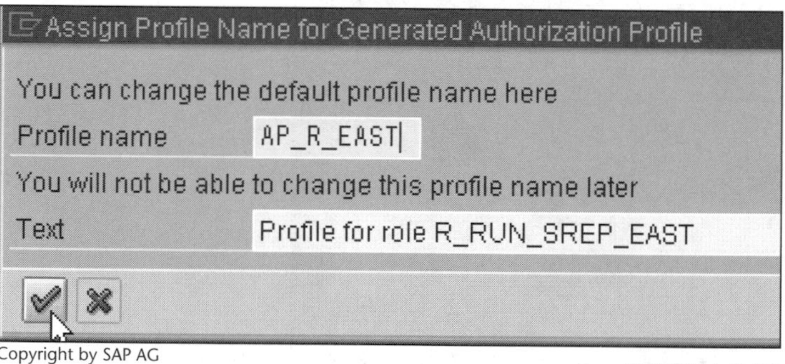

Copyright by SAP AG

SCREEN 6.39

Step 20 Notice that the status light of the *Authorizations* tab turns green. Click the *User* tab to assign user *U_EAST* to this role, and then click [User compare] to add the authorization profile to U_EAST's master data.

SCREEN 6.40

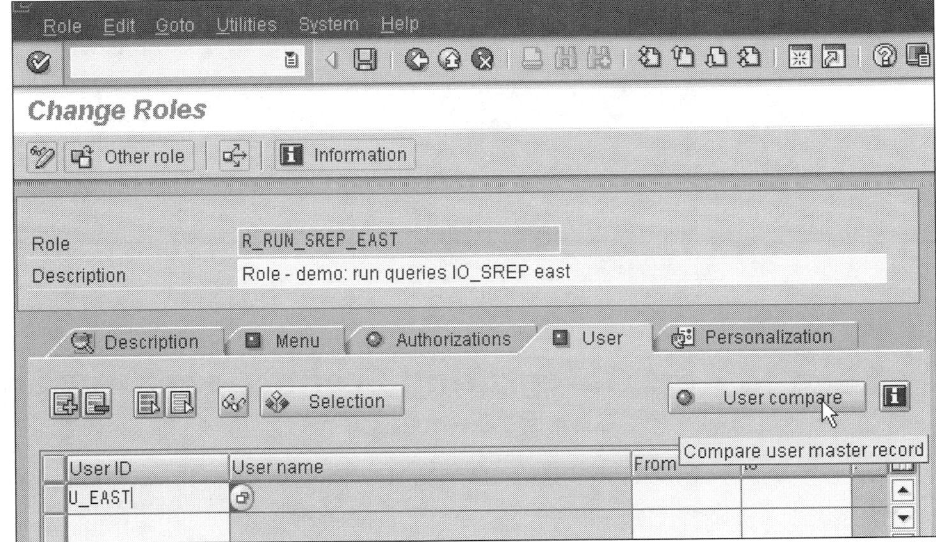

Copyright by SAP AG

Step 21 Repeat the steps from Screens 6.13 and 6.14. When they are complete, the status light of the *User* tab will turn green.

SCREEN 6.41

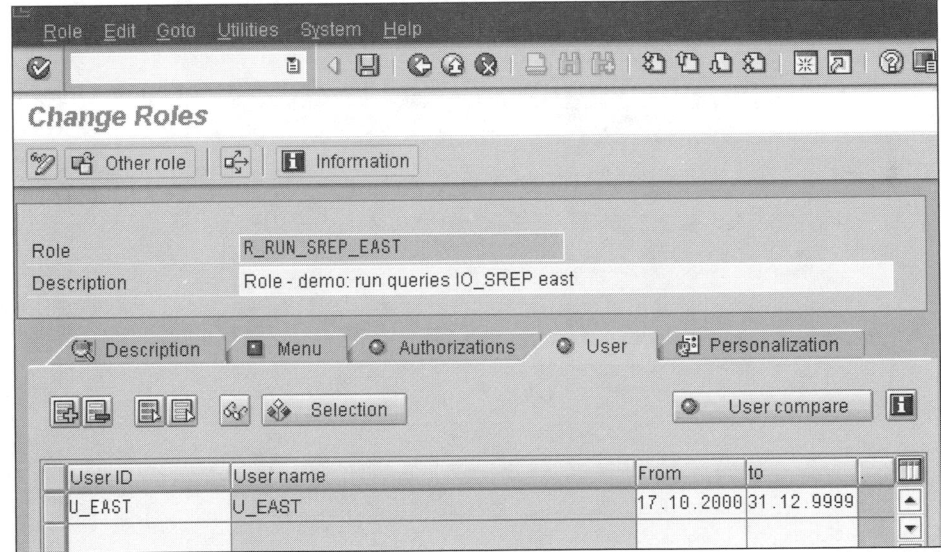

Copyright by SAP AG

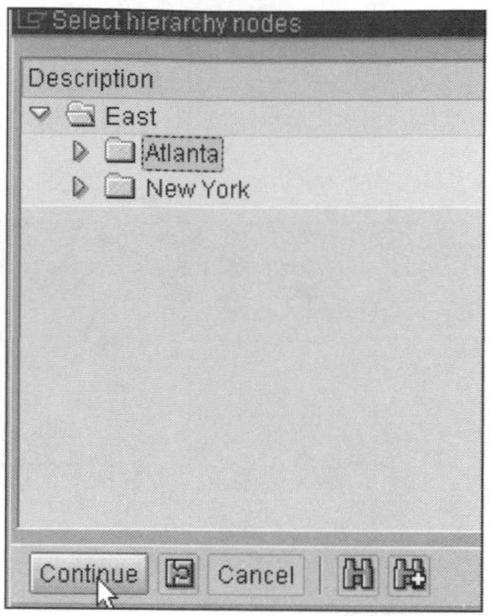

SCREEN 6.42

Copyright by SAP AG

Result

You have created the role *R_RUN_SREP_EAST* using a new authorization object. Users assigned to this role and the role created in Section 6.1 can only access the East region sales data. For example, when user U_EAST runs the query in Screen 5.31 again, the user will have only two cities from which to choose (Screen 6.42).

6.3 Integrating Profile Generator and BEx Browser

In Chapter 5, we learned that BEx Browser is a workbook organizer. To display query results, we use the BEx Analyzer. With Profile Generator, BEx Browser can truly serve as an information center for organizing all kinds of information resources in one place. The following procedure shows how to access a Web site and run an R/3 transaction from BEx Browser.

Work Instructions

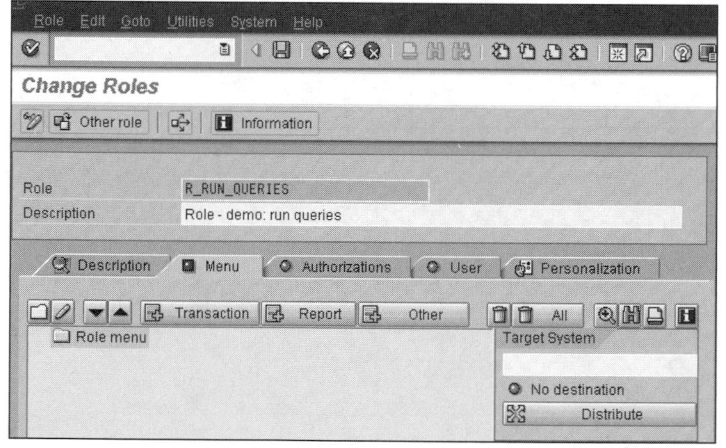

SCREEN 6.43

Copyright by SAP AG

Step 1 Open the role *R_RUN_QUERIES* that was created in Section 6.1. Click the *Menu* tab.

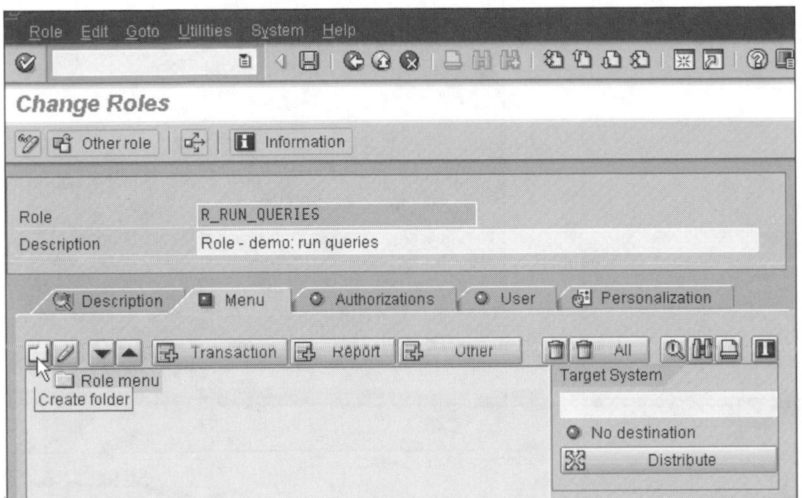

Copyright by SAP AG

SCREEN 6.44

Step 2 Click [icon] to create a new folder under *Role menu*.

Step 3 Enter a folder name, and then click [icon] to continue.

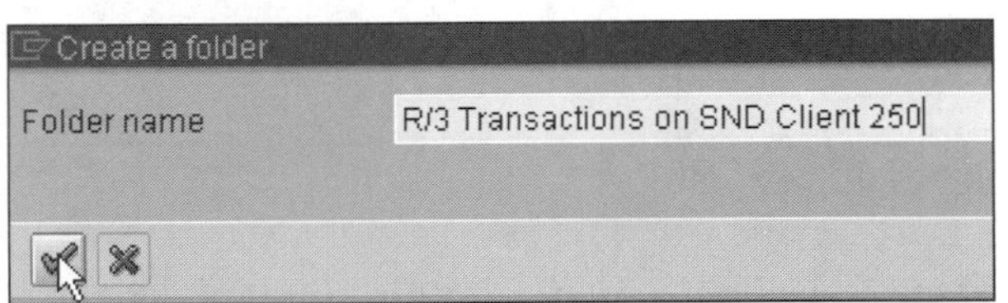

Copyright by SAP AG

SCREEN 6.45

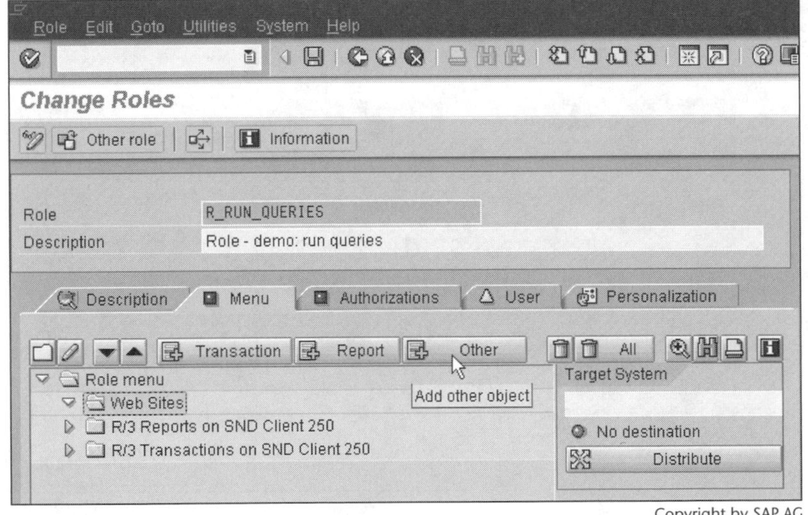

Copyright by SAP AG

SCREEN 6.46

Step 4 Repeat Steps 2 and 3 to create two more folders. The names of the new folders are shown in Screen 6.46.

To add a Web address to a folder, select the *Web Sites* folder, and then click [Other].

Step 5 Select the option *Web address or file*, and then click ✔ to continue.

Add additional objects

Select which type of object you want to add

- Web address or file
- Generischer BW Knotentyp
- Drag-and-Relate Component
- Knowledge Warehouse
- Aufruf der InfoSet Query aus dem BW Explorer

SCREEN 6.47

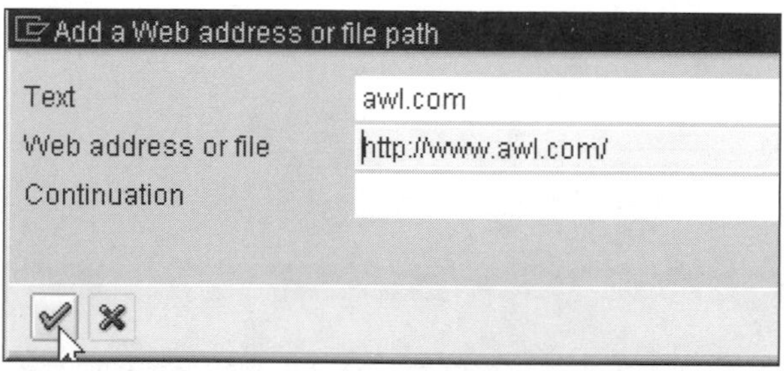

SCREEN 6.48

Step 6 Enter your text and a Web address beginning with *http://*, and then click ✔ to continue.

Step 7 To define an R/3 transaction that we can launch from BEx Browser, select a folder, and then click [Transaction] to add the transaction code.

Note: To run the R/3 transaction, we need to provide an **RFC (Remote Function Call) destination** in the *Target System* field. This RFC destination defines the R/3 system as a trusting system. That is, the R/3 system trusts the BW system, and selected BW users can run certain transactions or programs in the R/3 system without providing passwords.

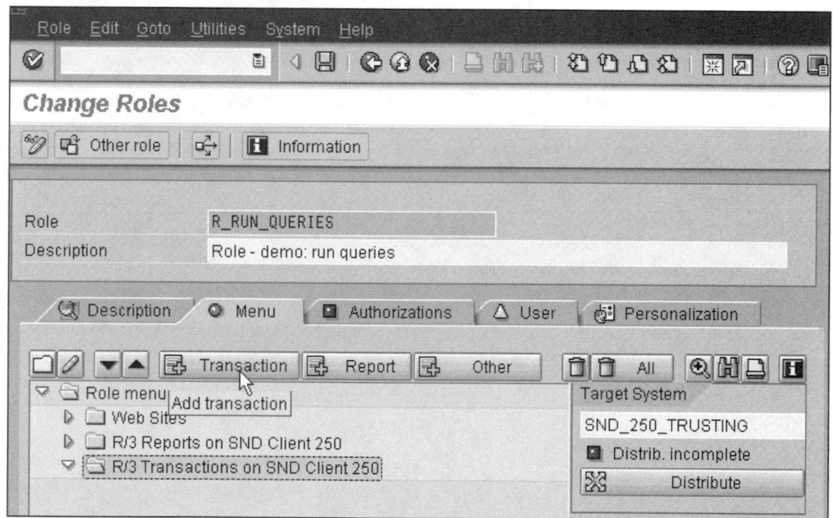

SCREEN 6.49

Step 8 Enter a transaction code, and then click [Assign transactions].

SCREEN 6.50

Step 9 Besides transactions, we can include R/3 reports. To do so, select a folder, and then click [Report].

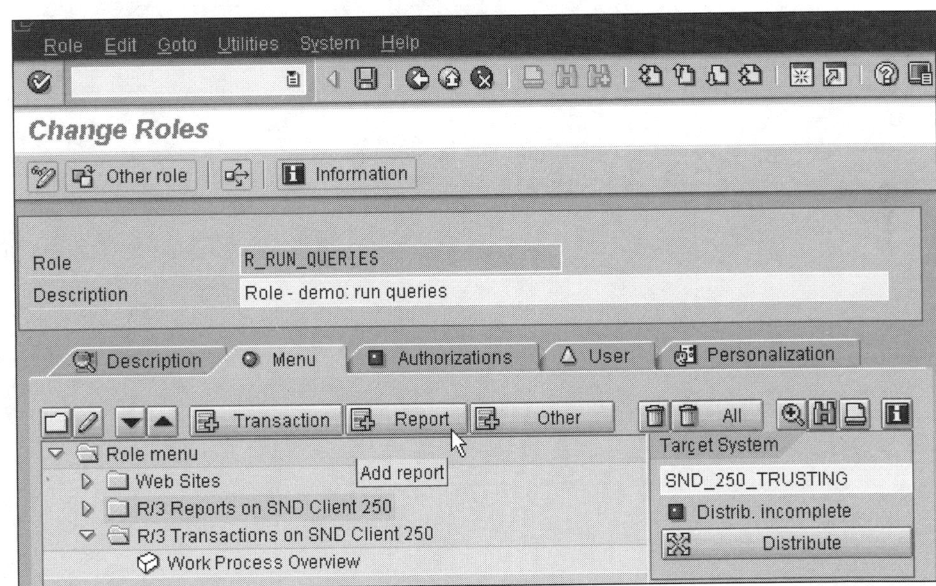

SCREEN 6.51

Step 10 The pop-up window shows the type of reports we can include. In this example, we do not include any reports. Click ✖ to cancel the operation and go back to the previous screen.

SCREEN 6.52

Step 11 Click [User compare] to update the user master data, and notice that all of the tab status lights are now green.

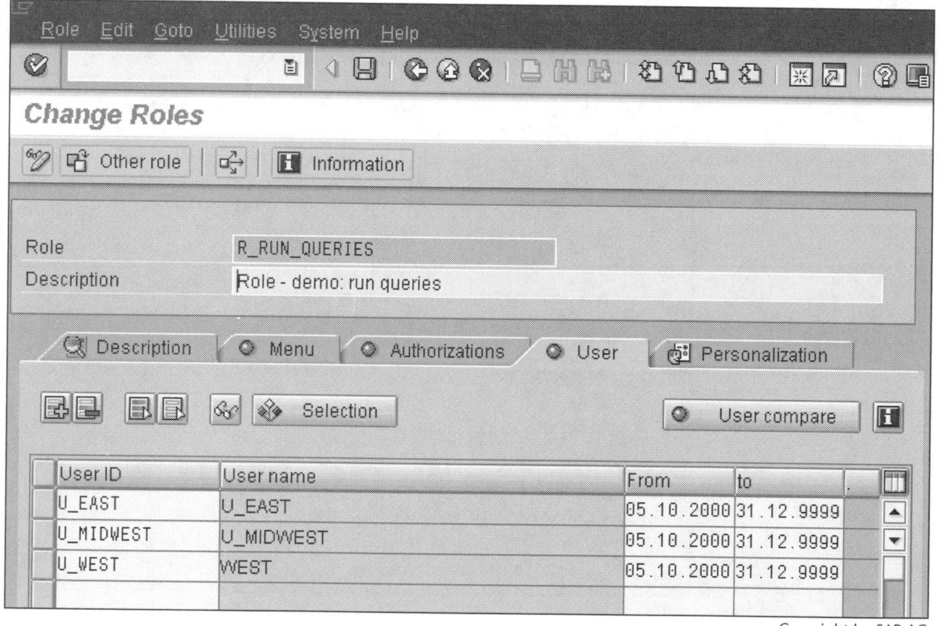

SCREEN 6.53

Result

Users with the *R_RUN_QUERIES* role can run the R/3 transaction SM50 and access the Web site www.awl.com.

Open BEx Browser and log on as U_EAST, then click folder *Role – demo: run queries* in the left panel. You will see Screen 6.54.

SCREEN 6.54

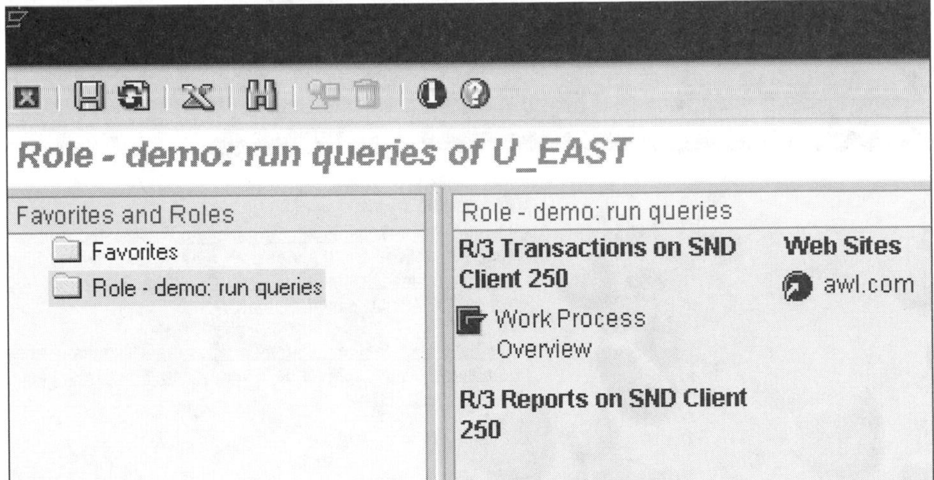

Copyright by SAP AG

Double-click the *Work Process Overview* icon. The BEx Browser opens an R/3 session. The session displays the result of transaction SM50 (Screen 6.55).

SCREEN 6.55

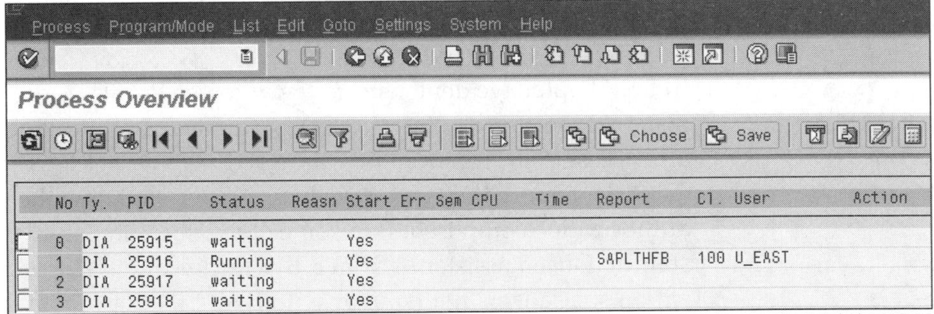

Copyright by SAP AG

Double-click the *awl.com* icon, and BEx Browser opens the www.awl.com Web page using the default Web browser, Internet Explorer (Screen 6.56).

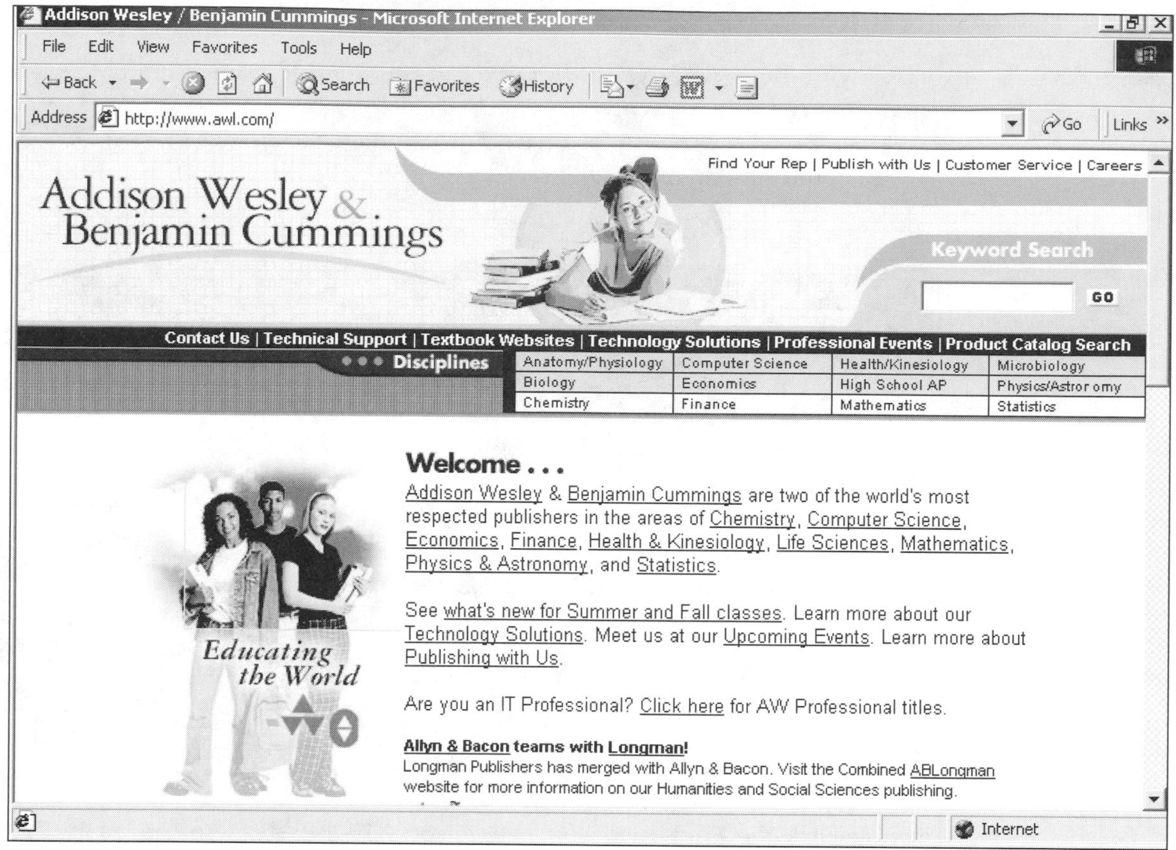

SCREEN 6.56

6.4 Summary

In this chapter, we demonstrated how to use Profile Generator to create authorization profiles and objects. We also learned how to launch R/3 transactions and access Web sites from BEx Browser.

A larger organization will likely have staff members who specialize in authorization setup issues. In some cases, such an organization's authorization staff may need assistance from a BW technical developer as well if its authorization specialist is not familiar with BW. Smaller organizations may routinely depend on BW technical developers to set up authorization profiles and objects.

Key Terms

Term	Description
Authorization	An authorization defines what a user can do, and to which SAP objects. For example, a user may be able to display and execute, but not change, a query. Authorizations are defined using authorization objects
Authorization object	An authorization object is used to define user authorizations. It has fields with values that specify authorized activities, such as display and execution, on authorized business objects, such as queries. The maximum number of characters allowed for the technical name is 10.
Authorization profile	An authorization profile is a combination of multiple authorizations. The maximum number of characters allowed for the technical name is 10.
Profile Generator	Profile Generator is a tool used to create authorization profiles.
Role	In Profile Generator, an authorization profile corresponds to a role. A user assigned to the role automatically has the corresponding authorization profile. A user can be assigned to multiple roles. The maximum number of characters allowed for the technical name is 30.
RFC	Remote Function Call (RFC) is a call to a function module in a system different from the caller's system, usually another SAP system on the local network.

For Further Information

- Book: *Authorizations Made Easy 4.6A/B,* by SAP Labs, Inc., Simplification Group. Johnson Printing Service, 1999. ISBN: 1893570231.
- OSS Note 0128447, "Trusted/Trusting Systems."
- OSS Note 0399704, "Calling SAP Transactions from within the BEx Browser."

Next . . .

We will discuss InfoCube design alternatives for the business scenario described in Chapter 1.

Part II

Contents

Advanced Topics

In Part II, we will discuss advanced topics that address issues such as the following:

- What other InfoCube design options are available besides the one discussed in Part I? How can we evaluate each option?
- Other than InfoCubes, are any other system design options better suited for cross-subject analysis and detail information drill-down?
- How can we use Business Content to streamline project time and effort? How can we extract any R/3 data using the BW tool called Generic Data Extraction?
- How can we maintain BW data and fine-tune system performance?
- How can we migrate (or *transport,* as the process is called in SAP) BW objects from a development system to a quality assurance system or a production system?

Also in Part II, we will see BW's flexibility and learn to design, develop, maintain, fine-tune, and support a BW system.

Chapter 7

InfoCube Design

InfoCube design not only determines business functionality, but also directly affects system performance.

In this chapter we will first look into the star schema implemented in BW. Next, we will analyze three InfoCube design alternatives for the same business scenario described in Chapter 1. Finally, we will briefly discuss two other InfoCube design techniques:

- Compound attributes
- Line item dimensions

Note: In BW, use of aggregates is a key technique for improving query performance. Therefore, when evaluating an InfoCube design, we must consider whether the design supports aggregates as critical criteria. See Chapter 8 for more information on aggregates.

7.1 BW Star Schema

In Chapter 1, we introduced the concept of a star schema. In Chapter 2, Screen 2.31 showed an InfoCube data model. Armed with this information, the question then becomes:

> What does the InfoCube data model look like at the database level?

In this section, we will explore the relationships between database tables. They will give us a clear idea of what the star schema looks like in BW. Again, we use a step-by-step procedure.

Work Instructions

Step 1 Run transaction *SE11*, enter */BIC/FIC_DEMOBC* as the fact table name, and then click Display.

Note: From Screen 4.3, we know that */BIC/FIC_DEMOBC* is the name of the fact table.

If we are interested in only the table contents, and not the table definition, we can run transaction *SE16* instead.

SCREEN 7.1

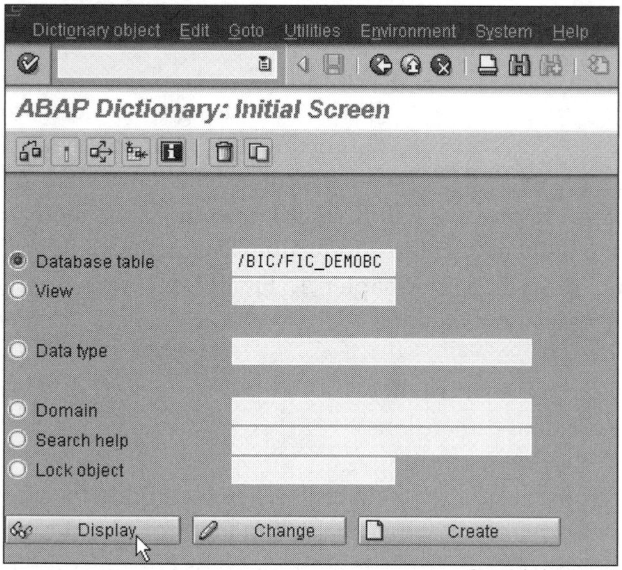

Step 2 The *Check table* column lists parent tables of the fact table. Double-click /BIC/DIC_DEMOBC3 to display the sales representative dimension table.

Note: BW uses </BIC/|/BIO/>D <InfoCube name><Number starting from 1> to name dimension tables.

- </BIC/|/BIO/>D<InfoCube name>P is for the data packet dimension. We will discuss its role in BW in Chapter 12.
- </BIC/|/BIO/>D<InfoCube name>T is for the time dimension.
- </BIC/|/BIO/>D<InfoCube name>U is for the unit dimension.

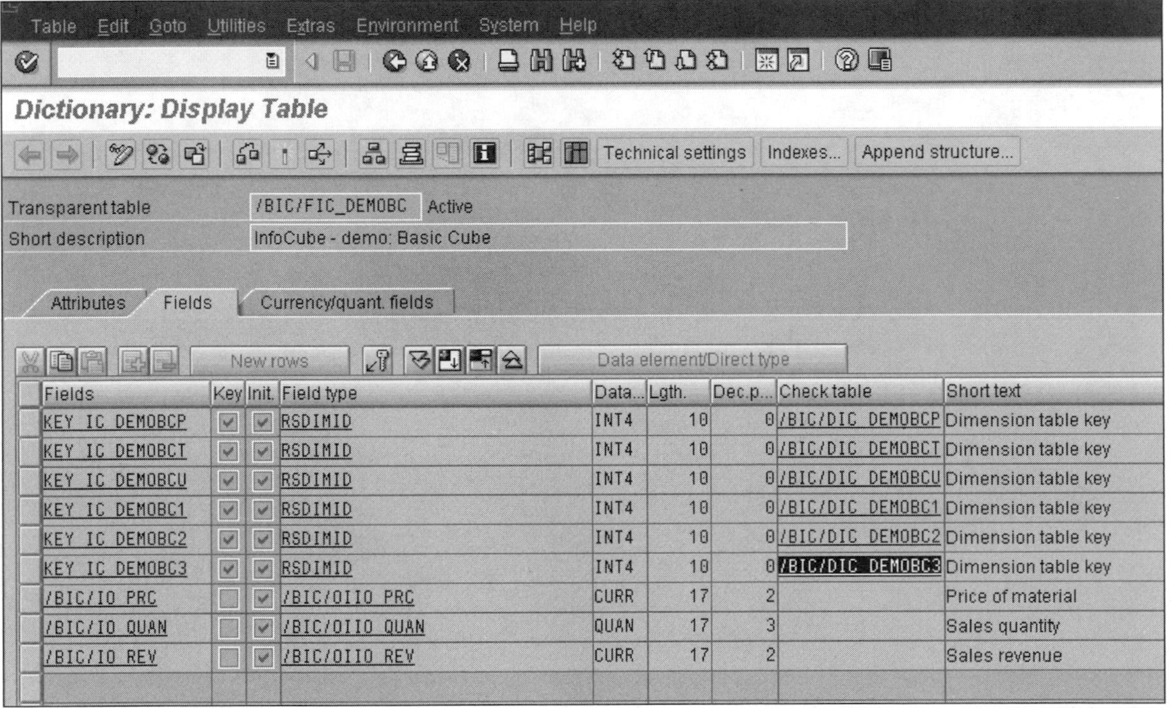

SCREEN 7.2

Step 3 The dimension table does not have any check tables, but it has a field called *SID_IO_SREP*. Click to display the table's contents.

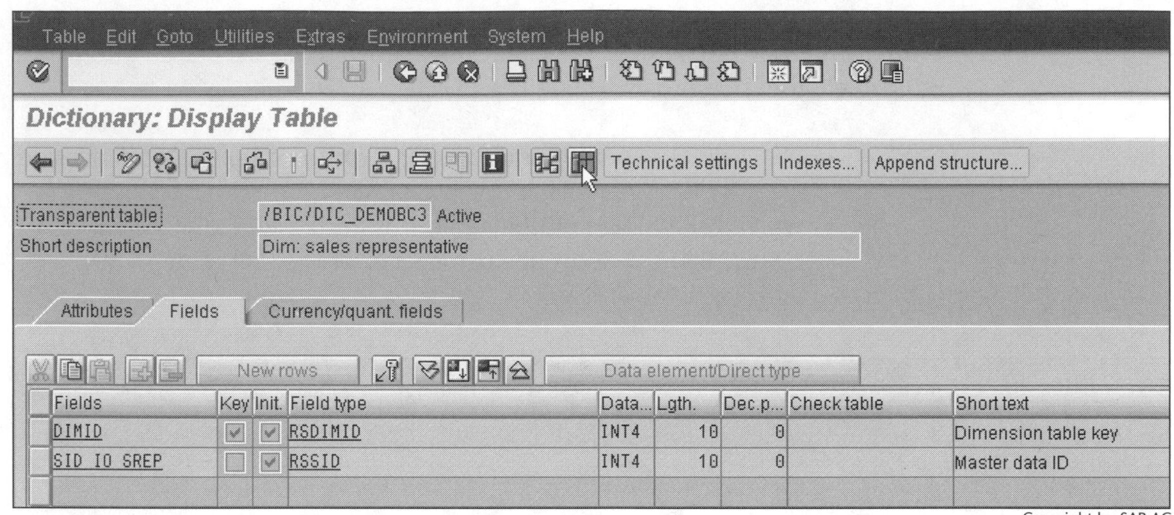

Copyright by SAP AG

SCREEN 7.3

Step 4 Click to execute.

SCREEN 7.4

Program Edit Goto Settings System Help

Data Browser: Table /BIC/DIC_DEMOBC3: Selection Screen

Number of entries

DIMID to

SID_IO_SREP to

Width of output list 250

Maximum no. of hits 500

Copyright by SAP AG

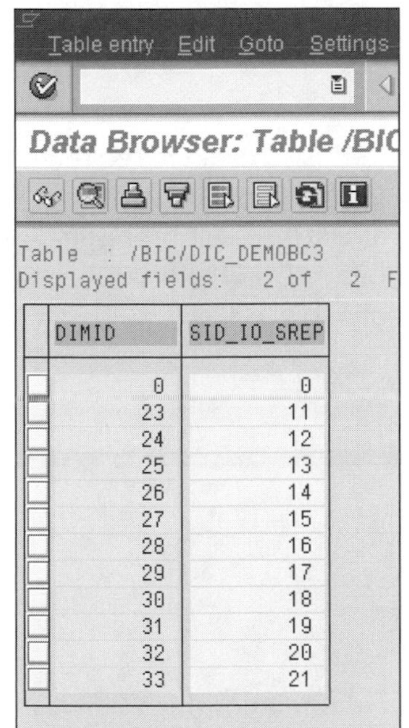

Data Browser: Table /BIC

Table : /BIC/DIC_DEMOBC3
Displayed fields: 2 of 2

DIMID	SID_IO_SREP
0	0
23	11
24	12
25	13
26	14
27	15
28	16
29	17
30	18
31	19
32	20
33	21

SCREEN 7.5

Step 5 Notice that SID_IO_SREP *11* corresponds to DIMID *23*.

From Screen 4.4, we know that DIMID *23* is the value of the field KEY_IC_DEMOBC3 in the first row of the table /BIC/FIC_DEMOBC.

Then what does SID_IO_SREP 11 represent?

Step 6 Repeat Step 1 to display the contents of IO_SREP's SID table, /BIC/SIO_SREP. This screen shows the SID table definition. Click ▦ to display the table's contents.

Dictionary: Display Table

Transparent table /BIC/SIO_SREP Active
Short description Master data IDs: InfoObject Sales rep. ID

Attributes | Fields | Currency/quant. fields

Fields	Key	Init.	Field type	Data...	Lgth.	Dec.p...	Check table	Short text
/BIC/IO_SREP	✓	✓	/BIC/OIIO_SREP	CHAR	15	0		Sales representative ID
.INCLUDE		✓	RSDSIDATTR		0	0		Attributes part of the SID table
SID			RSSID	INT4	10	0		Master data ID
CHCKFL			RSDCHCKFL	CHAR	1	0		Flag: Value in check tables
DATAFL			RSDDATAFL	CHAR	1	0		Flag: Value in dimension or available as attribute
INCFL			RSDINCFL	CHAR	1	0		Flag: Value is built into all inclusion tables

SCREEN 7.6

Note: Here SID is Surrogate-ID, not the System ID used to name an SAP system. BW uses </BIC/|/BIO/>S<characteristic name> to name a characteristic's SID table.

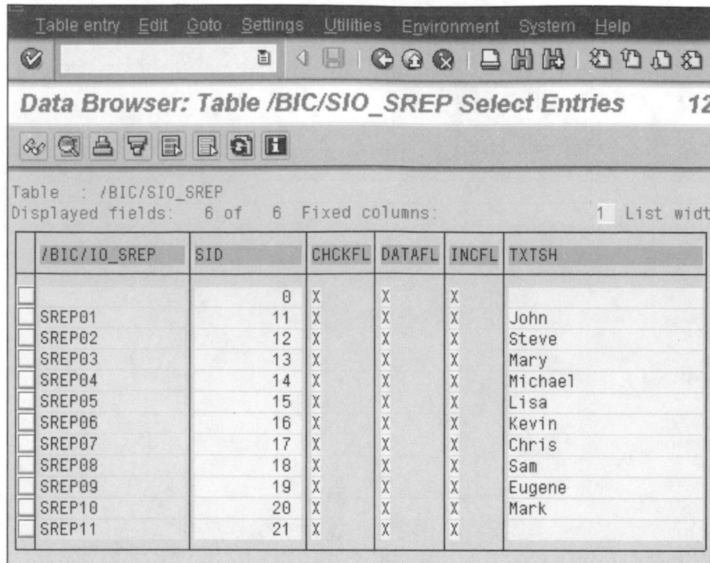
Table entry Edit Goto Settings Utilities Environment System Help

Data Browser: Table /BIC/SIO_SREP Select Entries

Table : /BIC/SIO_SREP
Displayed fields: 6 of 6 Fixed columns: 1 List widt

/BIC/IO_SREP	SID	CHCKFL	DATAFL	INCFL	TXTSH
	0	X	X	X	
SREP01	11	X	X	X	John
SREP02	12	X	X	X	Steve
SREP03	13	X	X	X	Mary
SREP04	14	X	X	X	Michael
SREP05	15	X	X	X	Lisa
SREP06	16	X	X	X	Kevin
SREP07	17	X	X	X	Chris
SREP08	18	X	X	X	Sam
SREP09	19	X	X	X	Eugene
SREP10	20	X	X	X	Mark
SREP11	21	X	X	X	

SCREEN 7.7

Step 7 The contents of the SID table /BIC/SIO_SREP are displayed.

In this screen, we see that SID *11* corresponds to *SREP01*, a sales representative ID in the first record of Table 3.3.

Following the same approach, we can discover the relationships between the SID table /BIC/SIO_SREP, the master data table /BIC/PIO_SREP, and the text table /BIC/TIO_SREP. The contents of the latter two tables are shown in Screens 7.8 and 7.9.

Step 8 Repeat Step 1 to display the contents of IO_SREP's master data table, /BIC/PIO_SREP. This screen shows the table's contents.

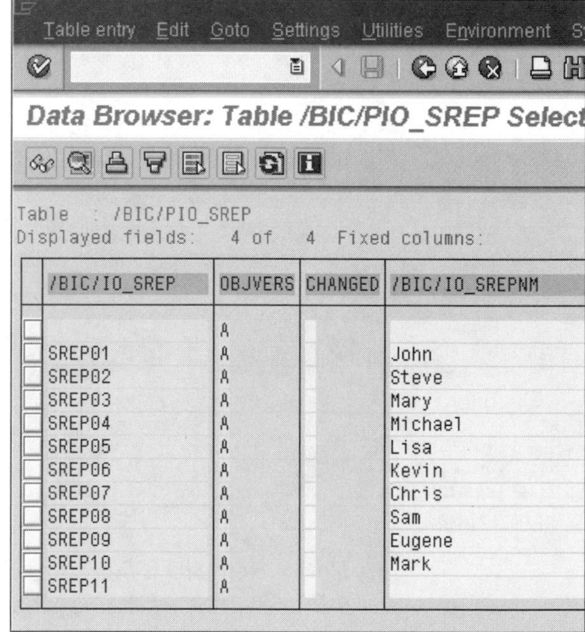
Table entry Edit Goto Settings Utilities Environment

Data Browser: Table /BIC/PIO_SREP Select

Table : /BIC/PIO_SREP
Displayed fields: 4 of 4 Fixed columns:

/BIC/IO_SREP	OBJVERS	CHANGED	/BIC/IO_SREPNM
	A		
SREP01	A		John
SREP02	A		Steve
SREP03	A		Mary
SREP04	A		Michael
SREP05	A		Lisa
SREP06	A		Kevin
SREP07	A		Chris
SREP08	A		Sam
SREP09	A		Eugene
SREP10	A		Mark
SREP11	A		

SCREEN 7.8

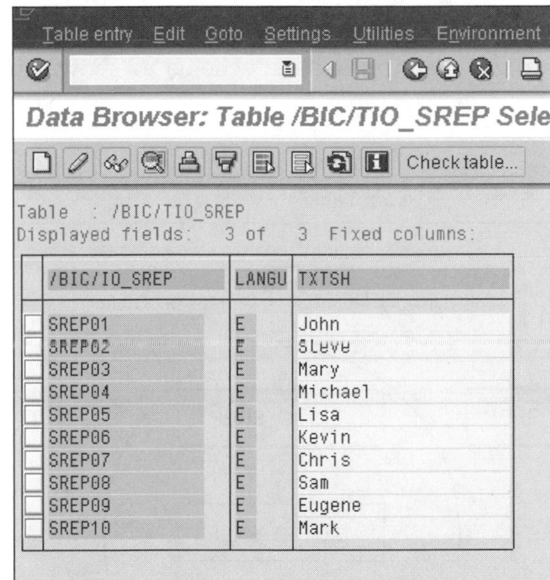
Data Browser: Table /BIC/TIO_SREP Sele

Table : /BIC/TIO_SREP
Displayed fields: 3 of 3 Fixed columns:

/BIC/IO_SREP	LANGU	TXTSH
SREP01	E	John
SREP02	E	Steve
SREP03	E	Mary
SREP04	E	Michael
SREP05	E	Lisa
SREP06	E	Kevin
SREP07	E	Chris
SREP08	E	Sam
SREP09	E	Eugene
SREP10	E	Mark

SCREEN 7.9

Step 9 Repeat Step 1 to display the contents of IO_SREP's text table, /BIC/TIO_SREP. Screen 7.9 shows the table's contents.

Step 10 Repeat Step 1 to display the contents of IO_SREP's hierarchy table, /BIC/HIO_SREP. Screen 7.10 shows the table's contents.

Note: Screen 7.10 shows the contents of the hierarchy table, /BIC/HIO_SREP. Unlike the master data table and the text table, the hierarchy table does not link to the SID table. BW builds the hierarchy based on the information in the tables /BIC/IIO_SREP, /BIC/KIO_SREP, and /BIC/SIO_SREP.

Data Browser: Table /BIC/HIO_SREP Select Entries 23

Table : /BIC/HIO_SREP
Fixed columns: 3 List width 0250

OBJVERS	NODEID	IOBJNM	NODENAME	TLEVEL	LINK	PARENTID	CHILDID	NEXTID	DATEFROM	DATETO
A	00000001	0HIER_NODE	ROOT	01		00000000	00000002	00000000	00.00.0000	31.12.9999
A	00000002	IO_SREG	EAST	02		00000001	00000003	00000004	01.01.1000	31.12.9999
A	00000003	IO_SOFF	ATLANTA	03		00000002	00000008	00000009	01.01.1000	31.12.9999
A	00000004	IO_SREG	MIDWEST	02		00000001	00000005	00000006	01.01.1000	31.12.9999
A	00000005	IO_SOFF	CHICAGO	03		00000004	00000011	00000012	01.01.1000	31.12.9999
A	00000006	IO_SREG	WEST	02		00000001	00000007	00000000	01.01.1000	31.12.9999
A	00000007	IO_SOFF	DENVER	03		00000006	00000016	00000017	01.01.2000	31.12.9999
A	00000008	IO_SREP	SREP01	04		00000003	00000000	00000000	01.01.1000	31.12.9999
A	00000009	IO_SOFF	NEW YORK	03		00000002	00000010	00000000	01.01.1000	31.12.9999
A	00000010	IO_SREP	SREP02	04		00000009	00000000	00000021	01.01.1000	31.12.9999
A	00000011	IO_SREP	SREP06	04		00000005	00000000	00000022	01.01.1000	31.12.9999
A	00000012	IO_SOFF	DALLAS	03		00000004	00000013	00000014	01.01.1000	31.12.9999
A	00000013	IO_SREP	SREP04	04		00000012	00000000	00000023	01.01.1000	31.12.9999
A	00000014	IO_SOFF	DENVER	03		00000004	00000015	00000000	01.01.1000	31.12.1999
A	00000015	IO_SREP	SREP08	04		00000014	00000000	00000000	01.01.1000	31.12.9999
A	00000016	IO_SREP	SREP08	04		00000007	00000000	00000000	01.01.1000	31.12.9999
A	00000017	IO_SOFF	LOS ANGLES	03		00000006	00000018	00000019	01.01.1000	31.12.9999
A	00000018	IO_SREP	SREP09	04		00000017	00000000	00000000	01.01.1000	31.12.9999
A	00000019	IO_SOFF	SEATTLE	03		00000006	00000020	00000000	01.01.1000	31.12.9999
A	00000020	IO_SREP	SREP10	04		00000019	00000000	00000000	01.01.1000	31.12.9999
A	00000021	IO_SREP	SREP03	04		00000009	00000000	00000000	01.01.1000	31.12.9999
A	00000022	IO_SREP	SREP07	04		00000005	00000000	00000000	01.01.1000	31.12.9999
A	00000023	IO_SREP	SREP05	04		00000012	00000000	00000000	01.01.1000	31.12.9999

SCREEN 7.10

Result

Based on our discussion, we can draw a simplified star schema as shown in Figure 7.1.

FIGURE 7.1 BW STAR SCHEMA FOR PART I INFOCUBE DESIGN

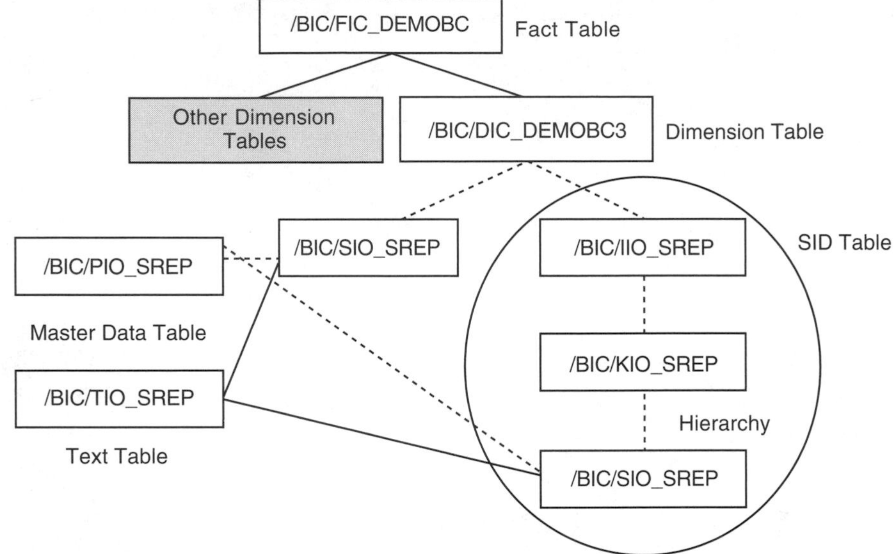

In Figure 7.1, the solid lines are the true master–detail relationships, reinforced by foreign keys. The dashed lines are relationships that are maintained by ABAP programs, but not reinforced by foreign keys.

The dashed-line relationships allow us to load transaction data even when the database does not contain any master data. Screen 7.11 shows the InfoPackage used in Section 3.9. Under the *Update parameters* tab, notice the *Always update data, even if no master data exists for the data* option.

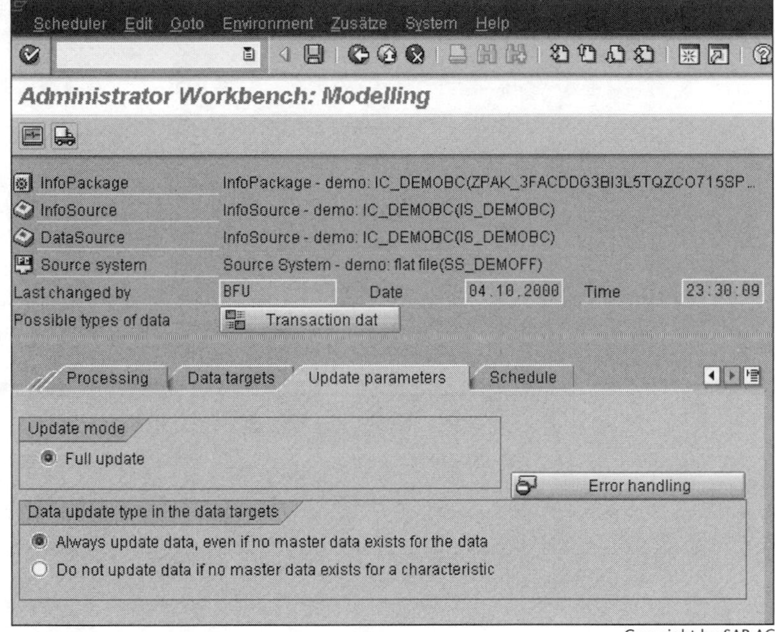

SCREEN 7.11

With this star schema in mind, let's look at three InfoCube design alternatives.

7.2 InfoCube Design Alternative I—Time-Dependent Navigational Attributes

In the Part I InfoCube design, IO_SREG and IO_SOFF are in a hierarchy of IO_SREP as the hierarchy's node values (Screen 3.46). In this section, we will discuss an alternative by putting IO_SREG and IO_SOFF into a new IO_SREP, or IO_SREPN1, as **time-dependent navigational attributes**.

First, we show how to build this new design.

Work Instructions

Step 1 In the definition of IO_SREPN1, append IO_SOFF and IO_SREG after the existing IO_SREPNM as attributes.

Make IO_SOFF and IO_SREG time-dependent by selecting the corresponding rows in the column *Time-Dependent*. Click [button] to switch them from display attributes to navigational attributes.

SCREEN 7.12

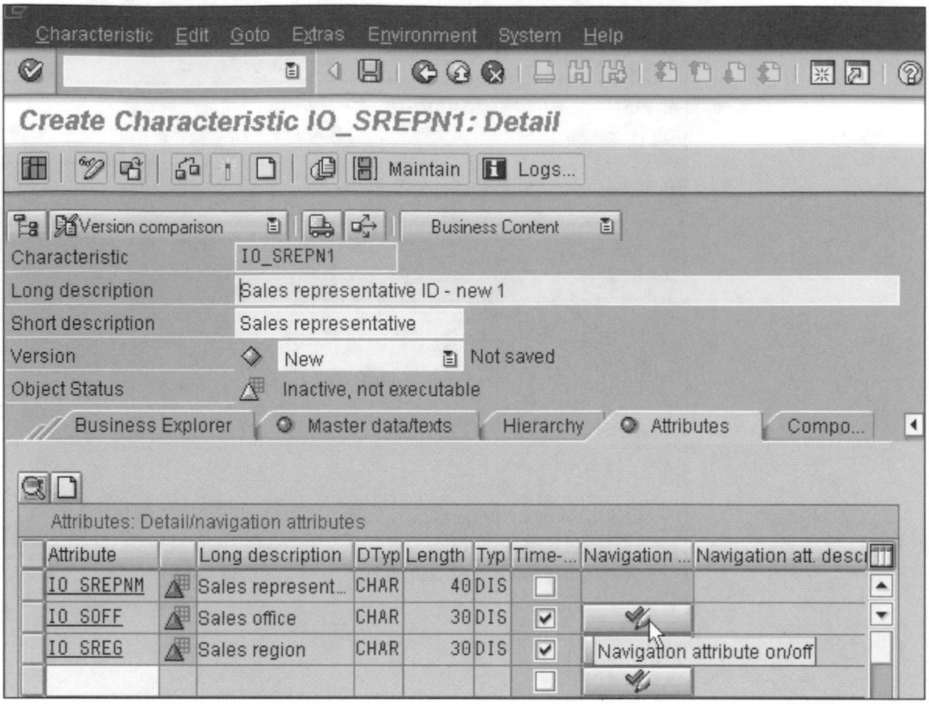

Copyright by SAP AG

Step 2 Enter the description *Sales office* for the navigational attribute IO_SOFF, and *Sales region* for IO_SREG.

(Screen 7.13 shows the description for IO_SOFF only.)

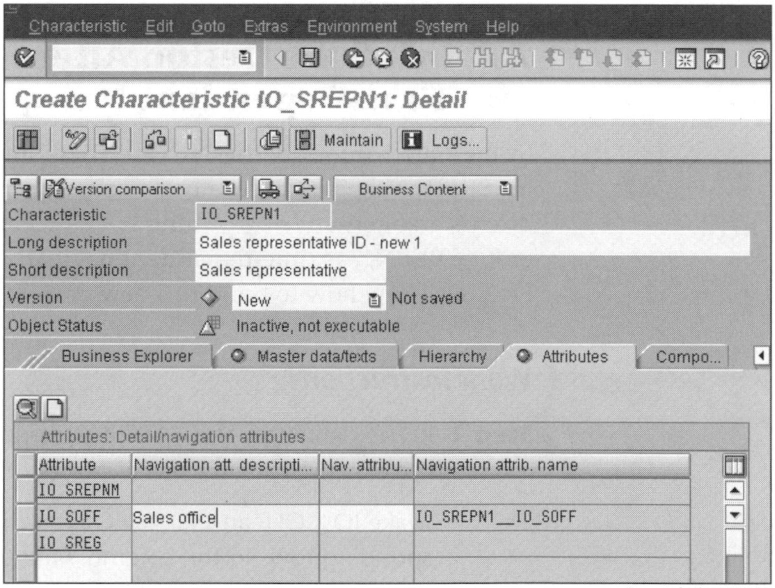

SCREEN 7.13

Copyright by SAP AG

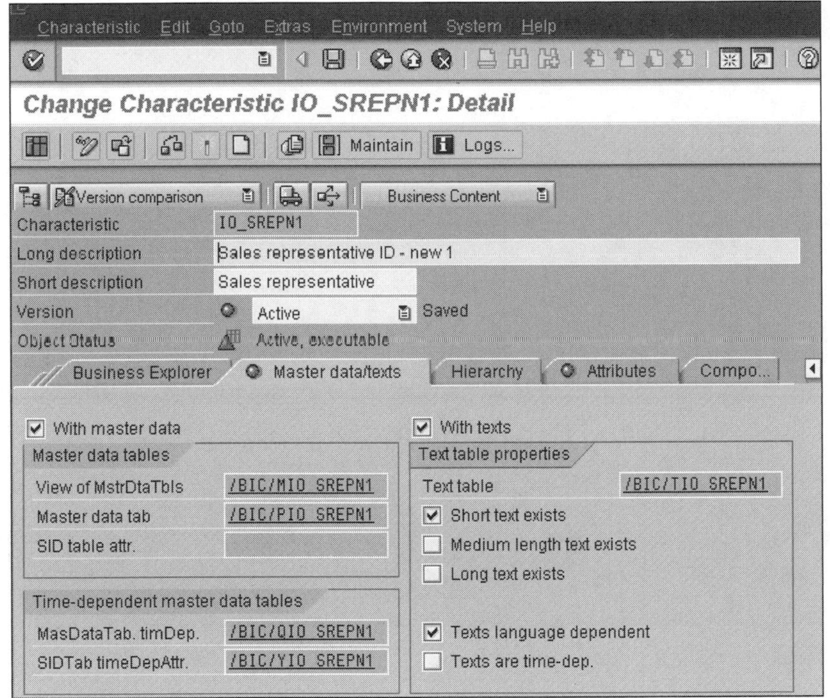

SCREEN 7.14

Step 3 Click to check the InfoObject. If it is valid, click to activate the InfoObject. The time-dependent master data table */BIC/QIO_SREPN1* and the time-dependent SID table */BIC/YIO_SREPN1* are created. Their names appear in the *Time-dependent master data tables* block.

Step 4 Double-click the SID table */BIC/YIO_SREPN1* to reach its definition screen.

Here we see two time-related fields, *DATETO* and *DATEFROM*. When we load data, we use these two fields to specify a record's valid period. DATETO is part of the key that makes a record unique.

We also see two other SID fields, *S__IO_SOFF* and *S__IO_SREG*. BW uses them to link IO_SREPN1 to IO_SOFF and IO_SREG, moving IO_SOFF and IO_SREG one more level away from the fact table. This layout will negatively affect query and load performance.

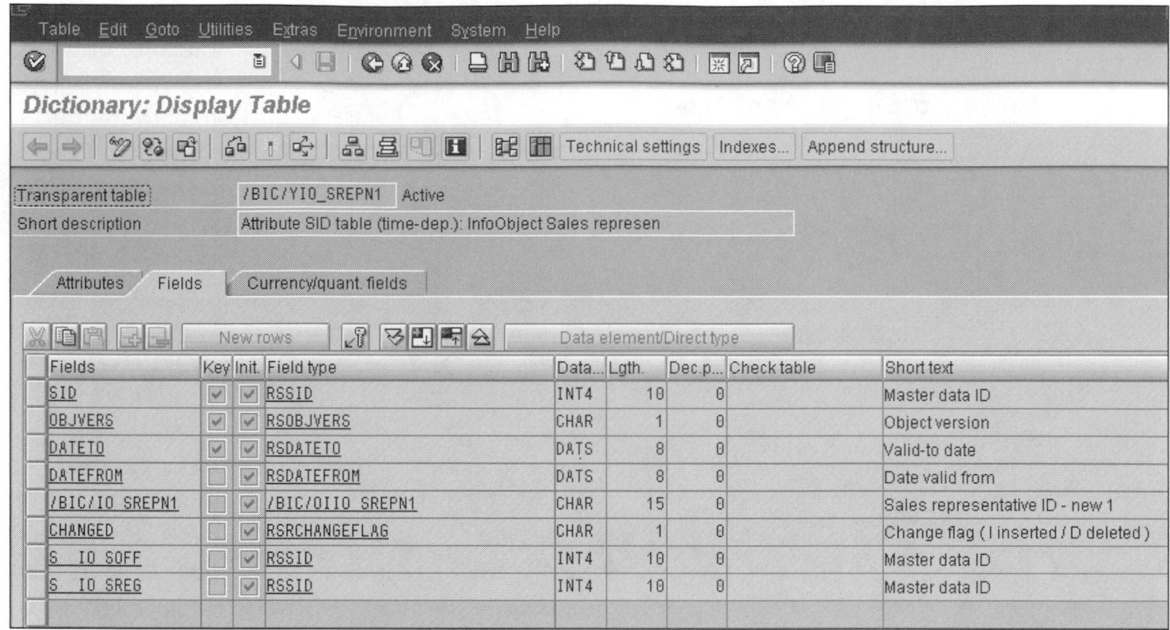

SCREEN 7.15

Step 5 Follow the work instructions in Section 2.5 to create a new InfoCube called IC_NEWBC1. In the InfoCube definition, click [Nav.attributes...] to specify the navigational attributes.

SCREEN 7.16

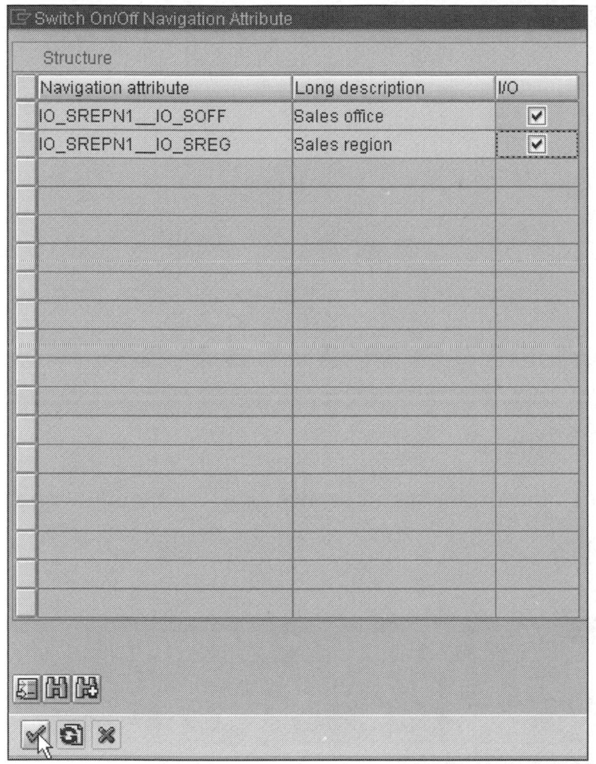

SCREEN 7.17

Step 6 In the pop-up window, check the I/O column to activate the two attributes, and then click ✔ to continue.

Step 7 After checking, activating, and loading data into the new InfoCube, we can create a query.

In the left panel, we see that *Sales office* (navigational attribute), *Sales region* (navigational attribute), and *Sales representative* (characteristic) all reside in the same dimension. From the query point of view, the navigational attributes are just like their characteristic, allowing for drill-down.

Click ▤ to specify a key date.

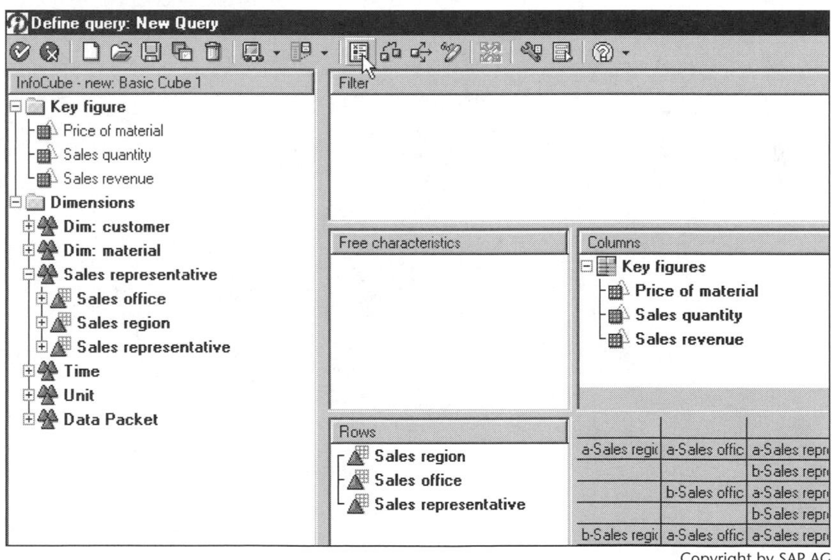

SCREEN 7.18

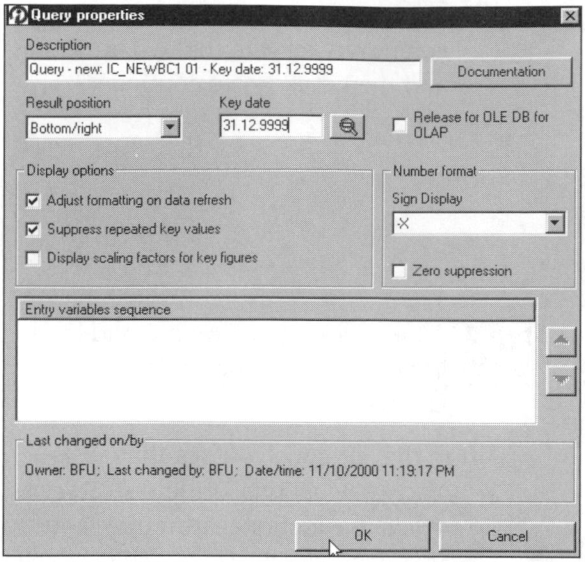

Query properties

Description: Query - new: IC_NEWBC1 01 - Key date: 31.12.9999 | Documentation

Result position: Bottom/right | Key date: 31.12.9999 | Release for OLE DB for OLAP

Display options: [x] Adjust formatting on data refresh; [x] Suppress repeated key values; [ ] Display scaling factors for key figures

Number format: Sign Display -X; [ ] Zero suppression

Entry variables sequence

Last changed on/by: Owner: BFU; Last changed by: BFU; Date/time: 11/10/2000 11:19:17 PM

OK | Cancel

SCREEN 7.19

Step 8 Enter *31.12.9999* as the key date, and then click OK to continue.

Result

The query result shows that the Denver office is located in the West region (Screen 7.20).

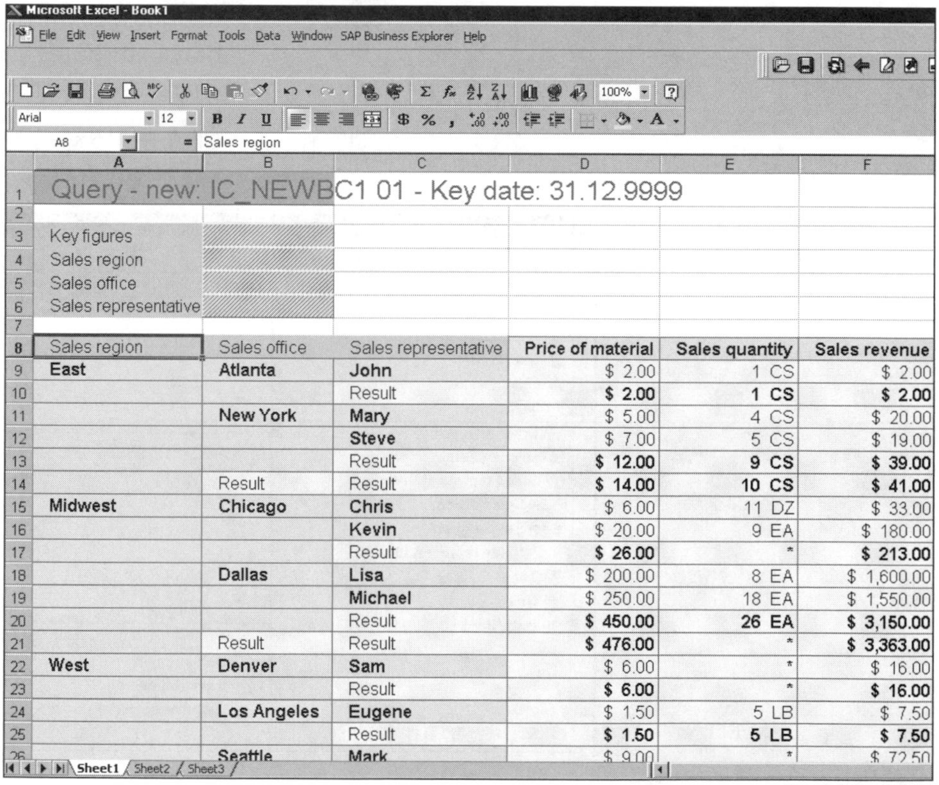

Microsoft Excel - Book1

Query - new: IC_NEWBC1 01 - Key date: 31.12.9999

Key figures
Sales region
Sales office
Sales representative

Sales region	Sales office	Sales representative	Price of material	Sales quantity	Sales revenue
East	**Atlanta**	**John**	$ 2.00	1 CS	$ 2.00
		Result	**$ 2.00**	**1 CS**	**$ 2.00**
	New York	**Mary**	$ 5.00	4 CS	$ 20.00
		Steve	$ 7.00	5 CS	$ 19.00
		Result	**$ 12.00**	**9 CS**	**$ 39.00**
	Result	Result	**$ 14.00**	**10 CS**	**$ 41.00**
Midwest	**Chicago**	**Chris**	$ 6.00	11 DZ	$ 33.00
		Kevin	$ 20.00	9 EA	$ 180.00
		Result	**$ 26.00**	*	**$ 213.00**
	Dallas	**Lisa**	$ 200.00	8 EA	$ 1,600.00
		Michael	$ 250.00	18 EA	$ 1,550.00
		Result	**$ 450.00**	**26 EA**	**$ 3,150.00**
	Result	Result	**$ 476.00**	*	**$ 3,363.00**
West	**Denver**	**Sam**	$ 6.00	*	$ 16.00
		Result	**$ 6.00**	*	**$ 16.00**
	Los Angeles	**Eugene**	$ 1.50	5 LB	$ 7.50
		Result	**$ 1.50**	**5 LB**	**$ 7.50**
	Seattle	**Mark**	$ 9.00	*	$ 72.50

SCREEN 7.20

Create another query, but this time enter *31.12.1999*, instead of *31.12.9999*, as the key date (Screen 7.19). Screen 7.21 displays the result of the new query, which shows that the Denver office is now located in the Midwest region.

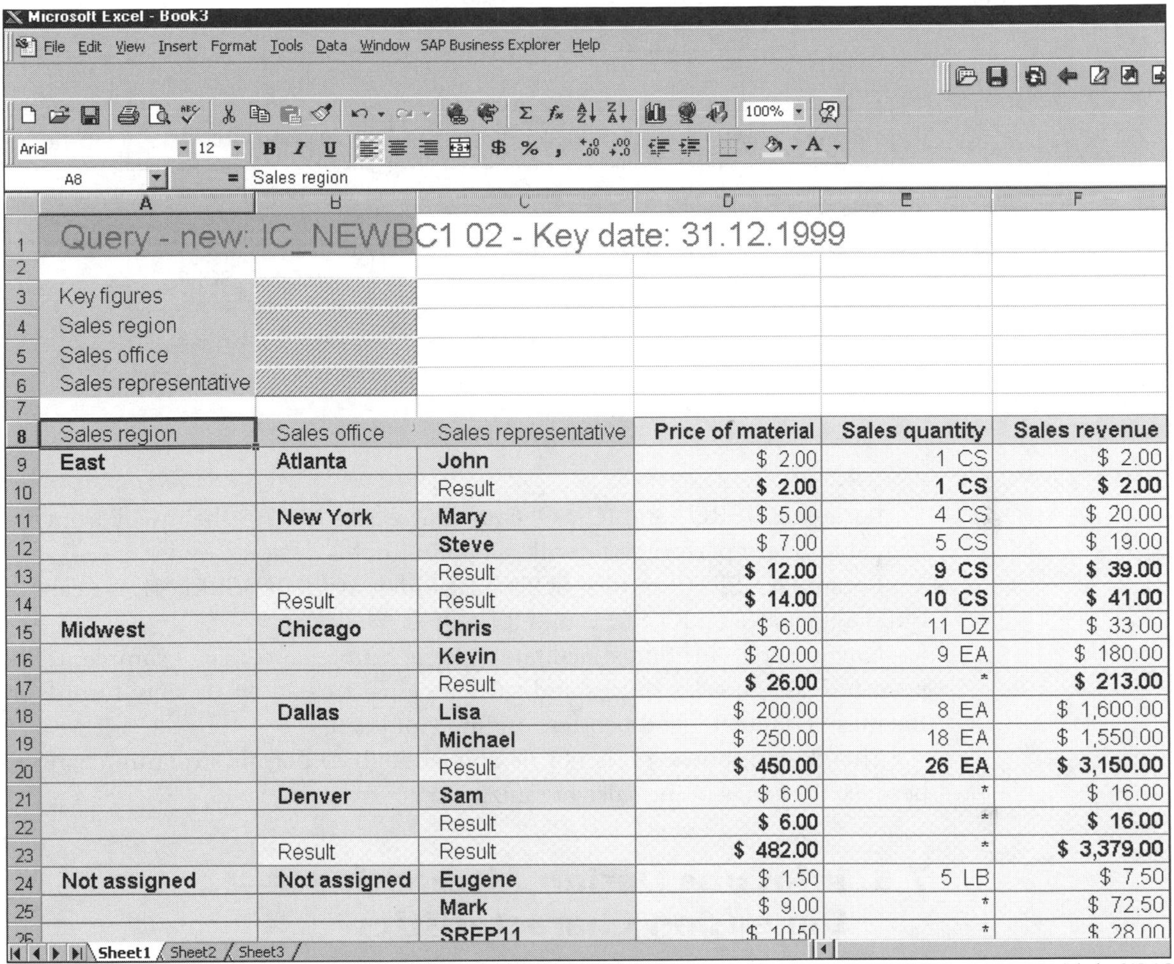

Microsoft Excel - Book3

Query - new: IC_NEWBC1 02 - Key date: 31.12.1999

Key figures
Sales region
Sales office
Sales representative

Sales region	Sales office	Sales representative	Price of material	Sales quantity	Sales revenue
East	**Atlanta**	**John**	$ 2.00	1 CS	$ 2.00
		Result	**$ 2.00**	**1 CS**	**$ 2.00**
	New York	**Mary**	$ 5.00	4 CS	$ 20.00
		Steve	$ 7.00	5 CS	$ 19.00
		Result	**$ 12.00**	**9 CS**	**$ 39.00**
	Result	Result	**$ 14.00**	**10 CS**	**$ 41.00**
Midwest	**Chicago**	**Chris**	$ 6.00	11 DZ	$ 33.00
		Kevin	$ 20.00	9 EA	$ 180.00
		Result	**$ 26.00**	*	**$ 213.00**
	Dallas	**Lisa**	$ 200.00	8 EA	$ 1,600.00
		Michael	$ 250.00	18 EA	$ 1,550.00
		Result	**$ 450.00**	**26 EA**	**$ 3,150.00**
	Denver	**Sam**	$ 6.00	*	$ 16.00
		Result	**$ 6.00**	*	**$ 16.00**
	Result	Result	**$ 482.00**	*	**$ 3,379.00**
Not assigned	**Not assigned**	**Eugene**	$ 1.50	5 LB	$ 7.50
		Mark	$ 9.00	*	$ 72.50
		SREP11	$ 10.50	*	$ 28.00

SCREEN 7.21

Note: Based on our discussion, we can draw a simplified star schema as shown in Figure 7.2 for this design alternative.

In Figure 7.2, /BIC/SIO_SREG and /BIC/SIO_SOFF have their own master data table and text table. These tables are not shown in the figure.

FIGURE 7.2 BW STAR SCHEMA OF ALTERNATIVE I INFOCUBE DESIGN

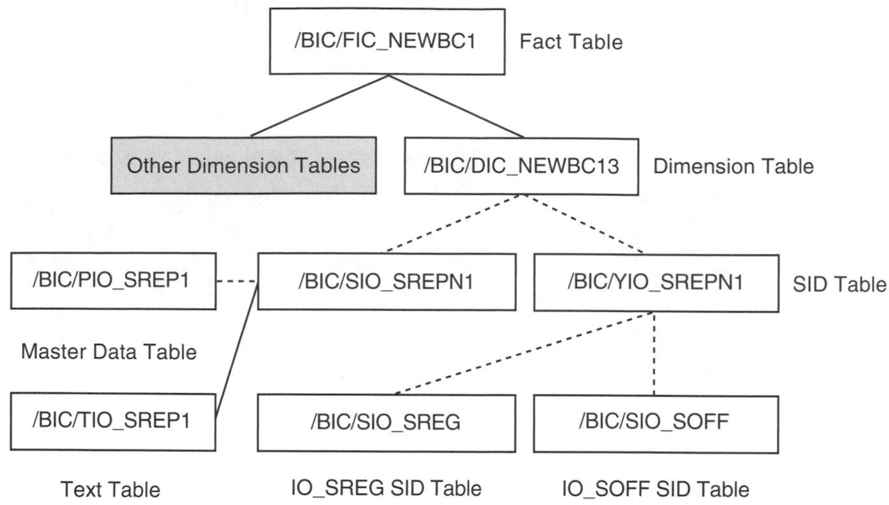

Because IO_SREG and IO_SOFF are placed one level farther away from the fact table, query performance will be poor with this design.

Because IO_SREG and IO_SOFF are hidden inside IO_SREPN1, we cannot build aggregates on IO_SREG and IO_SOFF.

Navigational attributes facilitate system maintenance. For example, if we need to reassign sales offices and sales regions, we can create new records in the master data table with corresponding valid dates.

This design, however, is not flexible enough to permit structure changes, because the levels of the sales organization are fixed.

7.3 InfoCube Design Alternative II—Dimension Characteristics

In this section, we discuss yet another design alternative. This time, we will create a new IO_SREP, called IO_SREPN2. We will treat IO_SREG and IO_SOFF as independent characteristics, just like IO_SREPN2, and put them all together in the same dimension. Figure 7.3 shows a simplified star schema for this design.

In Figure 7.3, /BIC/SIO_SREG and /BIC/SIO_SOFF have their own master data table and text table. These tables are not shown in the figure.

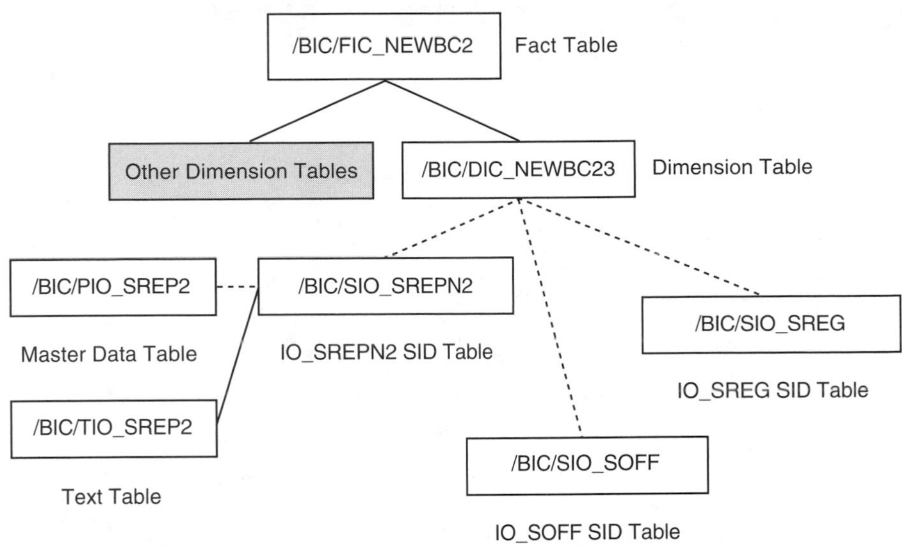

FIGURE 7.3 BW STAR SCHEMA OF ALTERNATIVE II INFOCUBE DESIGN

This design methodology is known as the **Dimension Characteristics** method. The following steps explain how to build this new design.

Work Instructions

Step 1 Repeat the Steps in Section 2.3 to create *IO_SREPN2*. It has no hierarchies.

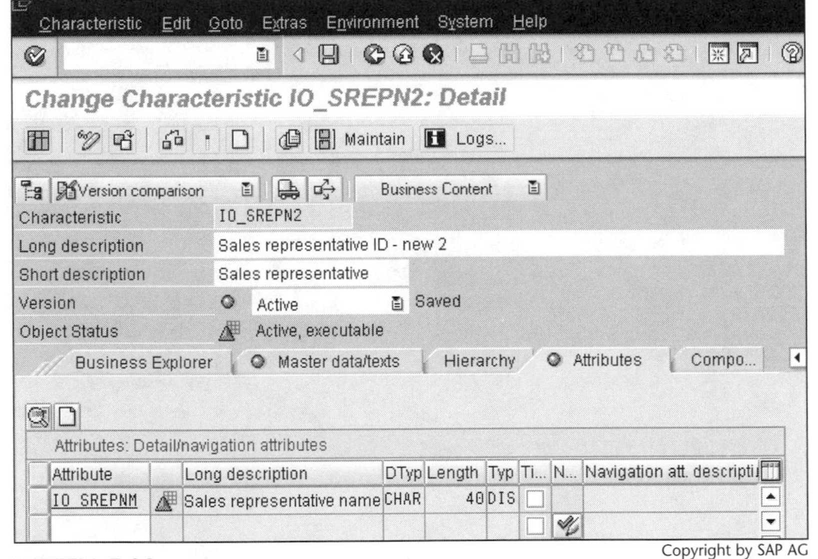

SCREEN 7.22

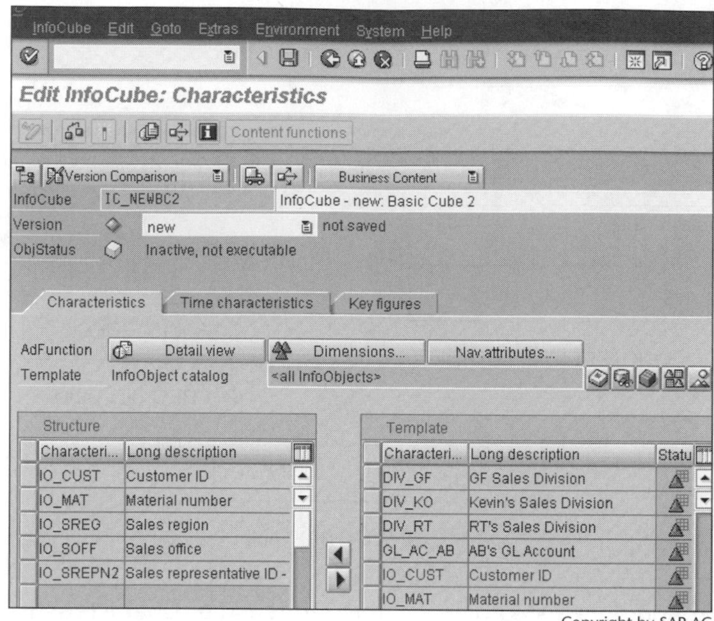

SCREEN 7.23

Step 2 Create an InfoCube and include *IO_SREG* and *IO_SOFF* as characteristics.

Step 3 Assign IO_SREG, IO_SOFF, and IO_SREPN2 to the same dimension as shown in this screen. (See Screen 2.27 for the difference.)

Click to check the new InfoCube. If it is valid, click to activate the new InfoCube.

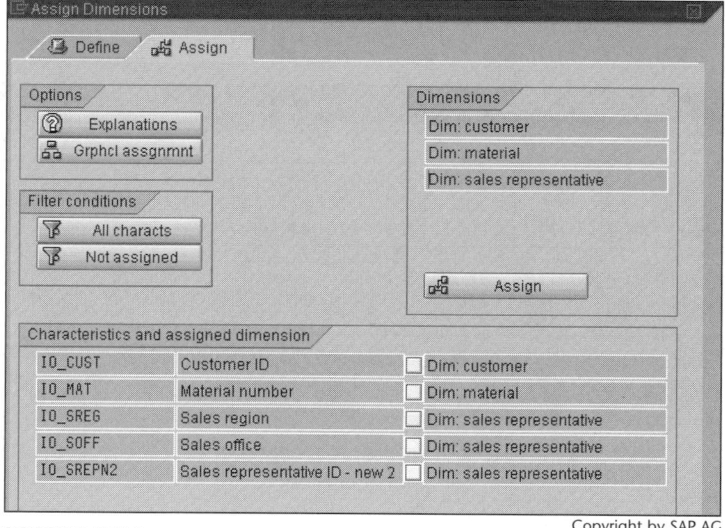

SCREEN 7.24

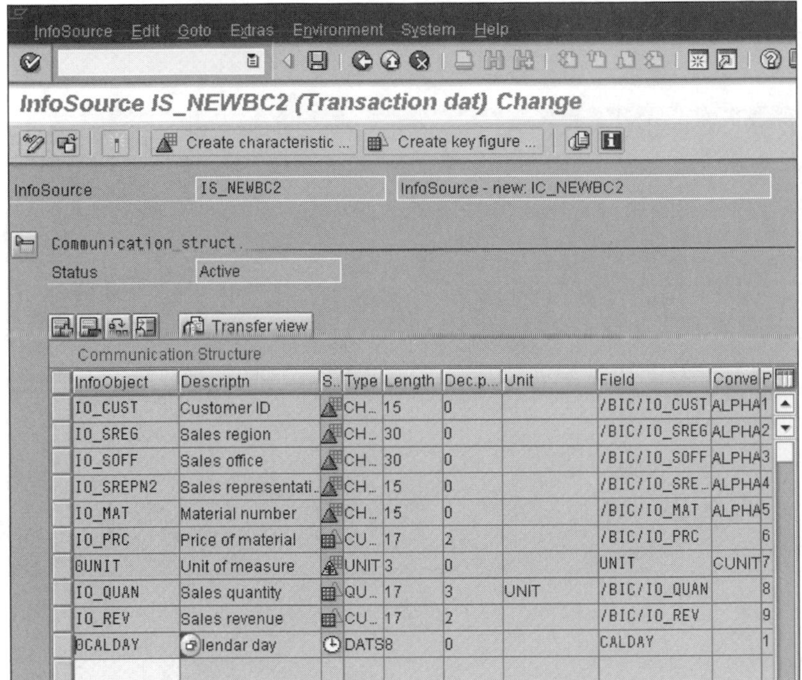

InfoObject	Descriptn	S..	Type	Length	Dec.p...	Unit	Field	Conve	P
IO_CUST	Customer ID		CH...	15	0		/BIC/IO_CUST	ALPHA	1
IO_SREG	Sales region		CH...	30	0		/BIC/IO_SREG	ALPHA	2
IO_SOFF	Sales office		CH...	30	0		/BIC/IO_SOFF	ALPHA	3
IO_SREPN2	Sales representati...		CH...	15	0		/BIC/IO_SRE...	ALPHA	4
IO_MAT	Material number		CH...	15	0		/BIC/IO_MAT	ALPHA	5
IO_PRC	Price of material		CU...	17	2		/BIC/IO_PRC		6
0UNIT	Unit of measure		UNIT	3	0		UNIT	CUNIT	7
IO_QUAN	Sales quantity		QU...	17	3	UNIT	/BIC/IO_QUAN		8
IO_REV	Sales revenue		CU...	17	2		/BIC/IO_REV		9
0CALDAY	lendar day		DATS	8	0		CALDAY		1

SCREEN 7.25

Step 4 We also need to include *IO_SREG* and *IO_SOFF* in the communication structure. (See Screen 3.52 for the difference.)

Step 5 Load data into the new InfoCube and create a query.

In the left panel, we see the three characteristics *Sales office*, *Sales region*, and *Sales representative.* They are all in the same dimension.

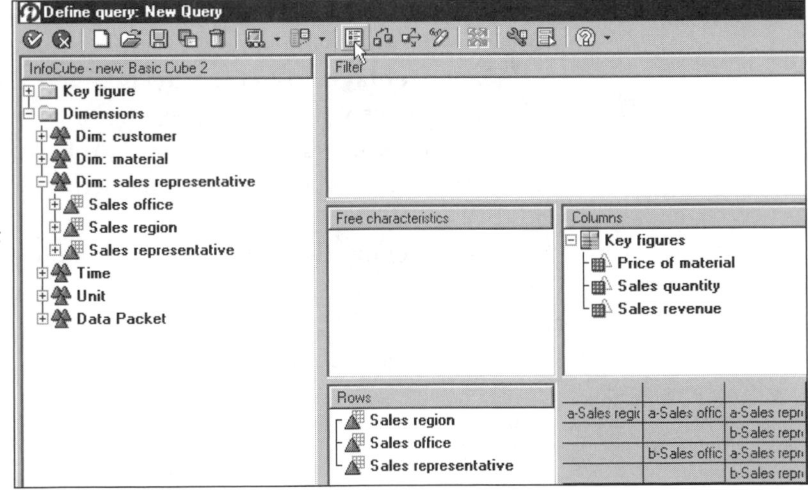

SCREEN 7.26

Step 6 As before, we specify *31.12.9999* as the key date, and run the query.

SCREEN 7.27

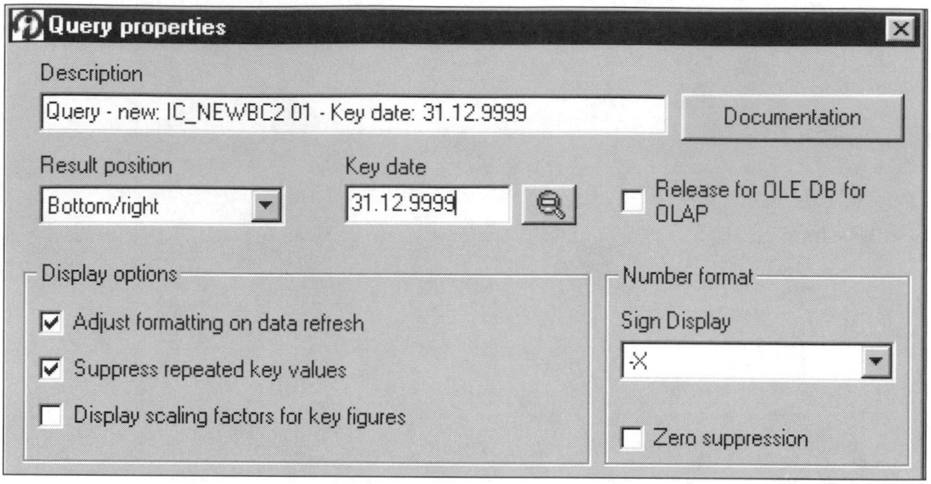

Query properties

Description

Query - new: IC_NEWBC2 01 - Key date: 31.12.9999

Documentation

Result position

Bottom/right

Key date

31.12.9999

Release for OLE DB for OLAP

Display options

Adjust formatting on data refresh

Suppress repeated key values

Display scaling factors for key figures

Number format

Sign Display

-X

Zero suppression

Result

Screen 7.28 shows the query result. The Denver office is listed under the Midwest region, instead of the West region, although we specified 31.12.9999 as the key date. This result arises because the sales transactions conducted by the Denver office all took place before January 1, 2000 (see Table 1.4). In the data warehousing world, this query result is referred to as a **yesterday-or-today** scenario—the data were valid when they were generated.

In a **yesterday-and-today** scenario, the data that were valid yesterday *and* today are displayed. In our example, we would not see the Denver office data in a yesterday-and-today scenario. For further information on this scenario, refer to ASAP for BW Accelerator, "Multi-Dimensional Modeling with BW."

Now we know that our new InfoCube design does not provide the two views of data that we saw earlier with the time-dependent hierarchy structure and time-dependent navigational attributes—namely, the today-is-yesterday scenario and the yesterday-is-today scenario.

Microsoft Excel - Book1

Query - new: IC_NEWBC2 01 - Key date: 31.12.9999

Key figures
Sales region
Sales office
Sales representative

Sales region	Sales office	Sales representative	Price of material	Sales quantity	Sales revenue
East	Atlanta	John	$ 2.00	1 CS	$ 2.00
		Result	**$ 2.00**	**1 CS**	**$ 2.00**
	New York	Mary	$ 5.00	4 CS	$ 20.00
		Steve	$ 7.00	5 CS	$ 19.00
		Result	**$ 12.00**	**9 CS**	**$ 39.00**
	Result	Result	**$ 14.00**	**10 CS**	**$ 41.00**
Midwest	Chicago	Chris	$ 6.00	11 DZ	$ 33.00
		Kevin	$ 20.00	9 EA	$ 180.00
		Lisa	$ 200.00	8 EA	$ 1,600.00
		Result	**$ 226.00**	*	**$ 1,813.00**
	Dallas	Michael	$ 250.00	18 EA	$ 1,550.00
		Result	**$ 250.00**	**18 EA**	**$ 1,550.00**
	Denver	Sam	$ 6.00	*	$ 16.00
		Result	**$ 6.00**	*	**$ 16.00**
	Result	Result	**$ 482.00**	*	**$ 3,379.00**
West	Los Angeles	Eugene	$ 1.50	5 LB	$ 7.50
		Result	**$ 1.50**	**5 LB**	**$ 7.50**
	Seattle	Mark	$ 9.00	*	$ 72.50

SCREEN 7.28

Note: From a performance point of view, this design improves upon the two earlier options, because it places IO_SREG and IO_SOFF closer to the fact table.

Performance is, of course, one of the major concerns in data warehousing. Here are some guidelines for dealing with this issue:

1. If IO_SREG and IO_SOFF data are included in the transaction data, as shown in Table 7.1, use IO_SREG and IO_SOFF as dimension characteristics instead of characteristic attributes.

TABLE 7.1 SALES DATA

IO_CUST	IO_SREG	IO_SOFF	IO_SREPN2	IO_MAT	IO_PRC	OUNIT	IO_QUAN	IO_REV	OCALDAY
CUST001	EAST	ATLANTA	SREP01	MAT001	2	CS	1	2	19980304
CUST002	EAST	NEW YORK	SREP02	MAT002	2	CS	2	4	19990526
CUST002	EAST	NEW YORK	SREP02	MAT003	5	CS	3	15	19990730
CUST003	EAST	NEW YORK	SREP03	MAT003	5	CS	4	20	20000101
CUST004	MIDWEST	DALLAS	SREP04	MAT004	50	EA	5	250	19991023
CUST004	MIDWEST	DALLAS	SREP04	MAT005	100	EA	6	600	19980904
CUST004	MIDWEST	DALLAS	SREP04	MAT005	100	EA	7	700	19980529
CUST005	MIDWEST	CHICAGO	SREP05	MAT006	200	EA	8	1600	19991108
CUST006	MIDWEST	CHICAGO	SREP06	MAT007	20	EA	9	180	20000408
CUST007	MIDWEST	CHICAGO	SREP07	MAT008	3	DZ	10	30	20000901
CUST007	MIDWEST	CHICAGO	SREP07	MAT008	3	DZ	1	3	19990424
CUST008	MIDWEST	DENVER	SREP08	MAT008	3	DZ	2	6	19980328
CUST008	MIDWEST	DENVER	SREP08	MAT009	2	CS	3	6	19980203
CUST008	MIDWEST	DENVER	SREP08	MAT010	1	LB	4	4	19991104
CUST009	WEST	LOS ANGLES	SREP09	MAT011	1.5	LB	5	7.5	20000407
CUST010	WEST	SEATTLE	SREP10	MAT011	1.5	LB	6	9	20000701
CUST010	WEST	SEATTLE	SREP10	MAT011	1.5	LB	7	10.5	19990924
CUST010	WEST	SEATTLE	SREP10	MAT012	2	LB	8	16	19991224
CUST010	WEST	SEATTLE	SREP10	MAT013	3	CS	9	27	20000308
CUST011	WEST	SEATTLE	SREP10	MAT014	1	LB	10	10	19980627
CUST012			SREP11	MAT014	2	LB	1	2	19991209
CUST012			SREP11	MAT015	3	CS	2	6	19980221
CUST012			SREP11	MAT015	2	CS	3	6	20000705
CUST012			SREP11	MAT015	3.5	CS	4	14	20001225

2. If IO_SREG and IO_SOFF are frequently used for navigation, use IO_SREG and IO_SOFF as dimension characteristics instead of characteristic attributes.

When considering the dimension in which a characteristic should be placed, follow these two guidelines:

1. If the characteristics, such as IO_SREG, IO_SOFF, and IO_SREPN2, have a one-to-many relationship, group them in the same dimension.
2. If the characteristics, such at IO_MAT and IO_CUST, have a many-to-many relationship, group them in different dimensions. In some special

cases, when the combinations of the relations are small, such as materials and colors, you might consider grouping them within one dimension.

Another advantage of this InfoCube design is that we can create aggregates on IO_SREG and IO_SOFF. As in Alternative I, however, the levels of the sales organization are fixed in Alternative II.

7.4 InfoCube Design Alternative III—Time-Dependent Entire Hierarchies

The original design in Section 3.6.2, "Hierarchy," uses a time-dependent hierarchy structure. Although that design performs more poorly than the alternative II InfoCube design, its sales organization hierarchy is very flexible. That is, we can easily add or delete levels in the sales organization. The major drawback of the Section 3.6.2 design, however, is that we cannot create aggregates on a time-dependent hierarchy structure.

This section introduces another type of hierarchy, called a **time-dependent entire hierarchy**, that does allow us to create aggregates. Figure 7.4 illustrates how it differs from the time-dependent hierarchy.

FIGURE 7.4 A COMPARISON OF TWO TYPES OF HIERARCHIES (continued on page 188)

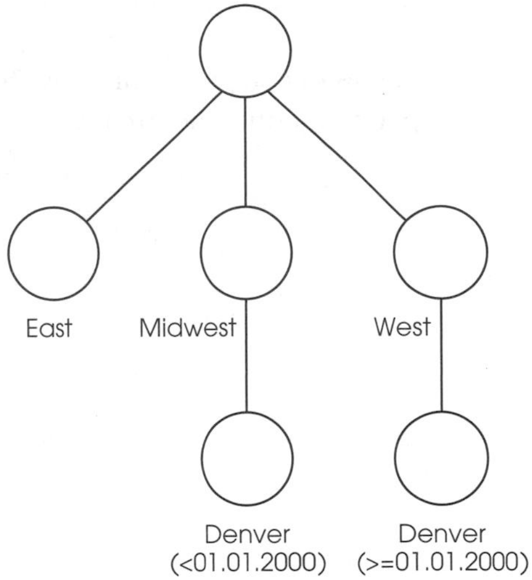

(a) Time-dependent hierarchy structures in the Part I example

FIGURE 7.4 (continued)

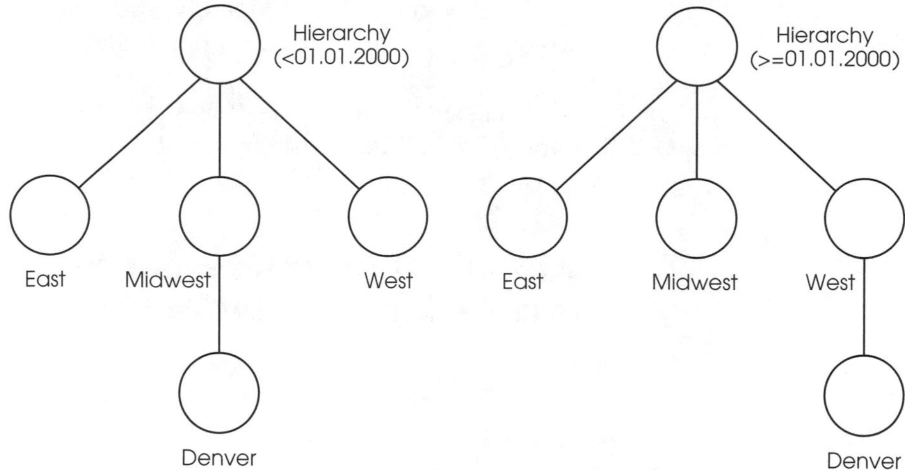

(b) Time-dependent entire hierarchies to be discussed in Section 7.4

As shown in Figure 7.4(a), time-dependent hierarchy structures consist of nodes or leaves that are time-dependent. The hierarchy itself is not time-dependent.

As shown in Figure 7.4(b), time-dependent entire hierarchies consist of nodes or leaves that are not time-dependent. The hierarchy itself is time-dependent.

The following steps explain how to build the design for our example with time-dependent entire hierarchies.

Work Instructions

Step 1 Create a new IO_SREP, called IO_SREPN3. Select the *Entire hierarchy is time-dependent* option.

SCREEN 7.29

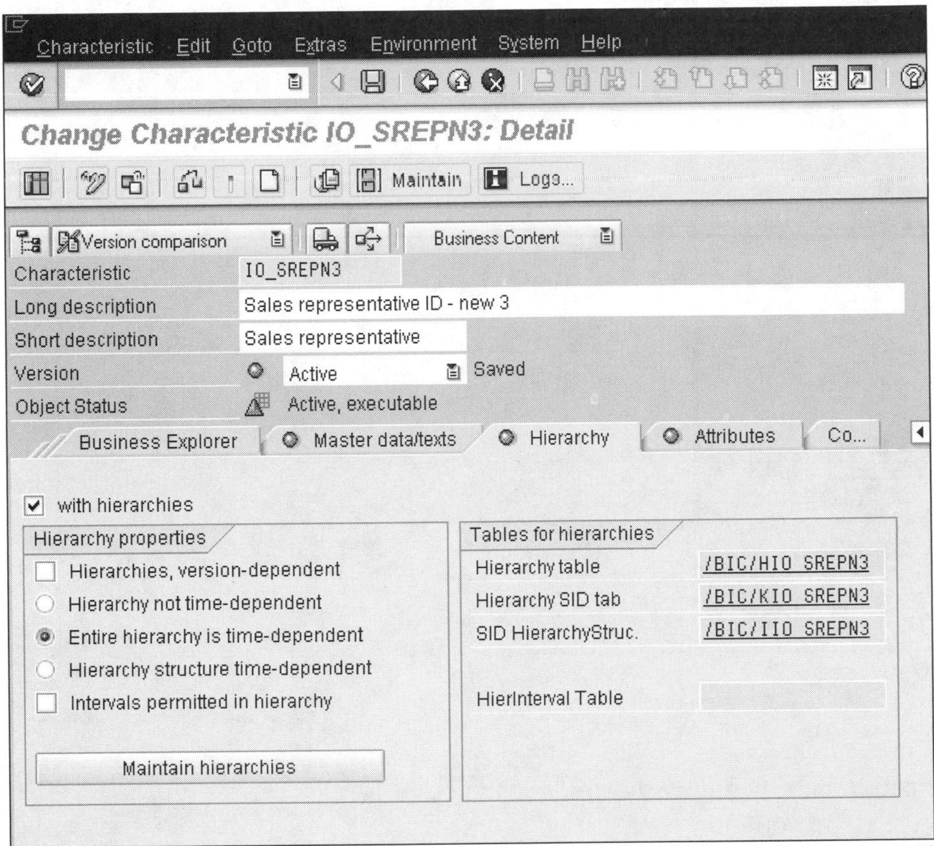

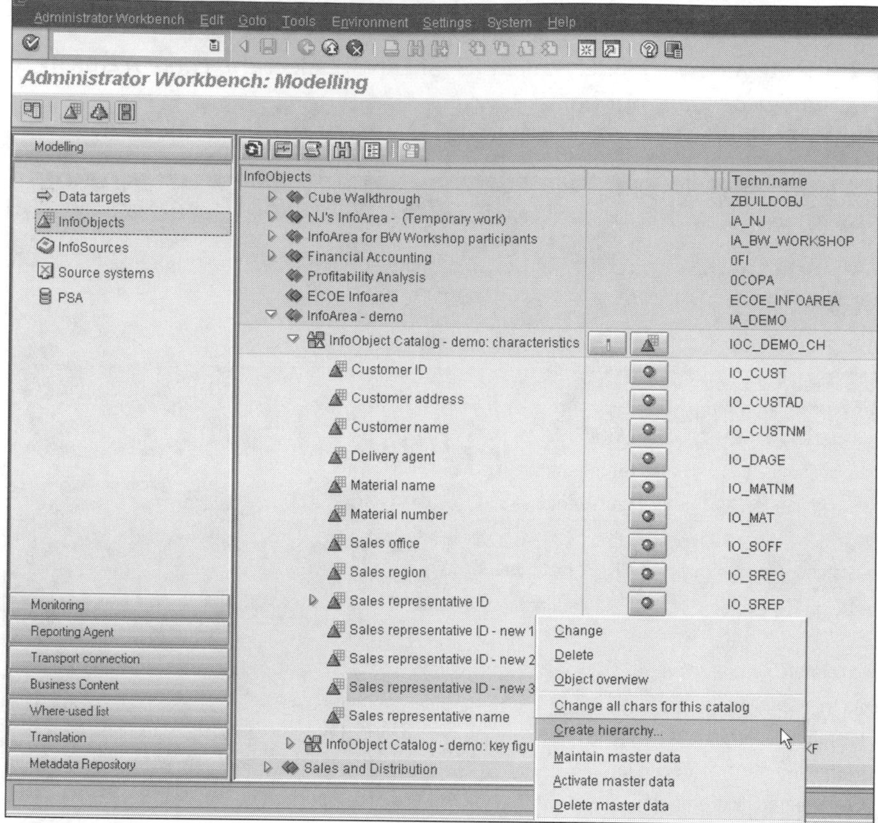

SCREEN 7.30

Step 2 Select *Create hierarchy* from the InfoObject menu.

Step 3 Specify the valid dates, and then click ✔ to continue.

Create Hierarchy

InfoObject: Sales representative
Hierarchy name: IO_SREPN3_H9999

Description
Short description: IO_SREPN3 hier 9999
Medium description:
Long description:

Validity
Valid from: 01.01.2000
To: 31.12.9999

SCREEN 7.31

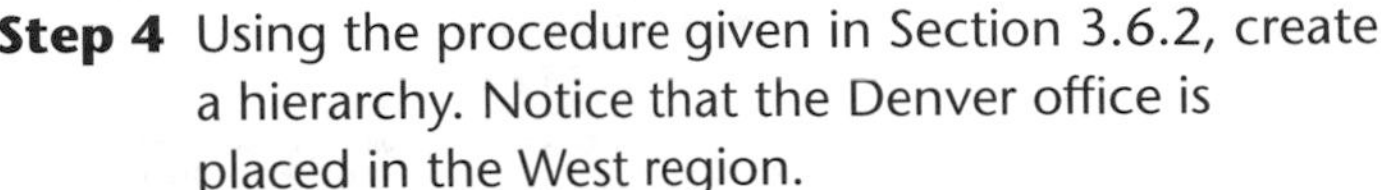

Step 4 Using the procedure given in Section 3.6.2, create a hierarchy. Notice that the Denver office is placed in the West region.

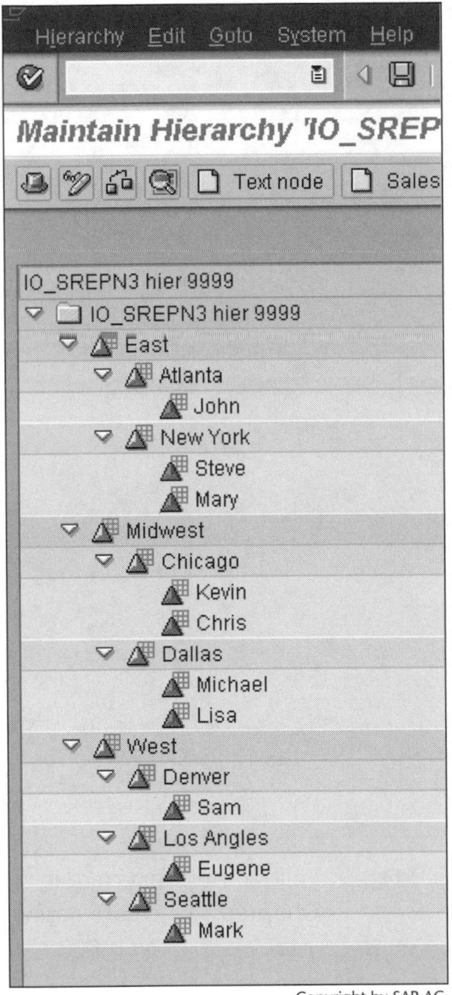

SCREEN 7.32

Step 5 Create another hierarchy, and specify its valid dates as being from *01.01.**1000*** to *31.12.**1999***. Now the Denver office appears in the Midwest region.

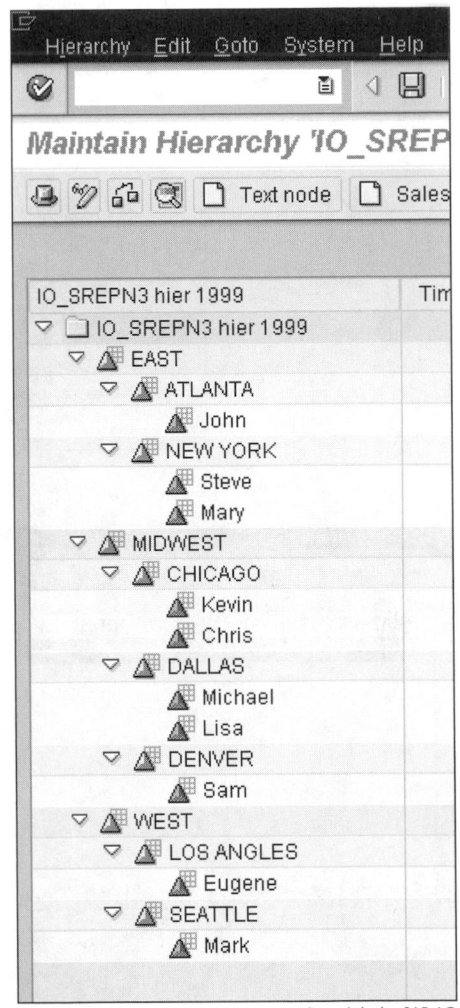

SCREEN 7.33

Step 6 Notice the two hierarchies. Each has an associated valid date.

SCREEN 7.34

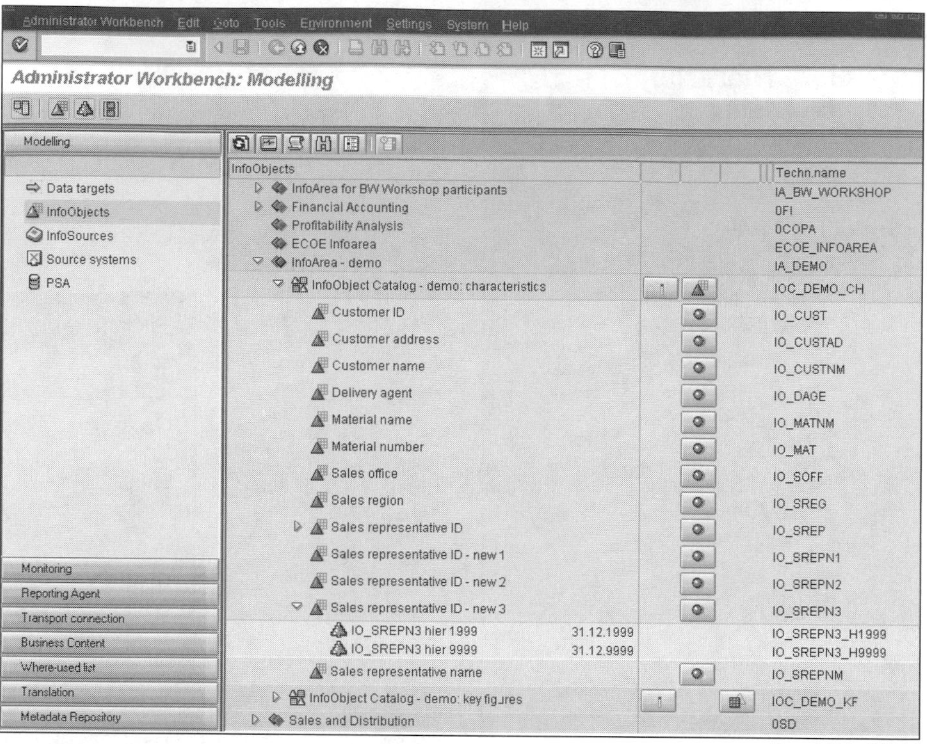

Copyright by SAP AG

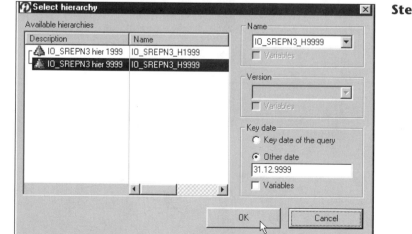

SCREEN 7.35

Copyright by SAP AG

Step 7 Follow the procedure in Chapter 2 to create a new InfoCube, *IC_NEWBC3.*

Follow the procedure in Chapter 5 to create a new query, *IC_NEWBC3_Q01.* When selecting hierarchies, we have two hierarchies, not just one as shown in Screen 5.10.

Select one hierarchy, and click OK. Save and run the query.

Result

The first query result shows that the Denver office is located in the West region (Screen 7.36).

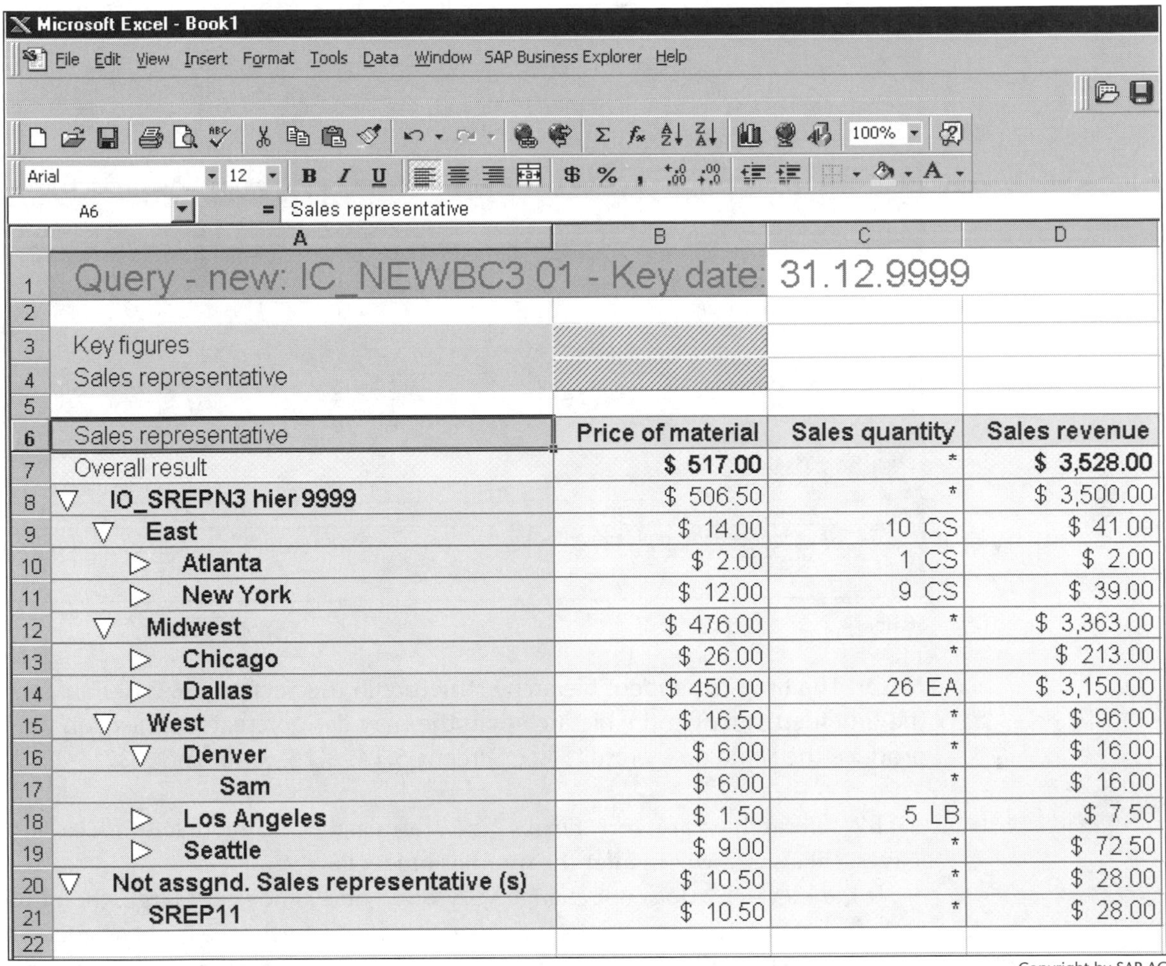

Microsoft Excel - Book1

	A	B	C	D
1	Query - new: IC_NEWBC3 01 - Key date:		31.12.9999	
2				
3	Key figures			
4	Sales representative			
5				
6	Sales representative	Price of material	Sales quantity	Sales revenue
7	Overall result	**$ 517.00**	*	**$ 3,528.00**
8	▽ IO_SREPN3 hier 9999	$ 506.50	*	$ 3,500.00
9	▽ East	$ 14.00	10 CS	$ 41.00
10	▷ Atlanta	$ 2.00	1 CS	$ 2.00
11	▷ New York	$ 12.00	9 CS	$ 39.00
12	▽ Midwest	$ 476.00	*	$ 3,363.00
13	▷ Chicago	$ 26.00	*	$ 213.00
14	▷ Dallas	$ 450.00	26 EA	$ 3,150.00
15	▽ West	$ 16.50	*	$ 96.00
16	▽ Denver	$ 6.00	*	$ 16.00
17	Sam	$ 6.00	*	$ 16.00
18	▷ Los Angeles	$ 1.50	5 LB	$ 7.50
19	▷ Seattle	$ 9.00	*	$ 72.50
20	▽ Not assgnd. Sales representative (s)	$ 10.50	*	$ 28.00
21	SREP11	$ 10.50	*	$ 28.00
22				

SCREEN 7.36

Create another query. This time, select IO_SREPN3_H1999 as the hierarchy (not IO_SREPN3_H9999, as shown in Screen 7.35). The result of this query puts the Denver office in the Midwest region (Screen 7.37).

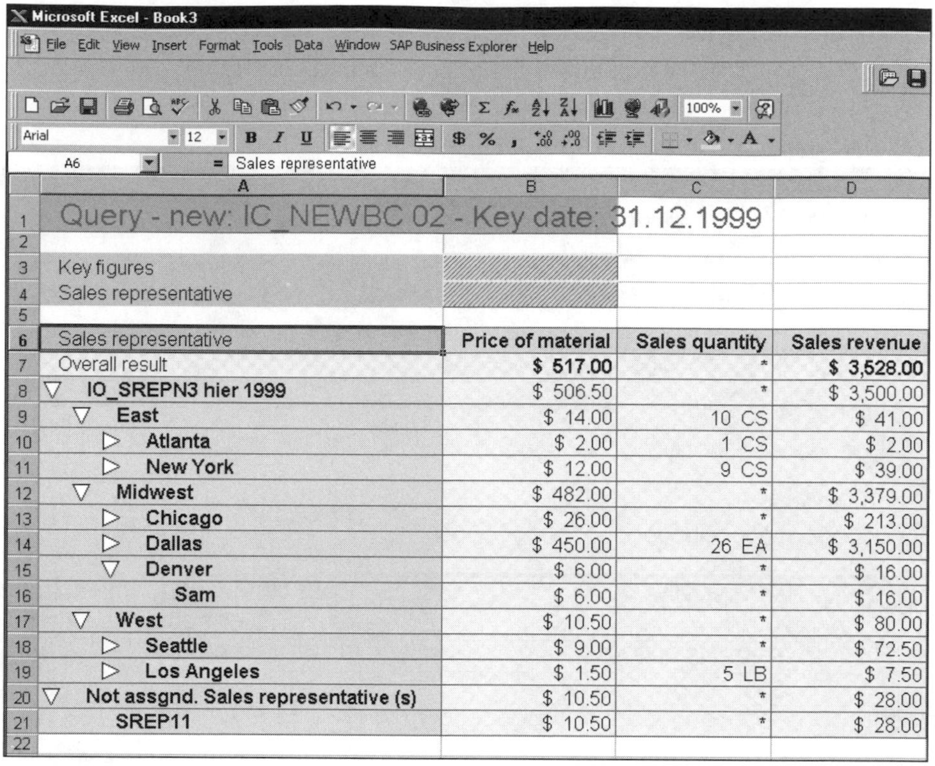

Microsoft Excel - Book3

File Edit View Insert Format Tools Data Window SAP Business Explorer Help

A6 = Sales representative

	A	B	C	D
1	Query - new: IC_NEWBC 02 - Key date: 31.12.1999			
2				
3	Key figures			
4	Sales representative			
5				
6	Sales representative	**Price of material**	**Sales quantity**	**Sales revenue**
7	Overall result	**$ 517.00**	*	**$ 3,528.00**
8	▽ **IO_SREPN3 hier 1999**	$ 506.50	*	$ 3,500.00
9	▽ **East**	$ 14.00	10 CS	$ 41.00
10	▷ **Atlanta**	$ 2.00	1 CS	$ 2.00
11	▷ **New York**	$ 12.00	9 CS	$ 39.00
12	▽ **Midwest**	$ 482.00	*	$ 3,379.00
13	▷ **Chicago**	$ 26.00	*	$ 213.00
14	▷ **Dallas**	$ 450.00	26 EA	$ 3,150.00
15	▽ **Denver**	$ 6.00	*	$ 16.00
16	**Sam**	$ 6.00	*	$ 16.00
17	▽ **West**	$ 10.50	*	$ 80.00
18	▷ **Seattle**	$ 9.00	*	$ 72.50
19	▷ **Los Angeles**	$ 1.50	5 LB	$ 7.50
20	▽ **Not assgnd. Sales representative (s)**	$ 10.50	*	$ 28.00
21	**SREP11**	$ 10.50	*	$ 28.00
22				

SCREEN 7.37

Note: The time-dependent hierarchy structure in the Section 3.6.2 design and the time-dependent entire hierarchies in the new design created in Section 7.4 produce the same query results (see Screens 5.14, 5.15, 7.36, and 7.37).

BW hierarchies are very flexible. We can easily add or delete nodes and leaves. Likewise, we can alter the number of levels.

If the hierarchy does not change very often and is not very large, then this new design is a good one. Note, however, that its performance is not as good as that of the Alternative II InfoCube design. We can create aggregates that compensate for the loss in performance to a certain extent.

7.5 Other InfoCube Design Techniques

Before closing this chapter, let's briefly discuss two other InfoCube design techniques:

- Compound attributes
- Line item dimensions

7.5.1 Compound Attributes

Compounding entities is an idea that BW borrows from R/3 to model coexistent entities. Compound attributes requires overhead, so you should not use them unless absolutely necessary.

Screen 7.38 shows that 0CO_AREA is a compound attribute of 0COSTCENTER as defined in Business Content.

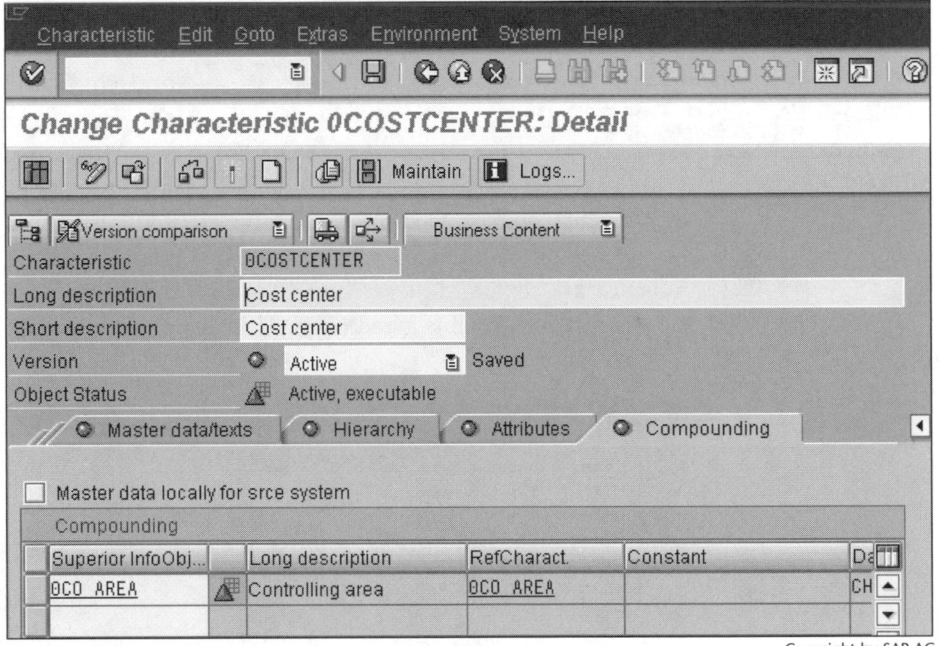

SCREEN 7.38

Sometimes the meaning of master data depends on the source of the data. In these cases, we need to compound the characteristic with the InfoObject 0SOURSYSTEM (Source system ID).

For example, suppose a characteristic IO_HOUSE has an entry called *White House.* The characteristic could mean the home of the U.S. President if it comes from a government source system, or it could mean a house painted white if it comes from a home improvement Web site. To handle cases such as this one, we need to compound IO_HOUSE with 0SOURCESYSTEM to clarify the meaning of the characteristic.

The 0SOURSYSTEM InfoObject is provided with Business Content.

7.5.2 Line Item Dimensions

Define Dimensions

Define | Assign

Dimension	Long description	Line Item
IC_DEMOBC1	Dim: customer	☐
IC_DEMOBC2	Dim: material	☐
IC_DEMOBC3	Dim: sales representative	☐
IC_DEMOBC4	Dim: sales transaction	☑

SCREEN 7.39

If a dimension has only one characteristic, we can make the dimension become a line item dimension. Consider the following example. For the InfoCube described in Chapter 2, we can create another dimension called *Dim: sales transaction*, and check the option *Line Item* as shown in Screen 7.39.

After checking and activating the InfoCube, Screen 7.40 reveals that the fact table has no dimension table created for the line item dimension. The key in the fact table is the SID of the SID table. Thus the fact table links to the master data, text, and hierarchy tables with the SID table, and one middle layer for the dimension table is removed. This design improves system performance.

SCREEN 7.40

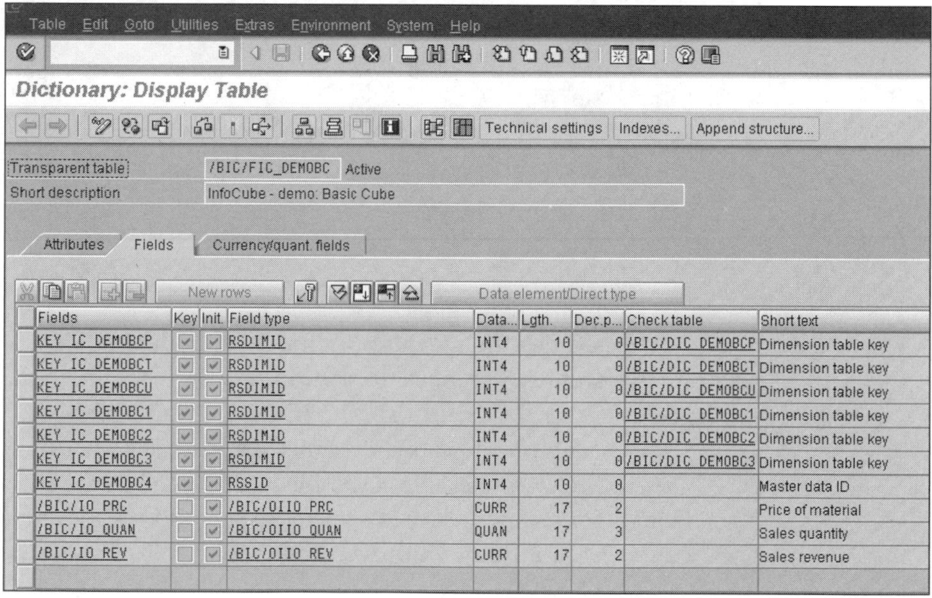

Dictionary: Display Table

Transparent table: /BIC/FIC_DEMOBC Active
Short description: InfoCube - demo: Basic Cube

Fields	Key	Init.	Field type	Data...	Lgth.	Dec.p...	Check table	Short text
KEY_IC_DEMOBCP	☑	☑	RSDIMID	INT4	10	0	/BIC/DIC_DEMOBCP	Dimension table key
KEY_IC_DEMOBCT	☑	☑	RSDIMID	INT4	10	0	/BIC/DIC_DEMOBCT	Dimension table key
KEY_IC_DEMOBCU	☑	☑	RSDIMID	INT4	10	0	/BIC/DIC_DEMOBCU	Dimension table key
KEY_IC_DEMOBC1	☑	☑	RSDIMID	INT4	10	0	/BIC/DIC_DEMOBC1	Dimension table key
KEY_IC_DEMOBC2	☑	☑	RSDIMID	INT4	10	0	/BIC/DIC_DEMOBC2	Dimension table key
KEY_IC_DEMOBC3	☑	☑	RSDIMID	INT4	10	0	/BIC/DIC_DEMOBC3	Dimension table key
KEY_IC_DEMOBC4	☑	☑	RSSID	INT4	10	0		Master data ID
/BIC/IO_PRC	☐	☑	/BIC/OIIO_PRC	CURR	17	2		Price of material
/BIC/IO_QUAN	☐	☑	/BIC/OIIO_QUAN	QUAN	17	3		Sales quantity
/BIC/IO_REV	☐	☑	/BIC/OIIO_REV	CURR	17	2		Sales revenue

Note The line item dimension derives its name from the need for detailed information reporting at the line item level. In Chapter 9, Operational Data Store (ODS), we will discuss another technique that allows us to build a multilayer structure for different levels of detail information reporting.

The level of detail found in a data warehouse is called its **granularity**. It is determined by business requirements and technology capabilities.

7.6 Summary

In this chapter, we discussed the BW star schema and analyzed three InfoCube design alternatives for the same business scenario described in Chapter 1. We also briefly discussed two other InfoCube design techniques: compound attributes and line item dimensions.

Key Terms

Term	Description
SID	Surrogate-ID (SID) translates a potentially long key for an InfoObject into a short four-bytes integer, which saves I/O and memory during OLAP.
Display attribute	A display attribute provides supplemental information to a characteristic. In our example, IO_CUSTNM (Customer name) and IO_CUSTAD (Customer address) are display attributes of IO_CUST (Customer ID).
Navigational attribute	A navigational attribute indicates a characteristic-to-characteristic relationship between two characteristics. It provides additional information about a characteristic and supports navigation from characteristic to characteristic during a query. In our example, IO_SOFF (Sales office) and IO_SREG (Sales region) are navigational attributes to IO_SREPN1 (Sales representative ID).
Compound attribute	A compound attribute differentiates a characteristic so as to make it uniquely identifiable. For example, if the same characteristic data from different source systems means different things, then we can add the compound

attribute 0SOURSYSTEM (Source system ID) to the characteristic. 0SOURSYSTEM is provided with the Business Content.

Time-dependent hierarchy structure — The time-dependent hierarchy structures consist of nodes or leaves that are time-dependent. The hierarchy itself is not time-dependent. In our Chapter 3 example, the Denver office is listed twice in the hierarchy: Before January 1, 2000, it belongs to the Midwest region; on and after January 1, 2000, it belongs to the West region.

Time-dependent entire hierarchy — A time-dependent entire hierarchy is a time-dependent hierarchy whose nodes and leaves are not time-dependent. The Chapter 7 example includes two hierarchies. One hierarchy is for the period January 1, 1000, to December 31, 1999; during this period, the Denver office belongs to the Midwest region. The other hierarchy is for the period January 1, 1999, to December 31, 9999; during this period, the Denver office belongs to the West region.

Line item dimension — A line item dimension in a fact table does not have the dimension table shown in the simple star schema. Rather, it connects directly with the SID table of its sole characteristic.

Granularity — Granularity describes the level of detail in a data warehouse. It is determined by business requirements and technology capabilities.

Next . . .

We will discuss aggregates and multi-cubes. Aggregates help improve query performance. Multi-cubes support cross-subject analysis.

Chapter 8

Aggregates and Multi-Cubes

Most users need to access only a subset of information in an InfoCube. In Section 6.2, for example, the East region users were not allowed to access other regions' data. In that case, we could create a new InfoCube, which contained only the East region sales data, a subset of the original InfoCube. Because the new InfoCube is smaller, the required disk I/O volume during query execution will be smaller, too, and the East region users would therefore see improved query performance.

SAP implements this idea in BW and calls the new InfoCube an **aggregate**. An InfoCube can have multiple aggregates, and the aggregates are transparent to users. It means that we create queries upon InfoCubes, not aggregates. For a query run or a navigation step, the BW OLAP processor is responsible for selecting an appropriate aggregate. If no appropriate aggregate exists, the BW OLAP processor will retrieve data from the original InfoCube.

Different from our need for aggregates, which are subsets of InfoCubes, we also often need to combine data from multiple InfoCubes to do cross-subject analysis, such as from sales to delivery. But from Chapter 5, we know that queries can be created on only one InfoCube. To overcome this limit using the techniques we have learned so far, we must build a larger InfoCube that contains both sales and delivery data.

Suppose we have only one delivery agent, DAGE02 (characteristic IO_DAGE), that can deliver only one unit per day. In that case, the combined sales (from Table 3.3) and delivery data should be as shown in Table 8.1.

TABLE 8.1 SALES (FROM TABLE 3.3) AND DELIVERY DATA

IO_CUST	IO_SREP	IO_MAT	IO_PRC	0UNIT	IO_QUAN	IO_REV	0CALDAY (Sales)	IO_DAGE	0UNIT	IO_DQUAN	0CALDAY (Delivery)
CUST001	SREP01	MAT001	2	CS	1		19980304	DAGE02	X	1	XX
CUST002	SREP02	MAT002	2	CS	2		19990526	DAGE02	X	1	XX
1 record here, with the same data as the above record except the delivery date.											
CUST002	SREP02	MAT003	5	CS	3		19990730	DAGE02	X	1	XX
2 records here, with the same data as the above record except the delivery dates.											
CUST003	SREP03	MAT003	5	CS	4		20000101	DAGE02	X	1	XX
3 records here, with the same data as the above record except the delivery dates.											
CUST004	SREP04	MAT004	50	EA	5		19991023	DAGE02	X	1	XX
4 records here, with the same data as the above record except the delivery dates.											
CUST004	SREP04	MAT005	100	EA	6		19980904	DAGE02	X	1	XX
5 records here, with the same data as the above record except the delivery dates.											
CUST004	SREP04	MAT005	100	EA	7		19980529	DAGE02	X	1	XX
6 records here, with the same data as the above record except the delivery dates.											
CUST005	SREP05	MAT006	200	EA	8		19991108	DAGE02	X	1	XX
7 records here, with the same data as the above record except the delivery dates.											
CUST006	SREP06	MAT007	20	EA	9		20000408	DAGE02	X	1	XX
8 records here, with the same data as the above record except the delivery dates.											
CUST007	SREP07	MAT008	3	DZ	10		20000901	DAGE02	X	1	XX
9 records here, with the same data as the above record except the delivery dates.											
CUST007	SREP07	MAT008	3	DZ	1		19990424	DAGE02	X	1	XX
CUST008	SREP08	MAT008	3	DZ	2		19980328	DAGE02	X	1	XX
1 record here, with the same data as the above record except the delivery date.											

IO_CUST	IO_SREP	IO_MAT	IO_PRC	0UNIT	IO_QUAN	IO_REV	0CALDAY (Sales)	IO_DAGE	0UNIT	IO_DQUAN	0CALDAY (Delivery)
CUST008	SREP08	MAT009	2	CS	3		19980203	DAGE02	X	1	XX
2 records here, with the same data as the above record except the delivery dates.											
CUST008	SREP08	MAT010	1	LB	4		19991104	DAGE02	X	1	XX
3 records here, with the same data as the above record except the delivery dates.											
CUST009	SREP09	MAT011	1.5	LB	5		20000407	DAGE02	X	1	XX
4 records here, with the same data as the above record except the delivery dates.											
CUST010	SREP10	MAT011	1.5	LB	6		20000701	DAGE02	X	1	XX
5 records here, with the same data as the above record except the delivery dates.											
CUST010	SREP10	MAT011	1.5	LB	7		19990924	DAGE02	X	1	XX
6 records here, with the same data as the above record except the delivery dates.											
CUST010	SREP10	MAT012	2	LB	8		19991224	DAGE02	X	1	XX
7 records here, with the same data as the above record except the delivery dates.											
CUST010	SREP10	MAT013	3	CS	9		20000308	DAGE02	X	1	XX
8 records here, with the same data as the above record except the delivery dates.											
CUST011	SREP10	MAT014	1	LB	10		19980627	DAGE02	X	1	XX
9 records here, with the same data as the above record except the delivery dates.											
CUST012	SREP11	MAT014	2	LB	1		19991209	DAGE02	X	1	XX
CUST012	SREP11	MAT015	3	CS	2		19980221	DAGE02	X	1	XX
1 record here, with the same data as the above record except the delivery date.											
CUST012	SREP11	MAT015	2	CS	3		20000705	DAGE02	X	1	XX
2 records here, with the same data as the above record except the delivery dates.											
CUST012	SREP11	MAT015	3.5	CS	4		20001225	DAGE02	X	1	XX
3 records here, with the same data as the above record except the delivery dates.											

This approach has a drawback: The InfoCube containing the sales and delivery data will be very large and the query performance will consequently be very slow. Also, imagine what would happen if we needed to do cross-subject analysis from purchase, to inventory, to sales, to delivery, and to billing. The InfoCube would become so large that we could not manage it, and query performance would degrade to such a level that we could not receive a report in an acceptable response time, even using aggregates.

To resolve this problem, BW offers a technique called the **multi-cube**. The InfoCubes we discussed previously are called **basic cubes**. The multi-cube contains no data, but rather simply links the basic cubes together. We can create queries on a multi-cube just as we did on a basic cube.

With the multi-cube technique, one basic cube is recommended to cover one subject area only. One benefit of this approach is that we save disk space. It should be easy for us to estimate the saved disk space after taking out the repeated sales data from Table 8.1, which is the data in 96 (1 + 2 + 3 + 4 + 5 + 6 + 7 + 8 + 9 + 1 + 2 + 3 + 4 + 5 + 6 + 7 + 8 + 9 + 1 + 2 + 3) rows of these 6 columns:

- IO_SREP
- IO_PRC
- 0UNIT
- IO_QUAN
- IO_REV
- 0CALDAY (Sales)

In this chapter, we will demonstrate how to create and use aggregates and multi-cubes.

8.1 Aggregates

In this section, we first show how to create an aggregate for the InfoCube design described in Section 7.3, "InfoCube Design Alternative II—Dimension Characteristics."

Work Instructions

Step 1 Right-click the InfoCube *IC_NEWBC2,* and then select *Maintain aggregates. . . .*

SCREEN 8.1

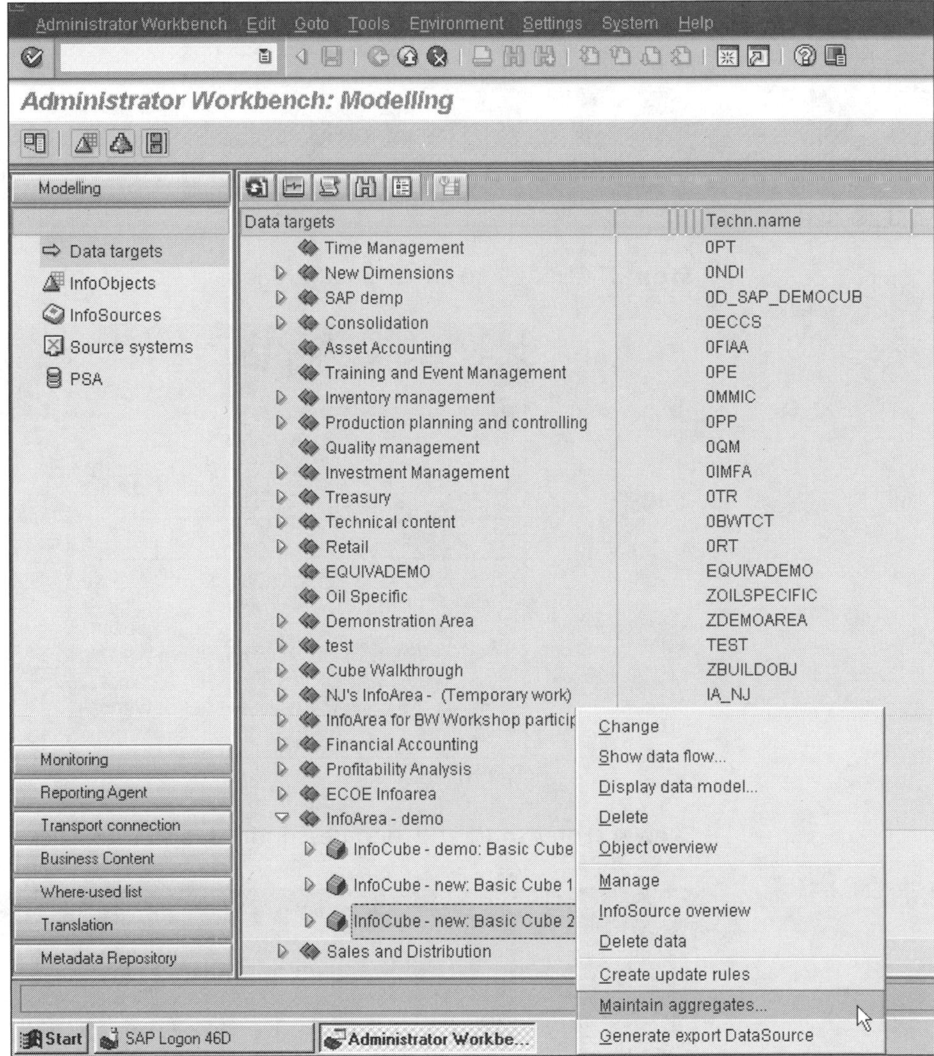
Administrator Workbench Edit Goto Tools Environment Settings System Help
Administrator Workbench: Modelling
Modelling
Data targets
InfoObjects
InfoSources
Source systems
PSA
Monitoring
Reporting Agent
Transport connection
Business Content
Where-used list
Translation
Metadata Repository
Data targets
Techn.name
Time Management 0PT
New Dimensions 0NDI
SAP demp 0D_SAP_DEMOCUB
Consolidation 0ECCS
Asset Accounting 0FIAA
Training and Event Management 0PE
Inventory management 0MMIC
Production planning and controlling 0PP
Quality management 0QM
Investment Management 0IMFA
Treasury 0TR
Technical content 0BWTCT
Retail 0RT
EQUIVADEMO EQUIVADEMO
Oil Specific ZOILSPECIFIC
Demonstration Area ZDEMOAREA
test TEST
Cube Walkthrough ZBUILDOBJ
NJ's InfoArea - (Temporary work) IA_NJ
InfoArea for BW Workshop particip
Financial Accounting
Profitability Analysis
ECOE Infoarea
InfoArea - demo
InfoCube - demo: Basic Cube
InfoCube - new: Basic Cube 1
InfoCube - new: Basic Cube 2
Sales and Distribution
Change
Show data flow...
Display data model...
Delete
Object overview
Manage
InfoSource overview
Delete data
Create update rules
Maintain aggregates...
Generate export DataSource
Start
SAP Logon 46D
Administrator Workbe...

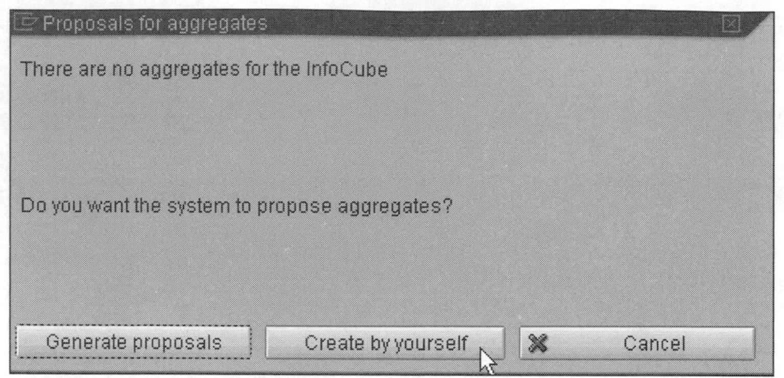

SCREEN 8.2

Step 2 Click [Create by yourself] as we know the aggregate we need to create.

Step 3 Click [new] to create an aggregate.

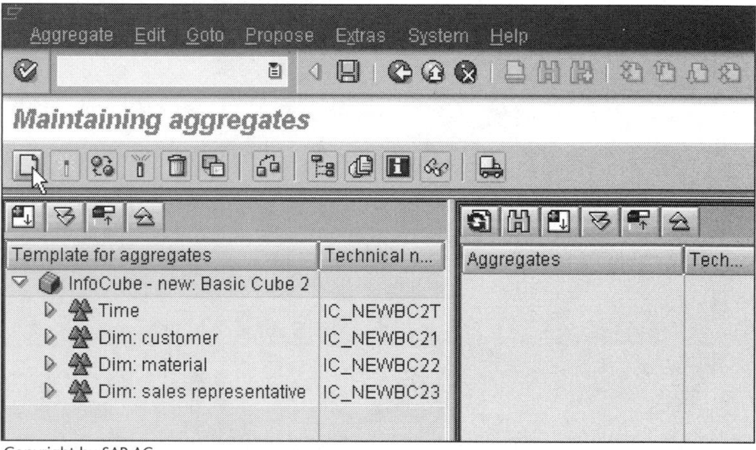

SCREEN 8.3

Step 4 Enter short and long descriptions, and then click [✔] to continue.

SCREEN 8.4

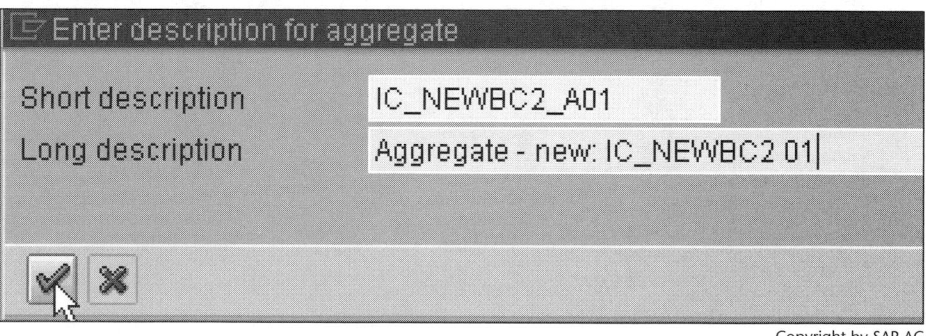

Step 5 Select *IO_SOFF*, *IO_SREG*, and *IO_SREPN2* from the left panel, and then drag and drop each into the right panel.

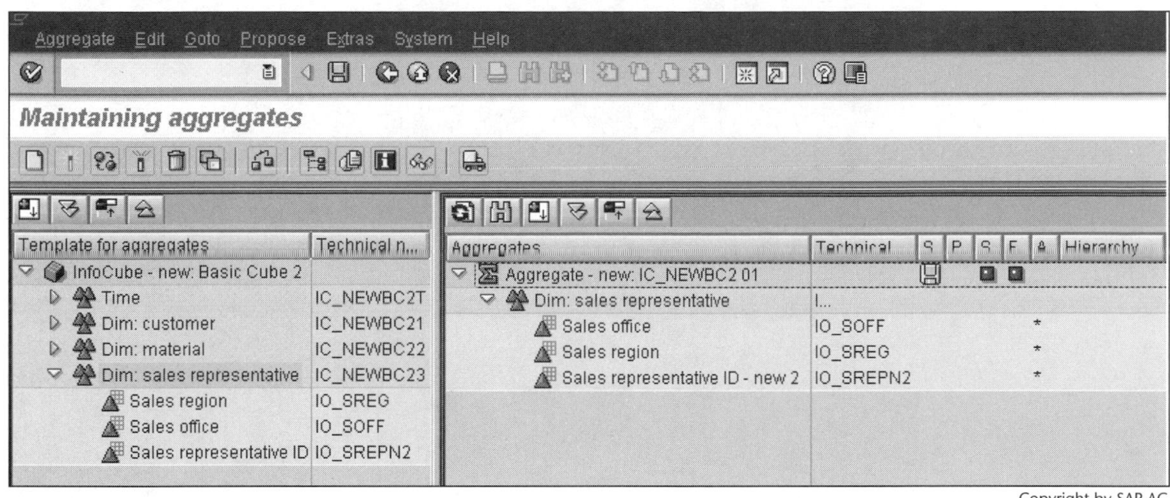

SCREEN 8.5

Step 6 Right-click *Sales region,* and then select *Fixed value.*

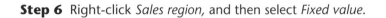

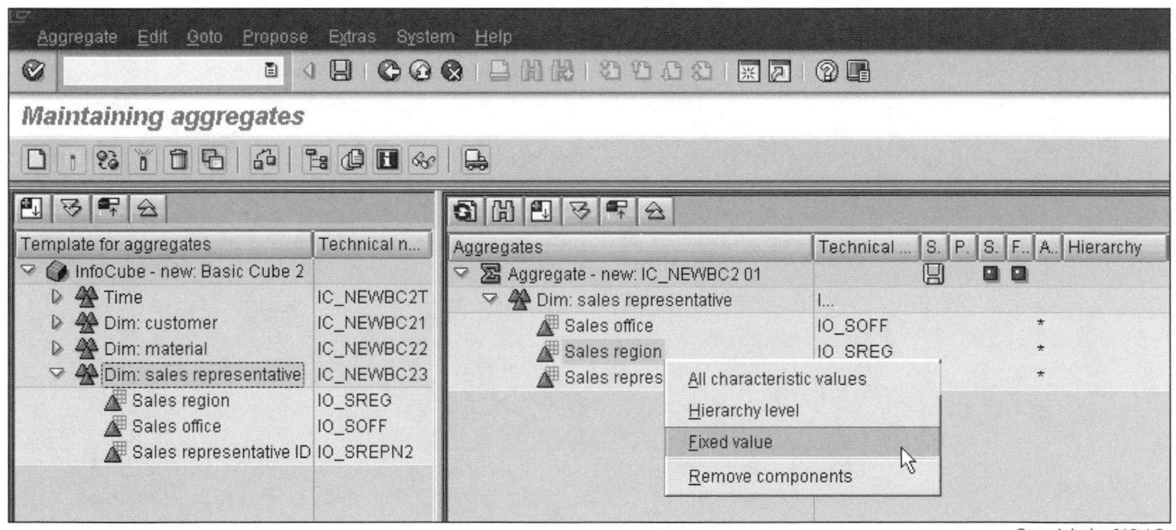

SCREEN 8.6

Step 7 Select *EAST*, and then click to continue.

SCREEN 8.7

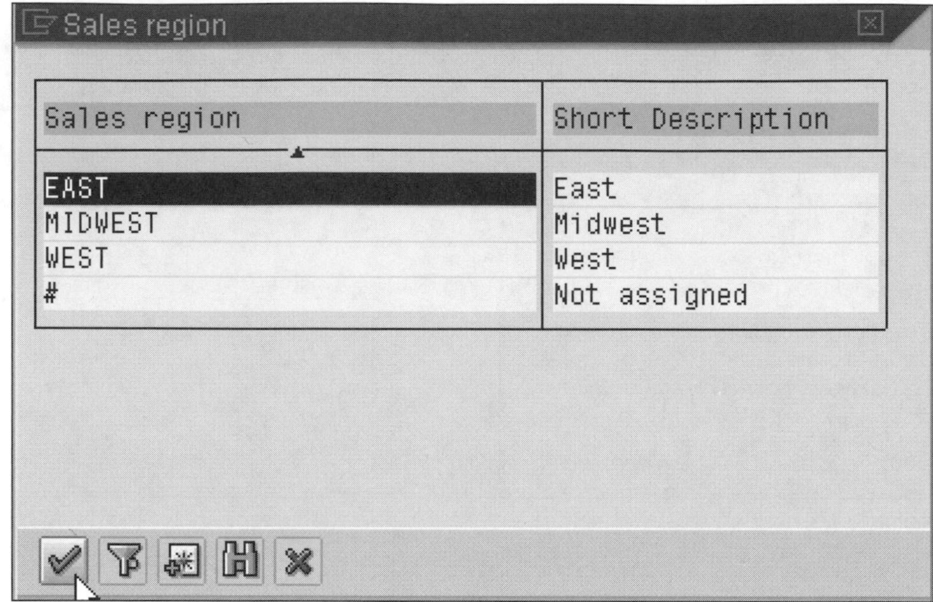

Step 8 Select the aggregate, and then click to create the aggregate and fill the aggregate with data.

SCREEN 8.8

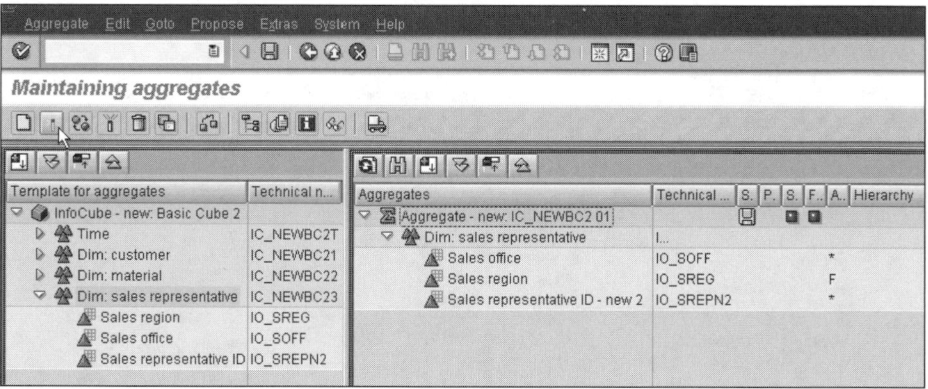

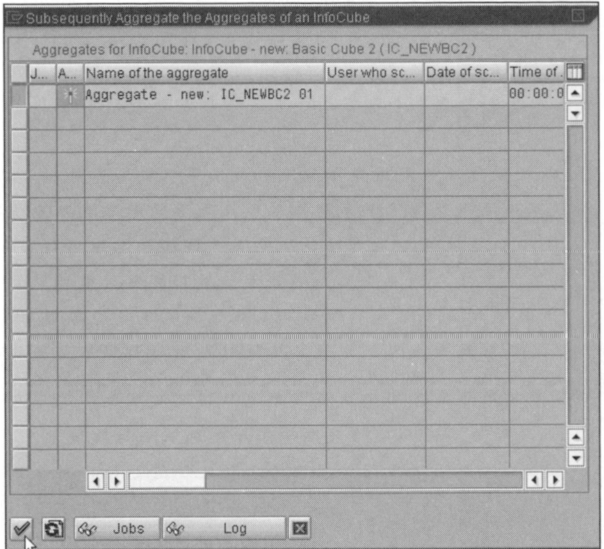

SCREEN 8.9

Step 9 To load the aggregate with aggregated data, click ✔ to launch a background job.

Step 10 To start the background job immediately, click Now.

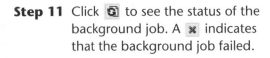

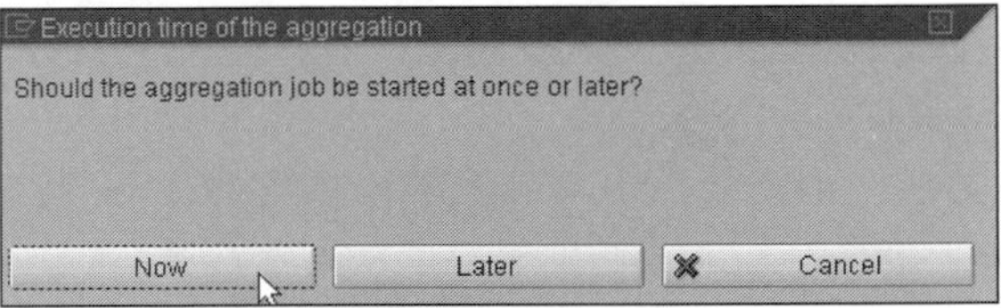

SCREEN 8.10

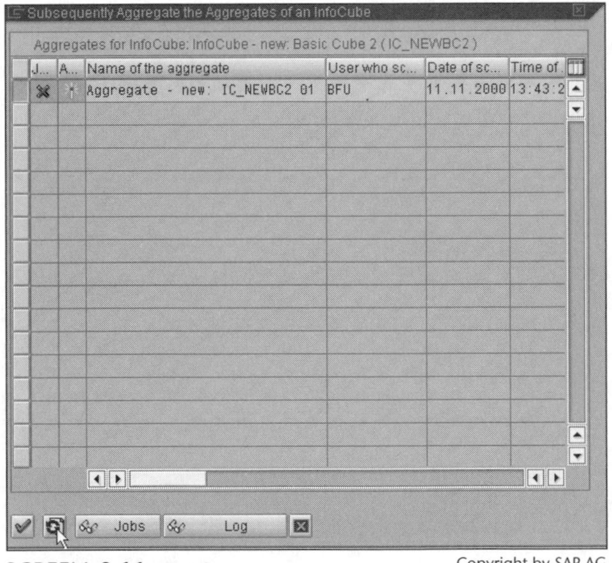

SCREEN 8.11

Step 11 Click the refresh icon to see the status of the background job. A ✖ indicates that the background job failed.

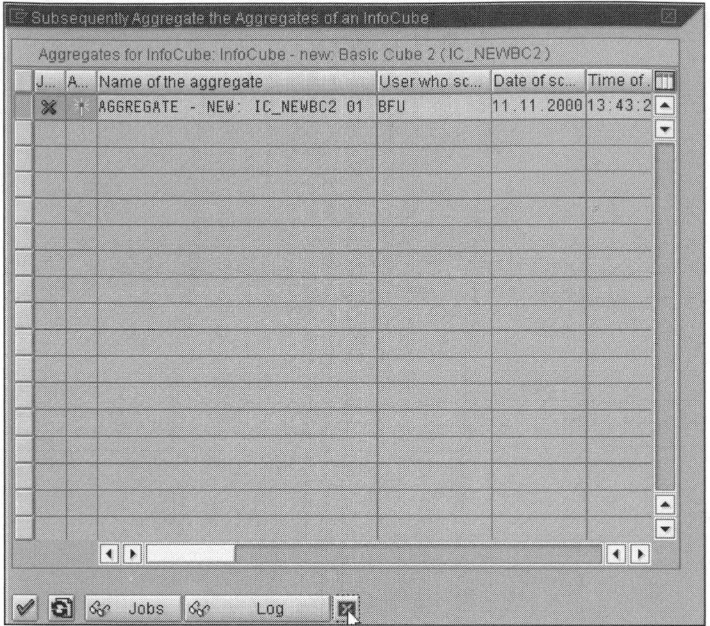

SCREEN 8.12

Step 12 Close the window, and return to the *Maintaining Aggregates* screen.

Step 13 BW opens a message text window in the lower-right corner, displaying the status of creating the aggregate and filling the aggregate with data.

Here we see the error message *Dimension IC_NEWBC2U: Error when writing the initial record to the DB table.*

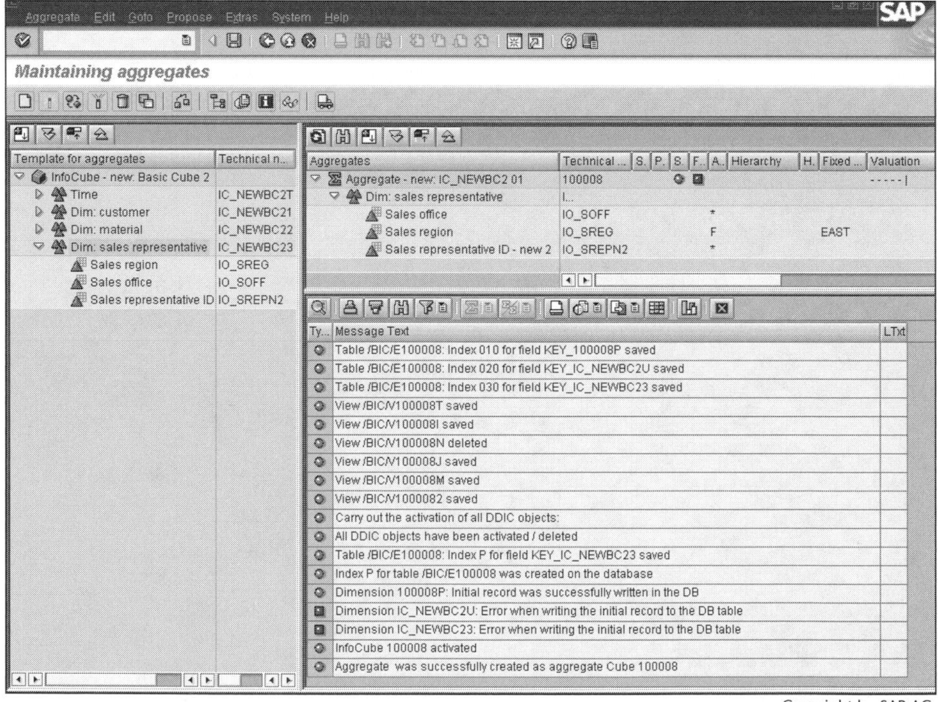

SCREEN 8.13

IC_NEWBC2U is the dimension for the units of measure. It is reasonable to believe that the error was caused by an aggregation of different units of measure. Let's prove our hypothesis.

Step 14 Return to the InfoCube, and then select *Delete data* from the menu.

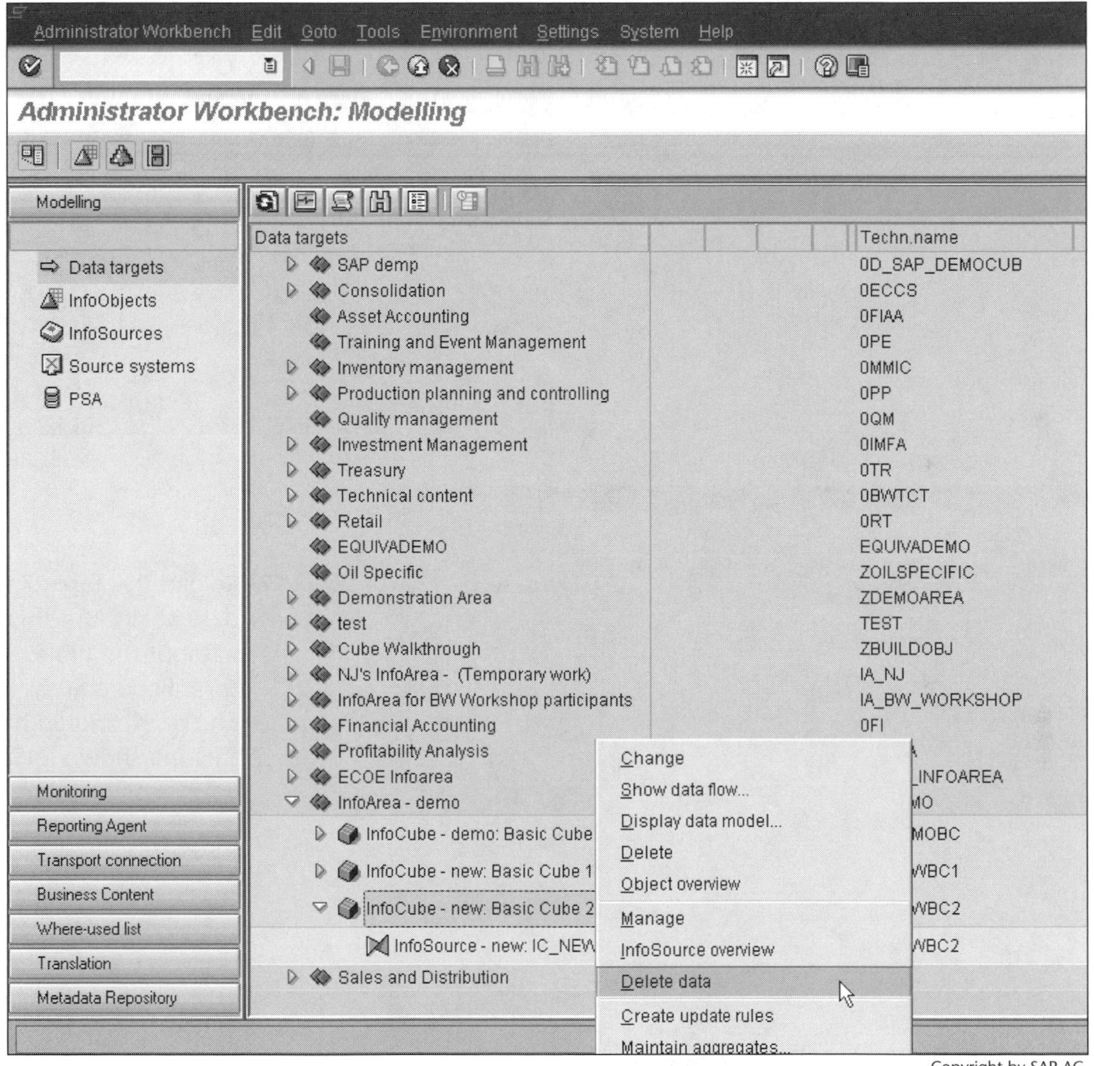

SCREEN 8.14

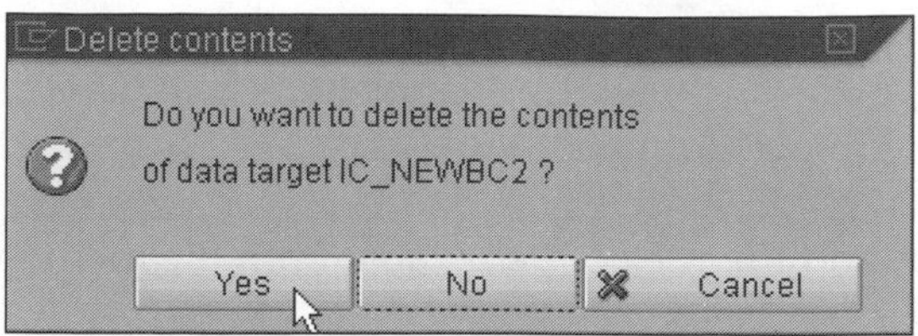

SCREEN 8.15

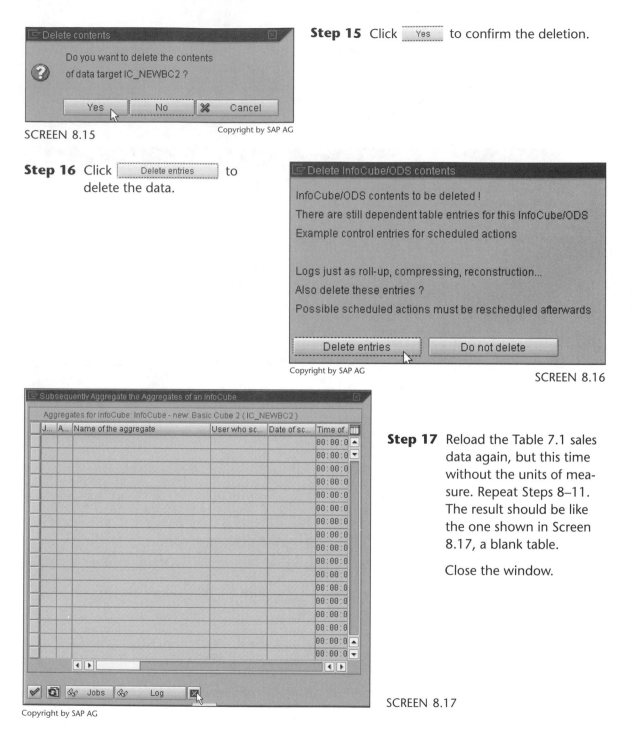

Step 15 Click [Yes] to confirm the deletion.

Step 16 Click [Delete entries] to delete the data.

Delete InfoCube/ODS contents

InfoCube/ODS contents to be deleted !

There are still dependent table entries for this InfoCube/ODS

Example control entries for scheduled actions

Logs just as roll-up, compressing, reconstruction...

Also delete these entries ?

Possible scheduled actions must be rescheduled afterwards

[Delete entries] [Do not delete]

SCREEN 8.16

Subsequently Aggregate the Aggregates of an InfoCube

Aggregates for InfoCube: InfoCube - new: Basic Cube 2 (IC_NEWBC2)

J...	A...	Name of the aggregate	User who sc...	Date of sc...	Time of
					00:00:0
					00:00:0
					00:00:0
					00:00:0
					00:00:0
					00:00:0
					00:00:0
					00:00:0
					00:00:0
					00:00:0
					00:00:0
					00:00:0
					00:00:0
					00:00:0
					00:00:0
					00:00:0
					00:00:0

Jobs Log

Step 17 Reload the Table 7.1 sales data again, but this time without the units of measure. Repeat Steps 8–11. The result should be like the one shown in Screen 8.17, a blank table.

Close the window.

SCREEN 8.17

Result

The aggregate has been created and filled with data.

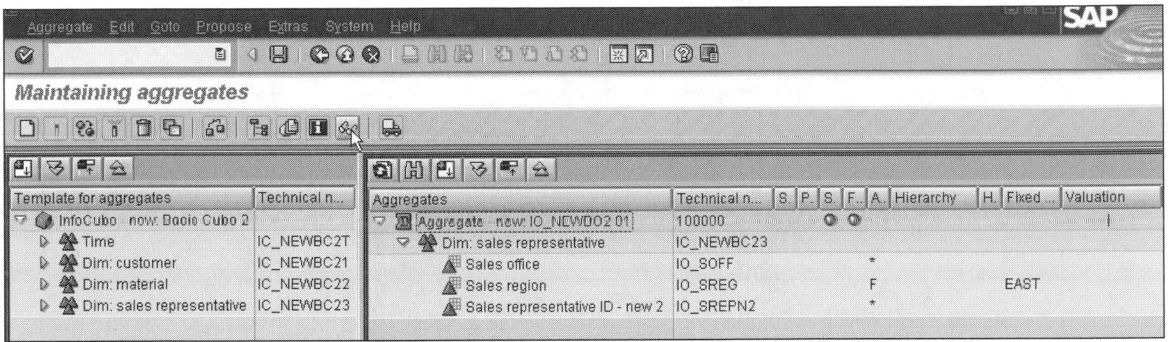

Copyright by SAP AG

SCREEN 8.18

As shown in the right panel of Screen 8.18, BW generated a number 100008 (next to the aggregate long description *Aggregate – new: IC_NEWBC2 01*) as the technical name of the aggregate. To display the aggregate contents, select the long description and click .

Click to display the aggregate contents. Screen 8.20 shows the result.

The result in Screen 8.20 is an aggregate of the East region sales data at the sales representative level, as specified by the aggregate definition in Screen 8.18. Tables 8.2 and 8.3 show how this result is calculated.

The number in the 0FACTCOUNT column of Screen 8.20 indicates how many fact table records are aggregated to generate a record of the aggregate.

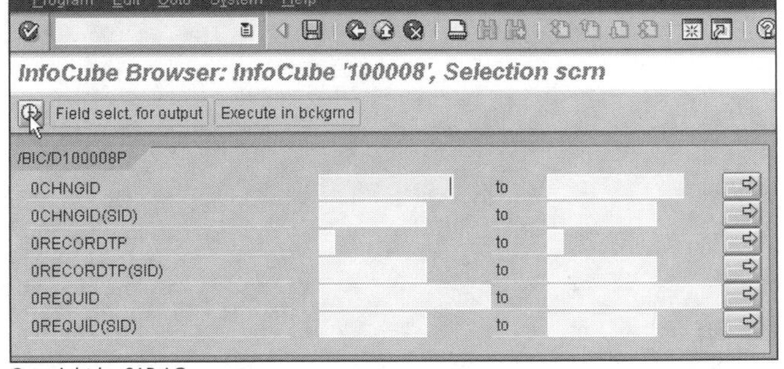

Copyright by SAP AG

SCREEN 8.19

In Screen 8.18, the *F* in the *Aggregation level* column for the *Sales region* characteristic indicates that the aggregate should be filled with the data of a specified region—in this case, *EAST*, as shown in the *Fixed value* column.

Create a query on IC_NEWBC2. This query works much like the one generated in Section 5.3 with the V_SREG variable. After running the query, selecting *East* when asked to enter a value for V_SREG, and then refreshing Screen 8.18, we

List Edit Goto Views Settings System Help

InfoCube Browser: InfoCube "100008",

0UNIT	0FACTCOUNT	IO_PRC	IO_QUAN	IO_REV
	1	2.00	1.000	2.00
	1	5.00	4.000	20.00
	2	7.00	5.000	19.00

Copyright by SAP AG

SCREEN 8.20

TABLE 8.2 AN EXCERPT OF THE EAST REGION SALES DATA FROM TABLE 7.1

IO_CUST	IO_SREG	IO_SOFF	IO_SREPN2	IO_MAT	IO_PRC	0UNIT	IO_QUAN	IO_REV	0CALDAY
CUST001	EAST	ATLANTA	SREP01	MAT001	2	CS	1	2	19980304
CUST002	EAST	NEW YORK	SREP02	MAT002	2	CS	2	4	19990526
CUST002	EAST	NEW YORK	SREP02	MAT003	5	CS	3	15	19990730
CUST003	EAST	NEW YORK	SREP03	MAT003	5	CS	4	20	20000101

TABLE 8.3 AN AGGREGATE OF THE EAST REGION SALES DATA AT THE SALES REPRESENTATIVE LEVEL

IO_CUST	IO_SREG	IO_SOFF	IO_SREPN2	IO_MAT	IO_PRC	0UNIT	IO_QUAN	IO_REV	0CALDAY
			SREP01		2		1	2	
			SREP02		7		5	19	
			SREP03		5		4	20	

see that the aggregate's *Usage* value increased by 1, and a time stamp was entered under *Last used* (Screen 8.21). This result means that the query used this aggregate, which is what we want.

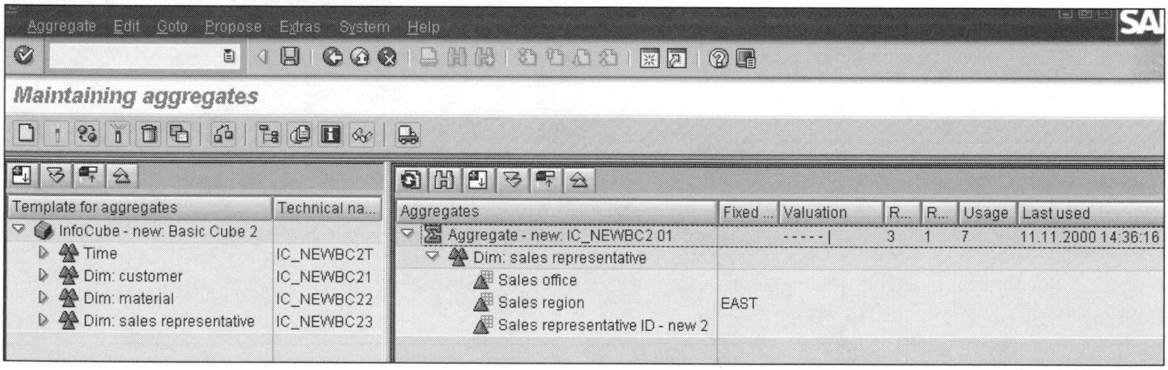

SCREEN 8.21

To find appropriate aggregates, you use the menu items shown under the *Propose* pull-down menu (Screen 8.22).

Note: After we run transaction *SE11* to display the */BIC/F100008* table definition, we see that the aggregate is a subset of the InfoCube (Screen 8.23). It has the same structure as an InfoCube, and it references the same dimension table.

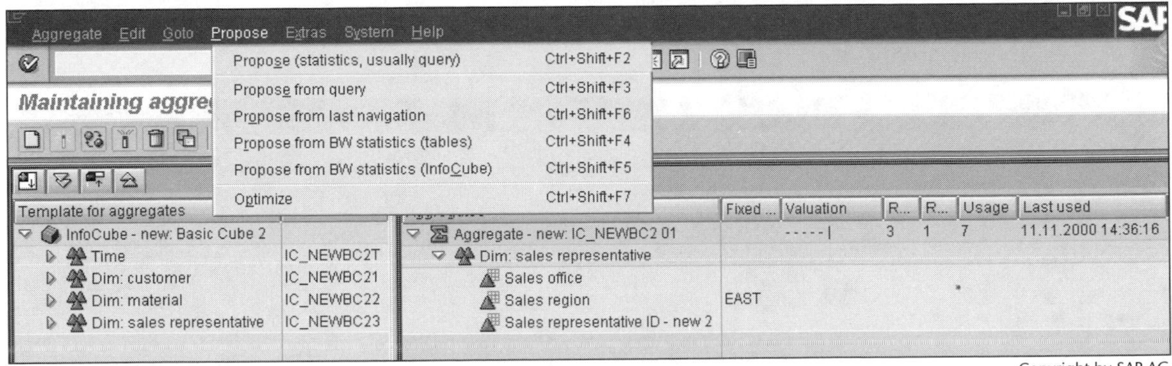

Copyright by SAP AG

SCREEN 8.22

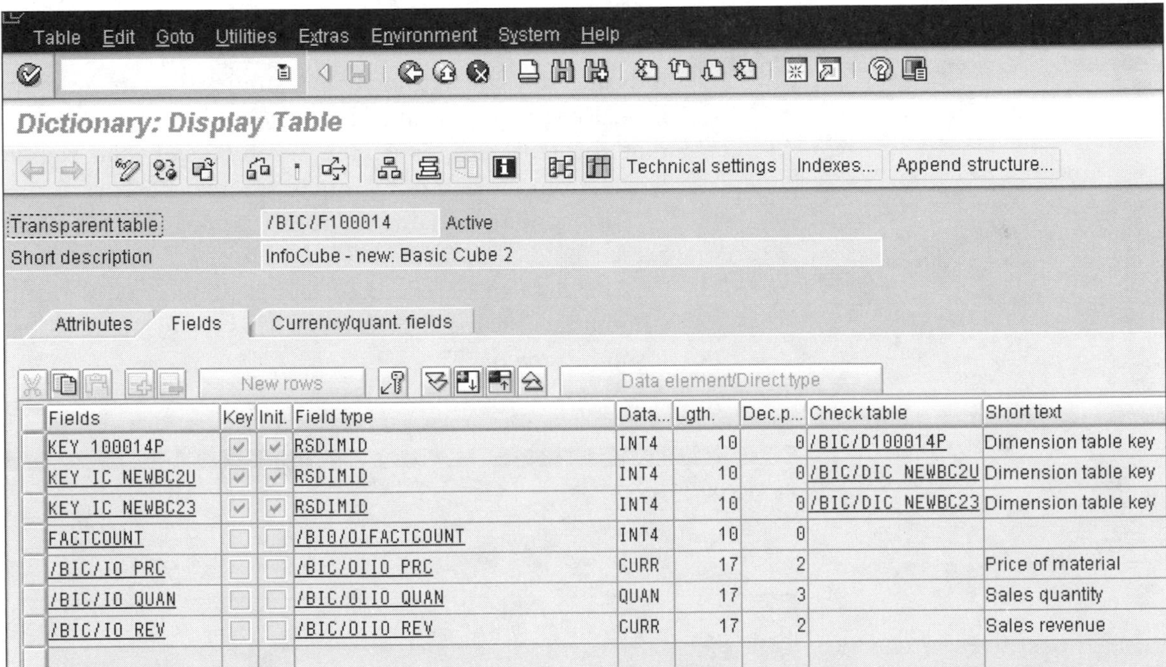

Copyright by SAP AG

SCREEN 8.23

This screen was captured after the aggregate was deleted and re-created several times. For each new aggregate, BW increased the number given to the aggregate's technical name by 1. Therefore, */BIC/F100014*, instead of */BIC/F100008*, appears in the *Transparent table* field.

In the same way, we can create an aggregate for the InfoCube created in Section 7.4.

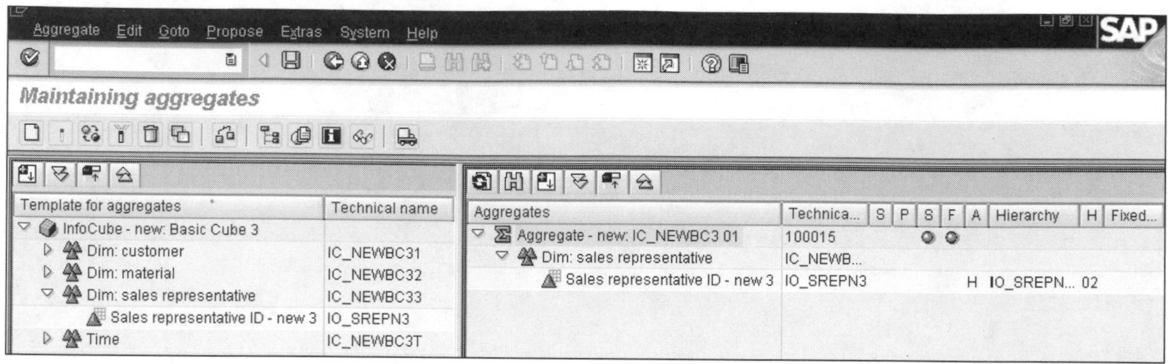

List Edit Goto Views Settings System Help

InfoCube Browser: InfoCube "100015"

0UNIT	0FACTCOUNT	IO_PRC	IO_QUAN	IO_REV
	4	14,00	10,000	41,00
	9	16,50	54,000	96,00
	4	10,50	10,000	28,00
	7	476,00	46,000	3.363,00

SCREEN 8.25

In Screen 8.24, the *H* in the *Aggregation level* column indicates that the aggregate is a summary at a hierarchy level. The value *02* in the *Hierarchy level* column indicates that the summary is at the second level—the region level—from the hierarchy root (see Screen 7.32 or 7.33).

The contents of this aggregate appear as shown in Screen 8.25.

The data in Screen 8.26 represent the query result summarized at the region level. This result matches the result in Screen 8.25.

Microsoft Excel - Book1

File Edit View Insert Format Tools Data Window SAP Business Explorer Help

A6 = Sales representative

Query - new: IC_NEWBC3 01 - Key date: 31.12.9999

Key figures
Sales representative

Sales representative	Price of material	Sales quantity	Sales revenue
Overall result	**$ 517.00**	**120.000**	**$ 3,528.00**
▽ **IO_SREPN3 hier 9999**	$ 506.50	110.000	$ 3,500.00
▷ **EAST**	$ 14.00	10.000	$ 41.00
▷ **MIDWEST**	$ 476.00	46.000	$ 3,363.00
▷ **WEST**	$ 16.50	54.000	$ 96.00
▷ **Not Assigned Sales representative (s)**	$ 10.50	10.000	$ 28.00

SCREEN 8.26

Note An aggregate can be created only for key figures for the SUM, MIN, and MAX operations, not the AVG operation.

Aggregates require additional disk space and system maintenance.

8.2 Multi-Cubes

Aggregates reduce data retrieval volume by creating small, virtual InfoCubes from the original InfoCube. A multi-cube seems to work in the opposite manner, by combining multiple InfoCubes to build a larger InfoCube. The larger InfoCube contains no data, however.

A good multi-cube example is BW Statistics, which will be discussed in Section 13.1.

The following steps show how to create a multi-cube.

Work Instructions

Step 1 Suppose we have another InfoCube for delivery, and its data model is as shown in Screen 8.27.

We would like to build a new InfoCube that brings the previous sales InfoCube and the new delivery InfoCube together to give a bigger picture of business, from sales to delivery.

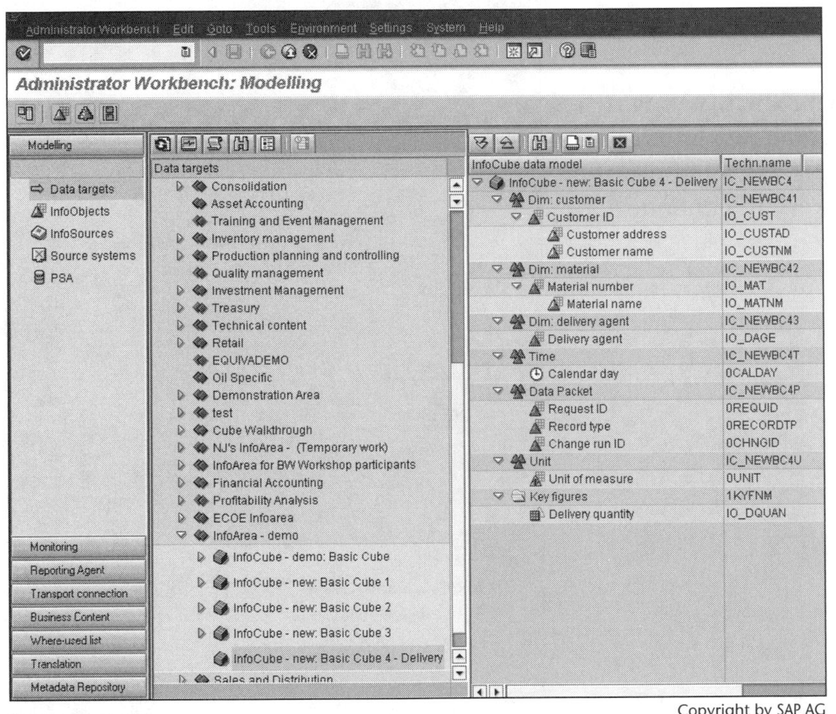

SCREEN 8.27

SCREEN 8.28

Step 2 Follow the procedure in Section 2.5 to create a new InfoCube.

Enter a name and a description, select the *MultiCube* option, and then click [create icon] to continue.

Step 3 The window in Screen 8.29 lists all available InfoCubes. Select the two InfoCubes IC_NEWBC2 and IC_NEWBC4 to build the new multi-cube. Click [check icon] to continue.

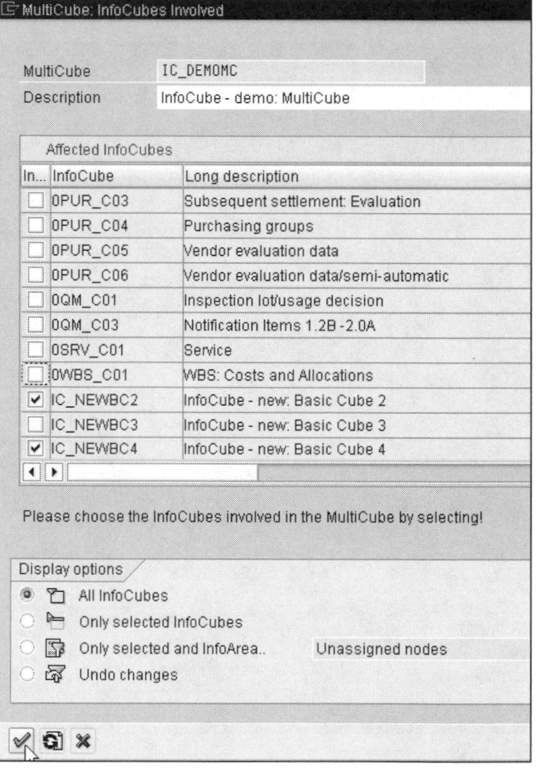

SCREEN 8.29

InfoCube Edit Goto Extras Environment System Help

Edit InfoCube: Characteristics

Content functions

Version Comparison Business Content

InfoCube IC_DEMOMC InfoCube - demo: MultiCube

Version new not saved

ObjStatus Inactive, not executable

Characteristics Time characteristics Key figures

AdFunction Detail view Dimensions... Nav.attributes... Identification

Template for MultiCube: <InfoObjects of the relevant InfoCubes>

Structure

Characteri...	Long description
IO_MAT	Material number
IO_CUST	Customer ID
IO_SREPN2	Sales representative ID -
IO_DAGE	Delivery agent

Template

Characteri...	Long description	Statu
IO_CUST	Customer ID	
IO_DAGE	Delivery agent	
IO_MAT	Material number	
IO_SOFF	Sales office	
IO_SREG	Sales region	
IO_SREPN2	Sales representative ID - n...	

SCREEN 8.30

Step 4 Select four characteristics from the *Template* table, and move them to the Structure table on the left, using ◀.

Step 5 Select a time characteristic from the *Template* table, and move it to the Structure table on the left, using ◀.

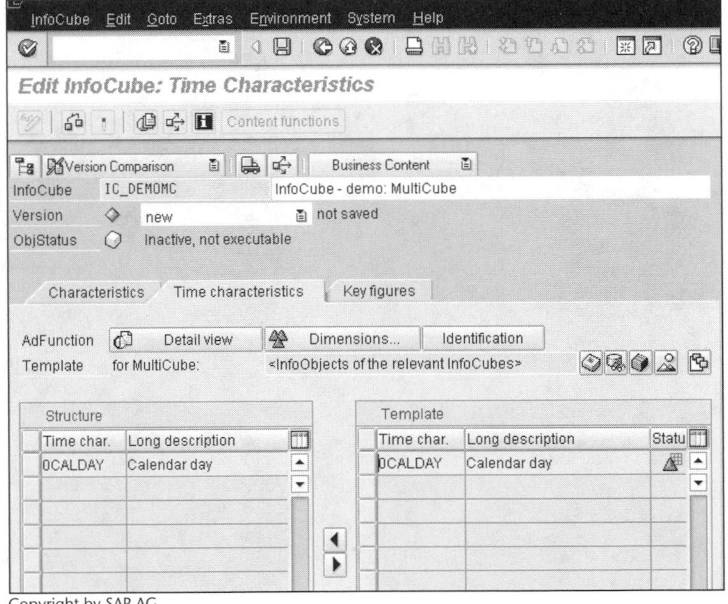

SCREEN 8.31

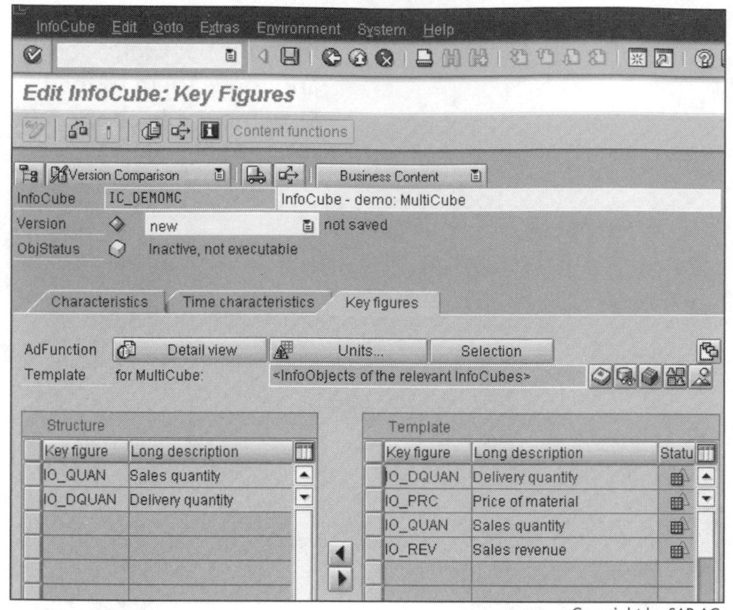

SCREEN 8.32

Step 6 Select two key figures from the *Template* table, and move them to the Structure table on the left, using ◄.

Step 7 Click Identification to set up the union conditions.

SCREEN 8.33

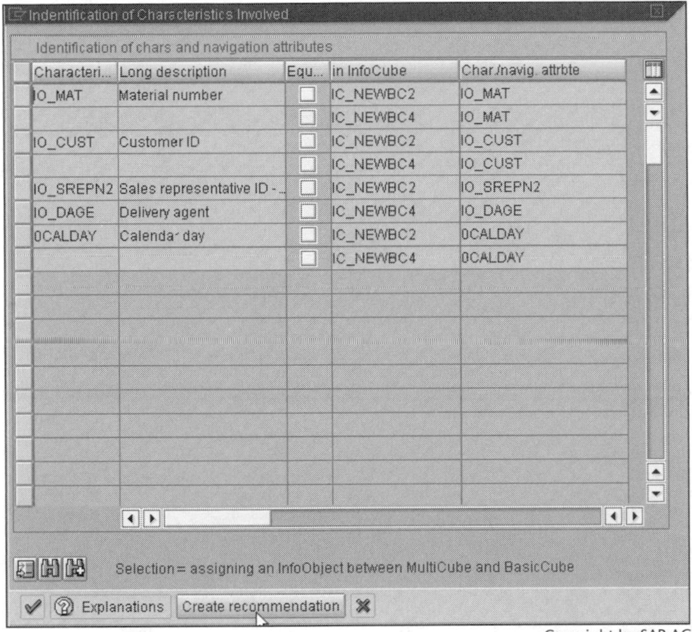

SCREEN 8.34

Step 8 Click Create recommendation to get help from BW.

Step 9 Accept the recommendation from BW, and then click ✔ to continue.

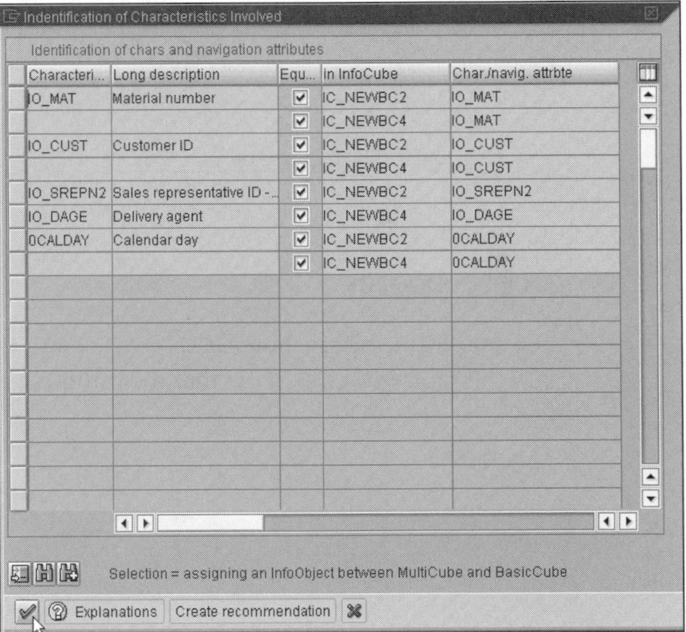

SCREEN 8.35

Step 10 After checking and activating the multi-cube, display its data model. As you see, it looks like a regular InfoCube.

SCREEN 8.36

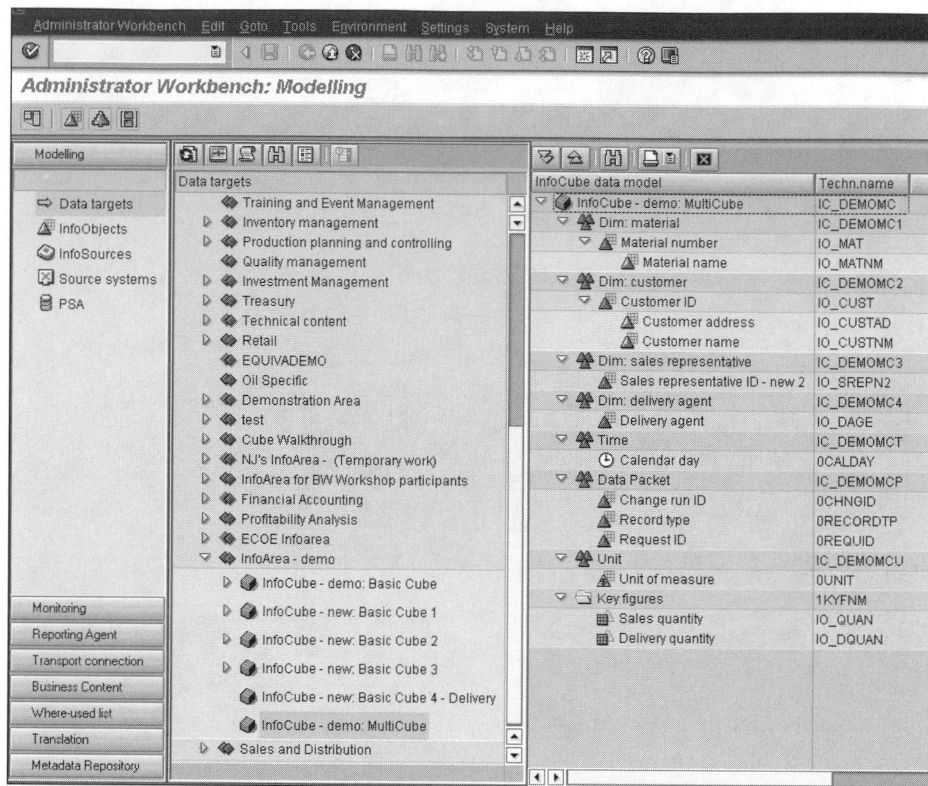

Result

Run transaction *SE11* to display the */BIC/FIC_DEMOMC* table definition (Screen 8.37). Note that the multi-cube is an ABAP structure.

SCREEN 8.37

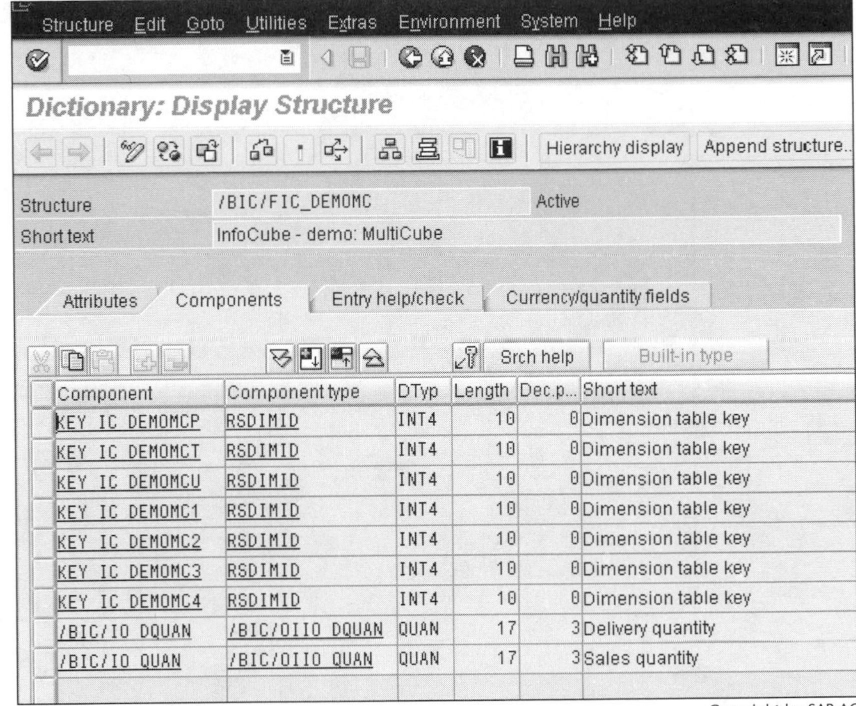

Component	Component type	DTyp	Length	Dec.p...	Short text
KEY_IC_DEMOMCP	RSDIMID	INT4	10	0	Dimension table key
KEY_IC_DEMOMCT	RSDIMID	INT4	10	0	Dimension table key
KEY_IC_DEMOMCU	RSDIMID	INT4	10	0	Dimension table key
KEY_IC_DEMOMC1	RSDIMID	INT4	10	0	Dimension table key
KEY_IC_DEMOMC2	RSDIMID	INT4	10	0	Dimension table key
KEY_IC_DEMOMC3	RSDIMID	INT4	10	0	Dimension table key
KEY_IC_DEMOMC4	RSDIMID	INT4	10	0	Dimension table key
/BIC/IO_DQUAN	/BIC/OIIO_DQUAN	QUAN	17	3	Delivery quantity
/BIC/IO_QUAN	/BIC/OIIO_QUAN	QUAN	17	3	Sales quantity

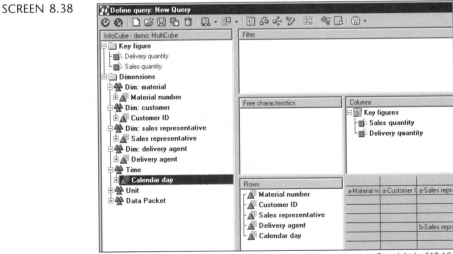

In the same way as we create queries for a basic cube, we can create queries for the multi-cube. Screen 8.38 shows the query definition, and Screen 8.39 shows its result.

SCREEN 8.38

SCREEN 8.39

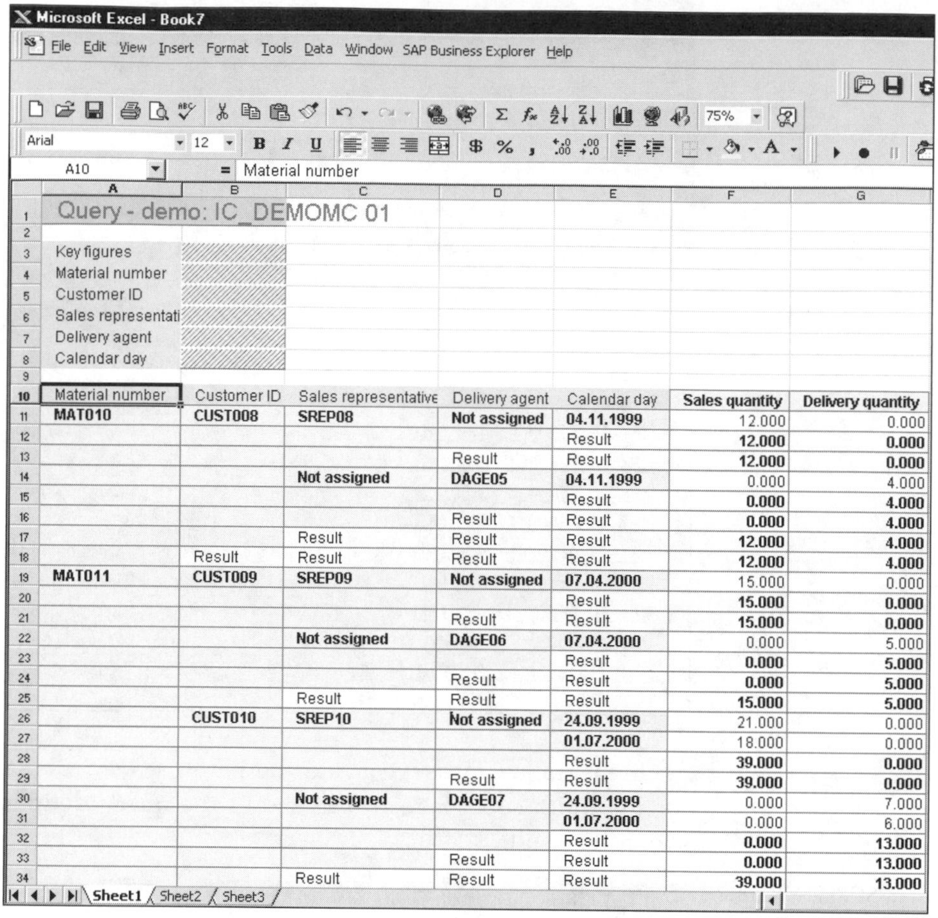

Microsoft Excel - Book7

Query - demo: IC_DEMOMC 01

Key figures	
Material number	
Customer ID	
Sales representati	
Delivery agent	
Calendar day	

Material number	Customer ID	Sales representative	Delivery agent	Calendar day	Sales quantity	Delivery quantity
MAT010	CUST008	SREP08	Not assigned	04.11.1999	12.000	0.000
				Result	12.000	0.000
			Result	Result	12.000	0.000
		Not assigned	DAGE05	04.11.1999	0.000	4.000
				Result	0.000	4.000
			Result	Result	0.000	4.000
		Result	Result	Result	12.000	4.000
	Result	Result	Result	Result	12.000	4.000
MAT011	CUST009	SREP09	Not assigned	07.04.2000	15.000	0.000
				Result	15.000	0.000
			Result	Result	15.000	0.000
		Not assigned	DAGE06	07.04.2000	0.000	5.000
				Result	0.000	5.000
			Result	Result	0.000	5.000
		Result	Result	Result	15.000	5.000
	CUST010	SREP10	Not assigned	24.09.1999	21.000	0.000
				01.07.2000	18.000	0.000
				Result	39.000	0.000
			Result	Result	39.000	0.000
		Not assigned	DAGE07	24.09.1999	0.000	7.000
				01.07.2000	0.000	6.000
				Result	0.000	13.000
			Result	Result	0.000	13.000
		Result	Result	Result	39.000	13.000

Sheet1 / Sheet2 / Sheet3

As shown in Screen 8.39, when the characteristics selected by a multi-cube query are not shared across all underlying basic cubes, the query result will produce multiple lines. This is one drawback of the multi-cube technique. In this example, we want SREP08 and DAGE05 to appear in the same line.

Tracing the SQL statements during the query execution, we find out our multi-cube query was split into two subqueries on the underlying basic cubes:

```
SELECT "DP"."SID_0RECORDTP" AS "S0002",
       "DU"."SID_0UNIT" AS "S0005",
       "DT"."SID_0CALDAY" AS "S0004",
       "D2"."SID_IO_MAT" AS "S0006",
```

```
        "D1"."SID_IO_CUST" AS "S0007",
        "D3"."SID_IO_SREPN2" AS "S0008",
        COUNT (*) AS "1ROWCOUNT",
        SUM ("E"."/BIC/IO_QUAN") AS "IO_QUAN"
FROM  "/BIC/E100014" "E",
      "/BIC/D100014P" "DP",
      "/BIC/DIC_NEWBC2U" "DU",
      "/BIC/DIC_NEWBC2T" "DT",
      "/BIC/DIC_NEWBC22" "D2",
      "/BIC/DIC_NEWBC21" "D1",
      "/BIC/D1000143" "D3"
WHERE  "E"."KEY_100014P" = "DP"."DIMID" AND
       "E"."KEY_IC_NEWBC2U" = "DU"."DIMID" AND
       "E"."KEY_IC_NEWBC2T" = "DT"."DIMID" AND
       "E"."KEY_IC_NEWBC22" = "D2"."DIMID" AND
       "E"."KEY_IC_NEWBC21" = "D1"."DIMID" AND
       "E"."KEY_1000143" = "D3"."DIMID" AND
   (((("DP"."SID_0CHNGID" = 0)) AND
     (("DP"."SID_0RECORDTP" = 0)) AND
     (("DP"."SID_0REQUID" <= 1099))))
GROUP BY "DP"."SID_0RECORDTP",
         "DU"."SID_0UNIT",
         "DT"."SID_0CALDAY",
         "D2"."SID_IO_MAT",
         "D1"."SID_IO_CUST",
         "D3"."SID_IO_SREPN2"
```

and

```
SELECT "DP"."SID_0RECORDTP" AS "S0002",
       "DU"."SID_0UNIT" AS "S0005",
       "DT"."SID_0CALDAY" AS "S0004",
       "D2"."SID_IO_MAT" AS "S0006",
       "D1"."SID_IO_CUST" AS "S0007",
       "D3"."SID_IO_DAGE" AS "S0009",
       COUNT (*) AS "1ROWCOUNT",
       SUM ("E"."/BIC/IO_DQUAN") AS "IO_DQUAN"
FROM  "/BIC/E100020" "E",
      "/BIC/D100020P" "DP",
      "/BIC/DIC_NEWBC4U" "DU",
```

```
        "/BIC/DIC_NEWBC4T" "DT",
        "/BIC/DIC_NEWBC42" "D2",
        "/BIC/DIC_NEWBC41" "D1",
        "/BIC/DIC_NEWBC43" "D3"
  WHERE  "E"."KEY_100020P" = "DP"."DIMID" AND
         "E"."KEY_IC_223
         "E"."KEY_IC_NEWBC42" = "D2"."DIMID" AND
         "E"."KEY_IC_NEWBC41" = "D1"."DIMID" AND
         "E"."KEY_IC_NEWBC43" = "D3"."DIMID" AND
     (((("DP"."SID_0CHNGID" = 0)) AND
      (("DP"."SID_0RECORDTP" = 0)) AND
      (("DP"."SID_0REQUID" <= 1101))))
  GROUP BY "DP"."SID_0RECORDTP",
           "DU"."SID_0UNIT",
           "DT"."SID_0CALDAY",
           "D2"."SID_IO_MAT",
           "D1"."SID_IO_CUST",
           "D3"."SID_IO_DAGE"
```

Each subquery used an aggregate: aggregate 100014 for the IC_NEWBC2 (sales) subquery, and aggregate 100020 for the IC_NEWBC4 (delivery) subquery.

Note: The aggregated data are stored in the E fact table, rather than the F fact table. Section 12.2.5, "InfoCube Compression," provides more information on the differences between these two types of fact tables.

The subqueries were processed in parallel. One work process sent the second subquery to the database without waiting for the database to return the result of the first subquery. After both subqueries received their data from the database, the same work process then presented the final result.

8.3 Summary

This chapter described the creation and use of aggregates and multi-cubes. Aggregates, a key technique for improving query performance, can be used in multi-cube queries. Without resorting to aggregates, a complex query on a large multi-cube may experience an unacceptable response time.

Key Terms

Term	Description
Aggregate	An aggregate is a subset of an InfoCube. The objective when using aggregates is to reduce I/O volume. The BW OLAP processor selects an appropriate aggregate during a query run or a navigation step. If no appropriate aggregate exists, the processor will retrieve data from the original InfoCube.
Multi-cube	A multi-cube is a union of basic cubes. The multi-cube itself does not contain any data; rather, the data reside in the basic cubes. To a user, the multi-cube resembles a basic cube. When creating a query, the user can select characteristics and key figures from different basic cubes.

For Further Information

- OSS Note 0175534, "Large BW Systems and Performance of Aggregate Build."
- OSS Note 0379736, "How Does a MultiCube Work?"
- OSS Note 0327876, "MultiCube Query and Using Several Aggregates."

Next . . .

Chapter 9 discusses the Operational Data Store (ODS).

Chapter 9

Operational Data Store (ODS)

In Section 7.5, we discussed line item dimensions as a technique for detail reporting. In this chapter, we will demonstrate another technique, **Operational Data Store (ODS)**. It allows us to build a multilayer structure for detail reporting at different levels, including the line item level.

Specifically, ODS is a BW architectural component located between PSA and InfoCube (Figure 9.1). The ODS layer itself can contain multiple ODS objects with data at different levels of detail.

As shown in Figure 9.1, there are many ways to send data to their destinations. If one destination is an ODS object, then as BW 2 releases the data, it must be loaded into PSA first, then from PSA to the ODS object. We will explain the reason for this in Section 9.3, "Loading Data into the ODS Object."

FIGURE 9.1
ODS IN BW

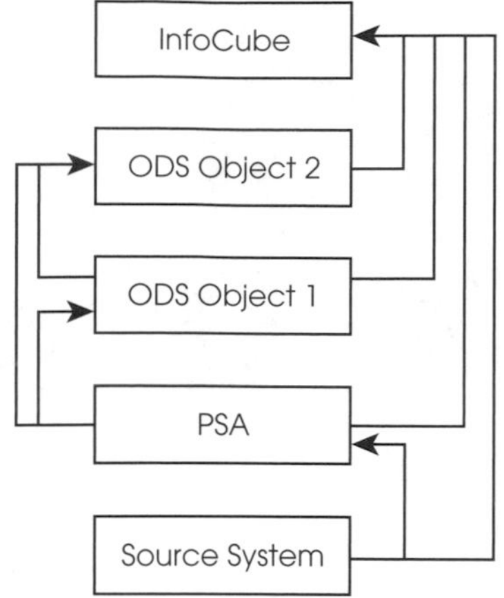

Like InfoCubes, ODS objects allow BEx reporting. Unlike InfoCubes, ODS objects are not based on the star schema and should not be used for multidimensional analysis. For the same reason, ODS objects do not aggregate data as InfoCubes do, cannot have aggregates, and cannot be included in a multi-cube. Other differences are described later in this chapter.

In this chapter, we will create an ODS object, load data into it, and then load the data from the ODS object into an InfoCube. The solid lines in Figure 9.2 represent this procedure.

FIGURE 9.2
DATA FLOW

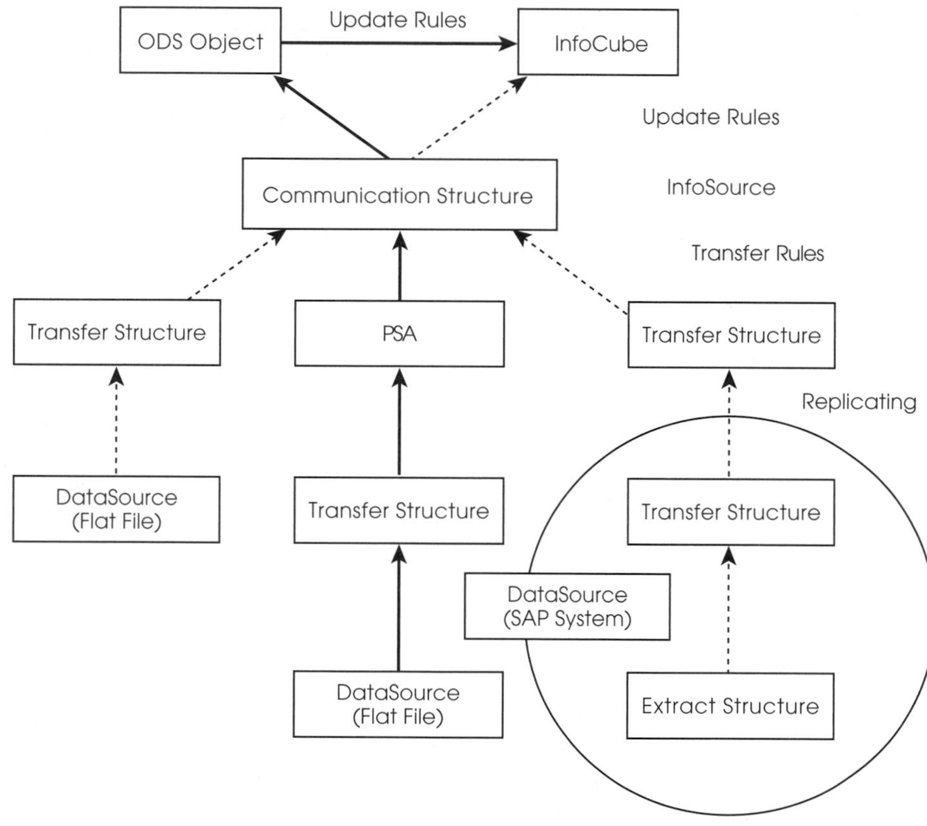

9.1 Creating an ODS Object

First, let's create an ODS object.

Work Instructions

Step 1 Right-click *InfoArea—demo,* and then select *Create ODS object. . . .*

SCREEN 9.1

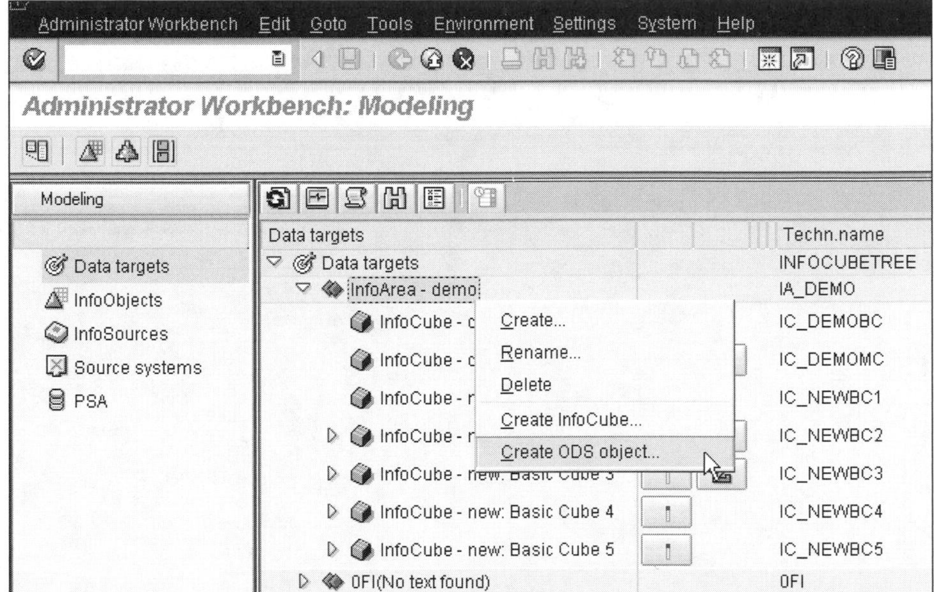

Step 2 Enter a name and a description, and then click [icon] to create the named ODS object.

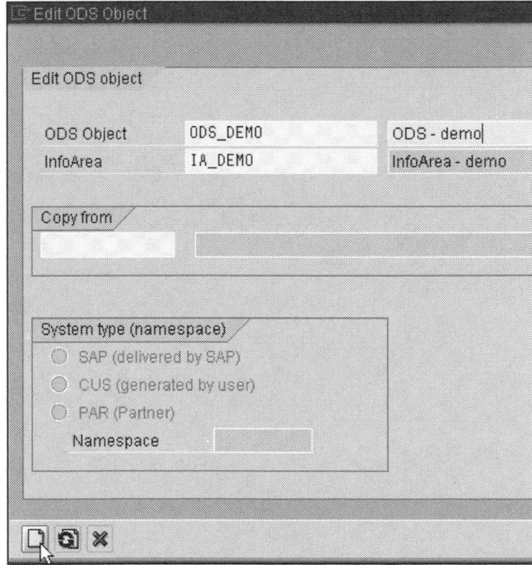

SCREEN 9.2

Step 3 Select the *BEx Reporting* option, allowing us to create queries on the ODS object from BEx Analyzer.

Note: We leave other options open so we have opportunities later to manually complete these tasks. It helps us to understand the data load process.

Next, click to get the necessary InfoObjects.

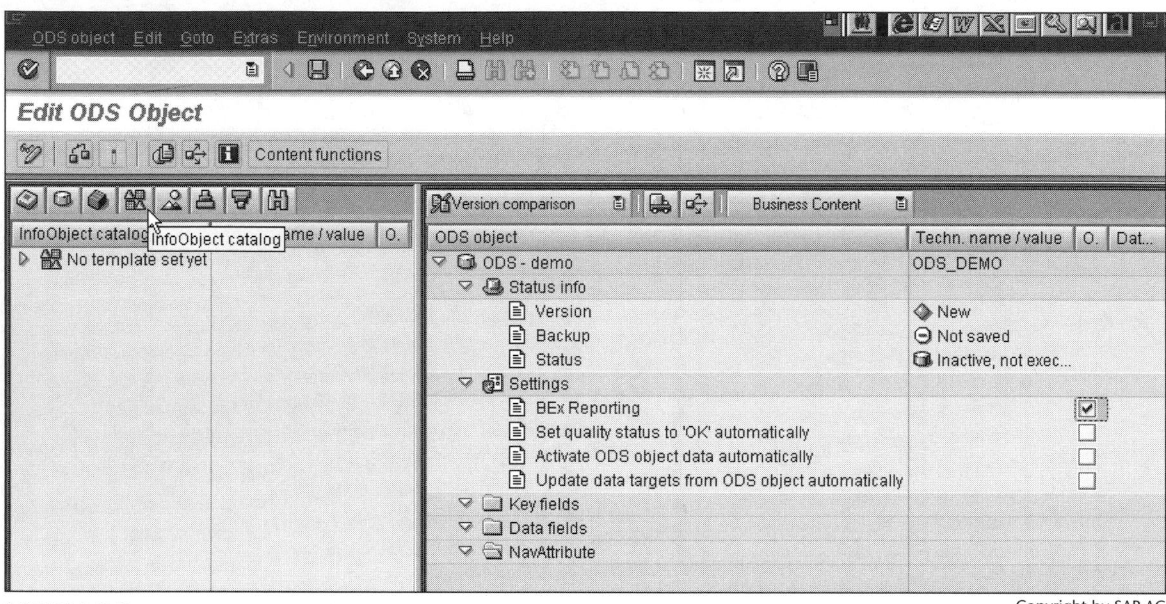

SCREEN 9.3

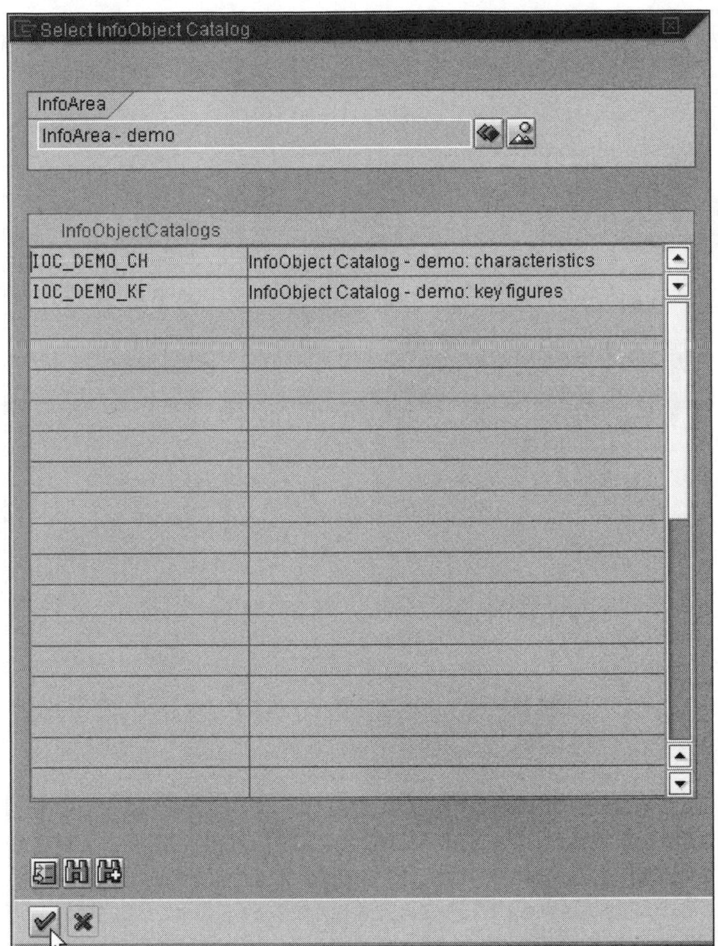

SCREEN 9.4

Step 4 Select *IOC_DEMO_CH,* which was created in Section 2.2. Click ✔ to continue.

Step 5 Drag *IO_ORD* (Order number), *IO_CUST* (Customer ID), *IO_SREG* (Sales region), *IO_SOFF* (Sales office), *IO_SREPN2* (Sales representative ID – new 2), and *IO_MAT* (Material number) from the left panel into the right panel and place them under the *Key fields* folder. Here *IO_ORD* is a newly created characteristic for sales orders.

SCREEN 9.5

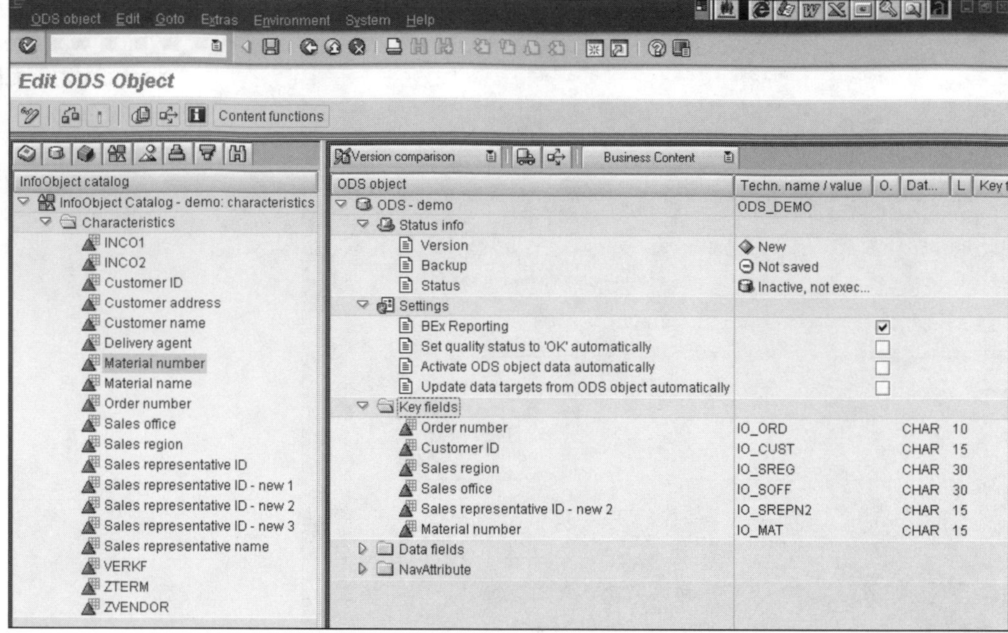

Copyright by SAP AG

Step 6 Repeat Steps 3–5 to add *IO_QUAN* and *IO_PRC* to the ODS object. Be sure to add them to the *Data fields* folder.

SCREEN 9.6

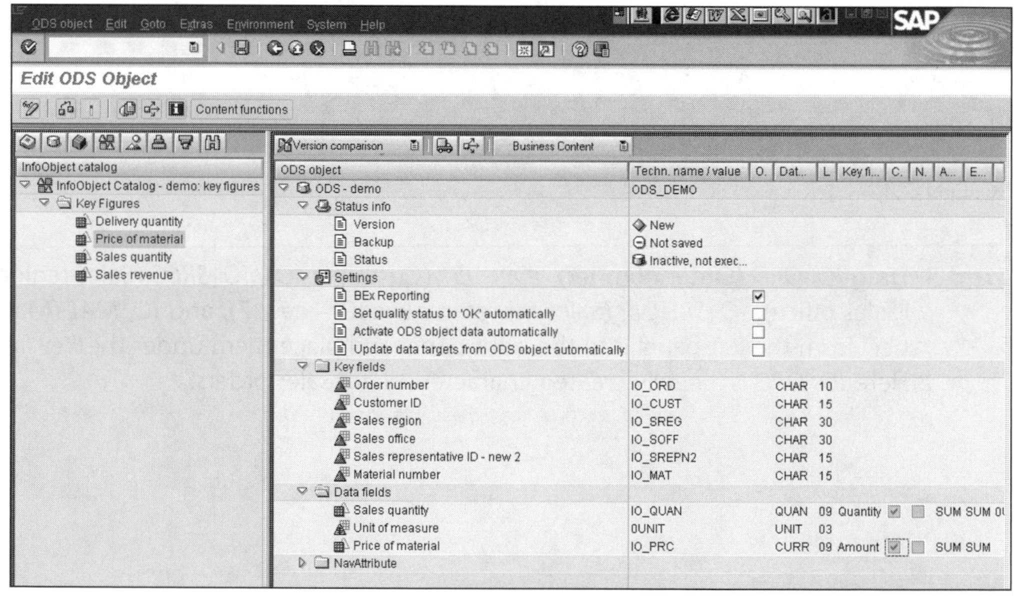

Copyright by SAP AG

Step 7 Repeat Steps 3–5 to add *0CALDAY* (Calendar day) to the ODS object. Be sure to add it to the *Key fields* folder.

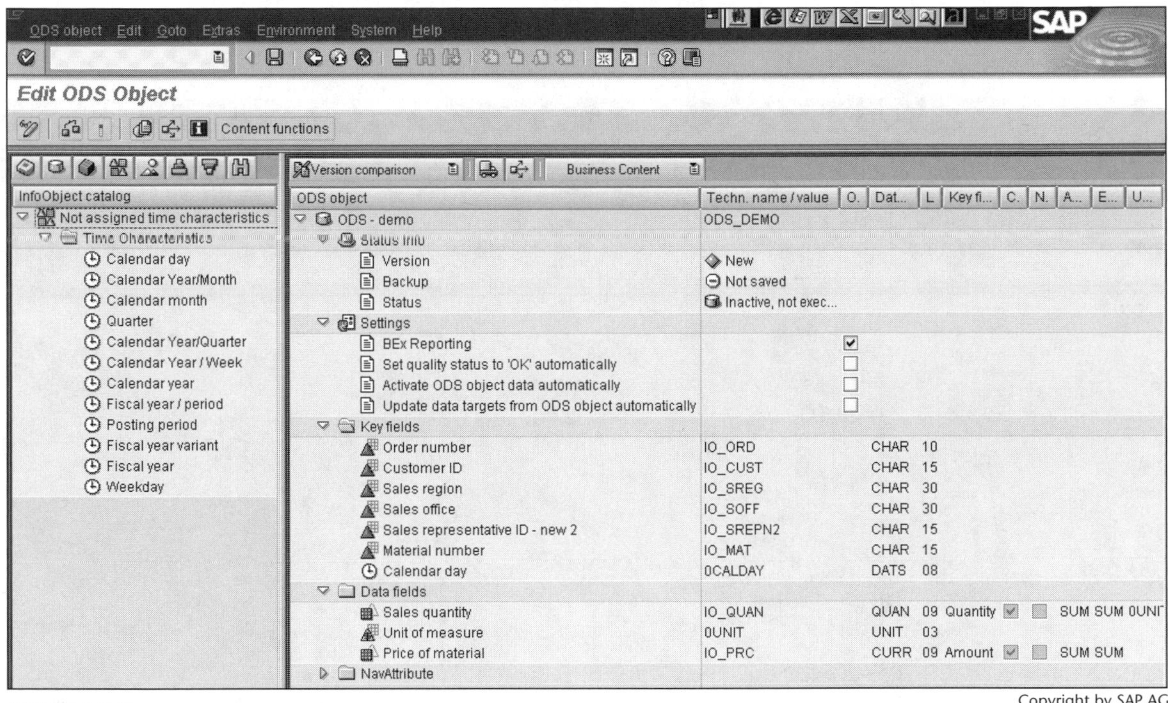
ODS object Edit Goto Extras Environment System Help
SAP
Edit ODS Object
Content functions
Version comparison
Business Content
InfoObject catalog
Not assigned time characteristics
Time Characteristics
Calendar day
Calendar Year/Month
Calendar month
Quarter
Calendar Year/Quarter
Calendar Year / Week
Calendar year
Fiscal year / period
Posting period
Fiscal year variant
Fiscal year
Weekday
ODS object
Techn. name / value O. Dat... L Key fi... C. N. A... E... U...
ODS - demo ODS_DEMO
Status Info
Version New
Backup Not saved
Status Inactive, not exec...
Settings
BEx Reporting
Set quality status to 'OK' automatically
Activate ODS object data automatically
Update data targets from ODS object automatically
Key fields
Order number IO_ORD CHAR 10
Customer ID IO_CUST CHAR 15
Sales region IO_SREG CHAR 30
Sales office IO_SOFF CHAR 30
Sales representative ID - new 2 IO_SREPN2 CHAR 15
Material number IO_MAT CHAR 15
Calendar day 0CALDAY DATS 08
Data fields
Sales quantity IO_QUAN QUAN 09 Quantity SUM SUM 0UNIT
Unit of measure 0UNIT UNIT 03
Price of material IO_PRC CURR 09 Amount SUM SUM
NavAttribute

SCREEN 9.7

Step 8 Click . A new InfoObject, *0RECORDMODE,* is added. In Section 9.5, we will learn how to use it in delta data loads.

Click to activate the ODS object.

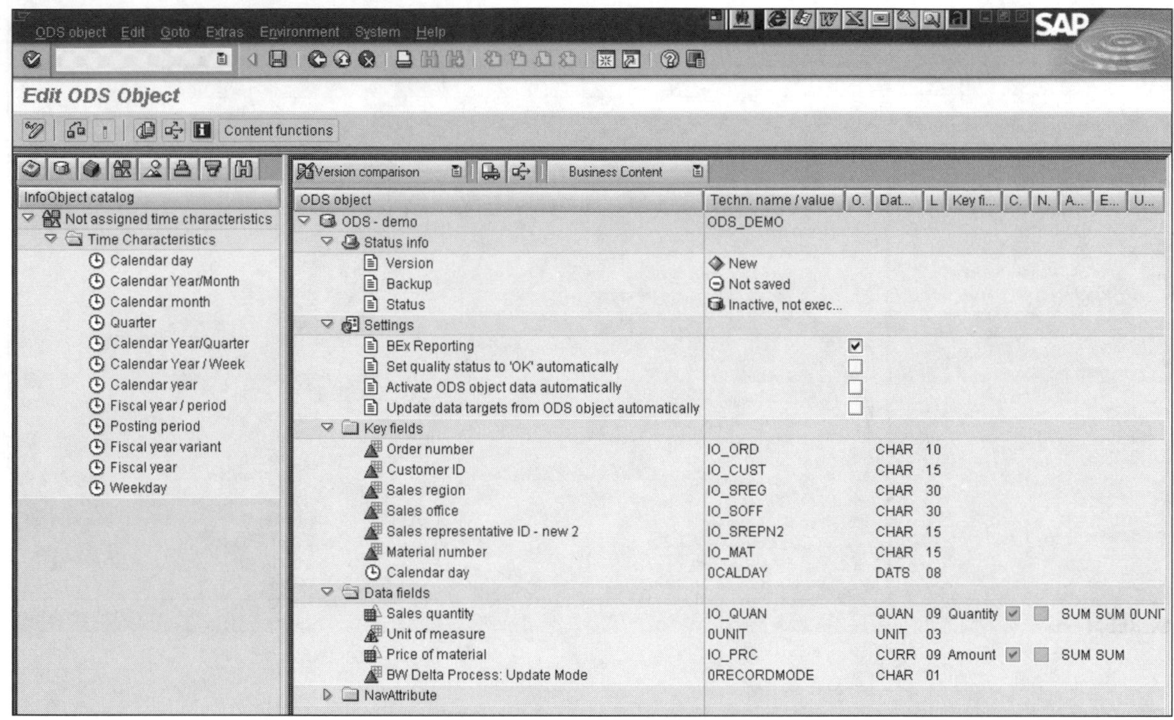

SCREEN 9.8

Result

You have created an ODS object that includes a new InfoObject, IO_ORD, for sales orders.

9.2 Preparing to Load Data into the ODS Object, Then into an InfoCube

To load data into the ODS object, we need to create an InfoSource, transfer rules, and update rules as we did in Chapter 3. After loading the data into the

ODS object, we will aggregate the data from the ODS object and load them into an InfoCube.

Prerequisites

A new InfoCube has been created that will accept the data from the ODS object. Screen 9.9 shows its data model.

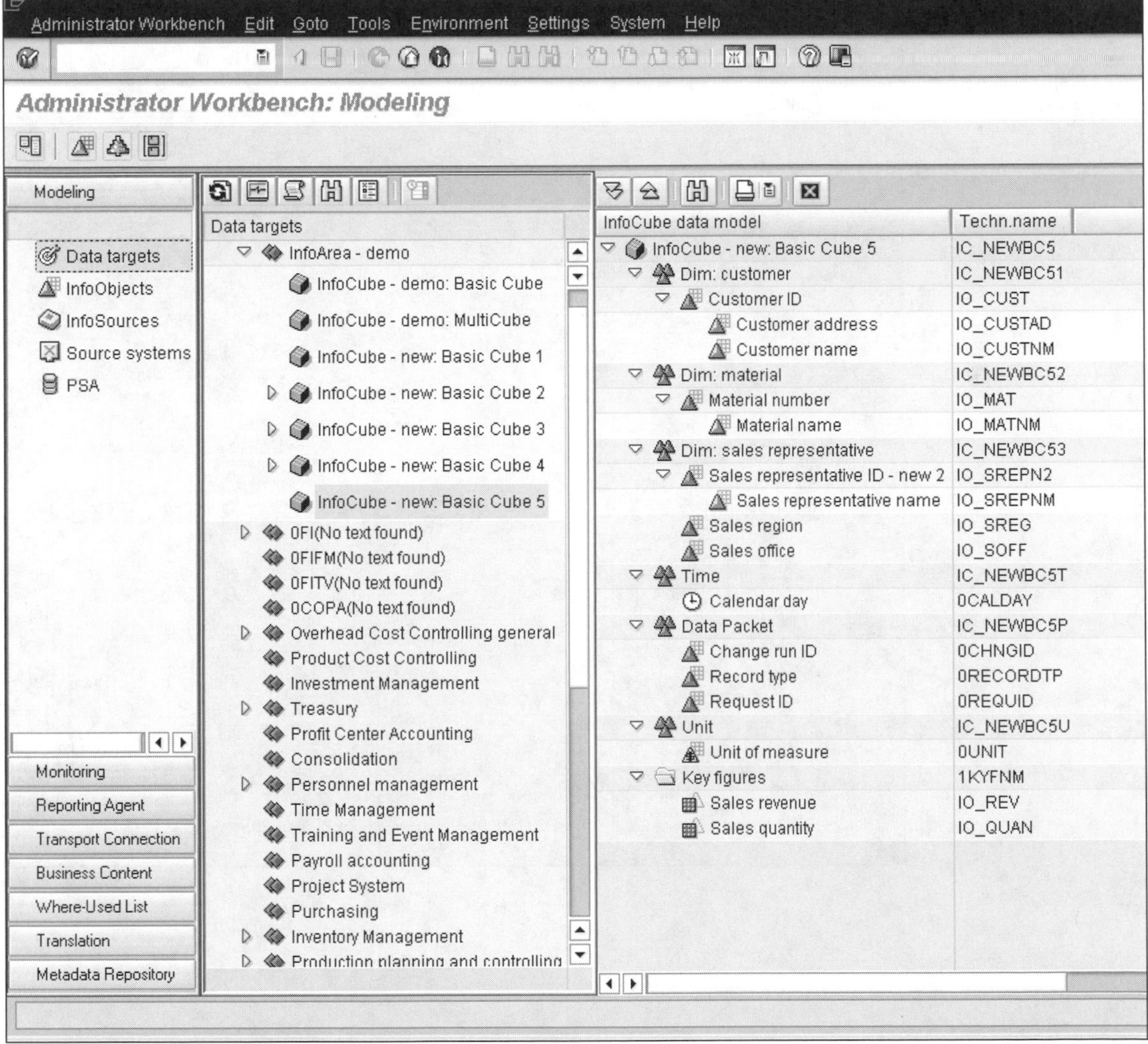

SCREEN 9.9

Work Instructions

Step 1 Repeat the procedure outlined in Section 3.7 to create an InfoSource, *IS_ODS_DEMO*, and then create transfer rules. Screen 9.10 shows the active transfer rules.

SCREEN 9.10

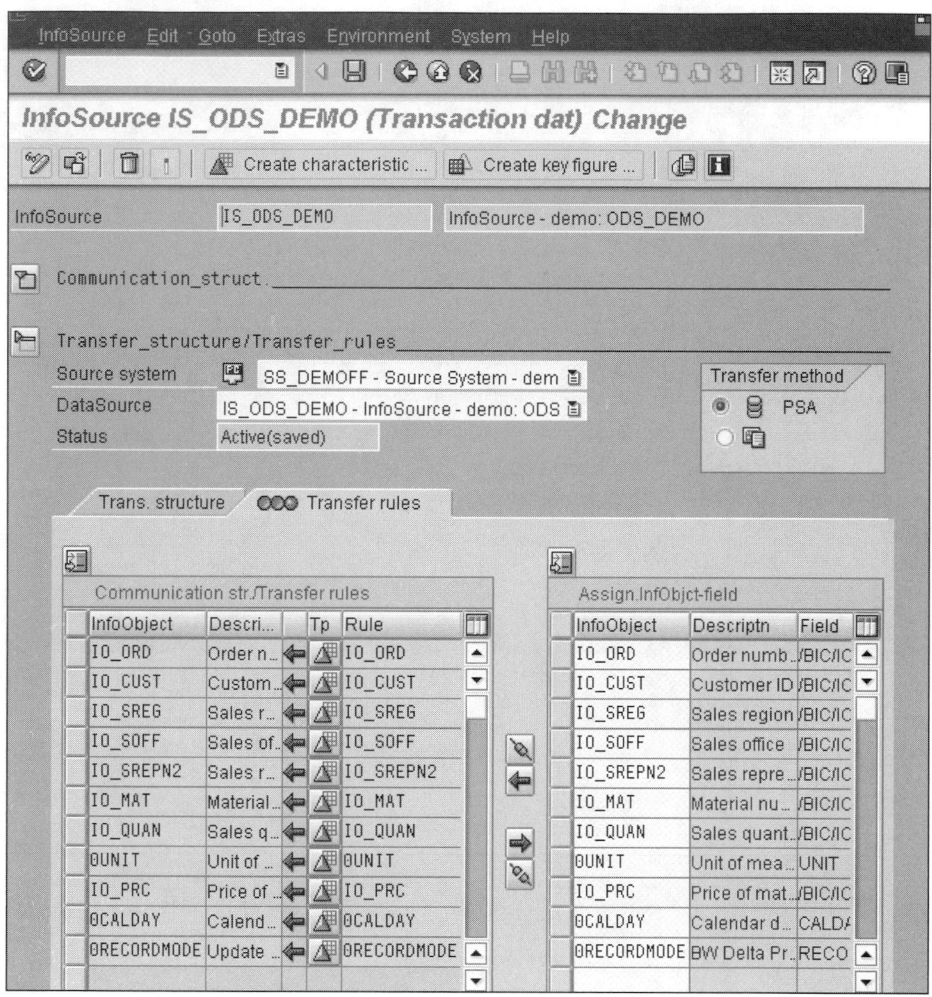

Step 2 Repeat the procedure outlined in Section 3.8 to create update rules. The InfoSource is *IS_ODS_DEMO*. Screen 9.11 shows the active update rules.

Let's check the update type for ODS data fields. To display the update type for *Sales quantity*, select *Sales quantity* and then click .

SCREEN 9.11

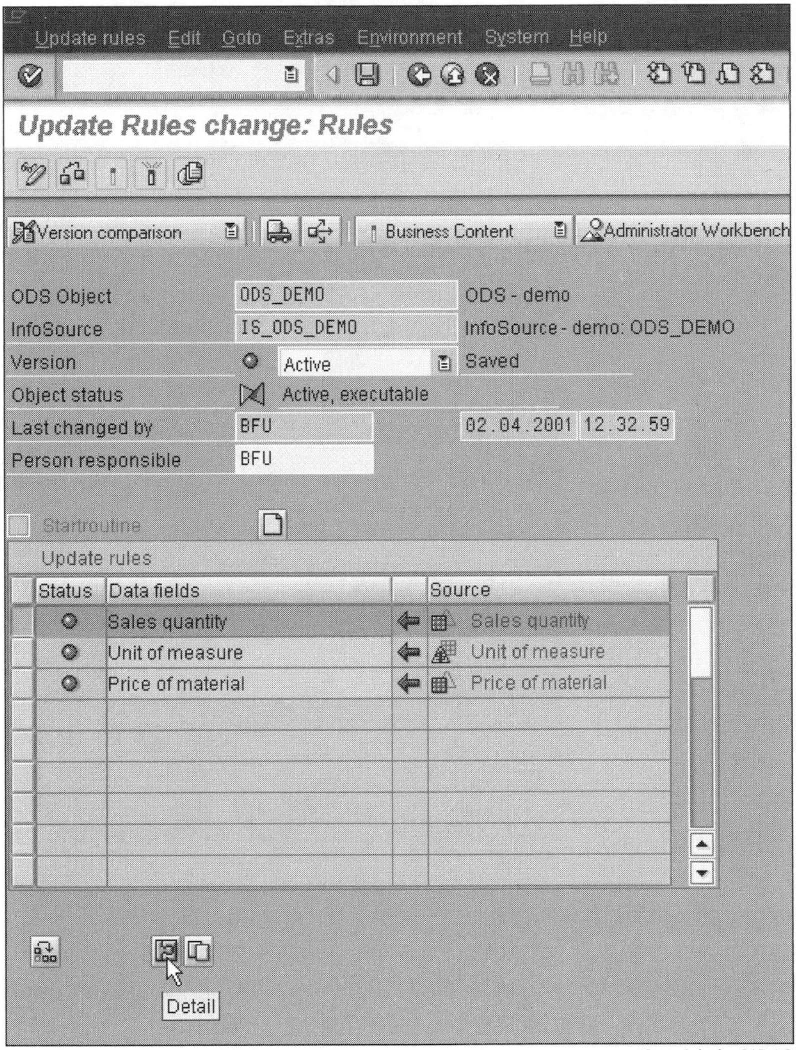

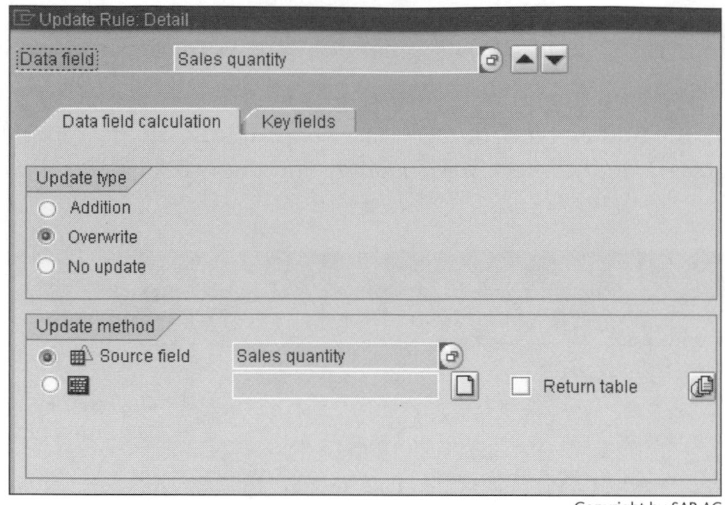

SCREEN 9.12

Step 3 Screen 9.12 shows one of the differences between ODS objects and InfoCubes: The default update type for an ODS object is *Overwrite,* and the default update type for an InfoCube is *Addition.*

Step 4 Repeat the procedure outlined in Section 3.8 to create update rules for the InfoCube shown in Figure 9.2. In this case, use the ODS object *ODS_DEMO* as the DataSource instead of the *InfoSource* as shown in Screen 3.64. Click [icon] to continue.

Step 5 After proposing update rules, BW finds out that one or more InfoCube key figures cannot have one-to-one mappings with the key figures in the ODS object. It therefore decides the update type for these key figures should be set to "no update."

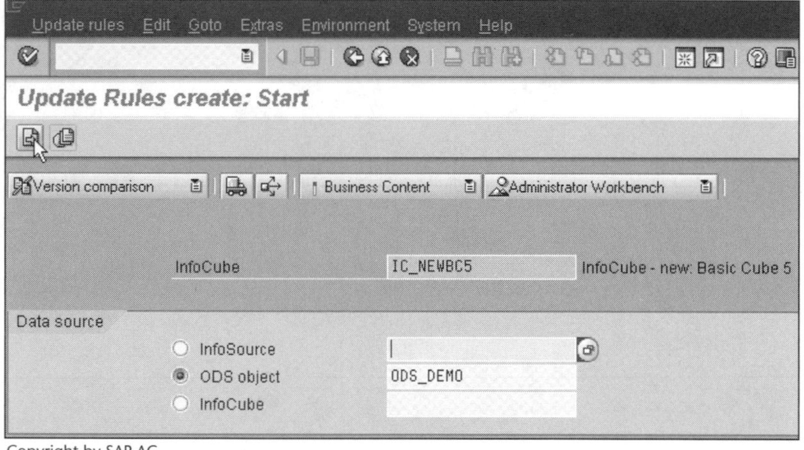

SCREEN 9.13

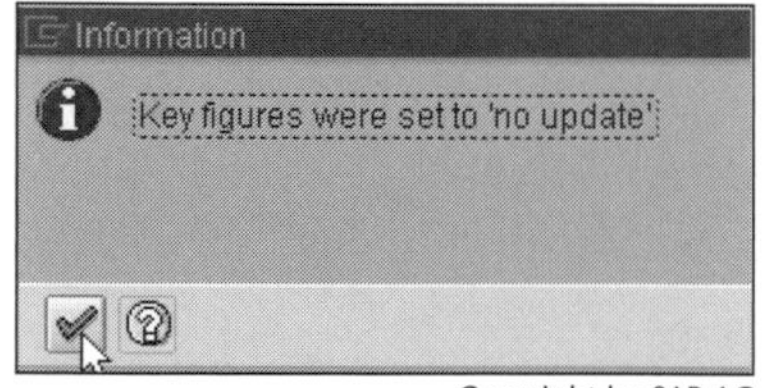

SCREEN 9.14

In Screen 9.15, we will find out which InfoCube key figures do not have the one-to-one mappings with the key figures in the ODS object. Click [icon] to continue.

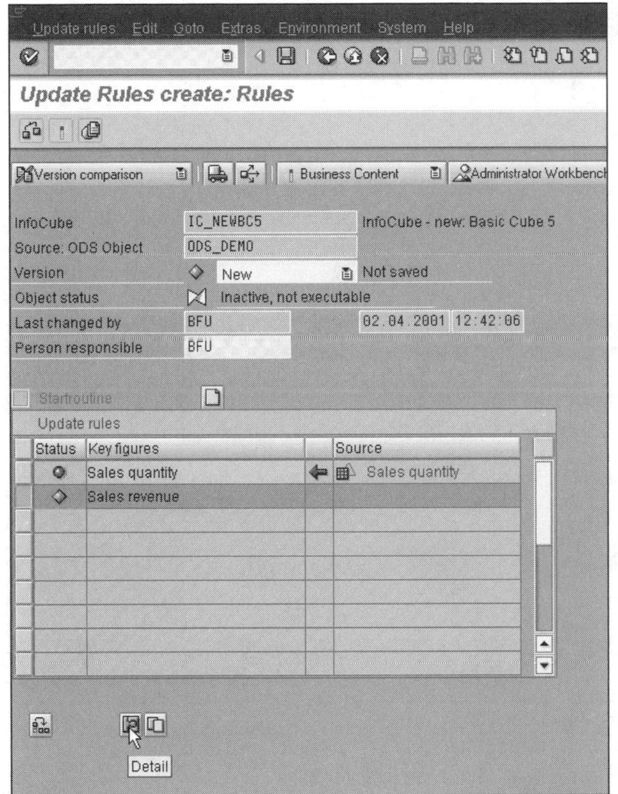

SCREEN 9.15

Step 6 Screen 9.15 shows that the key figure *Sales revenue* does not have a one-to-one mapping with a key figure in the ODS object. Let's create an update rule for it. Select *Sales revenue,* and then click [icon].

Step 7 Click [icon] to create an update rule.

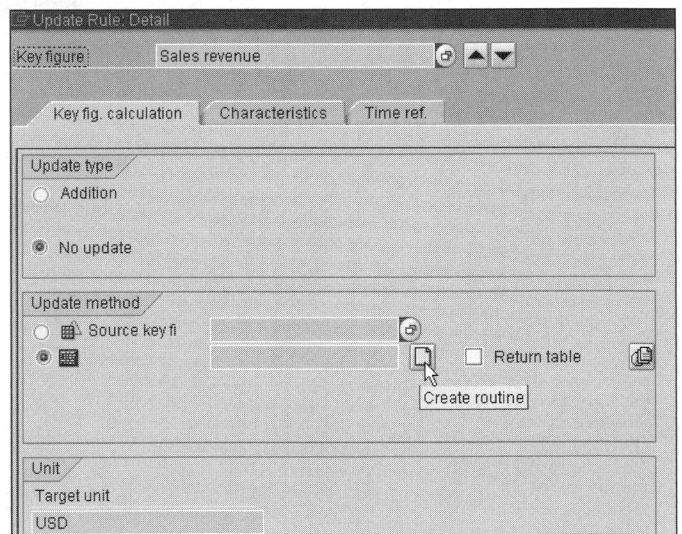

SCREEN 9.16

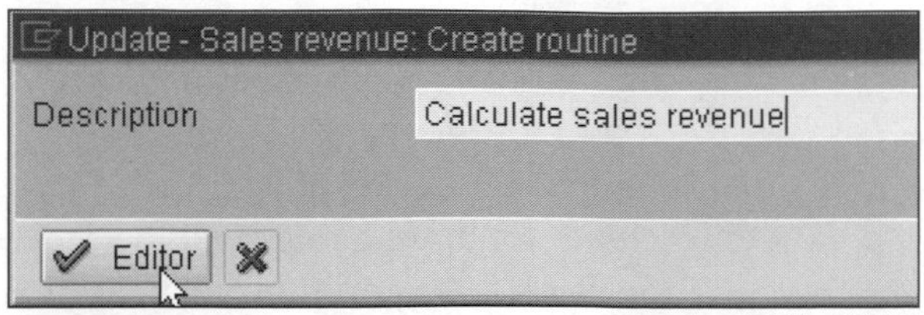

SCREEN 9.17

Step 8 Enter a description, and then click Editor to open the ABAP editor.

Step 9 Enter *RESULT = COMM_STRUCTURE-/BIC/IO_QUAN * COMM_STRUCTURE-/BIC/IO_PRC.* as shown on line 21, and then click to check the routine. If it is valid, click to save it and go back.

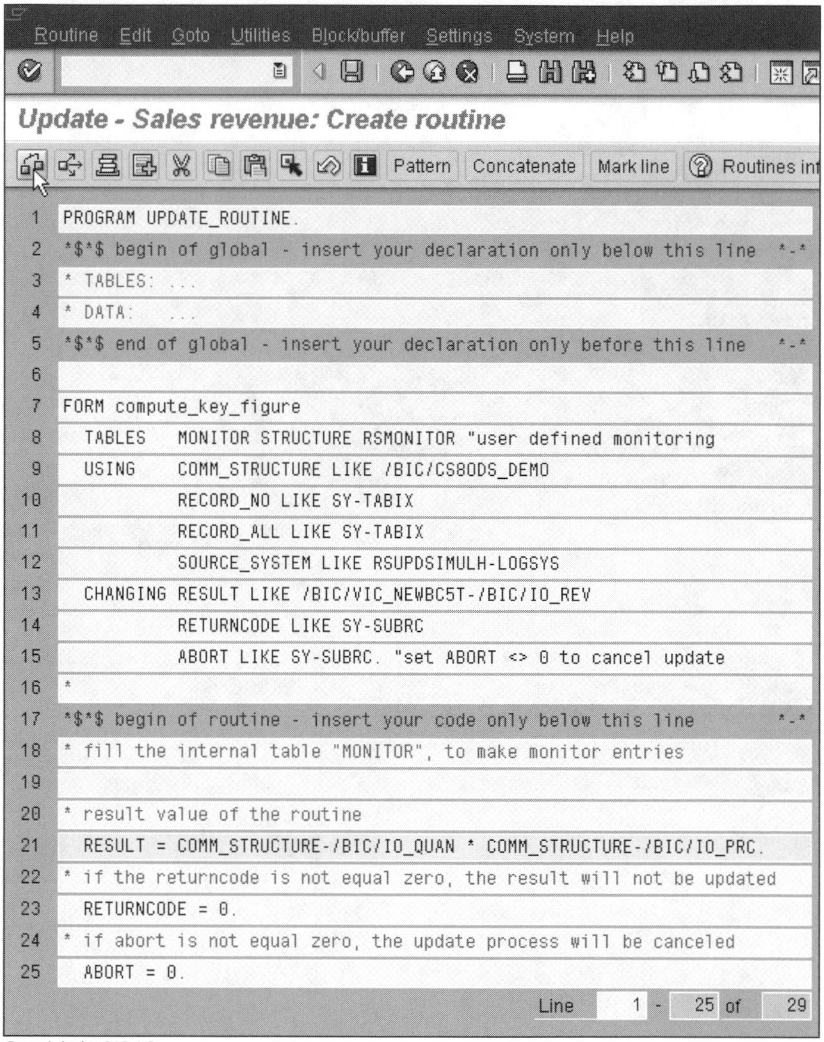

Routine Edit Goto Utilities Block/buffer Settings System Help

Update - Sales revenue: Create routine

Pattern Concatenate Mark line Routines inf

```
1  PROGRAM UPDATE_ROUTINE.
2  *$*$ begin of global - insert your declaration only below this line  *-*
3  * TABLES: ...
4  * DATA:   ...
5  *$*$ end of global - insert your declaration only before this line   *-*
6
7  FORM compute_key_figure
8    TABLES   MONITOR STRUCTURE RSMONITOR "user defined monitoring
9    USING    COMM_STRUCTURE LIKE /BIC/CS8ODS_DEMO
10            RECORD_NO LIKE SY-TABIX
11            RECORD_ALL LIKE SY-TABIX
12            SOURCE_SYSTEM LIKE RSUPDSIMULH-LOGSYS
13   CHANGING RESULT LIKE /BIC/VIC_NEWBC5T-/BIC/IO_REV
14            RETURNCODE LIKE SY-SUBRC
15            ABORT LIKE SY-SUBRC. "set ABORT <> 0 to cancel update
16 *
17 *$*$ begin of routine - insert your code only below this line        *-*
18 * fill the internal table "MONITOR", to make monitor entries
19
20 * result value of the routine
21   RESULT = COMM_STRUCTURE-/BIC/IO_QUAN * COMM_STRUCTURE-/BIC/IO_PRC.
22 * if the returncode is not equal zero, the result will not be updated
23   RETURNCODE = 0.
24 * if abort is not equal zero, the update process will be canceled
25   ABORT = 0.
```

Line 1 - 25 of 29

SCREEN 9.18

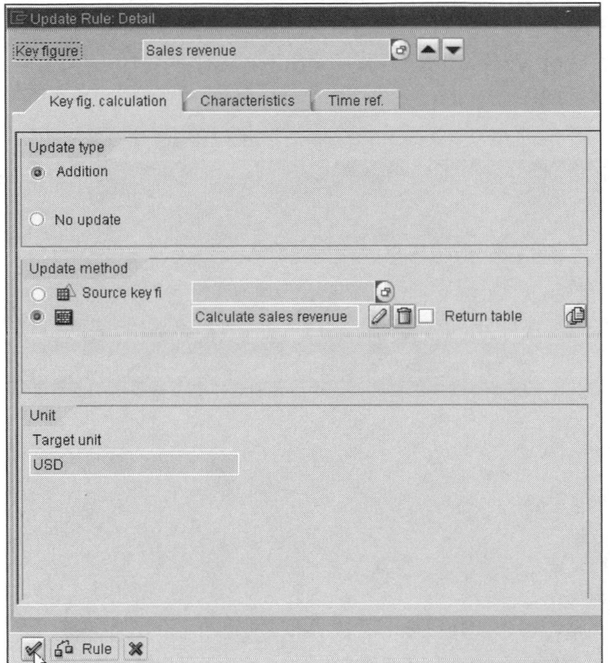

SCREEN 9.19

Step 10 Click to continue.

Step 11 Click to check the update rules. If they are valid, click to activate them.

Update rules Edit Goto Extras Environment System Help

Update Rules create: Rules

Version comparison | Business Content | Administrator Workbench

InfoCube	IC_NEWBC5	InfoCube - new: Basic Cube 5
Source: ODS Object	ODS_DEMO	
Version	Active	Saved
Object status	Active, executable	
Last changed by	BFU	02.04.2001 12:52:42
Person responsible	BFU	

Startroutine

Update rules

Status	Key figures		Source
	Sales quantity		Sales quantity
	Sales revenue		Calculate sales revenue

SCREEN 9.20

Result

Screen 9.21 shows you have achieved a data flow path from the flat file source system all the way to the InfoCube.

SCREEN 9.21

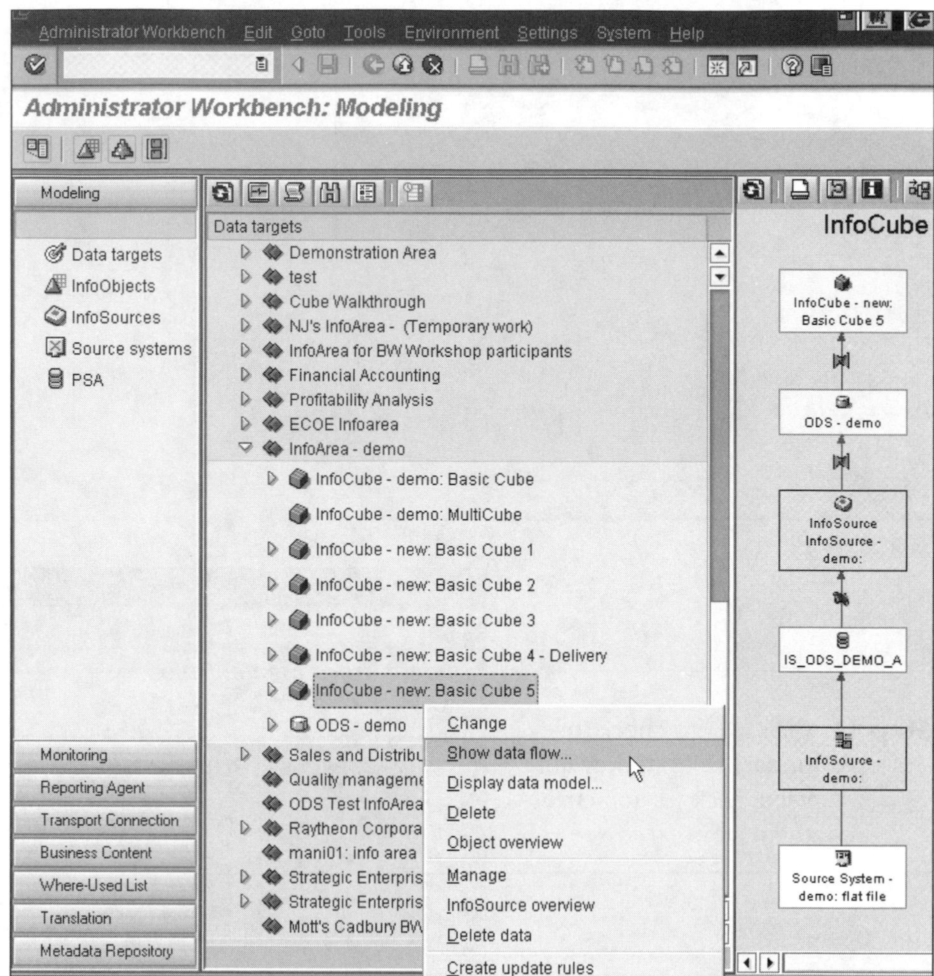

9.3 Loading Data into the ODS Object

Now we can load data into the ODS object.

Work Instructions

Step 1 Repeat the procedure outlined in Section 3.9 to create an InfoPackage. Select the *Only PSA* option in the InfoPackage.

Note: As of BW 2 releases, when loading data into ODS objects BW requires us to select the *Only PSA* option because ODS objects do not support parallel loads.

A load request can be processed in parallel when the data are sent in multiple packets from the source system. Each packet will use one SAP work process. This parallel processing generates an ORA-54 error when multiple processes compete for the same table lock on the ODS tables. This table lock is essential so that the *Overwrite* option selected in Screen 9.12 will not cause data consistency problems when the data load executes. Loading data from PSA to an ODS object or an InfoCube is handled by a single SAP work process, which prevents the table locking problem.

BW release 3.0A removes this restriction. Data can now be loaded into an ODS object in multiple packets, through parallel processing. The new release achieves this goal via a queuing mechanism. Data requests are identified uniquely by a combination of several key fields.

SCREEN 9.22

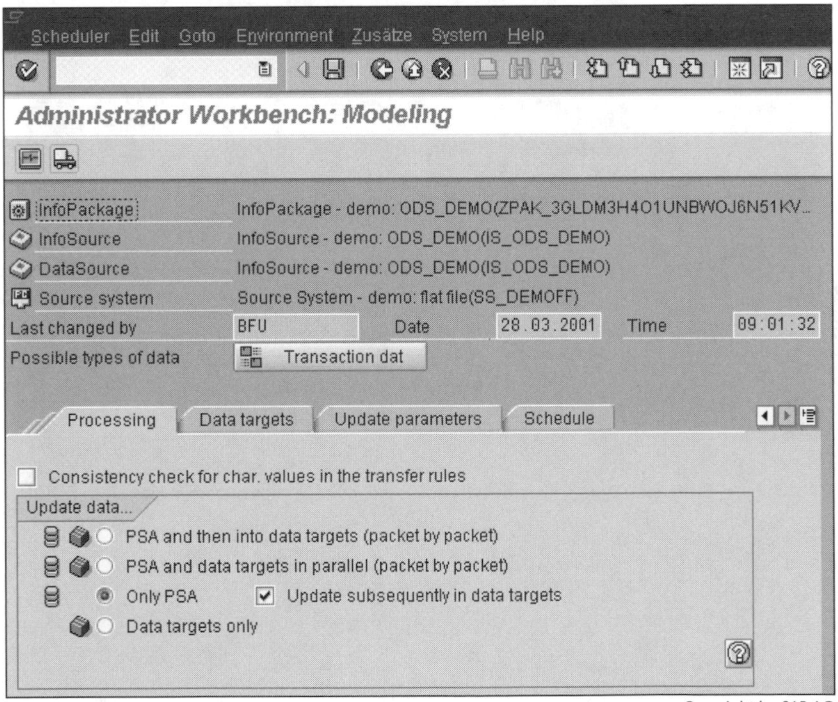

Step 2 Under the *Update parameters* tab, we see another difference between ODS objects and InfoCubes: We do not have the delta load option. In Section 9.5, we will see how to perform delta data loading into the ODS object using 0RECORDMODE.

SCREEN 9.23

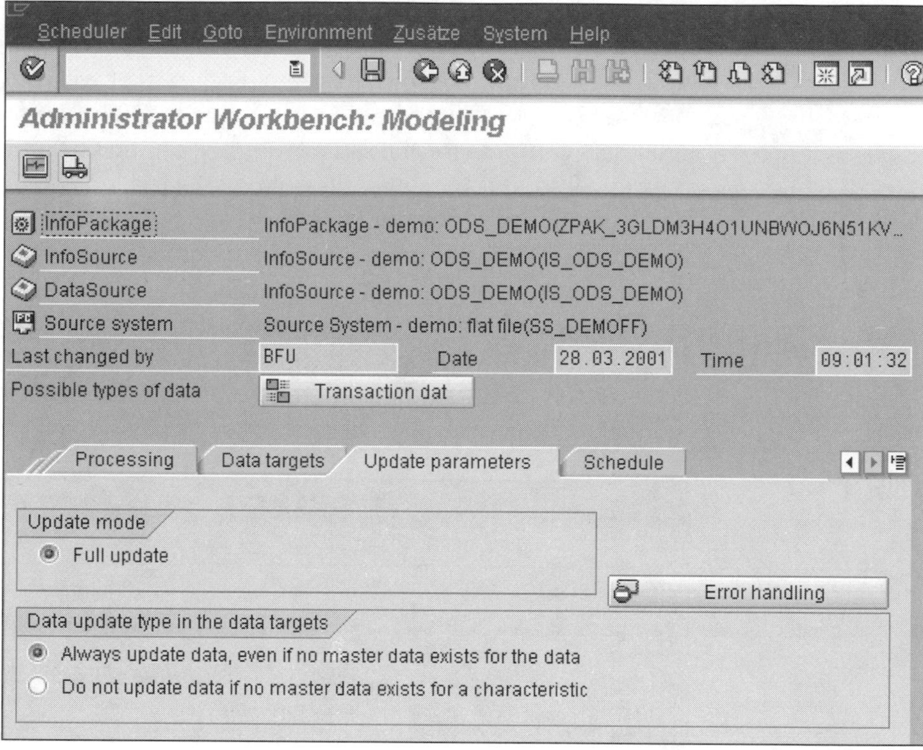

Step 3 After loading the data, go to PSA to check its contents using the procedure outlined in Section 4.3.

List Edit Goto Settings System Help

Maintenance of PSA data request REQU_3H8RA11I382LZZJUXDPS6XW

Data records to be edited

Status	Order numb	Customer I	Sales regi	Sales offi	Sales repr	Material n	Sales quan	Unit of me	Price of m	Calendar d	U
	ORD0000001	CUST001	EAST	ATLANTA	SREP01	MAT001	2	CS	1.00	19980304	
	ORD0000002	CUST001	EAST	ATLANTA	SREP01	MAT001	100	CS	0.75	19980305	
	ORD0000003	CUST001	EAST	ATLANTA	SREP01	MAT001	10	CS	0.50	19980306	
	ORD0000004	CUST002	EAST	NEW YORK	SREP02	MAT002	2	CS	2.00	19990526	
	ORD0000005	CUST002	EAST	NEW YORK	SREP02	MAT003	5	CS	3.00	19990730	
	ORD0000006	CUST003	EAST	NEW YORK	SREP03	MAT003	5	CS	4.00	20000101	
	ORD0000007	CUST004	MIDWEST	DALLAS	SREP04	MAT004	50	EA	5.00	19991023	
	ORD0000008	CUST004	MIDWEST	DALLAS	SREP04	MAT005	100	EA	6.00	19980904	
	ORD0000009	CUST004	MIDWEST	DALLAS	SREP04	MAT005	100	EA	7.00	19980529	
	ORD0000010	CUST005	MIDWEST	CHICAGO	SREP05	MAT006	200	EA	8.00	19991108	
	ORD0000011	CUST006	MIDWEST	CHICAGO	SREP06	MAT007	20	EA	9.00	20000408	
	ORD0000012	CUST007	MIDWEST	CHICAGO	SREP07	MAT008	3	DZ	10.00	20000901	
	ORD0000013	CUST007	MIDWEST	CHICAGO	SREP07	MAT008	3	DZ	1.00	19990424	
	ORD0000014	CUST008	MIDWEST	DENVER	SREP08	MAT008	3	DZ	2.00	19980328	
	ORD0000015	CUST008	MIDWEST	DENVER	SREP08	MAT009	2	CS	3.00	19980203	
	ORD0000016	CUST008	MIDWEST	DENVER	SREP08	MAT010	1	LB	4.00	19991104	
	ORD0000017	CUST009	WEST	LOS ANG...	SREP09	MAT011	1.5	LB	5.00	20000407	
	ORD0000018	CUST010	WEST	SEATTLE	SREP10	MAT011	1.5	LB	6.00	20000701	
	ORD0000019	CUST010	WEST	SEATTLE	SREP10	MAT011	1.5	LB	7.00	19990924	
	ORD0000020	CUST010	WEST	SEATTLE	SREP10	MAT012	2	LB	8.00	19991224	
	ORD0000021	CUST010	WEST	SEATTLE	SREP10	MAT013	3	CS	9.00	20000308	
	ORD0000022	CUST011	WEST	SEATTLE	SREP10	MAT014	1	LB	10.00	19980627	
	ORD0000023	CUST012			SREP11	MAT014	2	LB	1.00	19991209	
	ORD0000024	CUST012			SREP11	MAT015	3	CS	2.00	19980212	
	ORD0000025	CUST012			SREP11	MAT015	2	CS	3.00	20000705	
	ORD0000026	CUST012			SREP11	MAT015	3	CS	4.00	20001225	

SCREEN 9.24

Step 4 After checking the data in PSA, load it into the ODS object following the step shown in Screen 4.16.

Next, we need to check and set the data quality status. To do so, right-click the ODS and select *Manage*.

SCREEN 9.25

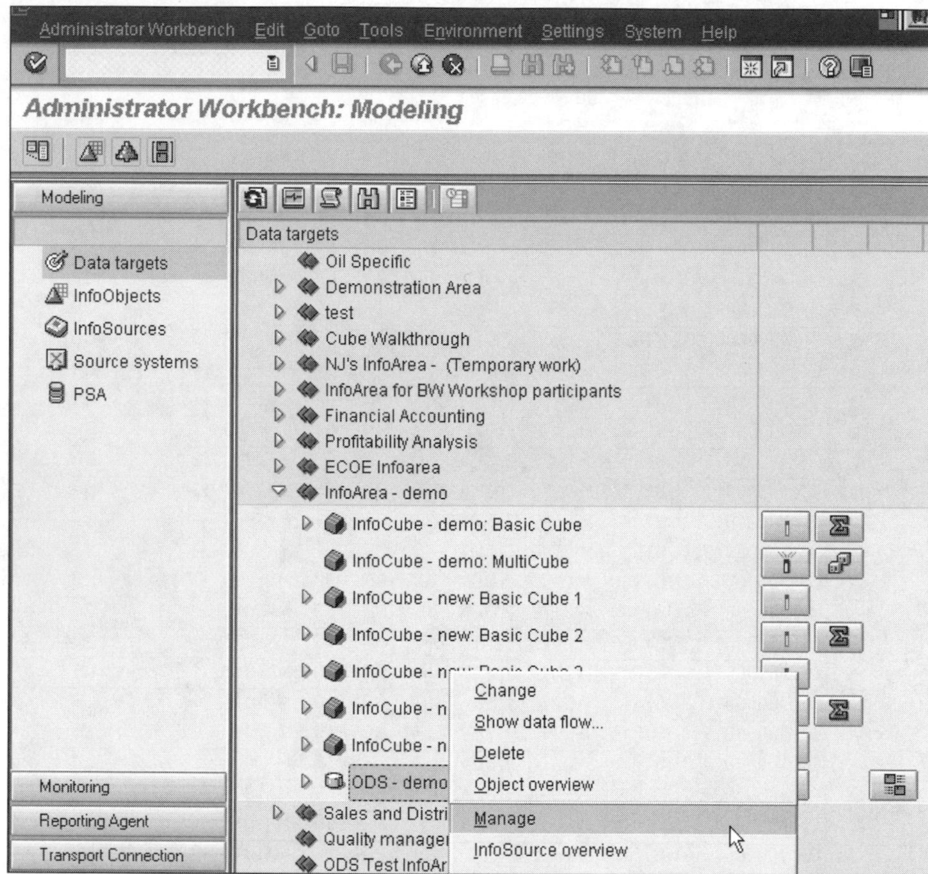

Step 5 Click [icon] in the *QM . . .* column.

Note: QM stands for "quality management." Before the loaded data will be available for reporting, the QM status must be set to "OK," as indicated by the green light on the right.

We could have skipped Step 5 if we had selected the option *Set quality status to 'OK' automatically* in Screen 9.3.

SCREEN 9.26

General Edit Goto Environment System Help

Manage Data Targets

Contents | Log

Name	D...	Technical name	Table type
ODS - demo		ODS_DEMO	ODS Object

Contents | Requests | Reconstruct

Request from ODS:ODS - demo(ODS_DEMO)

Requ...	R...	PSA I...	QM...	Te...	Dis...	Request d...	Update date	Selection conditions
1860		0				03.04.2001	03.04.2001	

Stil no QM release for this request complete

Step 6 Change the status from *Status indifferent; not yet f* to *Status OK*, and then click [save icon] to save the change.

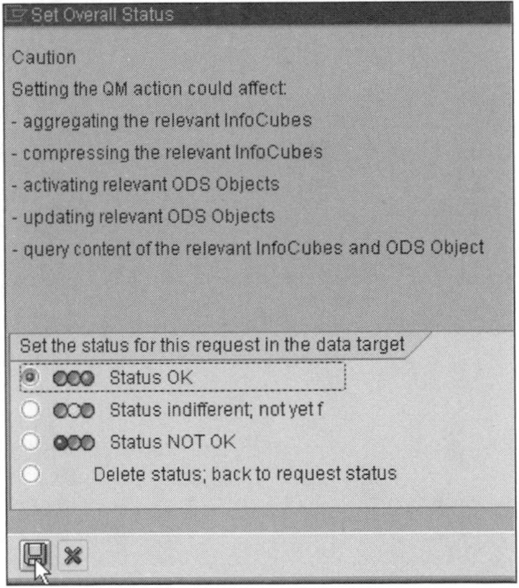

Set Overall Status
Caution
Setting the QM action could affect:
- aggregating the relevant InfoCubes
- compressing the relevant InfoCubes
- activating relevant ODS Objects
- updating relevant ODS Objects
- query content of the relevant InfoCubes and ODS Object
Set the status for this request in the data target
Status OK
Status indifferent; not yet f
Status NOT OK
Delete status; back to request status

SCREEN 9.27

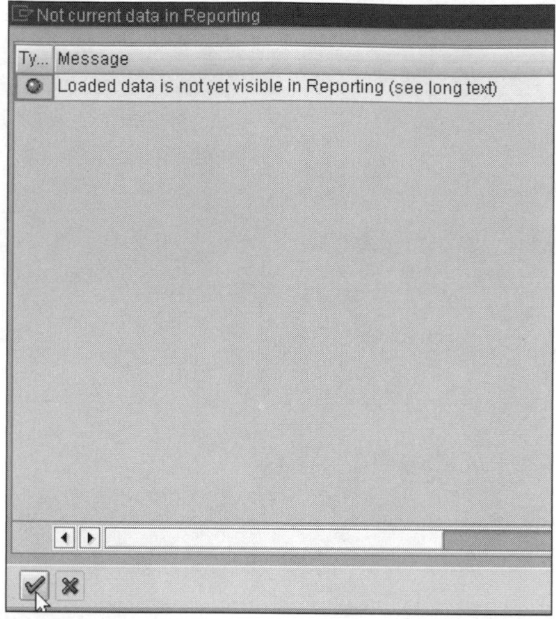

SCREEN 9.28

Step 7 Click ✔ to pass the message.

Note: The loaded data are available for reporting only after being activated, which takes place in Step 10.

Step 8 Click ✔ to pass the message.

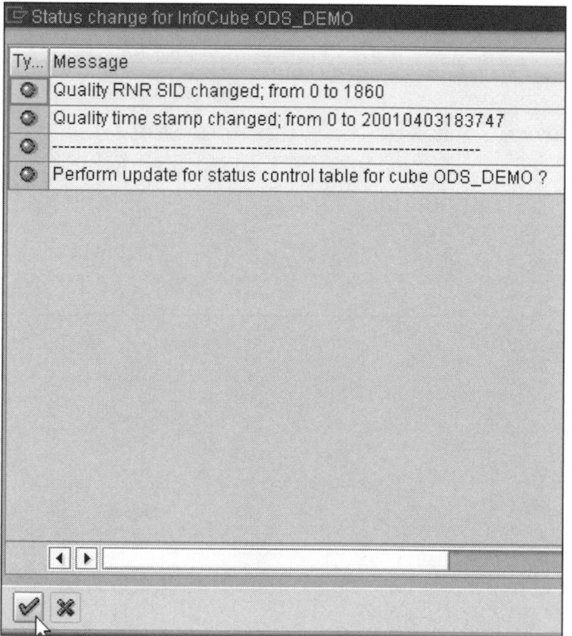

SCREEN 9.29

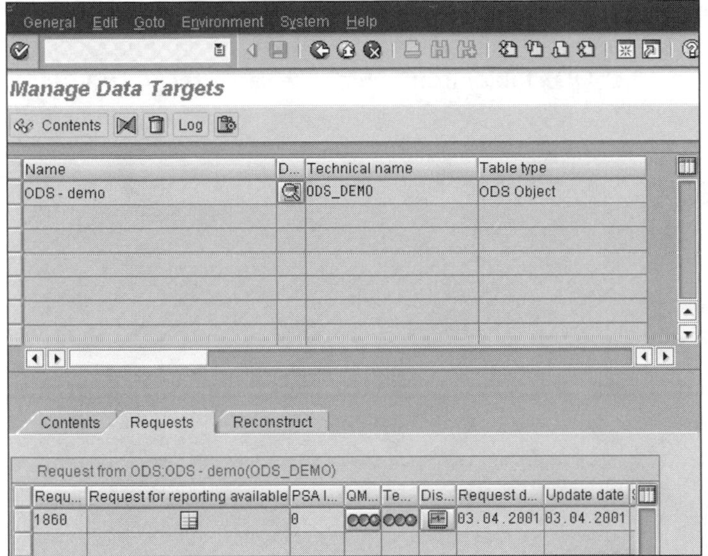

SCREEN 9.30

Step 9 The icon ▤ in the *Request for reporting available* column indicates that the loaded data are available for reporting, which is not correct. Screen 9.28 indicated that the data were not ready for reporting yet. As mentioned earlier, to make the data ready for reporting, we need to activate it.

Step 10 To make the data ready for reporting, right-click the ODS object, and then select *Activate data in ODS. . . .*

Note: We could have skipped Step 10 if we had selected the option *Activate ODS object data automatically* in Screen 9.3.

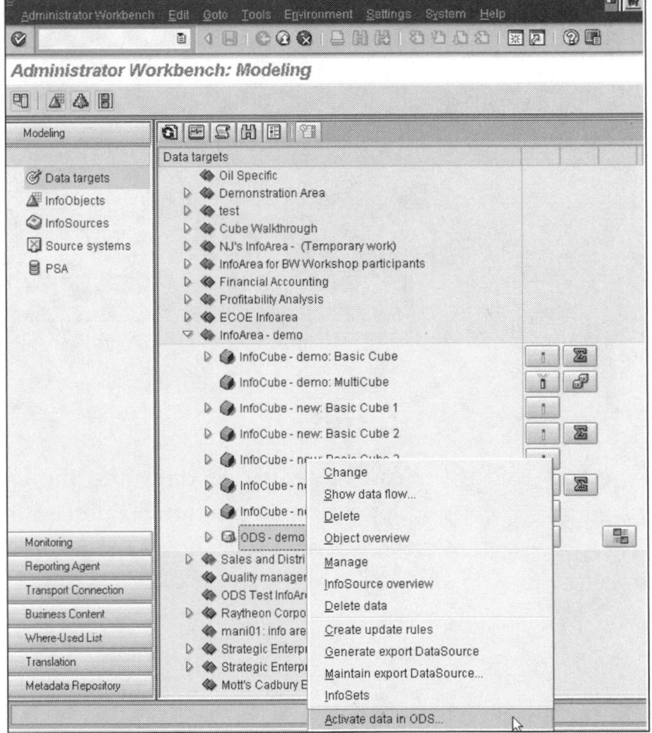

SCREEN 9.31

Step 11 Select the data load request, and then click Start. A background job is launched, which will move the data from one ODS table into another ODS table, from which we can display data using a BEx query.

SCREEN 9.32

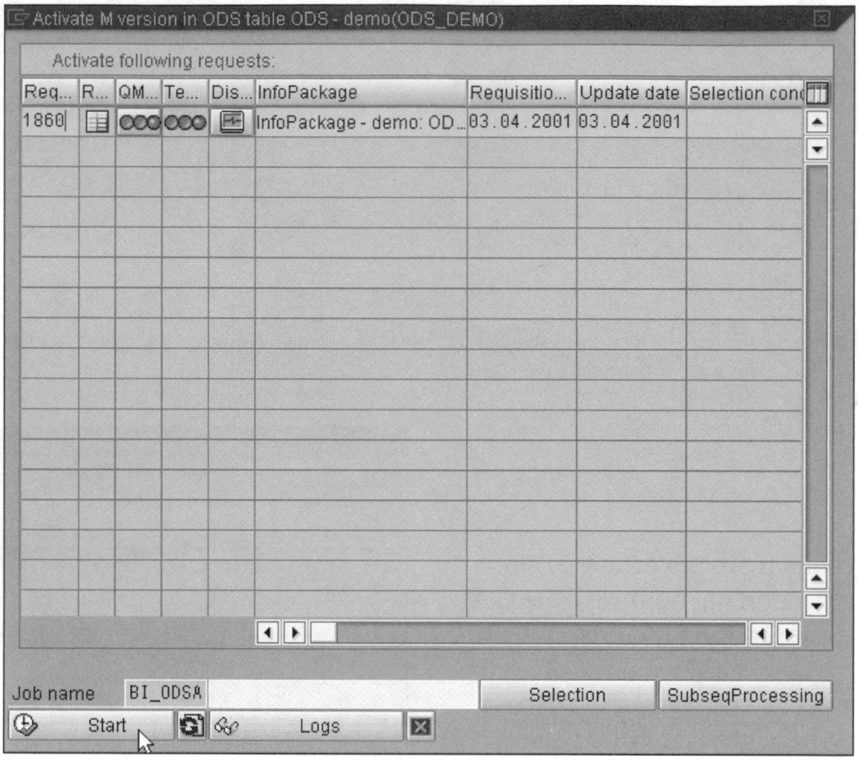

Activate M version in ODS table ODS - demo(ODS_DEMO)

Activate following requests:

Req...	R...	QM...	Te...	Dis...	InfoPackage	Requisitio...	Update date	Selection cond
1860					InfoPackage - demo: OD...	03.04.2001	03.04.2001	

Job name BI_ODSA Selection SubseqProcessing

Start Logs

Result

You have loaded data into the ODS object and made it ready for reporting. Repeating the Section 5.1 procedure, you can define a query as shown in Screen 9.33. Screen 9.34 shows the result of this query.

SCREEN 9.33

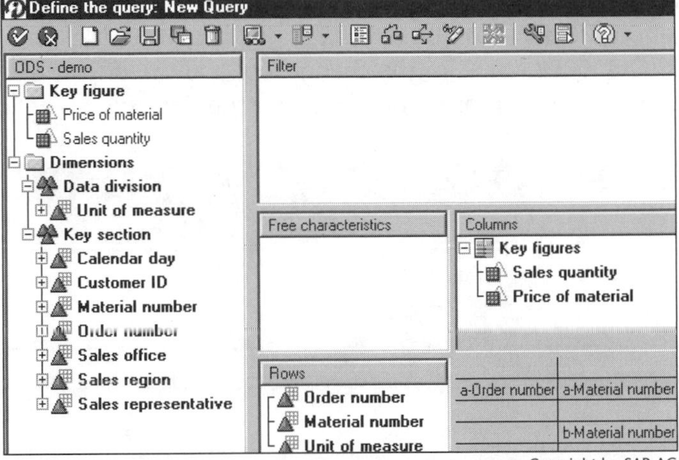

SCREEN 9.34

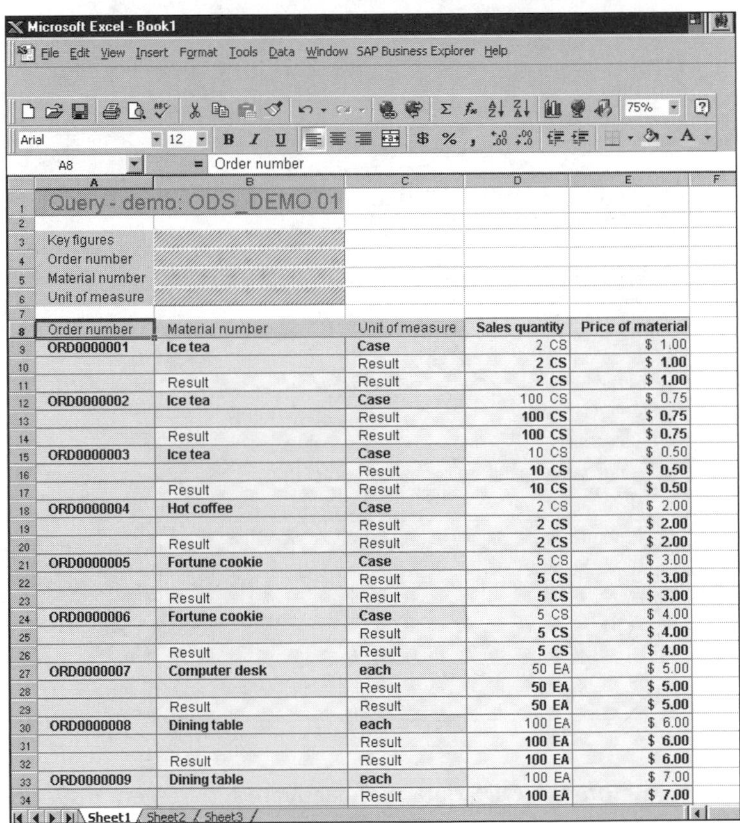

Order number	Material number	Unit of measure	Sales quantity	Price of material
ORD0000001	Ice tea	Case	2 CS	$ 1.00
		Result	2 CS	$ 1.00
	Result	Result	2 CS	$ 1.00
ORD0000002	Ice tea	Case	100 CS	$ 0.75
		Result	100 CS	$ 0.75
	Result	Result	100 CS	$ 0.75
ORD0000003	Ice tea	Case	10 CS	$ 0.50
		Result	10 CS	$ 0.50
	Result	Result	10 CS	$ 0.50
ORD0000004	Hot coffee	Case	2 CS	$ 2.00
		Result	2 CS	$ 2.00
	Result	Result	2 CS	$ 2.00
ORD0000005	Fortune cookie	Case	5 CS	$ 3.00
		Result	5 CS	$ 3.00
	Result	Result	5 CS	$ 3.00
ORD0000006	Fortune cookie	Case	5 CS	$ 4.00
		Result	5 CS	$ 4.00
	Result	Result	5 CS	$ 4.00
ORD0000007	Computer desk	each	50 EA	$ 5.00
		Result	50 EA	$ 5.00
	Result	Result	50 EA	$ 5.00
ORD0000008	Dining table	each	100 EA	$ 6.00
		Result	100 EA	$ 6.00
	Result	Result	100 EA	$ 6.00
ORD0000009	Dining table	each	100 EA	$ 7.00
		Result	100 EA	$ 7.00

Note: Each ODS object has three database tables. In our case, they are /BIC/AODS_DEMO10 for the new data, /BIC/AODS_DEMO00 for the active data, and /BIC/B0000842000 for the change log. You can display each table's contents by clicking the appropriate button under the *Contents* tab in Screen 9.35.

SCREEN 9.35

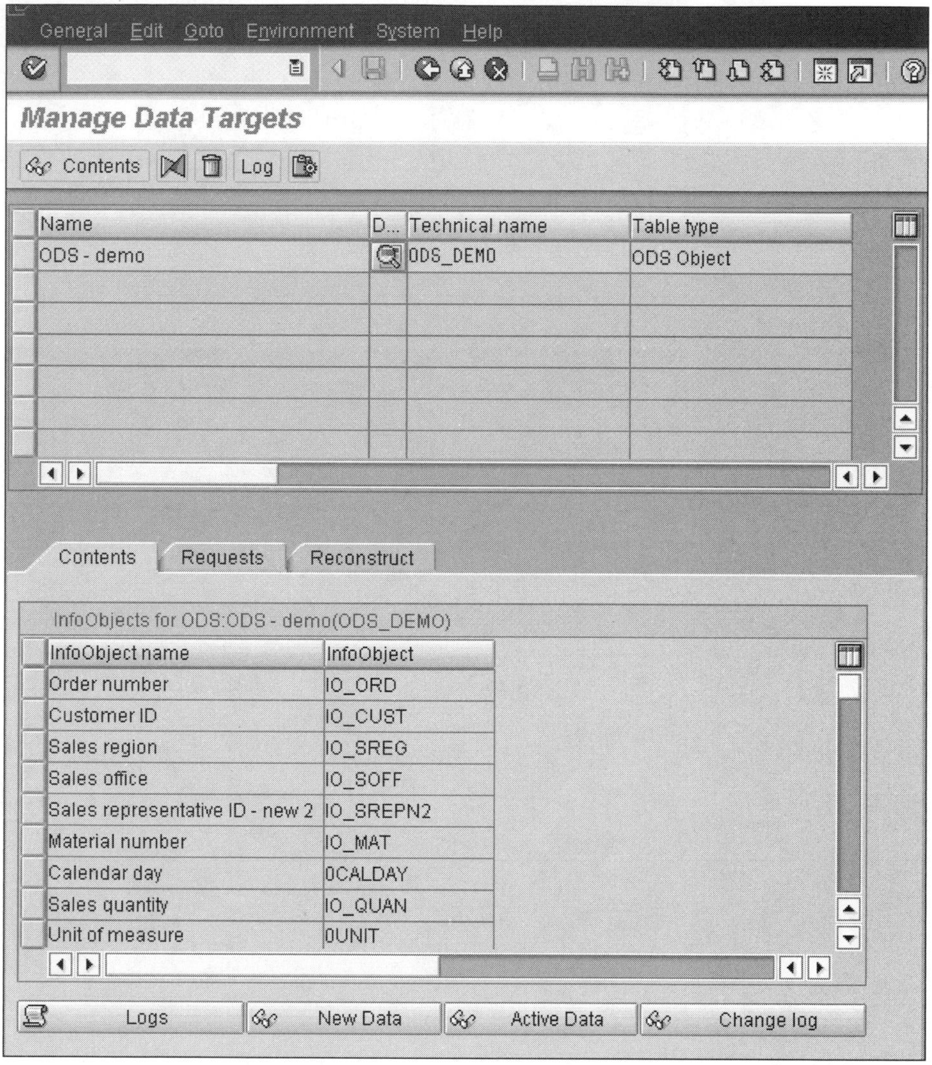

General Edit Goto Environment System Help

Manage Data Targets

Contents | Log

Name	D...	Technical name	Table type
ODS - demo		ODS_DEMO	ODS Object

Contents | Requests | Reconstruct

InfoObjects for ODS:ODS - demo(ODS_DEMO)

InfoObject name	InfoObject
Order number	IO_ORD
Customer ID	IO_CUST
Sales region	IO_SREG
Sales office	IO_SOFF
Sales representative ID - new 2	IO_SREPN2
Material number	IO_MAT
Calendar day	0CALDAY
Sales quantity	IO_QUAN
Unit of measure	0UNIT

Logs | New Data | Active Data | Change log

Before the ODS data were activated in Screen 9.30, only /BIC/AODS_DEMO10 had data. Clicking New Data, we can see its contents (Screen 9.36).

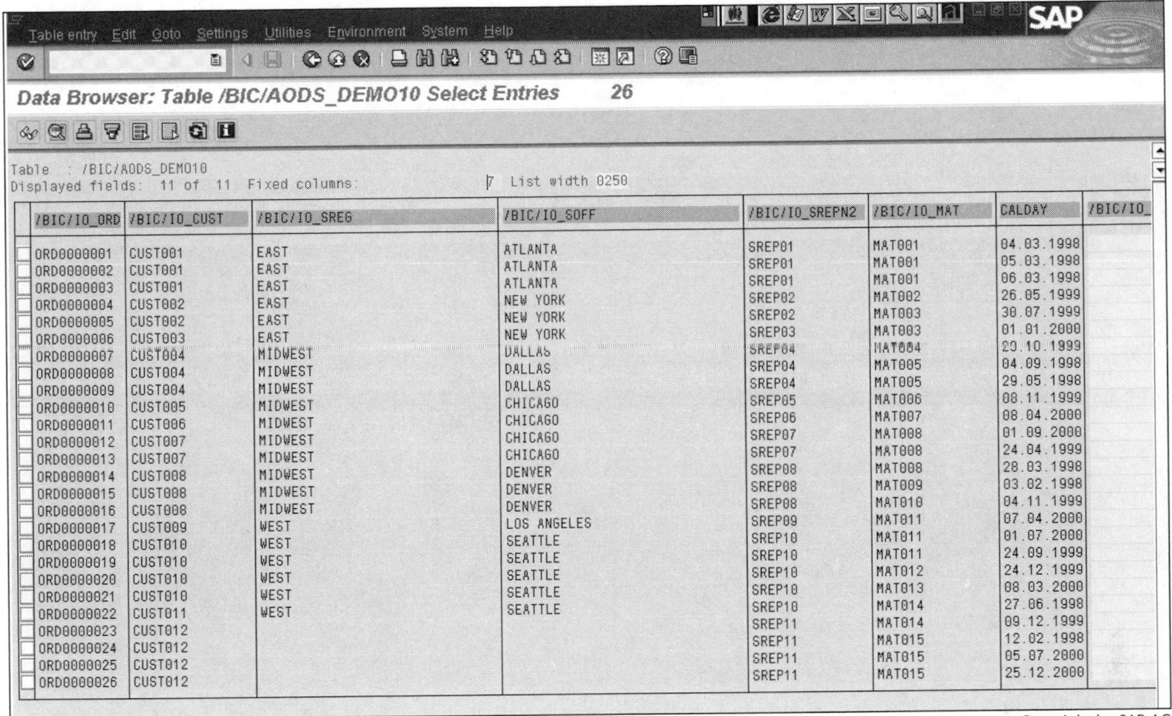

/BIC/IO_ORD	/BIC/IO_CUST	/BIC/IO_SREG	/BIC/IO_SOFF	/BIC/IO_SREPN2	/BIC/IO_MAT	CALDAY	/BIC/IO_
ORD0000001	CUST001	EAST	ATLANTA	SREP01	MAT001	04.03.1998	
ORD0000002	CUST001	EAST	ATLANTA	SREP01	MAT001	05.03.1998	
ORD0000003	CUST001	EAST	ATLANTA	SREP01	MAT001	06.03.1998	
ORD0000004	CUST002	EAST	NEW YORK	SREP02	MAT002	26.05.1999	
ORD0000005	CUST002	EAST	NEW YORK	SREP02	MAT003	30.07.1999	
ORD0000006	CUST003	EAST	NEW YORK	SREP03	MAT003	01.01.2000	
ORD0000007	CUST004	MIDWEST	DALLAS	SREP04	MAT004	20.10.1999	
ORD0000008	CUST004	MIDWEST	DALLAS	SREP04	MAT005	04.09.1998	
ORD0000009	CUST004	MIDWEST	DALLAS	SREP04	MAT005	29.05.1998	
ORD0000010	CUST005	MIDWEST	CHICAGO	SREP05	MAT006	08.11.1999	
ORD0000011	CUST006	MIDWEST	CHICAGO	SREP06	MAT007	08.04.2000	
ORD0000012	CUST007	MIDWEST	CHICAGO	SREP07	MAT008	01.09.2000	
ORD0000013	CUST007	MIDWEST	CHICAGO	SREP07	MAT008	24.04.1999	
ORD0000014	CUST008	MIDWEST	DENVER	SREP08	MAT008	28.03.1998	
ORD0000015	CUST008	MIDWEST	DENVER	SREP08	MAT009	03.02.1998	
ORD0000016	CUST008	MIDWEST	DENVER	SREP08	MAT010	04.11.1999	
ORD0000017	CUST009	WEST	LOS ANGELES	SREP09	MAT011	07.04.2000	
ORD0000018	CUST010	WEST	SEATTLE	SREP10	MAT011	01.07.2000	
ORD0000019	CUST010	WEST	SEATTLE	SREP10	MAT011	24.09.1999	
ORD0000020	CUST010	WEST	SEATTLE	SREP10	MAT012	24.12.1999	
ORD0000021	CUST010	WEST	SEATTLE	SREP10	MAT013	08.03.2000	
ORD0000022	CUST011	WEST	SEATTLE	SREP10	MAT014	27.06.1998	
ORD0000023	CUST012			SREP11	MAT014	09.12.1999	
ORD0000024	CUST012			SREP11	MAT015	12.02.1998	
ORD0000025	CUST012			SREP11	MAT015	05.07.2000	
ORD0000026	CUST012			SREP11	MAT015	25.12.2000	

SCREEN 9.36

After the ODS data were activated (see Screen 9.30), /BIC/AODS_DEMO10 no longer had data; the data had been moved into /BIC/B0000842000 and /BIC/AODS_DEMO00. Clicking [Change log] on Screen 9.35, we see the /BIC/B0000842000 contents (Screen 9.37). Clicking [Active Data], we see the /BIC/AODS_DEMO00 contents (Screen 9.38).

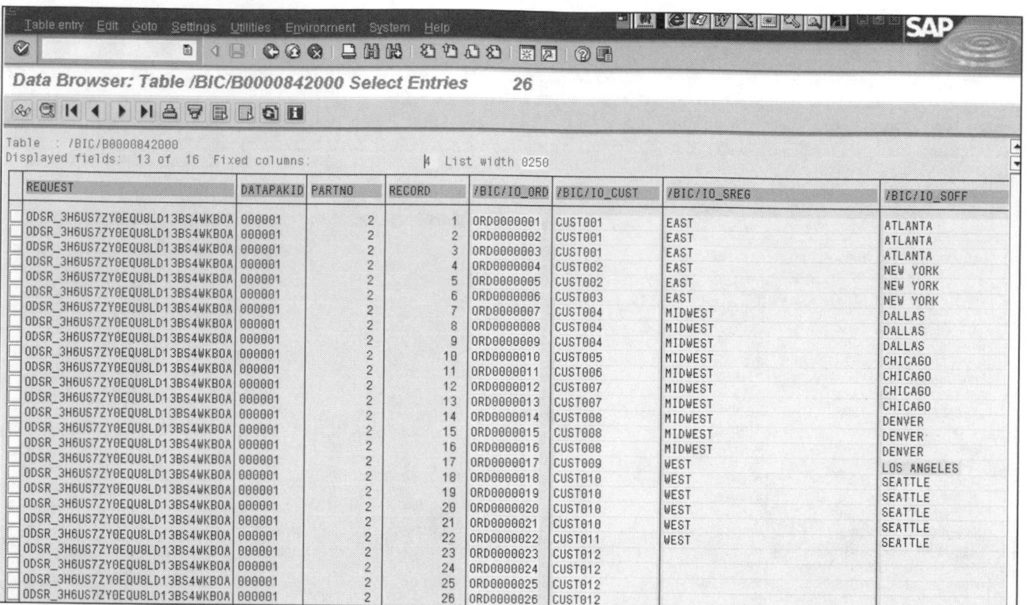

Table entry Edit Goto Settings Utilities Environment System Help

Data Browser: Table /BIC/B0000842000 Select Entries 26

Table : /BIC/B0000842000
Displayed fields: 13 of 16 Fixed columns: 4 List width 0250

REQUEST	DATAPAKID	PARTNO	RECORD	/BIC/IO_ORD	/BIC/IO_CUST	/BIC/IO_SREG	/BIC/IO_SOFF
ODSR_3H6US7ZY0EQU8LD13BS4WKBOA	000001	2	1	ORD0000001	CUST001	EAST	ATLANTA
ODSR_3H6US7ZY0EQU8LD13BS4WKBOA	000001	2	2	ORD0000002	CUST001	EAST	ATLANTA
ODSR_3H6US7ZY0EQU8LD13BS4WKBOA	000001	2	3	ORD0000003	CUST001	EAST	ATLANTA
ODSR_3H6US7ZY0EQU8LD13BS4WKBOA	000001	2	4	ORD0000004	CUST002	EAST	NEW YORK
ODSR_3H6US7ZY0EQU8LD13BS4WKBOA	000001	2	5	ORD0000005	CUST002	EAST	NEW YORK
ODSR_3H6US7ZY0EQU8LD13BS4WKBOA	000001	2	6	ORD0000006	CUST003	EAST	NEW YORK
ODSR_3H6US7ZY0EQU8LD13BS4WKBOA	000001	2	7	ORD0000007	CUST004	MIDWEST	DALLAS
ODSR_3H6US7ZY0EQU8LD13BS4WKBOA	000001	2	8	ORD0000008	CUST004	MIDWEST	DALLAS
ODSR_3H6US7ZY0EQU8LD13BS4WKBOA	000001	2	9	ORD0000009	CUST004	MIDWEST	DALLAS
ODSR_3H6US7ZY0EQU8LD13BS4WKBOA	000001	2	10	ORD0000010	CUST005	MIDWEST	CHICAGO
ODSR_3H6US7ZY0EQU8LD13BS4WKBOA	000001	2	11	ORD0000011	CUST006	MIDWEST	CHICAGO
ODSR_3H6US7ZY0EQU8LD13BS4WKBOA	000001	2	12	ORD0000012	CUST007	MIDWEST	CHICAGO
ODSR_3H6US7ZY0EQU8LD13BS4WKBOA	000001	2	13	ORD0000013	CUST007	MIDWEST	CHICAGO
ODSR_3H6US7ZY0EQU8LD13BS4WKBOA	000001	2	14	ORD0000014	CUST008	MIDWEST	DENVER
ODSR_3H6US7ZY0EQU8LD13BS4WKBOA	000001	2	15	ORD0000015	CUST008	MIDWEST	DENVER
ODSR_3H6US7ZY0EQU8LD13BS4WKBOA	000001	2	16	ORD0000016	CUST008	MIDWEST	DENVER
ODSR_3H6US7ZY0EQU8LD13BS4WKBOA	000001	2	17	ORD0000017	CUST009	WEST	LOS ANGELES
ODSR_3H6US7ZY0EQU8LD13BS4WKBOA	000001	2	18	ORD0000018	CUST010	WEST	SEATTLE
ODSR_3H6US7ZY0EQU8LD13BS4WKBOA	000001	2	19	ORD0000019	CUST010	WEST	SEATTLE
ODSR_3H6US7ZY0EQU8LD13BS4WKBOA	000001	2	20	ORD0000020	CUST010	WEST	SEATTLE
ODSR_3H6US7ZY0EQU8LD13BS4WKBOA	000001	2	21	ORD0000021	CUST010	WEST	SEATTLE
ODSR_3H6US7ZY0EQU8LD13BS4WKBOA	000001	2	22	ORD0000022	CUST011	WEST	SEATTLE
ODSR_3H6US7ZY0EQU8LD13BS4WKBOA	000001	2	23	ORD0000023	CUST012		
ODSR_3H6US7ZY0EQU8LD13BS4WKBOA	000001	2	24	ORD0000024	CUST012		
ODSR_3H6US7ZY0EQU8LD13BS4WKBOA	000001	2	25	ORD0000025	CUST012		
ODSR_3H6US7ZY0EQU8LD13BS4WKBOA	000001	2	26	ORD0000026	CUST012		

SCREEN 9.37

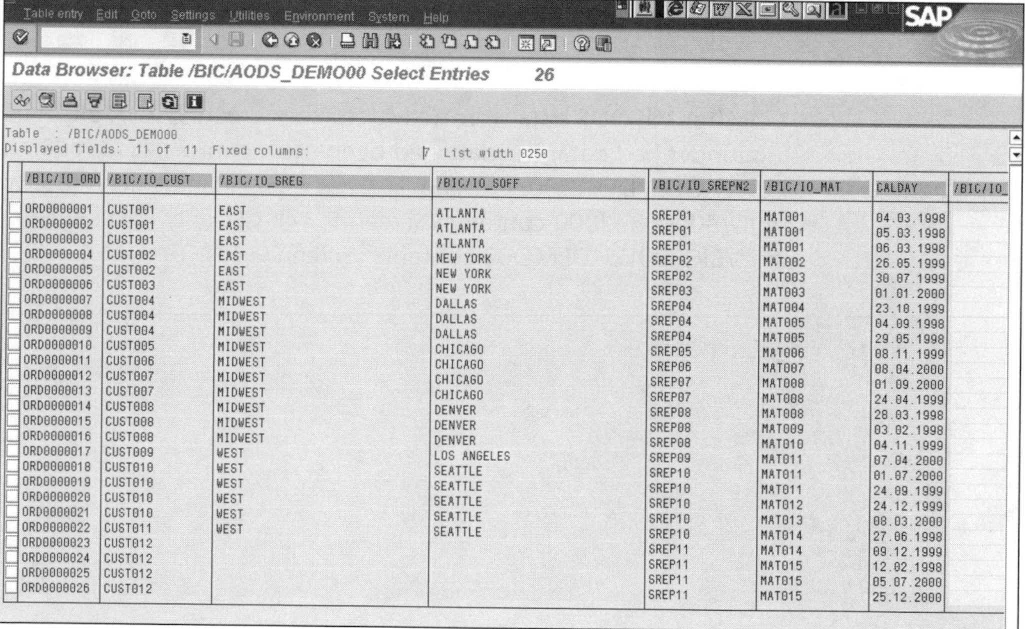

Table entry Edit Goto Settings Utilities Environment System Help

Data Browser: Table /BIC/AODS_DEMO00 Select Entries 26

Table : /BIC/AODS_DEMO00
Displayed fields: 11 of 11 Fixed columns: 7 List width 0250

/BIC/IO_ORD	/BIC/IO_CUST	/BIC/IO_SREG	/BIC/IO_SOFF	/BIC/IO_SREPN2	/BIC/IO_MAT	CALDAY	/BIC/IO_
ORD0000001	CUST001	EAST	ATLANTA	SREP01	MAT001	04.03.1998	
ORD0000002	CUST001	EAST	ATLANTA	SREP01	MAT001	05.03.1998	
ORD0000003	CUST001	EAST	ATLANTA	SREP01	MAT001	06.03.1998	
ORD0000004	CUST002	EAST	NEW YORK	SREP02	MAT002	26.05.1999	
ORD0000005	CUST002	EAST	NEW YORK	SREP02	MAT003	30.07.1999	
ORD0000006	CUST003	EAST	NEW YORK	SREP03	MAT003	01.01.2000	
ORD0000007	CUST004	MIDWEST	DALLAS	SREP04	MAT004	23.10.1999	
ORD0000008	CUST004	MIDWEST	DALLAS	SREP04	MAT005	04.09.1998	
ORD0000009	CUST004	MIDWEST	DALLAS	SREP04	MAT005	29.05.1998	
ORD0000010	CUST005	MIDWEST	CHICAGO	SREP05	MAT006	08.11.1999	
ORD0000011	CUST006	MIDWEST	CHICAGO	SREP06	MAT007	08.04.2000	
ORD0000012	CUST007	MIDWEST	CHICAGO	SREP07	MAT008	01.09.2000	
ORD0000013	CUST007	MIDWEST	CHICAGO	SREP07	MAT008	24.04.1999	
ORD0000014	CUST008	MIDWEST	DENVER	SREP08	MAT008	28.03.1998	
ORD0000015	CUST008	MIDWEST	DENVER	SREP08	MAT009	03.02.1998	
ORD0000016	CUST008	MIDWEST	DENVER	SREP08	MAT010	04.11.1999	
ORD0000017	CUST009	WEST	LOS ANGELES	SREP09	MAT011	07.04.2000	
ORD0000018	CUST010	WEST	SEATTLE	SREP10	MAT011	01.07.2000	
ORD0000019	CUST010	WEST	SEATTLE	SREP10	MAT011	24.09.1999	
ORD0000020	CUST010	WEST	SEATTLE	SREP10	MAT012	24.12.1999	
ORD0000021	CUST010	WEST	SEATTLE	SREP10	MAT013	08.03.2000	
ORD0000022	CUST011	WEST	SEATTLE	SREP10	MAT014	27.06.1998	
ORD0000023	CUST012			SREP11	MAT014	09.12.1999	
ORD0000024	CUST012			SREP11	MAT015	12.02.1998	
ORD0000025	CUST012			SREP11	MAT015	05.07.2000	
ORD0000026	CUST012			SREP11	MAT015	25.12.2000	

SCREEN 9.38

In BW release 3.0A, an ODS object will have an active table and a change log. The data are loaded directly to the change log and arrive in the active table when it becomes activated. This change shortens data loading time and makes data available for reporting more quickly.

9.4 Loading Data into the InfoCube

After loading and activating the ODS data, we can aggregate the ODS data and move the aggregated data into the InfoCube defined in Screen 9.9.

Note: We could have skipped this step if we had selected the option *Update data targets from ODS object automatically* in Screen 9.3.

Work Instructions

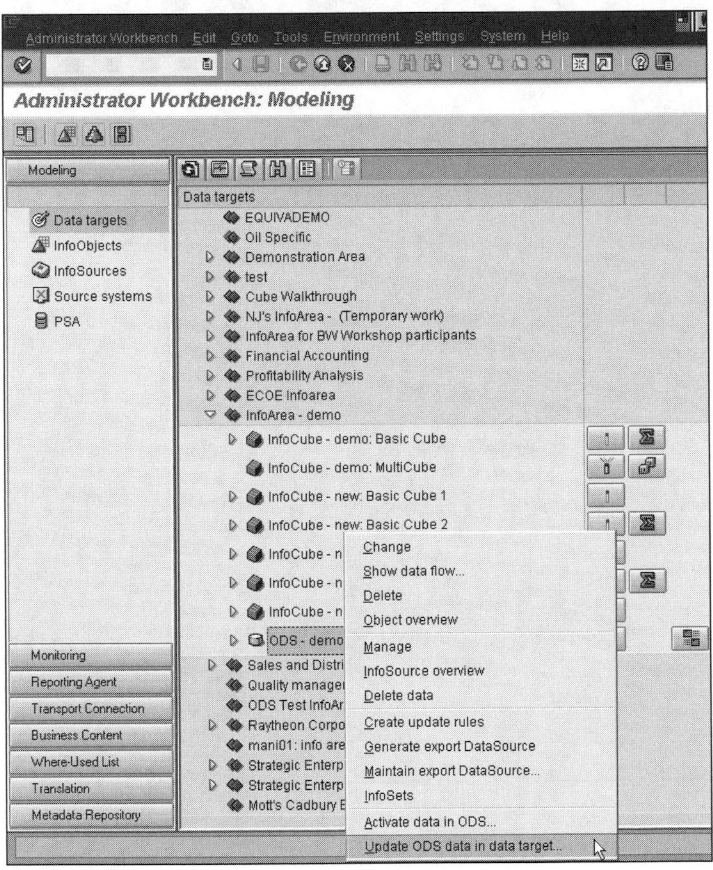

Step 1 To load the ODS data, right-click *ODS – demo,* and then select *Update ODS data in data target. . . .*

SCREEN 9.39

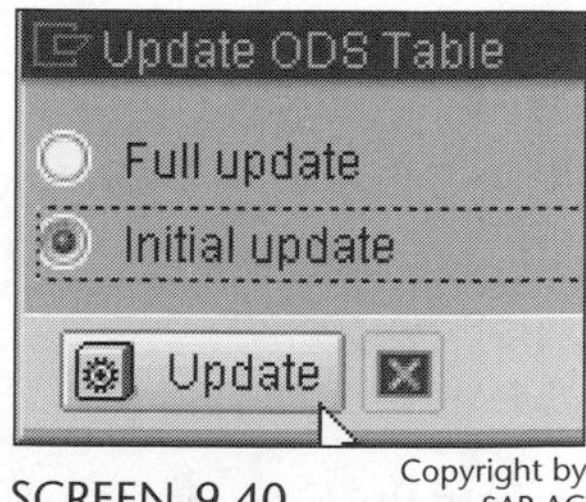

SCREEN 9.40

Step 2 Select the *Initial update* option. In the next section, we will see how to do delta data loads.

Step 3 BW opens an InfoPackage. Under the *Processing* tab, in the *Update data . . .* box, BW has selected *Data targets only* because it is the only choice allowed.

SCREEN 9.41

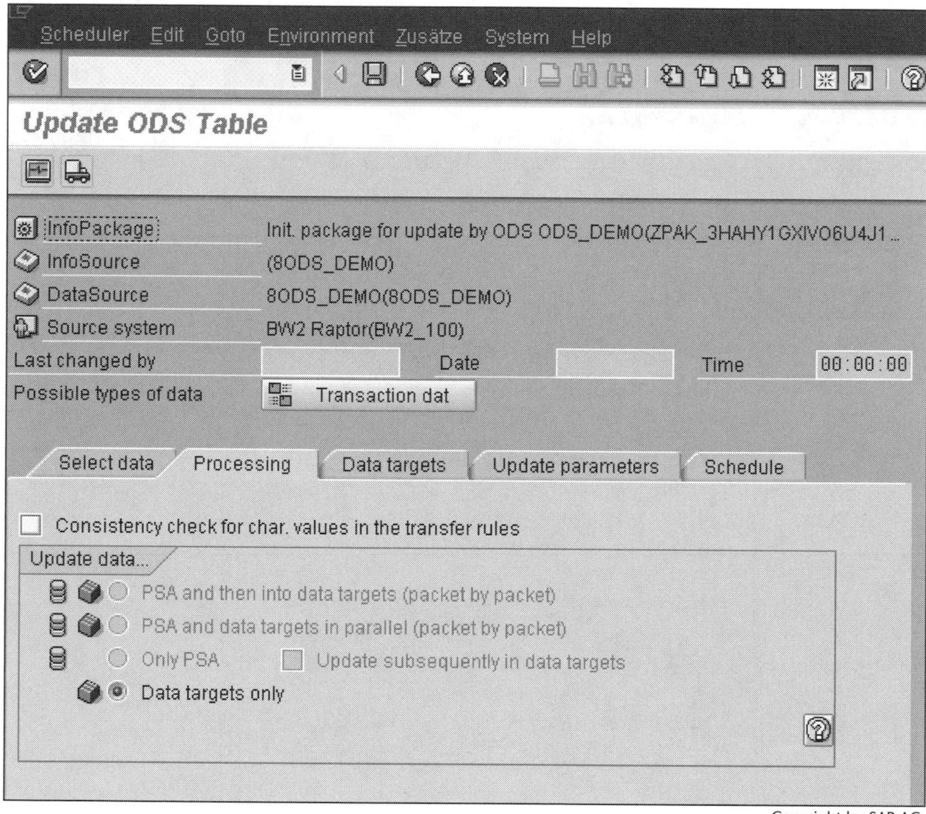

Step 4 Because we selected the *Initial update* option in Screen 9.40, the InfoPackage is set to *Initialize delta process*. Start the data load process from the *Schedule* tab.

SCREEN 9.42

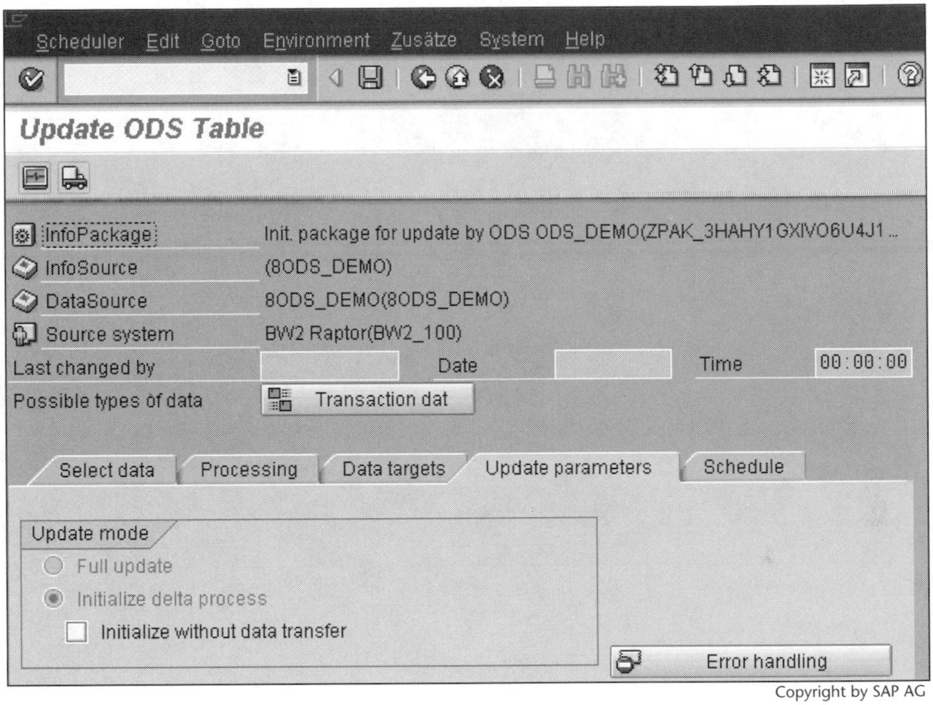

Scheduler	Edit	Goto	Environment	Zusätze	System	Help

Update ODS Table

InfoPackage	Init. package for update by ODS ODS_DEMO(ZPAK_3HAHY1GXIVO6U4J1 ...			
InfoSource	(8ODS_DEMO)			
DataSource	8ODS_DEMO(8ODS_DEMO)			
Source system	BW2 Raptor(BW2_100)			
Last changed by		Date	Time	00:00:00
Possible types of data	Transaction dat			

Select data | Processing | Data targets | Update parameters | Schedule

Update mode
- ○ Full update
- ◉ Initialize delta process
- ☐ Initialize without data transfer

Error handling

Result

The data have been loaded into the InfoCube. Screen 9.43 shows the fact table's contents.

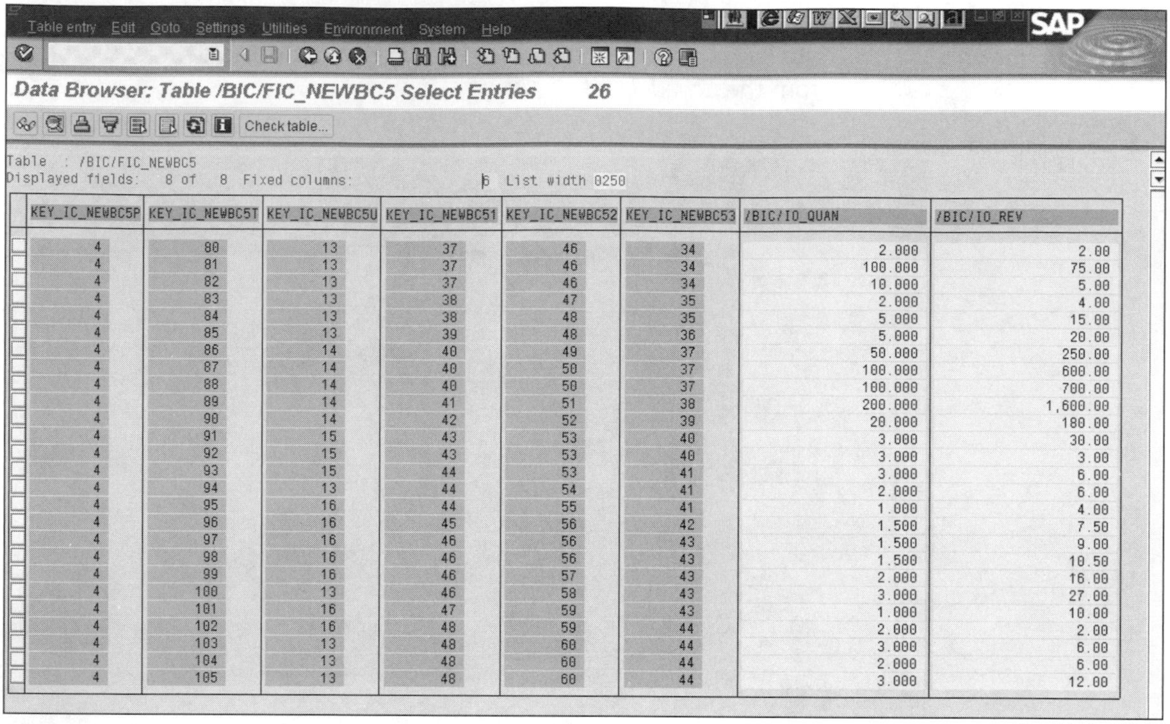

Table entry Edit Goto Settings Utilities Environment System Help

Data Browser: Table /BIC/FIC_NEWBC5 Select Entries 26

Check table...

Table : /BIC/FIC_NEWBC5
Displayed fields: 8 of 8 Fixed columns: 6 List width 0250

KEY_IC_NEWBC5P	KEY_IC_NEWBC5T	KEY_IC_NEWBC5U	KEY_IC_NEWBC51	KEY_IC_NEWBC52	KEY_IC_NEWBC53	/BIC/IO_QUAN	/BIC/IO_REV
4	80	13	37	46	34	2.000	2.00
4	81	13	37	46	34	100.000	75.00
4	82	13	37	46	34	10.000	5.00
4	83	13	38	47	35	2.000	4.00
4	84	13	38	48	35	5.000	15.00
4	85	13	39	48	36	5.000	20.00
4	86	14	40	49	37	50.000	250.00
4	87	14	40	50	37	100.000	600.00
4	88	14	40	50	37	100.000	700.00
4	89	14	41	51	38	200.000	1,600.00
4	90	14	42	52	39	20.000	180.00
4	91	15	43	53	40	3.000	30.00
4	92	15	43	53	40	3.000	3.00
4	93	15	44	53	41	3.000	6.00
4	94	13	44	54	41	2.000	6.00
4	95	16	44	55	41	1.000	4.00
4	96	16	45	56	42	1.500	7.50
4	97	16	46	56	43	1.500	9.00
4	98	16	46	56	43	1.500	10.50
4	99	16	46	57	43	2.000	16.00
4	100	13	46	58	43	3.000	27.00
4	101	16	47	59	43	1.000	10.00
4	102	16	48	59	44	2.000	2.00
4	103	13	48	60	44	3.000	6.00
4	104	13	48	60	44	2.000	6.00
4	105	13	48	60	44	3.000	12.00

SCREEN 9.43

9.5 Using 0RECORDMODE for Delta Load

In Sections 9.3 and 9.4, we loaded data first into the ODS object, and then into the InfoCube. The data in the InfoCube came from an initial loading process (Screen 9.40). Now let's see how ODS uses the characteristic 0RECORDMODE values—*X*, *D*, and *R*—to control consequent delta loading processes.

You use 0RECORDMODE value *X* to mark rows to be skipped in the delta data load. You use *D* and *R* to delete or remove rows, respectively, from the active ODS table if the rows can be identified by the table primary key. Otherwise, *D* and *R* work just like *X*—they do not affect either the change log or the active data table.

Now let's illustrate how the ODS delta load works.

Table 9.1 lists the first four rows of the original sales data from Table 7.1. What happens to the data in the ODS object and the InfoCube after loading the Table 9.2 data into them? Table 9.2 has an extra column that contains the 0RECORDMODE values. Also, the sales quantity is doubled.

TABLE 9.1 FIRST FOUR ROWS OF THE ORIGINAL DATA BEFORE CHANGES

IO_ORD	IO_CUST	IO_SREG	IO_SOFF	IO_SREP	IO_MAT	IO_QUAN	0UNIT	IO_PRC	0CALDAY
ORD0000001	CUST001	EAST	ATLANTA	SREP01	MAT001	**2**	CS	1	19980304
ORD0000002	CUST001	EAST	ATLANTA	SREP01	MAT001	**100**	CS	0.75	19980305
ORD0000003	CUST001	EAST	ATLANTA	SREP01	MAT001	**10**	CS	0.5	19980306
ORD0000004	CUST002	EAST	NEW YORK	SREP02	MAT002	**2**	CS	2	19990526

TABLE 9.2 FIRST FOUR ROWS OF THE DATA AFTER CHANGES

IO_ORD	IO_CUST	IO_SREG	IO_SOFF	IO_SREP	IO_MAT	IO_QUAN	0UNIT	IO_PRC	0CALDAY	0RECORD-MODE
ORD0000001	CUST001	EAST	ATLANTA	SREP01	MAT001	**4**	CS	1	19980304	
ORD0000002	CUST001	EAST	ATLANTA	SREP01	MAT001	**200**	CS	0.75	19980305	**X**
ORD0000003	CUST001	EAST	ATLANTA	SREP01	MAT001	**20**	CS	0.5	19980306	**D**
ORD0000004	CUST002	EAST	NEW YORK	SREP02	MAT002	**4**	CS	2	19990526	**R**

Repeating the procedure outlined in Section 9.3 for loading data into the ODS object, we see that the PSA data in Screen 9.44 match the data in Table 9.2. This result is expected.

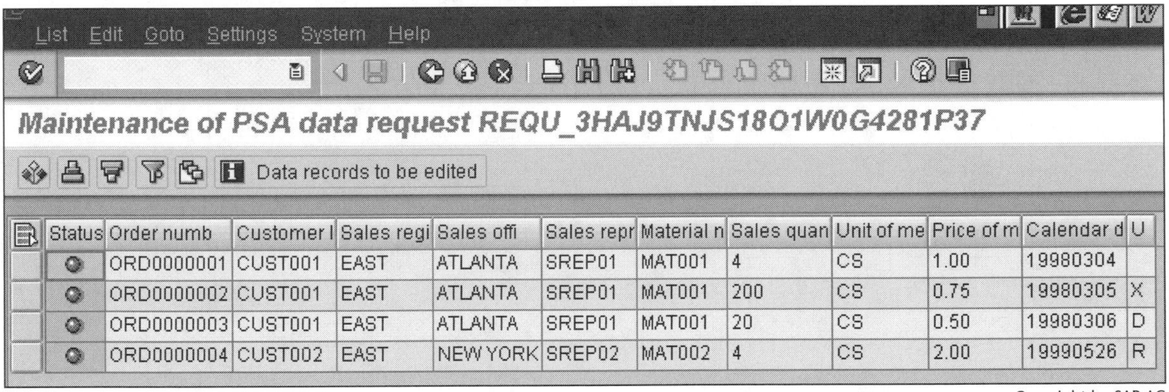

List Edit Goto Settings System Help

Maintenance of PSA data request REQU_3HAJ9TNJS18O1W0G4281P37

Data records to be edited

Status	Order numb	Customer I	Sales regi	Sales offi	Sales repr	Material n	Sales quan	Unit of me	Price of m	Calendar d	U
	ORD0000001	CUST001	EAST	ATLANTA	SREP01	MAT001	4	CS	1.00	19980304	
	ORD0000002	CUST001	EAST	ATLANTA	SREP01	MAT001	200	CS	0.75	19980305	X
	ORD0000003	CUST001	EAST	ATLANTA	SREP01	MAT001	20	CS	0.50	19980306	D
	ORD0000004	CUST002	EAST	NEW YORK	SREP02	MAT002	4	CS	2.00	19990526	R

SCREEN 9.44

After loading the PSA data into the ODS object, the table /BIC/AODS_DEMO10 contains the new data (Screen 9.45). The second row of Table 9.2 does not appear here, which indicates that BW detected the value *X* in the 0RECORDMODE column and then skipped the second row.

Table entry Edit Goto Settings Utilities Environment System Help

Data Browser: Table /BIC/AODS_DEMO10 Select Entries 3

Table : /BIC/AODS_DEMO10
List width 0250

/BIC/IO_SOFF	/BIC/IO_SREPN2	/BIC/IO_MAT	CALDAY	/BIC/IO_QUAN	UNIT	/BIC/IO_PRC	RECORDMODE
ATLANTA	SREP01	MAT001	04.03.1998	4.000	CS	1.00	
ATLANTA	SREP01	MAT001	06.03.1998	20.000	CS	0.50	D
NEW YORK	SREP02	MAT002	26.05.1999	4.000	CS	2.00	R

SCREEN 9.45

After activating the ODS data, Screen 9.46 shows that four rows are appended to the end of the change log table, /BIC/B0000842000. The first of these rows matches the first row in Table 9.2. The remaining three rows match the first, third, and fourth rows in the table /BIC/B0000842000, except that "-" is added to the /BIC/IO_QUAN value.

Table entry Edit Goto Settings Utilities Environment System Help

Data Browser: Table /BIC/B0000842000 Select Entries 30

Table : /BIC/B0000842000

CUST	/BIC/IO_SREG	/BIC/IO_SOFF	/BIC/IO_SREPN2	/BIC/IO_MAT	CALDAY	/BIC/IO_QUAN	UNIT
	EAST	ATLANTA	SREP01	MAT001	04.03.1998	2.000	CS
	EAST	ATLANTA	SREP01	MAT001	05.03.1998	100.000	CS
	EAST	ATLANTA	SREP01	MAT001	06.03.1998	10.000	CS
	EAST	NEW YORK	SREP02	MAT002	26.05.1999	2.000	CS
	EAST	NEW YORK	SREP02	MAT003	30.07.1999	5.000	CS
	EAST	NEW YORK	SREP03	MAT003	01.01.2000	5.000	CS
	MIDWEST	DALLAS	SREP04	MAT004	23.10.1999	50.000	EA
	MIDWEST	DALLAS	SREP04	MAT005	04.09.1998	100.000	EA
	MIDWEST	DALLAS	SREP04	MAT005	29.05.1998	100.000	EA
	MIDWEST	CHICAGO	SREP05	MAT006	08.11.1999	200.000	EA
	MIDWEST	CHICAGO	SREP06	MAT007	08.04.2000	20.000	EA
	MIDWEST	CHICAGO	SREP07	MAT008	01.09.2000	3.000	DZ
	MIDWEST	CHICAGO	SREP07	MAT008	24.04.1999	3.000	DZ
	MIDWEST	DENVER	SREP08	MAT008	28.03.1998	3.000	DZ
	MIDWEST	DENVER	SREP08	MAT009	03.02.1998	2.000	CS
	MIDWEST	DENVER	SREP08	MAT010	04.11.1999	1.000	LB
	WEST	LOS ANGELES	SREP09	MAT011	07.04.2000	1.500	LB
	WEST	SEATTLE	SREP10	MAT011	01.07.2000	1.500	LB
	WEST	SEATTLE	SREP10	MAT011	24.09.1999	1.500	LB
	WEST	SEATTLE	SREP10	MAT012	24.12.1999	2.000	LB
	WEST	SEATTLE	SREP10	MAT013	08.03.2000	3.000	CS
	WEST	SEATTLE	SREP10	MAT014	27.06.1998	1.000	LB
			SREP11	MAT014	09.12.1999	2.000	LB
			SREP11	MAT015	12.02.1998	3.000	CS
			SREP11	MAT015	05.07.2000	2.000	CS
			SREP11	MAT015	25.12.2000	3.000	CS
	EAST	ATLANTA	SREP01	MAT001	04.03.1998	4.000	CS
	EAST	ATLANTA	SREP01	MAT001	04.03.1998	2.000-	CS
	EAST	ATLANTA	SREP01	MAT001	06.03.1998	10.000-	CS
	EAST	NEW YORK	SREP02	MAT002	26.05.1999	2.000-	CS

SCREEN 9.46

Screen 9.47 shows the active data in the table /BIC/AODS_DEMO00. This result comes from compressing the change log; that is, the "-" sign actually makes the number on its left negative, and the result of the compression deleted the first, third, fourth, and last three rows from the change log.

LOS ANGELES
Table entry Edit Goto Settings Utilities Environment System Help

Data Browser: Table /BIC/AODS_DEMO00 Select Entries 24

Table : /BIC/AODS_DEMO00
List width 0250

/BIC/IO_SOFF	/BIC/IO_SREPN2	/BIC/IO_MAT	CALDAY	/BIC/IO_QUAN	UNIT	/BIC/IO_PRC	RECORDMODE
ATLANTA	SREP01	MAT001	04.03.1998	4.000	CS	1.00	
ATLANTA	SREP01	MAT001	05.03.1998	100.000	CS	0.75	
NEW YORK	SREP02	MAT003	30.07.1999	5.000	CS	3.00	
NEW YORK	SREP03	MAT003	01.01.2000	5.000	CS	4.00	
DALLAS	SREP04	MAT004	23.10.1999	50.000	EA	5.00	
DALLAS	SREP04	MAT005	04.09.1998	100.000	EA	6.00	
DALLAS	SREP04	MAT005	29.05.1998	100.000	EA	7.00	
CHICAGO	SREP05	MAT006	08.11.1999	200.000	EA	8.00	
CHICAGO	SREP06	MAT007	08.04.2000	20.000	EA	9.00	
CHICAGO	SREP07	MAT008	01.09.2000	3.000	DZ	10.00	
CHICAGO	SREP07	MAT008	24.04.1999	3.000	DZ	1.00	
DENVER	SREP08	MAT008	28.03.1998	3.000	DZ	2.00	
DENVER	SREP08	MAT009	03.02.1998	2.000	CS	3.00	
DENVER	SREP08	MAT010	04.11.1999	1.000	LB	4.00	
LOS ANGELES	SREP09	MAT011	07.04.2000	1.500	LB	5.00	
SEATTLE	SREP10	MAT011	01.07.2000	1.500	LB	6.00	
SEATTLE	SREP10	MAT011	24.09.1999	1.500	LB	7.00	
SEATTLE	SREP10	MAT012	24.12.1999	2.000	LB	8.00	
SEATTLE	SREP10	MAT013	08.03.2000	3.000	CS	9.00	
SEATTLE	SREP10	MAT014	27.06.1998	1.000	LB	10.00	
	SREP11	MAT014	09.12.1999	2.000	LB	1.00	
	SREP11	MAT015	12.02.1998	3.000	CS	2.00	
	SREP11	MAT015	05.07.2000	2.000	CS	3.00	
	SREP11	MAT015	25.12.2000	3.000	CS	4.00	

SCREEN 9.47

Now we load the ODS data into the InfoCube as shown in Screen 9.39. This time we select the *Delta Update* option (Screen 9.48).

SCREEN 9.48

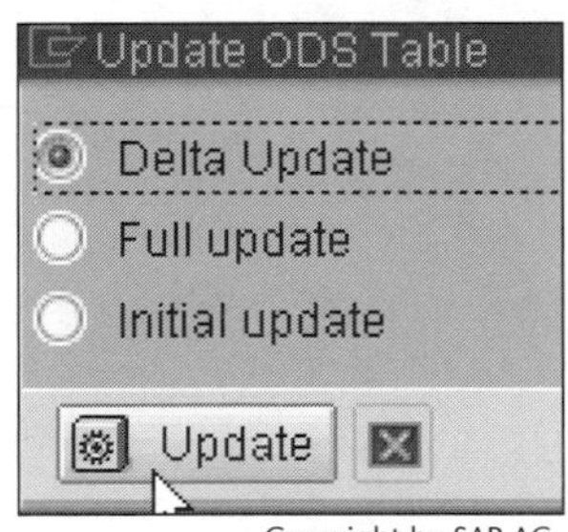

BW makes the corresponding selection automatically in the InfoPackage definition (Screen 9.49).

SCREEN 9.49

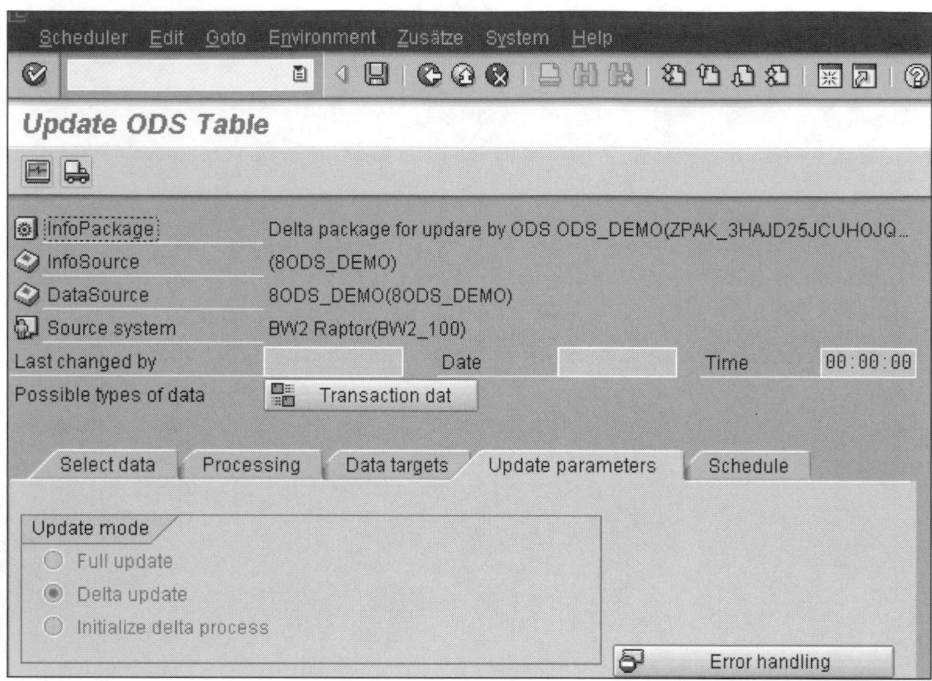

After we launch the delta load process, changes to the data appear in the InfoCube fact table (Screen 9.50). Three new rows are added as another data load request. The values in the three new rows are obtained by compressing the last four rows in Screen 9.46. The "-" sign has the same meaning—it makes the number on its left negative.

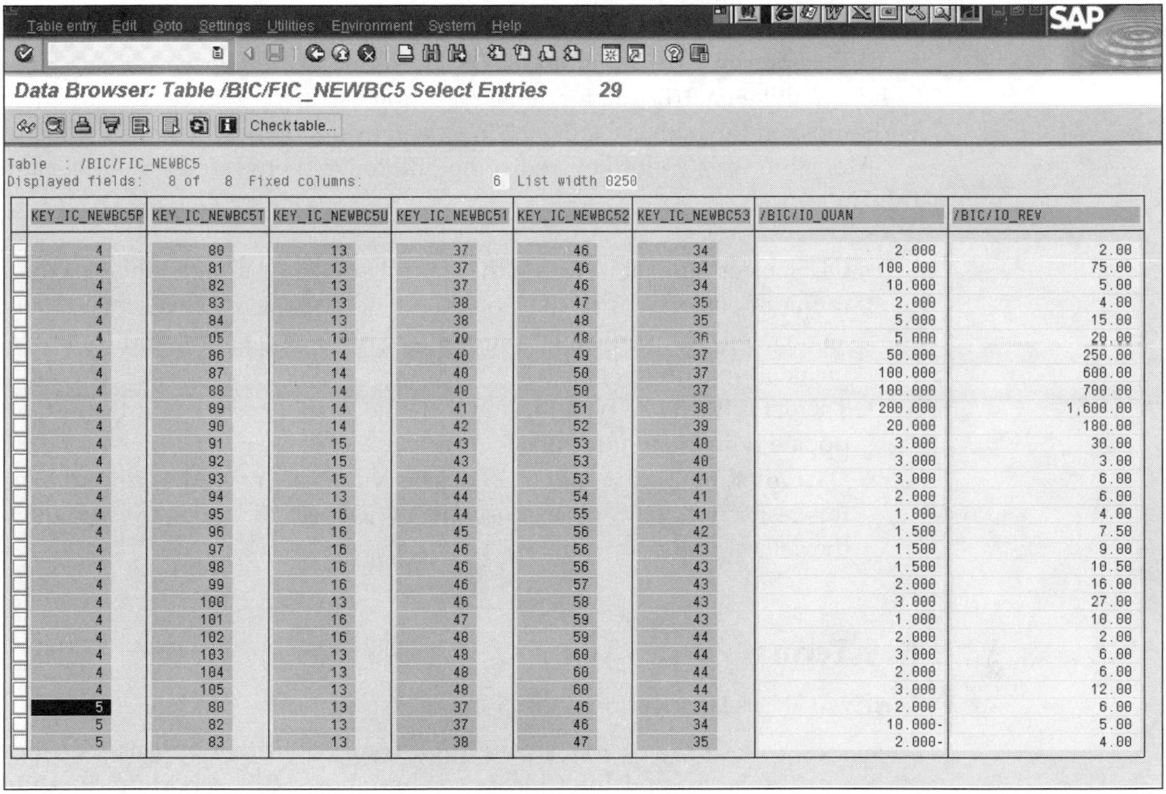

Table entry Edit Goto Settings Utilities Environment System Help

Data Browser: Table /BIC/FIC_NEWBC5 Select Entries 29

Check table...

Table : /BIC/FIC_NEWBC5
Displayed fields: 8 of 8 Fixed columns: 6 List width 0250

KEY_IC_NEWBC5P	KEY_IC_NEWBC5T	KEY_IC_NEWBC5U	KEY_IC_NEWBC51	KEY_IC_NEWBC52	KEY_IC_NEWBC53	/BIC/IO_QUAN	/BIC/IO_REV
4	80	13	37	46	34	2.000	2.00
4	81	13	37	46	34	100.000	75.00
4	82	13	37	46	34	10.000	5.00
4	83	13	38	47	35	2.000	4.00
4	84	13	38	48	35	5.000	15.00
4	85	13	39	48	36	5.000	20.00
4	86	14	40	49	37	50.000	250.00
4	87	14	40	50	37	100.000	600.00
4	88	14	40	50	37	100.000	700.00
4	89	14	41	51	38	200.000	1,600.00
4	90	14	42	52	39	20.000	180.00
4	91	15	43	53	40	3.000	30.00
4	92	15	43	53	40	3.000	3.00
4	93	15	44	53	41	3.000	6.00
4	94	13	44	54	41	2.000	6.00
4	95	16	44	55	41	1.000	4.00
4	96	16	45	56	42	1.500	7.50
4	97	16	46	56	43	1.500	9.00
4	98	16	46	56	43	1.500	10.50
4	99	16	46	57	43	2.000	16.00
4	100	13	46	58	43	3.000	27.00
4	101	16	47	59	43	1.000	10.00
4	102	16	48	59	44	2.000	2.00
4	103	13	48	60	44	3.000	6.00
4	104	13	48	60	44	2.000	6.00
4	105	13	48	60	44	3.000	12.00
5	80	13	37	46	34	2.000	6.00
5	82	13	37	46	34	10.000-	5.00
5	83	13	38	47	35	2.000-	4.00

SCREEN 9.50

Result

These steps prove what we said at the beginning of this section: You use 0RECORDMODE value *X* to mark rows to be skipped in the delta data load. You use *D* and *R* to delete or remove rows, respectively, from the active ODS table if the rows can be identified by the table primary key. Otherwise, *D* and *R* work just like *X*—they do not affect either the change log or the active data table.

9.6 Summary

In this chapter, we demonstrated ODS as a new technique that allows us to build a multilayer structure for detail reporting at different levels. In particular, we completed the path in Figure 9.2 indicated by solid lines.

Along the way, we discovered some differences between ODS objects and InfoCubes:

- ODS objects are not based on the star schema and should not be used for multidimensional analysis. For the same reason, ODS objects do not aggregate data as InfoCubes do, cannot have aggregates, and cannot be included in a multi-cube.
- The default update type for an ODS object is *Overwrite*, and the default update type for an InfoCube is *Addition*.
- Data must be loaded into ODS objects via PSA. InfoCubes do not have this restriction. ODS objects use 0RECORDMODE values to implement the delta update.

Key Terms

Term	Description
ODS	ODS is a BW architectural component that appears between PSA and InfoCubes and that allows BEx reporting. It is not based on the star schema and is used primarily for detail reporting, rather than for dimensional analysis. ODS objects do not aggregate data as InfoCubes do. Data are loaded into an ODS object by inserting new records, updating existing records, or deleting old records as specified by 0RECORD-MODE value.
Full update	The Full update option in the InfoPackage definition requests that BW load all data that meet the selection criteria specified under the *Select data* tab.
Delta update	The Delta update option in the InfoPackage definition requests that BW load only the data that have been accumulated since the last update. Before performing a delta update, the delta process must be initialized.

For Further Information

- OSS Note 0364577, "ODS: ORA-54 When Loading Data into the ODS."
- OSS Note 0384023, "Optimize Performance of ODS Objects."

Next . . .

We will discuss Business Content and learn how to use it.

Chapter 10

Business Content

One of the BW's strongest selling points is its Business Content. **Business Content** is a set of BW objects developed by SAP based on predefined business roles and their tasks. For example, a sales manager is a business role, and monitoring and forecasting sales demands and pricing trends is a task. To accomplish these tasks, the sales manager needs reports to get business information and conduct online analysis. In Part I of this book, we learned that reports are created from queries, queries are created from InfoCubes, and InfoCubes are created from InfoObjects. To load data, we need DataSources, transfer rules, InfoSources, and update rules. Business Content contains all of these objects for predefined business roles and their tasks.

As described in Chapter 3, DataSources relate to their source systems. In Business Content, the DataSources are defined for R/3. Considering the difficulties in the R/3 ETTL process, we can say that the R/3 DataSources in Business Content make data warehousing projects much easier and more manageable.

This chapter discusses how to load R/3 data using a R/3 DataSource for 0PLANT. 0PLANT is a standard InfoObject in Business Content. Put another way, we will implement the path paved by the solid lines in Figure 10.1. First, we need to create an R/3 source system.

FIGURE 10.1
DATA FLOW

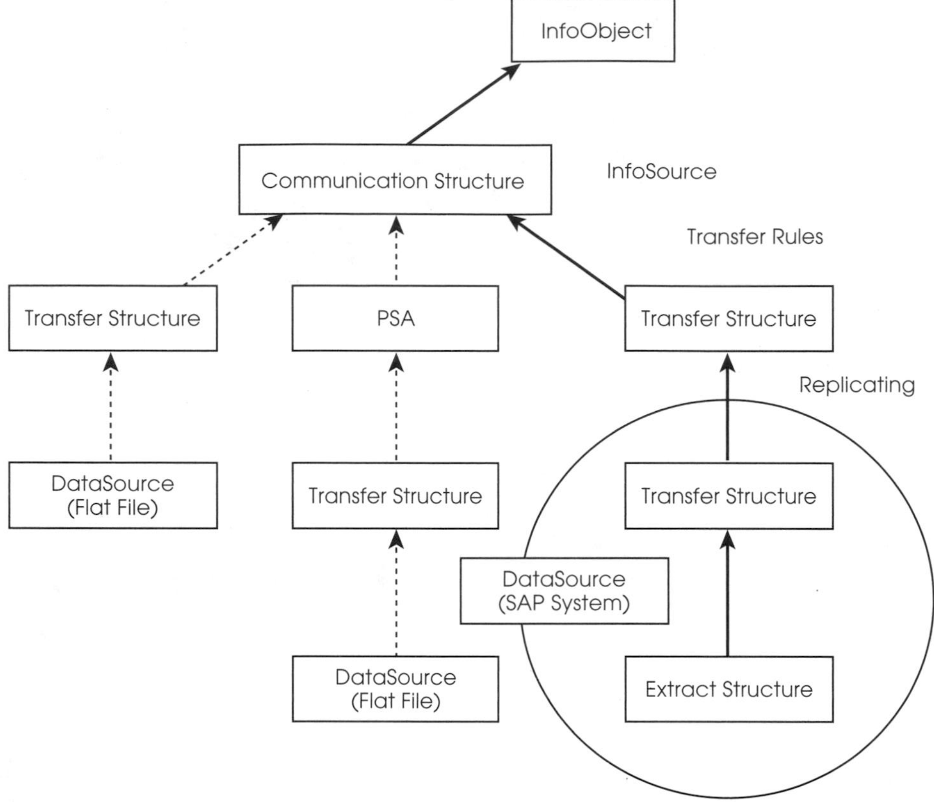

10.1 Creating an R/3 Source System

A high-level procedure for creating an R/3 source system involves the following steps:

1. Creating a logical system for the R/3 client
2. Creating a logical system for the BW client
3. Naming background users
4. Creating the R/3 source system in BW

Note: Some activities were carried out before the screens shown in this chapter were captured. Here we can only check their status.

10.1.1 Creating a Logical System for the R/3 Client

A **client** is a subset of the data in the SAP database. It belongs to a legally and organizationally independent function group. When a user logs on to an SAP system, he or she actually logs on to a particular client as specified in the logon screen. In Section 11.3, "Creating a Characteristic in BW," we will see how the client is defined at the database level.

A **logical system** identifies a client in an SAP system. SAP systems, whether R/3 or BW, communicate with one another using logical systems instead of clients. An R/3 system can have client 100, and a BW system can also have client 100. Logical systems allow us to distinguish between these two clients although both are numbered 100.

The following procedure shows how to create a logical system.

Work Instructions

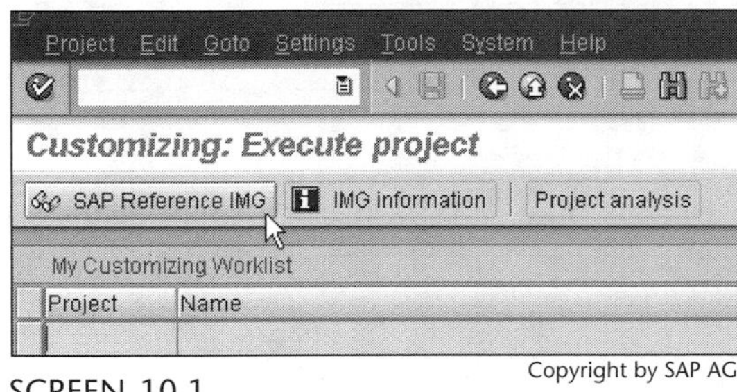

SCREEN 10.1

Step 1 Log on to the R/3 source system, run transaction *SPRO*, and then click SAP Reference IMG. IMG stands for **IMplementation Guide**.

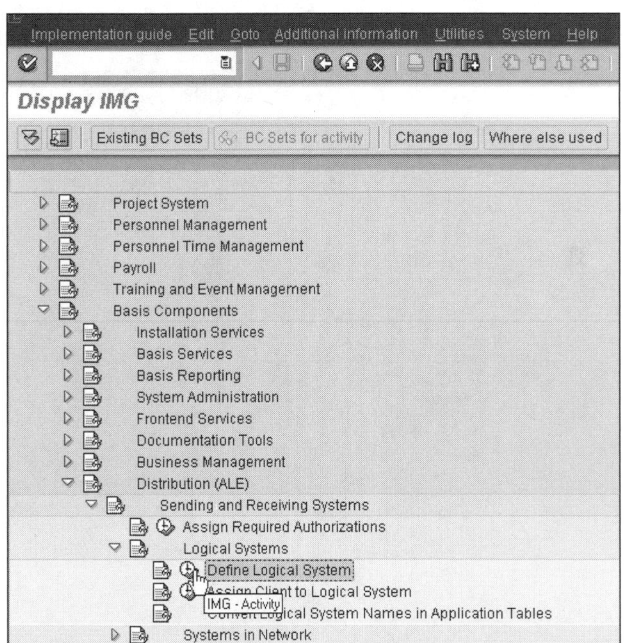

Step 2 Click the icon next to *Define Logical System* to execute the function.

SCREEN 10.2

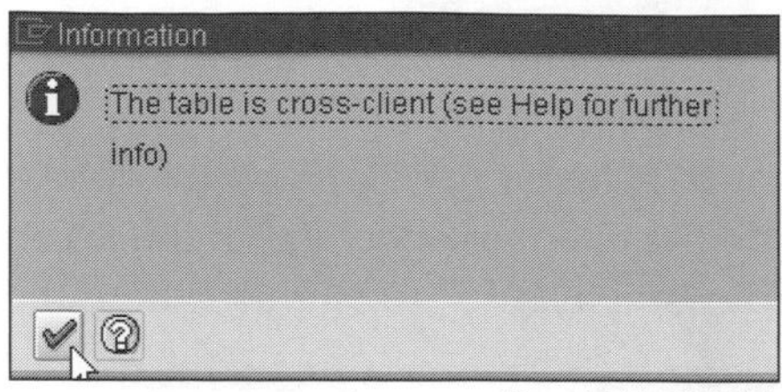

SCREEN 10.3 Copyright by SAP AG

Step 3 Click to continue.

Note: In either an R/3 or BW SAP system, some data are **client dependent**; other data are **client independent**. Client-independent data are also called **cross-client data**. The data about the logical system definition is client independent.

Step 4 We see a logical system named as *TC1_200*. We will soon find out that it represents system TC1 and client 200. TC1 is the R/3 system ID.

Note: To create a new logical system name, click New entries.

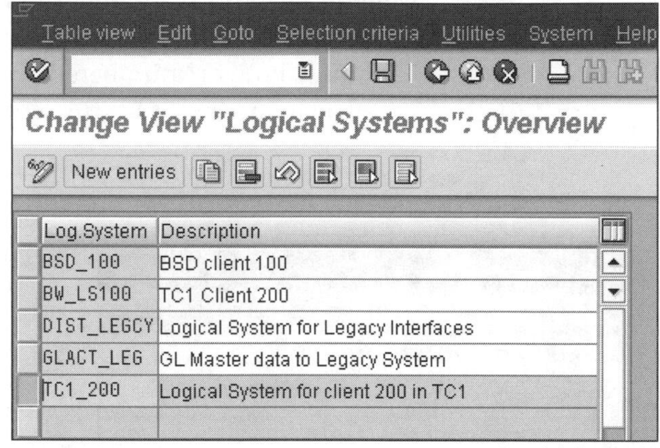

SCREEN 10.4 Copyright by SAP AG

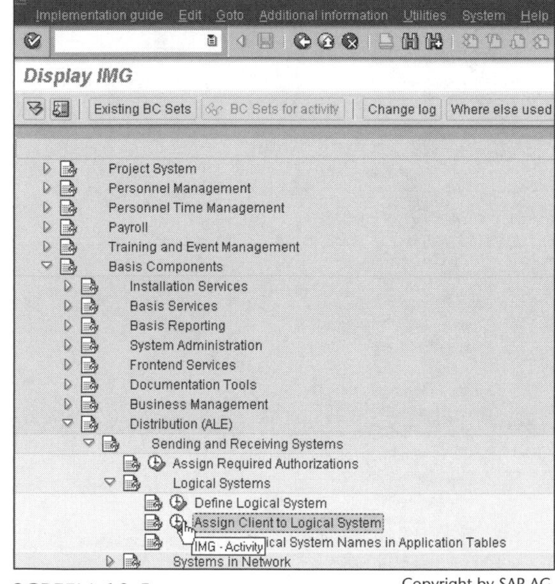

SCREEN 10.5 Copyright by SAP AG

Step 5 Return to Screen 10.2, and then click next to *Assign Client to Logical System* to execute the function.

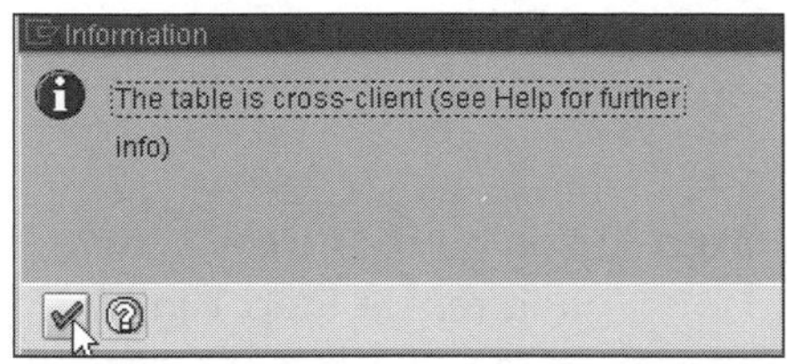

SCREEN 10.6 Copyright by SAP AG

Step 6 Click to continue.

Table view Edit Goto Selection criteria Utilities System Help

Change View "Clients": Overview

New entries

Client	Name	City	Crcy	Changed on
000	SAP AG	Walldorf	DEM	
001	Auslieferungsmandant R11	Kundstadt	USD	
066	EarlyWatch	Walldorf	DEM	
100	Production Gold Client	Houston	USD	08/03/2000
200	Production Load Test Cl	Houston	USD	08/03/2000
300	ABAP Training Cl	Houston	USD	09/18/2000
911	SAP E & P Testing client	Dallas	USD	08/31/2000
930	Temporary Copy from 200	Houston	USD	06/08/2000

Copyright by SAP AG SCREEN 10.7

Step 7 Select client *200*, and then click to view the client definition.

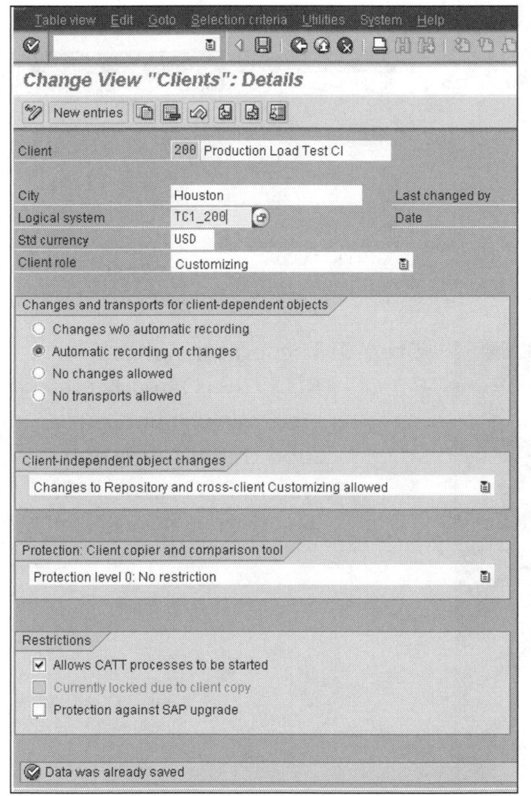

SCREEN 10.8 Copyright by SAP AG

Step 8 Note that logical system *TC1_200* is assigned to client 200.

Note: The *Changes to Repository and cross-client Customizing allowed* option in the *Client-independent object changes* block must be selected. The procedure of turning system TC1 client 200 into a source system in BW will create a background user and set up RFC (Remote Function Call) related configurations in R/3 and BW.

Tip: If system TC1 client 200 is a production client, we can switch off this option after creating the source system in BW.

Result

The logical system TC1_200 represents the system TC1 client 200.

10.1.2 Creating a Logical System for the BW Client

Work Instructions

Step 1 Log on to the BW system, and repeat Step 1 in Screen 10.1. Next, click [icon] next to *Define Logical System* to execute the function.

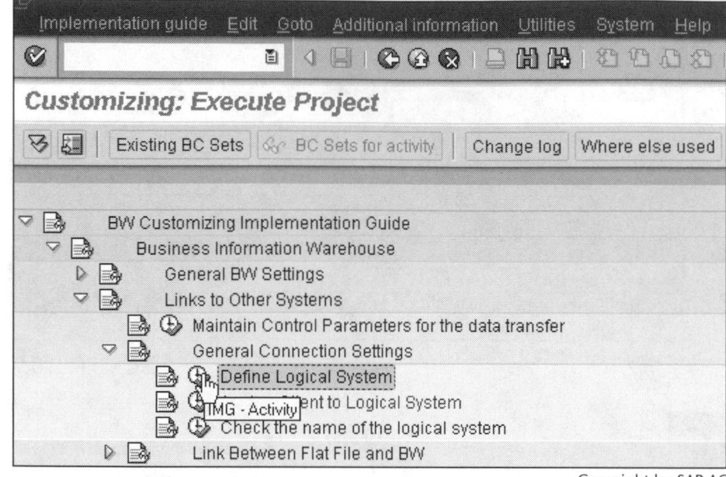

SCREEN 10.9

Step 2 Click [icon] to continue.

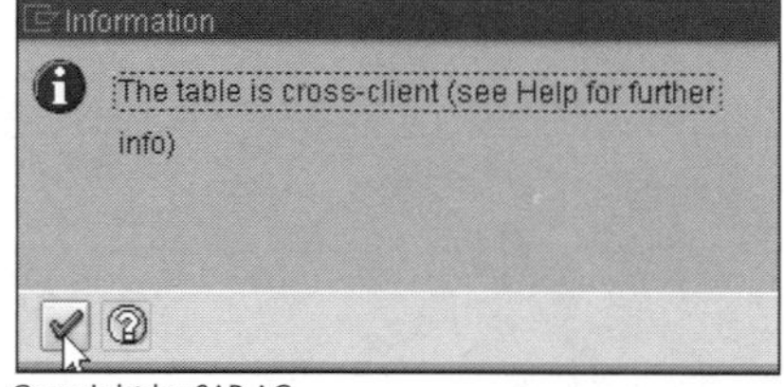

SCREEN 10.10

Step 3 The logical system *BTC_100* is already created. We will find out soon that it represents system BTC client 100. BTC is the BW system ID.

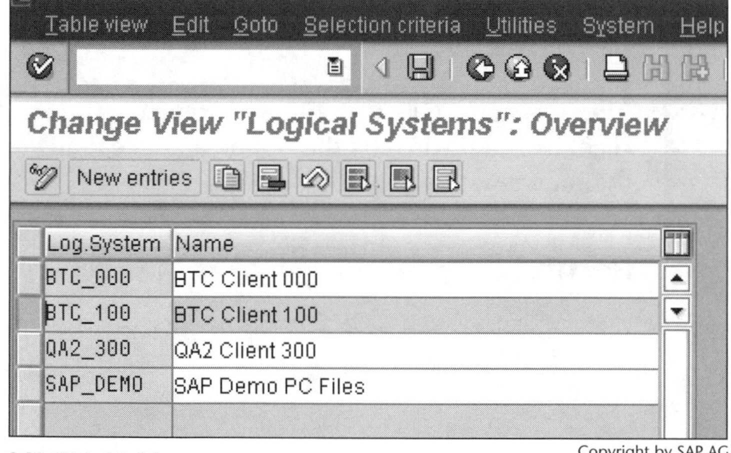

SCREEN 10.11

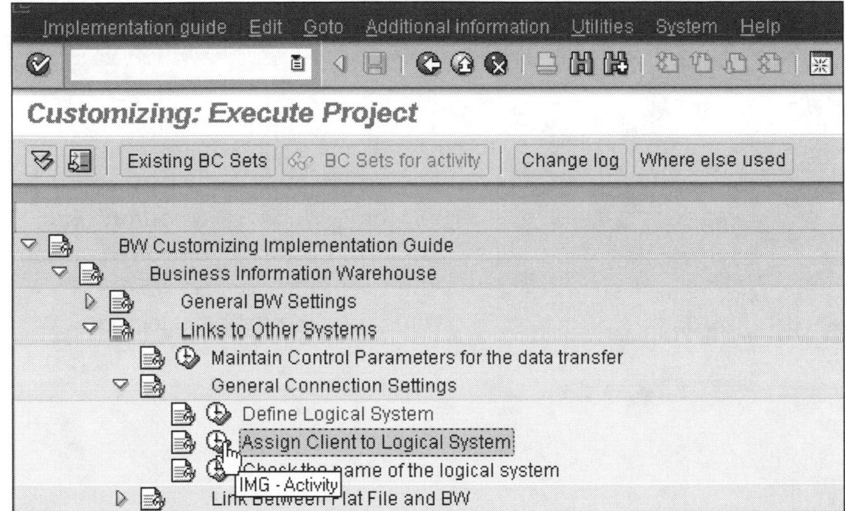

Copyright by SAP AG

SCREEN 10.12

Step 4 Return to Screen 10.9, and then click [icon] next to *Assign Client to Logical System* to execute the function.

Step 5 Click [icon] to continue.

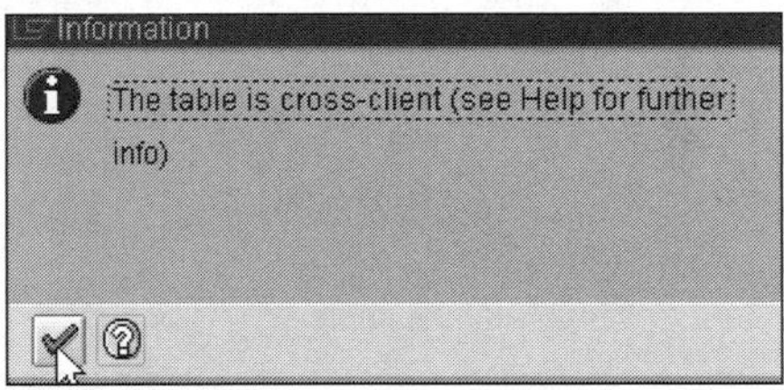

Copyright by SAP AG

SCREEN 10.13

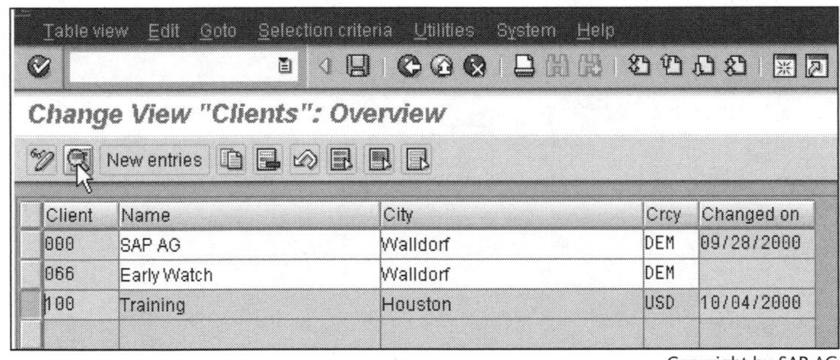

Copyright by SAP AG

SCREEN 10.14

Step 6 Select client *100*, and then click [icon] to view the client details.

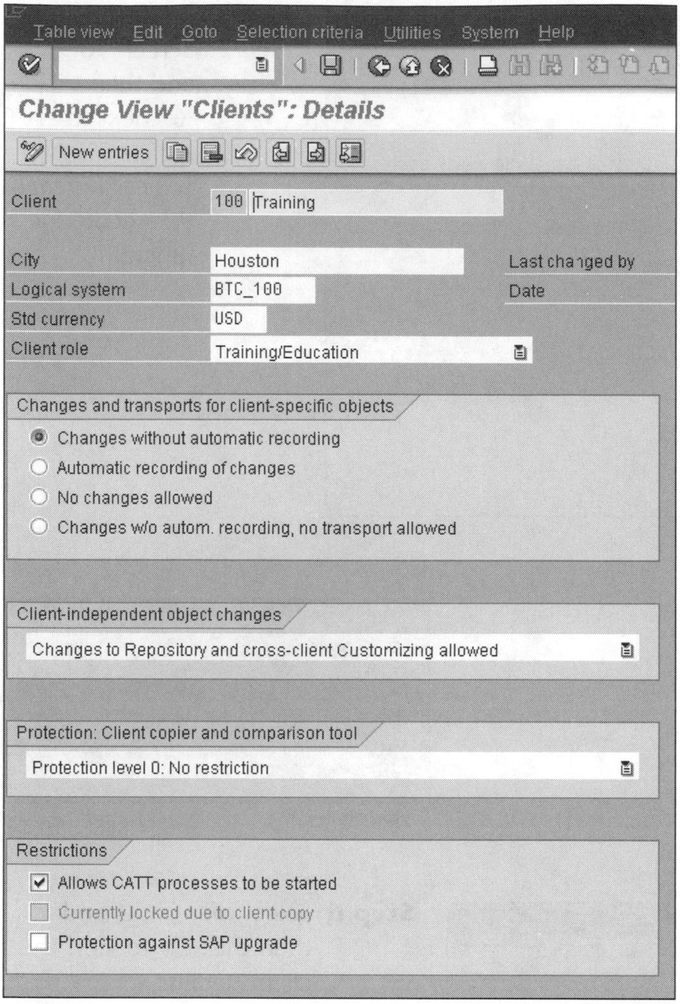

SCREEN 10.15

Copyright by SAP AG

Step 7 Note that the logical system *BTC_100* is assigned to client 100.

Note: For the same reason mentioned in conjunction with Screen 10.8, the *Changes to Repository and cross-client Customizing allowed* option in the *Client-independent object changes* block must be selected.

Result

The logical system BTC_100 represents system BTC client 100.

10.1.3 Naming Background Users

TC1_200 and BTC_100 communicate with each other through system users. For our example, we will name ALEREMOTE as the user in system TC1 client 200 and BWREMOTE as the user in system BTC client 100.

Work Instructions

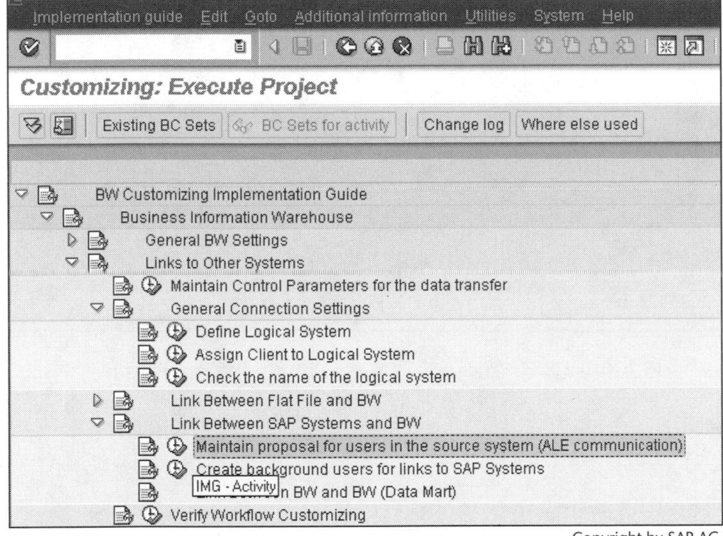

Copyright by SAP AG

SCREEN 10.16

Step 1 Return to Screen 10.12, and click next to *Maintain proposal for users in the source system (ALE communication)* to execute the function.

Step 2 *ALEREMOTE* is the default name. Accept it and return to the previous screen.

Table view Edit Goto Selection criteria

Change View "BW: User in SS

BW: User in SS for ALE Communicatio

SS user ALE ALEREMOTE

Copyright by SAP AG

SCREEN 10.17

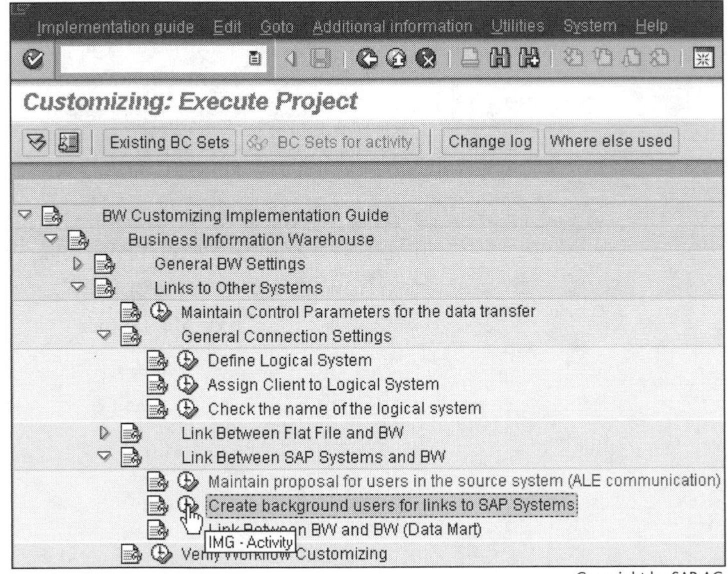

Copyright by SAP AG

SCREEN 10.18

Step 3 Click next to *Create background users for links to SAP Systems* to execute the function.

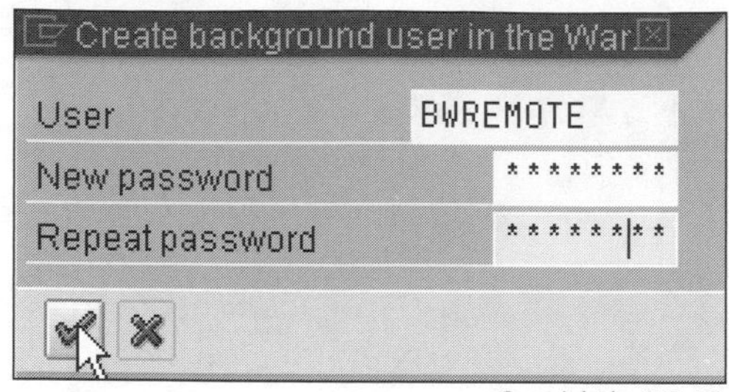

SCREEN 10.19 Copyright by SAP AG

Step 4 Enter *BWREMOTE* and a password, and then click ✔ to save the configuration.

Result

Two system users are named. You will create them next.

10.1.4 Creating an R/3 Source System in BW

Now we are ready to create TC1_200 as an R/3 source system in BTC.

Work Instructions

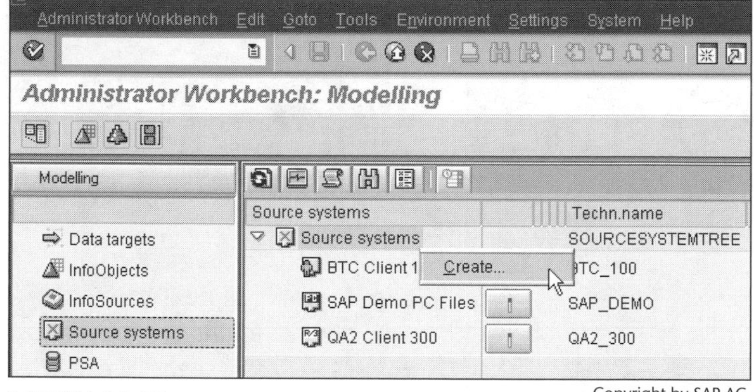

SCREEN 10.20 Copyright by SAP AG

Step 1 From the BTC BW Administrator Workbench, click *Source systems* in the left panel. In the right panel, right-click *Source systems*, and then select *Create. . . .*

Note: A BW system can serve itself as a source system. We will see how this process works in Section 13.1, "BW Statistics."

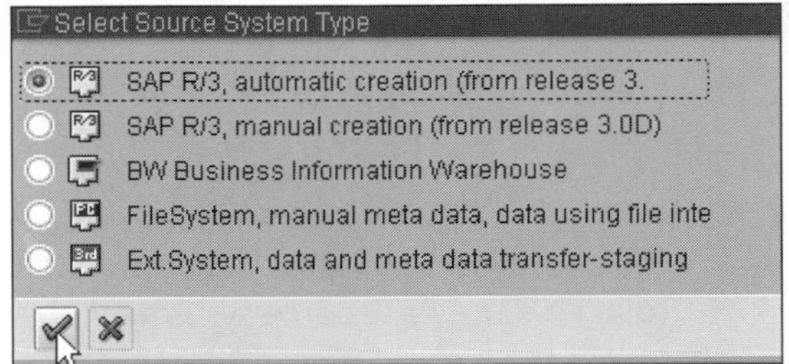

SCREEN 10.21

Step 2 Select the first option because TC1 is 4.6B, higher than 3.0D. Click ✔ to continue.

Step 3 Enter the application server host name of the R/3 source system, its system ID and system number, and the passwords for ALEREMOTE and BWREMOTE. Click ✔ to continue.

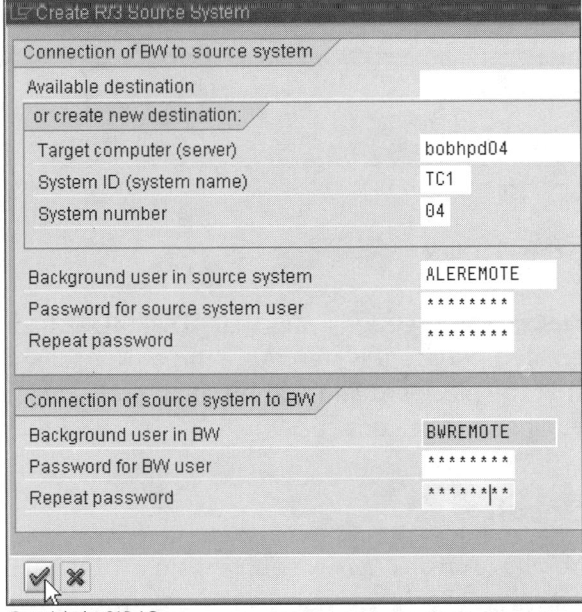

SCREEN 10.22

Information

Please log on as an administrator in the following screen

SCREEN 10.23

Step 4 Click ✔ to continue.

Note: BW will check the authorizations in the next screen. We need sufficient authorizations so that we can create the users ALEREMOTE and BWREMOTE and configure the system settings. We will see the result in Screen 10.27.

Step 5 Enter the user ID and password, and log on to TC1 client 200.

Note: This step is necessary to verify that we have the authorization needed to access the R/3 source system.

SCREEN 10.24

Step 6 Click Contine.

Note: This message notes that ALEREMOTE had been created prior to this step. Also, this message indicates that the password and authorization profile we set up earlier must be correct.

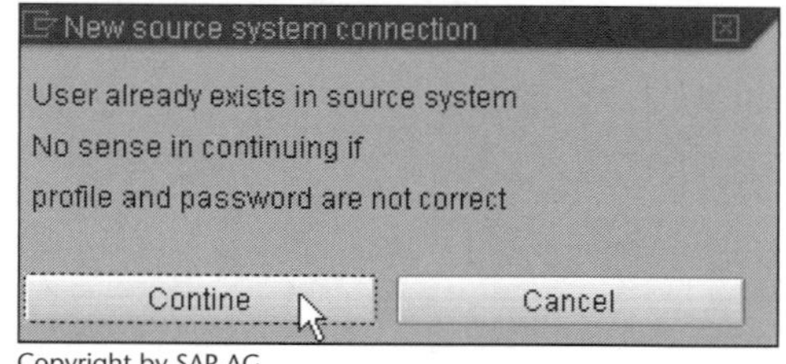

New source system connection
User already exists in source system
No sense in continuing if
profile and password are not correct
Contine
Cancel

SCREEN 10.25

Result

You have created a new source system TC1_200 in BW (Screen 10.26).

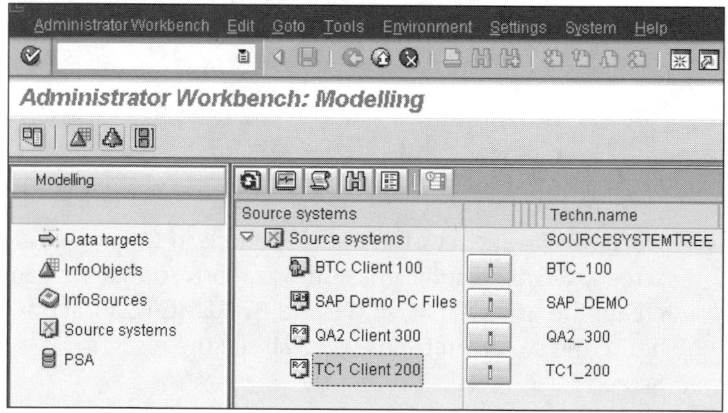

SCREEN 10.26

Note: This procedure would create the ALEREMOTE user in system TC1 client 200 and the BWREMOTE user in system BTC client 100, both with appropriate authorization, if they did not exist. It would also create two **RFC (Remote Function Call) destinations**, one in system TC1 and the other in system BTC.

To check the RFC destination information in BTC, run transaction *SM59.* In Screen 10.27, we see that the RFC destination TC1_200 contains the necessary information for user ALEREMOTE to log on to system TC1 client 200, such as the host machine name *bobhpd04* and the SAP system number *04*.

TC1_200 and BTC_100 locate each other by using the RFC destinations and log on to each other as the ALEREMOTE and BWREMOTE users.

SCREEN 10.27

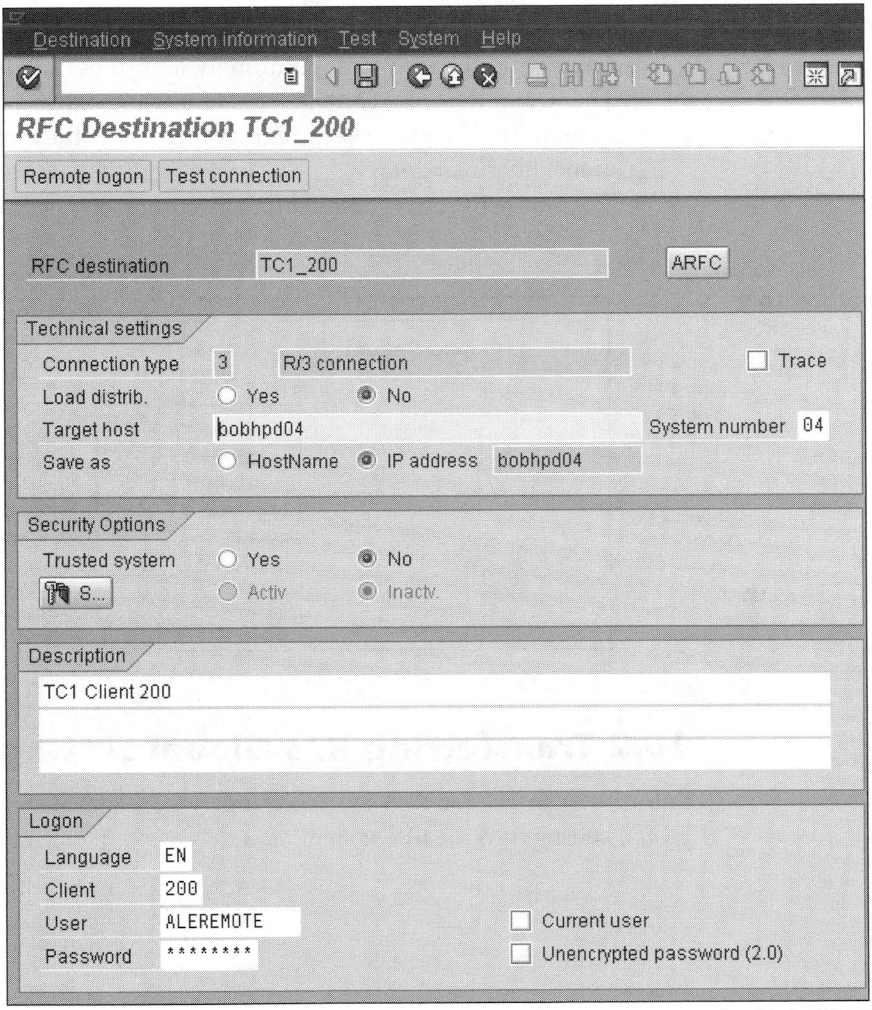

With RFC destinations, the following settings were also created:

- IDoc partner profiles
- IDoc port definitions
- IDoc types
- IDoc segments

IDoc (Intermediate Document) is a template that SAP systems use to exchange data with one another and with outside systems. An IDoc consists of three types of records (Figure 10.2):

- The Control Record contains administration information, such as the sender and the recipient. It uniquely identifies an IDoc.
- The Data Records contain segments and their administration information, such as the parent segment to which they are attached. The segments hold real data.
- The Status Records contain all of the processing status information.

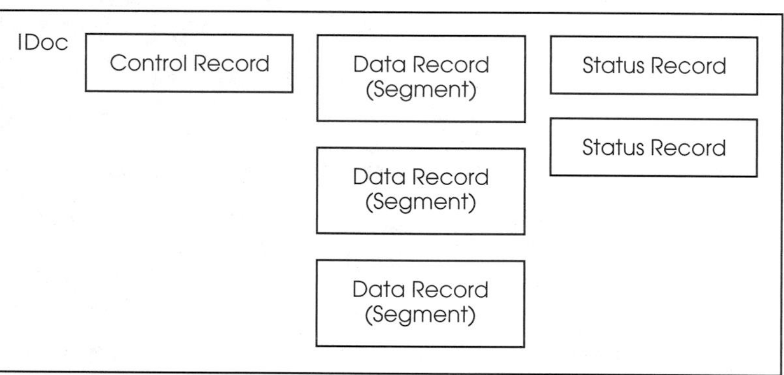

FIGURE 10.2 IDOC STRUCTURE

10.2 Transferring R/3 Global Settings

Before we can use the R/3 source system, we must transfer the source system's global setting into the BW system.

Work Instructions

Step 1 Right-click the newly created source system *TC1_200*, and then select *Transfer global settings.*

Note: If exchange rates are configured in TC1_200, select *Transfer exchange rates* and transfer this configuration as well.

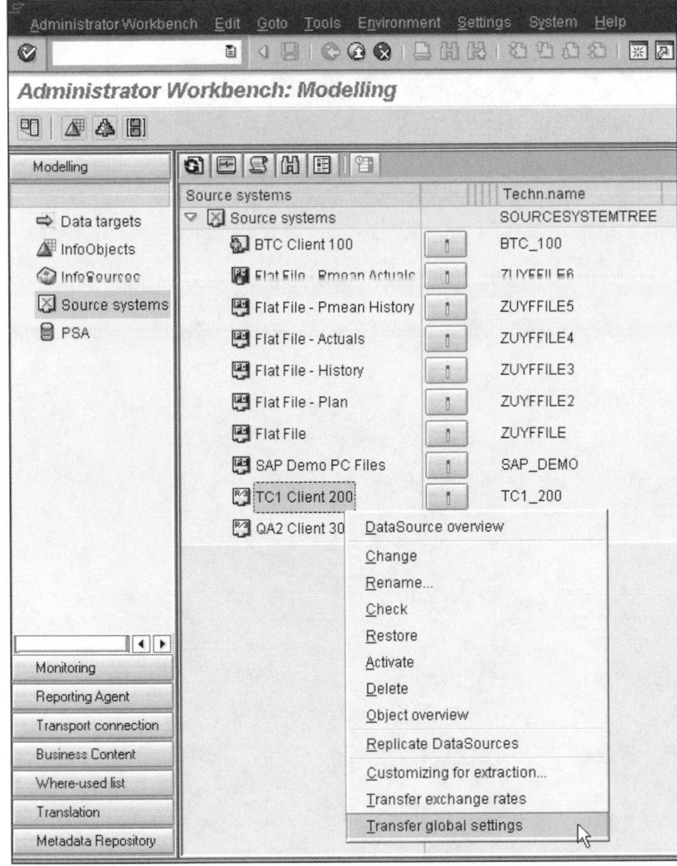

SCREEN 10.28

Copyright by SAP AG

Step 2 Check all options in the *Transfer global table contents* block, check the *Rebuild tables* option, and then click [execute icon] to execute the options.

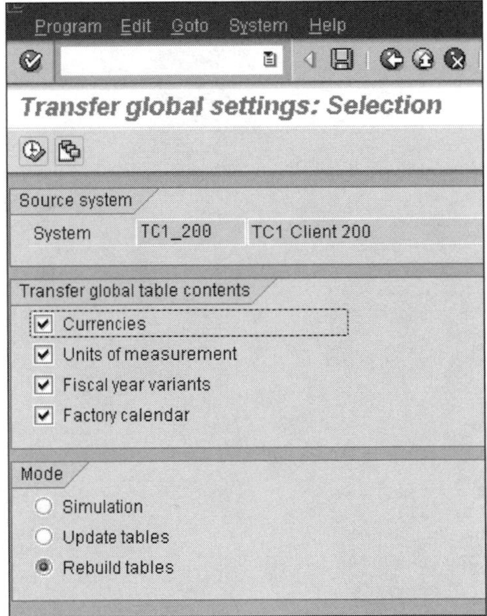

Copyright by SAP AG

SCREEN 10.29

Result

Screen 10.30 opens, listing what happened to each configuration table.

SCREEN 10.30

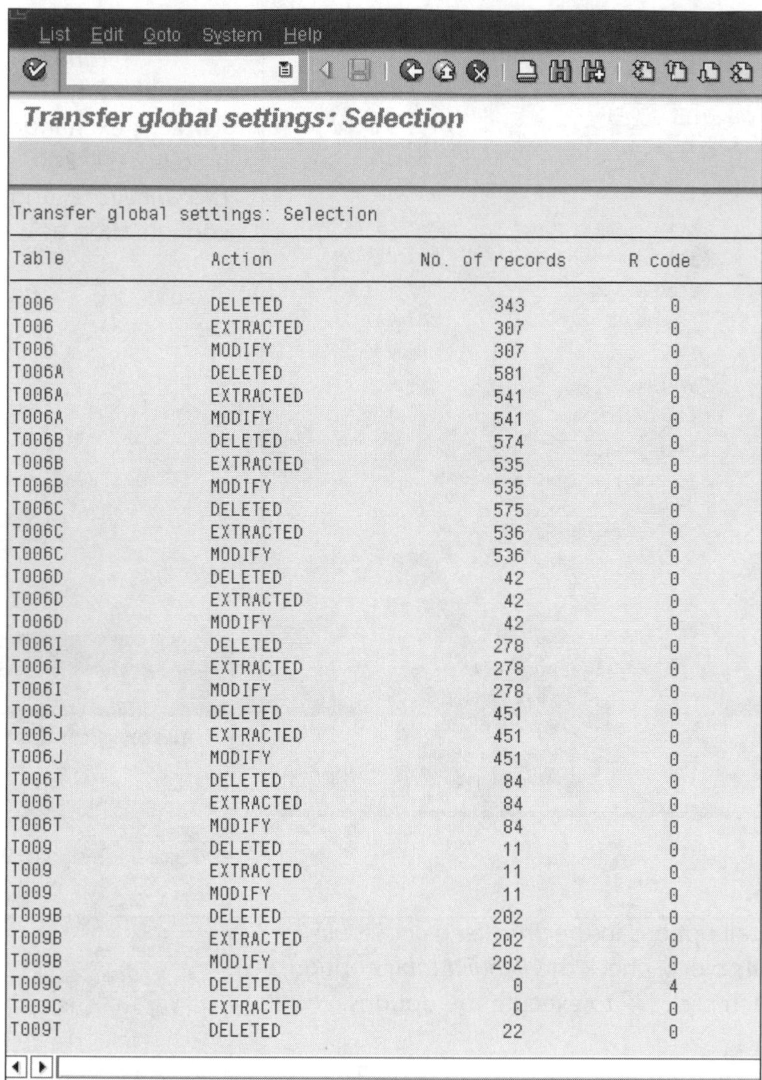

Table	Action	No. of records	R code
T006	DELETED	343	0
T006	EXTRACTED	307	0
T006	MODIFY	307	0
T006A	DELETED	581	0
T006A	EXTRACTED	541	0
T006A	MODIFY	541	0
T006B	DELETED	574	0
T006B	EXTRACTED	535	0
T006B	MODIFY	535	0
T006C	DELETED	575	0
T006C	EXTRACTED	536	0
T006C	MODIFY	536	0
T006D	DELETED	42	0
T006D	EXTRACTED	42	0
T006D	MODIFY	42	0
T006I	DELETED	278	0
T006I	EXTRACTED	278	0
T006I	MODIFY	278	0
T006J	DELETED	451	0
T006J	EXTRACTED	451	0
T006J	MODIFY	451	0
T006T	DELETED	84	0
T006T	EXTRACTED	84	0
T006T	MODIFY	84	0
T009	DELETED	11	0
T009	EXTRACTED	11	0
T009	MODIFY	11	0
T009B	DELETED	202	0
T009B	EXTRACTED	202	0
T009B	MODIFY	202	0
T009C	DELETED	0	4
T009C	EXTRACTED	0	0
T009T	DELETED	22	0

Before installing a Business Content object, we need to finish one more thing if the object uses DataSources: We must activate the DataSources in TC1_200 and replicate them into BTC_100. We will accomplish this task in the next section.

10.3 Replicating R/3 DataSources

First, we will demonstrate how to activate InfoObject 0PLANT's DataSources in the R/3 source system SND_250. Then, we will replicate those DataSources into BW2.

Note: In the rest of this book, we will use SND_250 as the R/3 source system and BW2 as the BW system.

The following steps show how to activate DataSources.

Prerequisites

The R/3 Plug-In (PI) must be installed in the source system. The Plug-In interface enables the exchange of data between SAP systems. Technically, the Plug-In contains ABAP objects, such as tables and programs, used for data extraction.

Caution: The Plug-In cannot be "plugged out" after its installation. Use the database backup to restore the system to its previous state if needed.

Work Instructions

Step 1 Check whether the DataSources have been activated. Log on to the R/3 source system, execute transaction *RSA6*, and then click [icon] to list the active DataSources.

SCREEN 10.31

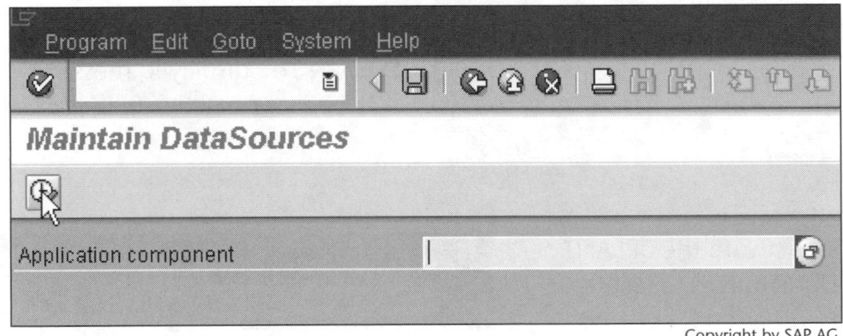

Note: DataSources in an R/3 source system come in two versions:

- D—SAP delivery version
- A—active version

The D version is the original definition from the Plug-In. The A version is used in data extraction.

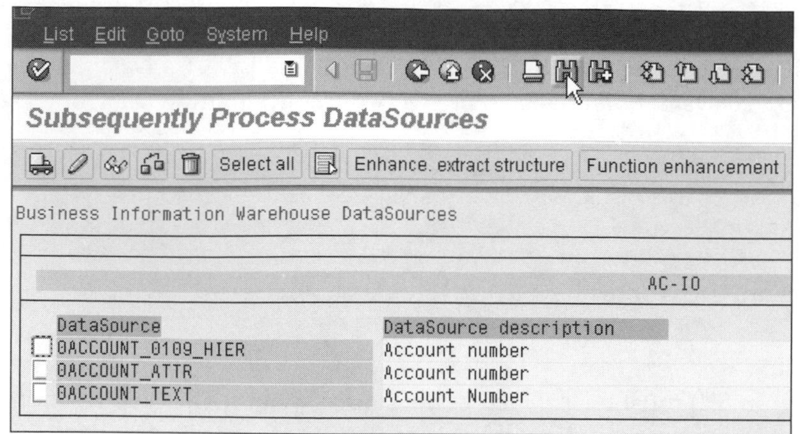

SCREEN 10.32

Step 2 Click to search for 0PLANT's DataSources.

Note: In Business Content, DataSources are named in the following format:

- <characteristic name>_ATTR for master data
- <characteristic name>_TEXT for texts
- <characteristic name>_<four letters>_HIER for hierarchies

Step 3 Enter *0PLANT,* and then click again.

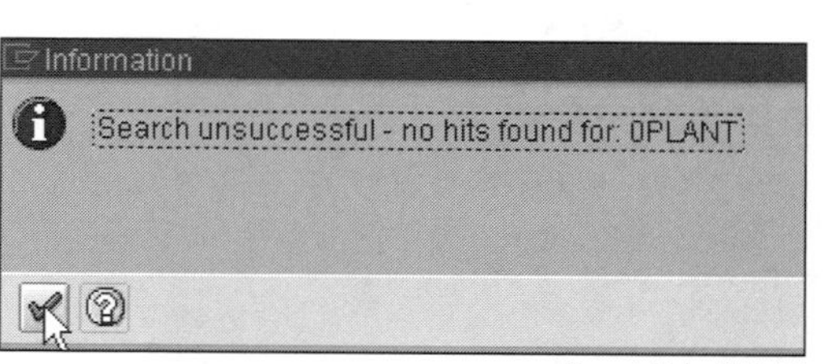

SCREEN 10.33

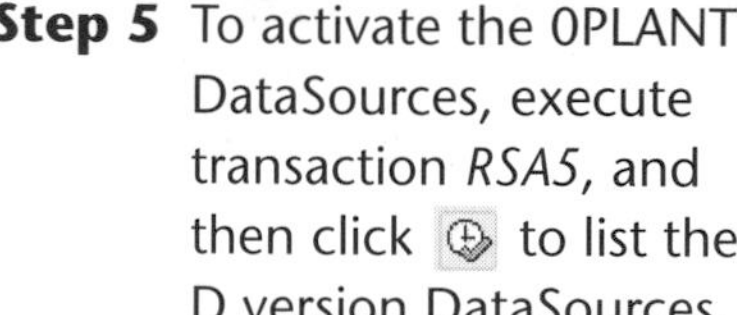

SCREEN 10.34

Step 4 The displayed message indicates that there are no active 0PLANT DataSources. Click to continue.

Step 5 To activate the 0PLANT DataSources, execute transaction *RSA5*, and then click to list the D version DataSources.

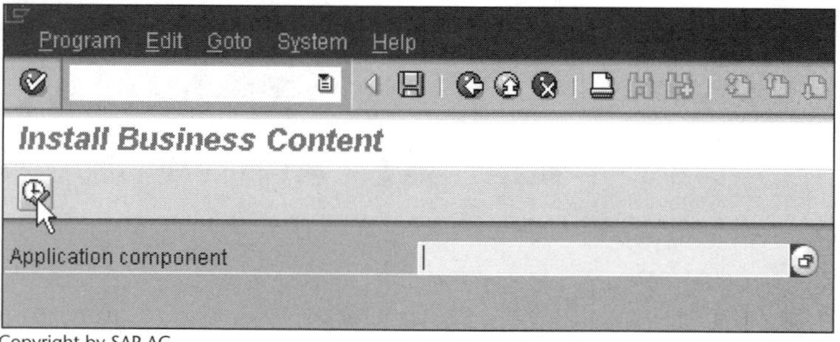

SCREEN 10.35

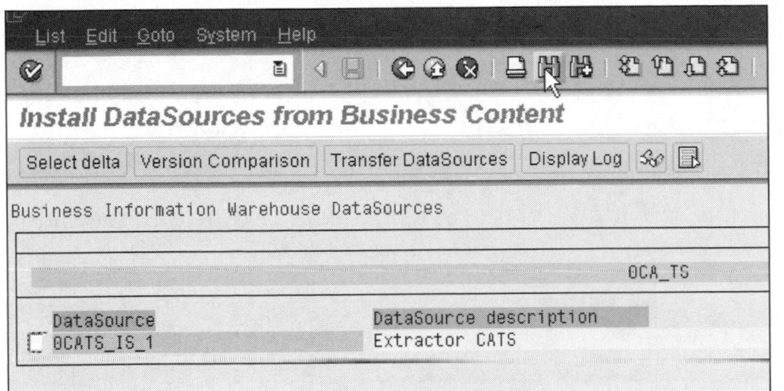

Copyright by SAP AG

SCREEN 10.36

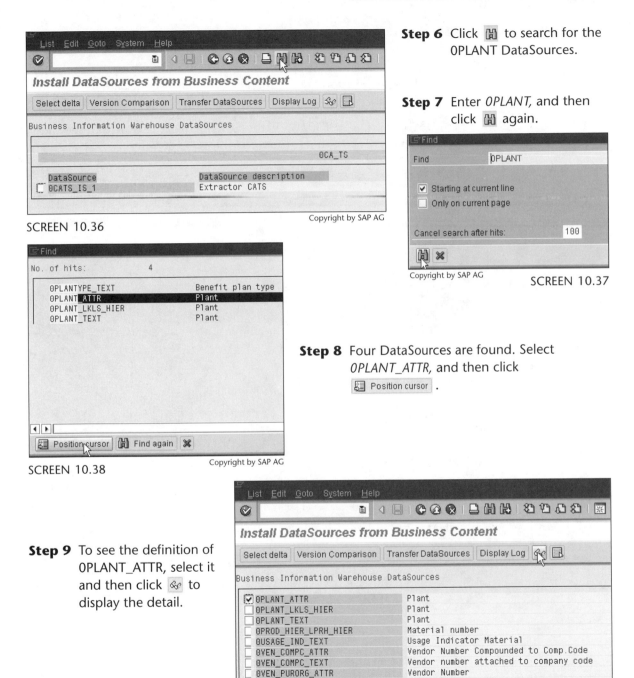

Step 6 Click [find icon] to search for the 0PLANT DataSources.

Step 7 Enter *0PLANT,* and then click [find icon] again.

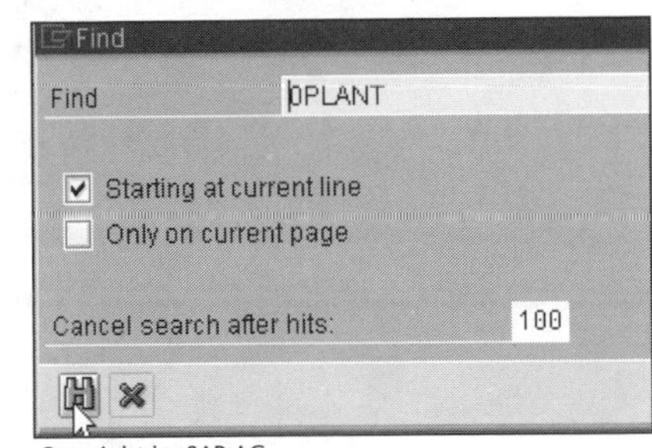

Copyright by SAP AG

SCREEN 10.37

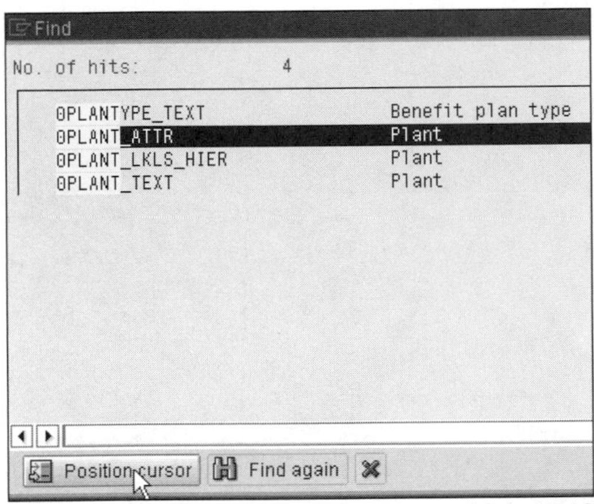

Copyright by SAP AG

SCREEN 10.38

Step 8 Four DataSources are found. Select *0PLANT_ATTR,* and then click [Position cursor].

Step 9 To see the definition of 0PLANT_ATTR, select it and then click [detail icon] to display the detail.

List Edit Goto System Help

Install DataSources from Business Content

Select delta | Version Comparison | Transfer DataSources | Display Log

Business Information Warehouse DataSources

0PLANT_ATTR	Plant
0PLANT_LKLS_HIER	Plant
0PLANT_TEXT	Plant
0PROD_HIER_LPRH_HIER	Material number
0USAGE_IND_TEXT	Usage Indicator Material
0VEN_COMPC_ATTR	Vendor Number Compounded to Comp.Code
0VEN_COMPC_TEXT	Vendor number attached to company code
0VEN_PURORG_ATTR	Vendor Number
0VEN_PURORG_TEXT	Vendor Number

Copyright by SAP AG

SCREEN 10.39

Step 10 Now we see a list of DataSource fields.

Note: Fields selected in the *Selection* column, such as *WERKS* in this case, will be used as the selection conditions when creating an InfoPackage to load 0PLANT master data.

Double-click *BIW_T001WS* in the *ExtractStruktur* text field to see the definition of the extract structure for this DataSource.

SCREEN 10.40

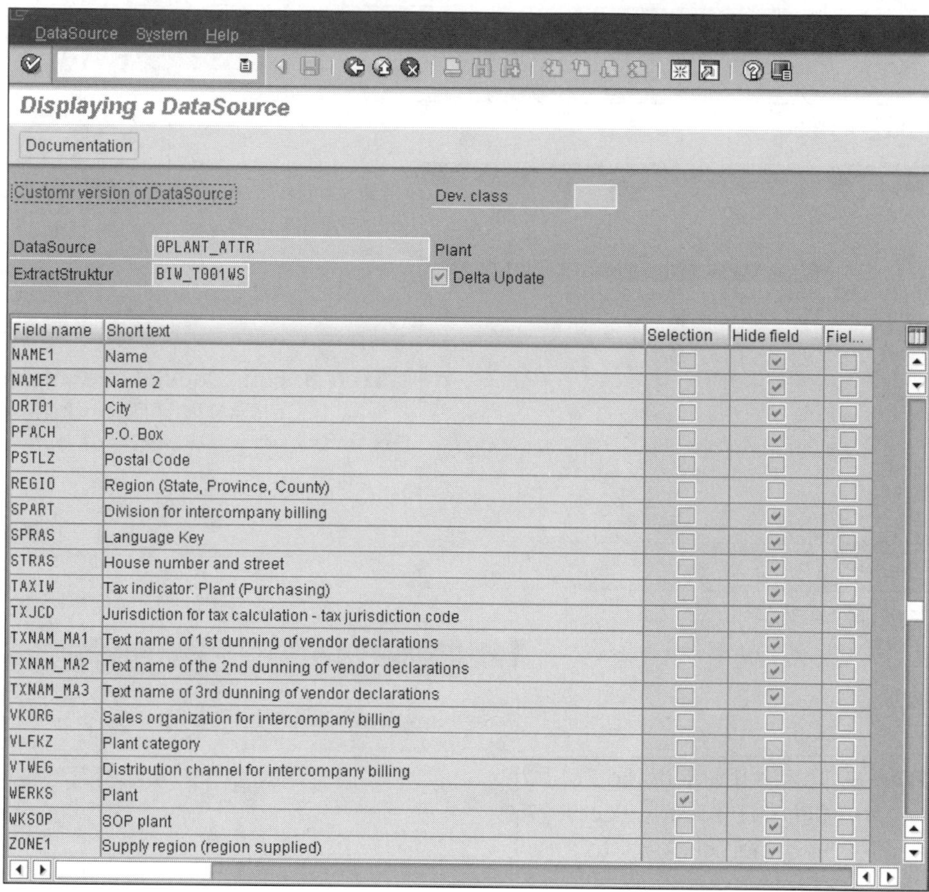

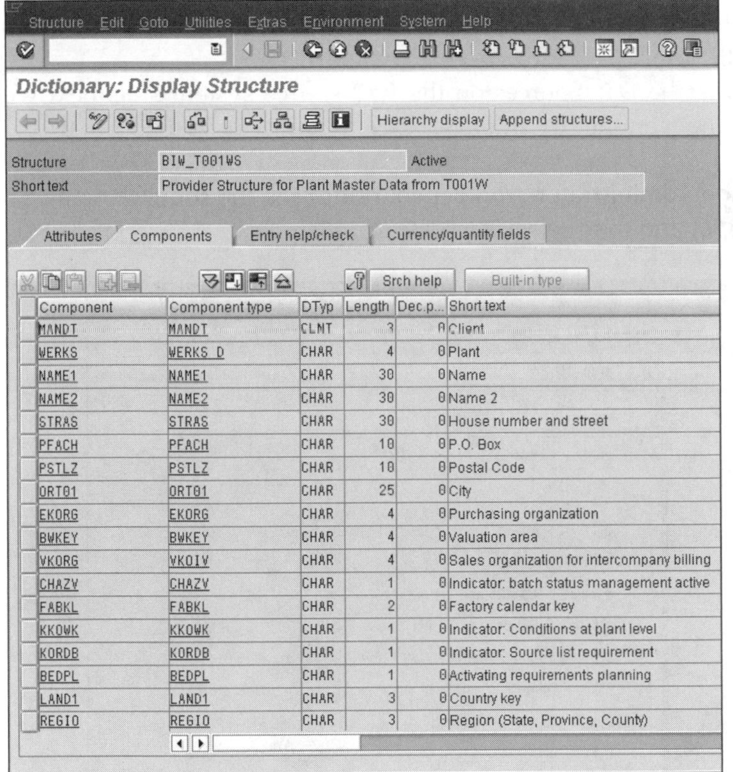

SCREEN 10.41

Step 11 Screen 10.41 shows an ABAP structure named *BIW_T001WS*.

Step 12 To activate the DataSource *0PLANT_ATTR*, select *0PLANT_ATTR* and then click Transfer DataSources .

List Edit Goto System Help

Install DataSources from Business Content

Select delta | Version Comparison | Transfer DataSources | Display Log

Business Information Warehouse DataSources

	DataSource	Description
☑	0PLANT_ATTR	Plant
☐	0PLANT_LKLS_HIER	Plant
☐	0PLANT_TEXT	Plant
☐	0PROD_HIER_LPRH_HIER	Material number
☐	0USAGE_IND_TEXT	Usage Indicator Material
☐	0VEN_COMPC_ATTR	Vendor Number Compounded to Comp.Code
☐	0VEN_COMPC_TEXT	Vendor number attached to company code
☐	0VEN_PURORG_ATTR	Vendor Number
☐	0VEN_PURORG_TEXT	Vendor Number

SCREEN 10.42

Result

The DataSource 0PLANT_ATTR has been activated.

After activating the DataSources on the R/3 source system side, next we need to replicate them on the BW side.

Step 13 From the Administrator Workbench, right-click the source system *SND_250*, and then select *Replicate DataSources.*

SCREEN 10.43

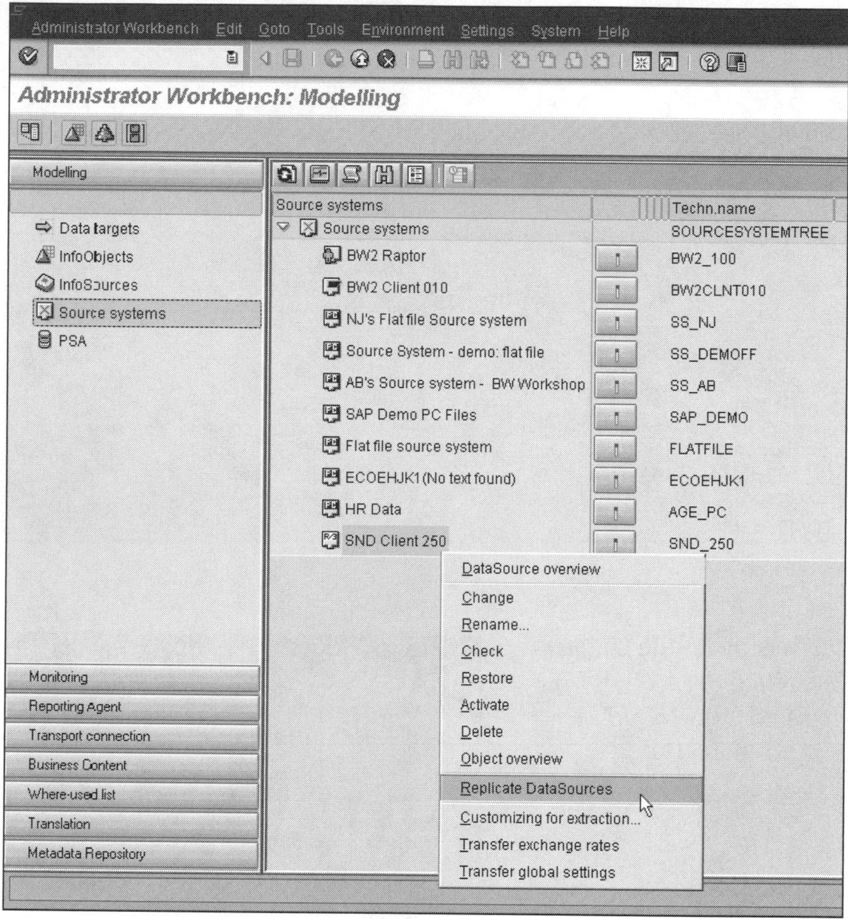

Result

When the procedure is finished, the status message *Tree data refreshed: Source system tree* appears at the bottom of Screen 10.44.

SCREEN 10.44

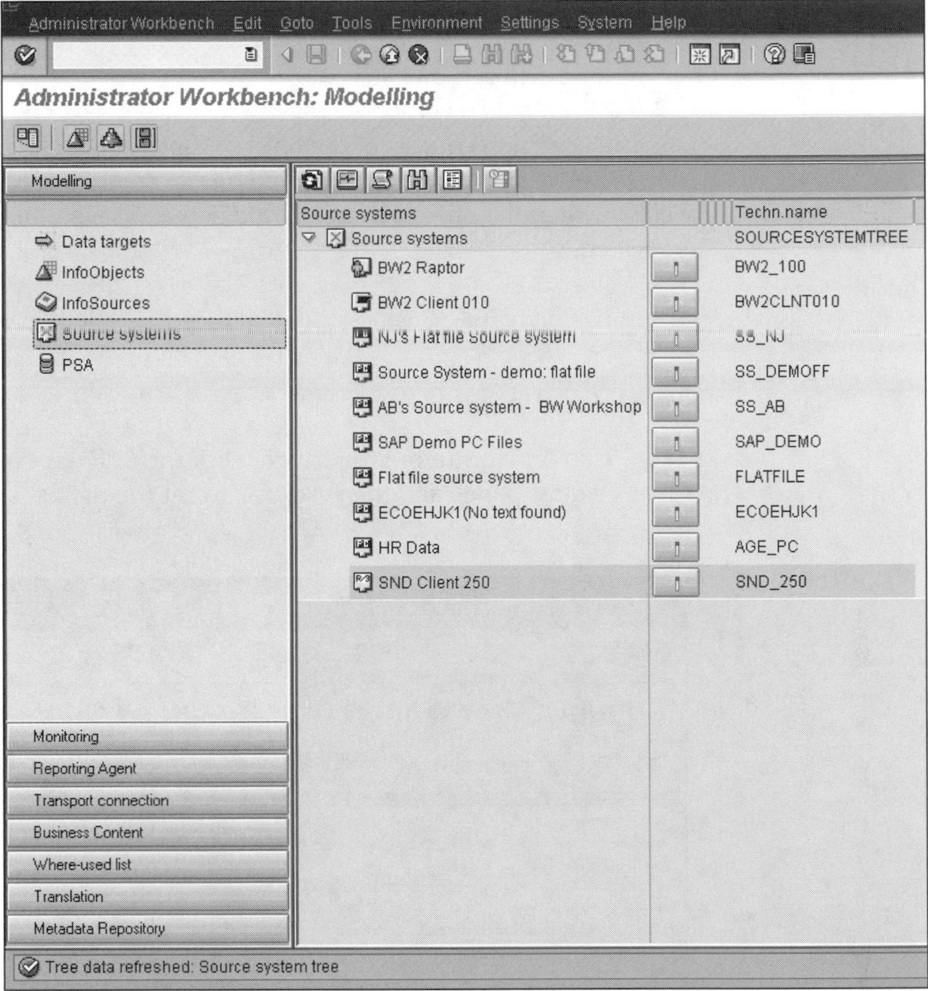

Note: Replicating DataSources from a source system will create identical DataSource structures in the BW system.

10.4 Installing Business Content Objects and Loading R/3 Data

Initially, all of the Business Content objects are set to the D version, so we must activate them before we can use them. This section provides the procedure for doing so, using 0PLANT as an example.

Note: Business Content objects come in three versions:

- D—SAP delivery version
- A—active version
- M—modified version

The D version consists of the object's meta-data defined in Business Content. An A version object has been physically created. It appears as an M version when the object has been modified and saved, but has not yet been activated.

In BW, activating Business Content object is called *Install(ing)* the object.

Work Instructions

Step 1 In Administrator Workbench, click the *Business Content* bar in the leftmost panel, and then click ⊠ to set the default source systems.

SCREEN 10.45

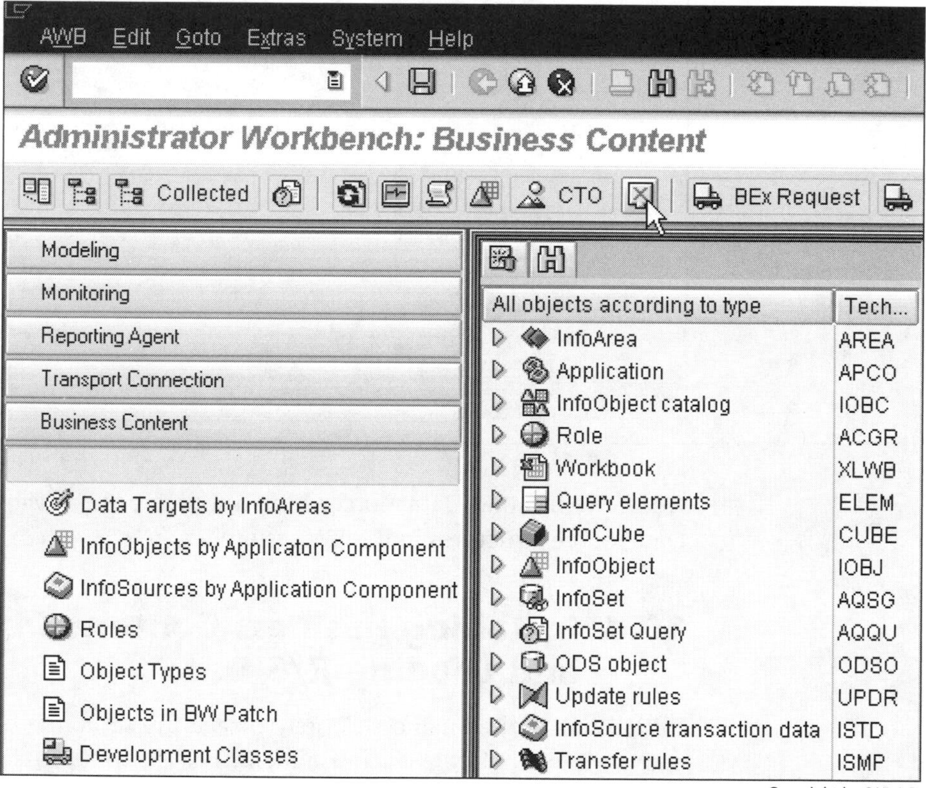

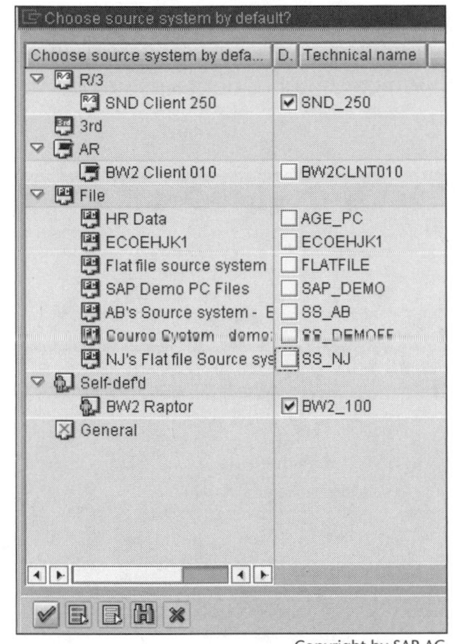

SCREEN 10.46

Step 2 The default source systems are displayed. Click ✔ to accept them and continue.

Step 3 Click [Collection mode], and then select the *collect automatically* option. The *collect automatically* option means that BW will collect related objects for us.

SCREEN 10.47

Note: A Business Content object cannot be activated if the objects on which it depends do not exist. Therefore, it is recommended that you select this option when installing a Business Content object.

Step 4 Click Grouping, and then select the *in dataflow before and aftrwds* option. With the *in dataflow before and aftrwds* option, objects that depend on 0PLANT and objects on which 0PLANT depends will be collected and activated together.

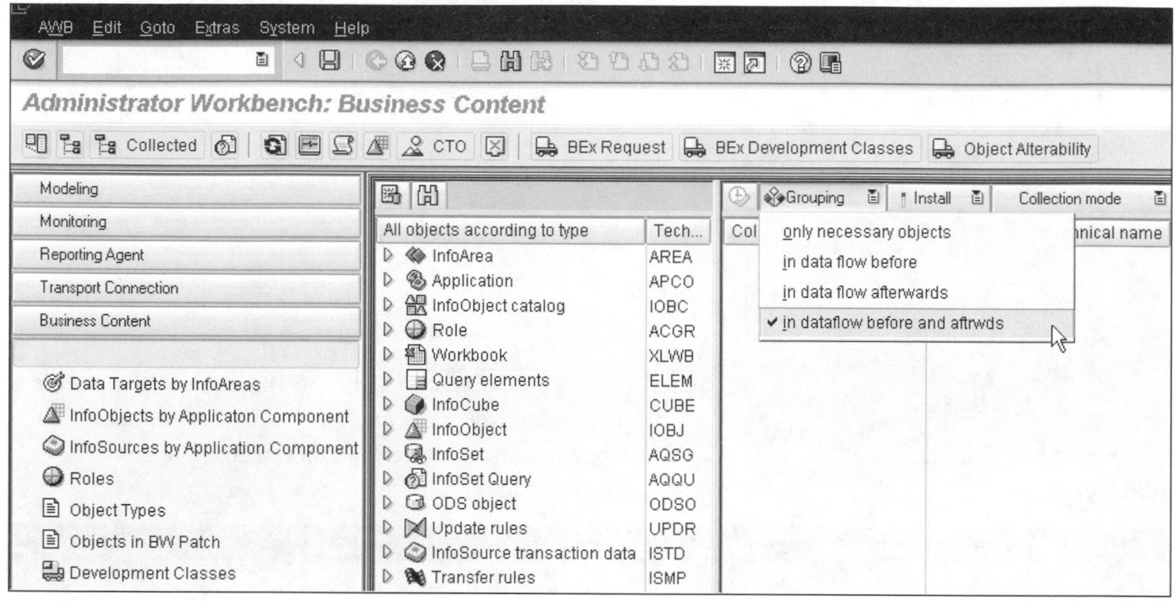

SCREEN 10.48

Step 5 Next, we will select a Business Content object and activate it. Click *Select objects* under *InfoObject* to locate 0PLANT.

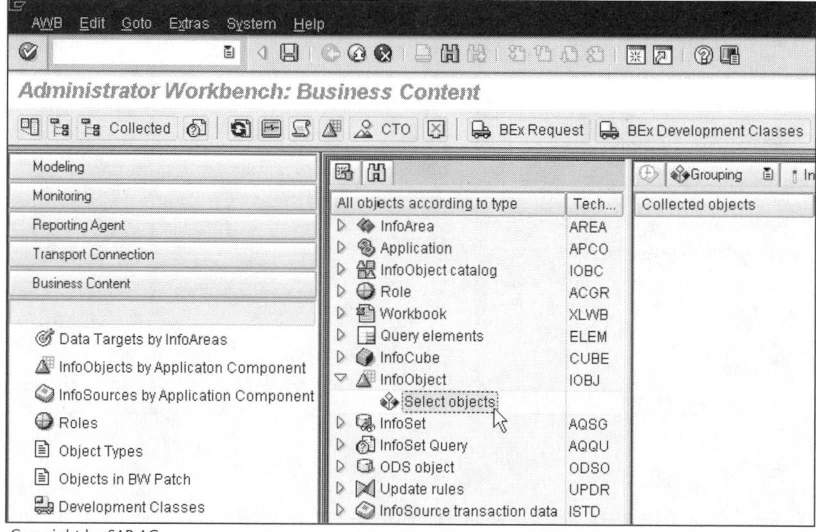

SCREEN 10.49

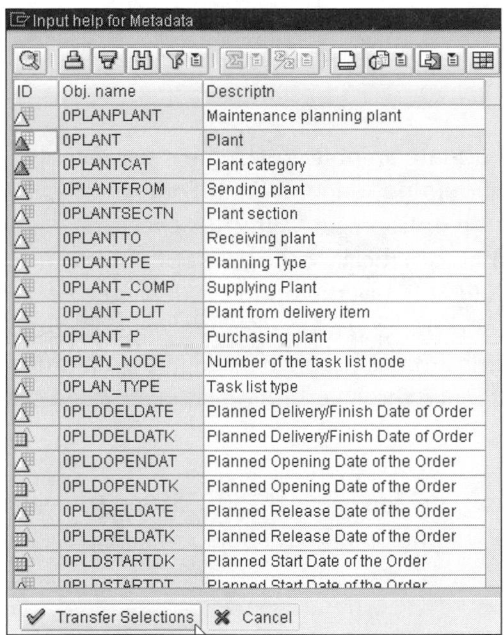

SCREEN 10.50

Step 6 Select *0PLANT*, and then click ✔ Transfer Selections .

Step 7 Notice that 0PLANT and the associated objects are listed in the rightmost panel.

Note: Next to column *Collected objects* are two columns, *Install* and *Match (X) or copy.* If 0PLANT has not been installed previously, then by default the collected objects will be checked only in *Install*, not *Match (X) or copy*. We can use the check boxes to select objects for installation.

If 0PLANT has been installed previously, Screen 10.51 displays, in which the collected objects are checked in *Match (X) or copy*, not *Install*. With this setting, the installation will do nothing to the object, keeping its A version untouched.

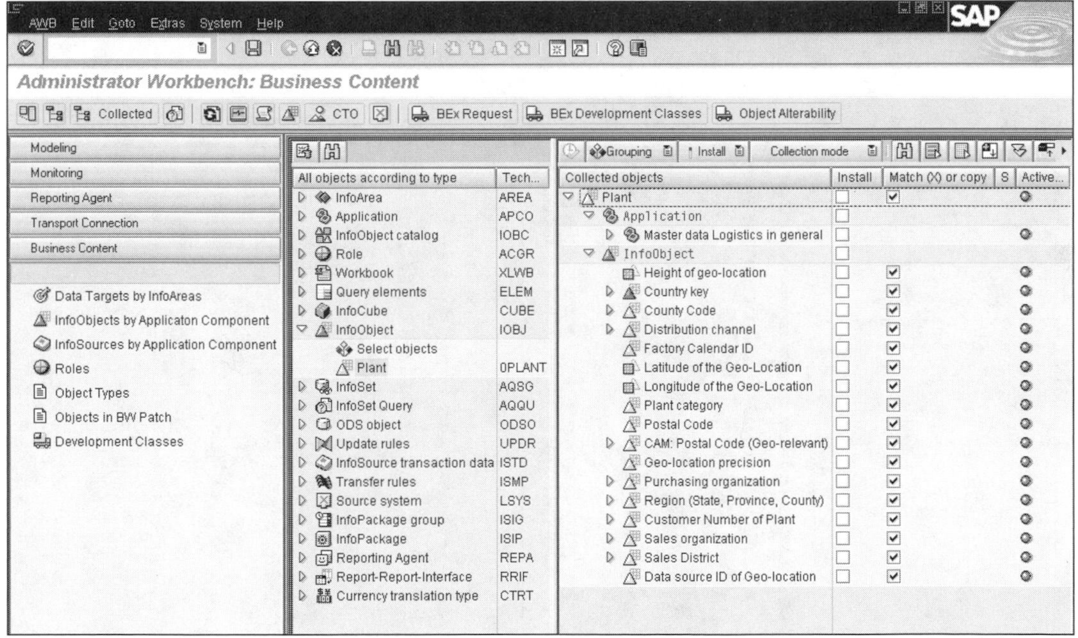

SCREEN 10.51

If an object is checked in both *Match (X) or copy* and *Install*, the installation process will open a new screen, asking us whether to merge the A version object with its D version definition.

Caution: You can use this feature to update an object with the most recently delivered Business Content, but you should not depend on it. For example, if the A version 0PLANT does not have the option *with hierarchies* checked (Screen 3.34), the installation will not automatically check the option *with hierarchies* although the D version of 0PLANT has the option *with hierarchies* checked. It means that the A version and the D version do not always merge.

If an object is checked in the column *Install* and unchecked in the column *Match (X) or copy*, the installation will make the A version object have its D version definition.

Caution: Without any warning, this setting can cause the installation to overwrite the A version object. Accordingly, some data in the object will be deleted, too.

Step 8 Click *Install,* and then select *Install* to activate 0PLANT and the associated objects.

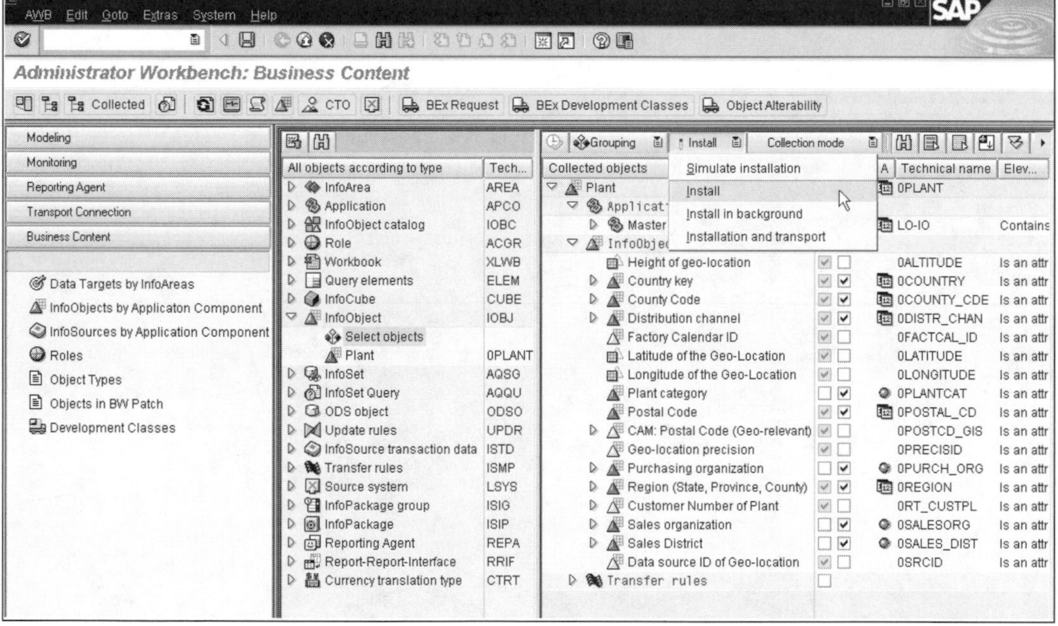

SCREEN 10.52

Note: BW takes care of the sequence of activating objects.

Tip: Use the *Install in background* option when activating a large object.

Result

0PLANT and the associated objects, including transfer rules, are activated.

Next, to load 0PLANT data from the SND_250 source system, we need to create InfoPackages (Screen 10.53).

As mentioned earlier in conjunction with Screen 10.40, Screen 10.53 includes an entry called *Plant* under the *Select data* tab. This entry is used as a data selection condition when extracting data from the SND_250 source system.

SCREEN 10.53

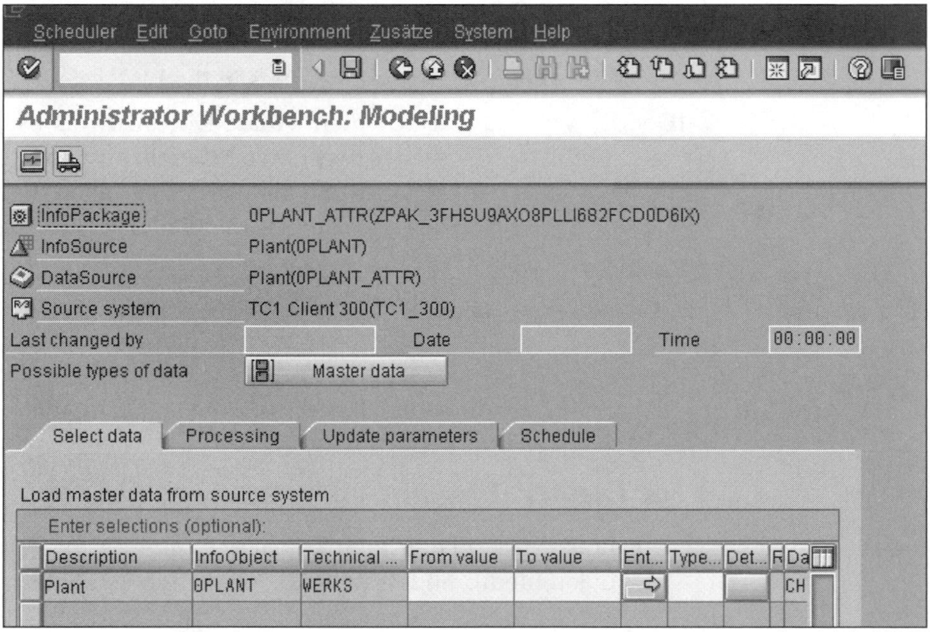

Following the same procedures in Sections 3.4 and 3.5, we can load and check 0PLANT data.

10.5 Summary

This chapter examined Business Content, demonstrating how to activate and use it to load R/3 data. Business Content includes extensive objects, and its functionality continues to expand in every new BW release.

Key Terms

Term	Description
Logical system	A logical system is the name of a client in an SAP system.
Client	A client is a subset of data in an SAP system. Data shared by all clients are called client-independent data, as compared with client-dependent data. When logging on to an SAP system, a user needs to specify which client to use. Once in the system, the user has access to both client-dependent data and client-independent data.
DataSource	A DataSource is a structure in the source system that specifies the method for transferring data out of the source system. If the source system is R/3, replicating DataSources from a source system will create identical DataSource structures in the BW system.
IDoc	IDoc (Intermediate Document) is used in SAP to transfer data between two different systems. IDoc itself is a specific instance of a data structure called the IDoc Type. The IDoc Interface defines the IDoc Type processing logic.
Business Content	Business Content is a complete set of BW objects developed by SAP to support OLAP tasks. It contains roles, workbooks, queries, InfoCubes, key figures, characteristics, update rules, InfoSources, extractors for SAP R/3, and other mySAP solutions.

For Further Information

- Book: *ALE, EDI & IDoc Technologies for SAP,* by Arvind Nagpal, Robert Lyfareff(ed.), and Gareth M. de Bruyn (ed.). Prima Publishing, 1999. ISBN: 0761519033.

Next . . .

Besides the standard R/3 DataSources, Business Content provides a function called **Generic Data Extraction**. When necessary, we can use this function to create a new DataSource, as described in Chapter 11.

Chapter 11

Generic R/3 Data Extraction

In Chapter 10, we discussed how to use Business Content's standard DataSources. In this chapter, we will describe how to use its generic R/3 data extraction capability. Generic R/3 data extraction allows us to extract virtually any R/3 data.

For example, the 0VENDOR characteristic in Business Content contains only vendor master data. The data are from R/3 table LFA1 (Screen 11.1).

If the information about a vendor in our business depends on the purchasing organization with which the vendor deals, then we must create a new vendor characteristic compounded with 0PURCH_ORG (Purchasing Organization). In R/3, the data will come from another table LFM1 (Screen 11.2). LFM1 is a join table containing vendor and purchasing organization data. It provides a reference from vendors to purchasing organizations, and vice versa.

Our goal in this chapter is to load the appropriate R/3 data into the new vendor characteristic called ZVENDOR. Its master data and text will be extracted from LFM1 and LFA1. Tables 11.1 and 11.2 list the necessary fields.

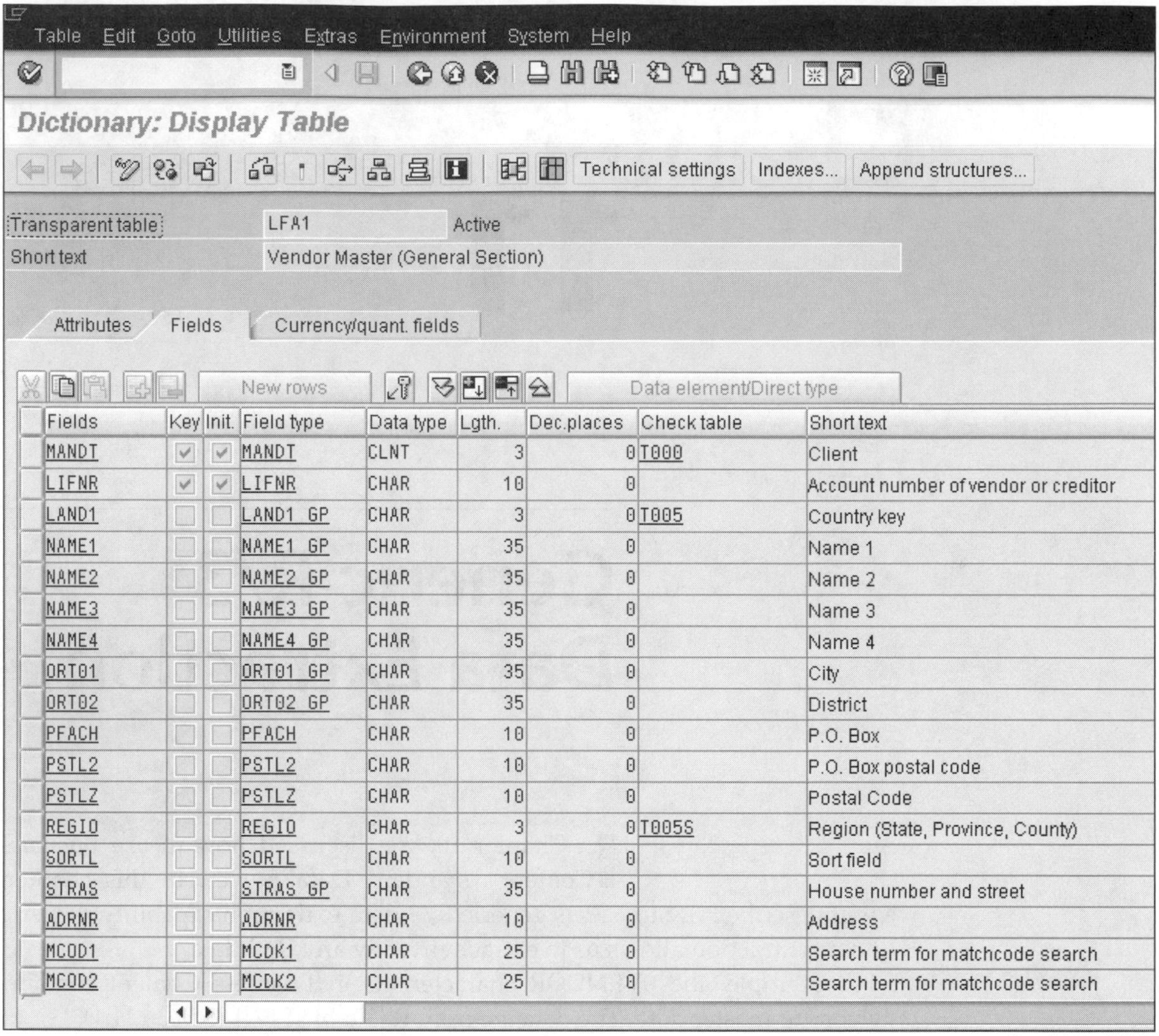

Table Edit Goto Utilities Extras Environment System Help

Dictionary: Display Table

Technical settings | Indexes... | Append structures...

Transparent table: LFA1 Active

Short text: Vendor Master (General Section)

Attributes | Fields | Currency/quant. fields

New rows | Data element/Direct type

Fields	Key	Init.	Field type	Data type	Lgth.	Dec.places	Check table	Short text
MANDT	✓	✓	MANDT	CLNT	3	0	T000	Client
LIFNR	✓	✓	LIFNR	CHAR	10	0		Account number of vendor or creditor
LAND1			LAND1_GP	CHAR	3	0	T005	Country key
NAME1			NAME1_GP	CHAR	35	0		Name 1
NAME2			NAME2_GP	CHAR	35	0		Name 2
NAME3			NAME3_GP	CHAR	35	0		Name 3
NAME4			NAME4_GP	CHAR	35	0		Name 4
ORT01			ORT01_GP	CHAR	35	0		City
ORT02			ORT02_GP	CHAR	35	0		District
PFACH			PFACH	CHAR	10	0		P.O. Box
PSTL2			PSTL2	CHAR	10	0		P.O. Box postal code
PSTLZ			PSTLZ	CHAR	10	0		Postal Code
REGIO			REGIO	CHAR	3	0	T005S	Region (State, Province, County)
SORTL			SORTL	CHAR	10	0		Sort field
STRAS			STRAS_GP	CHAR	35	0		House number and street
ADRNR			ADRNR	CHAR	10	0		Address
MCOD1			MCDK1	CHAR	25	0		Search term for matchcode search
MCOD2			MCDK2	CHAR	25	0		Search term for matchcode search

SCREEN 11.1

SCREEN 11.2

Table Edit Goto Utilities Extras Environment System Help

Dictionary: Display Table

Technical settings | Indexes... | Append structures...

Transparent table: LFM1 Active

Short text: Vendor master record purchasing organization data

Attributes | Fields | Currency/quant. fields

Fields	Key	Init.	Field type	Data type	Lgth.	Dec.places	Check table	Short text
MANDT	✓	✓	MANDT	CLNT	3	0	T000	Client
LIFNR	✓	✓	ELIFN	CHAR	10	0	LFA1	Vendor's account number
EKORG	✓	✓	EKORG	CHAR	4	0	T024E	Purchasing organization
.INCLUDE			LFM2I1		0	0		Include LFM1 LFM2
ERDAT			ERDAT	DATS	8	0		Date on which the record was created
ERNAM			ERNAM	CHAR	12	0		Name of Person who Created the Object
SPERM			SPERM_M	CHAR	1	0		Purchasing block at purchasing organization level
LOEVM			LOEVM_M	CHAR	1	0		Delete flag for vendor at purchasing level
LFABC			LFABC	CHAR	1	0		ABC indicator
WAERS			BSTWA	CUKY	5	0	TCURC	Purchase order currency
VERKF			EVERK	CHAR	30	0		Responsible salesperson at vendor's office
TELF1			TELFE	CHAR	16	0		Vendor's telephone number
MINBW			MINBW	CURR	13	2		Minimum order value
ZTERM			DZTERM	CHAR	4	0		Terms of payment key
INCO1			INCO1	CHAR	3	0	TINC	Incoterms (part 1)
INCO2			INCO2	CHAR	28	0		Incoterms (part 2)
WEBRE			WEBRE	CHAR	1	0		Indicator: GR-based invoice verification
KZABS			KZABS	CHAR	1	0		Order acknowledgment requirement

TABLE 11.1 NECESSARY LFM1 FIELDS FOR ZVENDOR MASTER DATA

Fields	Data Type	Length	Decimal Places	Check Table	Short Text
MANDT	CLNT	3	0	T000	Client
LIFNR	CHAR	10	0	LFA1	Vendor's account number
EKORG	CHAR	4	0	T024E	Purchasing organization
VERKF	CHAR	30	0		Responsible salesperson at vendor's office
MINBW	CURR	13	2		Minimum order value
ZTERM	CHAR	4	0		Terms of payment key
INCO1	CHAR	3	0	TINC	Incoterms (part 1)
INCO2	CHAR	28	0		Incoterms (part 2)
WAERS	CUKY	5	0	TCURC	Purchase order currency

TABLE 11.2 NECESSARY LFA1 FIELDS FOR ZVENDOR TEXT

Fields	Data Type	Length	Decimal Places	Check Table	Short Text
MANDT	CLNT	3	0	T000	Client
LIFNR	CHAR	10	0	LFA1	Vendor's account number
EKORG	CHAR	4	0	T024E	Purchasing organization
NAME1	CHAR	35			Name 1
NAME2	CHAR	35			Name 2
NAME3	CHAR	35			Name 3

To link the text with the master data, the field LIFNR of the table LFA1 must be equal to the field LIFNR of the table LFM1.

As before, we will use step-by-step work instructions to demonstrate this process. The R/3 source system used in our example is release 4.0B with R/3 Plug-In PI-A 1999_1_40B patch 0004.

Note: Like other SAP products, R/3 Plug-In has its own releases and patches. The feature discussed in this chapter has not been changed in the current R/3 Plug-In release and patch, although its screens may have a slightly different appearance from those of the screens shown here.

11.1 Creating Views in R/3

First we need to create two views: one for master data and one for texts.

Note: Views are ABAP dictionary objects. They are used to display data from multiple tables with specified table join conditions.

Work Instructions

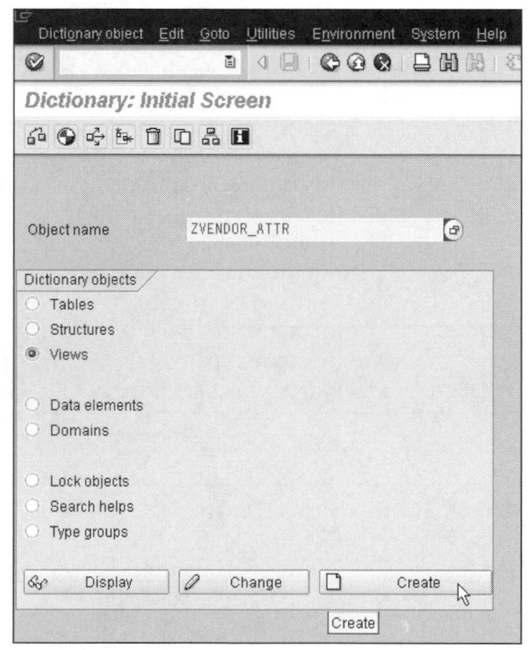

SCREEN 11.3

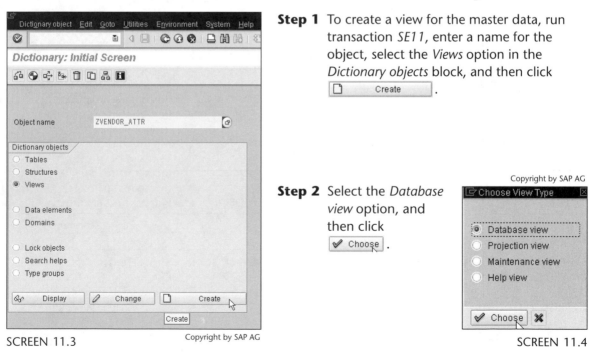

Step 1 To create a view for the master data, run transaction *SE11*, enter a name for the object, select the *Views* option in the *Dictionary objects* block, and then click Create.

Step 2 Select the *Database view* option, and then click Choose.

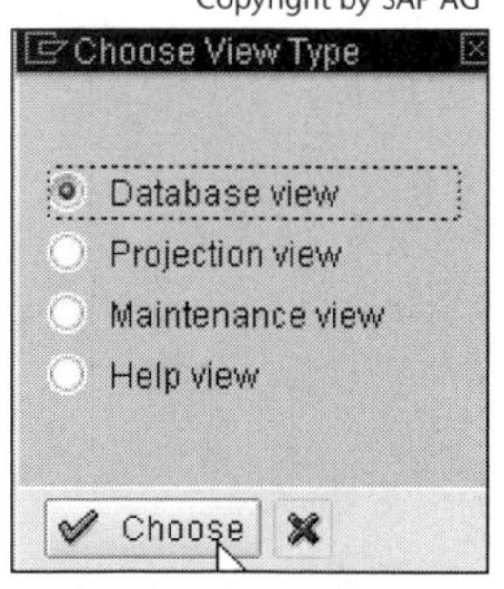

SCREEN 11.4

Create Object Directory Entry

Object R3TR VIEW ZVENDOR_ATTR

Attributes

Development class

Person responsible BFU

Original system SND

Original language EN English

Repair flag

Generation flag

Local object   Lock overview

Copyright by SAP AG

SCREEN 11.5

Step 3 The view needs to be included in a development class in order to be transported to other R/3 systems. In our example, we create views as local objects. Enter *$TMP* as the development class name and click the save icon, or simply click Local object to assign the object to $TMP. Click Local object to continue.

Note: A **development class** groups logically related objects, such as the objects that make up an accounting application. $TMP is a temporary local development class. Objects in $TMP cannot be transported into other systems.

See ABAP documents for more information on $TMP and non-$TMP development classes.

Step 4 This view consists of only one table, *LFM1* (Vendor master record purchasing organization data). Enter the names of the fields from which we will extract data (see Table 11.1).

Click the save icon to save the view definition.

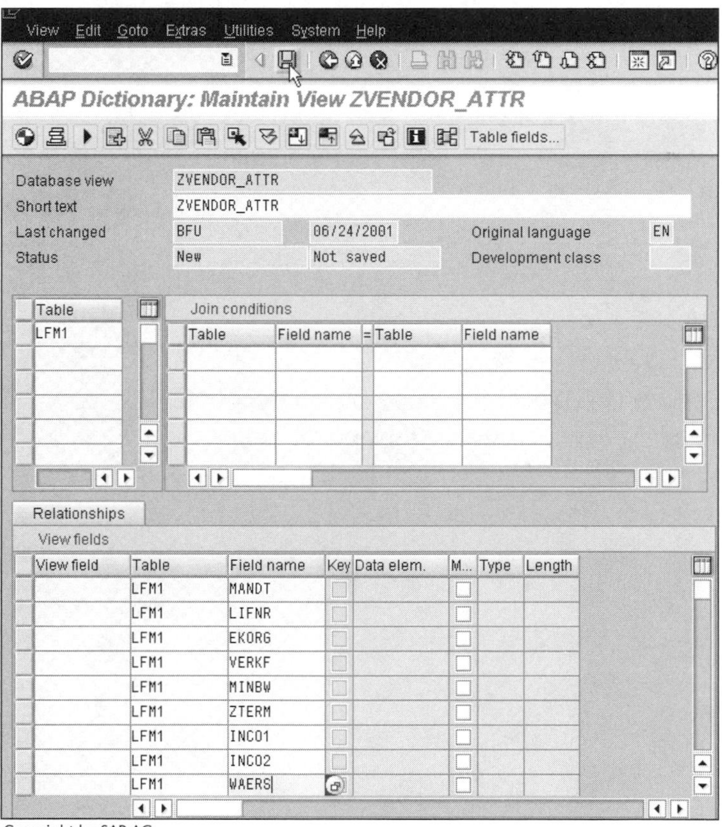

Copyright by SAP AG

SCREEN 11.6

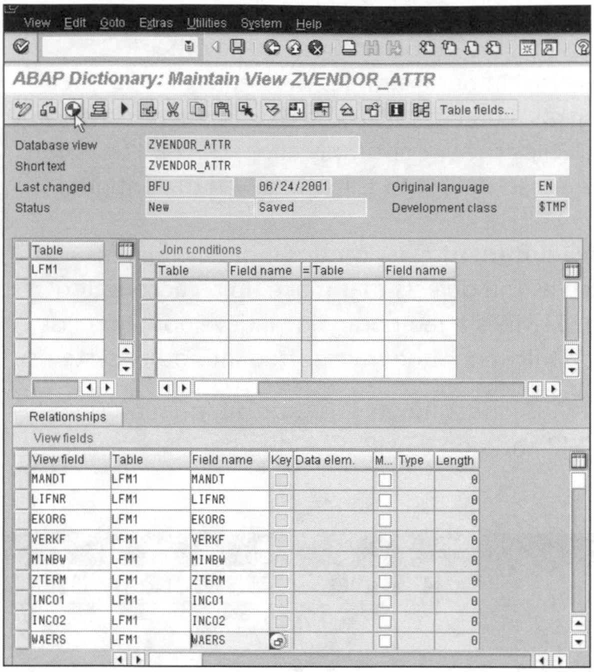

SCREEN 11.7

Step 5 Click [check icon] to check the view definition. If it is valid, click [generate icon] to generate the view.

Step 6 To display the data selected by this view, select the *Display data* option on the Utilities menu.

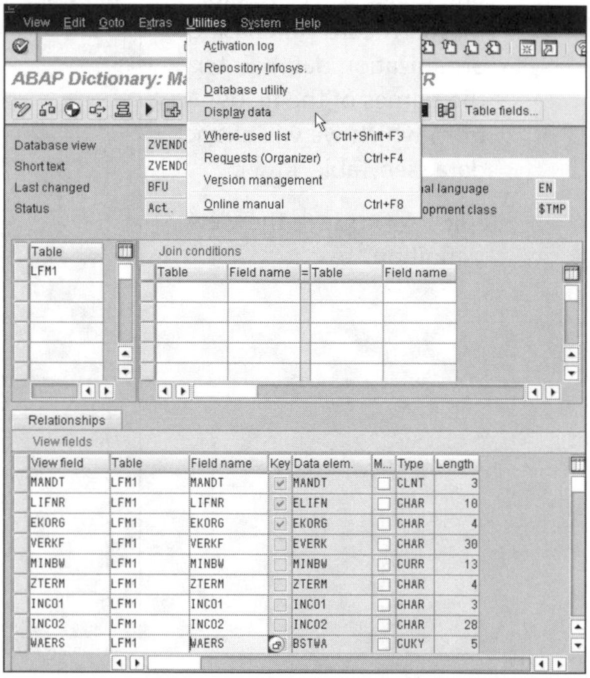

SCREEN 11.8

Program Edit Goto Settings System Help

Data Browser: Table ZVENDOR_ATTR: Selection Screen

Selection options Number of entries

LIFNR to
EKORG to
VERKF to
MINBW to
ZTERM to
INCO1 to
INCO2 to
WAERS to

Width of output list 250
Maximum no. of hits 500

SCREEN 11.9

Step 7 Click [icon] to display the data.

Result

The result, which is shown in Screen 11.10, has two entries.

SCREEN 11.10

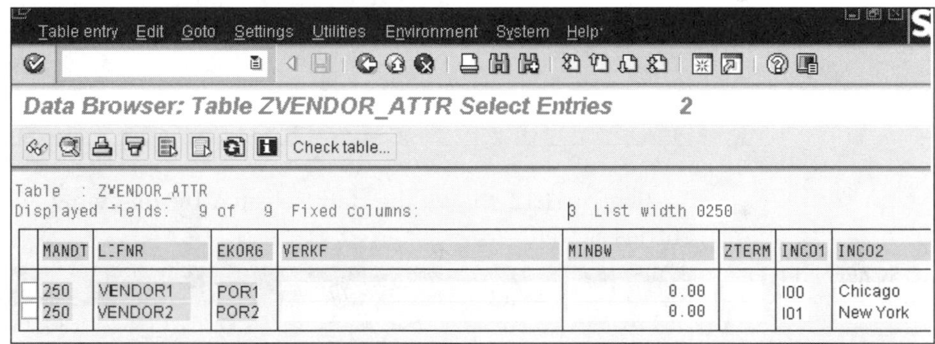

Table entry Edit Goto Settings Utilities Environment System Help

Data Browser: Table ZVENDOR_ATTR Select Entries 2

Check table...

Table : ZVENDOR_ATTR
Displayed fields: 9 of 9 Fixed columns: 3 List width 0250

MANDT	LIFNR	EKORG	VERKF	MINBW	ZTERM	INCO1	INCO2
250	VENDOR1	POR1		0.00		I00	Chicago
250	VENDOR2	POR2		0.00		I01	New York

We use the same procedure to create a view for the text data (see Screen 11.11). This view consists of data from two tables, *LFM1* (Vendor master record purchasing organization data) and LFA1 (Vendor master – general section). The text data come from the *LFA1* table.

SCREEN 11.11

View Edit Goto Extras Utilities System Help

ABAP Dictionary: Maintain View ZVENDOR_TEXT

Table fields...

Database view	ZVENDOR_TEXT
Short text	ZVENDOR_TEXT
Last changed	BFU 06/24/2001
Original language	EN
Status	Act. Saved
Development class	$TMP

Table
LFA1
LFM1

Join conditions

Table	Field name	=	Table	Field name
LFA1	MANDT	=	LFM1	MANDT
LFA1	LIFNR	=	LFM1	LIFNR

Relationships

View fields

View field	Table	Field name	Key	Data elem.	M...	Type	Length
MANDT	LFA1	MANDT	✓	MANDT	☐	CLNT	3
LIFNR	LFA1	LIFNR	✓	LIFNR	☐	CHAR	10
EKORG	LFM1	EKORG	✓	EKORG	☐	CHAR	4
NAME1	LFA1	NAME1		NAME1_GP	☐	CHAR	35
NAME2	LFA1	NAME2		NAME2_GP	☐	CHAR	35
NAME3	LFA1	NAME3		NAME3_GP	☐	CHAR	35

Screen 11.12 shows the data selected by this view, which consists of two entries as well.

SCREEN 11.12

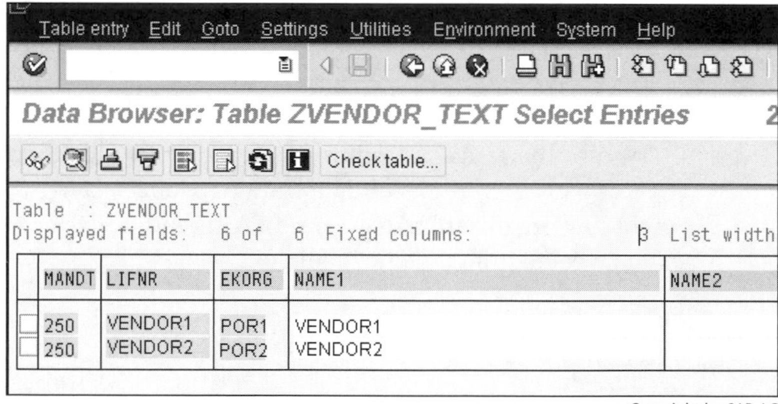

Table entry Edit Goto Settings Utilities Environment System Help

Data Browser: Table ZVENDOR_TEXT Select Entries 2

Check table...

Table : ZVENDOR_TEXT
Displayed fields: 6 of 6 Fixed columns: 3 List width

MANDT	LIFNR	EKORG	NAME1	NAME2
250	VENDOR1	POR1	VENDOR1	
250	VENDOR2	POR2	VENDOR2	

Now we have created two views, one for master data and one for texts. Next, we will create DataSources using these two views.

11.2 Creating DataSources in R/3 and Replicating Them to BW

DataSources consist of structures and objects that BW uses to extract data from source systems. Generic R/3 data extraction in Business Content allows us to create DataSources for the views created in Section 11.1. The procedure follows.

Work Instructions

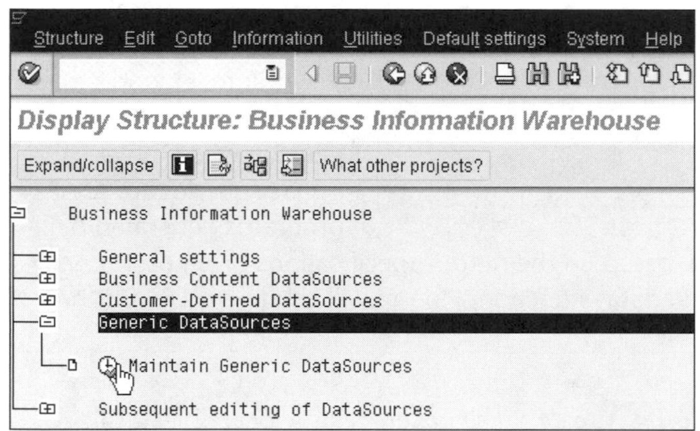

SCREEN 11.13

Step 1 Run transaction *SBIW* and click *Maintain Generic DataSources,* or run transaction *RSO2.*

Step 2 Because our BW system is 2.0B, click the *BW Release 2.0* button. Enter a name as the *Master data attributes*, and then click Create.

Note: Here *ZVENDOR_ATTR* is a DataSource name, not the name of the view ZVENDOR_ATTR created in Section 11.1.

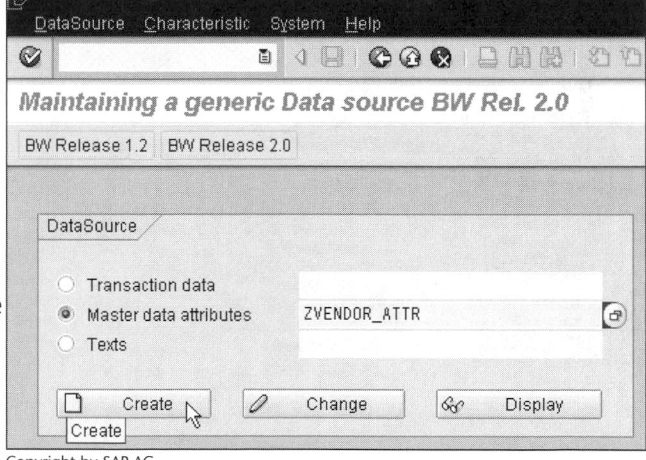

SCREEN 11.14

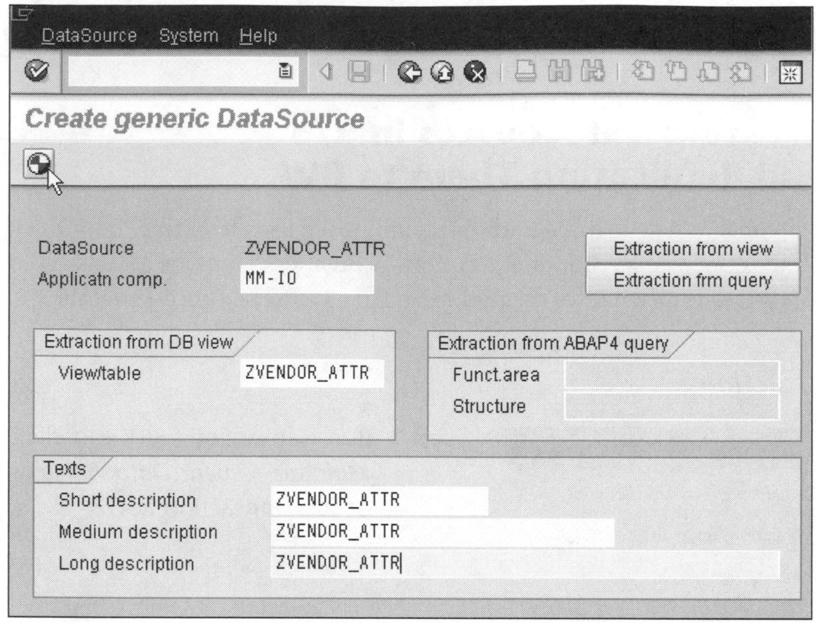

SCREEN 11.15

Copyright by SAP AG

Step 3 Enter *ZVENDOR_ATTR* as the *View/table* and other information as shown, and then click [generate icon] to generate the DataSource.

Note: Besides DB view, we can use ABAP queries to select R/3 data. ABAP queries are now called **InfoSet** queries.

An InfoSet works much like a view but allows outer joins between tables. InfoSet queries are ABAP programs generated by SAP (either R/3 or BW), based on the output specifications given by a user. When you use InfoSet in data extraction, Plug-In will create a query for the DataSource automatically.

Create Object Directory Entry
Object R3TR OSOA ZVENDOR_ATTR
Attributes
Development class
Person responsible BFU
Original system SND
Original language EN English
Local object Lock overview

SCREEN 11.16

Copyright by SAP AG

Step 4 Create the DataSource as a local object. Click Local object.

Step 5 In the new window, check two selection fields and click [save icon] to save the DataSource.

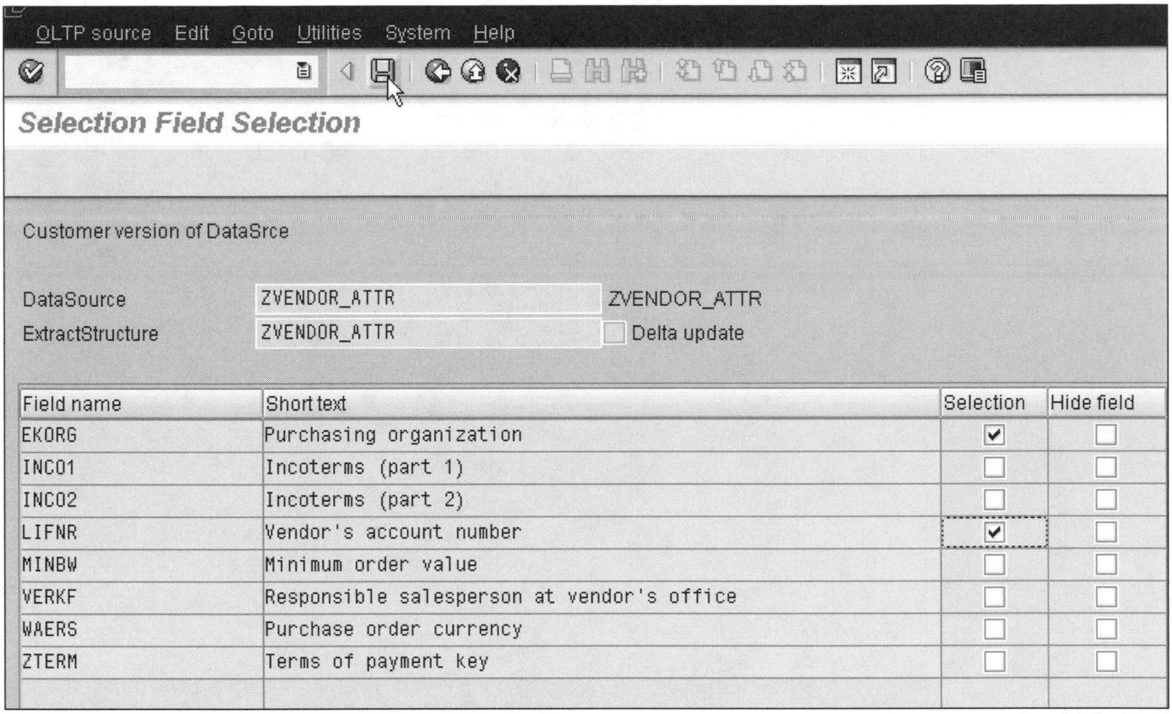

OLTP source Edit Goto Utilities System Help

Selection Field Selection

Customer version of DataSrce

DataSource ZVENDOR_ATTR ZVENDOR_ATTR

ExtractStructure ZVENDOR_ATTR ☐ Delta update

Field name	Short text	Selection	Hide field
EKORG	Purchasing organization	☑	☐
INCO1	Incoterms (part 1)	☐	☐
INCO2	Incoterms (part 2)	☐	☐
LIFNR	Vendor's account number	☑	☐
MINBW	Minimum order value	☐	☐
VERKF	Responsible salesperson at vendor's office	☐	☐
WAERS	Purchase order currency	☐	☐
ZTERM	Terms of payment key	☐	☐

SCREEN 11.17

Result

You have created the DataSource ZVENDOR_ATTR.

Repeating the preceding steps, we create DataSource ZVENDOR_TEXT for the view ZVENDOR_TEXT.

Now we need to replicate the DataSources so that identical structures of the DataSources will appear in the BW system (see Screen 11.18).

SCREEN 11.18

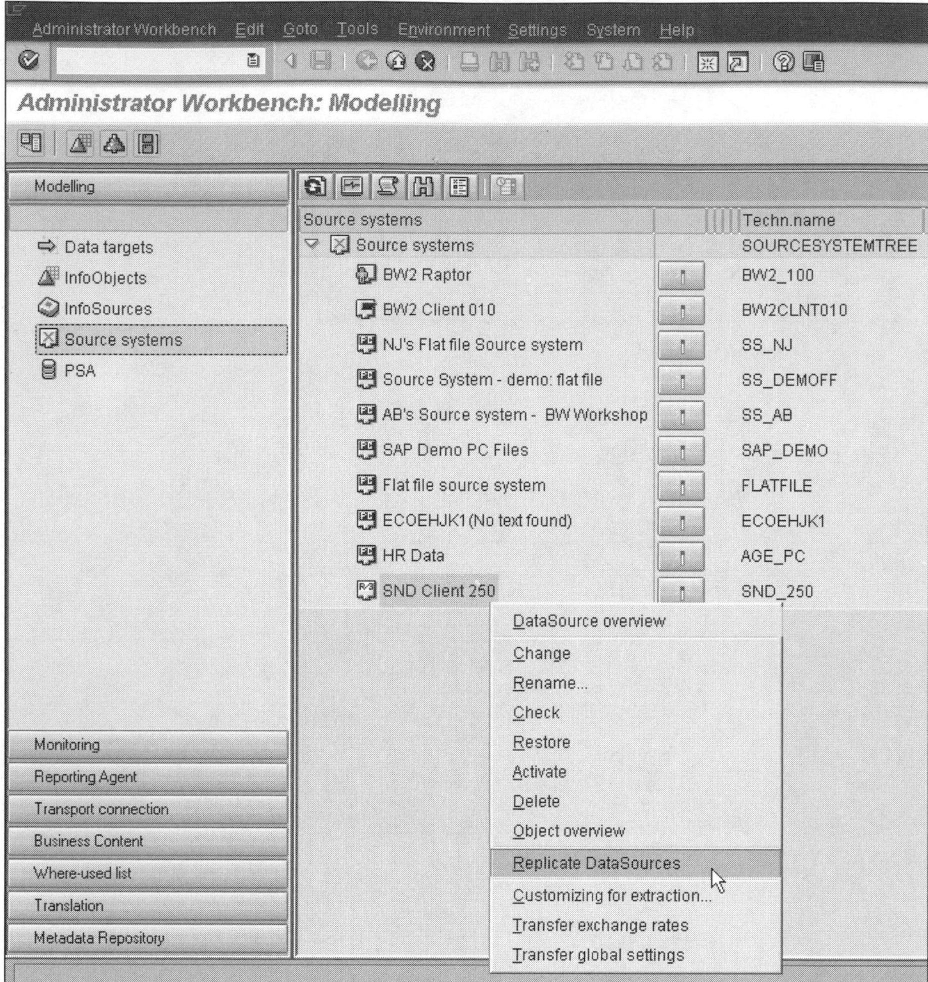

Next, we will create a characteristic in the BW system to receive and store the R/3 data.

11.3 Creating a Characteristic in BW

Now we need to create a characteristic, which we will name ZVENDOR. Table 11.3 shows how we match the R/3 table fields to the characteristic ZVENDOR and its attributes.

TABLE 11.3 CHARACTERISTIC ZVENDOR AND ITS ATTRIBUTES

Table LFM1 Field Attribute	Characteristic	Attribute	Compound
MANDT			
LIFNR	ZVENDOR		
EKORG			EKORG
VERKF		VERKF:	
MINBW		MINBW	
ZTERM		ZTERM	
INCO1		INCO1	
INCO2		INCO2	
WAERS		WAERS	

The characteristic ZVENDOR does not need to have an attribute for the field MANDT. The field MANDT is used to group the LFM1 data into **clients** (see Section 10.1.1). Our earlier replication of DataSources from the source system SND_250 (Screen 11.18) has already determined the client from which to extract data.

Section 2.3 provided the procedure for creating a characteristic. To save space, the work instructions here focus only on what is special to ZVENDOR.

Work Instructions

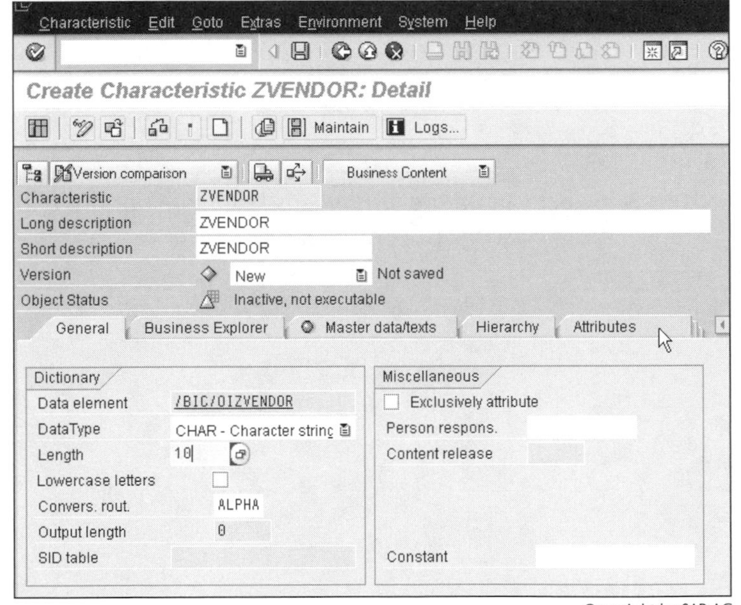

SCREEN 11.19

Step 1 Repeat the procedure in Section 2.3, "Creating InfoObjects—Characteristics," to create the *ZVENDOR* characteristic.

Select *CHAR* as the *DataType*, enter *10* as the field *Length*, and then click the *Attributes* tab to add the attributes.

Step 2 Create attributes as described in Section 2.3. Here, however, the attribute *MINBW* is of type currency, not type character.

Enter *MINBW* as the attribute name, and then click [create icon] to create the attribute.

SCREEN 11.20

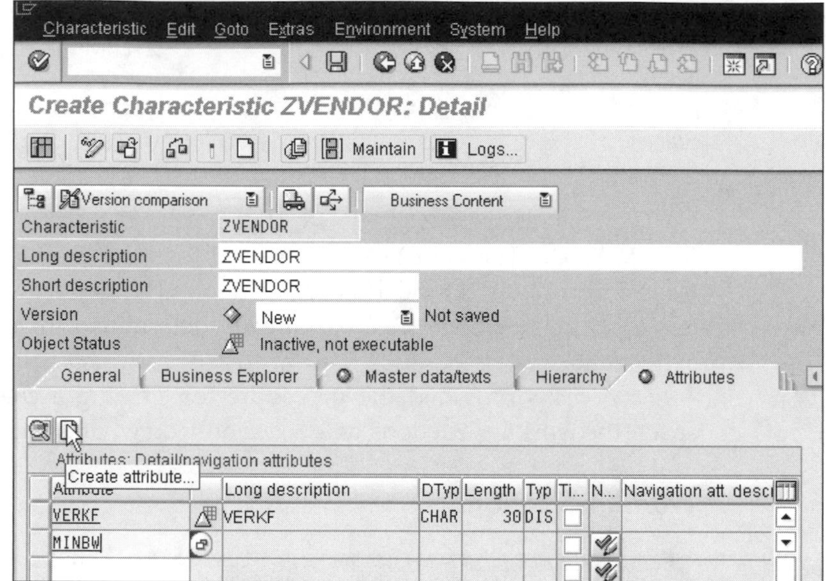

SCREEN 11.21

Step 3 Select the *Create attribute as key figure* option, and then click ✔ to continue.

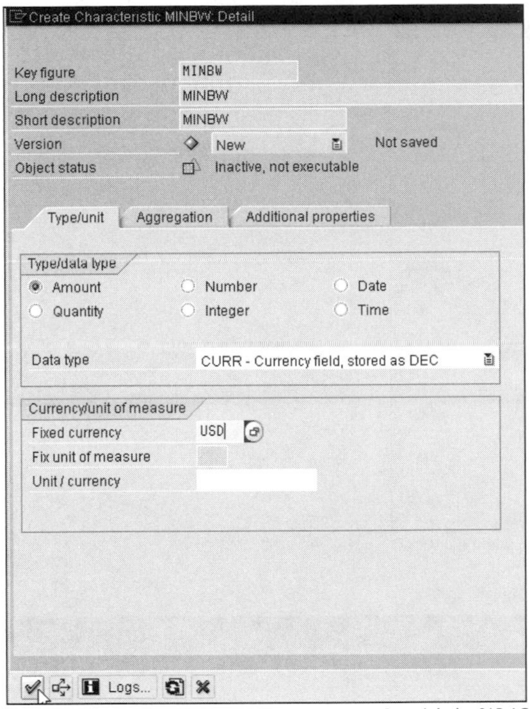
Create Characteristic MINBW: Detail
Key figure
MINBW
Long description
MINBW
Short description
MINBW
Version
New
Not saved
Object status
Inactive, not executable
Type/unit
Aggregation
Additional properties
Type/data type
Amount
Number
Date
Quantity
Integer
Time
Data type
CURR - Currency field, stored as DEC
Currency/unit of measure
Fixed currency
USD
Fix unit of measure
Unit / currency
Logs...

Copyright by SAP AG

SCREEN 11.22

Step 4 Make selections as shown in this screen, and then click ✓ to continue.

Step 5 After creating other attributes, go to the *Compounding* tab.

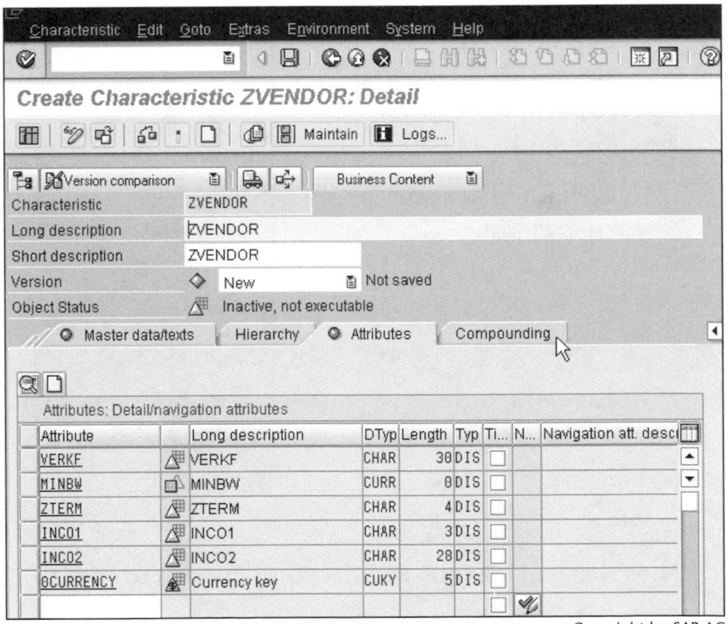
Characteristic Edit Goto Extras Environment System Help
Create Characteristic ZVENDOR: Detail
Maintain
Logs...
Version comparison
Business Content
Characteristic
ZVENDOR
Long description
ZVENDOR
Short description
ZVENDOR
Version
New
Not saved
Object Status
Inactive, not executable
Master data/texts
Hierarchy
Attributes
Compounding
Attributes: Detail/navigation attributes
Attribute
Long description
DTyp
Length
Typ
Ti...
N...
Navigation att. descr
VERKF
VERKF
CHAR
30
DIS
MINBW
MINBW
CURR
0
DIS
ZTERM
ZTERM
CHAR
4
DIS
INCO1
INCO1
CHAR
3
DIS
INCO2
INCO2
CHAR
28
DIS
0CURRENCY
Currency key
CUKY
5
DIS

SCREEN 11.23

Copyright by SAP AG

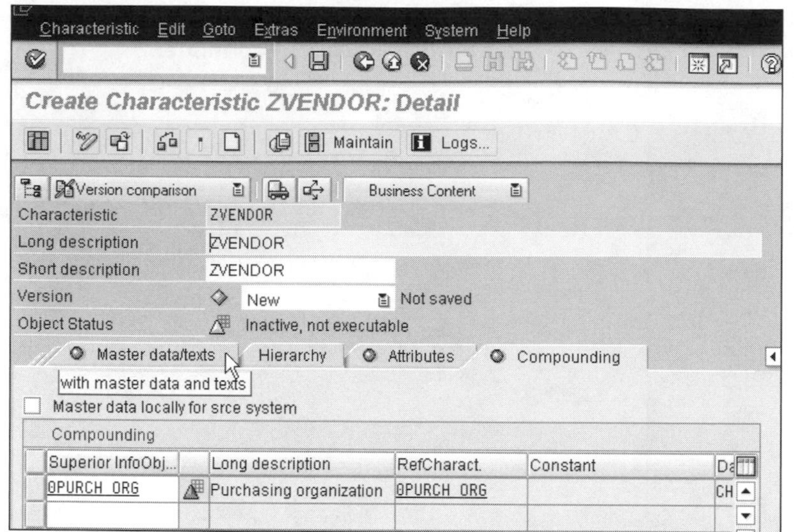

SCREEN 11.24

Step 6 Enter *0PURCH_ORG* as the compound attribute, and then go to the *Master data/texts* tab.

Step 7 Check off *Short*, *Medium*, and *Long* to create three fields in the text table /BIC/TZVENDOR; these fields will store the view ZVENDOR_TEXT's NAME1, NAME2, and NAME3, respectively (Screen 11.11).

Check and activate the characteristic.

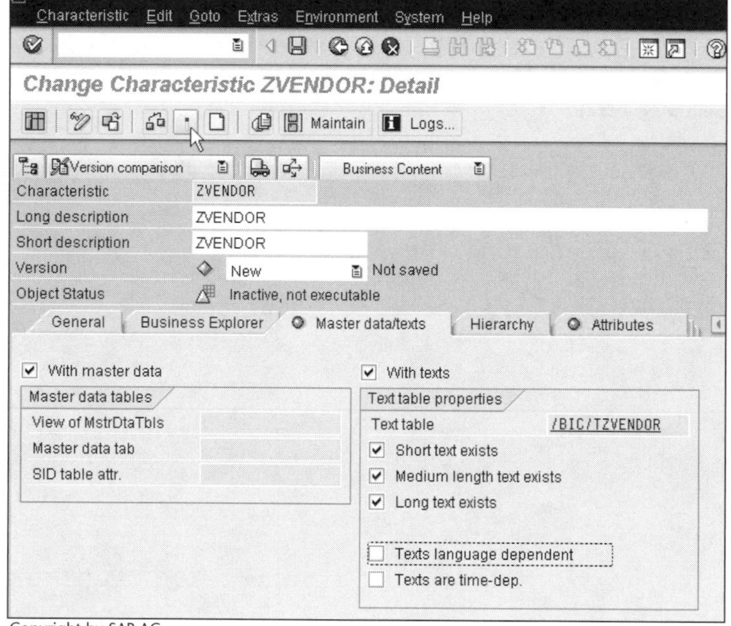

SCREEN 11.25

Next, we will load the R/3 data into the characteristic ZVENDOR.

11.4 Loading Data from R/3 into BW

Previously, we defined the characteristic ZVENDOR and its DataSources, ZVENDOR_ATTR and ZVENDOR_TEXT. Loading the source system data is relatively easy, as noted in Chapter 3. To save space, here we show only those procedures that are special to characteristic ZVENDOR.

This section also provides an example demonstrating how to use the BW Monitor to troubleshoot data load failures.

Work Instructions

Step 1 To load the master data, first we follow the procedure in Section 3.3, "Creating an InfoSource for Characteristic Data," to create transfer rules for the DataSource ZVENDOR_ATTR. Screen 11.26 shows the activated transfer rules.

SCREEN 11.26

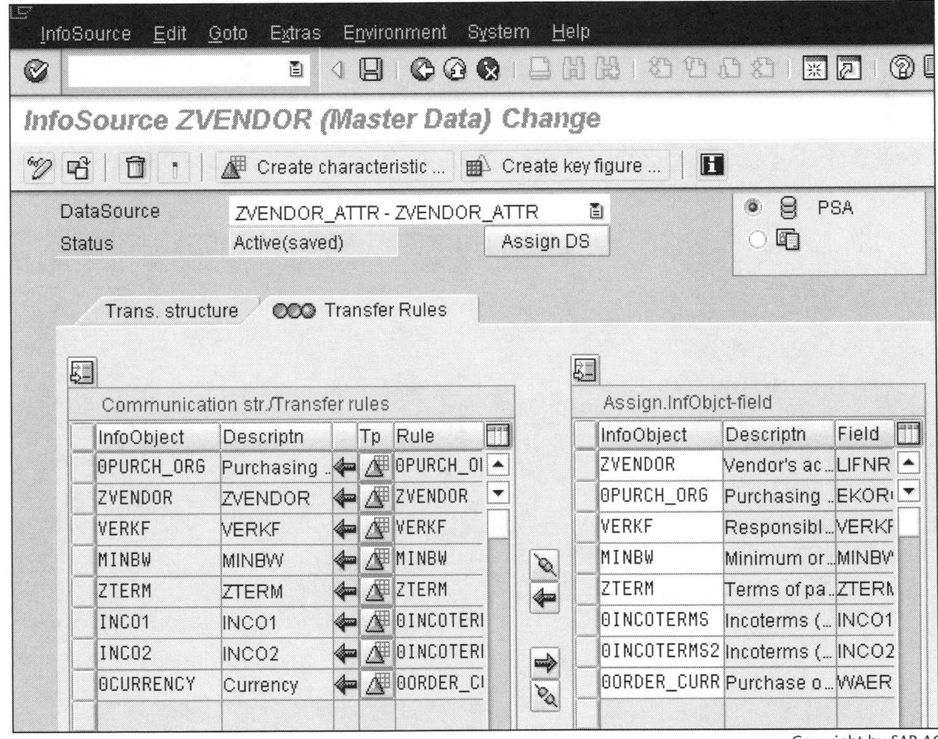

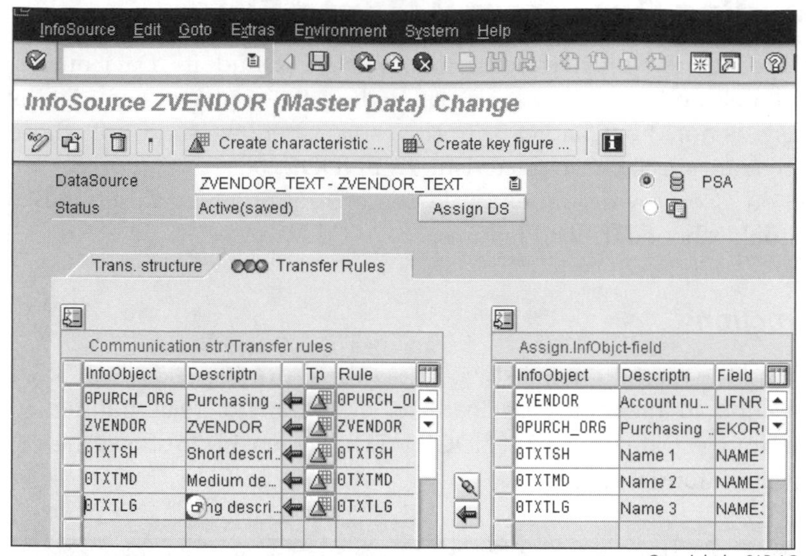

SCREEN 11.27

Step 2 To load the texts, follow the procedure in Section 3.3 again to create transfer rules for the DataSource ZVENDOR_TEXT. Screen 11.27 shows the activated transfer rules.

Step 3 Follow the procedure in Section 3.4, "Creating InfoPackages to Load Characteristic Data," to create InfoPackages.

Screen 11.28 shows the first InfoPackage for master data. Notice the two fields (LIFNR and EKORG) that we selected when we created the ZVENDOR_ATTR DataSource (Screen 11.17).

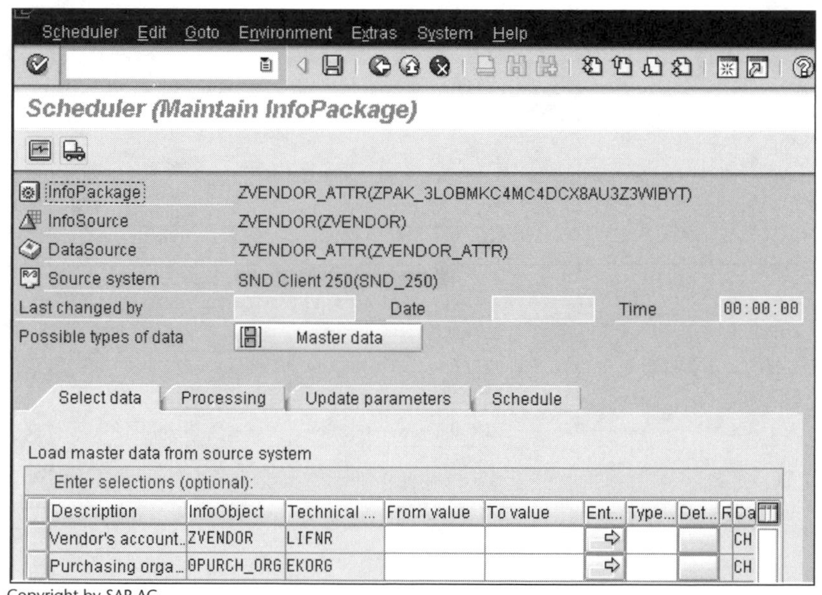

SCREEN 11.28

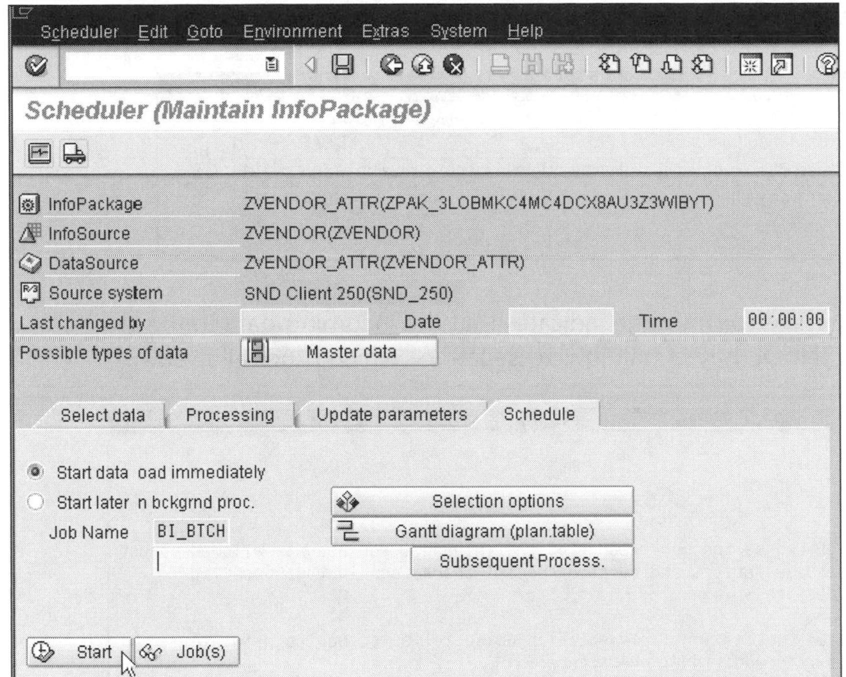

SCREEN 11.29

Step 4 Click Start to load the data immediately

Step 5 BW Monitor indicates that the load attempt failed. Click Error message to display the error.

SCREEN 11.30

Step 6 Click [icon] to display the error messages in detail.

SCREEN 11.31

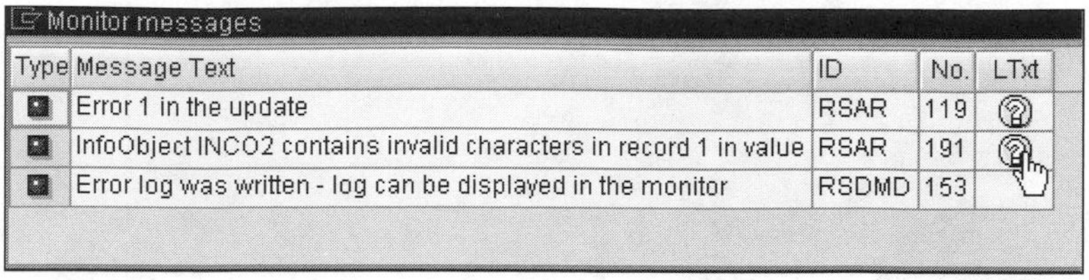

Monitor messages

Type	Message Text	ID	No.	LTxt
■	Error 1 in the update	RSAR	119	?
■	InfoObject INCO2 contains invalid characters in record 1 in value	RSAR	191	?
■	Error log was written - log can be displayed in the monitor	RSDMD	153	

Step 7 The error message indicates that the incoming data to the attribute INCO2 have small/lowercase letters, which is not allowed.

SCREEN 11.32

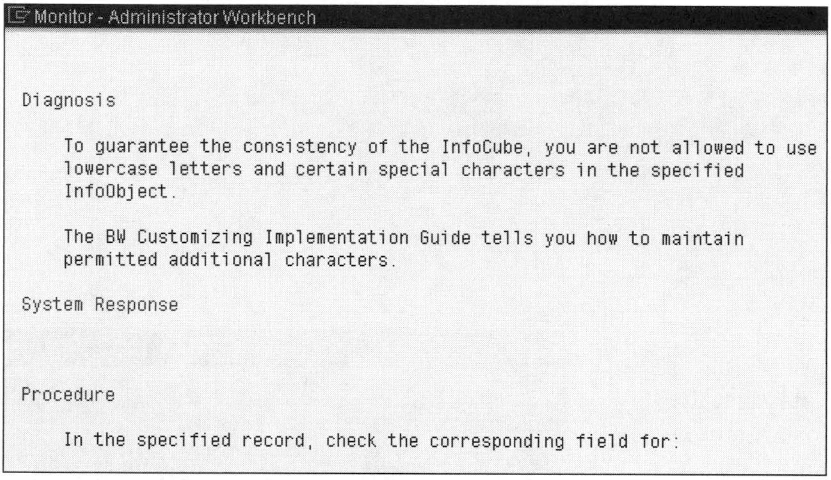

Monitor - Administrator Workbench

```
Diagnosis

    To guarantee the consistency of the InfoCube, you are not allowed to use
    lowercase letters and certain special characters in the specified
    InfoObject.

    The BW Customizing Implementation Guide tells you how to maintain
    permitted additional characters.

System Response


Procedure

    In the specified record, check the corresponding field for:
```

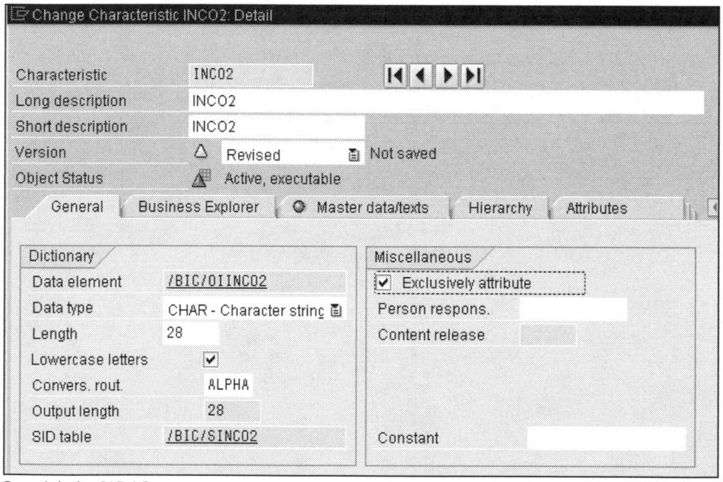

Change Characteristic INCO2: Detail

Characteristic: INCO2
Long description: INCO2
Short description: INCO2
Version: Revised — Not saved
Object Status: Active, executable

General | Business Explorer | Master data/texts | Hierarchy | Attributes

Dictionary
- Data element: /BIC/OIINCO2
- Data type: CHAR - Character string
- Length: 28
- Lowercase letters: ☑
- Convers. rout.: ALPHA
- Output length: 28
- SID table: /BIC/SINCO2

Miscellaneous
- ☑ Exclusively attribute
- Person respons.
- Content release
- Constant

Step 8 To allow small/lowercase letters in the upload, modify the attribute INCO2's definition. Under the *General* tab, check the *Lowercase letters* option.

SCREEN 11.33

Change Characteristic INCO2: Detail

Characteristic INCO2
Long description INCO2
Short description INCO2
Version Revised Not saved
Object Status Active, executable

General | Business Explorer | Master data/texts | Hierarchy | Compounding

☐ With master data
Master data tables
View of MstrDtaTbls /BIC/MINCO2
Master data tab /BIC/PINCO2
SID table attr.

☐ With texts
Text table properties
Text table
☑ Short text exists
☐ Medium length text exists
☐ Long text exists
☑ Texts language dependent
☐ Texts are time-dep.

SCREEN 11.34

Step 9 If we allow lowercase letters, the attribute INCO2 can no longer have its own master data and texts.

Result

If we load the data again, this time the operation will succeed. Screen 11.35 shows BW Monitor status.

SCREEN 11.35

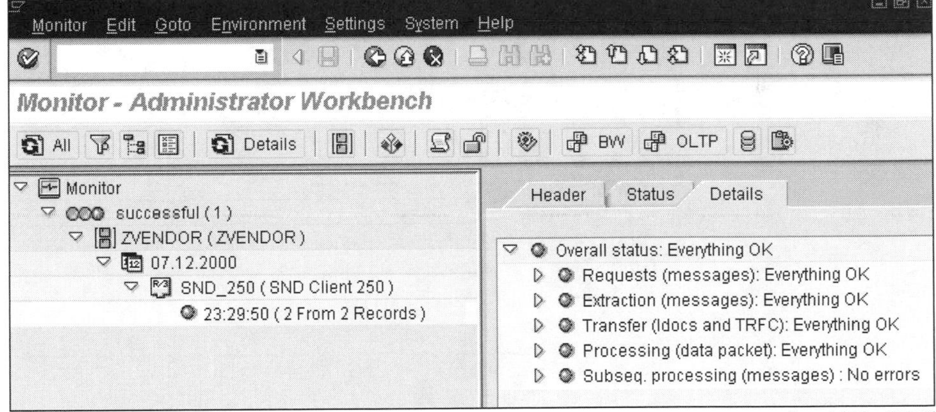

Compared with the data in the R/3 source system (Screen 11.10), the BW master data table /BIC/PZVENDOR contains correct contents (Screen 11.36).

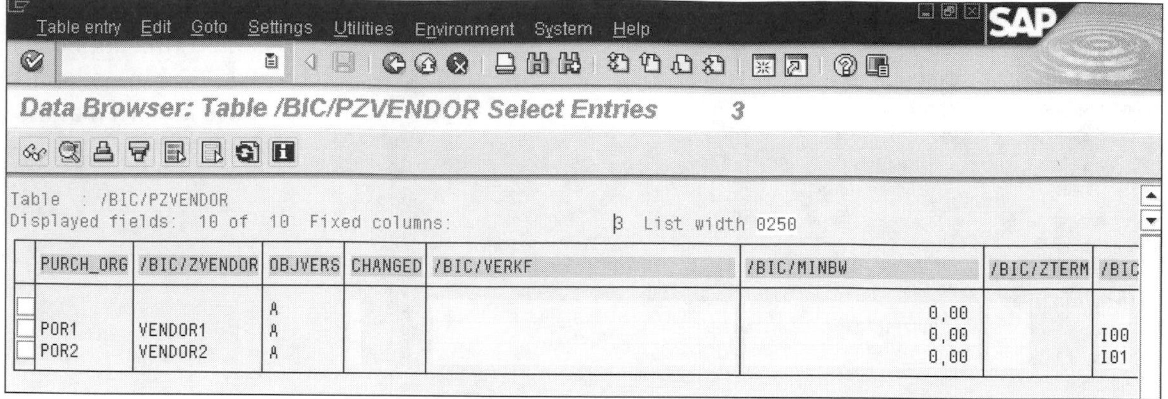
Table entry Edit Goto Settings Utilities Environment System Help

Data Browser: Table /BIC/PZVENDOR Select Entries 3

Table : /BIC/PZVENDOR
Displayed fields: 10 of 10 Fixed columns: 3 List width 0250

PURCH_ORG	/BIC/ZVENDOR	OBJVERS	CHANGED	/BIC/VERKF	/BIC/MINBW	/BIC/ZTERM	/BIC
		A			0,00		
POR1	VENDOR1	A			0,00		I00
POR2	VENDOR2	A			0,00		I01

SCREEN 11.36

Next, create an InfoPackage to load the texts. Compared with Screen 11.12, the text table /BIC/TZVENDOR contains the correct texts as well (Screen 11.37).

SCREEN 11.37

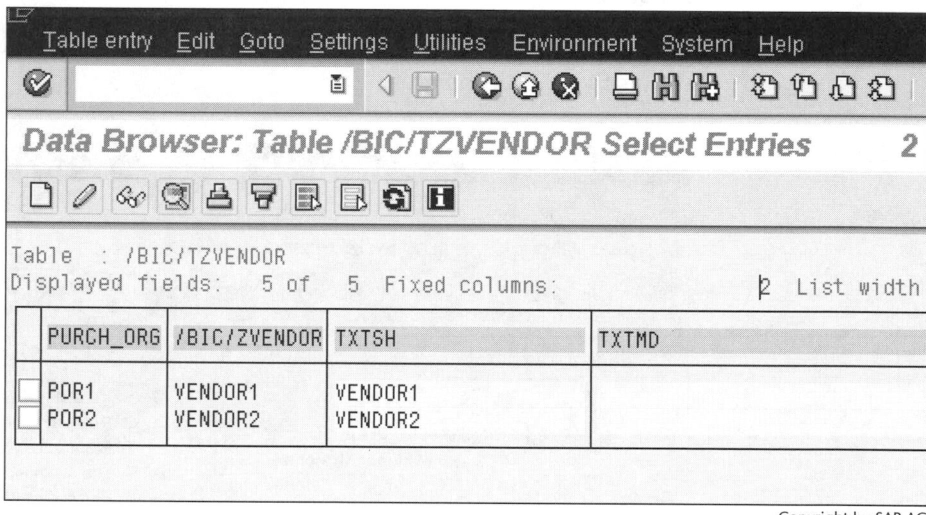
Table entry Edit Goto Settings Utilities Environment System Help

Data Browser: Table /BIC/TZVENDOR Select Entries 2

Table : /BIC/TZVENDOR
Displayed fields: 5 of 5 Fixed columns: 2 List width

PURCH_ORG	/BIC/ZVENDOR	TXTSH	TXTMD
POR1	VENDOR1	VENDOR1	
POR2	VENDOR2	VENDOR2	

At this point, we have achieved the goal set at the beginning of this chapter.

11.5 Summary

In this chapter, we demonstrated how easy it is to extract R/3 data using Business Content's generic data extraction function. Actually, of course, this process is not as easy as it looks. The very first question is, How do we know that the R/3 tables LFM1 and LFA1 contain the data we want? After all, an R/3 system has approximately 10,000 tables. The answer is very simple: The BW technical developer must know the R/3 database inside and out—a very big challenge.

Key Terms

Term	Description
Generic data extraction	Generic data extraction is a function in Business Content that supports the creation of DataSources based on database views or InfoSet queries. InfoSet is similar to a view but allows outer joins between tables.

Next . . .

We will demonstrate how to maintain data in BW.

Chapter 12

Data Maintenance

So far we have built a simple BW system and loaded data into it. Now suppose the business has changed, so that the characteristic data will change as well. If we modify the characteristic data, what will happen to the InfoCube, aggregate, and ODS object data that depend on the characteristic data? In this chapter we will answer this question and several others:

- How do we delete InfoCube data?
- How do we maintain indices and statistics?
- How do we manage individual data load requests?
- How do we automate aggregate rollup?
- Can we compress multiple data load requests into one request? How?

We start from the first question, how to deal with changed characteristic data.

12.1 Maintaining Characteristic Data

If characteristic data have been changed, we must activate the change before BEx Analyzer can display the new data. First we show how BW manages the history of characteristic data changes.

In Screen 12.1, we change material number MAT003's name and short description from *COOKIE* and *Fortune cookie,* to *SNACK* and *Popcorn,* respectively.

Note: To change a data entry, select the data entry and then click .

SCREEN 12.1

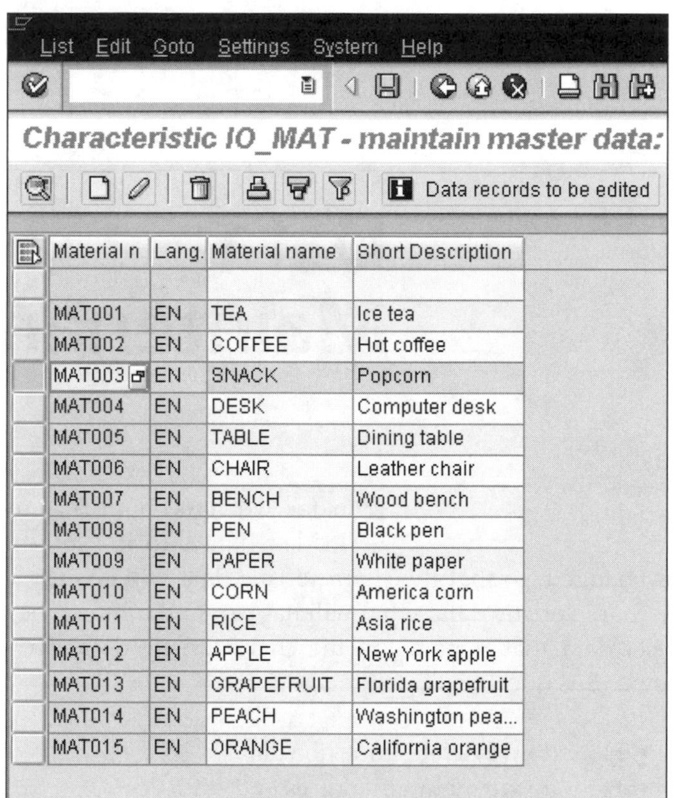

Material n	Lang.	Material name	Short Description
MAT001	EN	TEA	Ice tea
MAT002	EN	COFFEE	Hot coffee
MAT003	EN	SNACK	Popcorn
MAT004	EN	DESK	Computer desk
MAT005	EN	TABLE	Dining table
MAT006	EN	CHAIR	Leather chair
MAT007	EN	BENCH	Wood bench
MAT008	EN	PEN	Black pen
MAT009	EN	PAPER	White paper
MAT010	EN	CORN	America corn
MAT011	EN	RICE	Asia rice
MAT012	EN	APPLE	New York apple
MAT013	EN	GRAPEFRUIT	Florida grapefruit
MAT014	EN	PEACH	Washington pea...
MAT015	EN	ORANGE	California orange

The change we made in Screen 12.1 results in a new entry and a modified entry in the underlying database table /BIC/PIO_MAT (Screen 12.2). There, the *A* in the OBJVERS column indicates that the corresponding entry is active, and the *M* indicates that the corresponding entry is modified and to be activated. The *D* in the *CHANGED* column indicates that the corresponding entry is to be deleted, and the *I* indicates that the corresponding entry is a new one.

SCREEN 12.2

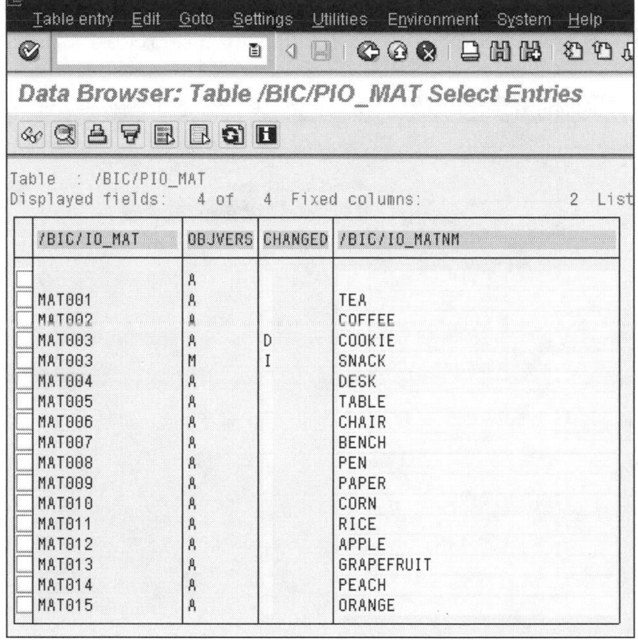

/BIC/IO_MAT	OBJVERS	CHANGED	/BIC/IO_MATNM
	A		
MAT001	A		TEA
MAT002	A		COFFEE
MAT003	A	D	COOKIE
MAT003	M	I	SNACK
MAT004	A		DESK
MAT005	A		TABLE
MAT006	A		CHAIR
MAT007	A		BENCH
MAT008	A		PEN
MAT009	A		PAPER
MAT010	A		CORN
MAT011	A		RICE
MAT012	A		APPLE
MAT013	A		GRAPEFRUIT
MAT014	A		PEACH
MAT015	A		ORANGE

Next, we create a query to display IO_MAT's attribute IO_MATNM. To do so, in the query definition window (Screen 12.3), right-click *Material number* and then select *Properties*.

SCREEN 12.3

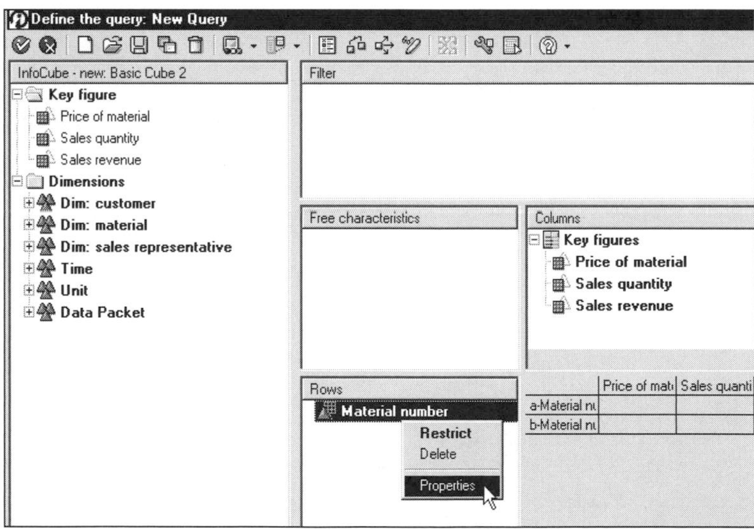

In the pop-up window, select and move *Material name* from the *Available attributes* area to the *Selected attributes* area (Screen 12.4).

SCREEN 12.4

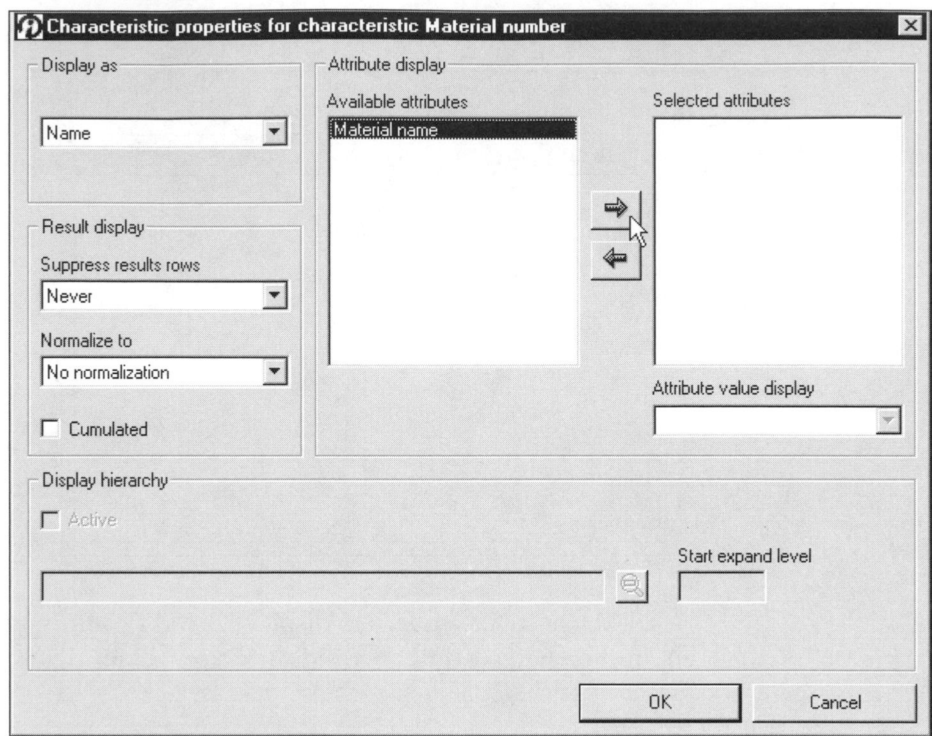

Click OK to return to Screen 12.3. After executing the query, we see the result shown in Screen 12.5.

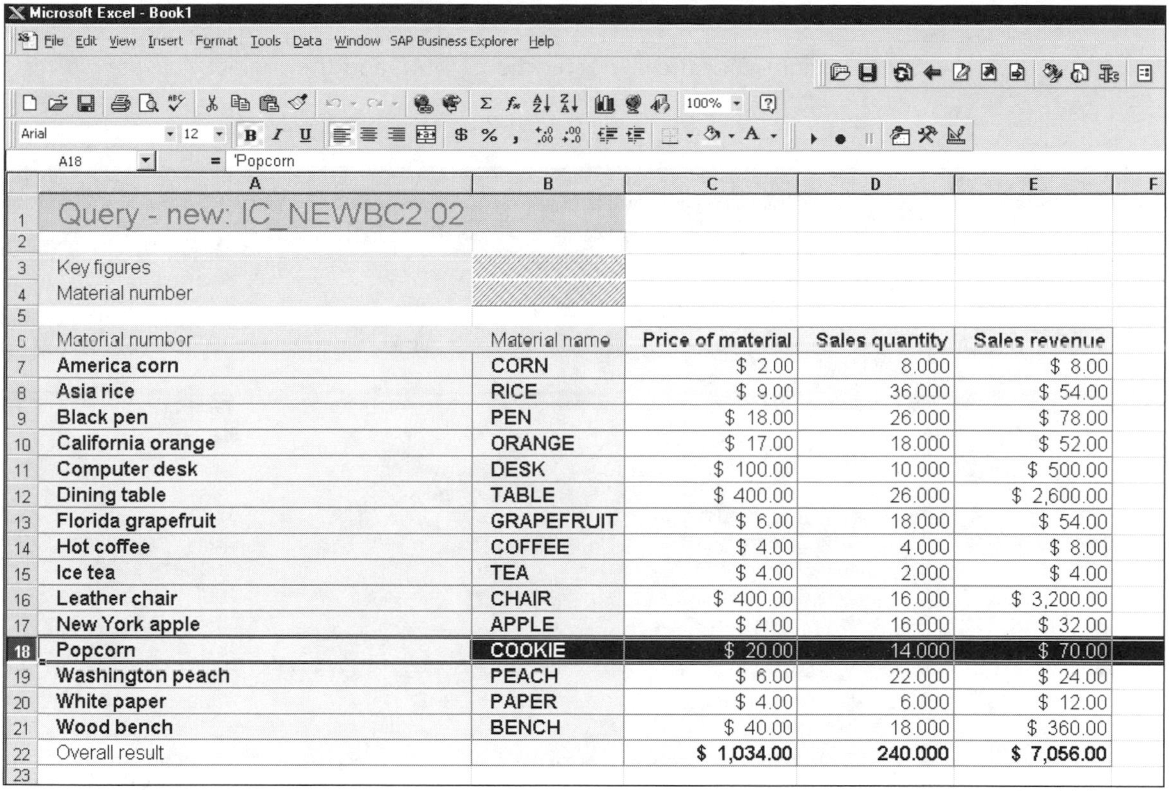

Microsoft Excel - Book1

File Edit View Insert Format Tools Data Window SAP Business Explorer Help

A18 = 'Popcorn

	A	B	C	D	E
1	Query - new: IC_NEWBC2 02				
2					
3	Key figures				
4	Material number				
5					
6	Material number	Material name	Price of material	Sales quantity	Sales revenue
7	**America corn**	CORN	$ 2.00	8.000	$ 8.00
8	**Asia rice**	RICE	$ 9.00	36.000	$ 54.00
9	**Black pen**	PEN	$ 18.00	26.000	$ 78.00
10	**California orange**	ORANGE	$ 17.00	18.000	$ 52.00
11	**Computer desk**	DESK	$ 100.00	10.000	$ 500.00
12	**Dining table**	TABLE	$ 400.00	26.000	$ 2,600.00
13	**Florida grapefruit**	GRAPEFRUIT	$ 6.00	18.000	$ 54.00
14	**Hot coffee**	COFFEE	$ 4.00	4.000	$ 8.00
15	**Ice tea**	TEA	$ 4.00	2.000	$ 4.00
16	**Leather chair**	CHAIR	$ 400.00	16.000	$ 3,200.00
17	**New York apple**	APPLE	$ 4.00	16.000	$ 32.00
18	**Popcorn**	COOKIE	$ 20.00	14.000	$ 70.00
19	**Washington peach**	PEACH	$ 6.00	22.000	$ 24.00
20	**White paper**	PAPER	$ 4.00	6.000	$ 12.00
21	**Wood bench**	BENCH	$ 40.00	18.000	$ 360.00
22	Overall result		**$ 1,034.00**	**240.000**	**$ 7,056.00**
23					

SCREEN 12.5

Here we see that the text short description has changed to *Popcorn*; however, the material name remains *COOKIE*. This phenomenon tells us two things:

1. A query always retrieves the current texts. The text table does not save the history of changes.
2. A query always retrieves active master data. In our case, *COOKIE* is the old but currently still active master data.

To make the Screen 12.1 change become reflected in this query, we need to activate the change. The procedure follows.

Work Instructions

Step 1 Right-click the characteristic *IO_MAT,* and then select *Activate master data.*

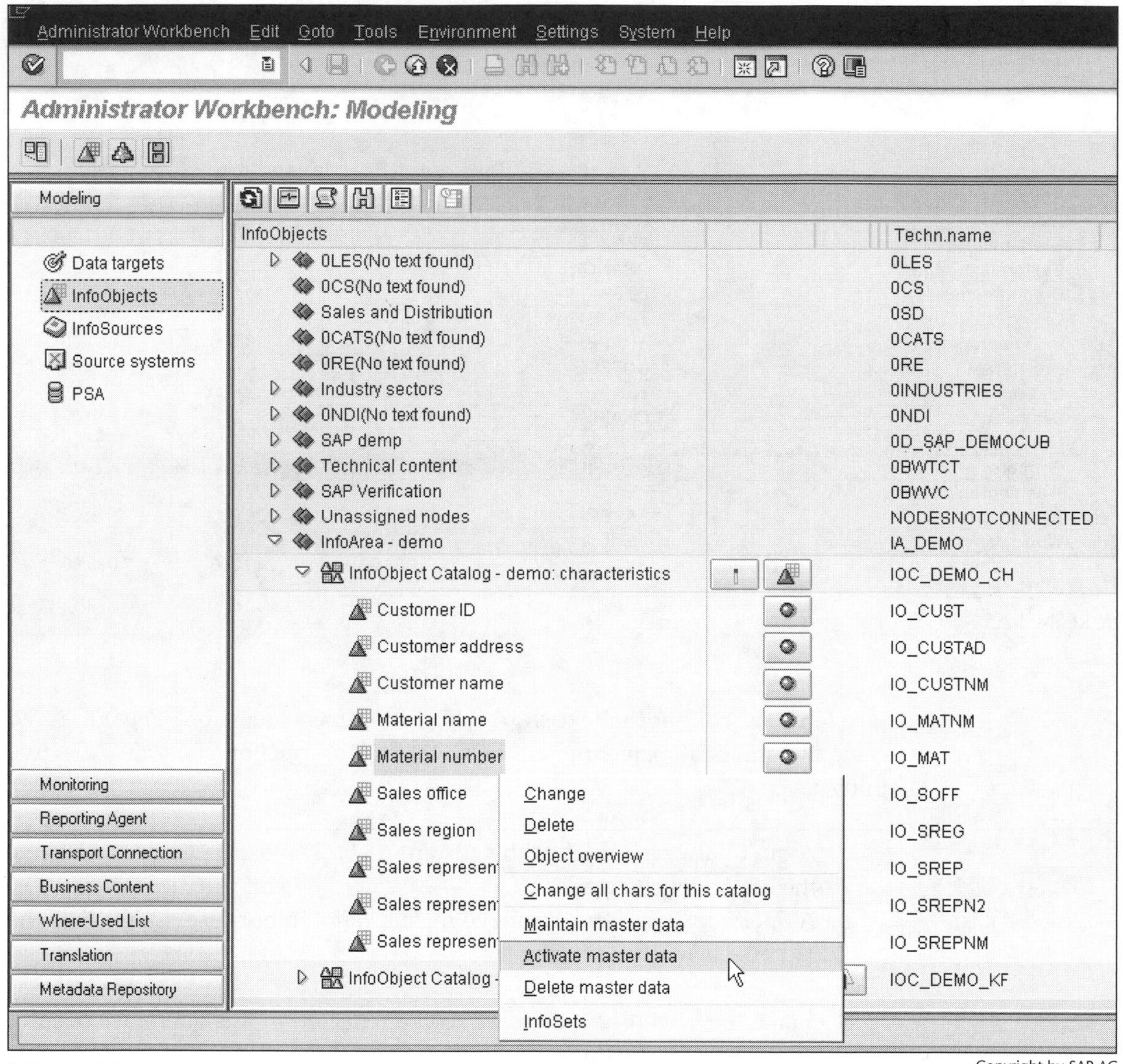

SCREEN 12.6

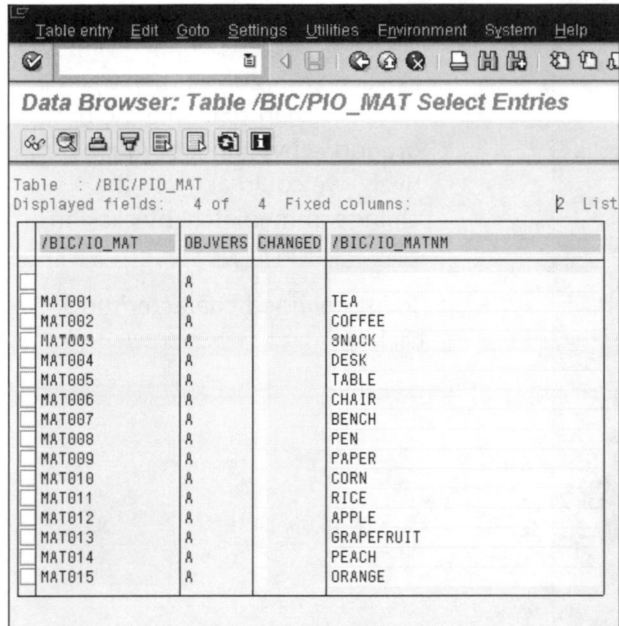

SCREEN 12.7

Result

After clicking in Screen 12.2 to refresh the table contents, we get the result shown in Screen 12.7. Now the change becomes active, and the old record is deleted. If we refresh the query result in Screen 12.5, we will see that the MAT003 material name has changed to *SNACK*.

The following procedure describes another way to activate characteristic data changes. The new procedure can be applied not only to master data changes, but also to hierarchy changes.

Work Instructions

Step 1 From the Administrator Workbench screen, select the *Apply Hierarchy/Attribute change . . .* item on the Tools menu.

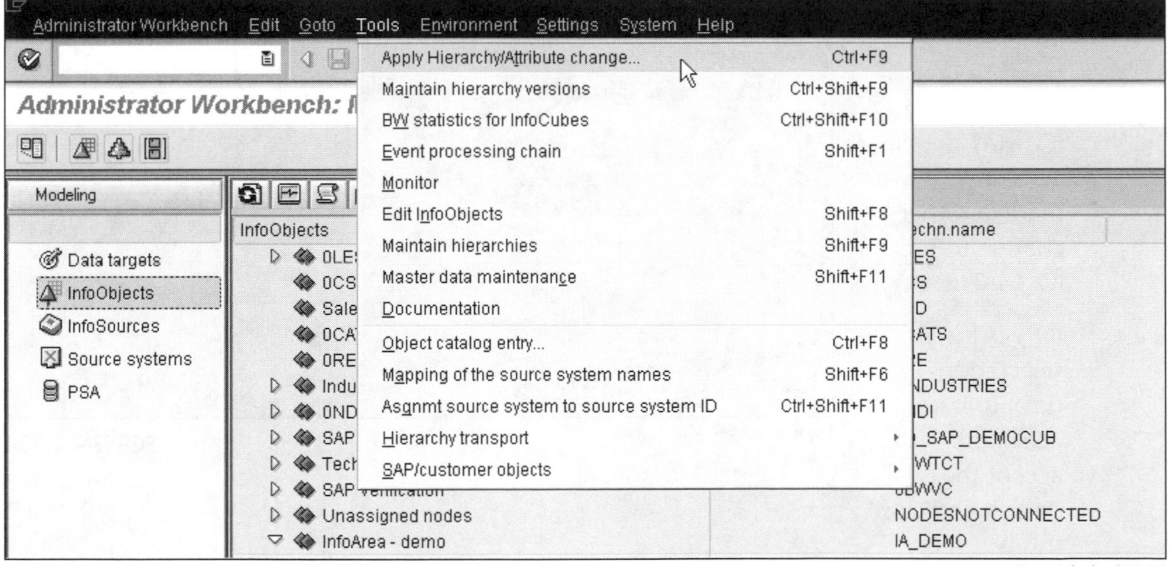

SCREEN 12.8

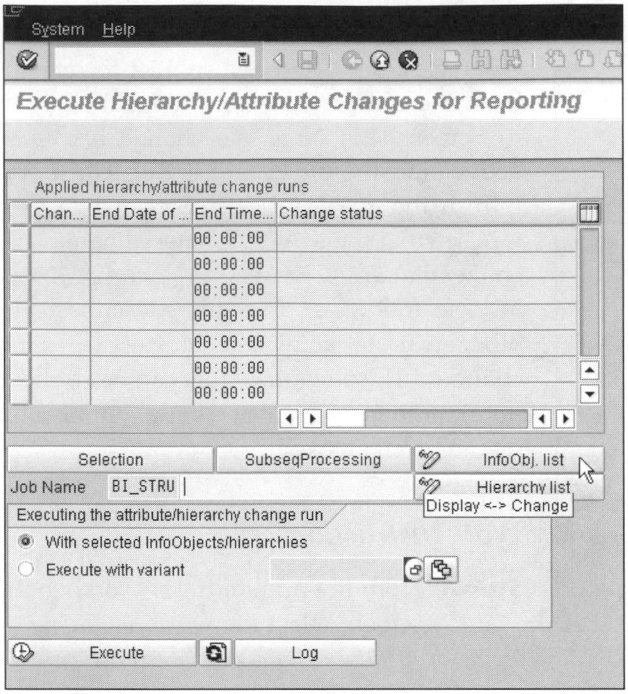

SCREEN 12.9

Step 2 We can schedule the activation by clicking Selection. A new window like Screen 3.20 will then open in which we can schedule the background activation job. Alternatively, we could activate the change immediately by clicking Execute.

To list changed characteristics, click InfoObj. list.

Step 3 IO_MAT is listed in Screen 12.10 because, after activating the IO_MAT data in Screen 12.6, we made another change to the IO_MAT data.

IO_MAT is selected by default to be activated. We accept the default and close this window.

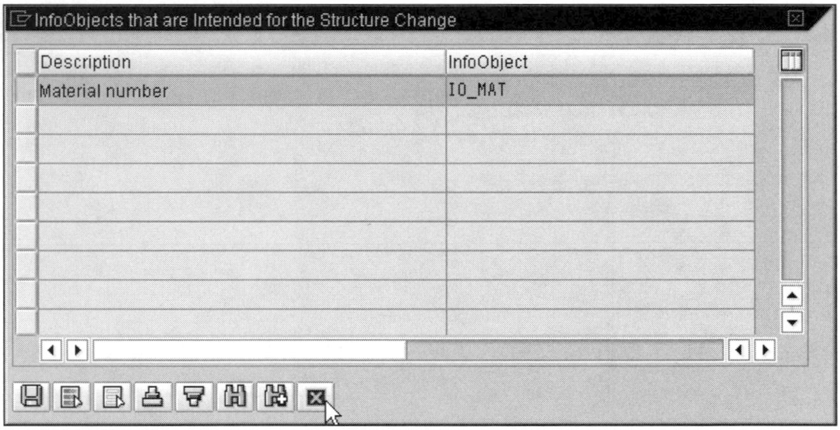

SCREEN 12.10

Result

If we click [Execute] in Screen 12.9, a background job will start immediately to activate the new change to the IO_MAT data.

We have now answered the first question raised at the beginning of this chapter.

Note: You cannot delete characteristic data if they are used by other BW objects. SID table contents can reveal the status of characteristic data. The X in column DATAFL indicates that an InfoCube uses the corresponding entry, and the X in column INCFL indicates that a hierarchy uses the entry (Screen 12.11).

SCREEN 12.11

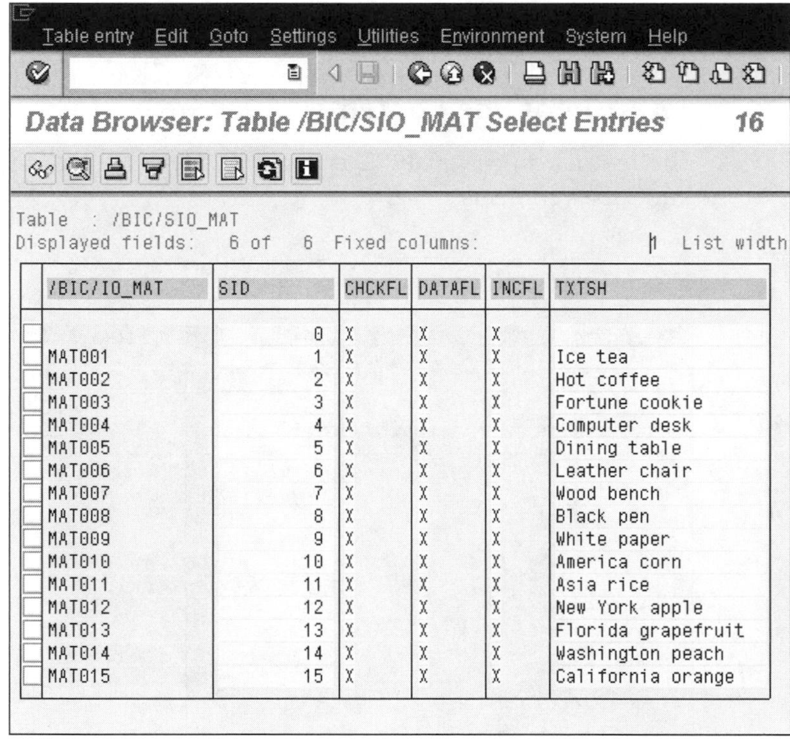

/BIC/IO_MAT	SID	CHCKFL	DATAFL	INCFL	TXTSH
	0	X	X	X	
MAT001	1	X	X	X	Ice tea
MAT002	2	X	X	X	Hot coffee
MAT003	3	X	X	X	Fortune cookie
MAT004	4	X	X	X	Computer desk
MAT005	5	X	X	X	Dining table
MAT006	6	X	X	X	Leather chair
MAT007	7	X	X	X	Wood bench
MAT008	8	X	X	X	Black pen
MAT009	9	X	X	X	White paper
MAT010	10	X	X	X	America corn
MAT011	11	X	X	X	Asia rice
MAT012	12	X	X	X	New York apple
MAT013	13	X	X	X	Florida grapefruit
MAT014	14	X	X	X	Washington peach
MAT015	15	X	X	X	California orange

12.2 Maintaining InfoCube Data

To answer the other questions raised at the beginning of this chapter, from Administrator Workbench right-click the concerned InfoCube (IC_NEWBC2 in our example), and then select *Manage*. Screen 12.12 appears.

Screen 12.12 contains six areas:

- Contents, where we can display and delete InfoCube data
- Performance, where we can check, delete, and create indices and statistics
- Requests, where we can manage individual data load requests
- Rollup, where we can roll up data per load requests into aggregates
- Collapse, where we can compress data in multiple load requests into a single request
- Reconstruct, where we can reconstruct the InfoCube using load requests in PSA

We will discuss each of these topics in turn.

12.2.1 InfoCube Contents

The first tab in Screen 12.12 is *Contents*. Here we can display and delete the InfoCube's contents.

Work Instructions

SCREEN 12.12

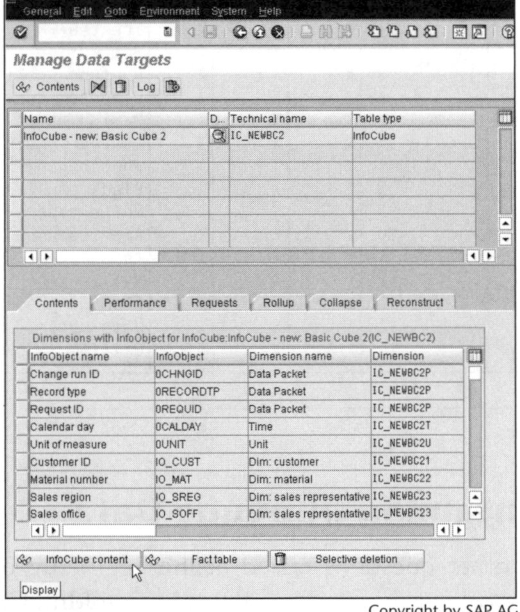

Step 1 To display the InfoCube contents, click InfoCube content.

Step 2 In Screen 12.13, we specify conditions regarding what contents to be displayed. Here are some options:

- Choose *Do not use any conversion* to display the data in the database formats.
- Choose *Use mat. aggregates* to display the data from an aggregate instead of the fact table if an appropriate aggregate exists.
- Choose *Use DB aggregation* to allow aggregation on the fields that are not the selection conditions.
- Choose *Output number of hits* to add a new column in the display to show how many records in the fact table are used to produce each display row.
- Choose *Display modified structures* to display the M version master data. Use this option to check how the result would look in BEx should the characteristic data be activated.

SCREEN 12.13

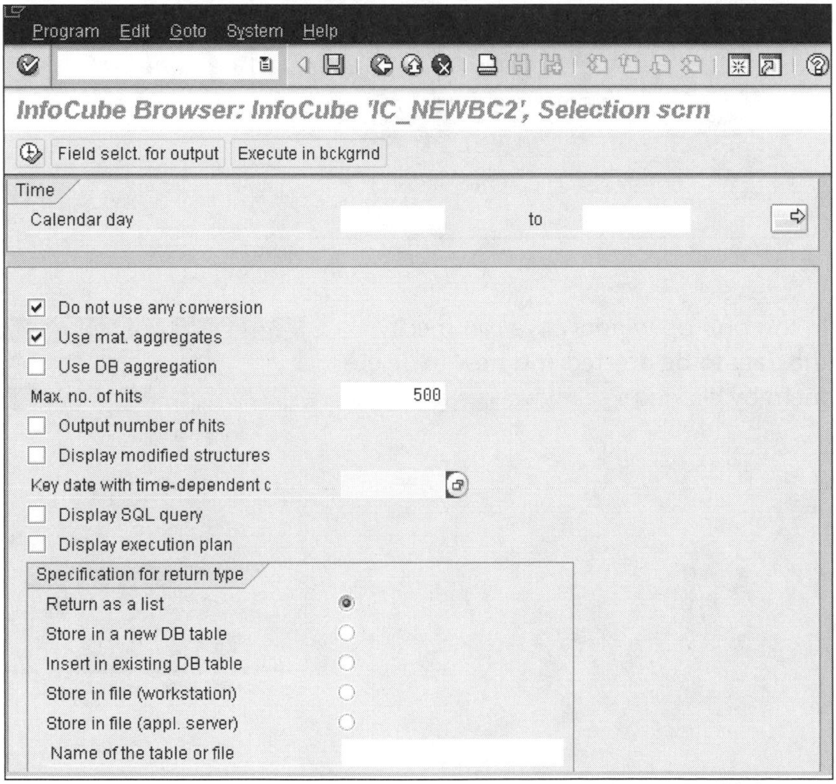

Program Edit Goto System Help

InfoCube Browser: InfoCube 'IC_NEWBC2', Selection scrn

Field selct. for output | Execute in bckgrnd

Time

Calendar day to

Do not use any conversion

Use mat. aggregates

Use DB aggregation

Max. no. of hits 500

Output number of hits

Display modified structures

Key date with time-dependent c

Display SQL query

Display execution plan

Specification for return type

Return as a list

Store in a new DB table

Insert in existing DB table

Store in file (workstation)

Store in file (appl. server)

Name of the table or file

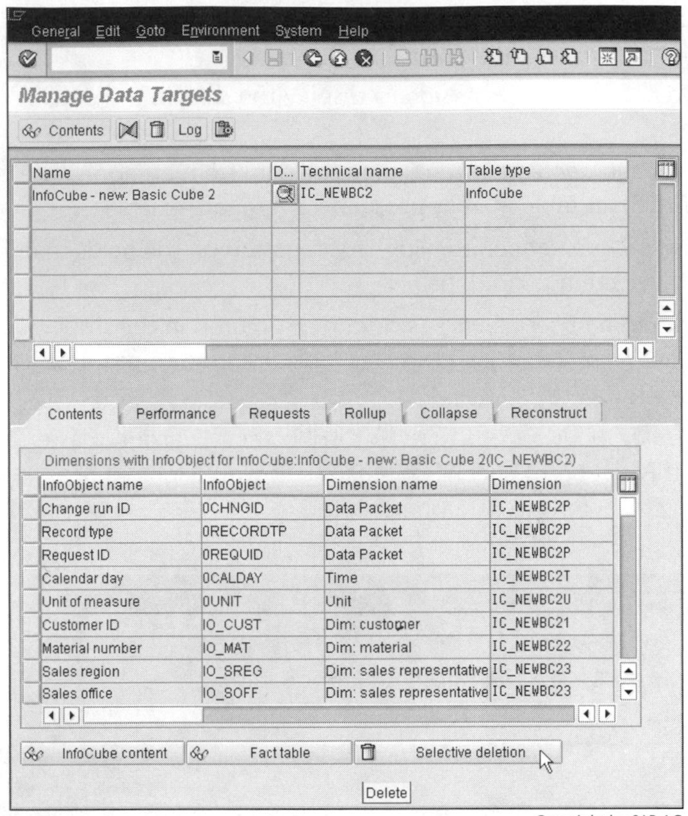

SCREEN 12.14

Step 3 To delete data from the InfoCube, click [Selective deletion].

Step 4 In this pop-up window, we can specify the data to be deleted and how to delete them by clicking [DeleteSelections].

Selective deletion for InfoCube IC_NEWBC2
DeleteSelections | Log
Deletion report
Start in the background
Selection | SubseqProcessing
Job Name BI_INDX
Start

SCREEN 12.15

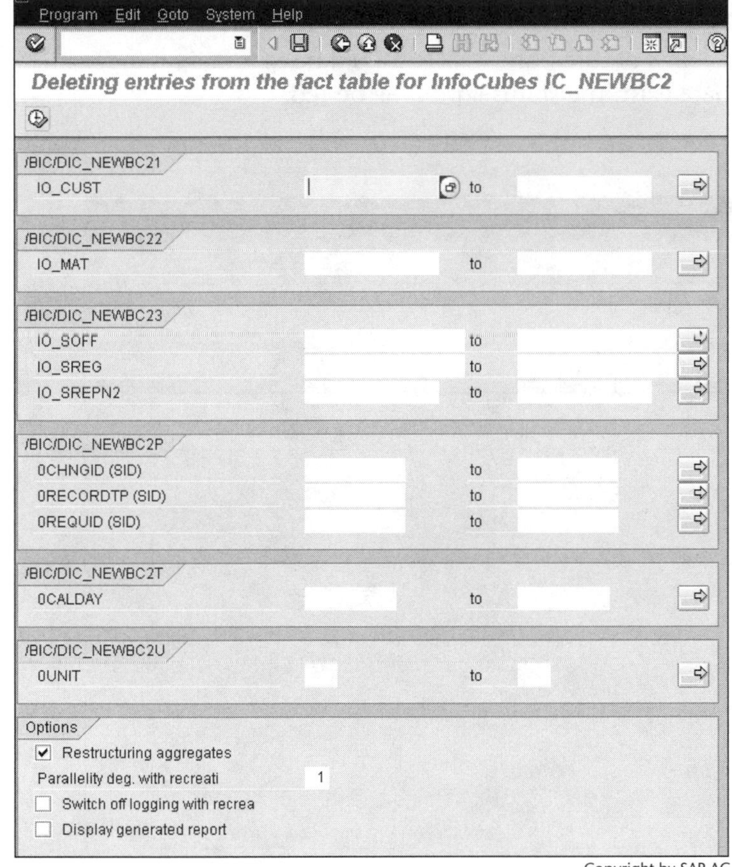

SCREEN 12.16

Step 5 Besides the conditions used to specify the data to be deleted, in this window, we can also do the following:

- Select *Restructuring aggregates* to rebuild aggregates after the data are deleted.
- Select *Parallelity deg. with recreati* field to enter the number of parallel processes to be used in reconstructing the table.
- Select *Switch off logging when recrea* to improve performance without logging the changes.
- Select *Display generated report* to display the ABAP program used to delete the data.

12.2.2 Indices and Statistics

The second tab in Screen 12.12 is related to performance. Here we can check, delete, and create indices and statistics.

Work Instructions

Step 1 The status lights on the right should be green. If no index/statistics data exist, the status lights will be red.

To delete indices from the fact table, click Delete indexes .

SCREEN 12.17

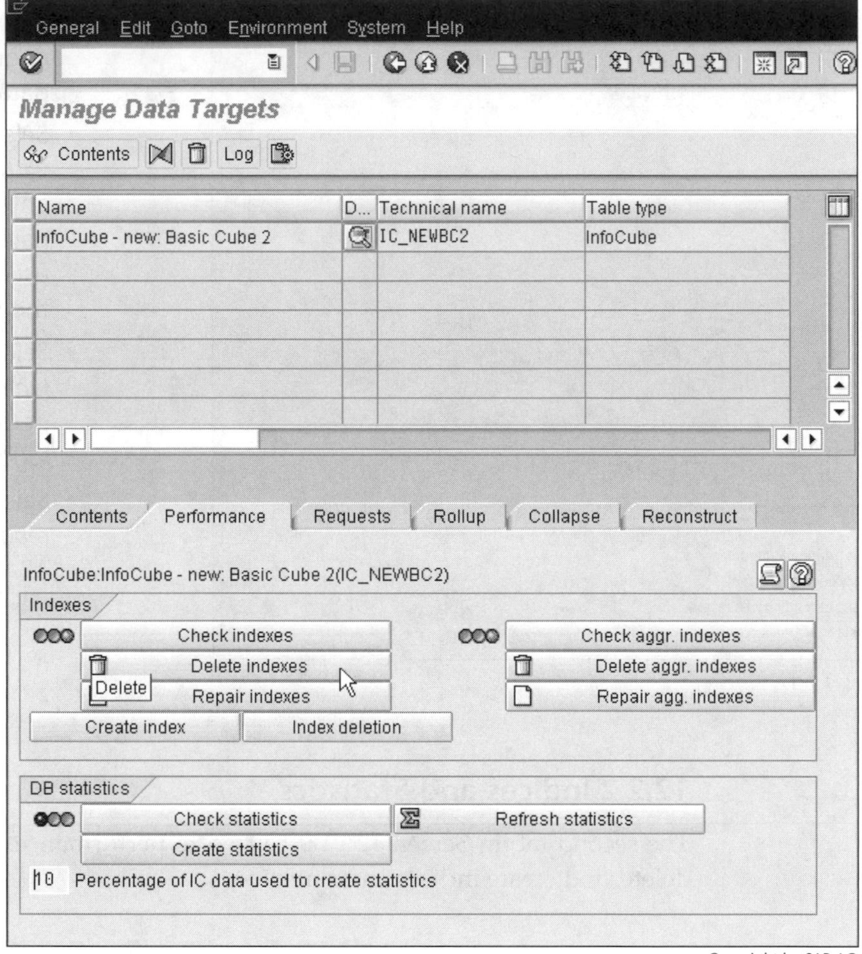

Step 2 Now the left status light turns red. To create the indices, click Repair indexes.

SCREEN 12.18

Copyright by SAP AG

Step 3 Click ✔ to continue.

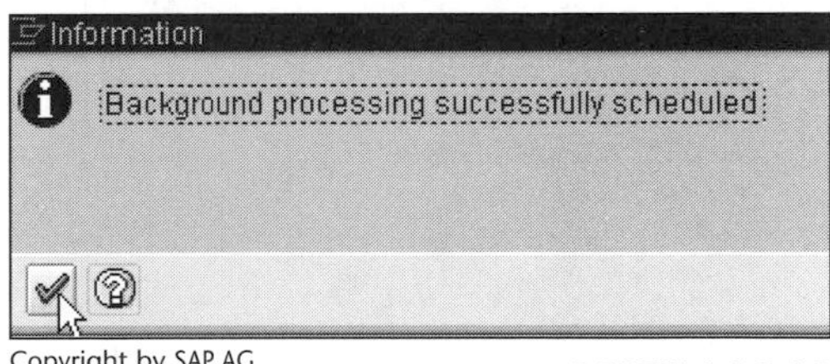

Copyright by SAP AG

SCREEN 12.19

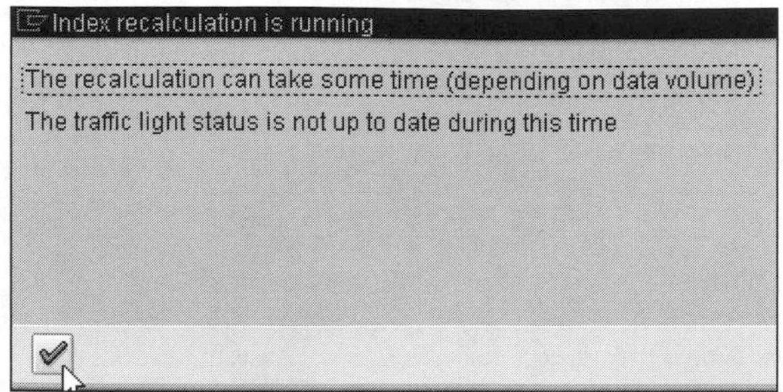

SCREEN 12.20

Step 4 Click ✓ to continue.

Step 5 Depending on the size of the InfoCube, it may take a while for the status light to turn green.

To improve data loading performance, it is a good practice to delete the indices, load the data, and then recreate the indices. To automate this job, click Create index .

Note: Rolling up aggregates will automatically repair the aggregates' indices.

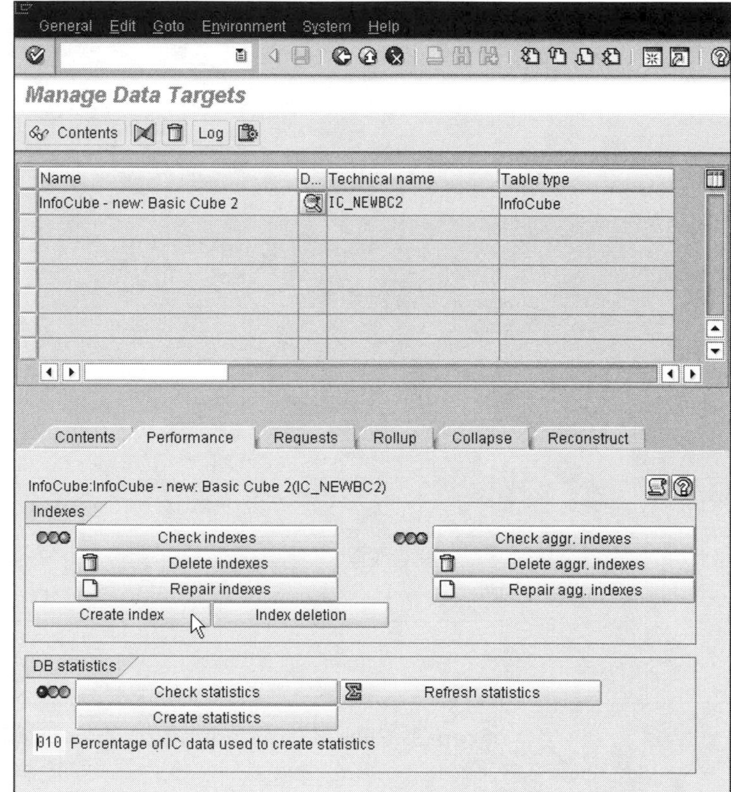

SCREEN 12.21

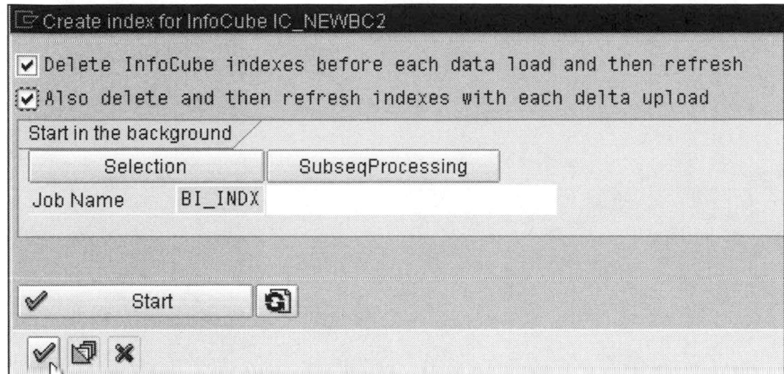

SCREEN 12.22

Step 6 Check all options, and then click ✔ to save the settings and continue.

Result

The next time when we load data into this InfoCube, we will receive a message like the one in Screen 12.23. To continue the data loading operation, click Yes .

SCREEN 12.23

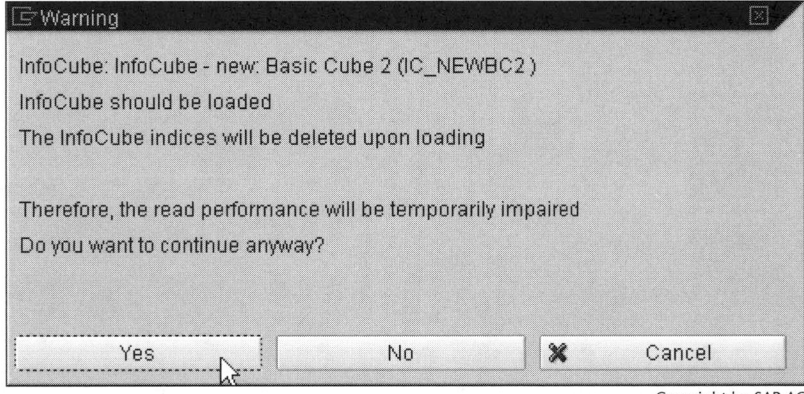

In the same way, we can check, delete, and create the BW statistics.

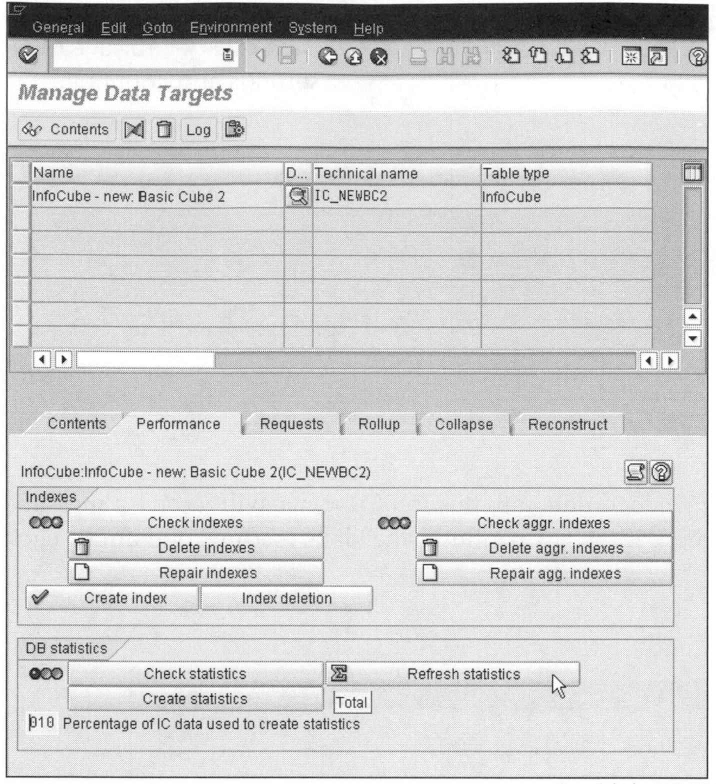

SCREEN 12.24

Copyright by SAP AG

Step 7 If the *DB statistics* status light is red, click Refresh statistics.

Step 8 Click ✔ to continue.

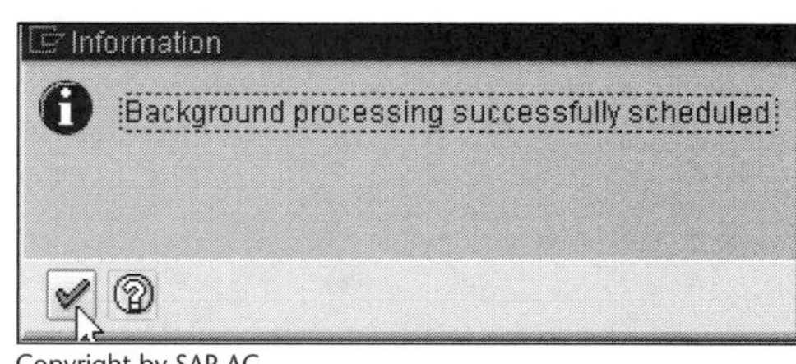

Copyright by SAP AG

SCREEN 12.25

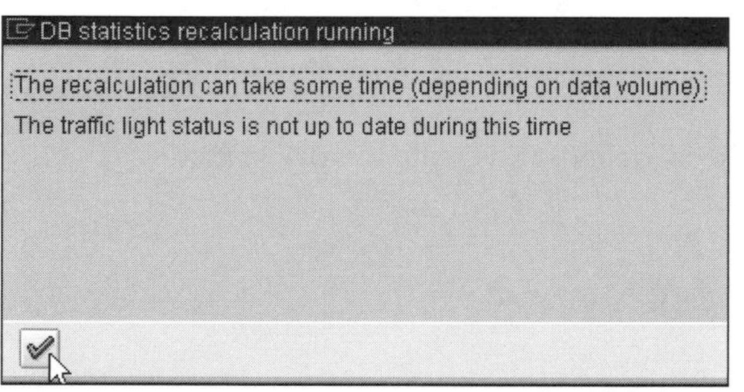

DB statistics recalculation running
The recalculation can take some time (depending on data volume)
The traffic light status is not up to date during this time

SCREEN 12.26

Copyright by SAP AG

Step 9 Click ✔ to continue.

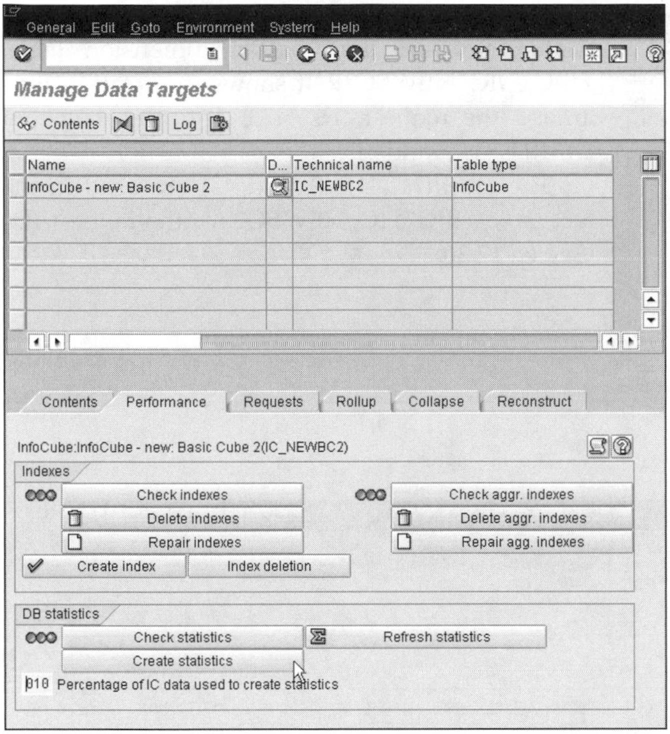

SCREEN 12.27

Copyright by SAP AG

Step 10 Depending on the size of the InfoCube, it may take a while for the status light to turn green.

Each time when new data are loaded into the fact table, statistics should be refreshed. To automate this process, click Create statistics.

Step 11 Check both options, and then click ✔ to save the settings and continue.

From now on, the DB statistics will be refreshed after each data load and each delta load.

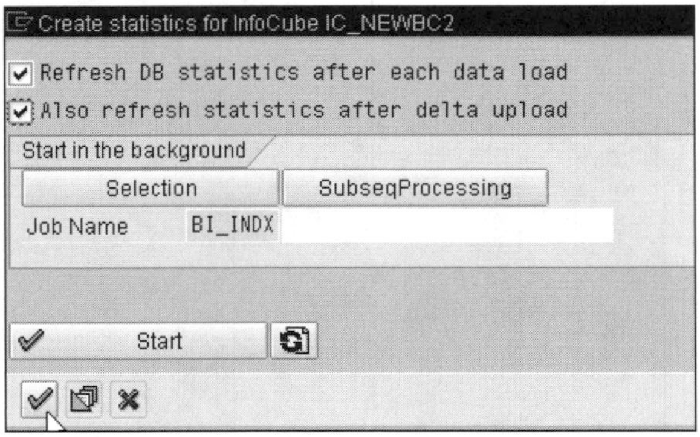

Copyright by SAP AG

SCREEN 12.28

12.2.3 Data Load Requests

The third tab in Screen 12.12, *Requests,* allows us to manage individual data load requests.

In BW, each data load from BW Scheduler counts as a request and is assigned a unique request number consisting of 30 characters. This request number is stored as an integer value called a **request ID**, in the data packet dimension of the InfoCube.

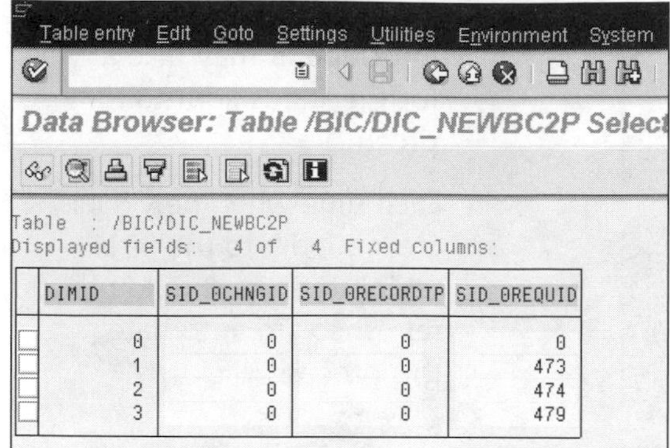

Table entry Edit Goto Settings Utilities Environment System

Data Browser: Table /BIC/DIC_NEWBC2P Select

Table : /BIC/DIC_NEWBC2P
Displayed fields: 4 of 4 Fixed columns:

DIMID	SID_0CHNGID	SID_0RECORDTP	SID_0REQUID
0	0	0	0
1	0	0	473
2	0	0	474
3	0	0	479

SCREEN 12.29

As an example, Screen 12.29 displays the contents of the data packet dimension table, /BIC/DIC_NEWBC2P. It shows the relationships among the request IDs (473, 474, and 479) and DIMIDs (1, 2, and 3).

The DIMIDs (41, 42, and 43) are used in the fact table /BIC/FIC_NEWBC2 for the request IDs (Screen 12.30).

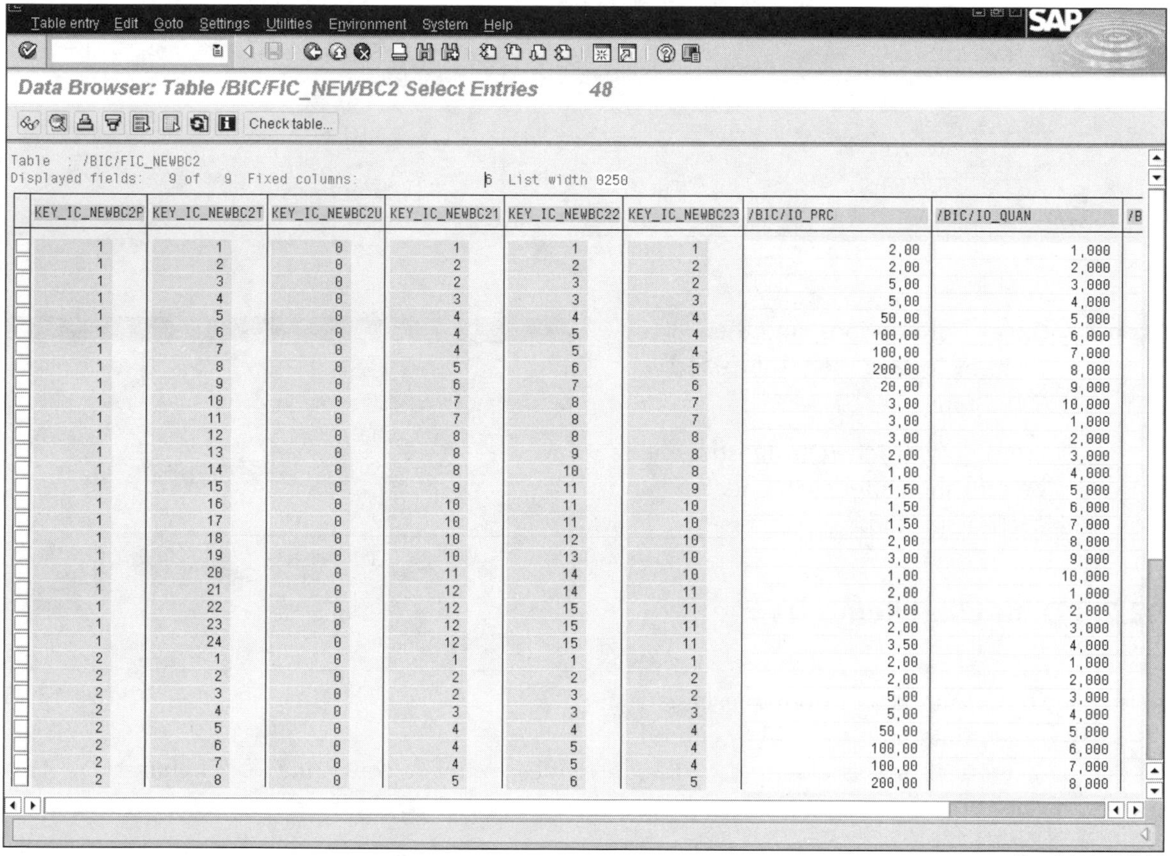

Table entry Edit Goto Settings Utilities Environment System Help

Data Browser: Table /BIC/FIC_NEWBC2 Select Entries 48

Check table...

Table : /BIC/FIC_NEWBC2
Displayed fields: 9 of 9 Fixed columns: 6 List width 0250

KEY_IC_NEWBC2P	KEY_IC_NEWBC2T	KEY_IC_NEWBC2U	KEY_IC_NEWBC21	KEY_IC_NEWBC22	KEY_IC_NEWBC23	/BIC/IO_PRC	/BIC/IO_QUAN	/B
1	1	0	1	1	1	2,00	1,000	
1	2	0	2	2	2	2,00	2,000	
1	3	0	2	3	2	5,00	3,000	
1	4	0	3	3	3	5,00	4,000	
1	5	0	4	4	4	50,00	5,000	
1	6	0	4	5	4	100,00	6,000	
1	7	0	4	5	4	100,00	7,000	
1	8	0	5	6	5	200,00	8,000	
1	9	0	6	7	6	20,00	9,000	
1	10	0	7	8	7	3,00	10,000	
1	11	0	7	8	7	3,00	1,000	
1	12	0	8	8	8	3,00	2,000	
1	13	0	8	9	8	2,00	3,000	
1	14	0	8	10	8	1,00	4,000	
1	15	0	9	11	9	1,50	5,000	
1	16	0	10	11	10	1,50	6,000	
1	17	0	10	11	10	1,50	7,000	
1	18	0	10	12	10	2,00	8,000	
1	19	0	10	13	10	3,00	9,000	
1	20	0	11	14	10	1,00	10,000	
1	21	0	12	14	11	2,00	1,000	
1	22	0	12	15	11	3,00	2,000	
1	23	0	12	15	11	2,00	3,000	
1	24	0	12	15	11	3,50	4,000	
2	1	0	1	1	1	2,00	1,000	
2	2	0	2	2	2	2,00	2,000	
2	3	0	2	3	2	5,00	3,000	
2	4	0	3	3	3	5,00	4,000	
2	5	0	4	4	4	50,00	5,000	
2	6	0	4	5	4	100,00	6,000	
2	7	0	4	5	4	100,00	7,000	
2	8	0	5	6	5	200,00	8,000	

SCREEN 12.30

As shown in Screen 12.31, if an InfoCube has aggregates, then a request is not available for reporting until it is rolled up into the aggregates.

To delete a request from the InfoCube, click [Delete]. If the request has been rolled up into an aggregate or compressed, however, then you cannot delete it. If it has been rolled up, then the aggregate must be deactivated first. If it has been compressed, then all data in the fact table must be deleted first.

SCREEN 12.31

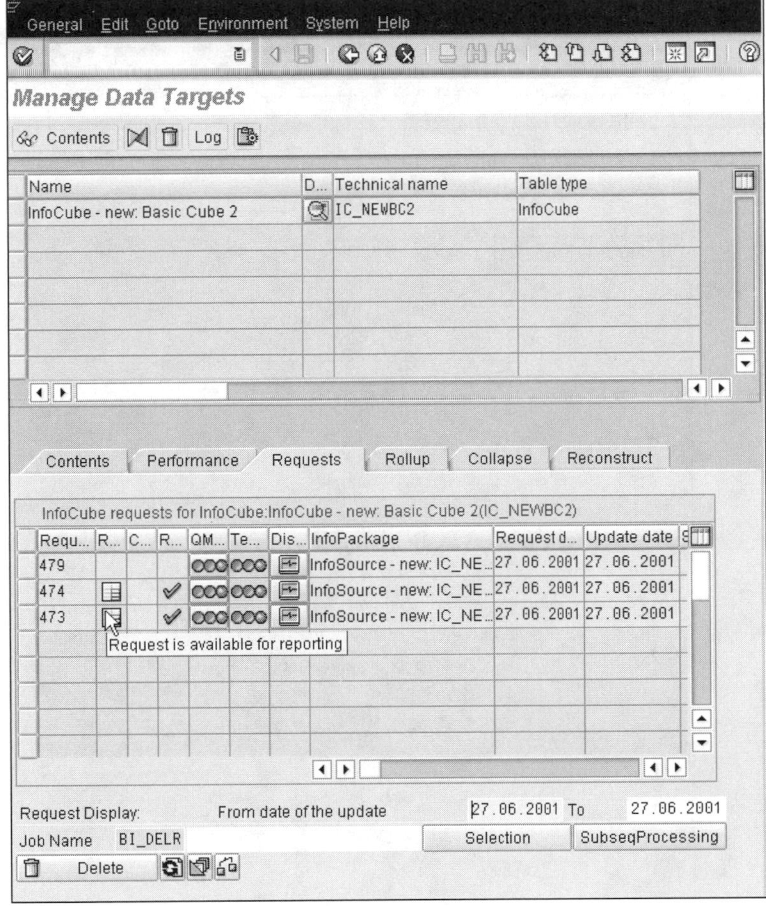

BW provides a useful function that allows us to check whether one data load request overlaps with another. The following is an example for request 474.

Work Instructions

Step 1 Select request *474*, and then click [icon].

SCREEN 12.32

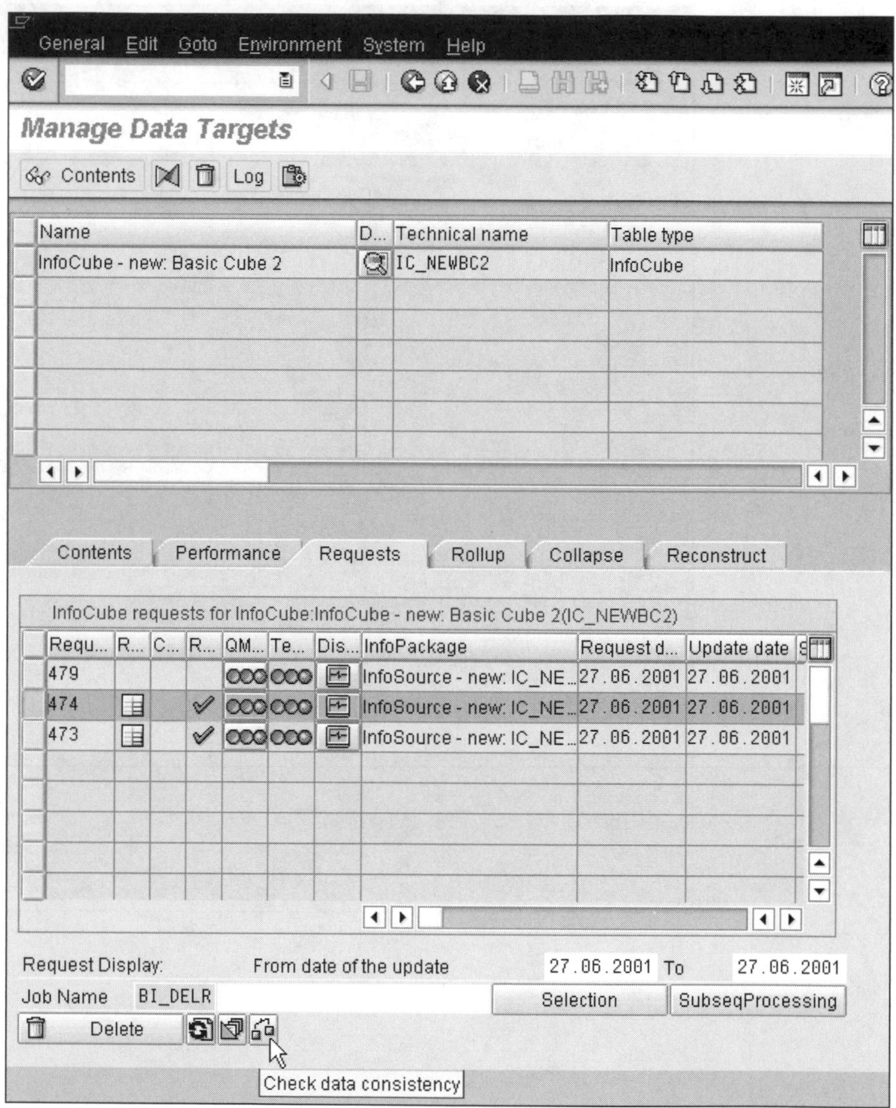

Step 2 A new session window opens and displays the request's 30-character request number,-REQU_3I4VT73UXJDCQIO47YE4Q4QAI.

Click [icon] to check the overlapping.

SCREEN 12.33

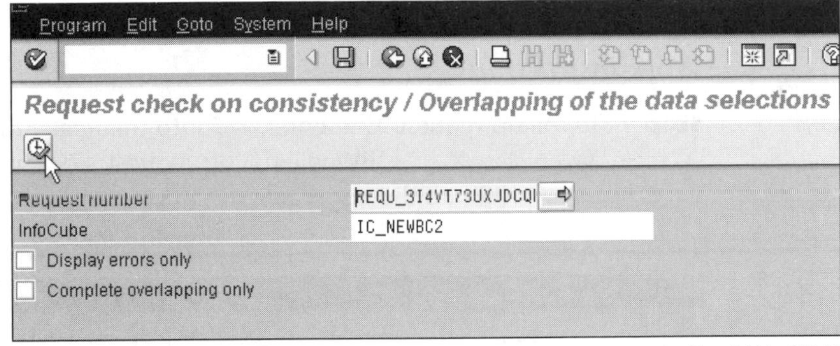

Result

The result contains information about the overlapping. If overlapping is present, the result also tells us whether we can delete the request (Screen 12.34).

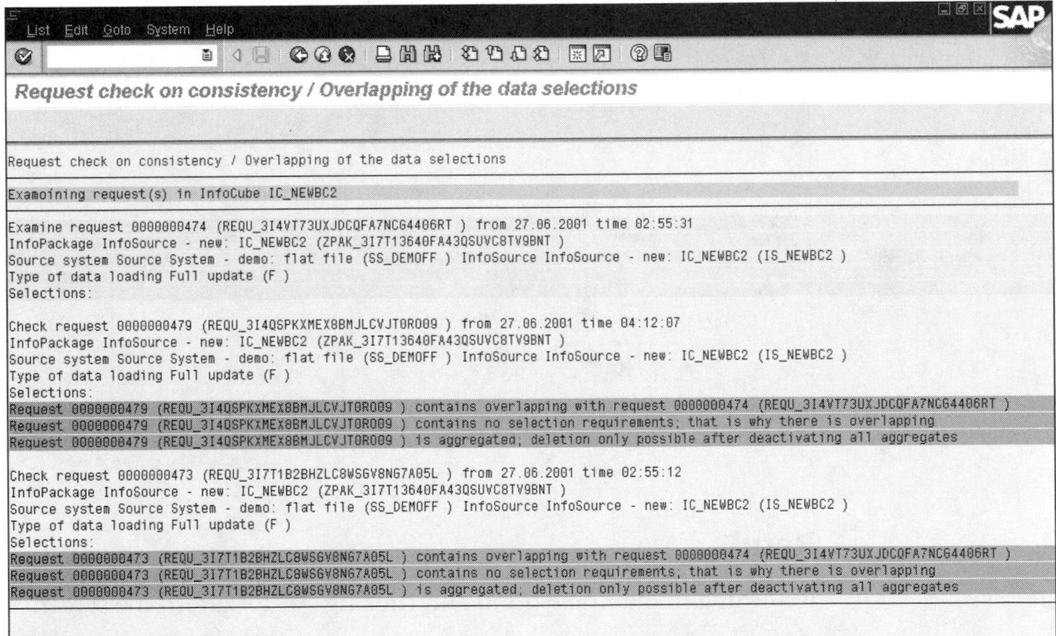

SCREEN 12.34

12.2.4 Aggregate Rollup

The fourth tab, *Rollup,* in Screen 12.12 deals with the aggregate rollup. When we roll up data load requests, we roll them up into all the aggregates of the InfoCube.

Work Instructions

Step 1 To roll up request 479, enter *479* into the *Request ID* and then click Execute. BW will roll up request 479 and other requests below 479 into the aggregates.

SCREEN 12.35

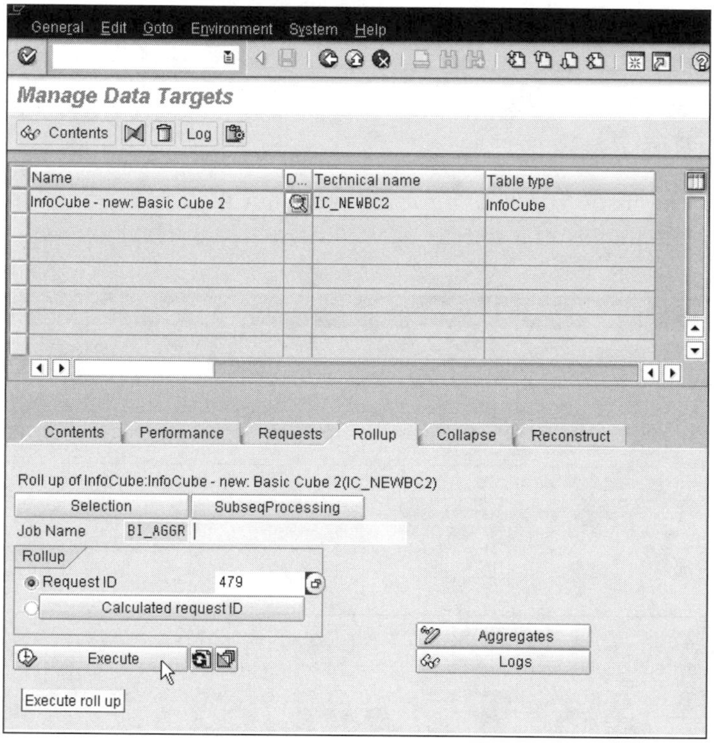

Result

Returning to the *Requests* tab and clicking to refresh the screen, notice that request 479 has been rolled up. Now it is available for reporting (Screen 12.36).

SCREEN 12.36

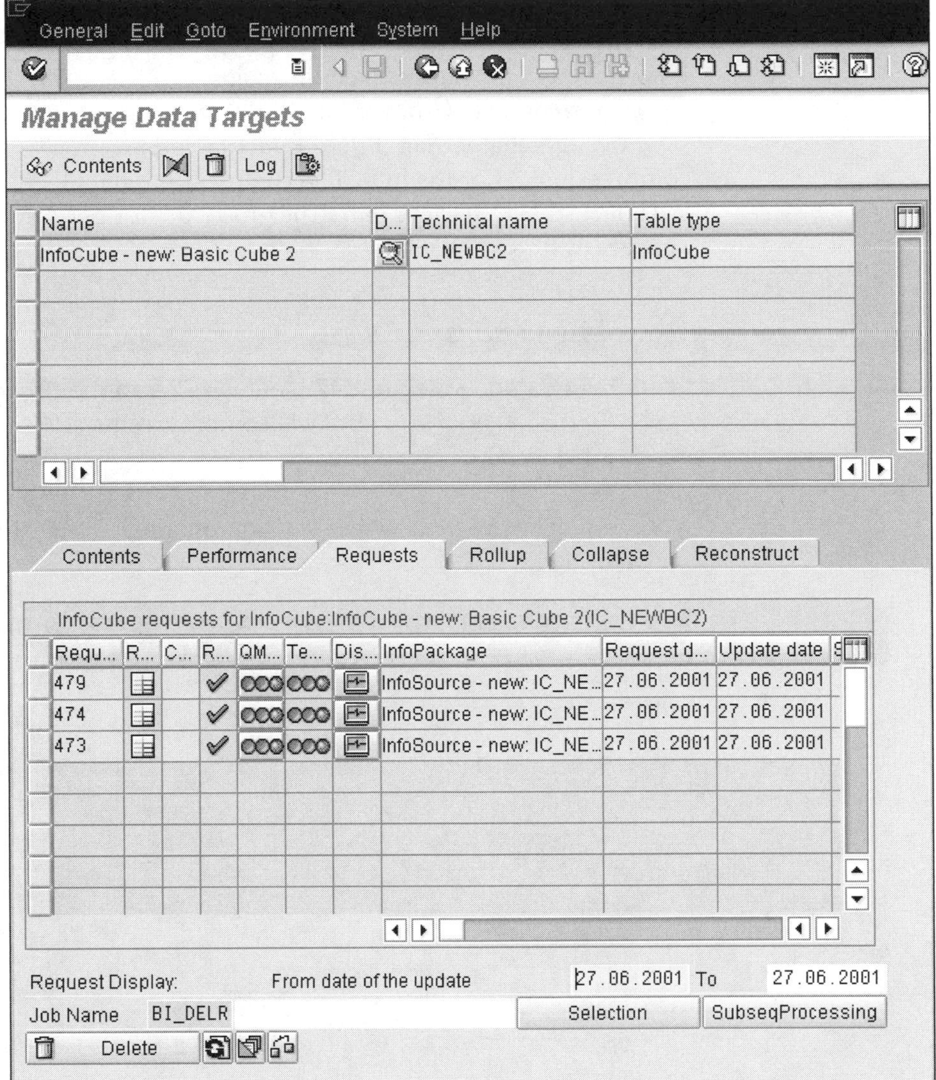

12.2.5 InfoCube Compression

The fifth tab in Screen 12.12, *Collapse,* focuses on the InfoCube compression.

Each InfoCube has two fact tables: the F fact table and the E fact table. We load data into the F fact table, where the data are grouped according to the individual load among requests. The F table allows us to check for overlapping requests and to delete unnecessary requests.

The F fact table degrades query performance, however. When executing a query, the OLAP processor must aggregate key figures to eliminate the request information in the data packet dimension.

To overcome this drawback, BW allows us to aggregate the F fact table and save the aggregated data in the E fact table in a process called the **InfoCube compression**. After the InfoCube compression, the OLAP processor will go to the E fact table to retrieve data. The procedure for performing this compression appears next.

Work Instructions

Step 1 To compress request 479, enter *479* into the *Request ID* and then click [Release]. BW will compress request 479 and other requests below 479.

Note: To delete records whose key figures are all 0, select the *With zero elimination* option.

SCREEN 12.37

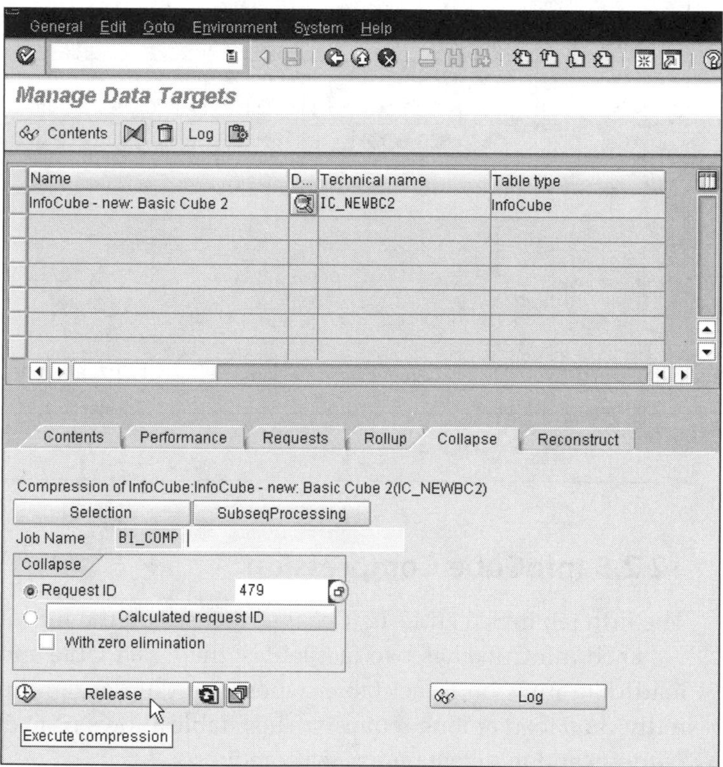

Result

After the compression, the F fact table /BIC/FIC_NEWBC2 contains no more data. Instead, the compressed data now appear in the E fact table, /BIC/EIC_NEWBC2. The E fact table has only 24 records of data, instead of 72 as shown in Screen 12.30. The data packet dimension column KEY_IC_NEWBC2P contains only zeros.

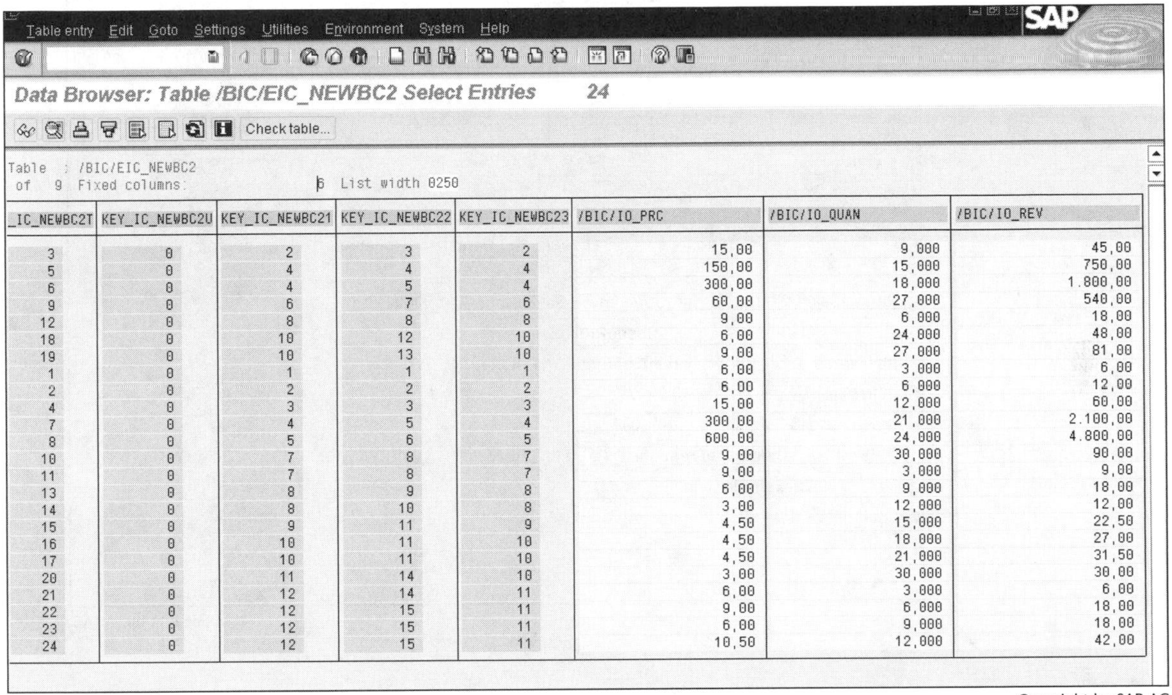

Table entry Edit Goto Settings Utilities Environment System Help

Data Browser: Table /BIC/EIC_NEWBC2 Select Entries 24

Check table...

Table : /BIC/EIC_NEWBC2
of 9 Fixed columns: 6 List width 0250

_IC_NEWBC2T	KEY_IC_NEWBC2U	KEY_IC_NEWBC21	KEY_IC_NEWBC22	KEY_IC_NEWBC23	/BIC/IO_PRC	/BIC/IO_QUAN	/BIC/IO_REV
3	0	2	3	2	15,00	9,000	45,00
5	0	4	4	4	150,00	15,000	750,00
6	0	4	5	4	300,00	18,000	1.800,00
9	0	6	7	6	60,00	27,000	540,00
12	0	8	8	8	9,00	6,000	18,00
18	0	10	12	10	6,00	24,000	48,00
19	0	10	13	10	9,00	27,000	81,00
1	0	1	1	1	6,00	3,000	6,00
2	0	2	2	2	6,00	6,000	12,00
4	0	3	3	3	15,00	12,000	60,00
7	0	4	5	4	300,00	21,000	2.100,00
8	0	5	6	5	600,00	24,000	4.800,00
10	0	7	8	7	9,00	30,000	90,00
11	0	7	8	7	9,00	3,000	9,00
13	0	8	9	8	6,00	9,000	18,00
14	0	8	10	8	3,00	12,000	12,00
15	0	9	11	9	4,50	15,000	22,50
16	0	10	11	10	4,50	18,000	27,00
17	0	10	11	10	4,50	21,000	31,50
20	0	11	14	10	3,00	30,000	30,00
21	0	12	14	11	6,00	3,000	6,00
22	0	12	15	11	9,00	6,000	18,00
23	0	12	15	11	6,00	9,000	18,00
24	0	12	15	11	10,50	12,000	42,00

SCREEN 12.38

Note: For performance and disk space reasons, it is recommended that you roll up a request as soon as possible and then compress the InfoCube.

To roll up or compress a request automatically when data are loaded into an InfoCube, select the *Automatic request processing . . .* item from the *Environment* menu on the InfoCube definition screen (see Screen 12.39).

SCREEN 12.39

In the pop-up window (Screen 12.40), check all options and click .

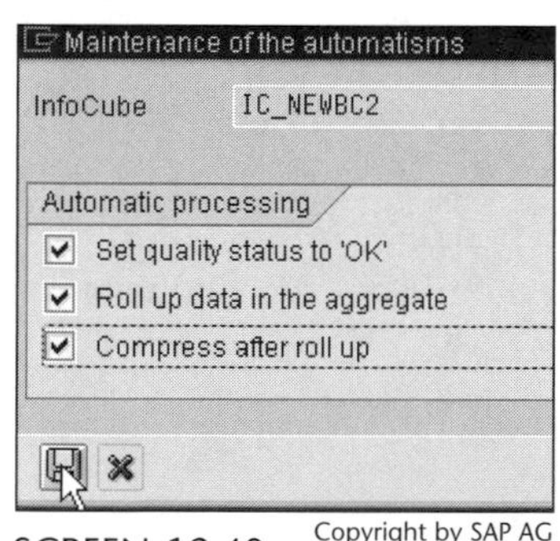

SCREEN 12.40

Caution: The order in which requests are rolled up and compressed is very important. After their compression into the E table, requests are no longer available in the F fact table and therefore cannot be rolled up into the aggregates. If we roll up requests after compressing them, the status under the Requests tab will indicate these requests are now in the aggregates—that is not true.

To delete a compressed request, we must either delete all of the E fact table data or use the *request reverse posting* function in Screen 4.8 by clicking .

12.2.6 InfoCube Reconstruction

The last tab in Screen 12.12, *Reconstruct*, allows us to reconstruct InfoCubes. Here we can reinsert the requests in PSA back into the InfoCube. The procedure follows.

Note: Using this feature, we can also fill other InfoCubes with the requests, as long as the requests remain in PSA. This feature is particularly useful when the requests call for delta loads because we cannot request the same delta loads again from the source system.

Work Instructions

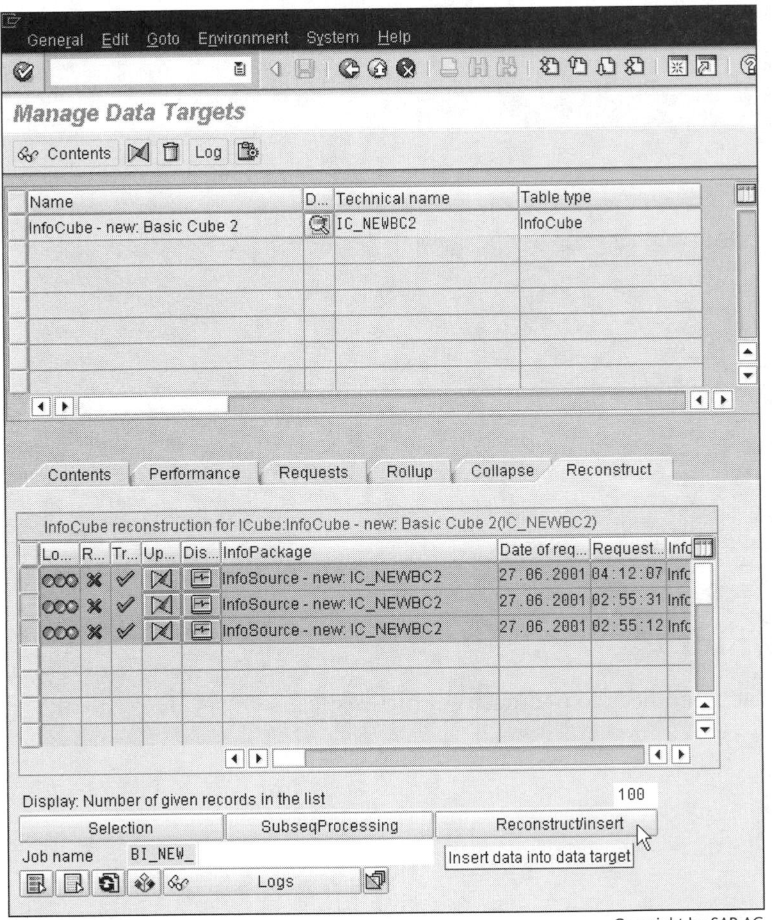

SCREEN 12.41

Step 1 Repeat the Screen 8.14 step to delete the IC_NEWBC2 data. BW removes all three requests (473, 474, and 479) from Screen 12.36.

To reconstruct the InfoCube using the requests (473, 474, and 479) that remain in PSA, select the requests and click Reconstruct/insert .

Result

Returning to the *Requests* tab and clicking [refresh icon] to refresh the view, we see that the three requests have returned to the InfoCube. They are not rolled up and compressed, but are available for reporting.

SCREEN 12.42

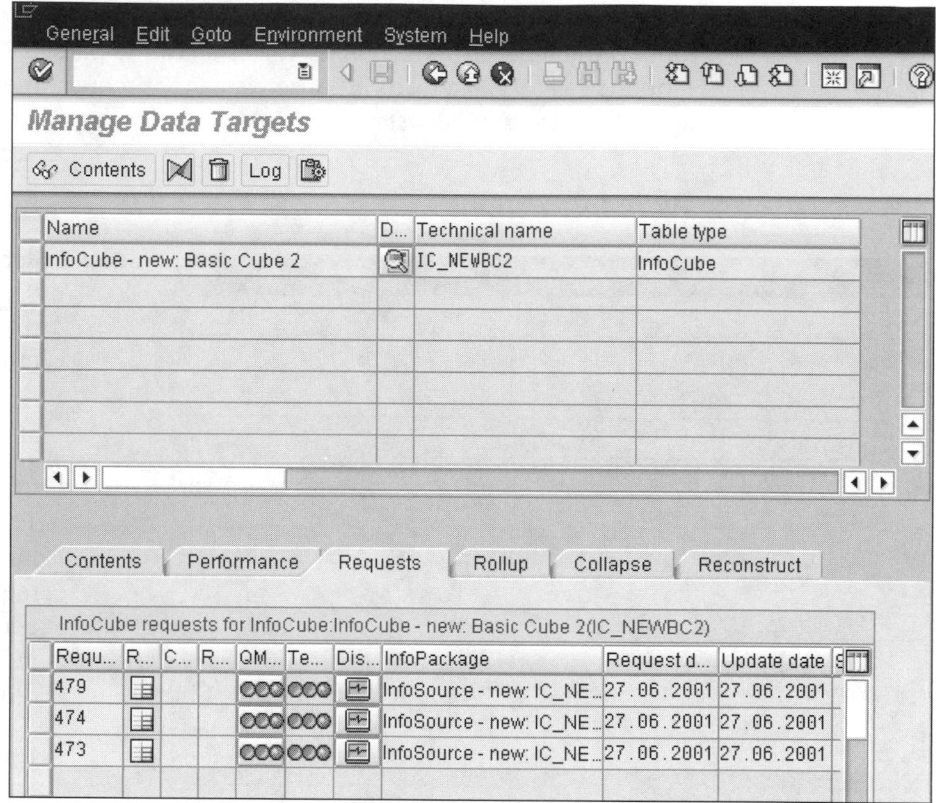

12.3 Summary

This chapter discussed how to maintain characteristic and InfoCube data in BW.

Key Terms

Term	Description
Change run	The change run procedure activates characteristic data changes.

Request	A request is a data load request from BW Scheduler. Each time that the BW Scheduler loads data into an InfoCube, a unique request ID is created in the data packet dimension table of the InfoCube.
Aggregate rollup	The aggregate rollup procedure updates aggregates with new data loads.
InfoCube compression	InfoCube compression aggregates multiple data loads at the request level.
Reconstruct	The reconstruct procedure restores load requests from PSA.
Index	Indices are used to locate needed records in a database table quickly. BW uses two types of indices, B-tree indices for regular database tables and bitmap indices for fact tables and aggregate tables. See Chapter 13 for more information on bitmap indices.
Statistics	For a SQL statement, many execution plans are possible. The database optimizer generates the most efficient execution plan based on either the heuristic ranking of available execution plans or the cost calculation of available execution plans. The cost-based optimizer uses statistics to calculate the cost of available execution plans and select the most appropriate one for execution. BW uses the cost-base optimizer for Oracle databases.

For Further Information

- OSS Note 0181944, "Accelerate Hierarchy Attribute Change Run."
- OSS Note 0397403, "Aggregate Rollup Runs Slowly."

Next . . .

We will discuss how to tune query performance and load performance.

Chapter 13

Performance Tuning

Performance is a critical issue in developing a data warehouse because of the size of data in the system. Earlier in this book, we explicitly discussed techniques to help improve performance. For example, in Chapter 7, we considered how to design an InfoCube so that its queries will have better performance.

Two types of performance measurements exist: system throughput and response time. System throughput usually applies to OLTP systems, which are designed to process thousands or even millions of small transactions per day. In contrast, response time typically applies to OLAP systems, which are designed to process massive parallel queries that fetch and sort hundreds of thousands of records from various tables.

The following tactics have proved very effective when tuning performance and are recommended by Oracle:

1. Set clear goals for tuning.
2. Create minimum repeatable tests.

3. Test hypotheses.
4. Keep records.
5. Avoid common errors.
6. Stop tuning when the objectives are met.
7. Demonstrate meeting the objectives.

In this chapter, we will first show how to install and use BW Statistics, a BW tool for performance measurement. We will also briefly discuss System Administration Assistant, an SAP function for general system performance monitoring. Finally, we will discuss techniques for tuning query performance and load performance.

Note: The discussion in this chapter applies to Oracle on HP-UX. Refer to the BW documentation for information on other platforms.

13.1 BW Statistics

BW Statistics is a multi-cube named 0BWTC_C10. It contains six basic cubes, each of which stores specific system performance information (Screen 13.1).

SCREEN 13.1

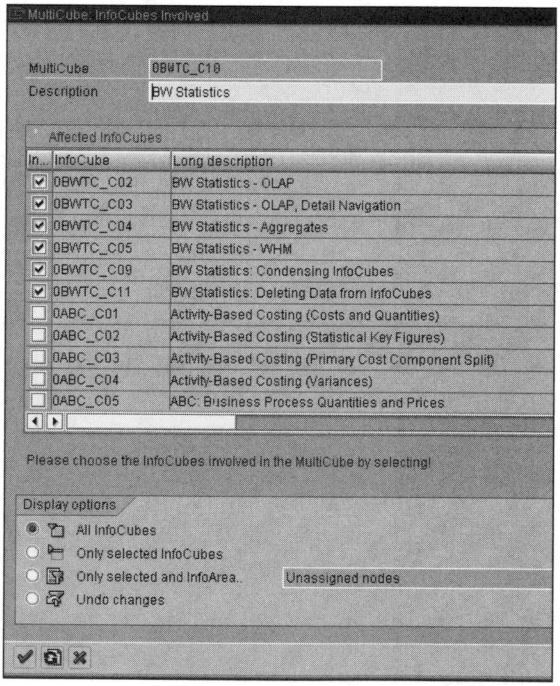

BW Statistics works as follows:

1. The raw statistical data are collected in database tables, such as RSDDSTAT, RSDDSTATWHM, and RSDDSTATAGGR.
2. The raw statistical data are loaded into the basic cubes through the regular BW data load procedure.
3. We run queries on the multi-cube to obtain BW performance information.

To specify the InfoCubes for which we want to collect statistical data, follow these steps:

Work Instructions

Step 1 In Administrator Workbench, select *BW statistics for InfoCubes* from the Tools menu.

SCREEN 13.2

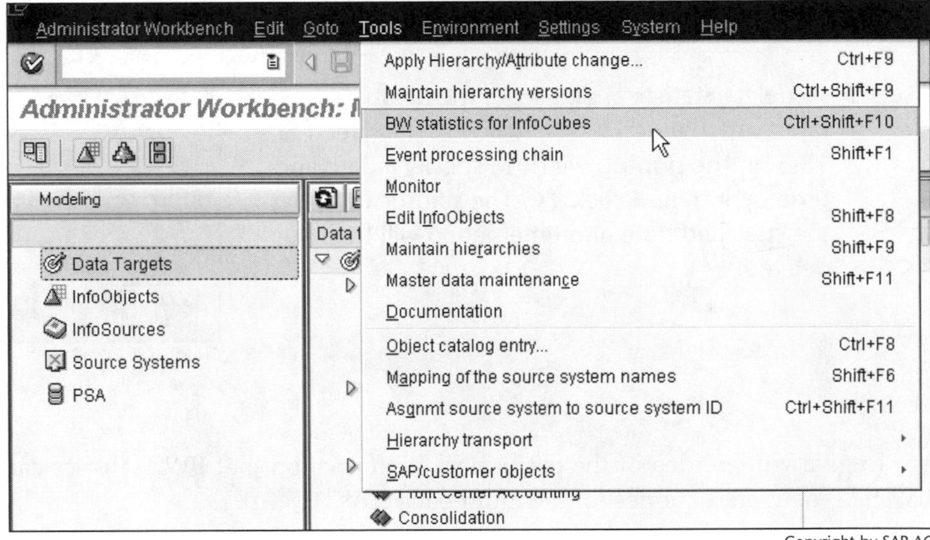

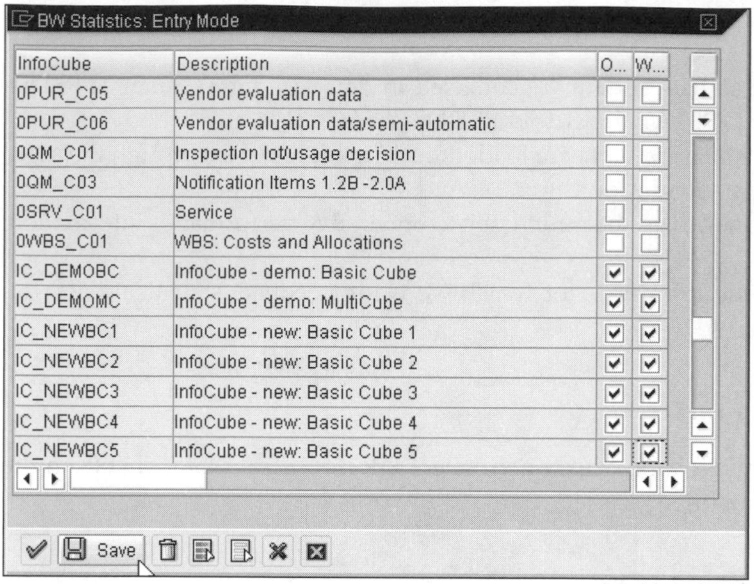

BW Statistics: Entry Mode

InfoCube	Description	O...	W...
0PUR_C05	Vendor evaluation data	☐	☐
0PUR_C06	Vendor evaluation data/semi-automatic	☐	☐
0QM_C01	Inspection lot/usage decision	☐	☐
0QM_C03	Notification Items 1.2B -2.0A	☐	☐
0SRV_C01	Service	☐	☐
0WBS_C01	WBS: Costs and Allocations	☐	☐
IC_DEMOBC	InfoCube - demo: Basic Cube	☑	☑
IC_DEMOMC	InfoCube - demo: MultiCube	☑	☑
IC_NEWBC1	InfoCube - new: Basic Cube 1	☑	☑
IC_NEWBC2	InfoCube - new: Basic Cube 2	☑	☑
IC_NEWBC3	InfoCube - new: Basic Cube 3	☑	☑
IC_NEWBC4	InfoCube - new: Basic Cube 4	☑	☑
IC_NEWBC5	InfoCube - new: Basic Cube 5	☑	☑

Save

SCREEN 13.3

Step 2 Select the InfoCubes for which we need to collect statistic data, and then click Save.

Note: Check column *OLAP* to collect OLAP-related statistical data, such as the number of records retrieved from the database. Check column *WHM* (WareHouse Management) to collect ETTL and data management-related statistical data, such as the number of records loaded into an InfoCube.

Step 3 To delete statistical data from the database tables, such as RSDDSTAT, click [delete icon] in Screen 13.3. In the pop-up window, specify a date and time period, and click [delete icon]. The statistical data in the specified date and time period will then be deleted.

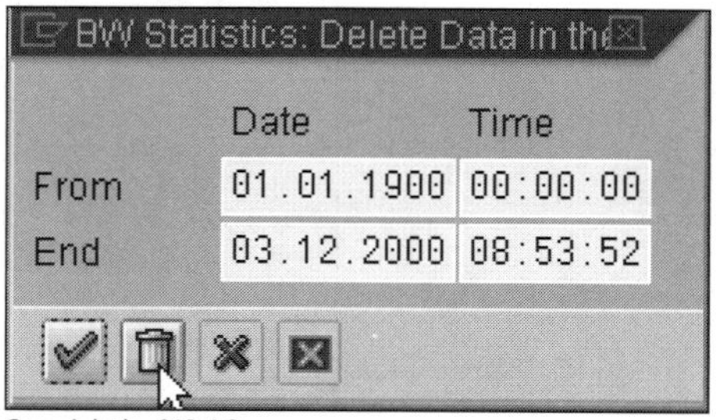

BW Statistics: Delete Data in th

	Date	Time
From	01.01.1900	00:00:00
End	03.12.2000	08:53:52

SCREEN 13.4

To give you an idea of the performance information that BW Statistics can provide, Table 13.1 lists SAP-delivered queries for the multi-cube 0BWTC_C10.

TABLE 13.1 BW STATISTICS QUERIES

Query	Characteristics	Key Figures
Chart: Records OLAP per InfoCube	BW system InfoCube	Overall time (OLAP) Records, selected on database Records, transferred from the database Cells, transferred to front end Formatting, transferred to front end Number, read texts
Chart: Times OLAP per InfoCube	BW system InfoCube	Time, initializing the OLAP processor Time, OLAP processor Time, read on the database Time, front end Time, authorization check Time, read texts/master data
Mean time per query	BW system User InfoCube Aggregate Query (UID)	Number of navigations Overall time (OLAP) Mean overall time (OLAP) Mean time, initializing OLAP Mean time, OLAP processor Mean time, reading database Mean time, front end Mean time, authorization check Mean time, reading texts/master data Mean number of records, selected on the database Mean number of records, transferred from the database Mean number of cells, transferred to front end Mean number of formatting, transferred to front end Mean number of texts, read
OLAP performance with/without reading on demand/aggregates	BW system User InfoCube Query OLAP read on/off Aggregate	Number of navigations Overall time (OLAP) Mean overall time (OLAP) Mean time, initializing OLAP Mean time, OLAP processor Mean time, reading database Mean time, front end Mean time, authorization check

TABLE 13.1 (continued)

Query	Characteristics	Key Figures
		Mean time, reading texts/master data Mean number of records, selected on the database Mean number of records, transferred from the database Mean number of cells, transferred to front end Mean number of formatting, transferred to front end Mean number of texts, read
Rolling up aggregates	BW system InfoCube User Superior cube Aggregate cube Aggregate	Number of navigations Last used (day) Last used (time of day)
Run-time query	BW system User InfoCube Query Validity period category	Number of navigations Mean overall time (OLAP) Overall time (OLAP) Time, initializing the OLAP processor Time, OLAP processor Time, read on the database Time, front end Time, authorization check Time, read texts/master data Overall number (OLAP) Records, selected on database Records, transferred from the database Cells, transferred to front end Formatting, transferred to front end Number, read texts
Transfer method loading data	BW system Automatically/manually posted Calendar day Source system Transfer type (WHM) Times and records (WHM)	Transfer type (WHM) Time (procedure WHM) Records (procedure WHM)

Query	Characteristics	Key Figures
	InfoSource InfoPackage ID Transfer type WHM Data request (SID)	
Use of InfoObjects	BW system Characteristic value Hierarchy Aggregation level InfoObject type InfoObject	Number of navigations Last used (day) Last used (time of day)
Use of InfoObjects in navigation	BW system Statistical data UID Navigation step Front-end session Characteristic value Hierarchy level Hierarchy Aggregation level Aggregate OLAP read on/off InfoCube User Query InfoObject	Frequency
Using aggregates (OLAP)	BW system InfoCube Aggregate	Number of navigations Last used (day) Last used (time of day)
Using hierarchies	BW system InfoObject Characteristic value Aggregation level InfoObject type Hierarchy	Number of navigations Last used (day) Last used (time of day)
Using InfoCube OLAP/WHM	BW system InfoCube	Time (OLAP/WHM) Total load time (WHM) Overall time (OLAP) Records (OLAP/WHM) Overall number (OLAP) Total number of records (WHM)

TABLE 13.1 (continued)

Query	Characteristics	Key Figures
Using InfoCubes	BW system InfoCube	Number of navigations Last used (day) Last used (time of day)
Utilizing OLAP	BW system User Time Calendar day Validity period category OLAP read on/off Navigation step Database read mode Aggregate UTC time stamp InfoCube Query	Number of navigations Mean overall time (OLAP) Overall time (OLAP) Time, initializing OLAP processor Time, OLAP processor Time, read on the database Time, front end Time, authorization check Time, read texts/master data Overall number (OLAP) Records, selected on database Records, transferred from the database Cells, transferred to front end Formatting, transferred to front end Number, read texts
Utilizing OLAP according to date	Calendar day	Overall time (OLAP) Overall number (OLAP)
Utilizing OLAP according to time of day	Time	Overall time (OLAP) Overall number (OLAP)
Utilizing OLAP per InfoCube	BW system InfoCube	Number of navigations Mean overall time (OLAP) Overall time (OLAP) Time, initializing OLAP processor Time, OLAP processor Time, read on the database Time, front end Time, authorization check Time, read texts/master data Overall number (OLAP) Records, selected on database Records, transferred from the database Cells, transferred to front end Formatting, transferred to front end Number, read texts

Query	Characteristics	Key Figures
Utilizing OLAP per query	BW system Query	Number of navigations Mean overall time (OLAP) Overall time (OLAP) Time, initializing OLAP processor Time, OLAP processor Time, read on the database Time, front end Time, authorization check Time, read texts/master data Overall number (OLAP) Records, selected on database Records, transferred from the database Cells, transferred to front end Formatting, transferred to front end Number, read texts
Utilizing OLAP per user	BW system User	Number of navigations Mean overall time (OLAP) Overall time (OLAP) Time, initializing OLAP processor Time, OLAP processor Time, read on the database Time, front end Time, authorization check Time, read texts/master data Overall number (OLAP) Records, selected on database Records, transferred from the database Cells, transferred to front end Formatting, transferred to front end Number, read texts
Utilizing WHM per InfoCube	BW system InfoCube	Time (procedure WHM) Records (procedure WHM)
Utilizing WHM per InfoSource	BW system InfoSource	Time (procedure WHM) Records (procedure WHM)
WHM usage per day	Calendar day	Time (procedure WHM) Records (procedure WHM)
WHM usage per hour	Time	Time (procedure WHM) Records (procedure WHM)

Screen 13.5 shows an example of the query *Mean Time per Query*.

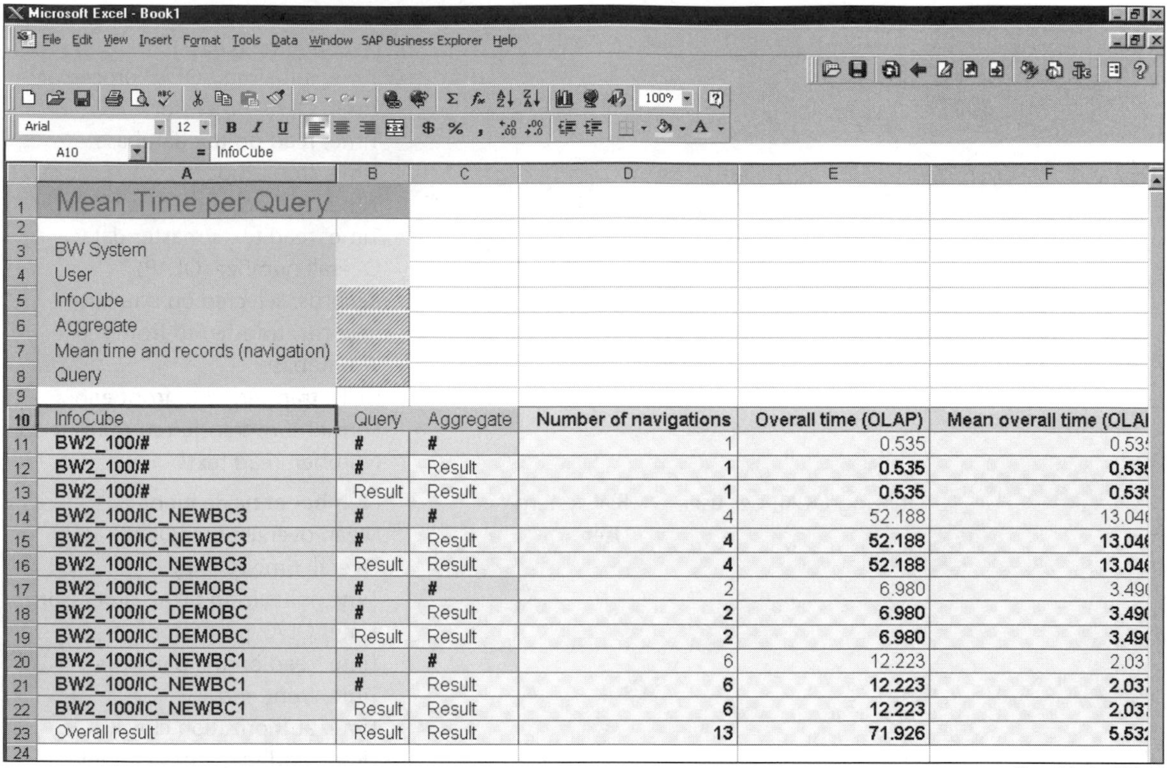

Microsoft Excel - Book1

File Edit View Insert Format Tools Data Window SAP Business Explorer Help

A10 = InfoCube

Mean Time per Query

BW System
User
InfoCube
Aggregate
Mean time and records (navigation)
Query

InfoCube	Query	Aggregate	Number of navigations	Overall time (OLAP)	Mean overall time (OLAI
BW2_100/#	#	#	1	0.535	0.53
BW2_100/#	#	Result	1	0.535	0.53
BW2_100/#	Result	Result	1	0.535	0.53
BW2_100/IC_NEWBC3	#	#	4	52.188	13.04
BW2_100/IC_NEWBC3	#	Result	4	52.188	13.04
BW2_100/IC_NEWBC3	Result	Result	4	52.188	13.04
BW2_100/IC_DEMOBC	#	#	2	6.980	3.49
BW2_100/IC_DEMOBC	#	Result	2	6.980	3.49
BW2_100/IC_DEMOBC	Result	Result	2	6.980	3.49
BW2_100/IC_NEWBC1	#	#	6	12.223	2.03
BW2_100/IC_NEWBC1	#	Result	6	12.223	2.03
BW2_100/IC_NEWBC1	Result	Result	6	12.223	2.03
Overall result	Result	Result	13	71.926	5.53

SCREEN 13.5

Note: When Screen 13.5 was produced, BW Statistics still needed some work. For example, the query did not give query and aggregate information. Later patches fixed most of the bugs.

The following procedure shows how to install BW Statistics and load statistics data into the basic cubes.

Work Instructions

Step 1 Repeat the procedure in Section 10.4, "Installing Business Content Objects and Loading R/3 Data," to activate the multi-cube 0BWTC_C10 and its six basic cubes from Business Content.

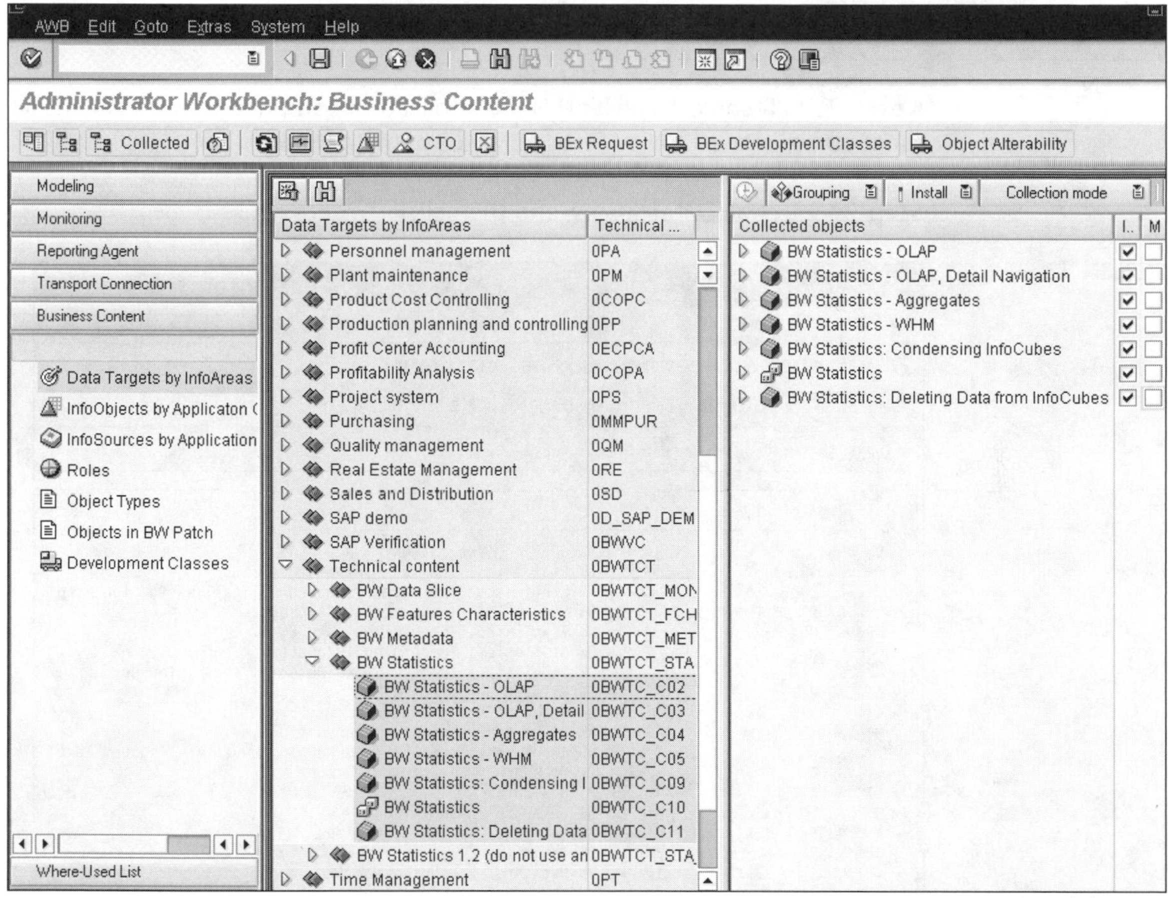

SCREEN 13.6

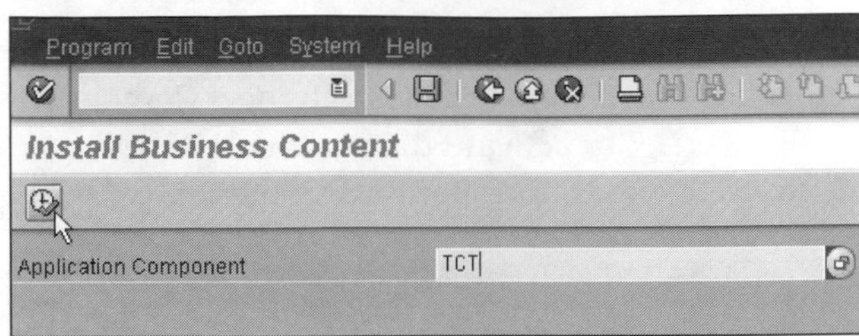

SCREEN 13.7

Step 2 To load data, we must transfer and replicate DataSources.

On the same BW system, run transaction *RSA5*, enter *TCT* in the *Application Component* field, and then click to continue.

Note: *TCT* (Technical ConTent) is the application component that contains all DataSources related to BW Statistics and BW meta-data.

Step 3 Select all DataSources, and then click Transfer DataSources .

SCREEN 13.8

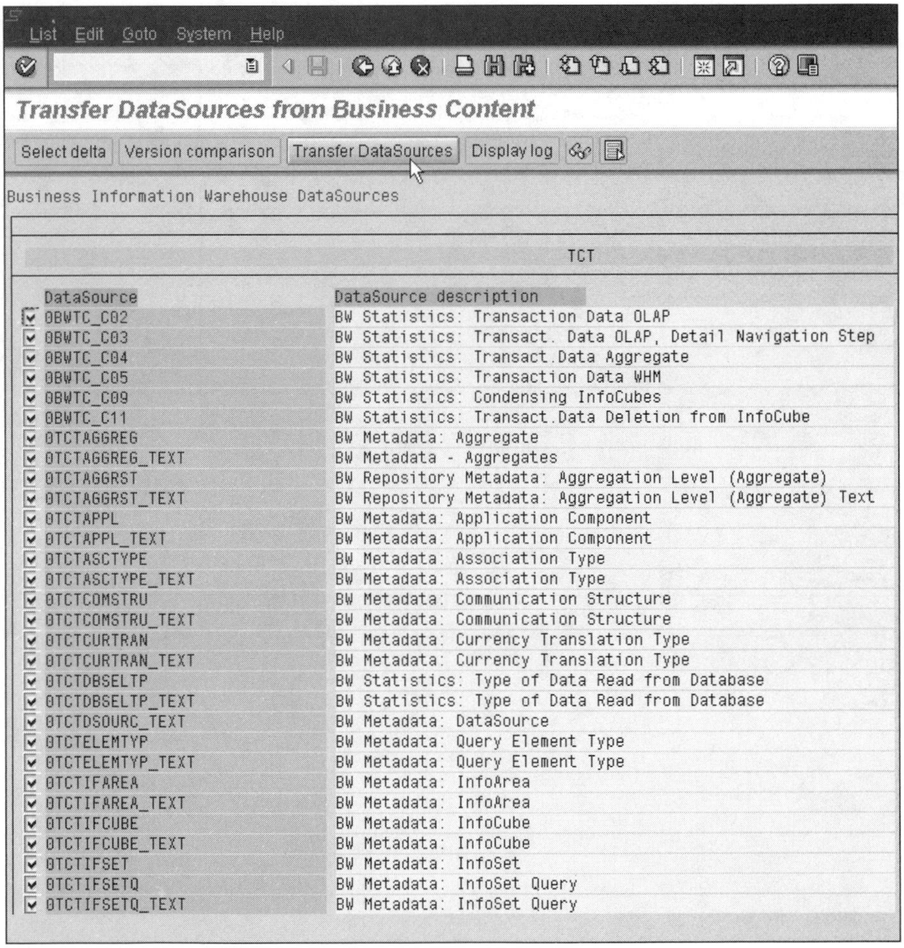

List Edit Goto System Help

Transfer DataSources from Business Content

Select delta | Version comparison | Transfer DataSources | Display log

Business Information Warehouse DataSources

TCT

DataSource	DataSource description
0BWTC_C02	BW Statistics: Transaction Data OLAP
0BWTC_C03	BW Statistics: Transact. Data OLAP, Detail Navigation Step
0BWTC_C04	BW Statistics: Transact.Data Aggregate
0BWTC_C05	BW Statistics: Transaction Data WHM
0BWTC_C09	BW Statistics: Condensing InfoCubes
0BWTC_C11	BW Statistics: Transact.Data Deletion from InfoCube
0TCTAGGREG	BW Metadata: Aggregate
0TCTAGGREG_TEXT	BW Metadata - Aggregates
0TCTAGGRST	BW Repository Metadata: Aggregation Level (Aggregate)
0TCTAGGRST_TEXT	BW Repository Metadata: Aggregation Level (Aggregate) Text
0TCTAPPL	BW Metadata: Application Component
0TCTAPPL_TEXT	BW Metadata: Application Component
0TCTASCTYPE	BW Metadata: Association Type
0TCTASCTYPE_TEXT	BW Metadata: Association Type
0TCTCOMSTRU	BW Metadata: Communication Structure
0TCTCOMSTRU_TEXT	BW Metadata: Communication Structure
0TCTCURTRAN	BW Metadata: Currency Translation Type
0TCTCURTRAN_TEXT	BW Metadata: Currency Translation Type
0TCTDBSELTP	BW Statistics: Type of Data Read from Database
0TCTDBSELTP_TEXT	BW Statistics: Type of Data Read from Database
0TCTDSOURC_TEXT	BW Metadata: DataSource
0TCTELEMTYP	BW Metadata: Query Element Type
0TCTELEMTYP_TEXT	BW Metadata: Query Element Type
0TCTIFAREA	BW Metadata: InfoArea
0TCTIFAREA_TEXT	BW Metadata: InfoArea
0TCTIFCUBE	BW Metadata: InfoCube
0TCTIFCUBE_TEXT	BW Metadata: InfoCube
0TCTIFSET	BW Metadata: InfoSet
0TCTIFSETQ	BW Metadata: InfoSet Query
0TCTIFSETQ_TEXT	BW Metadata: InfoSet Query

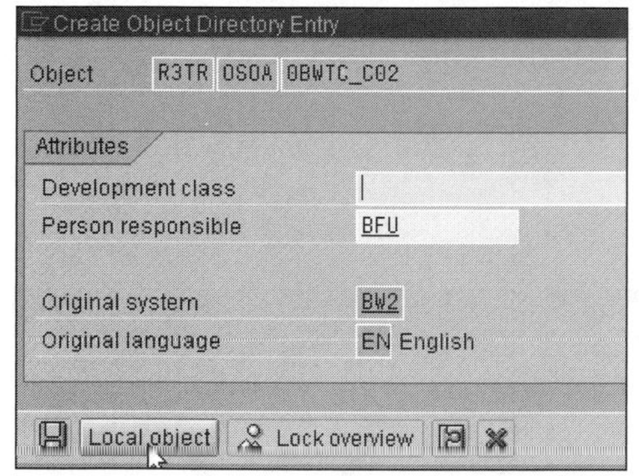

SCREEN 13.9

Step 4 The DataSources must be included in a development class to be transported to other BW systems. Here we create them as local objects.

Enter *$TMP* as the development class name and click [save icon], or simply click [Local object] to assign the object to $TMP. Click [Local object] to continue.

Step 5 Next, we need to replicate the DataSources.

In Administrator Workbench, right-click the BW system, and then select *Replicate DataSources*.

Note: The BW system is its own source system here.

SCREEN 13.10

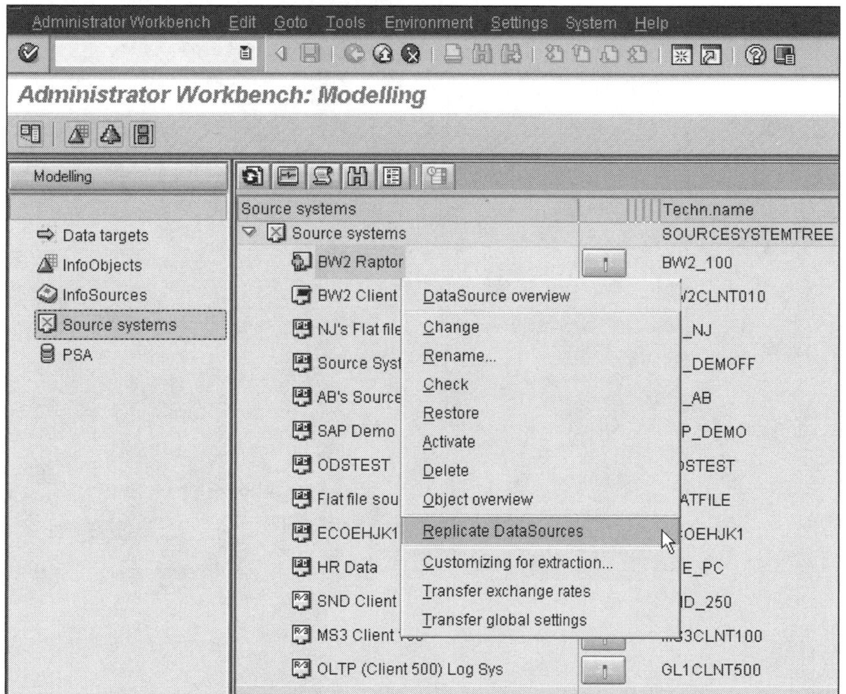

Next, we load the statistical data into the basic cubes. The following steps provide an example of loading data into a basic cube, 0BWTC_C02.

Step 6 Right-click the InfoSource *0BWTC_C02,* and then select *Assign DataSource. . . .*

SCREEN 13.11

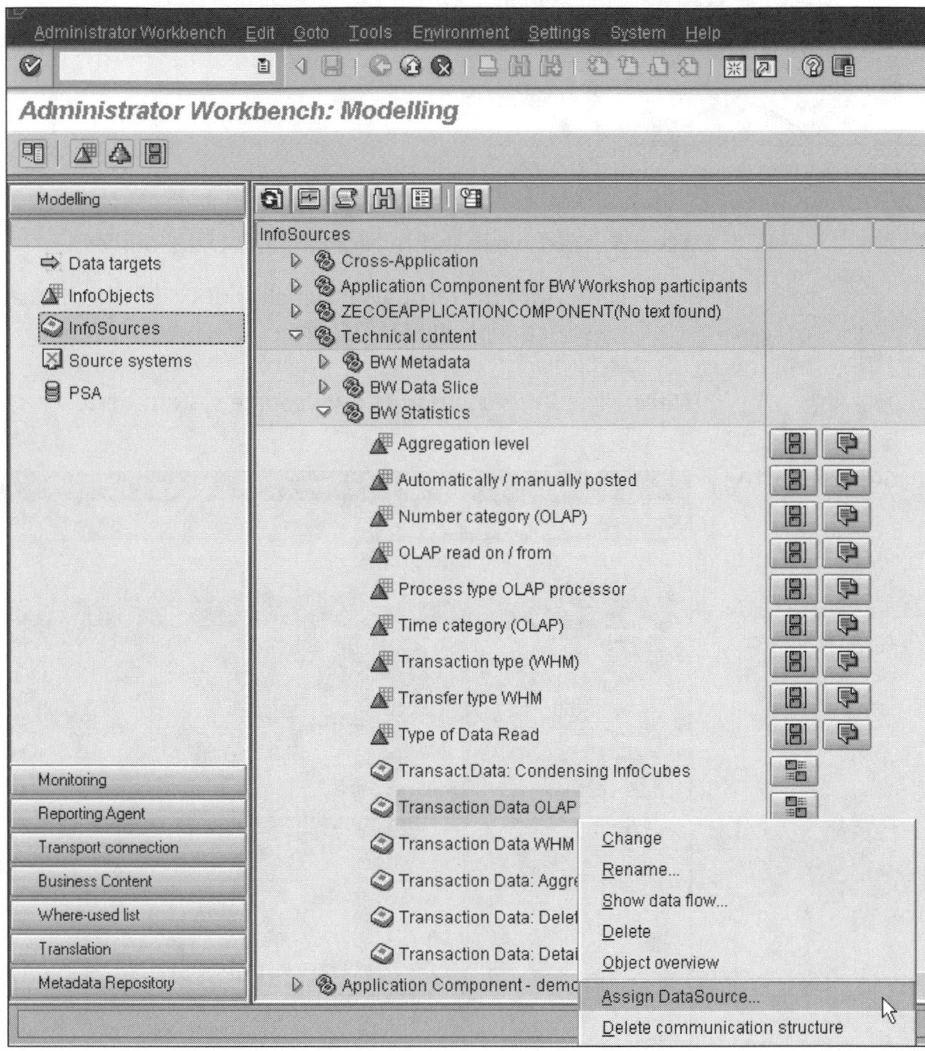

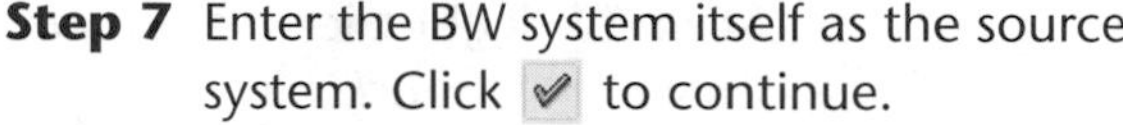

Step 7 Enter the BW system itself as the source system. Click ✔ to continue.

SCREEN 13.12

Step 8 Select the corresponding DataSource. Click ✔ to continue.

SCREEN 13.13

Step 9 Click Yes to continue.

SCREEN 13.14

Step 10 Click to activate the transfer rules, and then go back to Screen 13.16.

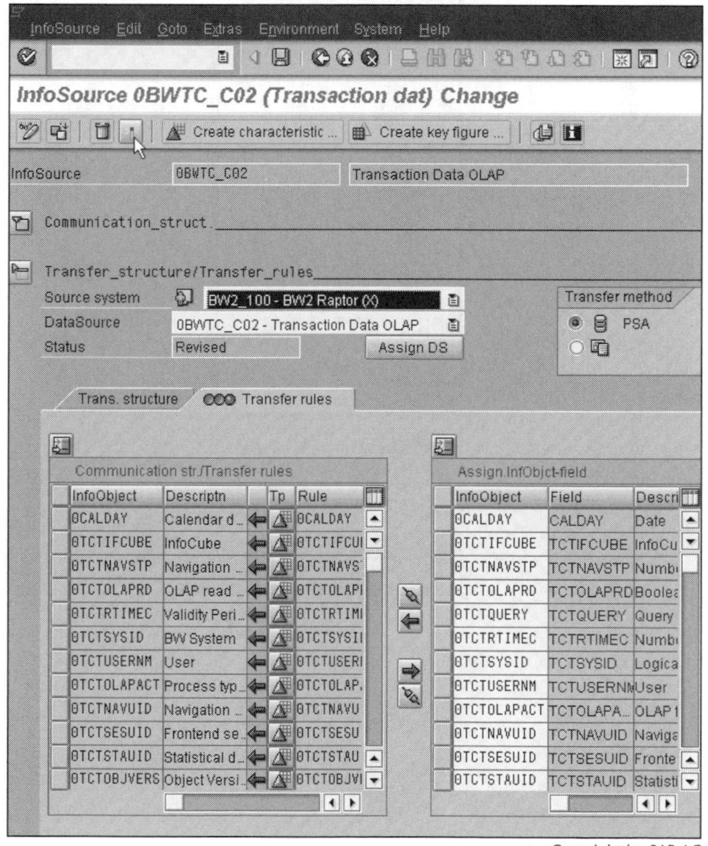

SCREEN 13.15

Step 11 Right-click the source system, and then select *Create InfoPackage. . . .*

SCREEN 13.16

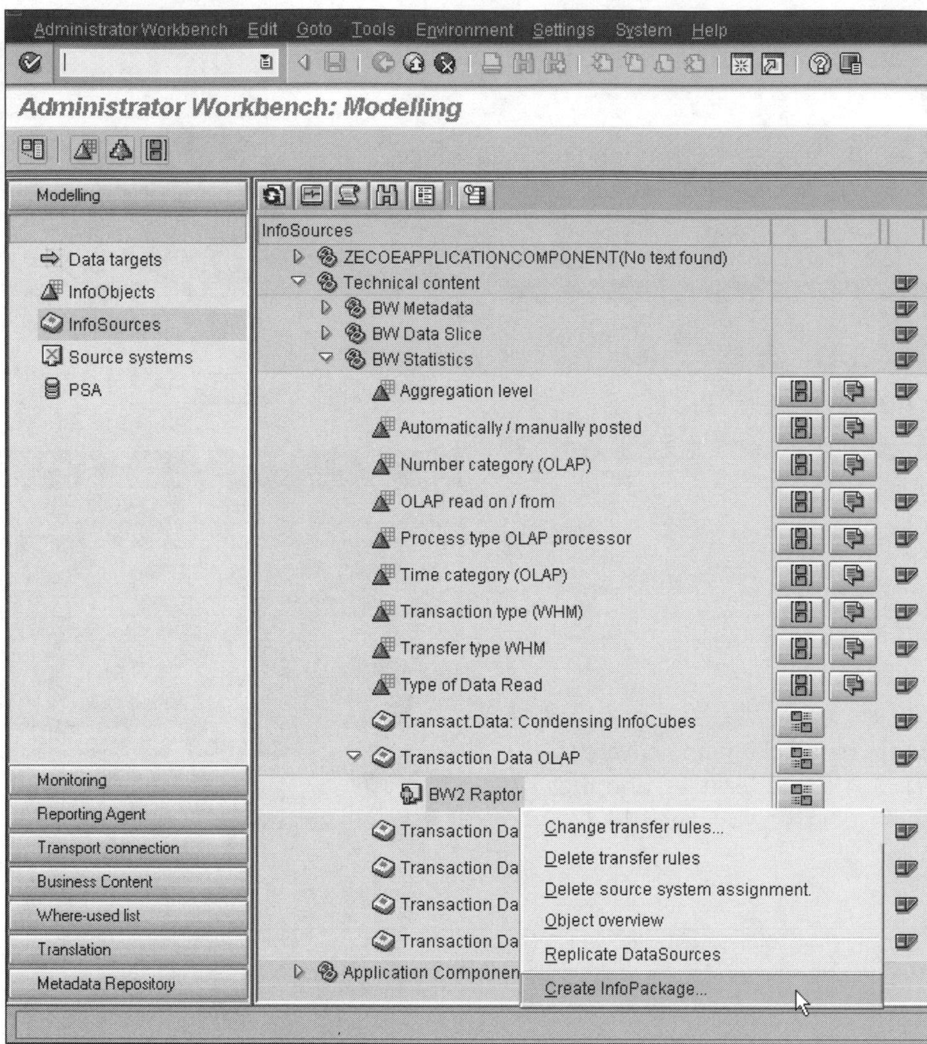

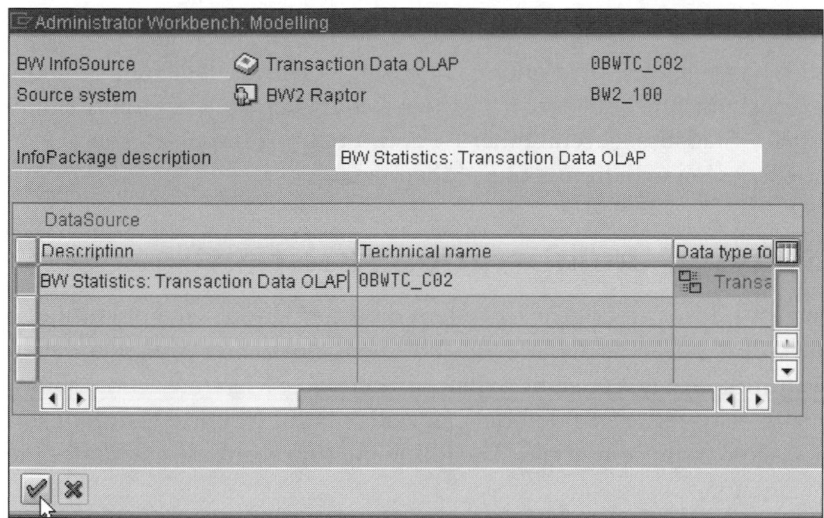

SCREEN 13.17

Step 12 Select the DataSource, enter a description, and then click ✔ to continue.

Step 13 Click Start to start the data load.

Scheduler Edit Goto Environment Zusätze System Help

Administrator Workbench: Modelling

InfoPackage BW Statistics: Transaction Data OLAP(ZPAK_3FJNU114Y9GIWLXY7EQ5Q...
InfoSource Transaction Data OLAP(0BWTC_C02)
DataSource BW Statistics: Transaction Data OLAP(0BWTC_C02)
Source system BW2 Raptor(BW2_100)
Last changed by Date Time 00:00:00
Possible types of data Transaction dat

Select data | Processing | Data targets | Update parameters | Schedule

Start data load immediately
Start later in bckgrnd proc.
Job Name BI_BTCH
Selection options
Gantt diagram (plan.table)
SubseqProcessing
Start
Job(s)
Execute; schedule

SCREEN 13.18

Result

BW Statistics has been activated and loaded with statistical data. You can now run any query against the multi-cube to obtain system performance information.

Besides BW Statistics, several other tools can help us monitor general system performance. We will discuss one of them next.

13.2 System Administration Assistant

This section introduces other general system monitoring tools, mainly from the Basis point of view. These tools come bundled in an SAP function called **System Administration Assistant**, which is accessible via transaction SSAA. SSAA contains SAP-recommended daily, weekly, monthly, nonscheduled, and occasional system monitoring tasks. The following procedure demonstrates the use of this function.

Work Instructions

Step 1 Run transaction *SSAA*. Click [icon] to get basic ideas about what this tool is and how it works.

SCREEN 13.19

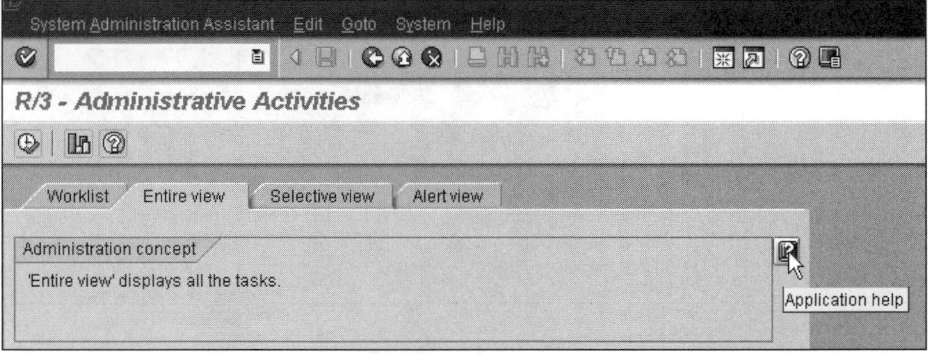

Step 2 The opened *Application help* file indicates that SSAA is System Administration Assistant, an administration concept implemented by SAP for system administrators.

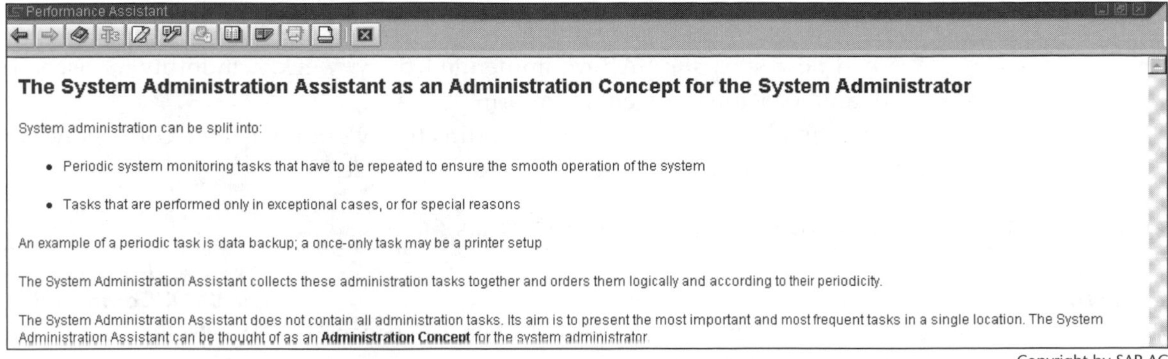

The System Administration Assistant as an Administration Concept for the System Administrator

System administration can be split into:

- Periodic system monitoring tasks that have to be repeated to ensure the smooth operation of the system
- Tasks that are performed only in exceptional cases, or for special reasons

An example of a periodic task is data backup; a once-only task may be a printer setup

The System Administration Assistant collects these administration tasks together and orders them logically and according to their periodicity.

The System Administration Assistant does not contain all administration tasks. Its aim is to present the most important and most frequent tasks in a single location. The System Administration Assistant can be thought of as an **Administration Concept** for the system administrator.

SCREEN 13.20

Step 3 Click [icon] in Screen 13.19 to reach Screen 13.21.

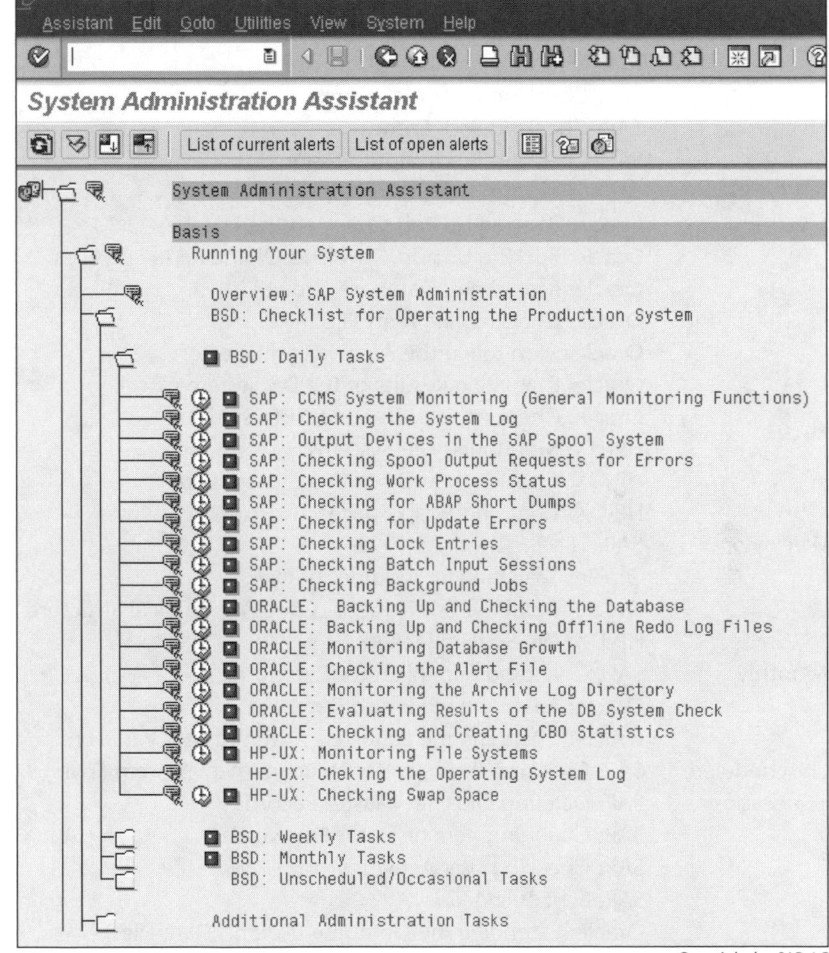

SCREEN 13.21

Result

We can now start the SAP-recommended daily, weekly, monthly, nonscheduled, and occasional system monitoring tasks.

We can also perform these tasks directly by running their corresponding transaction codes and UNIX commands (see Table 13.2).

TABLE 13.2 SAP-RECOMMENDED SYSTEM MONITORING TASKS

Frequency	**Task**	**Transaction Code or UNIX Command**
Daily	SAP: CCMS System Monitoring (General Monitoring Functions)	(See Note)
	SAP: Checking the System Log	SM21
	SAP: Output Devices in the SAP Spool System	SPAD
	SAP: Checking Spool Output Requests for Errors	SP01
	SAP: Checking Work Process Status	SM51
	SAP: Checking for ABAP Short Dumps	ST22
	SAP: Checking for Update Errors	SM13
	SAP: Checking Lock Entries	SM12
	SAP: Checking Batch Input Sessions	SM35
	SAP: Checking Background Jobs	SM37
	Oracle: Backing Up and Checking the Database	DB13
	Oracle: Backing Up and Checking Offline Redo Log Files	DB13
	Oracle: Monitoring Database Growth	DB02
	Oracle: Checking the Alert File	ST04
	Oracle: Monitoring the Archive Log Directory	DB12
	Oracle: Evaluating Results of the DB System Check	DB16B
	Oracle: Checking and Creating CBO Statistics	DB13
	HP-UX: Monitoring File Systems	ST06
	HP-UX: Checking the Operating System Log	(See HP-UX documents)
	HP-UX: Checking Swap Space	ST06
Weekly	SAP: TEMSE Check	SP12
	Oracle: Searching for Missing Indexes	DB02
	Oracle: Database Verification—Checking Physical Structure	sapdba
	HP-UX: File System Backup	tar
Monthly	SAP: Changing Administrator Passwords	SU01
	Oracle: Analyzing the Entire Database	analyze.cmd
	Oracle: Changing the Database Administrator Password	svrmgr30
Unscheduled/ occasional	SAP: Checking the Transport Management System (TMS)	STMS
	SAP: Deleting Old User Master Records	SU01
	SAP: Changing Administrator Passwords	SU01
	SAP: Checking User Activities	SM04
	SAP: Scheduling Jobs	SM36
	Oracle: Extending the Database (Adding Data Files)	sapdba

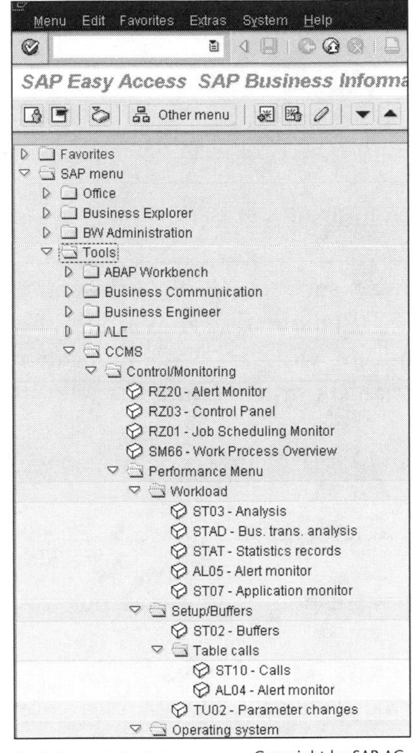

SCREEN 13.22

Note: CCMS stands for Computer Center Management System. As shown in Screen 13.22, CCMS itself collects together many monitoring tasks.

Each monitoring task in Screen 13.21 has three icons. Table 13.3 describes how to use these icons.

TABLE 13.3 FUNCTION ICONS IN SCREEN 13.21

Name	Icon	Meaning
Documentation		Click this icon to open a help file about this monitoring task.
Execute		Click this icon to start the monitoring task.
Status		The task has not been started. This icon will change to after you click , even though the task has not finished yet.

For example, if we click next to *SAP: CCMS System Monitoring (General Monitoring Functions)* in Screen 13.21, we get another SAP session (Screen 13.23).

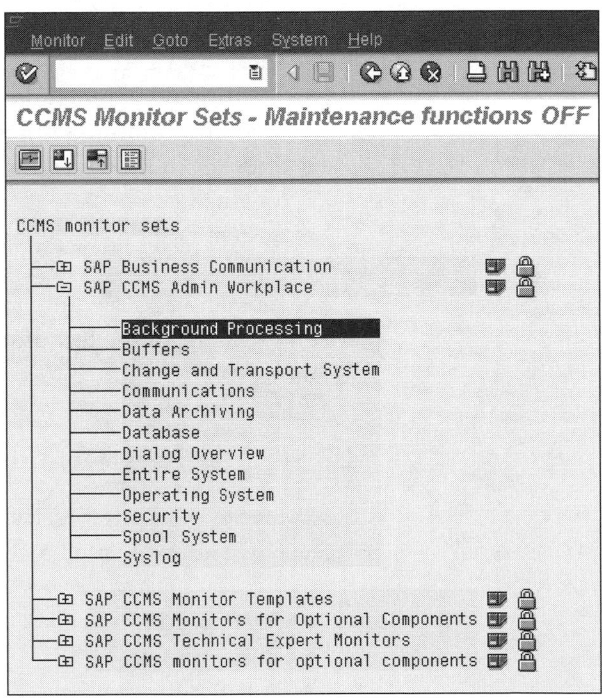

SCREEN 13.23

From this screen, we can monitor the following items:

- Background Processing, which includes background work processes and background jobs.
- Buffers, which include memory buffers for SAP objects, such as programs, table definitions, and table entries.
- Change and Transport System, which includes the object export/import and transport environment.
- Communications, which include gateway services, ALE (Application Link Enabling), and transactional RFC (Remote Function Call). BEx requires gateway services to communicate with an SAP application server. BW requires ALE and transactional RFC to communicate with its R/3 source systems.
- Data Archiving, which was introduced in BW 3.0A and is not available in 2.0B.
- Database, which includes space, performance, and backup/restore operations.
- Dialog Overview, which includes dialog response time and network time.
- Entire System, which duplicates other functions listed here.
- Operating System, which includes the file systems, CPU, paging, swap space, and LAN.
- Security, which includes security checks and audit logs of CPI-C (Common Programming Interface—Communications) and RFC logons.
- Spool System, which includes spool work processes and the spool queue length.
- System Log.

Now that we know how to monitor a BW system and measure its performance, we can examine techniques to improve query performance and load performance.

13.3 Tuning Query Performance

How queries perform directly affects the system's users. In this section, we will discuss five query-related techniques:

- Query read mode
- Bitmap index
- Statistics for cost-based optimizer

- Partition
- Parallel query option

We do not have enough space to discuss techniques that involve the configuration of hardware and operating system. Refer to the documentation from SAP and hardware vendors to find out more about these strategies.

13.3.1 Query Read Mode

Each query has one of the following three **read modes** (see Screen 13.25):

1. Query should import everything in one go.

In this read mode, when we run the query, the fact table data needed for all possible navigational steps are read into the main memory area of the OLAP processor. Therefore, subsequent navigational steps do not require any additional database reads.

This read mode takes a long time to present the initial query result.

2. Query should read during navigation.

In this read mode, when we run the query, the fact table data needed only for the current navigational step are read into the main memory area of the OLAP processor. As a consequence, later navigation steps may need additional database reads. The data for identical navigational states are buffered in the OLAP processor.

If the query involves a hierarchy, the data for the entire hierarchy are read into the main memory area of the OLAP processor.

This read mode is recommended for queries with many free characteristics.

3. Query should select data on demand in nav./expanding hier.

In this read mode, when we run the query, if a hierarchy is involved, the data needed only for the current node, such as the *EAST* region in Screen 5.34, are read into the main memory area of the OLAP processor. As a consequence, additional database reads are needed when expanding a lower-level node.

This read mode is very helpful for a query involving large hierarchies with many nodes. Aggregates should be created at a middle level of the hierarchies, and the start level of the query should be smaller than or the same as this aggregate level.

The procedure used to set the read mode for a query follows.

Work Instructions

Step 1 Run transaction *RSRT*, select a query from the lookup, and then click Read mode .

SCREEN 13.24

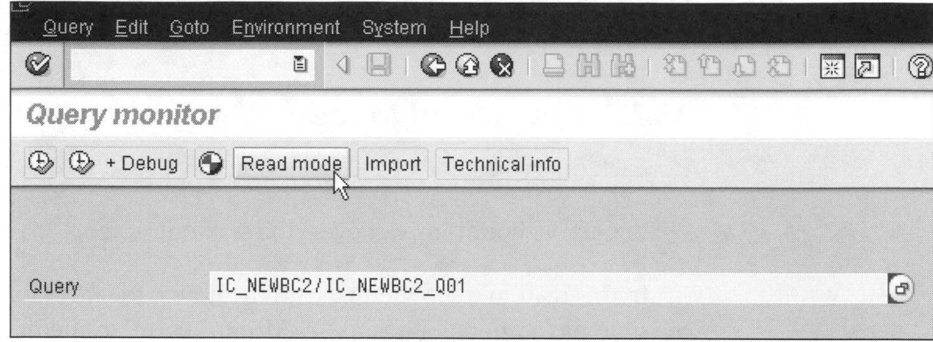

Copyright by SAP AG

Step 2 Select a read mode for this query, and then click ✔ to save the setting.

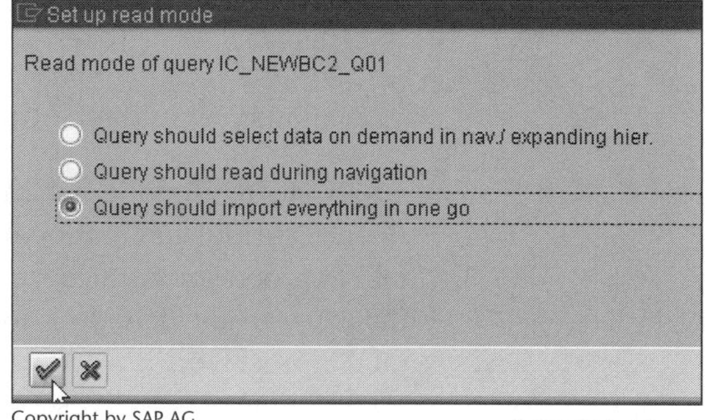

Copyright by SAP AG

SCREEN 13.25

Result

A read mode has been set for the query.

Note: To set a read mode for all queries, select *All queries read mode* from the *Environment* menu item from Screen 13.24.

To set a default read mode for future queries, run transaction *RDMD*.

13.3.2 Bitmap Index

Bitmap indices can dramatically improve query performance when table columns contain few distinct values. The ratio of the number of distinct values to the number of total rows in a table is called its **cardinality**. A column is a good candidate for a bitmap index when its cardinality is less than 0.01. Otherwise, you should consider using a B-tree index. For this reason, line item dimensions use B-tree indices, whereas other dimensions use bitmap indices.

Table 13.4 gives an example of a bitmap index—in this case, for the IO_SREG column in Table 7.1. It consists of four distinct bitmaps: 1000 for EAST, 0100 for MIDWEST, 0010 for WEST, and 0001 for blank.

TABLE 13.4 BITMAP INDEX FOR IO_SREG COLUMN IN TABLE 7.1

	Bitmap Index			
Region	**EAST**	**MIDWEST**	**WEST**	**blank**
EAST	1	0	0	0
EAST	1	0	0	0
EAST	1	0	0	0
EAST	1	0	0	0
MIDWEST	0	1	0	0
MIDWEST	0	1	0	0
MIDWEST	0	1	0	0
MIDWEST	0	1	0	0
MIDWEST	0	1	0	0
MIDWEST	0	1	0	0
MIDWEST	0	1	0	0
MIDWEST	0	1	0	0
MIDWEST	0	1	0	0
MIDWEST	0	1	0	0
WEST	0	0	1	0
WEST	0	0	1	0
WEST	0	0	1	0
WEST	0	0	1	0
WEST	0	0	1	0
WEST	0	0	1	0
	0	0	0	1
	0	0	0	1
	0	0	0	1
	0	0	0	1

When we run a query to display the sales revenue in the EAST and MIDWEST regions, the database will select and summarize sales revenue of all rows that contain the value 1 in the Result column of Table 13.5.

TABLE 13.5 BITMAP BOOLEAN OPERATION

EAST	OR MIDWEST	Result EAST OR MIDWEST
1	0	1
1	0	1
1	0	1
1	0	1
0	1	1
0	1	1
0	1	1
0	1	1
0	1	1
0	1	1
0	1	1
0	1	1
0	1	1
0	1	1
0	0	0
0	0	0
0	0	0
0	0	0
0	0	0
0	0	0
0	0	0
0	0	0
0	0	0
0	0	0

From this example, we make the following observations:

- Logical AND and OR conditions in the WHERE clause of a query can be quickly resolved by performing the corresponding Boolean operations directly on the bitmaps.
- Bitmap indices are small compared with B-tree indices, which reduces the I/O volume.

The procedure to check bitmap indices in BW follows.

Work Instructions

Step 1 Run transaction *SE11*, display the */BIC/IC_NEWBC2* table definition, and then click Indexes... .

SCREEN 13.26

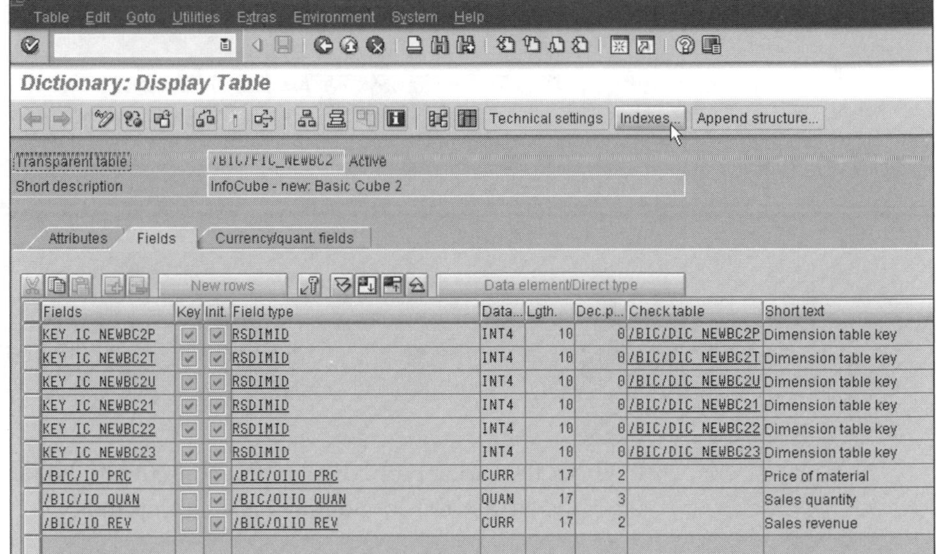

Copyright by SAP AG

Step 2 The indices for this table are listed. Select the first one, and then click Choose .

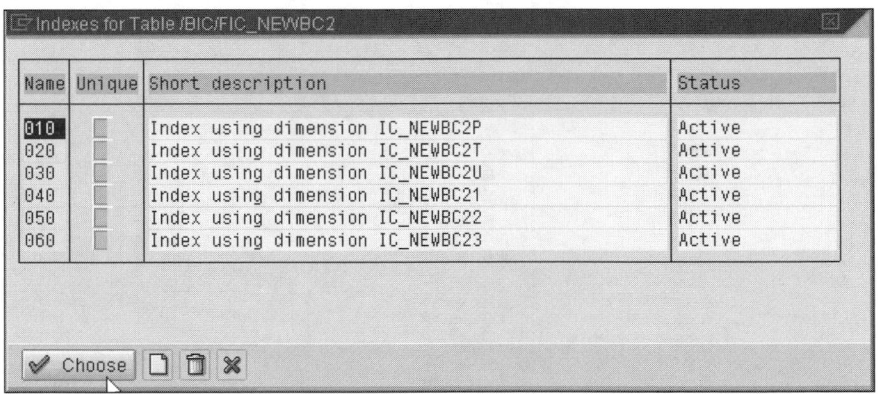

Copyright by SAP AG

SCREEN 13.27

Result

Information about this index appears in Screen 13.28.

SCREEN 13.28

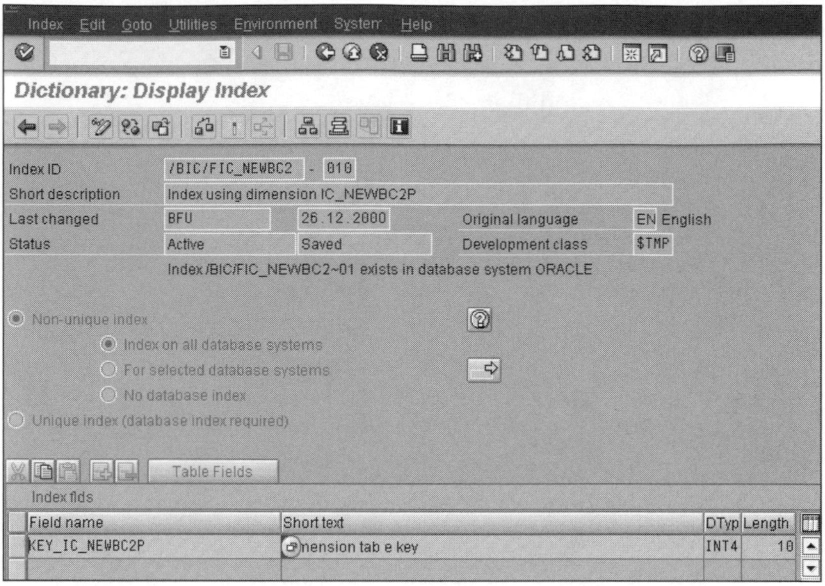

Index Edit Goto Utilities Environment System Help

Dictionary: Display Index

Index ID /BIC/FIC_NEWBC2 - 010
Short description Index using dimension IC_NEWBC2P
Last changed BFU 26.12.2000 Original language EN English
Status Active Saved Development class $TMP
Index /BIC/FIC_NEWBC2~01 exists in database system ORACLE

Non-unique index
Index on all database systems
For selected database systems
No database index
Unique index (database index required)

Table Fields

Index flds

Field name	Short text	DTyp	Length
KEY_IC_NEWBC2P	Dimension table key	INT4	10

To check the index type, display the contents of the table DDSTORAGE. In Screen 13.29, we see the above index is a bitmap index.

SCREEN 13.29

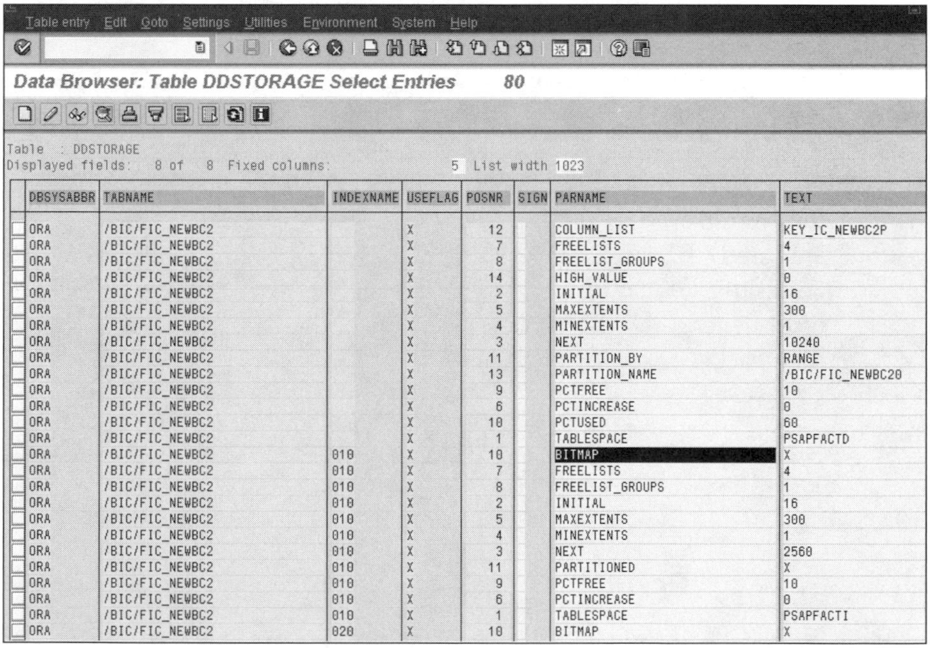

Table entry Edit Goto Settings Utilities Environment System Help

Data Browser: Table DDSTORAGE Select Entries 80

Table : DDSTORAGE
Displayed fields: 8 of 8 Fixed columns: 5 List width 1023

DBSYSABBR	TABNAME	INDEXNAME	USEFLAG	POSNR	SIGN	PARNAME	TEXT
ORA	/BIC/FIC_NEWBC2		X	12		COLUMN_LIST	KEY_IC_NEWBC2P
ORA	/BIC/FIC_NEWBC2		X	7		FREELISTS	4
ORA	/BIC/FIC_NEWBC2		X	8		FREELIST_GROUPS	1
ORA	/BIC/FIC_NEWBC2		X	14		HIGH_VALUE	0
ORA	/BIC/FIC_NEWBC2		X	2		INITIAL	16
ORA	/BIC/FIC_NEWBC2		X	5		MAXEXTENTS	300
ORA	/BIC/FIC_NEWBC2		X	4		MINEXTENTS	1
ORA	/BIC/FIC_NEWBC2		X	3		NEXT	10240
ORA	/BIC/FIC_NEWBC2		X	11		PARTITION_BY	RANGE
ORA	/BIC/FIC_NEWBC2		X	13		PARTITION_NAME	/BIC/FIC_NEWBC20
ORA	/BIC/FIC_NEWBC2		X	9		PCTFREE	10
ORA	/BIC/FIC_NEWBC2		X	6		PCTINCREASE	0
ORA	/BIC/FIC_NEWBC2		X	10		PCTUSED	60
ORA	/BIC/FIC_NEWBC2		X	1		TABLESPACE	PSAPFACTD
ORA	/BIC/FIC_NEWBC2	010	X	10		BITMAP	X
ORA	/BIC/FIC_NEWBC2	010	X	7		FREELISTS	4
ORA	/BIC/FIC_NEWBC2	010	X	8		FREELIST_GROUPS	1
ORA	/BIC/FIC_NEWBC2	010	X	2		INITIAL	16
ORA	/BIC/FIC_NEWBC2	010	X	5		MAXEXTENTS	300
ORA	/BIC/FIC_NEWBC2	010	X	4		MINEXTENTS	1
ORA	/BIC/FIC_NEWBC2	010	X	3		NEXT	2560
ORA	/BIC/FIC_NEWBC2	010	X	11		PARTITIONED	X
ORA	/BIC/FIC_NEWBC2	010	X	9		PCTFREE	10
ORA	/BIC/FIC_NEWBC2	010	X	6		PCTINCREASE	0
ORA	/BIC/FIC_NEWBC2	010	X	1		TABLESPACE	PSAPFACTI
ORA	/BIC/FIC_NEWBC2	020	X	10		BITMAP	X

Note: The same information can be obtained from Screen 13.35 under the folder *indexes*.

In BW, we cannot change the index type.

13.3.3 Statistics for the Cost-Based Optimizer

The cost-based optimizer decides the most appropriate query execution plan based on available statistical information. For this reason, it is very important to have up-to-date statistical information.

In Section 12.2.2, "Indices and Statistics," we discussed ways to automate the process so as to refresh the statistical information for each new data load. In Screen 12.24 in that section, at the bottom of the *DB statistics* block, we need to specify a percentage that indicates how much of the InfoCube data will be used to calculate the statistics. The default value is 10.

In addition to this method, BW provides a program called SAP_ANALYZE_ALL_INFOCUBES that gathers statistical information for all tables related to InfoCubes, including master data and aggregates. When running this program, we need to give a percentage, which specifies how much of the InfoCube data will be used to calculate the statistics.

Both methods use an ABAP statement like the following:

```
IF percentage <= 20%
   ANALYZE TABLE /BIC/FIC_NEWBC2
   ESTIMATE STATISTICS
   SAMPLE 10 PERCENT
   FOR TABLE
   FOR ALL INDEXED COLUMNS
   FOR ALL INDEXES
ELSE
   ANALYZE TABLE /BIC/FIC_NEWBC2
   COMPUTE STATISTICS
   FOR TABLE
   FOR ALL INDEXED COLUMNS
   FOR ALL INDEXES
```

With this statement, both methods will produce the same statistical information. If the input percentage is less or equal to 20, BW will use 10 percent of the InfoCube data to estimate the statistics. Otherwise, BW will compute the *exact* statistics.

The biggest drawback of using ANALYZE in both methods is that the statistics will be calculated sequentially. In such a case, the Oracle PL/SQL package DBMS_STATS represents a better choice. Whenever possible, DBMS_STATS calls a parallel query to gather statistics; otherwise, it calls a sequential query or uses the ANALYZE statement. Index statistics are not gathered in parallel.

Refer to the Oracle document "Designing and Tuning for Performance" to obtain more information on database statistics.

The following procedure checks the status of a table's statistical information.

Work Instructions

Step 1 Run transaction *DB20*, enter the table name, and then click Refresh information.

SCREEN 13.30

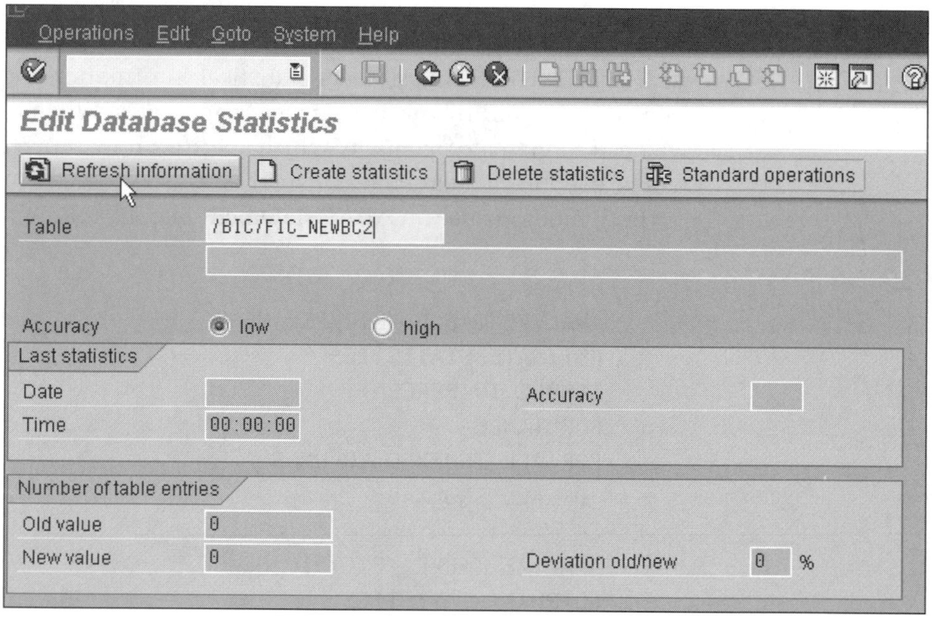

Result

Screen 13.31 displays the status.

SCREEN 13.31

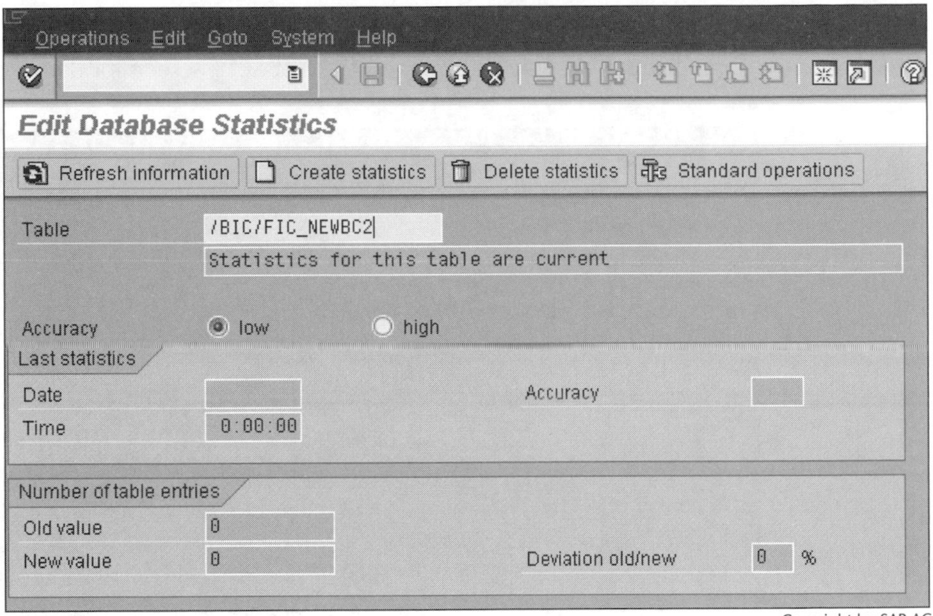

Copyright by SAP AG

13.3.4 Partition

A partition is a piece of physical storage for database tables and indices. If the needed data reside in one or a few partitions, then only those partitions will be selected and examined for a SQL statement, thereby significantly reducing I/O volume. This benefit, which substantially improves query performance, is called **partition pruning**. For a better result, it is recommended that you spread each partition over several disk devices.

Next, let's look at a partition example in BW. We already know how to check the table contents by running transaction SE11. SE11 also tells us how the table contents are stored in the database. The relevant procedure follows.

Work Instructions

Step 1 Screen 13.32 shows the first SE11 screen for the */BIC/FIC_NEWBC2* table.

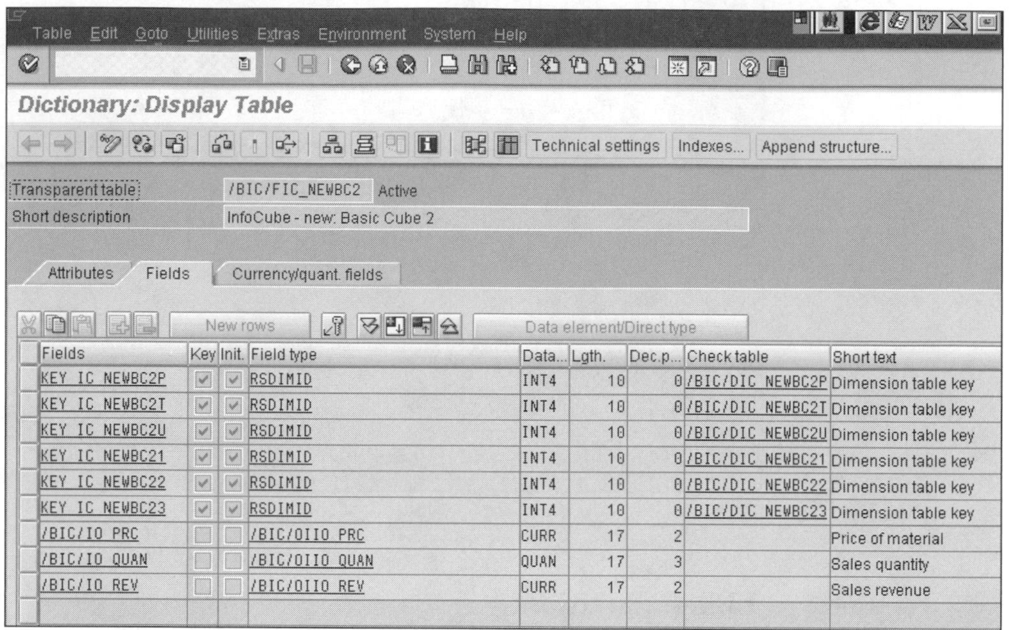

SCREEN 13.32

Step 2 Select Database utility from the Utilities menu item.

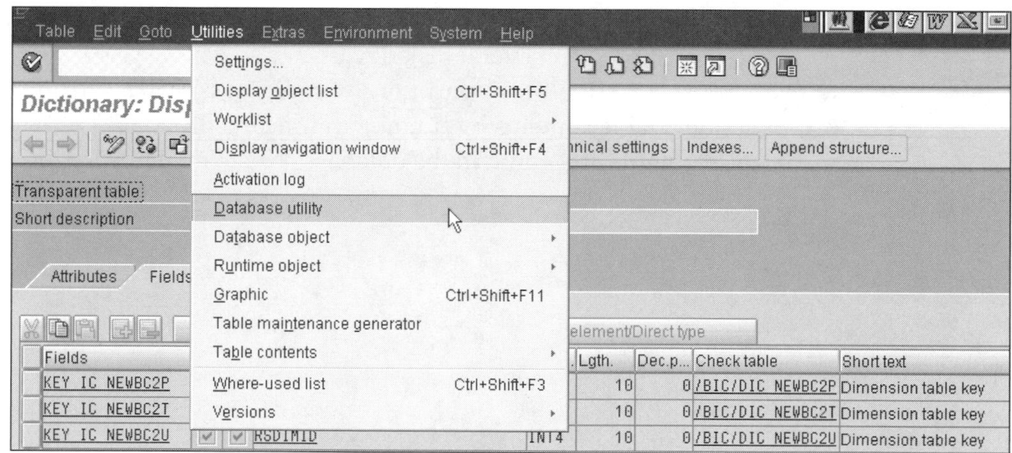

SCREEN 13.33

Step 3 Click Storage parameters .

SCREEN 13.34

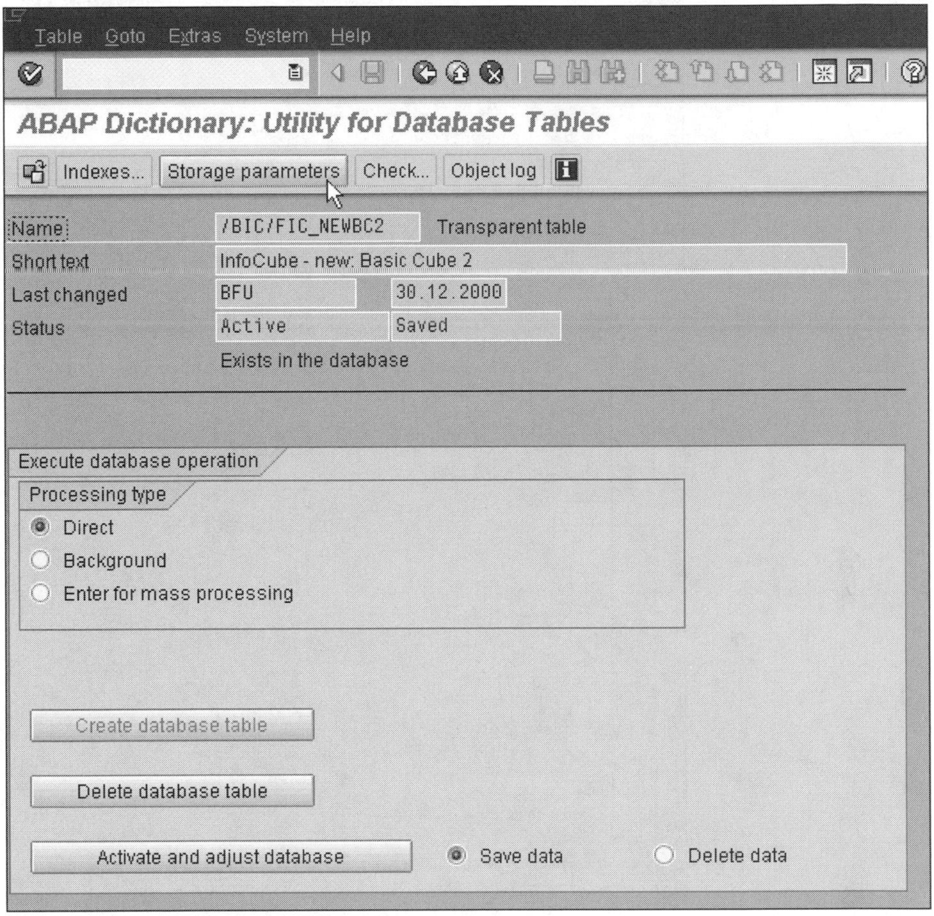

Result

Screen 13.35 indicates that the contents of /BIC/FIC_NEWBC2 are stored in three partitions. The argument used in partitioning the table is column KEY_IC_NEWBC2P. Because the first partition has a HIGH VALUE 0, only the second and third partitions hold data, and each contains the data from one load request.

SCREEN 13.35

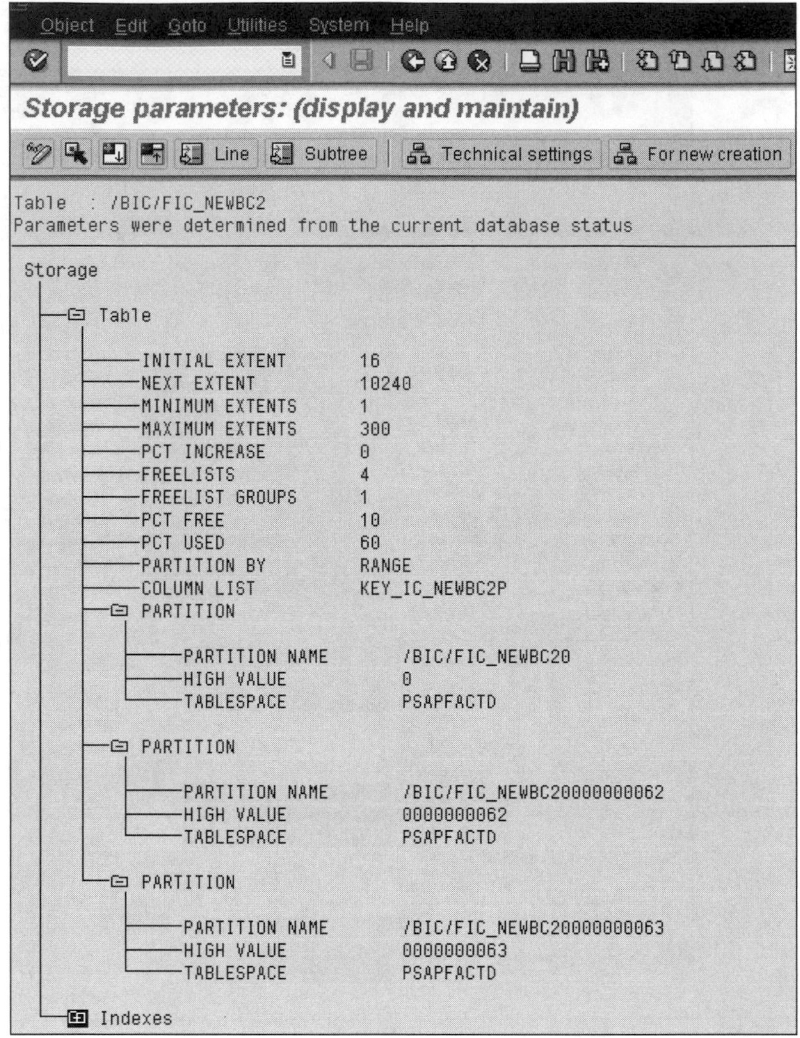

With E fact tables, we can partition each table by time. The procedure follows.

Work Instructions

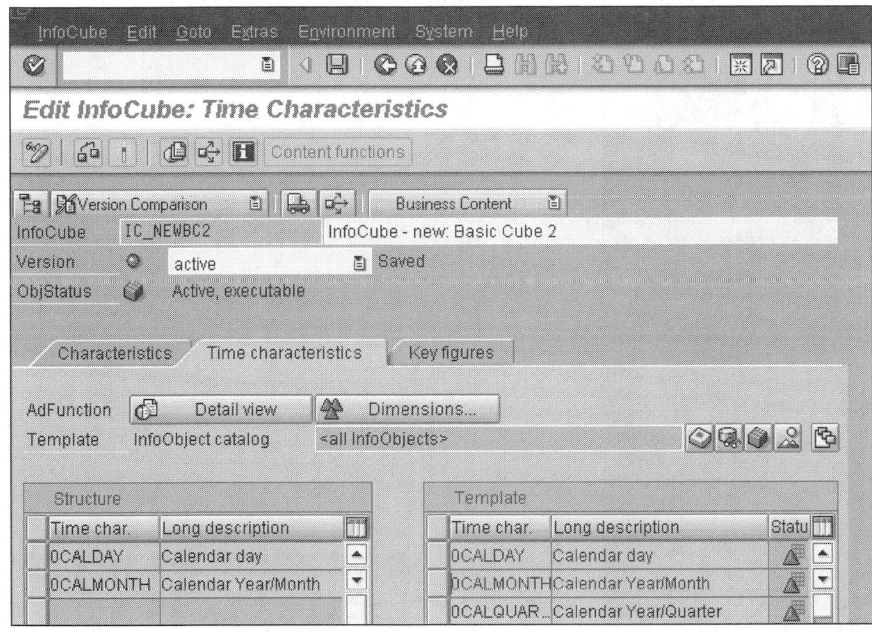

SCREEN 13.36

Step 1 After compressing InfoCube IC_NEWBC2, we open its definition.

Step 2 Select Partitioning from the Extras menu item.

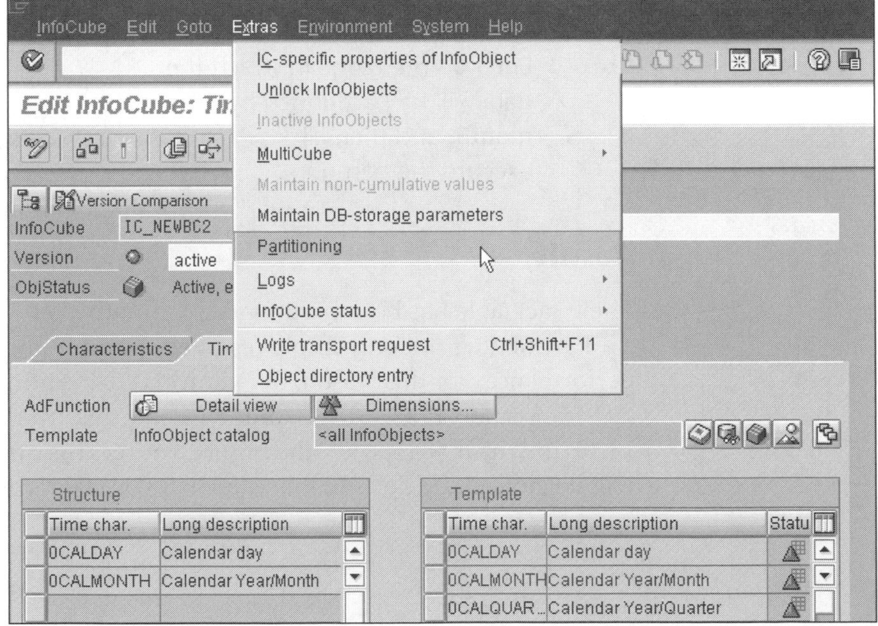

SCREEN 13.37

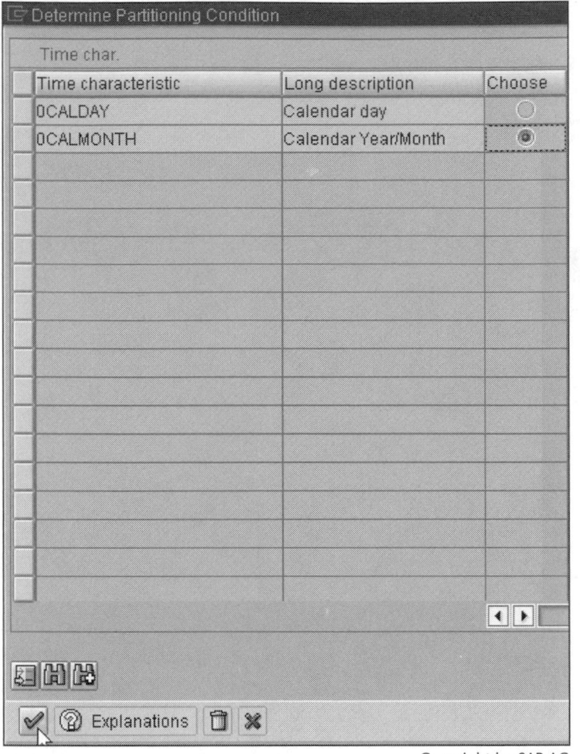

Copyright by SAP AG

SCREEN 13.38

Step 3 Partition the table by calendar month, and then click ✓ to continue.

Step 4 Enter a time range in which the data will be partitioned by month, and then click ✓ to execute the partition.

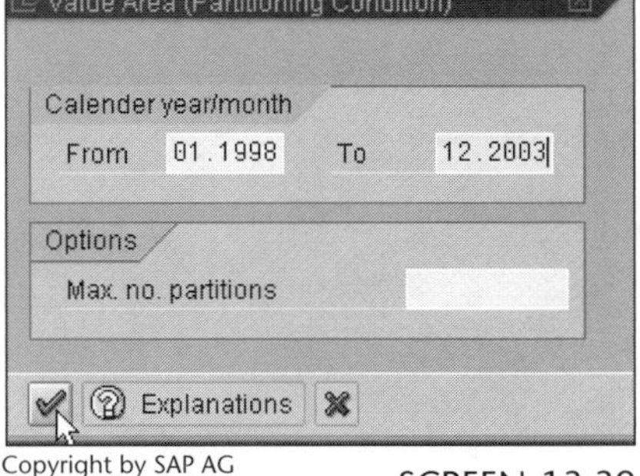

Copyright by SAP AG

SCREEN 13.39

Result

The E fact table has been partitioned by month.

Partitioning not only improves query performance, but also enhances load performance. For this reason, BW allows us to partition PSA tables using a special transaction RSCUSTV6. After running this transaction, we obtain Screen 13.40, in which we specify the number of records after which a new partition will be created. By default, this value is 1,000,000 records.

SCREEN 13.40

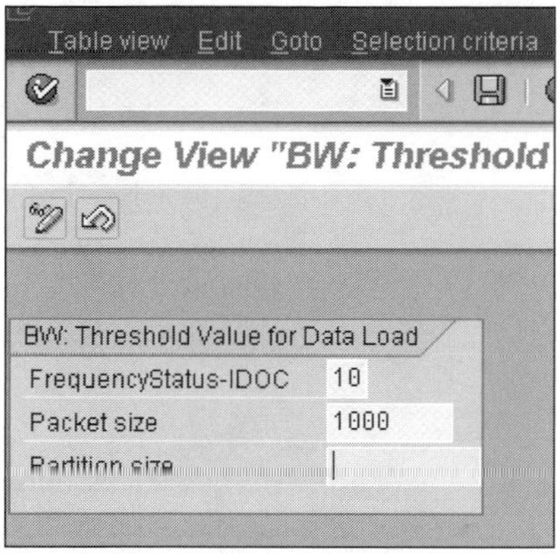

13.3.5 Parallel Query Option (PQO)

Parallel processing can dramatically improve query performance when multiple processes work together simultaneously to execute a single SQL statement. The number of parallel processes assigned to the execution is called the **degree of parallelism (DOP)**. The Oracle database determines DOP by following three steps:

1. It checks for hints or the PARALLEL clause specified in the SQL statement itself.
2. It looks at the table or index definition.
3. It checks for the default DOP.

Note: DOP cannot be specified within BW yet. You must use database tools to perform this task.

The Oracle initialization parameter PARALLEL_MIN_SERVERS specifies the number of parallel processes that an instance will have after start-up. A parallel query can obtain additional processes as specified, or they can be set by default. Whichever method is used, the total cannot exceed the value of PARALLEL_MAX_SERVERS. Table 13.6 lists other initialization parameters and their BW and R/3 default values.

TABLE 13.6 PQO-RELATED INITIALIZATION PARAMETERS

Initialization Parameter	**Description**
OPTIMIZER_PERCENT_PARALLEL BW default value: 100	Specifies how much the optimizer attempts to process a query in parallel.
R/3 default value: 0	The default values in BW and R/3 tell the difference.
PARALLEL_MIN_SERVERS BW default value: 0	Specifies the number of parallel processes that an instance will have after start-up.
R/3 default value: 0	
PARALLEL_MAX_SERVERS BW default value: 5	Specifies the maximum number of parallel processes at any time.
R/3 default value: 5	The value 5 may not be large enough for BW, especially for multi-cube queries. As noted in Section 8.2, a multi-cube query is split into multiple subqueries, one for each underlying basic cube. When enough database processes are available, every subquery can be processed in parallel, which means that we can achieve two levels of parallelism. If PARALLEL_AUTOMATIC_TUNING is set to TRUE as recommended by Oracle, PARALLEL_MAX_SERVERS will be set to CPU*10.
PARALLEL_MIN_PERCENT BW default value: 0	Specifies the desired minimum percentage of requested parallel processes.
R/3 default value: 0	For example, if we specify 50 for this parameter, then at least 50% of the parallel processes specified for a query must be available for the parallel execution to start. If the value is set to 0, then a query will be processed in parallel as long as at least two processes are available.
PARALLEL_ADAPTIVE_MULTI_USER BW default value: FALSE R/3 default value: FALSE	If the value of this parameter is TRUE, Oracle will reduce DOP as the load on the system increases. In BW, because we have only one Oracle user (SAPR3), SAP sets this value to FALSE.

Initialization Parameter	**Description**
PARALLEL_AUTOMATIC_TUNING BW default value: FALSE R/3 default value: FALSE	Oracle recommends a value of TRUE for this parameter. When PARALLEL_AUTOMATIC_TUNING is set to TRUE, the database will automatically set all PQO-related specifications, such as DOP, the adaptive multi-user feature, and memory sizing, based on the number of CPUs and the value of PARALLEL_THREADS_PER_CPU.
PARALLEL_THREADS_PER_CPU BW default value: 2 R/3 default value: 2	Specifies the number of parallel execution processes or threads that a CPU can handle during parallel processing. The default value is platform dependent (usually 2) and is adequate in most cases. We should decrease the value of this parameter if the machine appears to be overloaded.

PQO is a database feature. Increasing the CPU power in the application server machines in the SAP Basis 3-tier architecture will not improve database parallel processing, although it may improve OLAP performance.

Do not use PQO on a single-CPU machine.

A server that has already exhausted its CPU or I/O resources will not benefit from PQO.

To achieve optimal performance, all parallel processes should have equal workloads. Skewing occurs when some parallel processes perform significantly more work than the other processes.

PQO works best on partitions that are spread or striped across many disk devices.

13.4 Tuning Load Performance

When tuning load performance, you should follow a few simple rules:

- If possible, carry out data transformation in transfer rules rather than in update rules. The transformation made in transfer rules applies to all InfoCubes.

- Optimize ABAP programs in transfer rules and update rules, as they will be applied to every record during data loading.
- If the data come from flat files, place them in an application server host machine.
- If the data come from an R/3 system, optimize the extractor.
- Set the instance profile parameter rdisp/max_wprun_time to 0 to allow unlimited CPU time for dialog work processes.
- Consider using the database NOARCHIVELOG mode.

When loading transaction data, you should follow this procedure:

1. Load all master data.
2. Delete the indices of the InfoCube and its aggregates.
3. Turn on number range buffering.
4. Set an appropriate data packet size.
5. Load the transaction data.
6. Re-create the indices.
7. Turn off number range buffering.
8. Refresh the statistics.

Indices and statistics were discussed in both Section 13.3 and Section 12.2.2. Here, we discuss how to buffer the number range and set the data packet size.

13.4.1 Number Range Buffering

When loading data into an InfoCube, BW assigns DIMIDs to dimension tables (see Screen 7.5). To improve load performance, a range of numbers should be buffered. Then, after one number has been assigned to a record in the dimension table, a new number becomes available in memory for the next new record. This technique saves trips to the database, thereby improving load performance. Called **number range buffering**, it is used widely in SAP. Number range buffering occurs through **number range objects**.

In this section, we demonstrate first how to find the number range object for an InfoCube dimension and then how to configure a range of numbers.

Work Instructions

Step 1 Run transaction *SE37*. Enter a function module called *RSD_CUBE_GET*, and then click to run it.

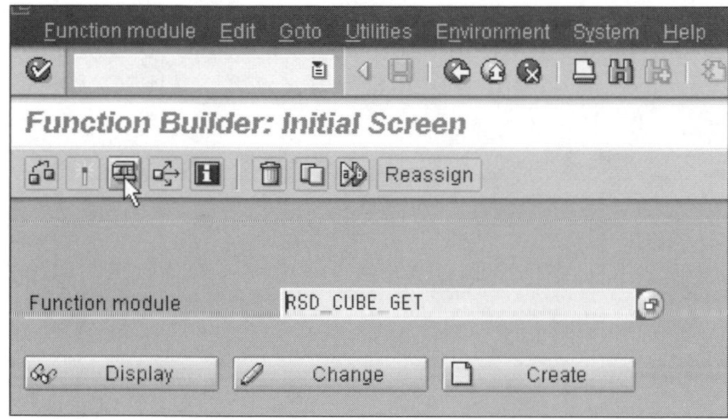

SCREEN 13.41 Copyright by SAP AG

Note: The function module *RSD_CUBE_GET* is an ABAP object used extensively in BW to provide InfoCube-related information. In our example, it will tell us the dimensions of an InfoCube and the number range objects used by these dimensions.

Step 2 Enter the InfoCube name *IC_NEWBC2* and other information as shown in Screen 13.42, and then click to continue.

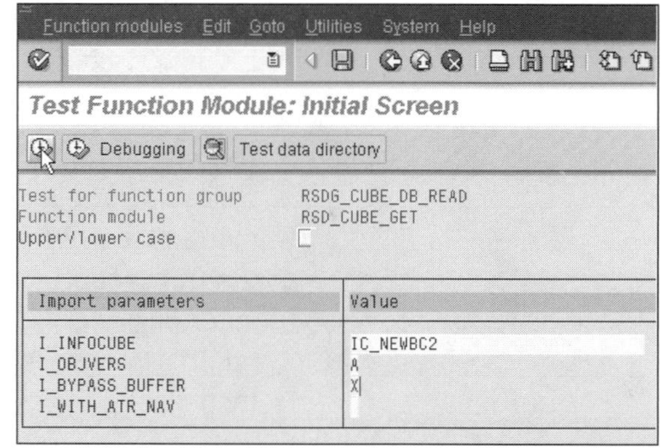

SCREEN 13.42 Copyright by SAP AG

Step 3 Screen 13.43 shows the output from the function module. The entry *E_T_DIME* under the column *Export parameters* is a table that contains the InfoCube dimension information. It has six entries. Double-click the *E_T_DIME* entry to display the table contents.

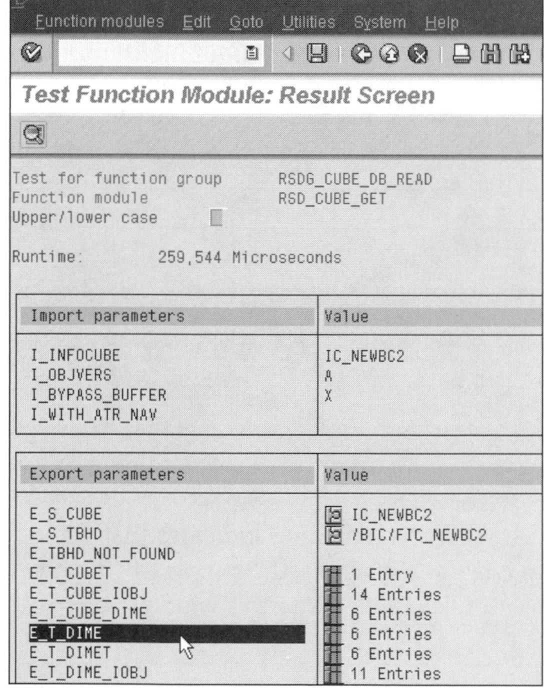

SCREEN 13.43 Copyright by SAP AG

Step 4 The *NOBJECT* column lists the number range objects, one for each dimension.

In this example, we will use the number range object *BID0001770* to buffer a range of numbers for the dimension */BIC/DIC_NEWBC21*.

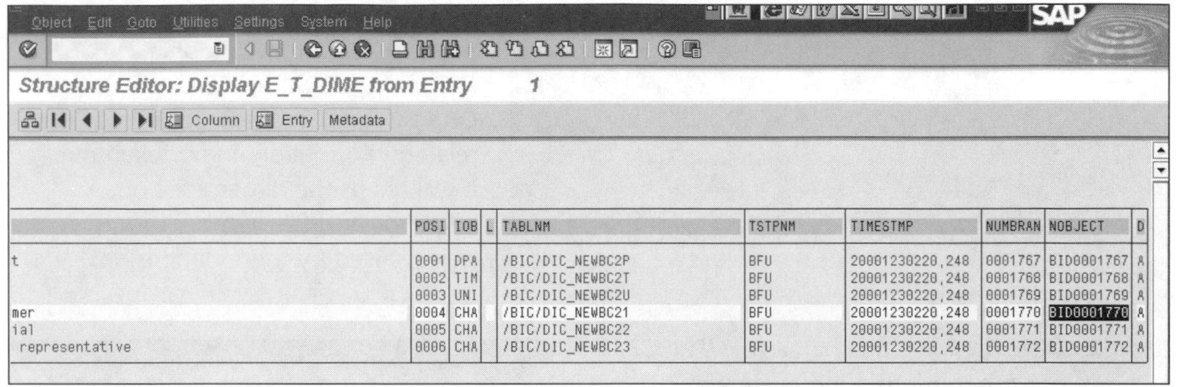

SCREEN 13.44

Step 5 To buffer a range of numbers using the number range object *BID0001770*, run transaction *SNRO*, enter *BID0001770* as the number range object, and then click [change button].

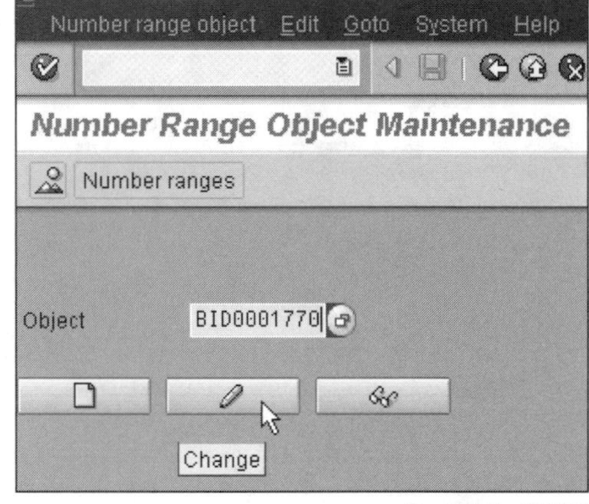

SCREEN 13.45

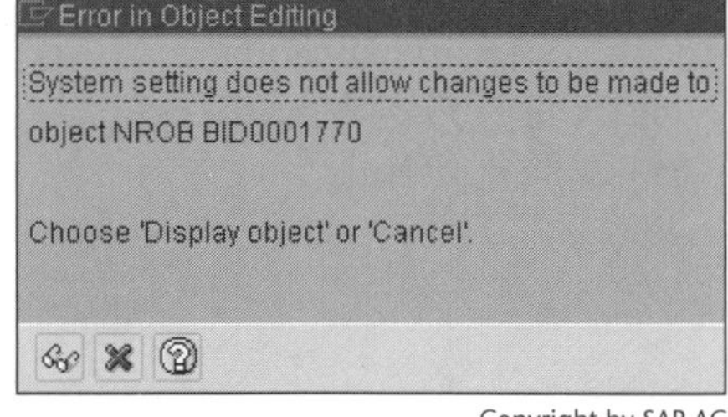

SCREEN 13.46

Step 6 The message in Screen 13.46 indicates that we need to change a system setting so as to change this object. Click [cancel icon] to close this window.

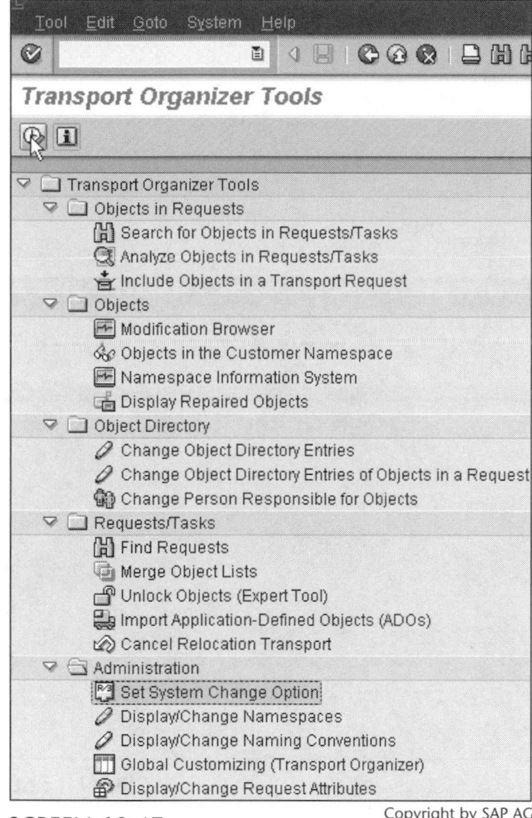

SCREEN 13.47

Step 7 To implement this change, run transaction *SE03*. Select the *Set System Change* Option, and then click [execute icon] to execute the function.

Note: Transaction SE03 is called Transport Organizer Tools. It lists functions we can use to configure system behaviors, as well as to display and change ABAP objects in transport requests. A **transport request** is the vehicle that transports ABAP objects from the development system, to the test system, and/or to the production system. We will discuss this topic further in Chapter 14.

Step 8 Change *Not modifiable* to *Modifiable* for *General SAP name range*. Click [save icon] to save the change.

Settings Edit Goto System Help

System Change Option

Client setting

Global setting: Modifiable

Software component	Technical name	Modifiable
Customer developments	HOME	Modifiable
Local developments (no automatic trans..	LOCAL	Modifiable
Cross-Application Component	SAP_ABA	Restricted modifi
SAP Basis Component	SAP_BASIS	Restricted modifi
Business Information Warehouse	SAP_BW	Modifiable
SEM-BW 2.0B: Installation.	SEM-BW	Modifiable

Namespace/name range	Prefix	Modifiable
Customer name range		Modifiable
General SAP name range		Modifiable
	/1APO/	Not modifiable

SCREEN 13.48

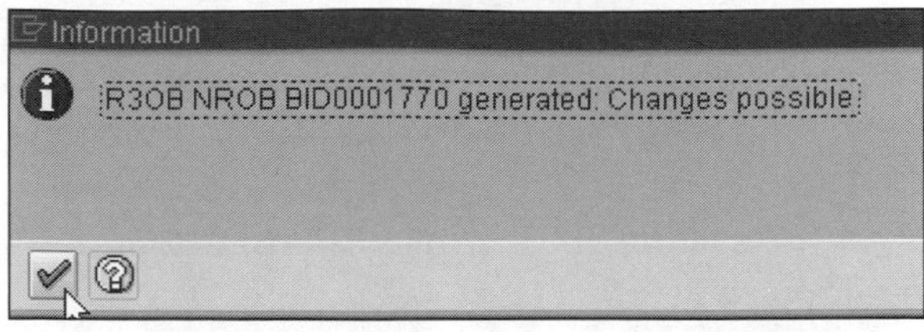

SCREEN 13.49

Step 9 Click ✔ to continue.

Step 10 Repeat Step 5; Screen 13.50 should appear as the result.

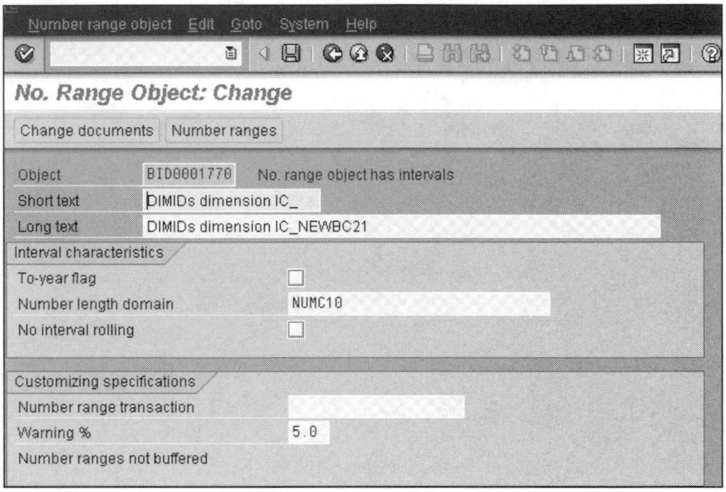

SCREEN 13.50

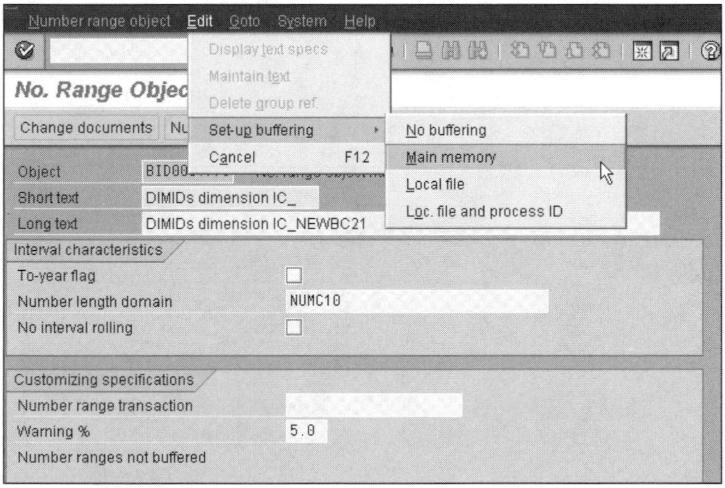

Step 11 Select Main memory from the Edit/Set-up buffering menu item.

SCREEN 13.51

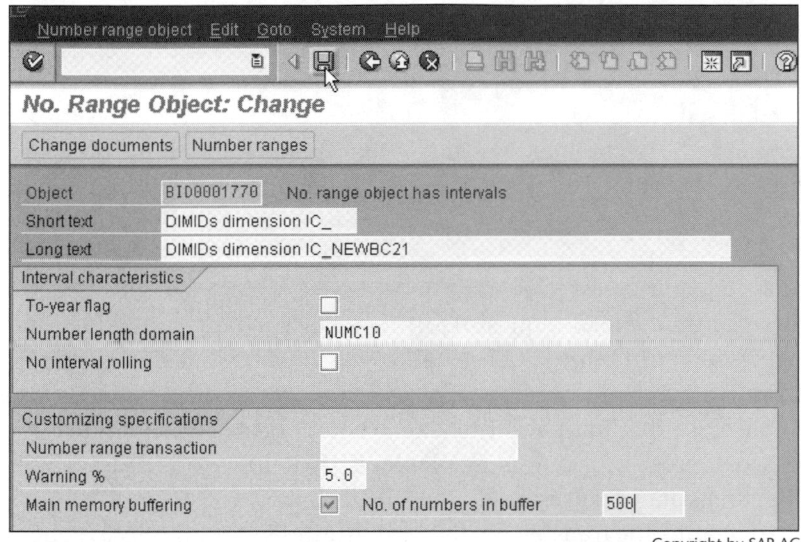

Copyright by SAP AG

SCREEN 13.52

Step 12 Enter a number range, such as *500*, in the *No. of numbers in buffer* field. Click [save icon] to save it.

Note: This step ensures that BW will keep 500 numbers in the main memory buffer for /BIC/DIC_NEWBC21. Setting the number range too low will not help load performance significantly, whereas setting it too high will consume a lot of memory on the application server machine, which will affect other applications on the same machine. Monitor the memory usage during data loading to find an appropriate number range.

Step 13 Click [Yes] to continue.

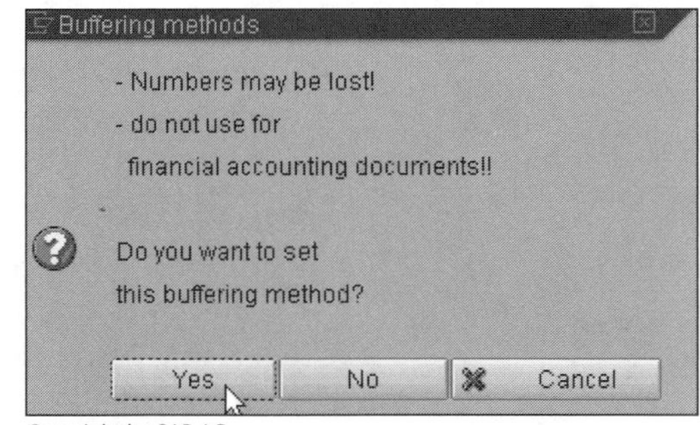

Copyright by SAP AG

SCREEN 13.53

Result

A status message *Number range object BID0001770 saved* will appear at the bottom of Screen 13.52.

13.4.2 Data Packet Sizing

When loading data into BW, we need to specify which one of the following transfer methods to use (Screens 3.15 and 3.56):

- **PSA:** With this method, data are transferred in the unit of packets as shown in Screen 4.10. This method uses the transfer structure defined for PSA, although it does not mean the data must stay there.
- **IDoc:** With this method, data are transferred in the unit of IDocs (Figure 10.2). The data must stop by the ALE inbox before proceeding to their targets. This method has a notable limitation: The transfer structure cannot be wider than 1000 bytes in the character format.

For these reasons, the PSA method is safer and more straightforward than the IDoc method; its use is recommended by SAP. In this section we discuss how to size the data packet to improve load performance when the PSA method is used in data loading.

To understand the technique, we must first understand how data are loaded. If the source system is R/3, BW uses the following procedure to collect and transfer data:

1. BW sends a load request IDoc to R/3.
2. As triggered by the load request IDoc, R/3 starts a background job. The job collects data from the database and saves them in packets of a predefined size.
3. After collecting the first packet of data, the background job launches a dialog work process, if one is available. The dialog work process will send the first data packet from R/3 to BW.
4. If more data must be transferred, the background job continues to collect the second packet of data without waiting for the first data packet to finish its transfer. Once it is complete, the background job will launch another dialog work process, if one is available. The new dialog work process will send the second data packet from R/3 to BW.
5. During the preceding steps, R/3 sends information IDocs to BW to notify it of the data extraction and transfer status.
6. The process continues in this fashion until all requested data have been selected and transferred.

Based on this understanding, we can readily discover why the size of data packets affects load performance.

For the same amount of data, if packets are small, then we will have many packets. They could potentially proliferate to such a degree that data packets use up all available dialog work processes in R/3. Without available dialog processes, later packets will frequently trigger the dispatcher to obtain a free dialog work process, which will greatly affect R/3 performance as a whole.

If packets are large, then we will have few packets. Each will take a long time to complete the transfer process. In such a case, we will have fewer dialog work processes participating in the parallel processing, and the loading operation will take a long time as well.

The procedure to set the size of packets follows.

Work Instructions

Step 1 Run transaction *SBIW* in the R/3 source system, and then click [icon] next to *Maintain Control Parameters for the data transfer* to execute the function.

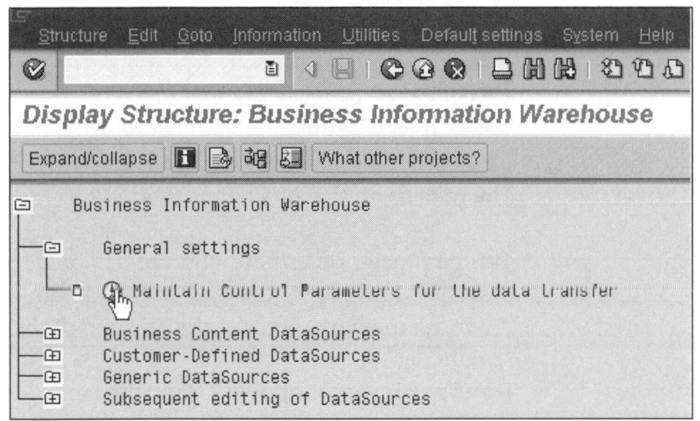

SCREEN 13.54 Copyright by SAP AG

Step 2 Click [icon] to continue.

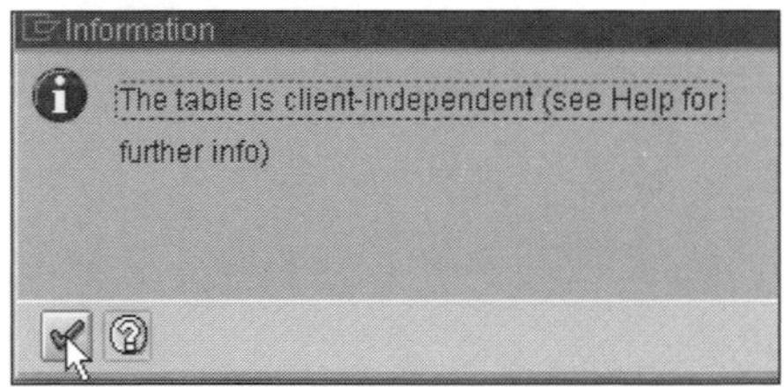

SCREEN 13.55 Copyright by SAP AG

Step 3 Click the *New entries* button to insert an entry.

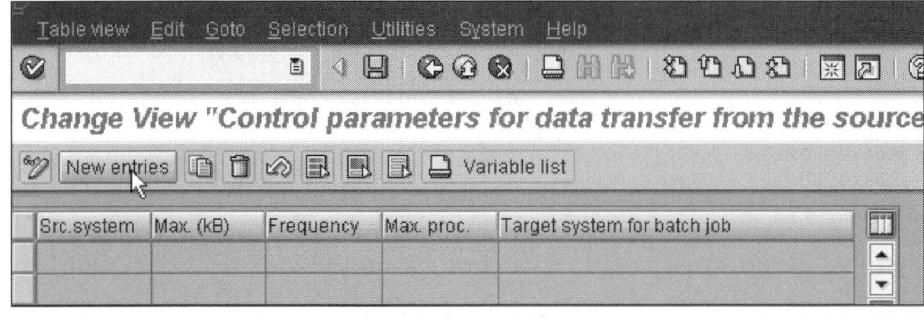

SCREEN 13.56 Copyright by SAP AG

Step 4 Enter the specifications, and then click [icon] to save the settings.

Table view Edit Goto Selection criteria Utilities System Help

New Entries: Overview of Added Entries

Src.system	Size (KB)	Max. lines	Frequency	Max. proc.	Target system for batch job
SND_250	20000	100000	10	3	raptor

Copyright by SAP AG SCREEN 13.57

The specifications are saved in the table ROIDOCPRMS. Its fields are explained in Table 13.7.

TABLE 13.7
FIELDS IN TABLE ROIDOCPRMS

Column	Description
SLOGSYS (Source system)	The logical system name of the R/3 source system.
MAXSIZE (Size in KB)	The maximum size of a data packet in KB. This parameter determines the size of a data packet, and consequently the requirement for the main memory for the creation of the data packet. For the same amount of R/3 data, the larger this parameter, the smaller the number of data packets employed. SAP recommends a value between 10,000 and 50,000 KB. The default value is 10,000 KB.
MAXLINES (Maximum number of lines)	The upper limit for the number of data records in a packet. The default value is 100,000.
STATFRQU (Frequency)	The number of data packets whose status an information IDoc will report. It determines the frequency with which information IDocs are sent. The default value is 1.
MAXPROCS (Maximum number of process)	The maximum number of parallel dialog work processes to be used for data transfer.
BTCSYSTEM (Target system for batch job)	The host machine name of the application server to run the background job. This field is very useful when we want to dedicate an R/3 application server to the extraction job.

To determine the number of data records in a data packet, Plug-In extractor uses the following simple algorithm:

```
PACKET_SIZE = MAXSIZE * 1000 / TRANSFER_STRUCTURE_WIDTH.
IF PACKET_SIZE > 999999, PACKET_SIZE = 999999.
IF PACKET_SIZE >= MAXLINES, PACKET_SIZE = MAXLINES.
```

Note: Refer to OSS Note 0157652, "Main Memory Requirement for Extraction from R/3," for details on how to size R/3 main memory.

13.5 Summary

BW needs much more performance tuning effort than R/3 does. To achieve acceptable performance, you must have a good understanding of the application and database design as well as the use of many advanced features provided with the underlying database.

Key Terms

Term	Description
BW Statistics	BW Statistics is a tool for recording and reporting system activity and performance information.
System Administration Assistant	System Administration Assistant is a collection of tools used to monitor and analyze general system operation conditions.
Read mode	The read mode for a query determines the size and frequency of data retrievals from the database: all data at once, as needed per navigation step, or as needed per hierarchy node.
Bitmap index	A bitmap index uses maps of bits to locate records in a table. Bitmap indices are very effective for Boolean operations in the WHERE clause of a SELECT statement. When the cardinality of a column is low, a bitmap index size will likewise be small, reducing I/O volume.
Partition	A partition is a piece of physical storage for database tables and indices. If the needed data reside in one or a few partitions, then only those partitions will be selected and examined for a SQL statement, thereby significantly reducing I/O volume.
Parallel query	A parallel query uses multiple database processes, when available, to execute a query.
Number range	A number range is a group of numbers that resides in application server memory and is available for quick number assignments.

Data packet size	For the same amount of data, the data packet size determines how work processes will be used in data transfer. The smaller data packet size, the more work processes needed.

For Further Information

SAP frequently updates the following two OSS Notes, which contain the most current information about performance tuning:

- OSS Note 0184905, "Collective Note Performance BW 2.0."
- OSS Note 0130253, "Notes on Upload of Transaction Data into the BW."

Other helpful OSS Notes include the following:

- OSS Note 0309955, "BW Statistics in 2.0B—Questions, Answers, Errors."
- OSS Note 0356801, "Performance Problems Based on a Wrong Optimizer Dec."
- OSS Note 0408532, "Using the DBMS_STATS Package for Collecting Stats."
- OSS Note 0351163, "Creating ORACLE DB Statistics Using DBMS_STATS."
- OSS Note 0156784, "Additional tablespaces for BW tables."
- OSS Note 0325839, "Considerable Increase of tablespace PSAPODSD."
- OSS Note 0339896, "ORACLE ERROR 14400" on Oracle partitions and parallel loads.

Next . . .

We will discuss how to transport BW objects from the development system to the quality assurance system and to the production system.

Chapter 14

Object Transport

BW uses the same architecture, tools, and programs to transport objects as R/3 does. The following high-level SAP procedure explains how you transport objects from the development system to other systems (Figure 14.1):

1. Develop and test objects in the development system. When the objects are ready for extensive and pre-production testing, export and save them in a common transport directory in the operating system.
2. Import the objects into the quality assurance system and conduct pre-production testing.
3. If the objects pass the test, import them into the production system. Otherwise, repeat Steps 1–2.

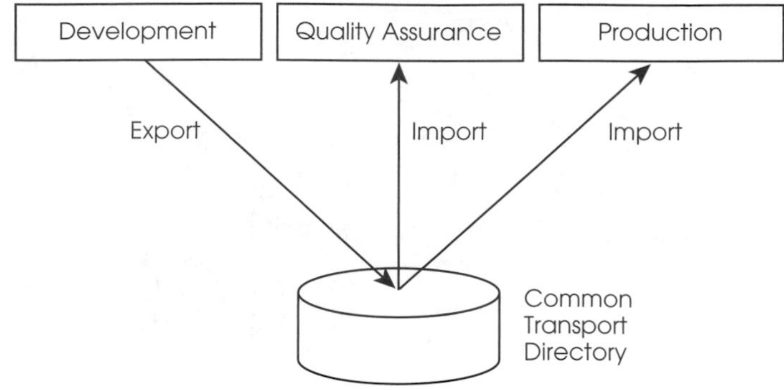

FIGURE 14.1 SAP CHANGE AND TRANSPORT SYSTEM

In this chapter, we will discuss how to transport BW objects in the transport environment depicted in Figure 14.1. Refer to the SAP Basis documentation for information on how to build a transport system.

14.1 System Landscape

Figure 14.2 shows the SAP recommended system landscape. In the figure, any of the three BW systems can interact with any of the three R/3 systems; this interaction does not have to occur in precisely the way shown in Figure 14.2, however.

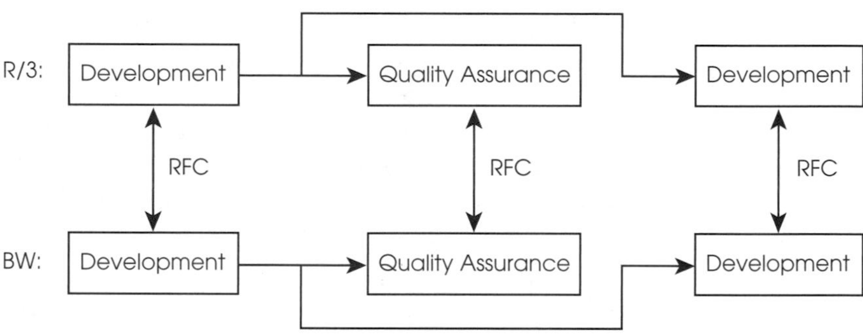

FIGURE 14.2 SYSTEM LANDSCAPE

Before transporting a BW object, we need to complete three tasks:

- Install the release-dependent Plug-In in the R/3 systems by following the instructions in SAP's 84-page installation document. Always back up the database before installing the Plug-In.

- Replicate the DataSources. BW does not allow us to transport replicated DataSources from the development system to other systems. Without the replicated DataSources in the quality assurance system, we cannot transport transfer rules from the development system to the quality assurance system because of the object dependency.
- Map the source systems. Note that the transfer rules are source system dependent. We must specify a new source system for the transported transfer rules in the new system. The next procedure explains how to do so.

Work Instructions

Step 1 In the target BW system, from Administrator Workbench, select Mapping of the source system names from the Tools menu item .

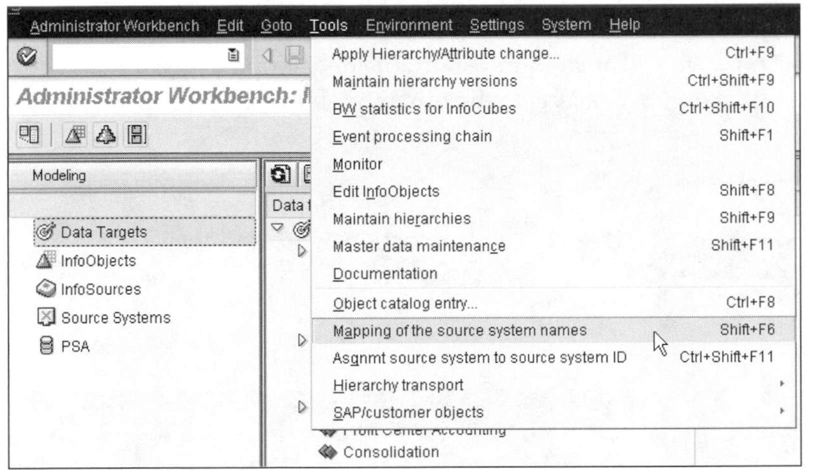

SCREEN 14.1

Step 2 Enter and save the source system names. In our case, we use the same source system name, *SND_250,* in the target system.

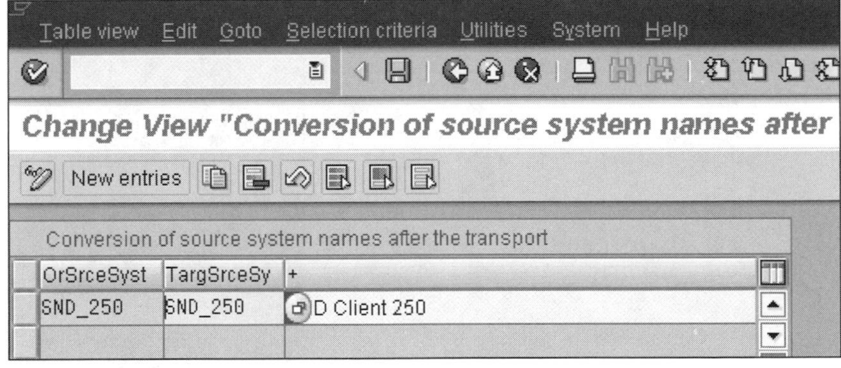

SCREEN 14.2

Result

When transfer rules are transported into the target system, they will have a new source system.

14.2 Development Class

BW objects are created as local objects and are saved in the development class $TMP. A **development class** is a group of objects that are logically related—that is, objects that must be developed, maintained, and transported together.

$TMP is a temporary local development class. Objects in $TMP cannot be transported into other systems. The names of development classes that we create must begin with "Y" or "Z".

In this section, we will create a transportable development class. In the next section, we will assign BW objects to the transportable development class.

Work Instructions

Step 1 Run transaction *SE80*, and then click

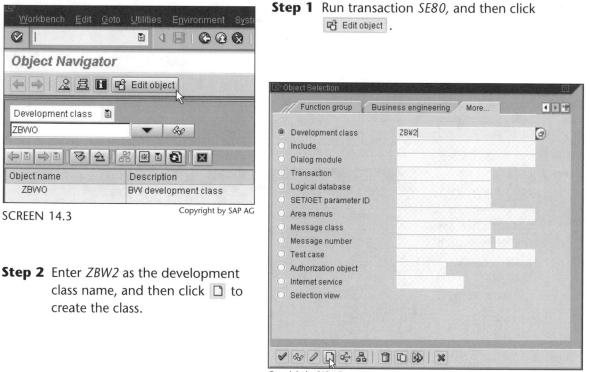

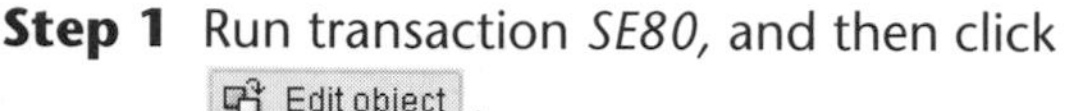

.

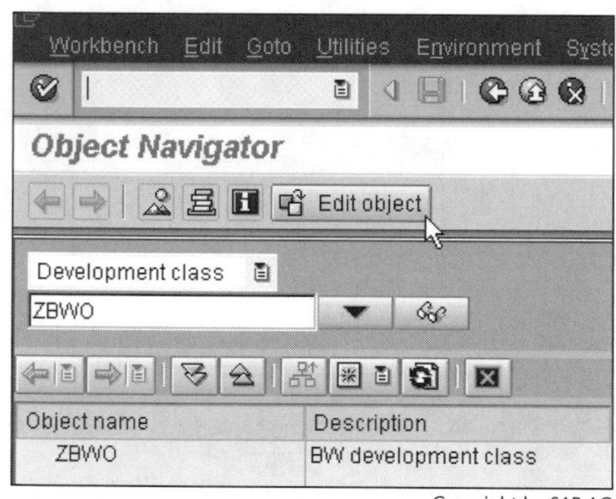

SCREEN 14.3

Step 2 Enter *ZBW2* as the development class name, and then click [icon] to create the class.

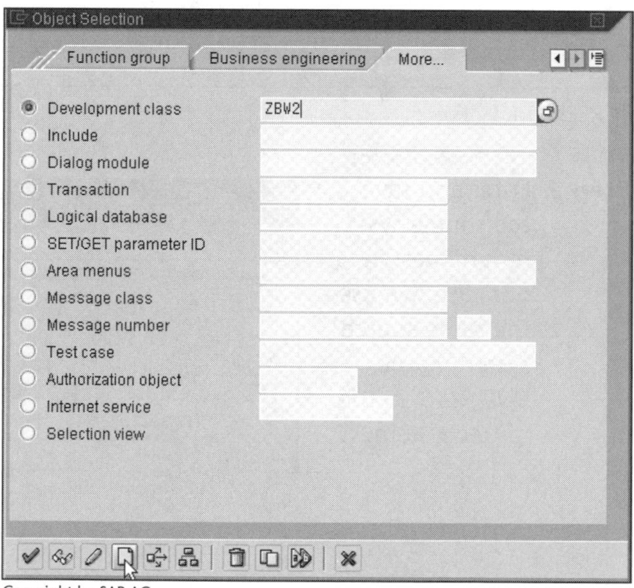

SCREEN 14.4

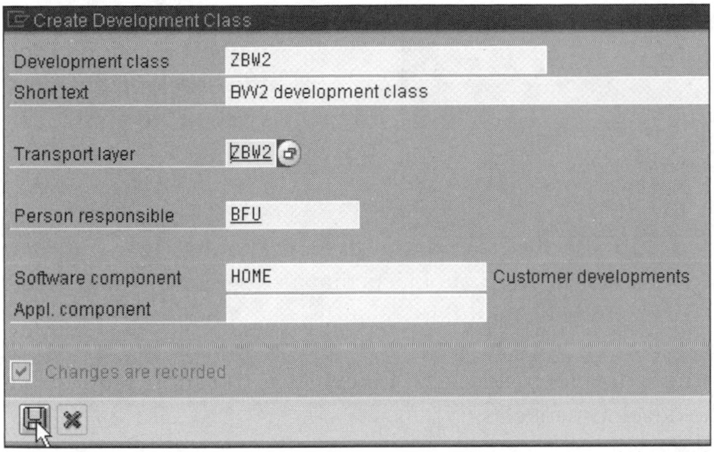

Step 3 Select a transport layer, and then click to save it.

Note: A **transport layer** links development classes with a **transport route.** The transport route specifies where to transport objects.

In our example, these routes have already been set up.

SCREEN 14.5

Step 4 We are prompted to enter a transport request for this development class so that it can be transported to other systems. We can either create a new transport request or use an existing one. Click to create a new one.

SCREEN 14.6

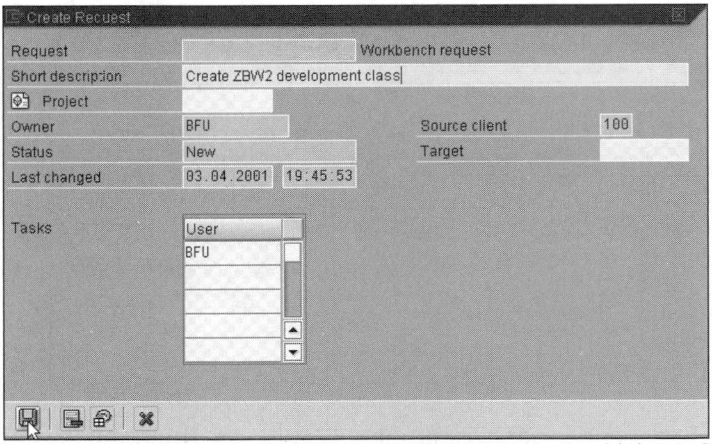

Step 5 Enter a short description for the transport request, and then click to save the transport request.

SCREEN 14.7

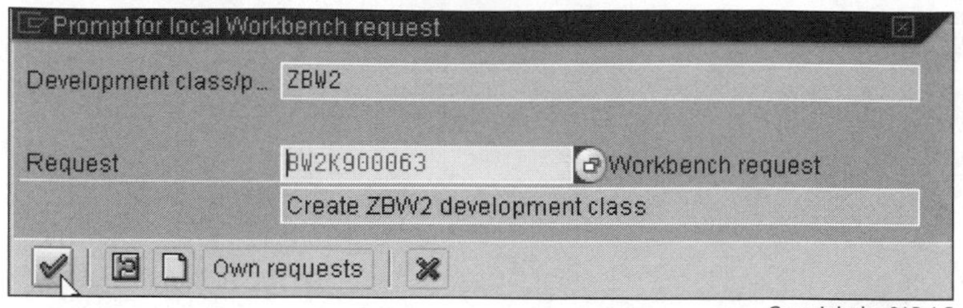

SCREEN 14.8

Step 6 The new transport request is assigned to the development class. Click ✔ to finish.

Result

We have created a new development class. Likewise, a transport request has been created for the development class.

14.3 Object Transport

Now we are ready to transport BW objects. Use the following procedure.

Work Instructions

Step 1 From Administrator Workbench, click the *Transport Connection* bar in the leftmost panel.

Click [Grouping] and select how BW should group the associated objects. We have seen this window before in Screen 10.48. In our example, we select *in dataflow before and aftrwds.*

SCREEN 14.9

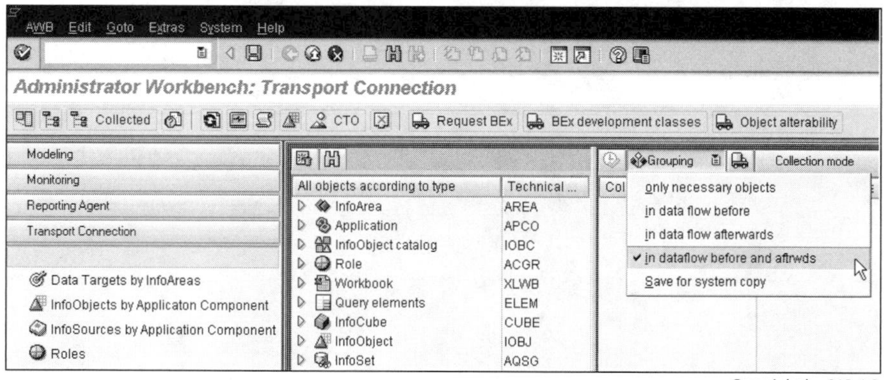

Note: We know that dependencies exist among BW objects. Using this option, we can group relevant objects and transport them together.

Step 2 Drag and drop InfoCube *IC_NEWBC5* to the rightmost panel, and then click [icon] to transport the objects.

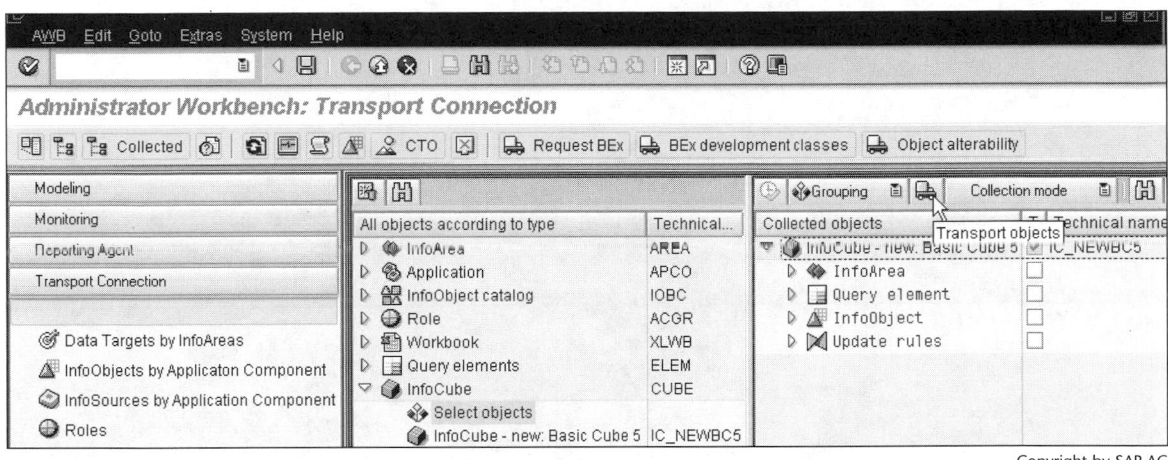

SCREEN 14.10

Step 3 BW asks us to change the development class for the objects selected in Screen 14.10. Screen 14.11 shows the original development class, which is *$TMP*. In Screen 14.12, we will change the development class from $TMP to ZBW2, the development class we created in Section 14.2.

Change Object Directory Entry
Object R3TR CUBE IC_NEWBC5
Attributes
Development class $TMP
Person responsible BFU
Original system BW2
Original language EN English
Lock overview

SCREEN 14.11

Change Object Directory Entry
Object R3TR CUBE IC_NEWBC5
Attributes
Development class ZBW2
Person responsible BFU
Original system BW2
Original language EN English
Lock overview

SCREEN 14.12

Step 4 Enter *ZBW2*, the development class we created in Section 14.2. Click [icon] to save the change and continue.

Prompt for local Workbench request
InfoCube IC_NEWBC5
Request BW2K900063 Workbench request
Create ZBW2 development class
Own requests

SCREEN 14.13

Step 5 Click [icon] to create a transport request.

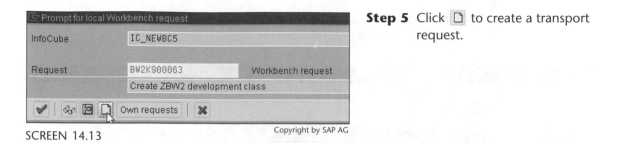

Step 6 Enter a *Short description* for the transport request, and then click [icon] to save the transport request.

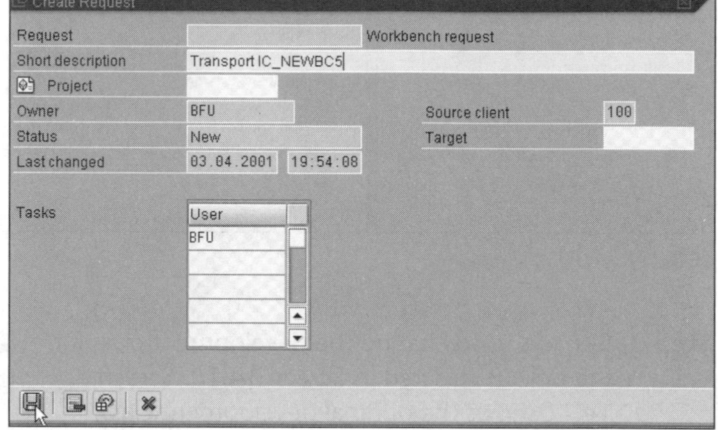

SCREEN 14.14

Prompt for local Workbench request
InfoCube IC_NEWBC5
Request BW2K900065 Workbench request
Transport IC_NEWBC5
Own requests

SCREEN 14.15

Step 7 Click [icon] to continue.

Step 8 Green lights in the lower-middle status panel indicate that we have successfully created a transport request for the InfoCube IC_NEWBC5 and its associated objects.

SCREEN 14.16

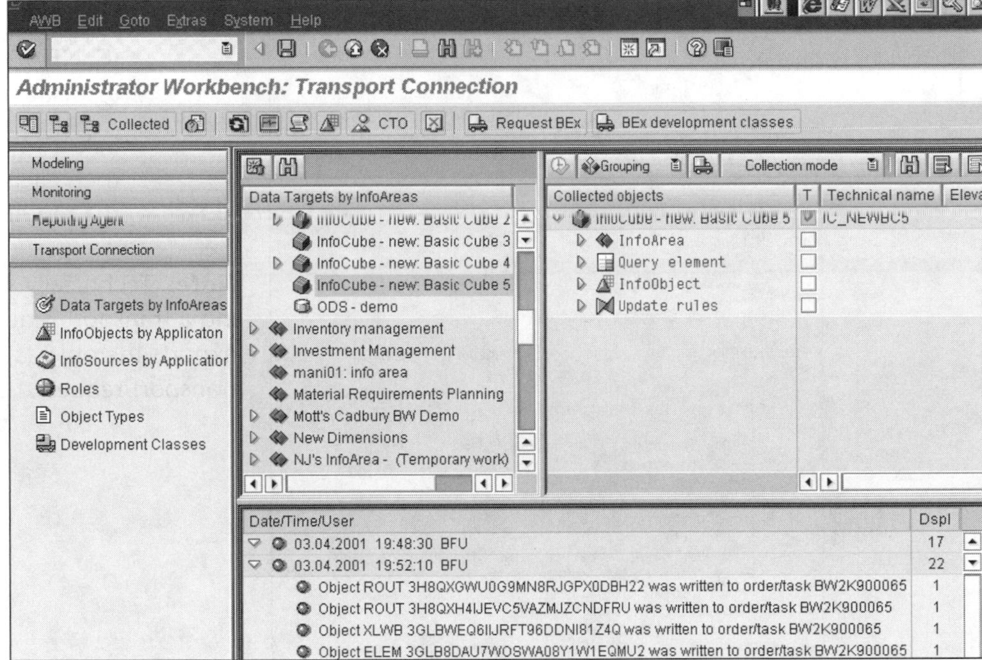

Step 9 Now we need to release the transport requests.

Run transaction *SE09*, and then click Display.

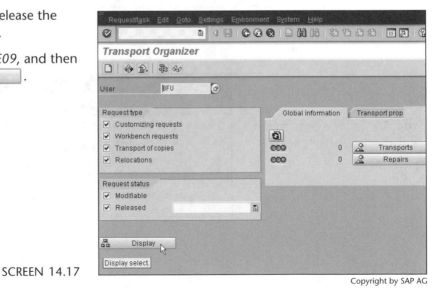

SCREEN 14.17

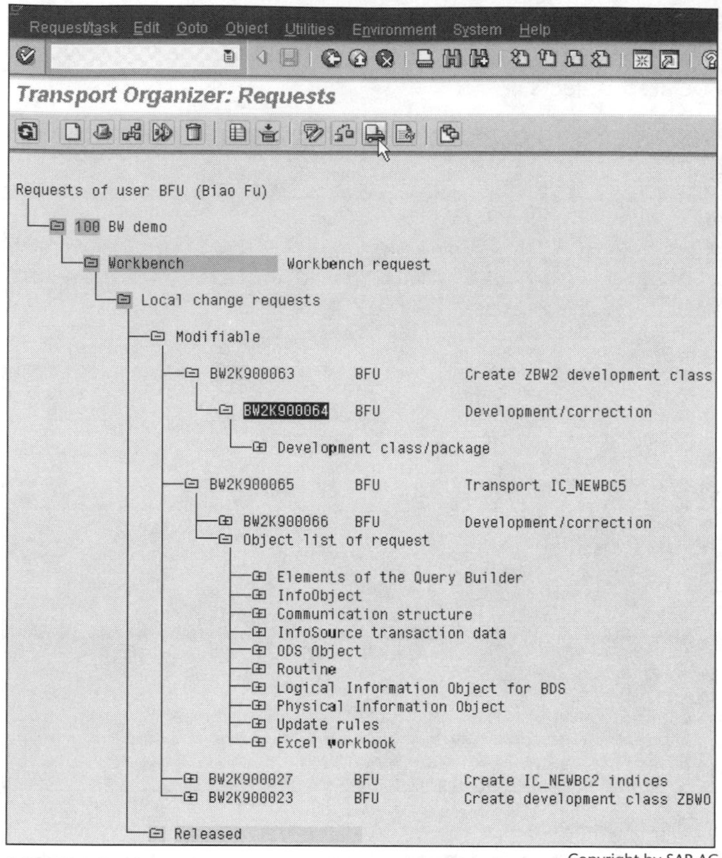

SCREEN 14.18

Step 10 The transport request *BW2K900063* applies to the development class ZBW2, and *BW2K900065* applies to the InfoCube IC_NEWBC5 and its associated objects.

Select *BW2K900064*, and then click [icon] to release the request.

Note: Technically speaking, releasing a transport request actually exports the objects in the transport request.

Step 11 Enter a description, and then click [icon] to save it.

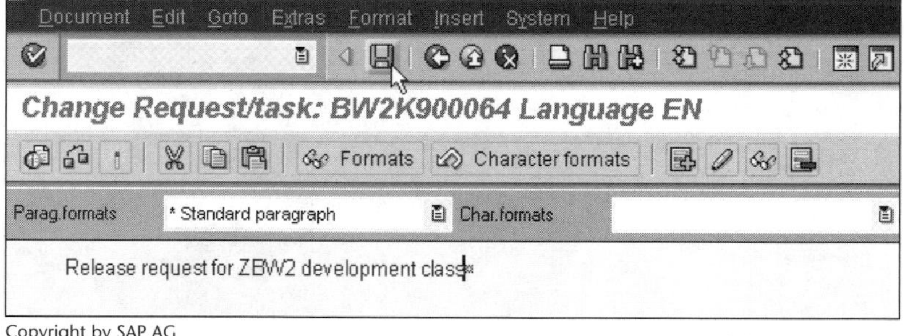

SCREEN 14.19

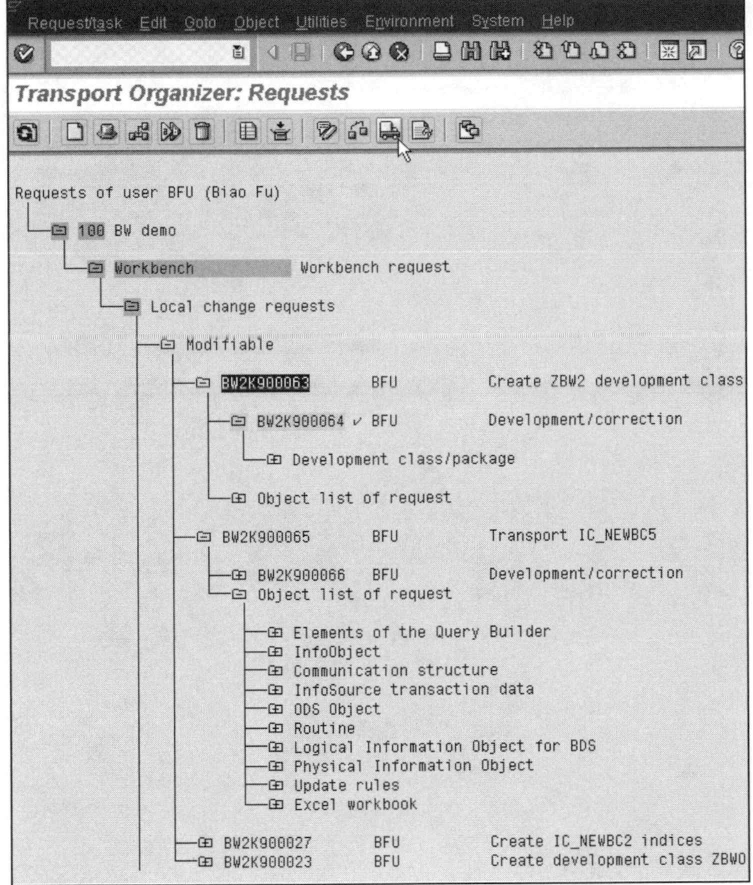

SCREEN 14.20

Step 12 Select *BW2K900063,* and then click to release the request.

Result

A check mark appears on the right of BW2K000923 and BW2K000924. It indicates that the development class has been exported (Screen 14.21).

SCREEN 14.21

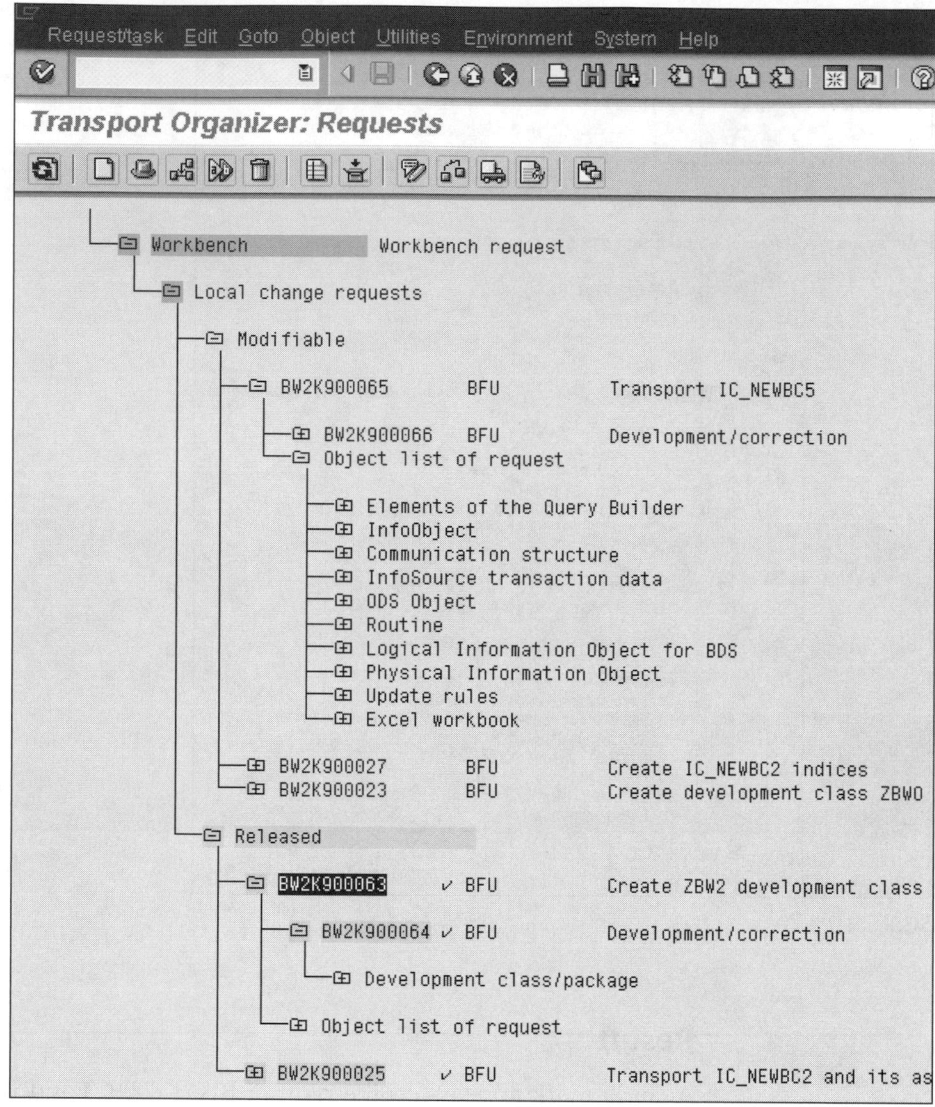

In the same way, we can release the transport request BW2K00065 (Screen 14.22).

SCREEN 14.22

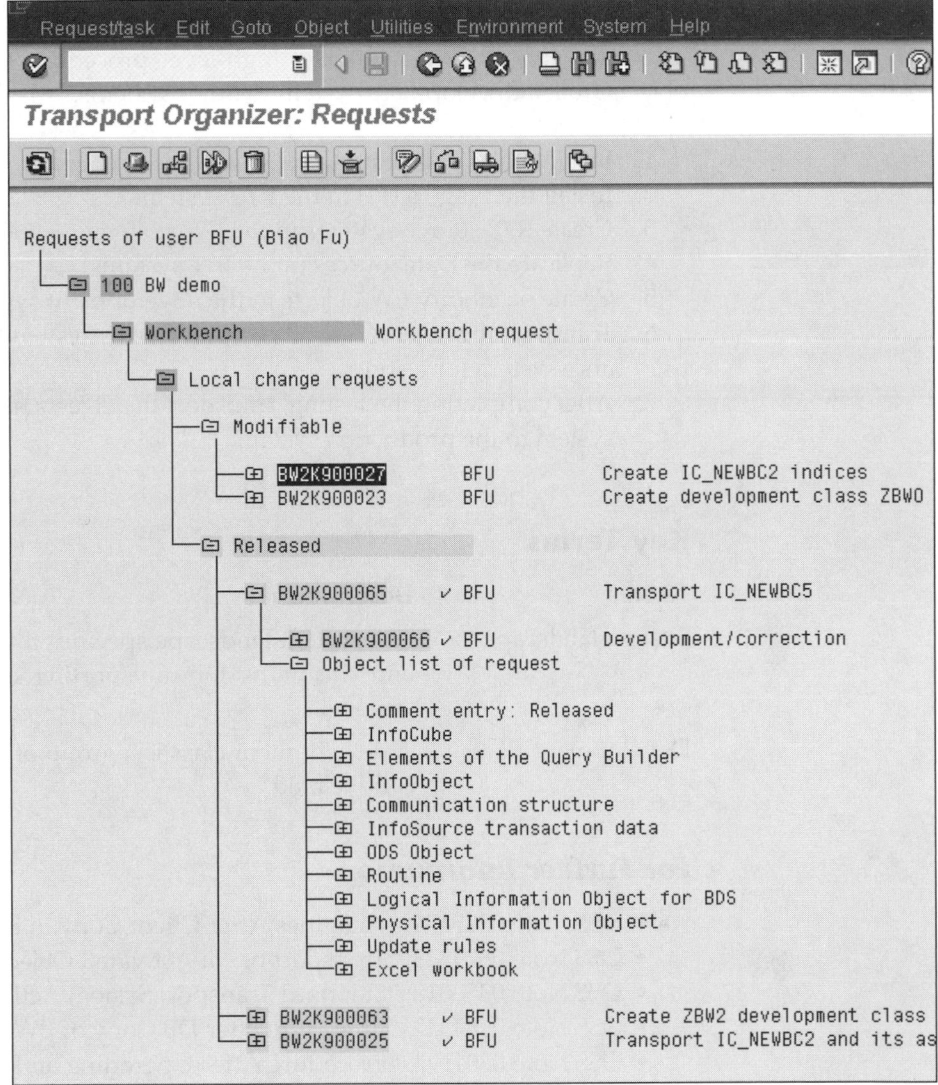

To import these previously exported objects, we would run transaction *STMS* in the target system. Because we have only one BW system, we cannot demonstrate this operation, however. Refer to the SAP Basis documentation for further information.

14.4 Summary

The following steps constitute a high-level procedure for transporting BW objects from a development system to other systems:

1. Install the BW systems.
2. Install the Plug-In (PI) in the R/3 systems.
3. Create R/3 source systems in the BW systems.
4. Replicate the DataSources in the BW systems.
5. Create or modify BW objects in the development system.
6. Transport the objects from the development system to the quality assurance system for testing.
7. After completing the testing, transport the objects from the development system to the production system.

Key Terms

Term	Description
System landscape	The system landscape specifies the role of each system and the paths for transporting objects among those systems.
Development class	A development class is a group of objects that are logically related.

For Further Information

- OSS Note 0325470, "Activities After Client Copy in BW Source Systems."
- OSS Note 0323323, "Transport of All Activated Objects of a System."
- OSS Note 0356018, "Standard Transport System Activation in BW."
- OSS Note 0184322, "Procedure after DB Copy of BW Source Systems."
- OSS Note 0301192, "Procedure After Upgrading an R/3 Source System."
- OSS Note 0325525, "Copying and Renaming Systems in a BW Environment."

Next . . .

So far we have covered most BW topics, but not all. Appendix A introduces ASAP for BW, a BW implementation methodology developed by SAP. Appendix B gives an overview of the SAP Basis 3-tier architecture.

Appendix A

BW Implementation Methodology

A methodology is the best practice for performing a job. SAP provides such a methodology for BW implementation, called **ASAP for BW**. It includes documents, templates, and tips and tricks intended to reduce implementation time and cost. Each document, template, or tip and trick is called an **Accelerator**.

You can download ASAP for BW from http://service.sap.com/bw/. An OSS (Online Service System) ID from SAP is required to access this Web site.

In this appendix, we will list all ASAP for BW Accelerators and then examine a simplified project plan.

A.1 ASAP for BW

Tables A.1, A.2, and A.3 list ASAP for BW project plans and Accelerators. These documents contain a vast amount of information and are very helpful in BW implementation, although some Accelerators are not updated at the same pace at which BW evolves.

Note: Tables A.1, A.2, and A.3 are adapted from the file called OverviewASAP.xls in ASAP for BW.

TABLE A.1 BW 1.2B/2.0A PROJECT PLANS

Title	File Name
High Level BW Project Plan	ETBWPP01.ppt
High Level BW Project Plan	ETBWPP01.doc
Mid Level BW Project Plan	ETBWPP02.ppt
Mid Level BW Project Plan	ETBWPP02.doc
Detailed Level BW Project Plan	ETBWPP03.ppt
Detailed Level BW Project Plan	ETBWPP03.doc
BW Project Plan—Delivered Content Only	ETBWPP04.ppt
BW Project Plan—Delivered Content Only	ETBWPP04.doc

TABLE A.2 BW 1.2B/2.0A ACCELERATORS

Title	File Name
Roles and Skills for BW Projects	bwroles.doc
Performance and Sizing	ETBMW009.DOC
Performance Tuning	ETBMW010.DOC
Correction and Transport System	ETBMW033.DOC
Data Modeling with BW	ETBMW012.DOC
Project Charter	ETBMW024.DOC
Sample Project Charter	ETBMW027.DOC
BW Operational Support	ETBMW040.DOC
InfoCube Sizer	ETBMW043.XLS
BW and Excel	ETBMW042.DOC
Business Content Check Template	ETBMW068.XLS
BW InfoCube Documentation Example	ETBMW069.DOC
BW Project Start-Up	ETBMW070.PPT
Data Flow Documentation Template	ETBMW071.XLS
Frequently Asked Questions	ETBMW072.DOC
Business Requirements Glossary	ETBMW073.XLS
Report Requirements Documentation Template	ETBMW074.DOC
Business Blueprint Methodology	ETBMW075.PPT
Data Modeling with BW	ETBMW012.DOC
Authorization Template for BW Authorizations	ETBMW076.XLS
Authorization in BW	ETBMW064.DOC
BW Statistics	ETBMW032.DOC
SD as an InfoSource	ETBMW035.DOC

Title	File Name
Characteristics and Versioning	ETBMW006.DOC
Loading InfoSource Data via Flat Files	ETBMW011.DOC
Compound InfoObjects	ETBMW014.DOC
Staging BAPIs for SAP BW	ETBMW015.DOC
Modeling Queries and Using Variables	ETBMW016.DOC
Production Support in SAP BW	ETBMW018.DOC
OLE DB for OLAP	ETBMW019.DOC
Consultants Guide	ETBMW020.DOC
Cross-Module Update	ETBMW021.DOC
Exits in SAP BW	ETBMW022.DOC
Extractions from CO	ETBMW028.DOC
BW Glossary	ETBMW030.doc
Enhancements of BW Content	ETBMW031.DOC
BW and mySAP.com	ETBMW056.DOC
Performance Test Queries	ETBMW057.DOC
Multiple Currencies in BW	ETBMW058.DOC
BW Specific Extensions of OLE DB for OLAP	ETBMW059.DOC
Packet for Generic Data Extraction	ETBMW060.DOC
InfoObject Assignment and Maintenance in R/3 OLTP	ETBMW061.DOC
Enhancements to BW Content Using the Generic Extractor	ETBMW062.DOC
InfoObject Assignment and Maintenance	ETBMW065.DOC
BW Extensions of OLE DB for OLAP	ETBMW066.DOC
Packet for Generic Data Extraction	ETBMW067.DOC

TABLE A.3 BW 2.0B ACCELERATORS

Title	File Name
BW Implementation Experiences and Methodology Overview	BW_Method_overview.doc
Phase 1: Project Charter for SAP BW Projects	ProjectCharter.doc
Phase 1: Project Start-Up (Workshop Template)	BW_StartUp.ppt
Phase 1: Roles and Skills in SAP BW Projects	BW_Roles_skills.doc
Phase 2: Detailed Guide through Business Blueprint Phase	BW_Bbstepbystep.doc
Phase 2: Authorizations in SAP BW	BW_Authorizations.doc
Phase 2: Business Blueprint Overview	BW_BusinessBlueprint_Ovw.ppt
Phase 2: Business Blueprint Templates (Zip)	Business_Blueprint_Templ.zip
Phase 2: Documentation Template for SAP BW Authorizations	BWAuthorizations_template.zip
Phase 2: Multidimensional Data Modeling with SAP BW	MDDatamodeling.doc
Phase 2: SAP BW Hardware Sizing	Sizing.doc
Phase 2: SAP BW System Landscape and Transport	SystemLandscape.doc
Phase 2: Sizing Tool	SizingTool.zip
Phase 3: Frequently Asked Questions	FAQ.doc
Phase 3: Hierarchies in SAP BW	Hierarchies.doc

TABLE A.3 (continued)

Title	File Name
Phase 3: Performance Tuning for Queries with BW Aggregates	Aggregates.doc
Phase 3: SAP BW MS Excel Features	BW_How_to_Excel.doc
Phase 4: SAP BW Performance Tuning	Performance.doc
SAP BW Strategy: How to Create an Enterprise-wide Strategy	BW_strategy.doc
SAP BW Strategy: SAP BW—APO Interface Considerations	SAP_BW_APO.doc
SAP BW Strategy: SAP BW and SEM Interface Considerations	SAP_BW_SEM.doc

A.2 A Simplified BW Project Plan

An ideal project team would include the following personnel:

- A data warehouse architect who oversees the entire project with focus on architecture design and system integration
- Business analysts who understand the business requirements and know data models in source systems, particularly in the R/3 systems
- Technical developers who know BW, ABAP, ALE/IDoc, and Visual Basic and are able to create BW objects and user-friendly reports
- Basis and database administrators who install and maintain BW systems, the system landscape, and communications between BW systems and their source systems

A simplified BW project plan appears next.

Phase I. Design

Number	Task	Resource
1	Define enterprise reporting and OLAP requirements, including technical requirements, such as the expected response time	Data warehouse architect, business analysts, technical developers
2	Design enterprise reporting and OLAP architecture, considering the use of data marts, multi-cubes, InfoCubes, ODS objects, and R/3 reporting functionality	

Number	Task	Resource
3	Check how much Business Content can be used	
4	Define user authorization requirements	
5	Develop BW object naming conventions	
6	Conduct design walkthrough	

Phase II. Development

Number	Task	Resource
1	Install a BW sandbox with minimum hardware requirements as given by the BW installation guide	Basis and database administrators
2	Use the sandbox for proof-of-concept testing and project team training	All team members
3	Size a development system using the sandbox as a baseline and the ASAP sizing document as a reference	Data warehouse architect, Basis and database administrators
4	Install the BW development system	Basis and database administrators
5	Create BW objects and build the data warehouse in the development system	Technical developers
6	Load OLTP data, including R/3 data, into the system	
7	Tune data loading performance	All team members
8	Create, test, and tune queries	
9	Check the built data warehouse against the design document	Data warehouse architect, business analysts, technical developers

Phase III. Test

Number	Task	Resource
1	Size a quality assurance system using the development system as a baseline and the ASAP sizing document as a reference	Data warehouse architect, Basis and database administrators
2	Install the quality assurance system	Basis and database administrators
3	Transport the BW objects to the quality assurance system	Technical developers, Basis and database administrators

Phase III. (continued)

Number	Task	Resource
4	Conduct function testing and performance testing; tools such as LoadRunner and WinRunner from Mercury Interactive can be very helpful.	All team members
5	If necessary, modify BW objects in the development system and transport them to the quality assurance system	Technical developers
6	Verify the test result against the design document	All team members

Phase IV. Training

Number	Task	Resource
1	Develop end-user training materials based on the design document	Business analysts
2	If the production system has not been built yet, build a training system as a copy of the quality assurance system; otherwise, build a training system as a copy of the production system	Basis and database administrators
3	Tune query performance in the training system during training sessions	All team members
4	Test authorizations created for user roles	

Phase V. Production

Number	Task	Resource
1	Size a production system using the training system as a baseline and the ASAP sizing document as a reference	Data warehouse architect, Basis and database administrators
2	Install the production system	Basis and database administrators
3	Transport the BW objects from the development system to the production system	Technical developers, Basis and database administrators
	Load production OLTP data, including R/3 data, into the production system	Technical developers

4	Tune query and load performance based on the experience from the quality assurance and training systems	All team members
5	Set up a help desk to provide end-user support	
6	Go live	
7	Monitor production operation and identify hot spots	

Repeat the development → test → training → production cycle when needed.

A.3 For Further Information

Check SAP's Web site at http://service.sap.com/bw/.

Appendix B

SAP Basis Overview

BW uses the same R/3 Basis 3-tier architecture. In this overview, we introduce basic concepts of SAP Basis 3-tier architecture, such as work processes and memory management.

B.1 SAP Basis 3-Tier Architecture

The SAP Basis 3-tier architecture consists of presentation front ends, application servers, and a database server, as shown in Figure B.1.

B.1.1 Presentation Interface

The SAPGUI interacts with an application server using an SAP presentation protocol, where generic GUI descriptions, instead of prepared screen images, are exchanged. This interaction results in a compact data stream, consisting of 1 to 2 kilobytes of data. Thus, the interface through WAN can be easily achieved without performance problems.

FIGURE B.1
SAP BASIS 3-TIER ARCHITECTURE

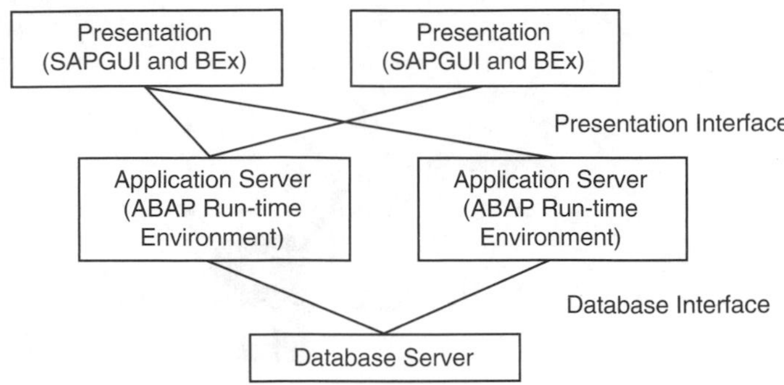

BEx communicates with an application server through the SAPGUI.

B.1.2 Application Server

SAP applications are written in ABAP or ABAP/4 (Advanced Business Application Programming, a fourth-generation language). ABAP runs on application servers. ABAP programs and flow logic for each screen are processed interpretatively by the R/3 run-time environment. The ABAP run-time environment is written in C and C++.

We used ABAP when writing transfer rules and update rules earlier in this book.

B.1.3 Database Interface

A remote SQL protocol is used for data transfer. The buffer, as shown in Figure B.2, stores often-used data. Changes to buffer contents are transmitted immediately to the database and broadcast at short time intervals by a message service to all other application servers.

We will discuss the message service later in this section.

FIGURE B.2
DATABASE INTERFACE

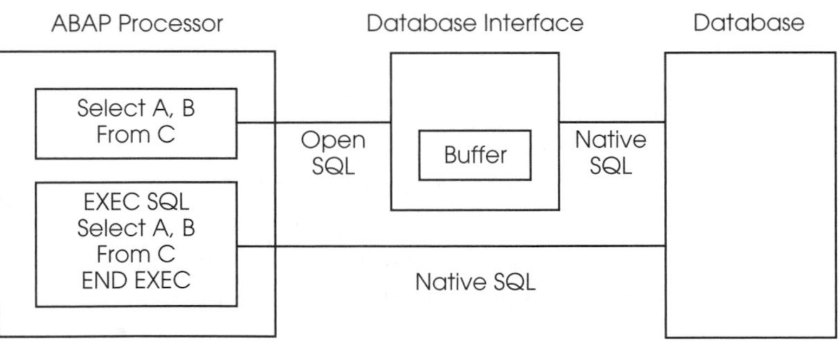

B.1.4 Open SQL

ABAP programs written in Open SQL are portable across different database systems. Along the way, the buffer mechanism enhances performance. Open SQL doesn't support the relational join operation. Instead, you can use views in ABAP. The database interface checks and converts Open SQL statements into Native SQL statements; it also detects syntax errors before run time.

B.1.5 Native SQL

Although programs written in Native SQL are not portable, all features of the database, including proprietary expansions of the standard SQL, are available for use. Obviously, Native SQL supports the relational join operation, but the DBMS cannot recognize an error in Native SQL until run time.

BW uses more Native SQL than R/3 does. For example, when the database is Oracle, BW uses many Oracle proprietary features designed for data warehousing. These features may not be available in other DBMSs.

B.2 Dispatcher, Work Processes, and Services

The Basis run-time environment has one dispatcher as well as several work processes and services. The dispatcher shown in Figure B.3 gathers user requests and assigns them to work processes for processing. After the processing ends, the dispatcher sends responses back to users. The Dispatcher also manages the communications between SAP and external systems.

FIGURE B.3 DISPATCHER AND WORK PROCESSES

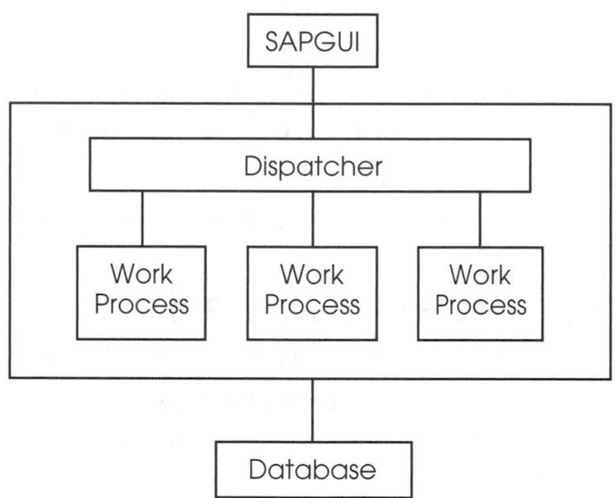

There are five types of work processes:

- Dialog
- Update
- Enqueue
- Background
- Spool

There are two types of services:

- Message
- Gateway

Each type of process or service has a special purpose.

B.2.1 Dialog Work Process

Dialog work processes take charge of the dialog steps involved in user sessions. If a screen is ready for processing after user input, for example, the dispatcher adds this job request to a queue. As soon as a dialog work process becomes available, the first job request waiting in the queue is submitted to it for processing.

An application server can have multiple dialog work processes.

B.2.2 Update Work Process

The update work process handles database update operations. An SAP transaction usually consists of several dialog steps. That is, it creates a log record for the dialog steps in an SAP transaction in the VBLOG table for the database update. An update work process later processes the log record at the end of the SAP transaction.

An application server can have multiple update work processes.

B.2.3 Enqueue Work Process

Each dialog step is a database LUW (logical unit of work). Because an update work process can execute more than one database LUW, the locking mechanism at database level is not sufficient in SAP.

An SAP LUW is an SAP transaction plus the database update. An enqueue work process manages this LUW. The update and enqueue work processes can run on different application servers.

A BW system has one and only one enqueue work process.

B.2.4 Background Work Process

The background work process executes ABAP/4 programs and reports at a scheduled time or in response to an event.

An application server can have multiple background work processes.

B.2.5 Spool Work Process

A spool work process generates a print-ready output stream for a variety of supported output devices and passes it to the host spool system. It relies on host spooling and printing services to transmit the print-ready output stream to a target output device. The output device can be a printer, fax, telex, or archiving device.

B.2.6 Message Service

The message service, or message handler, coordinates the internal message exchange between work processes in the same application server, and between dispatchers of different application servers. It performs load balancing among different application servers when users log on to BW.

A BW system has one and only one message service.

B.2.7 Gateway Service

The gateway service is for CPI-C (Common Programming Interface—Communications). It is used for the exchange of large amounts of data between application servers of the same SAP system or different SAP systems, and between SAP systems (via application servers) and non-SAP systems. BW BEx communicates with an application server using the gateway service.

A BW system has one and only one gateway service.

In BW, when a user logs on to a BW system through the BEx Browser, one gateway session is required to set up the communication link between the BEx Browser and the BW system. When the user fetches a workbook, four more gateway sessions are needed.

B.3 Memory Management

Memory management determines for a particular system activity when, and what type and size of memory is allocated. Figure B.4 shows the components involved in SAP memory management.

FIGURE B.4
SAP MEMORY MANAGEMENT

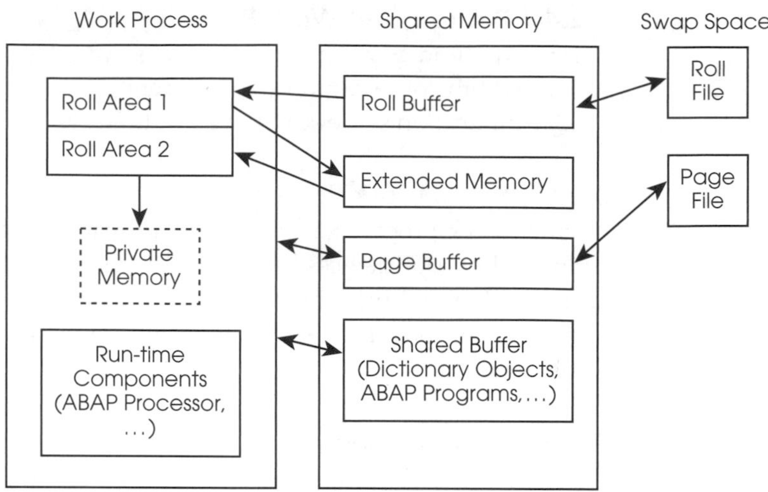

In the figure, Shared Memory represents memory space accessible by all work processes. Roll Buffer memory is used to queue user dialog requests. When the Roll Buffer becomes full, user dialog requests are swapped to the Roll File. Extended Memory stores user context (i.e., user data), such as the authorization and session context for each SAP session. Page Buffer memory holds large lists and long internal tables. When the Page Buffer becomes full, data are swapped to the Page File. Shared Buffer memory stores business objects and data. A dialog work process checks the Shared Buffer first for required business objects and data before searching the BW database. We will discuss the Shared Buffer later.

When a dialog work process becomes available to process the first user dialog request in Roll Buffer, it allocates memory in the following order:

1. The user dialog request, including the initial user context, is moved from the Roll Buffer into Roll Area 1. There the dialog work process can access the required data directly.
2. If Roll Area 1 is insufficient, more memory is allocated from the Extended Memory.
3. If the Extended Memory is also insufficient, more memory is allocated from Roll Area 2.
4. If Roll Area 2 is still insufficient, more memory is allocated from the Private Memory. Once this allocation takes place, the current dialog work process will no longer be available to process other user dialog requests.

To make Private Memory available again to process other user dialog requests, the operating system must restart the dialog work process.

5. If the Private Memory is still insufficient, the dialog work process is restarted, and the user dialog request is terminated.

After the user dialog request has been processed, the user context rolls into the Extended Memory and is ready for use by the next dialog request. In addition, the Roll Area and Private Memory allocated for the current dialog work process are released.

This procedure is repeated for each user dialog request in an SAP transaction. At the end of the SAP transaction, the last dialog work process copies the modified user dialog request back to the Roll Area, and eventually back to the end user.

B.3.1 SAP Buffer

The SAP Buffer stores frequently used business objects and data. With the SAP Buffer, work processes don't need to access the database if the buffer already contains the required information. This strategy helps to reduce database access, the load on the database server, and network traffic, thereby improving overall system performance. If the required information is not available in the buffer, it must be paged into the buffer before it can be used, resulting in slower performance.

If the SAP Buffer is too small, it cannot hold all of the required information. This shortage of space results in the information being swapped out of the buffers.

If the SAP Buffer is too large, the native operating system will start paging because too much memory is taken away and given to SAP, database, or other applications.

Ten types of buffers exist:

- The Repository Buffer, also called the nametab (NTAB) buffer, contains the table and field definitions
- The Program Buffer contains the compiled executable versions of ABAP programs
- The CUA Buffer contains the GUI objects, such as menus and push buttons
- The Screen Buffer contains the generated ABAP screens
- The Calendar Buffer contains all defined factory and public holiday calendars
- The Generic Key Table Buffer contains a range of table entries; it can also hold all the entries in a table

- The Single Record Table Buffer contains the single table entries.
- The Import/Export Buffers contain data that must be available to several work processes.
- The Roll and Paging Buffers were discussed earlier in this section.
- The Cursor Cache contains parsed SQL statements.

For Further Information

- Book: *SAP R/3 Administrator's Handbook,* by Jose Antonio Hernandez (ed.). McGraw-Hill Professional Publishing, 1999. ISBN: 0071354131.
- Book: *SAP R/3 System: A Client/Server Technology,* by Rudiger Buck-Emden, Jurgen Galimow, SAP AG. Addison-Wesley, 1996. ISBN: 0201403501.
- OSS Note 0039412, "How Many Work Processes to Configure."
- OSS Note 0021636, "RAM Extension: Which Changes to Profile?"
- OSS Note 0016223, "Problems with Roll Memory."

Appendix C

Glossary

Term	Description
Aggregate	An aggregate is a subset of an InfoCube. The objective when using aggregates is to reduce I/O volume. The BW OLAP processor selects an appropriate aggregate during a query run or a navigation step. If no appropriate aggregate exists, the BW OLAP processor retrieves data from the original InfoCube instead.
Aggregate rollup	Aggregate rollup is a procedure to update aggregates with new data loads.
Application component	Application components are used to organize InfoSources. They are similar to the InfoAreas used with InfoCubes. The maximum number of characters allowed for the technical name is 32.
Authorization	An authorization defines what a user can do, and to which SAP objects. For example, a user with an authorization can display and execute, but not

	change, a query. Authorizations are defined using authorization objects.
Authorization object	An authorization object is used to define user authorizations. It has fields with values to specify authorized activities, such as display and execution, on authorized business objects, such as queries. The maximum number of characters allowed for the technical name is 10.
Authorization profile	An authorization profile is made up of multiple authorizations. The maximum number of characters allowed for the technical name is 10.
Bitmap index	A bitmap index uses maps of bits to locate records in a table. Bitmap indices are very effective for Boolean operations of the WHERE clause of a SELECT statement. When the cardinality of a column is low, a bitmap index size will be small, thereby reducing I/O volume.
Business Content	Business Content is a complete set of BW objects developed by SAP to support the OLAP tasks. It contains roles, workbooks, queries, InfoCubes, key figures, characteristics, update rules, InfoSources, and extractors for SAP R/3, and other mySAP solutions.
BW	BW is a data warehousing solution from SAP.
BW Monitor	BW Monitor displays data loading status and provides assistance in troubleshooting if errors occur.
BW Scheduler	BW Scheduler specifies when to load data. It is based on the same techniques used for scheduling R/3 background jobs.
BW Statistics	BW Statistics is a tool for recording and reporting system activity and performance information.
Change run	Change run is a procedure used to activate characteristic data changes.
Characteristic	Characteristics are descriptions of key figures, such as Customer ID, Material Number, Sales Representative ID, Unit of Measure, and Transaction Date. The

	maximum number of characters allowed for the technical name is 9.
Client	A client is a subset of data in an SAP system. Data shared by all clients is called client-independent data, as compared with client-dependent data. When logging on to an SAP system, a user must specify which client to use. Once in the system, the user has access to both client-dependent data and client-independent data.
Communication structure	The communication structure is the structure underlying the InfoSource.
Compound attribute	A compound attribute differentiates a characteristic to make the characteristic uniquely identifiable. For example, if the same characteristic data from different source systems mean different things, then we can add the compound attribute 0SOURSYSTEM (source system ID) to the characteristic; 0SOURSYSTEM is provided with the Business Content.
Data packet size	For the same amount of data, the data packet size determines how work processes will be used in data loading. The smaller the data packet size, the more work processes needed.
Data Warehouse	Data Warehouse is a dedicated reporting and analysis environment based on the star schema database design technique and requiring special attention to the data ETTL process.
DataSource	A DataSource is not only a structure in which source system fields are logically grouped together, but also an object that contains ETTL-related information. Four types of DataSources exist: • DataSources for transaction data • DataSources for characteristic attributes • DataSources for characteristic texts • DataSources for characteristic hierarchies If the source system is R/3, replicating DataSources from a source system will create identical

	DataSource structures in the BW system. The maximum number of characters allowed for a DataSource's technical name is 32.
Delta update	The Delta update option in the InfoPackage definition requests BW to load only the data that have been accumulated since the last update. Before a delta update occurs, the delta process must be initialized.
Development class	A development class is a group of objects that are logically related.
Display attribute	A display attribute provides supplemental information to a characteristic.
Drill-down	Drill-down is a user navigation step intended to get further detailed information.
ETTL	ETTL, one of the most challenging tasks in building a data warehouse, is the process of extracting, transforming, transferring, and loading data correctly and quickly.
Free characteristic	A free characteristic is a characteristic in a query used for drill-downs. It is not displayed in the initial result of a query run.
Full update	The Full update option in the InfoPackage definition requests BW to load all data that meet the selection criteria specified via the Select data tab.
Generic data extraction	Generic data extraction is a function in Business Content that allows us to create DataSources based on database views or InfoSet queries. InfoSet is similar to a view but allows outer joins between tables.
Granularity	Granularity describes the level of detail in a data warehouse. It is determined by business requirements and technology capabilities.
IDoc	IDoc (Intermediate Document) is used in SAP to transfer data between two systems. It is a specific instance of a data structure called the IDoc Type, whose processing logic is defined in the IDoc Interface.

Index	An index is a technique used to locate needed records in a database table quickly. BW uses two types of indices: B-tree indices for regular database tables and bitmap indices for fact tables and aggregate tables.
InfoArea	InfoAreas are used to organize InfoCubes and InfoObjects. Each InfoCube is assigned to an InfoArea. Through an InfoObject Catalog, each InfoObject is assigned to an InfoArea as well. The maximum number of characters allowed for the technical name is 30.
InfoCube	An InfoCube is a fact table and its associated dimension tables in the star schema. The maximum number of characters allowed for the technical name is 30.
InfoCube compression	InfoCube compression is a procedure used to aggregate multiple data loads at the request level.
InfoObject	In BW, key figures and characteristics are collectively called InfoObjects.
InfoObject Catalog	InfoObject Catalogs organize InfoObjects. Two types of InfoObject Catalogs exist: one for characteristics, and one for key figures. The maximum number of characters allowed for the technical name is 30.
InfoPackage	An InfoPackage specifies when and how to load data from a given source system. BW generates a 30-digit code starting with ZPAK as an InfoPackage's technical name.
InfoSource	An InfoSource is a structure in which InfoObjects are logically grouped together. InfoCubes and characteristics interact with InfoSources to get source system data. The maximum number of characters allowed for the technical name is 32.
Key figure	Key figures are numeric values or quantities, such as Per Unit Sales Price, Quantity Sold, and Sales Revenue. The maximum number of characters allowed for the technical name is 9.

Line item dimension	A line item dimension in a fact table connects directly with the SID table of its sole characteristic.
Logical system	A logical system is the name of a client in an SAP system.
Multi-cube	A multi-cube is a union of basic cubes. The multi-cube itself does not contain any data; rather, data reside in the basic cubes. To a user, the multi-cube is similar to a basic cube. When creating a query, the user can select characteristics and key figures from different basic cubes.
Navigational attribute	A navigational attribute indicates a characteristic-to-characteristic relationship between two characteristics. It provides supplemental information about a characteristic and enables navigation from characteristic to characteristic during a query.
Number range	A number range is a range of numbers that resides in application server memory for quick number assignments.
ODS	ODS is a BW architectural component located between PSA and InfoCubes that allows BEx reporting. It is not based on the star schema and is used primarily for detail reporting, rather than for dimensional analysis. ODS objects do not aggregate data as InfoCubes do. Instead, data are loaded into an ODS object by inserting new records, updating existing records, or deleting old records, as specified by the 0RECORDMODE value.
Parallel query	A parallel query uses multiple database processes, when available, to execute a query.
Partition	A partition is a piece of physical storage for database tables and indices. If the needed data reside in one or a few partitions, then only those partitions will be selected and examined by a SQL statement, thereby significantly reducing I/O volume.
Profile Generator	Profile Generator is a tool used to create authorization profiles.

PSA	PSA is a data staging area in BW. It allows us to check data in an intermediate location, before the data are sent to its destinations in BW.
Query	A BW query is a selection of characteristics and key figures for the analysis of the data in an InfoCube. A query refers to only one InfoCube, and its result is presented in a BEx Excel sheet. The maximum number of characters allowed for the technical name is 30.
Read mode	Read mode for a query determines the size and frequency of data retrievals from database: all data at once, as needed per navigation step, or as needed per hierarchy node.
Reconstruct	Reconstruct is a procedure used to restore load requests from PSA.
Request	A request is a data load request from BW Scheduler. Each time that BW Scheduler loads data into an InfoCube, a unique request ID is created in the data packet dimension table of the InfoCube.
RFC	RFC (Remote Function Call) is a call to a function module in a system different from the caller's—usually another SAP system on the local network.
Role	In Profile Generator, an authorization profile corresponds to a role. A user assigned to that role also has the corresponding authorization profile. A user can be assigned to multiple roles. The maximum number of characters allowed for the technical name is 30.
SID	SID (Surrogate-ID) translates a potentially long key for an InfoObject into a short four-byte integer, which saves I/O and memory during OLAP.
Source system	A source system is a protocol that BW uses to find and extract data. When the source system is a non-SAP system, such as a flat file or a third-party tool, the maximum number of characters allowed for the technical name is 10. When the source system is an SAP system, either R/3 or BW, the technical name matches the logical system name. The maximum

number of characters allowed for the technical name is 32.

Star schema	A star schema is a technique used in the data warehouse database design to help data retrieval for online analytical processing.
Statistics	For a SQL statement, many execution plans are possible. The database optimizer generates the most efficient execution plan based on either the heuristic ranking of available execution plans or the cost calculation of available execution plans. Statistics is the information that the cost-based optimizer uses to calculate the cost of available execution plans and select the most appropriate one for execution. BW uses the cost-base optimizer for Oracle databases.
System Administration Assistant	System Administration Assistant is a collection of tools used to monitor and analyze general system operation conditions.
System landscape	The system landscape specifies the role of each system and the paths used in transporting objects among the various systems.
Time-dependent entire hierarchy	A time-dependent entire hierarchy is a time-dependent hierarchy whose nodes and leaves are not time-dependent.
Time-dependent hierarchy structure	A time-dependent hierarchy structure consists of nodes or leaves that are time-dependent, but the hierarchy itself is not time-dependent.
Transfer rule	Transfer rules specify how DataSource fields are mapped to InfoSource InfoObjects.
Transfer structure	A transfer structure maps DataSource fields to InfoSource InfoObjects.
Update rule	An update rule specifies how data will be updated into their targets. The data target can be an InfoCube or an ODS object. If the update rule is applied to data from an InfoSource, the update rule's technical name will match the InfoSource's technical name. If the update rule is applied to data from an ODS

	object, the update rule's technical name will match the ODS object's technical name prefixed with number 8.
Variable	A variable is a query parameter. It gets its value from user input or takes a default value set by the variable creator.
Workbook	A BW workbook is an Excel file with a BEx query result saved in BDS. BW assigns a 25-digit ID to each workbook. Users need merely name a workbook's title.

Appendix D

Bibliography

Books

- *ALE, EDI & IDoc Technologies for SAP,* by Arvind Nagpal, Robert Lyfareff (ed.), and Gareth M. de Bruyn (ed.). Prima Publishing, 1999. ISBN: 0761519033.
- *Authorizations Made Easy 4.6A/B,* by SAP Labs, Inc., Simplification Group. Johnson Printing Service, 1999. ISBN: 1893570231.
- *Business Information Warehouse for SAP,* by Naeem Hashmi. Prima Publishing, 2000. ISBN: 0761523359.
- *SAP BW Reporting Made Easy 2.0B/2.1C,* by SAP Labs, Inc., Simplification Group. Johnson Printing Service, 2001. ISBN: 1-893570-66-5.
- *SAP R/3 Administrator's Handbook,* by Jose Antonio Hernandez (ed.). McGraw-Hill Professional Publishing, 1999. ISBN: 0071354131.
- *SAP R/3 System: A Client/Server Technology,* by Rudiger Buck-Emden, Jurgen Galimow, and SAP AG. Addison-Wesley, 1996. ISBN: 0201403501.
- *The Data Warehouse Lifecycle Toolkit: Expert Methods for Designing, Developing, and Deploying Data Warehouses,* Ralph Kimball. John Wiley & Sons, 1998. ISBN: 0471255475.

BW Methodology

- ASAP for BW Accelerators can be downloaded from http://service.sap.com/bw/.

BW Online Documentation

- SAP Library: Business Information Warehouse comes with the BW installation CDs.

Helpful OSS Notes

- 0128447, "Trusted/Trusting Systems."
- 0130253, "Notes on Upload of Transaction Data into the BW."
- 0156784, "Additional Tablespaces for BW tables."
- 0175534, "Large BW-Systems and Performance of Aggregate Build."
- 0181944, "Accelerate Hierarchy Attribute Change Run."
- 0184322, "Procedure after DB Copy of BW Source Systems."
- 0184905, "Collective Note Performance BW 2.0."
- 0301192, "Procedure After Upgrading an R/3 Source System."
- 0309955, "BW Statistics in 2.0B—Questions, Answers, Errors."
- 0323323, "Transport of All Activated Objects of a System."
- 0325470, "Activities After Client Copy in BW Source Systems."
- 0325525, "Copying and Renaming Systems in a BW Environment."
- 0325839, "Considerable Increase of Tablespace PSAPODSD."
- 0327876, "MultiCube Query and Using Several Aggregates."
- 0339896, "ORACLE ERROR 14400."
- 0351163, "Creating ORACLE DB Statistics Using DBMS_STATS."
- 0356018, "Standard Transport System Activation in BW."
- 0356801, "Performance Problems Based on a Wrong Optimizer Dec."
- 0364577, "ODS: ORA-54 When Loading Data into the ODS."
- 0379736, "How Does a MultiCube Work?"
- 0384023, "Optimize Performance of ODS Objects."
- 0397403, "Aggregate Rollup Runs Slowly."
- 0399704, "Calling SAP Transactions from within the BEx Browser."
- 0408532, "Using the DBMS_STATS Package for Collecting Stats."

SAP White Papers

- "mySAP Technology for Open E-Business Integration—Overview," available at http://www.sap.com/
- "Portal Infrastructure: People-Centric Collaboration," available at http://www.sap.com/
- "mySAP Business Intelligence," available at http://www.sap.com/

Working Papers

Index